HEADLINES 2:
HALACHIC DEBATES
OF CURRENT EVENTS

HEADLINES 2:
Halachic Debates of Current Events

Dovid Lichtenstein

OU**PRESS**

NEW YORK

Copyright © 2017 Dovid Lichtenstein
Headlines: Halachic Debates of Current Events
ISBN: **978-0-692-85871-4**

All rights reserved. No part of this book may be used or reproduced in any manner whatsoever without written permission from the publisher, except in the case of brief quotations embodied in reviews and articles.

Design & Layout by Marzel A.S. — Jerusalem

Cover design by Rachel First

Published by
OU Press
An imprint of the Orthodox Union
11 Broadway
New York, NY 10004
www.oupress.org
oupress@ou.org

Contents

Publisher's Preface 15
Foreword 17

SOCIETY

1. Apple vs. the FBI
   Accessing and Disclosing Private Information 23
2. DNA as Halachic Evidence 49
3. What if Kim Davis Were an Orthodox Jew?
   Issuing Marriage Licenses to Same-Sex Couples 69
4. Who is a Believer? 81
5. The Disgraced Rabbi 95
6. Light Unto the Nations, or None of Our Business?
   Influencing Gentiles to Observe the Noachide Laws 121
7. Criminals in Shul:
   Should Convicted Felons be Welcomed in Our Communities? 137
8. Fraud and Deceit in the Contemporary Marketplace 163

FAMILY & HEALTH

9. Fathering a Child After Death 187
10. Is Artificial Insemination an Option for Unmarried Women? 211
11. Why is it Forbidden to Steal a Kidney? 239
12. Maintaining Good Health as a Halachic Imperative 255
13. Ebola: May a Doctor Endanger Himself by Treating Patients? . . . 269
14. Aborting a Fetus Infected With the Zika Virus 285
15. Suspending *Mitzva* Observance to Treat OCD 311

ISRAEL

16. Seducing the Enemy 329
17. Killing a Neutralized Terrorist 343

SHABBOS & YOM TOV

18. How Kosher is the Kosher Switch?............367
19. Adjusting "Sabbath Mode" Ovens on Yom Tov..............383
20. Bioplastic *Sechach*............395

KASHRUT

21. Is *Ben Pekua* Meat the Solution to Prohibitive Kosher Meat Prices?... 405
22. Genetically Modified Organisms:
    Will this be the Greatest *Kashrus* Challenge of Modern Times?......419
23. Is Sherry Cask Whiskey Kosher?.................. 439
24. Are *Treif* Utensils Really *Treif*?............ 459

בס"ד

ישיבת בית יוסף ברוקלין, בידידות כבוד והערכה

מיסודו של
מרן הגאון רבי אברהם יפהן זצוק"ל
ומרן הגאון רבי יעקב חיים יפהן זצוק"ל
ראשי ישיבות בית יוסף נובהרדוק
1502 Ave. N
Brooklyn, New York 11230

Rabbi Mordechai Jofen
Rosh Hayeshiva

מרדכי זאב יפה'ן
ראש הישיבה

עש"ק פ' בשלח ט' שבט תשע"ד

הנה ידיד נפשי הרה"ג ר' דוד ליכטנשטיין שליט"א שלח לי חבור שעומד להוציא על שאלות ובעיות חדשות העומדות על הפרק, דברים שהרב המחבר השמיע ברבים לפני שומעי לקחו מדי שבת בשבתו. ואין כוונת המחבר לקבוע הלכה בשאלות חמורות אלו, אלא להעמיד אותן בקרן אורה ולהאיר עליהם מאור תורתו והבנתו הישרה והבהירה כיד ה' הטובה עליו בתקוה שבעקבותיו יבאו מורי הוראה מובהקים להתעסק בשאלות אלו.

ודבר גדול עשה ידידי שליט"א ואני מברכו שיזכה לישב באהלו של תורה שידוע לי שזה מגמת נפשו ללמוד וללמד לפלפל ולחדש מתוך הרחבת הדעת.

בידידות כבוד והערכה,

מרדכי זאב יפה'ן

Mailing address:
Yeshiva Beth Joseph
P.O.Box 191001
Brooklyn, NY 11219

דוד קאהן

ביחמ"ד גבול יעבץ
ברוקלין, נוא יארק

ב"ה

To whom it may concern:

At the insistance of my good friend Reb Dovid Lichtenstein, I am stating that this is not a haskomo, but a michtav brocho; thusly I remove from my shoulders any responsibility if one wants to rely on the "rulings" of Reb Dovid.

The sefer which he sent me to peruse has, as yet, no name but it highly original and a delightful study of various halachic questions. My blessings that כל אשר יפנה ישכיל

בנן קלון
כן מנון שליט"א

הרב נתן שערמאן
Rabbi Nosson Scherman
1181 East Ninth Street
Brooklyn, New York 11230

ב' דר"ח אלול תשע"ג

כבוד ידידי הגאון המובהק אי"א מו"ה
הרה"ג ר' דוד פאלק שליט"א

Thank you for sharing with me your manuscript on complex modern halachic issues. These are questions that engage thinking people, but rarely do the disputants delve into halachic sources. As you show in your brilliant and far-reaching discourses, Chazal and poskim through the centuries have shown how halachic principles relate to all sorts of "new" situations, although it is easy to think that because the questions occur in a modern setting, eternal Halachah has nothing to say about them.

The range of your sources and your skill in showing how they apply to the questions you discuss are extremely enlightening and stimulating, especially to those of us whose learning concentrates on Shas and poskim without attempting to apply our learning to what might be called "practical Halachah." It is important and constructive to show, as you do in this work, that the Torah speaks authoritatively to every age and every question.

I appreciate, as you stress in your introduction, that your intention is not to issue final rulings, but to show the range and depth of שיטות התורה and their teachings and how there is no modern situation that cannot be resolved through Torah.

הנה כן יהי רצון שחפץ ה' בידו יצלח והספר הזה יפוצו מעינותיו חוצה להגדיל תורה ולהאדירה, וזכה להגדיל תורה ולהאדירה, ויזכה לעלות עוד במעלות התורה והיראה.

ידידו ומוקירו בהוקרה ובאהבה רבה

Nosson Scherman

הרב צבי שכטר
ראש ישיבה ורב כולל
ישיבת רבינו יצחק אלחנן

Rabbi Hershel Schachter
24 Bennett Avenue
New York, New York 10033
(212) 795-0630

מכתב ברכה

כבוד ידידנו הרה"ג לדוד לוכנשטיין
נ"י עושה רבר גדול להוצאות לאור
שהגדולה. וסלר מרד לומר לו ולסופרים
הקלאסיים הכותבים על הבריך, אשר נהנה
כבודה של תורה ואהל של צורה
של תורה — לגדלות ולהאדיר את הרב
אשר זכה בעל החמישה ספר יקרה
ויקרה הללו שהמה נותנו להגדיל ולהאדיר ספה הקדוש
מקרא של מסיורחא, ומתלמוני, שהספרי ובואל
כבלבלוי לתורה
הברכת והחכמ הרבי ה פ' תורה
רבני ספר
יום ב' חשון תשע"ה

Approbations for the Author's Mishna Acharona

Rabbi Azriel Auerbach
Rabbi of "Chanice Hayeshivot"
53 Hapisga St., Bayit Vegan, Jerusalem

בס"ד

הרב עזריאל אויערבאך
רב בית הכנסת "חניכי הישיבות", בית וגן
רחוב הפסגה 53, בית וגן, ירושלים

כ"א למבנ"י תשע"ב

שמחתי מאד כאשר ראיתי את הספר הנכבד משנה אחרונה שהוא איסוף וליקוט של הרבה תשובות בשאלות שנשאלו מאת גדולי הלכה וביניהם מדברי אאמו"ר ז"ל בהלכות שבת המצויות ובדברי המשנה ברורה בהלכות שבת. והדברים מפורטים בספר עם ציון המקורות שע"י יהי' לתועלת המעיינים.

וכל זה ליקט ואסף הרב החשוב רבי דוד ליכטנשטיין שליט"א ברב עמל ויגיעה וזכה להוציא מתחת ידיו דבר נאה ומתוקן בכלי מפואר.

והנני בברכה נאמנה להרב המחבר שליט"א שיזכה לישב תמיד באהלה של תורה בבריות גופא ונהורא מעליא, ולזכות הרבים בספרים מועילים שרבים יהנו לאורם, וירבה כבוד שמים על ידו.

RABBI J. J. NEUWIRTH
10 Bergman St. Bayit Vegan
Jerusalem, 96467

הרב יהושע י. נויבירט
רח׳ ברגמן 10, בית וגן
ירושלים 96467

בס״ד ט״ו טבת תשס״ו

מנחת בינה
_____

הנני בזה״ג את אוהבי הנחמד של הרה״ג
ר׳ קלמן עפשטיין שליט״א בשם "מנחת אהרן" ירום
הודו וישאו, זכרי בעיני דורנו על דרך "השגה כחוה"
לברך אתכל עמלה הרב הגדול אותם של מעלה בזה לגדול של
כל התכריך אגל מורה מחותי שתה ברכה לעושי רצונו כמו
מוטף אחת ידו.

יאור ה׳ פניהם וישא שלום גדולות יתגדל ויגדל להתגדל
כאות נפשם ונפש ה׳ ידידו.

החותם לכבוד של אורה
ולכבוד לבני קדש

יהושע י. נויבירט

RABBI Z. N. GOLDBERG

Abbad Badatz & Bies Horaa'h "Hayashar Vehatov"

Member Of Supreme Rabbinical Court

הרב זלמן נחמיה גולדברג

אב״ד בד״ץ ובית הוראה לדיני ממונות **״הישר והטוב״**

חבר בית הדין הרבני הגדול

ב״ה, יום ה׳ טבת תשע״ד

הראוני ספר חשוב מאוד ותועלתו מרובה למען ישמרו בני ישראל
את השבת לפי הדין בספר משנה אחרונה שהוא דיונים בשאלות
חדשות שנתעוררו בדור שאחר המשנה ברורה
על ידי גדולי עולם והמחבר ברוב חכמה הצליח להביא כל הדעות
ברב כמות ורב איכות
וכל זה חיבר הרב המאור הגדול ר׳ דוד ליכטנשטיין
ויזכה ויהי נכון להמשיך להוציא שאר חלקי המשנה ברורה
ובודאי מצוה גדולה לסייעו בכל מה שניתן שיתאפשר לו
להמשיך בפעלו הטוב

הכותב לכבוד התורה ושמירת המצוות

זלמן נחמיה גולדברג

רפאל שמואלביץ

ראש ישיבה
מיר ירושלים

ב"ה ט"ז אדר א' תשע"א

לידידי הרב ר' דוד ליכטנשטין שליט"א

שלום ורב ברכה,

שמחתי מאוד לראות גליונות נדפסים מתוך ספרך הגדול "משנה אחרונה", ובו איסוף התשובות של גדולי הדורות הללו, שנתחברו לאחר המשנה ברורה, והן עוסקות בשאלות אשר לא שייך שתהא להן התייחסות במשנה ברורה, כיון שהן שאלות שנתחדשו לפי תנאי החיים בדורות הללו, ועניין גדול מאד להביא לפני לומדי תורה את המקורות לתשובות לשאלות הללו, כדי שתהא להם האפשרות לברר את כל פרטי הדינים, ללמוד מהתשובות במקורותיהן, את הדרך ילכו בה ואת המעשה אשר יעשון בעניינים הללו, ומצוה רבה בידך להביא לאור עולם ספר גדול זה. ותועלת גדולה מזה לכל אלו המסוגלים לרדת לעומקם של דברי הפוסקים.

שמחה כפולה ומכופלת יש לי באופן אישי לראות את ספרך הגדול, וזאת לאור הטעם המתוק שנשאר בפי משנות הלימוד בחברותא בשנים בו למדת בישיבתינו, ישיבת מיר הק'. והנני לברך אותך, שספרך הגדול יתקבל ברעוא אצל קהל מבקשי תורת השם, ועוד תוסיף אומץ ותגביר חיל לפתוח הרבה שערי תורה, ולהנות את עולם התורה גם בספריך הבאים, אשר רבים ישוטטו בהם לבקש דעת ולהוסיף חכמה.

השמח בשמחתך

Publisher's Preface

In *Headlines 2: Halachic Debates of Current Events*, the sequel to the exceedingly popular first volume of the series, Dovid Lichtenstein continues his masterful application of *halacha* to some of the most controversial questions which face us today. On issues ranging from privacy rights and DNA evidence to technological innovations affecting Shabbos and *kashrus*, *Headlines 2* breaks new ground in its trenchant analysis of new halachic dilemmas.

On the *pasuk* in the first chapter of *Kerias Shema*, והיו הדברים האלה אשר אנכי מצוך היום על לבבך, "These words which I command you today shall be on your heart," Rashi cites the *Sifrei*: לא יהיו בעיניך כדיוטגמא ישנה שאין אדם סופנה, אלא כחדשה שהכל רצין לקראתה — "They should not be in your eyes as an old ordinance which no one regards, but as a new one which all rush to read." Rashi defines דיוטגמא as the edicts contained in a letter from the king (in the pre-Twitter era). In other words, we should treat the Torah not like yesterday's news, but with the same degree of relevance as today's headlines.

The plain meaning of *Chazal*'s words is that we must approach the Torah with vitality and freshness, always seeking new insight and greater understanding. But there is an additional message contained in these words as well. The ability to view the Torah as if it was given today is possible only because we have faith that the Torah encompasses the wisdom to address the problems of today. This faith in the applicability of the Torah's principles and values to our contemporary challenges is what enables us to appreciate the Torah anew each day.

Dovid Lichtenstein, a successful businessman who is a genuine *talmid chacham* possessed of great scholarship, excels in this arena — he displays a passion for the truth as he sees it and demonstrates great creativity in utilizing the halachic literature spanning the generations to address issues literally drawn from newspaper headlines. Confronting societal, medical, and technological questions and innovations, Reb Dovid marshals sources with great skill to discover *halacha*'s response.

Determining what *halacha* has to say about many of these issues is often a difficult task. I remember hearing from Rav Soloveitchik that many of the modern *shaylos* are so complex that it would have required weeks for Rav Chaim Ozer to have formulated responses. This volume displays the necessary scholarship and sensitivity in addressing such questions, and, after thoroughly examining the sources, does not shy away from staking out strongly articulated positions. Whether or not one agrees with the conclusions reached, the discussion is inevitably thought-provoking and provides a helpful framework to analyze the issue at hand. The present book is thus a significant contribution in furthering our appreciation for the unceasing relevance of the Torah's message.

Finally, I would like to acknowledge my colleagues at OU Press for their dedicated work on this volume: Rabbi Gad Buchbinder, for his meticulous oversight of the myriad details of this project, Rabbi Simon Posner, Executive Editor of OU Press, for his overall supervision of the project, and Eliyahu Krakowski for his careful review of drafts of the manuscript.

Menachem Genack
General Editor
OU Press

Foreword

ומי גוי גדול אשר לו חוקים ומשפטים צדיקים ככל התורה הזאת (דברים ד:ה)

For centuries, English Common Law, the legal system upon which American law is founded, denied a person the right to self-defense. Killing an assailant who had launched a life-threatening attack was deemed illegal, and tantamount to ordinary manslaughter. It was only in the 17th century when the right to self-defense was first recognized, and later, English law recognized the "Castle Doctrine," which affirms a property owner's right to protect his "castle" rather than flee from an intruder and surrender his property.

This is but one example of how Torah law was millennia ahead of other systems in terms of establishing a just, moral legal code. Today, nobody questions the right of an assault victim to fight back to protect his life, and to defend his property against an intruder, a right explicitly affirmed by Torah law. Our ancient legal code was way ahead of its time, and it took millennia for the others to catch up.

In the first volume of *Headlines*, we explored — among many other topics — the controversial case of George Zimmerman, who in 2012 killed suspected criminal Trayvon Martin, who apparently had assaulted him. We showed how the question surrounding the right to kill the assailant under these circumstances was discussed by Torah sages centuries ago, and how there is a vast literature of ancient rabbinic scholarship directly relevant to the 21st century debate regarding the parameters of the right to self-defense, and whether one has a "duty to retreat" to avoid violent self-defense.

In this second volume, we address, among many other fascinating contemporary halachic questions, the halachic issue surrounding the Law of Necessity, which permits one to violate laws to protect human life. The basic principle that conventional laws are suspended in the interest of saving human life is well-established and undisputed in the Talmud, even if its precise limits and parameters are subject to a great deal of debate, as we painstakingly discuss. As recently as the 1970s, English law forbade a fire engine from running a red light to rescue people from a burning home, due to concern about abuse of exceptions to the law. What is now universally recognized as a basic, intuitive legal doctrine, and which has, in fact, been indisputably recognized as such in Torah law ever since it was given to Moshe atop Mount Sinai, was rejected by other legal systems less than half a century ago. Once again, *halacha* was millennia ahead of the rest.

These volumes, which explore the application of our ancient Torah tradition to cutting-edge contemporary questions, are presented, at least in part, as chronicles of the תורה שבעל פה, as compelling evidence of the eternal relevance of Torah. If nothing else, these essays demonstrate that our sacred tradition continues to provide guidance and instruction for modern life, and will continue doing so, forever.

ותן חלקנו בתורתך

In one of the conversations I was privileged to have with Rav Moshe Shapiro zt"l, he asked the following question. If a person is with a group of people and tells them a humorous joke, they will laugh heartily. If he repeats it a bit later, they might still chuckle. If he says it a third time, they will think he is strange. A joke repeated several times is no longer funny. Yet, if a person tells a joke and then goes somewhere else, to a different group of people, and he tells the joke there, he will laugh together with them. He'll laugh each time he tells the joke to a new group of people, even though he has already heard it numerous times. Why? Why doesn't the joke become stale to the one telling it after repeating it so many times?

The reason, Rav Shapiro explained, is that the person finds himself, so-to-speak, in the joke. The content of the joke may not bring him amusement after the first several times, but it nevertheless evokes excitement because he "owns" this joke, it is part of him, it is something to which he connects very deeply.

This, Rav Shapiro explained, is the meaning of the *tefila* that we recite several times each day, ותן חלקנו בתורתך — "Grant us our portion in Your Torah." Each and every Jew, whether he is a seasoned *talmid chacham*, a budding young yeshiva student, or a layman, has his "portion" in the Torah. There is an area of Torah with which he can deeply connect, where he feels at home, which touches his soul. Needless to say, we ought to aspire to master כל התורה כולה, and we shouldn't ignore the areas of Torah which don't excite us. However, we are encouraged to identify our חלק, the portion of Torah with which we can connect, and nurture that sacred bond.

I have experienced this phenomenon firsthand. After I entered the business world, I would come home at night, weary after a long, tense day of בזעת אפך תאכל לחם, toiling to earn a living, and I would open a Gemara and *mefarshim* and try poring over difficult *sugyos*. Very often, I found it difficult to muster the enthusiasm and rigor I needed to keep myself going. I found this enthusiasm when I found my חלק — when I began exploring contemporary questions through the lenses of the *Tannaim*, *Amoraim*, *Geonim*, *Rishonim* and *Acharonim*. I found this to be an exciting and rewarding enterprise, and this newfound excitement led me to publish these volumes, a labor of love which I have undertaken in order to share this treasure with Jews across the world.

Many articles appearing in this book were originally written by me in Hebrew, the language used by the Poskim that I quote throughout this book. Rabbi David Silverberg, a brilliant and erudite talmid chochom, translated those articles into English, and I thank him for his meticulous attention to detail.

I hope and pray that this material will inspire and motivate others — scholars and laymen alike — to find, as I did, their חלק in Torah, the area with which they can forge a special emotional bond, so we can all grow מחיל אל חיל, climbing from one rung to the next in our passionate pursuit of Torah knowledge.

Judge Forces Apple to Help Unlock San Bernardino Shooter iPhone

February 16, 2016
by Andrew Blankfein

A federal judge on Tuesday ordered Apple to give investigators access to encrypted data on the iPhone used by one of the San Bernardino shooters, assistance the computer giant "declined to provide voluntarily," according to court papers.

In a 40-page filing, the U.S. Attorney's Office in Los Angeles argued that it needed Apple to help it find the password and access "relevant, critical…data" on the locked cellphone of Syed Farook, who with his wife Tashfeen Malik murdered 14 people in San Bernardino, California on December 2.

"Despite…a warrant authorizing the search," said prosecutors, "the government has been unable to complete the search because it cannot access the iPhone's encrypted content. Apple has the exclusive technical means which would assist the government in completing its search, but has declined to provide that assistance voluntarily."

Prosecutors said they needed Apple's help accessing the phone's data to find out who the shooters were communicating with and who may have helped plan and carry out the massacre, as well as where they traveled prior to the incident.

The judge ruled Tuesday that the Cupertino-based company had to provide "reasonable technical assistance" to the government in recovering data from the iPhone 5c, including bypassing the auto-erase function and allowing investigators to submit an unlimited number of passwords in their attempts to unlock the phone. Apple has five days to respond to the court if it believes that compliance would be "unreasonably burdensome."

Syed Farook and Tashfeen Malik arrive in Chicago on July 27, 2014. U.S. Government

In a statement, United States Attorney Eileen M. Decker called the move an "important step."

"Since the terrorist attack in San Bernardino on December 2, 2015, that took the lives of 14 innocent Americans and shattered the lives of numerous families, my office and our law enforcement partners have worked tirelessly to exhaust every investigative lead in the case," said Decker. "We have made a solemn commitment to the victims and their families that we will leave no stone unturned as we gather as much information and evidence as possible. These victims and families deserve nothing less. The application filed today in federal court is another step — a potentially important step — in the process of learning everything we possibly can about the attack in San Bernardino."

After the shooting at the Inland Regional Center in San Bernardino, authorities said they recovered several cell phones Farook and Malik had tried to destroy and had dropped in a waste bin. The iPhone referenced in the judge's ruling was found in a black Lexus belonging to Farook's family.

An iPhone 5C is displayed during an Apple product announcement at the Apple campus on September 10, 2013 in Cupertino, California. Justin Sullivan / Getty Images file

The iPhone is owned by Farook's employer, the San Bernardino County Department of Public Health, which assigned it to him. The county consented to investigators' requests to search its contents.

Prosecutors argued evidence in Farook's iCloud account indicates that he was in communication with victims whom he and his wife later shot, and phone records show Farook communicated with Malik using his iPhone.

Prosecutors alleged in their filing that Farook may have disabled the iCloud data feature to hide evidence. Although investigators have been able to obtain several backup versions of Farook's iCloud data, the most recent version they've been able to access dates from about a month and a half before the shooting. They said this showed Farook "may have disabled the feature to hide evidence."

Last week FBI Director James Comey referenced the San Bernardino shootings when testifying before Congress about the challenges posed by technology that allows cell phones to lock with no apparent means of override. The new court documents give some details about those hurdles and the ongoing investigation.

Apple did not immediately respond to a request for comment.

Copyright © nbcnews.com

Apple vs. the FBI
Accessing and Disclosing Private Information

On December 2, 2015, the United States — and the world — was shaken by a devastating, deadly terror attack perpetrated by a married couple who killed fourteen people and seriously injured twenty-two others at the Inland Regional Center in San Bernardino, California. The perpetrators — Syed Farook and Tashfeen Malik — were found and killed by police in a shootout that same day.

Two months later, on February 9th, the FBI, which had taken over the investigation of the attack, announced that it had recovered Syed Farook's iPhone, but was unable to unlock the device in order to find clues of the shooter's possible accomplices and other important contacts. This information, the FBI claimed, was vital to the Bureau's ongoing investigation into the terrorists' motives and modes of operation. The FBI asked that Apple disable the phone's security system to enable them to access Mr. Farook's information, but the company refused, arguing that it needed to strictly uphold its commitments not to compromise its customers' security. The FBI then appealed to a federal judge, and a court order was issued ordering Apple to comply with the FBI's demands by February 26th. The brief legal battle came to an anticlimactic end on March 28th, when the Department of Justice announced that it had succeeded in unlocking the device.

This unfortunate incident brings to the fore the broader question as to the limits of a person's right to have personal information kept private, a question that has implications for even more common situations than terrorism. For example, if a person wishes to find out about a prospective business partner or spouse, and he is able to "hack" that individual's email account or other sources of personal information, would Halacha sanction such prying? For that matter, may a hacker access confidential information purely out of curiosity or for amusement, without sharing that information with anyone else?

This question also arises with regard to wiretapping. May one place a hidden recorder near a yeshiva student's seat in the *beis midrash*, for example, to determine his level of seriousness when considering him as a *shidduch*? Similarly, would it be permissible to secretly check his computer's internet browsing history to see if he accesses inappropriate material? Another example would be obtaining medical information to learn of a prospective *shidduch*'s family history. If a person somehow has the ability to access someone's confidential medical records, are there any circumstances in which this would be allowed?

These questions force us to explore the origins of the halachic prohibition against invading a person's privacy, and then to determine the limits to this prohibition and the exceptions that might apply under certain circumstances. In this essay, we will examine: 1) the prohibition against sharing with others someone's personal information of which we have knowledge; 2) the prohibition against accessing someone's personal information without sharing it; and 3) situations in which breaches of privacy are permissible.

I. Sharing Someone's Personal Information

הרי הוא בבל יאמר

The Gemara in *Maseches Yoma* (4b) explicitly establishes that one may not share a conversation he had with someone without that person's consent. In the Gemara's words, הרי הוא בבל יאמר — the contents of the conversation may not be shared until permission is granted. The Gemara infers this concept from the fact that God related His commands to Moshe לאמר — to then be told to *Bnei Yisrael*. God expressly instructed Moshe to relay His commands to *Bnei Yisrael* because otherwise he would have had to keep this information to himself. This demonstrates that when someone is told something by his fellow, he may not pass it on to others without that person's express permission.[1]

The Chafetz Chayim (*Hilchos Lashon Ha-Ra* 2:13; *Be'er Mayim Chayim* 27) notes that since this law is inferred from Moshe's prophecies, it must apply even when the disclosed information will not cause any harm to the individual. After all, God cannot be "harmed" in any way, but it nevertheless would have been forbidden for Moshe to relay the information given to him to by God if God had not explicitly authorized him to do so. Necessarily, then, the law of הרי הוא בבל יאמר applies to everything told to a person, even if sharing it would not cause any harm to the speaker.

The question arises as to the relationship between this prohibition and the more famous prohibition of לשון הרע. The Rambam (*Hilchos Dei'os* 7:5) defines

---

1. There is some discussion among the *Acharonim* as to whether this inference is made from the oft-repeated Biblical verse, וידבר ה' אל משה לאמר, or, as indicated by the version found in common editions of the Talmud, from the opening verse of *Sefer Vayikra*: וידבר ה' אל משה מאהל מועד לאמר.

לשון הרע as spreading information about someone that could cause him harm or distress:

> המספר דברים שגורמים אם נשמעו איש מפי איש להזיק חבירו בגופו או בממונו ואפילו להצר לו או להפחידו, הרי זה לשון הרע.

One who relates matters that cause, if heard by word of mouth, physical or monetary damage to his fellow, or even cause him distress or to be frightened — this constitutes לשון הרע.

Why did the Torah introduce a separate prohibition of לשון הרע if sharing private information of any kind is already forbidden by force of the law of הרי הוא בבל יאמר? Once telling any personal information about someone is forbidden, what is added by the special prohibition against spreading negative information?

The Chafetz Chayim suggests that the rule of הרי הוא בבל יאמר was not stated as an outright prohibition, but rather as a guideline of etiquette and propriety (מידה טובה בעלמא). The Torah prohibition of לשון הרע applies only to information that could cause a person harm or distress, but basic courtesy dictates that even other personal information should not be shared. The Chafetz Chayim observes that the Rambam makes no mention of הרי הוא בבל יאמר in his code of law, likely because he did not regard this rule as a bona fide halachic prohibition.[2]

The Chafetz Chayim also suggests a second approach, proposing that even if the law of הרי הוא בבל יאמר constitutes an outright halachic prohibition, it perhaps applies only when the information was shared in private, indicating the speaker's desire for confidentiality. God conveyed His laws to Moshe inside the *Mishkan* and ensured that His voice would not be heard outside.[3] Under such circumstances, when a person made a point of speaking to his fellow in private, expressing his desire for secrecy, his fellow may not share the information with others, even if the information would not pose any risk of harm or distress. The prohibition of לשון הרע, by contrast, applies even when the information was not conveyed secretly; according to the rules of לשון הרע it is forbidden to share anything that would cause the speaker any sort of damage or angst.

It thus emerges that sharing the content of personal correspondence may be halachically forbidden if there is reason to assume that the individual wants the content to remain private, and it might be deemed inappropriate (albeit not halachically forbidden) even if there is no reason to make such an assumption.

---

2. Indeed, the Meiri, who generally adheres to the Rambam's rulings, writes explicitly in his commentary to *Maseches Yoma* that this rule was intended as a guideline for refined conduct, and not as an actual halachic prohibition.
3. Rashi, *Vayikra* 1:1.

לא תלך רכיל בעמך

Revealing private information may also likely fall under the halachic prohibition of לא תלך רכיל בעמך ("You shall not go about gossiping among your people" — *Vayikra* 19:16), which the *Semag* (*lo sa'aseh* 9) defines as, המגלה לחבירו דברים שדיבר ממנו אדם אחר בסתר — revealing information spoken to a person in private. It stands to reason that according to the *Semag*, this would apply not only to information that was told to someone, but also to information that one discovered through other means, such as by searching through his computer or overhearing his private conversations.

This also appears to be the view of the Rambam in *Hilchos Dei'os* (7:2), where he defines the term רכיל:

> זה שטוען דברים והולך מזה לזה ואומר כך אמר פלוני, כך וכך שמעתי על פלוני, אע"פ שהוא אמת.

> This refers to one who carries information and goes from one person to another saying, 'So-and-so said such-and-such'; 'I heard such-and-such about so-and-so' — even though it is true.

According to the Rambam, spreading private information about people transgresses the Torah prohibition of לא תלך רכיל בעמך.[4]

Similarly, the Meiri (*Sanhedrin* 31a) writes:

> אף בכל דבר שמחבירו לחבירו, חייב אדם שלא לגלותו ושלא להביא דבר מזה לזה, ועל כלם נאמר לא תלך רכיל בעמך.

> Also in every matter from one person to his fellow, a person is obligated not to reveal it and not to bring information from one person to another. Regarding all of these it is said, לא תלך רכיל בעמך.

Rashi likewise seems to adopt this understanding of the prohibition לא תלך רכיל בעמך. Commenting on the term לישנא תליתאי with which the Gemara in *Maseches Arachin* (15b) refers to gossip, Rashi writes: לשון הרכיל שהיא שלישית בין אדם לחבירו לגלות לו סוד — "The tongue of the gossiper, who is the third party, coming in between a person and his fellow to reveal secrets to him." The term רכיל, according to Rashi, refers to a person who reveals other people's secrets, and thus revealing private information would seemingly violate the prohibition of לא תלך רכיל בעמך.

---

4. Surprisingly, the Chafetz Chayim (*Hilchos Lashon Ha-Ra* 1:1, *Be'er Mayim Chayim* 4) understands the Rambam as referring specifically to someone who tells people what others have said about them, as opposed to general personal information. This does not, however, appear to be the implication of the Rambam's remarks.

However, a different conclusion appears to emerge from Rashi's Torah commentary (*Vayikra* 19:16), where he interprets רכיל as referring to הולכים בבתי רעיהם לרגל מה יראו רע או מה ישמעו רע לספר בשוק — "those who go to their friends' homes to check what negative information they can see or hear to tell in the marketplace." Here, Rashi appears to limit רכילות to negative personal information, such that disclosing neutral personal information would not fall under the prohibition of לא תלך רכיל.

In any event, according to the aforementioned *Rishonim*, disclosing a person's private information would violate the Torah prohibition of לא תלך רכיל בעמך. Support for this view may, at first glance, be drawn from the Mishna's ruling in *Maseches Sanhedrin* (29a) that after a *Beis Din* issues its decision, a judge should not publicize the fact that he felt the defendant was innocent while the majority determined that he was guilty. Although this announcement does not entail negative information about his colleagues, a judge should not publicize this fact, as his colleagues likely prefer keeping their decisions private. The Gemara (31a) cites as the source of this prohibition the verse לא תלך רכיל בעמך, clearly indicating that this verse forbids disclosing other people's personal information that they prefer keeping secret.[5]

We may, however, refute this proof, and distinguish between the case of a judge revealing his colleagues' decisions and other cases of רכילות. Publicizing a judge's opinion could evoke the ire of the defendant or losing party, thereby potentially endangering the judge. Hence, the application of לא תלך רכיל בעמך in such a case does not necessarily dictate that it applies to information that poses no harm to the individual. Second, the Rambam, in his commentary to the Mishna (*Sanhedrin* ad loc.), explains this *halacha* as intended to ensure that people look upon judges fondly and admiringly. As such, no conclusions can be reached on the basis of this *halacha* with respect to general situations of disclosure of private information.

Regardless, at least according to several *Rishonim*, one who discloses

---

5. The Mishna and Gemara also cite a second source for this prohibition, namely, the verse in *Mishlei* (11:13), הולך רכיל מגלה סוד ("One who goes around gossiping reveals secrets"). The citation of two Scriptural sources challenges us to identify the precise relationship between them. One possibility emerges from the Vilna Gaon's interpretation of הולך רגיל מגלה סוד in his commentary to *Mishlei*: המגלה סוד הוא דומה להולך רכיל, ועוונם שוה — "One who reveals secrets resembles one who goes around gossiping, and their iniquity is equal." This might mean that the verse in *Mishlei* introduces a new prohibition against disclosing private information, which is likened in severity to the prohibition of רכילות. Accordingly, we might explain that the Gemara cites both verses because the actual prohibition that one violates is הולך רכיל מגלה סוד, but it is considered as grievous an infraction as a violation of לא תלך רכיל בעמך.

someone's personal information that he presumably wishes to be kept private transgresses the Torah prohibition of לא תלך רכיל בעמך.[6]

Revealing Secrets as an Ethical Breach

Beyond the strict halachic prohibitions entailed, numerous sources indicate that disclosing private information constitutes a severe breach of Torah ethics.

Rabbeinu Yona writes in *Sha'arei Teshuva* (3:228):

> וחייב אדם להסתיר הסוד אשר יגלה אליו חברו דרך סתר אעפ"י שאין בגילוי ההוא ענין רכילות, כי יש בגילוי הסוד נזק לבעליו וסבה להפר מחשבתו...והשנית כי מגלה הסוד אך יצא יצא מדרך הצניעות והנה הוא מעביר על דעת בעל הסוד.

> A person is obligated to conceal a secret revealed to him by his fellow in a secretive manner, even if revealing it would not involve רכילות, because revealing the secret causes damage to the owner and results in the foiling of his plan... and, second, one who reveals a secret deviates from the path of modesty and violates the wish of the secret's owner.

Rabbeinu Yona writes explicitly that irrespective of any practical harm caused by disclosing private information, it constitutes a breach of trust and violates appropriate standards of צניעות ("modesty" or discretion).

Another relevant source is a responsum of Rav Menachem Mi-Rizbork (*Nimukei Rav Menachem Mi-Rizbork, Dinei Boshes*, printed in the responsa of Mahari Weil) addressing the case of a person who revealed to a number of people disparaging information about his wife, and then strictly ordered them not to disclose the information. Mahari Weil ruled that those who heard the report were required to come testify before *beis din* to testify against the husband for slandering his wife, because דברי הרב ודברי התלמיד דברי מי שומעין — their obligations to the Almighty supersede their pledge to the husband. The underlying assumption, of course, is that their pledge of secrecy was binding, but it was overridden by the halachic requirement to give testimony. Clearly, then, disclosing information about a person that he wants kept secret is forbidden, either as a strict halachic prohibition or on the level of general ethical conduct.

Perhaps the most striking expression of *Chazal*'s condemnation of spreading private information appears in a Midrashic passage (*Bamidbar Rabba, Masei* 23) discussing the disturbing story of King David and Uriya, a soldier in his army. As

---

6. The *Midrash Gadol U-Gedula* (published by Aharon Jellinek, *Beis Ha-Midrash*, vol. 3, pp. 126–127) likewise comments, "Concealing a secret is of great importance, for whoever reveals his fellow's secret is considered as though he shed blood, as it says, לא תלך רכיל בעמך."

we read in *Sefer Shemuel II* (11), King David ordered his general, Yoav, to assign Uriya to the front lines during a fierce war against Amon, so that Uriya would be killed. After Uriya's death, the *midrash* relates, the military officers were incensed at Yoav for causing Uriya's death, and they threatened to kill him. Yoav defended himself by showing them the note he had received from David, ordering him to place Uriya on the front lines. The Midrash comments that Yoav deserved to be punished for publicizing a personal letter from the king. Although this was done in self-defense, the Midrash nevertheless censures Yoav for disclosing personal information. This underscores the severity with which *Chazal* viewed violating one's fellow's trust by sharing personal information with others.[7]

II. Uncovering One's Personal Information Without Sharing It

Let us now turn our attention to the issue of uncovering another person's private information for his own knowledge, without making it public or sharing it with anyone. Intuitively, we understand that it is inappropriate to pry into another person's private affairs, such as by searching through his computer or personal documents or listening to his private conversations, but is this truly forbidden by *halacha*?

In this section, we will attempt to identify the source and nature of this prohibition and determine which precise Torah laws are transgressed when one violates his fellow's privacy.

ואהבת לרעך כמוך

It seems clear that respecting privacy is required by force of the general command of ואהבת לרעך כמוך, which requires one to treat others the way he would want them to treat him.[8] Quite obviously, no one wishes to have his privacy violated, even if the information does not become public, and, as such, the obligation of ואהבת לרעך כמוך would require us to respect other people's privacy just as we would want them to respect ours.[9]

---

7. We will discuss below the question of whether this is indeed forbidden even if disclosing the information is necessary for the sake of self-defense, as this Midrash seems to suggest.
8. See Rambam, *Hilchos Dei'os* 6:6 and *Sefer Ha-Mitzvos*, asei 206; *Sefer Ha-Chinuch*, mitzva 243; and *Semag*, asei 9.
9. This point is made by Rav Chayim Palagi in his *Chikekei Leiv*, Y.D. 1:49.

שואל שלא מדעת

Another possible basis for such a prohibition is the notion that a person "owns" his private information. According to many halachic authorities, *halacha* recognizes the concept of legal ownership over one's intellectual property.[10] Perhaps one is similarly considered the legal owner of his private information. As such, peering into a person's home, viewing medical records, or reading his personal correspondence would be forbidden on the grounds of שואל שלא מדעת — "borrowing" someone's property without his permission, which *halacha* equates with theft.

This theory was advanced by Rav Chaim Shabtai of Salonica (the "Maharchash") in *Toras Chayim* (3:47), in reference to reading someone else's personal correspondence. He writes that reading someone's letter without his consent constitutes שאילה שלא מדעת, as the writer has legal ownership over the letter he wrote to be read by a particular individual. Some have suggested applying the *Toras Chayim*'s theory to all situations of accessing private information, claiming that a person has legal ownership over all of his private information, and therefore obtaining such information without the "owner's" consent would constitute theft.[11]

The concept that violating someone's privacy constitutes theft may be reflected in the *Siach Yitzchak* commentary to the *siddur*, which asserts that when we confess גזלנו ("We have stolen") in the *Vidui* prayer, this includes חטאנו בהיזק ראייה — that we "stole" people's privacy by peering into their personal property. Classifying privacy violation under the category of theft might suggest that this prohibition stems from the unauthorized "use" of a person's "property."[12]

לא תלך רכיל בעמך

A particularly intriguing approach is taken by Rav Yaakov Chagiz in *Halachos Ketanos* (1:276), where he writes:

---

10. See *Headlines*, vol. 1, chapter 33.
11. Professor Nachum Rakover, in *Ha-Hagana Al Tzinas Ha-Prat* (pp. 114–115), cites a ruling of the Tel-Aviv Rabbinical Court written by Rav Avraham Sherman, in which Rav Sherman interprets the *Toras Chayim*'s responsum to mean that a person legally owns all of his private information: שכל מידע אישי של אדם יש לו בעלות עליו ואין רשות לזולתו לקחת מידע זו בניגוד לרצונו ובלא ידיעתו, ויש בזה איסור של שואל שלא מדעת. Professor Rakover dismisses this claim, arguing that the *Toras Chayim* referred only to a person's ownership over his letter, not ownership over all private information. Likewise, Rabbi J. David Bleich (*Bioethical Dilemmas*, vol. 1, p. 176) writes that Rav Sherman's "statement is conclusory and goes far beyond any statement found in the comments of *Torat Hayyim*."
12. This source was cited by Rav Yitzchak Zilberstein, *Shoshanas Ha-Amakim, Ve-Rapo Yerapei*, 58.

> נראה שיש איסור לבקש ולחפש מסתוריו של חבירו, ומה לי לא תלך רכיל לאחרים או לעצמו.
>
> It would seem that it is forbidden to seek and search for one's fellow's secrets. What difference is there between "Do not go around gossiping" for others or for oneself?

According to Rav Yaakov Chagiz, the prohibition of רכילות forbids not only sharing one's fellow's private information with others, but also accessing it for oneself. He contends that there is no difference between sharing confidential information with another person and accessing such information for oneself. After all, both have the same effect: someone who did not previously have personal information about another person is now privy to such information. Therefore, the prohibition of לא תלך רכיל forbids accessing someone's private information for oneself, just as it forbids sharing with another person such information that one already has.[13]

This is also implied by the *Tzava'as Rabbi Eliezer Ha-Gadol*, cited by the Chafetz Chayim:[14]

> בני אל תשב בחבורת האומרים גנאי מחבריהם כי כשהדברים עולים למעלה בספר נכתבים וכל העומדים שם נכתבין בשם חבורת רשע ובעלי לשון הרע.
>
> My son, do not sit in groups of people who speak of their fellow's disgrace, for when the words rise upwards, they are written in the book, and the ones standing there are recorded as an evil group and people who speak לשון הרע.

The Chafetz Chayim infers from this that simply sitting in the company of people who share unflattering information about others, even if one does not actively participate or necessarily believe what they say, constitutes לשון הרע. The implication, seemingly, is that accessing unflattering personal information itself qualifies as forbidden gossip, as Rav Yaakov Chagiz claimed.

היזק ראייה

The Mishnayos in *Maseches Bava Basra* (59b–60a) forbid neighbors from constructing windows from which they could peer into their neighbors' yards or that are facing their neighbors' windows. The Gemara (60a) famously cites as

---

13. Rav Asher Weiss, in a letter to Professor Rakover (printed as an appendix to the latter's *Ha-Hagana Al Tzinas Ha-Prat*, p. 316), claims that Rav Yaakov Chagiz did not actually intend to classify disclosing private information under the halachic category of רכילות, but rather sought to compare the severity of violating people's privacy in this fashion to the severity of gossip.
14. Introduction to *Chafetz Chayim*, lavin 4.

the source of this *halacha* the Torah's description of Bilaam being overcome by רוח אלקים ("the spirit of God") when he saw the way *Bnei Yisrael*'s tents were arranged as they encamped in the wilderness.[15] Bilaam noticed that אין פתחי אהליהם מכוונין זה לזה — the tents were arranged such that the entrances did not face one another, so that people could not peer into each other's tents. On this basis, the Gemara established the rule that neighbors may not have windows through which they can peer into each other's homes or yards.

The question arises as to whether the Mishnayos here establish a specific *halacha* relevant to neighbors or a general prohibition against violating people's privacy. On the one hand, we might approach this *halacha* as a "zoning law" of sorts, which dictates a policy relevant to neighboring residences. *Chazal* inferred from Bilaam's reaction to the Israelite camp the proper way that neighboring residences are to be constructed, but not a halachic prohibition against peering into another person's property. Indeed, the Gemara states that Bilaam noticed that the tents were arranged in such a way that the people could not peer into each other's tents, not that the people avoided peering. Alternatively, however, we may interpret the Gemara as viewing this verse as a Biblical source of a person's right to privacy. The fact that *Bnei Yisrael* ensured that their entrances did not face one another reveals that the Torah forbids looking upon people as they conduct their private affairs, and it is for this reason that *Chazal* forbid constructing windows from which one can peer into a neighbor's property.

The Ramban (commentary to *Bava Basra* 59a) seems to take a very clear stance on this issue. He writes that if a person built windows overlooking his neighbor's property, even with his neighbor's permission, he is halachically required to seal them. He explains:

> כיון דודאי אסור הוא למזיק להזיקו בראיה ולהסתכל בו לדעת, ואין אדם יכול ליזהר בכך לעמוד כל היום בעצימת עינים, על כרחנו נאמר לזה סתום חלונך ואל תחטא תדיר.

> Since it is certainly forbidden to cause damage by looking and to knowingly look at him, and since a person is unable to avoid this and spend the entire day with his eyes closed, we necessarily say to him: Seal your window so you do not sin all the time.

The Ramban here explicitly speaks of היזק ראייה as a halachic prohibition, and not merely as a matter of policy when building neighboring properties.

The Rambam (*Hilchos Shecheinim* 6:7, 11:4) disagrees and maintains that if a window was built with the neighbor's consent, the owner does not have to seal the window, even if the neighbor later rescinds his agreement. This ruling

---

15. וישא בלעם את עיניו וירא את ישראל שוכן לשבטיו ותהי עליו רוח אלקים (*Bamidbar* 24:2).

is codified by the *Shulchan Aruch* (C.M. 154:7), but the Rama adds that even in such a case, one must ensure that he will not peer into his neighbor's property:

אפילו למאן דאמר יש לו חזקה – היינו לגופו של חלון, דלא יוכל בעל החצר לסתמו או למחות בו, אבל הוא אסור לעמוד בחלון ולראות בחצר חבירו כדי שלא יזיקנו בראייתו, ובזה איסורא קעביד ולא מהני ליה חזקה, וזה יוכל בעל החצר למחות בו.

> Even according to the opinion that one can obtain a presumptive right [to have a window overlooking a neighbor's yard] — this applies only to the window itself, as the yard's owner cannot seal it or protest it [once it had been built with his consent]. However, it is forbidden for him to stand by the window and view his fellow's yard, so that he does not cause him damage through his viewing, as he thereby commits a violation, and there is no presumptive right for this, and the yard's owner can protest it.

The source of the Rama's comments is a responsum of the Rashba (2:1) concerning the case of a person who for twenty-five years had a window in his second floor overlooking his neighbor's yard. The man occasionally stood by the window to oversee the work in his vineyards, and his neighbor demanded that he stop looking through his window, as he thereby viewed the neighbor's yard. The Rashba ruled that even according to the opinion that the neighbor cannot demand that the window be sealed, it is nevertheless forbidden to look through the window into the neighbor's yard:

דבר ברור שאין שמעון יכול לעמוד בחלון כדי שלא יזיק בראייתו לראובן...אין לו להציץ ממנו לחצר ראובן כדי שלא יזיקנו בראייתו, ואין זה צריך לפנים.

> It is clear that Shimon may not stand by the window, so that he does not cause Reuven damage through his viewing... He may not peer through the window into Reuven's yard, so that he does not cause him damage through his viewing, and this does not require in-depth discussion.

Accordingly, all *poskim* agree that one may not peer into his fellow's property. The aforementioned debate revolves around the question of whether a person may keep a window that his neighbor had approved, trusting that the person would not peer into his home.

Similarly, the *Shulchan Aruch Ha-Rav* (*Hilchos Nizkei Mamon* 11) writes in the context of היזק ראייה that there is an outright prohibition to look into someone else's property:

אסור להסתכל בעסקיו ומעשיו של חבירו... שאם עושה אדם עסקיו בביתו וברשותו, אסור לראותו שלא מדעתו, שמא אינו חפץ שידעו ממעשיו ועסקיו.

> It is forbidden to look upon one's fellow's affairs and actions... For if a

person conducts his affairs in his home and in his property, it is forbidden to look at him against his will, because perhaps he does not want people to know about his actions and his affairs.

Later (13), the *Shulchan Aruch Ha-Rav* writes that this applies — albeit with one minor exception — even to a person walking in a public area from which he can see into people's private property through their windows:

אף בני רשות הרבים אינם רשאים לעמוד ולהסתכל אלא כשרואים ראיה קלה דרך הילוכם אין לחוש שהרי מזה אין יכול להזהר וצריך להיות צנוע בתשמישיו שראיה קלה בהם קשה עליו.

> People in the public domain are also not permitted to stand and look [into someone's property], but there is no concern when they glance briefly as they walk, as this cannot be avoided, and a person must conduct himself modestly in affairs regarding which [another's] brief glance would disturb him.

Pedestrians do not have to make a special effort to avoid glancing into the windows on the side of the street, but it is forbidden for them to stop and peer into people's private property.[16]

In any event, it seems quite clear from the aforementioned halachic sources that the law of היזק ראייה not only dictates protocol for constructing windows, but also entails a halachic prohibition against looking into other people's property.[17]

The question then becomes as to whether this prohibition applies specifically to viewing another person's property or to any invasion of a person's privacy.

The Ramban (*Bava Basra* 59b) defines the "damage" of היזק ראייה as consisting of three elements:

אי משום עין הרע, אי משום לישנא בישא, אי משום צניעותא.

Seeing another person as he conducts his private affairs causes damage through עין הרע (the "evil eye");[18] לשון הרע — by enabling, or perhaps instigating, the

---

16. By the same token, Rav Yitzchak Zilberstein notes that people in hospitals must ensure not to look into patients' rooms, which violates their privacy and thus violates the prohibition of היזק ראייה (*Shoshanas Ha-Amakim Be-Inyanei Halacha U-Refua*, p. 117).
17. This *halacha* yields vital contemporary importance with regard to the looming question surrounding the commercial use of drones for delivering goods, which is anticipated to become widespread in the near future. On May 22, 2016, the *Wall Street Journal* featured a debate between two legal experts as to whether companies should be allowed to fly their drones over people's properties without their consent. From the viewpoint of Halacha, it seems clear that the prohibition of היזק ראייה would certainly forbid one from operating an airborne camera recording one's yard from the air.
18. This refers to the Gemara's comment (*Bava Metzia* 107a; *Bava Basra* 2b) that it is

dissemination of unflattering information about him;[19] and צניעותא — the embarrassment of being seen tending to personal and private matters.[20]

Whereas the first factor (עין הרע) may likely apply only when one actually views a person's property, the other two are relevant to any form of privacy violation. If one violates his fellow's privacy by listening to his personal conversations or accessing private information through hacking and the like, he causes the same kind of damage as one who peers into his fellow's living room. As such, this would presumably be forbidden on the grounds of היזק ראייה.[21]

חרם דרבנו גרשום

A number of *poskim* addressed the question of whether accessing someone's personal information violates חרם דרבנו גרשום, the famous enactment issued by Rabbeinu Gershom forbidding reading other people's correspondence. As cited at the end of the responsa of the Maharam Mei-Rotenberg, Rabbeinu Gershom legislated שלא לראות בכתב חבירו ששולח לחבירו בלא ידיעתו — that one may not look upon that which his fellow wrote to someone else, without that person's consent. The text of the edict concludes, ואם זרקו מותר — once the letter has been discarded, we may presume that the parties no longer consider its content confidential, and thus it may be read.

This enactment was codified as *halacha* in *Be'er Ha-Gola* (end of Y.D. 334) and other sources.[22]

---

forbidden to gaze upon a person's field when it is laden with fresh produce, as one thereby casts an "evil eye" upon his property.

19. It is unclear what precisely the Ramban means by לישנא בישא, whether this refers to the concern that the viewer might be tempted to tell others what he saw or if the viewing itself constitutes a form of gossip. See Rav Rafael Stern's *Nizkei Shecheinim*, p. 136. Most likely, the Ramban refers here to the natural human tendency to reveal negative information about other people, and astutely observes that the process of לשון הרע often begins when one happens to be privy to secret, unflattering information about his fellow.

20. Others have noted that one who knows he can be seen is forced to limit his activity, and this, too, constitutes damage. See *Sema* 378:4; *Even Ha-Azel, Hilchos Shecheinim* 2:16; and *Kehillos Yaakov, Bava Basra* 5.

21. This point is made by Rav Yaakov Avraham Cohen in *Emek Ha-Mishpat* 3:26.

22. See, for example, *Kenesses Ha-Gedola*, Y.D. 334; *Birkei Yosef*, Y.D. 334:14. Significantly, as noted by Professor Rakover (*Ha-Hagana Al Tzin'as Ha-Prat*, p. 109, note 9), this enactment, as opposed to other measures legislated by Rabbeinu Gershom, was accepted as binding even by Sephardic communities.

The question has been asked as to why Rabbeinu Gershom felt compelled to enact a prohibition against reading other people's private correspondence, given that, as we have seen, this is in any event forbidden for several reasons. One possible answer is that Rabbeinu Gershom did not, in fact, introduce a new prohibition, but rather established

There is considerable discussion among recent and contemporary *poskim* as to whether Rabbeinu Gershom's edict extends to other forms of privacy violation, such as wiretapping and the like. Several authorities maintain that since there is no substantive difference between obtaining a person's private information by reading his letter and by secretly recording his conversations, there is no reason not to apply חרם דרבנו גרשום to the latter case.[23] Others, however, argue that a rabbinic edict cannot be expanded beyond its original parameters, even to situations in which the edict's rationale is applicable. Hence, since Rabbeinu Gershom specifically banned viewing written correspondence and said nothing about eavesdropping (not to mention wiretapping, which, quite obviously, was not available when the edict was issued one thousand years ago), his ban cannot be applied to listening to people's private conversations.[24]

With regard to email, however, it stands to reason that reading electronic communication is identical to reading written letters, and would thus fall under the חרם דרבנו גרשום even according to the minimalist approach to the ban. Even though the material is delivered digitally and not on paper, nevertheless, since Rabbeinu Gershom's edict speaks of written correspondence, it seems likely that this would include email.[25]

---

a חרם, condemning violators to excommunication. Alternatively, Rabbeinu Gershom perhaps extended this law even to situations in which the writer does not necessarily insist on secrecy, and thus reading the letter would not constitute a breach of privacy. An example would be postcards, which are not closed and sealed. According to this theory, reading postcards would not violate the standard prohibition of invading privacy, but would be forbidden by force of חרם דרבנו גרשום. (The question of whether postcards are included under the חרם דרבנו גרשום is addressed by, among others, the *Aruch Ha-Shulchan*, Y.D. 334:21.)

Rabbi Bleich (*Bioethical Dilemmas*, vol. 1, p. 177) suggests that Rabbeinu Gershom viewed violation of privacy not as a technical halachic prohibition, but rather as a general ethical breach, and therefore found it necessary to enact his ban. As we have seen, however, there appears to be ample evidence of a strict halachic prohibition against accessing private information.

23. These authorities include Rav Shlomo Daichovsky and Rav Tzvi Spitz, cited by Professor Rakover, p. 117. Rav Yaakov Avraham Cohen (*Emek Ha-Mishpat* 3:26) argues that if Rabbeinu Gershom banned reading a private letter, then *a fortiori* he would ban directly intercepting a person's communication through wiretapping and the like.

24. Rabbi Bleich (*Bioethical Dilemmas*, p. 177) writes: "If a formal ban was indeed necessary to engender a prohibition, there is no reason to assume that eavesdropping, either natural or electronic, was included in Rabbeinu Gershom's edict." Likewise, Rav Eliezer Shinkolovsky, writing in the journal *Ha-Ma'ayan* (37), writes: "לענ״ד לשונו של החרם "בכתב" ברורה ואינה מותירה מקום לספק שמדובר דווקא על קריאה בכתב של חבירו, והבא להרחיב את האיסור עליו הראייה.

25. This point was made by Rav Re'em Ha-Kohen of Otniel (http://archive.is/keqE): ביחס

Respecting Privacy as an Ethical Mandate

Irrespective of the potential halachic violations entailed in accessing someone's private information, a number of sources underscore the ethical mandate to respect people's privacy and to avoid accessing personal information that they presumably wish to keep private.

The *Sefer Chasidim* (461) writes that it is preferable to pray privately if attending the synagogue service would result in hearing confidential information. If a person knows that if he attends the *minyan* he will hear people gossiping and sharing private information, then he should remain at home in order to avoid hearing of other people's private affairs. Clearly, the *Sefer Chasidim* regards the discovery of private information as a grave matter, even if one has no intention of spreading it.

The unique severity of prying into people's private affairs is noted by Rav Eliezer Papo in *Pele Yoetz* (ערך סוד):

> וכמה מהגנות והדופי ואיסורי ואישורא מגיע על אותם המחטטים ומחפשים לידע סוד אחר על ידי שמיעה אחרי הכותל או גניבת דעת או פתיחת איגרות...וגם מזה נפיק חורבא ושנאה וקטטה ואש להבת המחלוקת עולה לאין מרפא. לכן שומר נפשו ירחק כל אלה כי תועבת ה׳ כל עושה אלה ואשרי תמימי דרך.

> How much disgrace, guilt, and sin fall upon those who investigate and search to find out another person's secret by listening behind a wall, or by deception, or by opening letters… Additionally, this can have disastrous consequences — hatred, fighting, and the raging fire of strife rising without a cure. Therefore, one who wishes to protect his soul should distance himself from all this, for anyone who does this is abominable to God, and fortunate are those who follow the path of innocence.

להודעת טקסט ולדואר אלקטרוני ברור שאין כל הבדל ממכתב מוסתר ואין שום היתר לקרא מייל והודעה של הזולת והעובר על זה עובר בחרם. One might have argued that given the insecure nature of digital communication, which can be accessed and disseminated far more easily than print material, one who sends an email anticipates the possibility of its public exposure, and thus it may be read or passed along unless the sender specifically requested confidentiality. It seems more likely, however, that people do not expect electronic correspondence to be spread without their consent. To the contrary, whereas printed letters are handled by the postal service, email is sent directly to the recipient without any intermediary, and thus there may be even a greater expectation of privacy when sending an email than when mailing a letter. As such, email correspondence should certainly fall under the חרם דרבנו גרשום.

Halachically Sanctioned Snooping

Notwithstanding the importance of respecting privacy, it is clear that there are instances in which certain forms of information-gathering are permissible.

One such situation is when a person is considering a purchase or entering into a relationship with another person. One who sells merchandise is halachically obligated to notify the buyer of any defects,[26] and before a woman is betrothed, she must inform the suitor of any physical deformities.[27] By the same token, it is permissible for the prospective buyer or husband to perform "due diligence" and inquire about potential defects. In fact, under certain circumstances, one who failed to perform due diligence is denied the right to void the transaction or to divorce the woman, as the failure to research in advance amounts to implicit acceptance of any and all subsequently discovered defects. Thus, for example, the *Shulchan Aruch* (E.H. 117:5–6) rules that when it is possible for a man to have his female relatives inspect a prospective spouse's body for defects, failure to do so before betrothal constitutes implicit acceptance.[28] Therefore, if he later decides to divorce the woman upon discovering the defects, he must pay the *kesuba*.[29] Certainly, then, a person is permitted to "dig" for relevant information before entering into a marriage or any kind of commercial relationship.

However, a clear distinction exists between this kind of information-gathering and "snooping" into a person's private affairs. In the example noted above, the person "inspects" a prospective mate by asking people close to her for relevant and readily accessible information. This is far different than "spying" on her private life or accessing private information that she presumably desires to be kept secret.

The question is thus under what circumstances it would be permissible to violate someone's privacy to uncover personal information that is relevant to the decision of whether or not to enter into a relationship with that person.[30]

---

26. *Shulchan Aruch*, C.M. 228:6.
27. *Maggid Mishneh*, *Hilchos Ishus* 28:8, cited by *Chelkas Mechokek* and *Beis Shmuel*, E.H. 117:1.
28. See also E.H. 39:4.
29. The *Perisha* writes that even if the prospective bride does not normally bathe in a public bathhouse, such that the prospective groom cannot ask his female relatives to check her for defects, nevertheless, it is expected that he check through some other means, and if he did not, he cannot later divorce without paying the *kesuba*.
30. It goes without saying that this question is asked only with regard to information that is indeed relevant to the decision. Any process of "digging" for information must begin with the understanding the all people are imperfect; not every stain on a person's record or flaw in his character renders him ineligible as a marriage partner or employee. As such, we cannot speak of even a possibility of allowing accessing personal information

It seems clear that when it comes to the general ethical issue of respecting privacy, there is greater room for exceptions when the information is necessary for a legitimate constructive purpose. Certainly, if a person is making a fateful decision such as whether to marry or hire a certain individual, it would not strike us as unethical to access information that is relevant to that person's eligibility.[31] This is not the case, however, with regard to strict halachic prohibitions of שאילה שלא מדעת (which constitutes theft) or היזק ראייה. Nowhere do we find *halacha* permitting stealing or causing damage to one's fellow for a constructive purpose (other than self-defense). Hence, since it seems quite clear, as noted above, that accessing private information that someone clearly wishes to keep private transgresses the prohibition of היזק ראייה, and it is possible that it may also constitute שאילה שלא מדעת — a form of theft — this would seem to be forbidden even when that person is being considered for marriage or any other type of relationship. Although it is certainly acceptable to try to access readily available information about the person — such as, for example, by examining his public posts and comments on social media sites, and asking friends and acquaintances about his character — it would be forbidden to secretly access information that he clearly wishes to keep private, such as email correspondences, medical records, browsing history, and private conversations.[32]

Opening a Letter to Save One's Life

To illustrate the severity with which Halacha treats the issue of privacy, let us examine a striking responsum of Rav Yaakov Chagiz earlier in *Halachos Ketanos* (173). There he addresses the case of a person given a letter to deliver to someone, and the messenger has reason to suspect that the content of the letter could

---

when considering entering into a relationship with someone unless that information is clearly relevant.
31. This would also be true if we build solely upon the prohibition of לא תלך רכיל בעמך, as רכילות is permitted when the information is needed for a legitimate purpose.
32. Rav Yitzchak Zilberstein (*Aleinu Leshabei'ach, Bamidbar, Teshuvos*, 52) addresses the situation of a boy who underwent a blood test, and the lab technician happened to be a girl for whom he was suggested as a prospective *shidduch*. The question arose whether the girl was entitled to check the blood for conditions beyond those for which he was being tested, as part of her attempt to determine his eligibility. Rav Zilberstein briefly considered allowing her to perform the extra tests, because the boy, knowing that he was suggested as a potential marriage partner for her, might expect her to do so. In the end, Rav Zilberstein dismisses this argument and forbids conducting the additional examinations. In any event, the underlying assumption is clearly that even though the patient was suggested as a *shidduch*, she may not access personal information about him that he would presumably not agree to disclose.

endanger him. Rav Chagiz does not specify the kind of danger entailed, but he compares the situation to the aforementioned story of Uriya, the soldier in David's army with whom David sent a letter to the general, Yoav, instructing Yoav to station Uriya in the front lines so that he would be killed. This comparison leads us to believe that Rav Chagiz speaks of a case in which the messenger faced mortal danger if he delivered the letter — just as Uriya lost his life by delivering King David's note to Yoav.

If so, we would certainly assume that the messenger would be allowed to open the letter to see if, indeed, it posed a risk to his life, so that he could protect himself. Yet this is not how Rav Chagiz rules in this case. He writes: אין לו תקנה אלא פורר וזורק לרוח או מטיל לים — the only solution is to destroy the letter. Oddly, Rav Chagiz forbids the messenger to violate the dispatcher's privacy and open the letter, despite the potential risk to his life, but he does allow the messenger to destroy the letter.

How can we explain this seemingly peculiar ruling? Why would this prohibition override a threat to human life, and why is destroying the letter different from reading it?

The answer can be found, perhaps, in a number of sources that point to the possibility that theft, under certain circumstances, is forbidden even when it is necessary to save one's life.

The Gemara in *Bava Kama* (60b) establishes that אסור להציל עצמו בממון חבירו — one may not use someone else's money or property to save his life. The Rosh (*Bava Kama* 6:12) explains this to mean that one who uses his fellow's assets to save his life must then repay the money that he used.[33] This is the view codified by the *Shulchan Aruch* (C.M. 359:4), who writes that one may seize another person's possessions to save his life, but he must then repay his fellow for his loss.

Rashi, however, seems to imply otherwise. According to Rashi's reading of the Gemara,[34] King David refused to permit setting fire to a field in which Philistine warriors were hiding, because it is forbidden to save oneself with someone else's property, אסור להציל עצמו בממון חבירו. Despite the fact that these enemy soldiers clearly posed a threat to his life, David nevertheless forbade burning the field, and he did not allow his men to destroy it even with the intention of compensating the owner. Apparently, as noted by the *Parshas Derachim* (19), Rashi maintains that one must sacrifice his life rather than take or destroy someone else's property. The *Parshas Derachim* leaves open the question of why

---

33. See also *Tosfos*, ד"ה מהו.
34. ד"ה ויצילה: שלא ישרפוה הואיל ואסור להציל את עצמו בממון חבירו.

the concern for human life does not override the prohibition of theft. How could Rashi require surrendering one's life to avoid stealing?[35]

In truth, this question may arise even according to the Rosh's position. The *Tur* (C.M. 359) codifies the Rosh's view as follows:

> אפילו אם הוא בסכנת מות ובא לגזול את חבירו ולהציל את נפשו אסור לו לגזול אם לא על דעת לשלם, דודאי אין לך דבר העומד בפני פיקוח נפש. לכך הוא רשאי ליטלו ולהציל נפשו, אבל לא יקחנו אלא על דעת לשלם.

> Even if one faces the risk of death, and he comes to steal from his friend to save his life, it is forbidden for him to steal unless he does so with the intent of repaying, for certainly nothing stands in the way of concern for life. Therefore, he is allowed to take it to save his life, but he should not take it unless he does so with the intention of repaying.

Rav Yaakov Ettlinger (*Binyan Tziyon* 167–169, 171) notes that the *Tur* does not formulate this *halacha* as a law that unconditionally permits saving oneself with another person's possessions and then requires repaying. Rather, the *Tur* presents the intent to repay as a precondition to the halachic license to steal. In other words, the *Tur* understood that even according to the Rosh, the prohibition of theft is not overridden by the concern for human life, except if one steals with the intent to repay. We might thus conclude that in a situation in which one knows from the outset that he will be unable to repay the money he wishes to seize to protect himself, it is forbidden for him to take the money, and he must instead surrender his life.

---

35. The Maharatz Chayos (*Bava Kama* ad loc.) suggests that according to Rashi, the *gemara*'s discussion follows the minority view cited in the Yerushalmi (*Avoda Zara* 2) that the prohibition against theft is not overridden by the concern for human life. This view in the Yerushalmi, the Maharatz Chayos adds, likely refers to Rabbi Meir, who ruled that witnesses may not falsely sign a written piece of testimony even under the threat of death (*Kesubos* 19a). The Ramban (*Kesubos* ad loc.) cites a source stating explicitly that Rabbi Meir included theft together with murder, idolatry, and sexual immorality as violations that must be avoided even at the expense of one's life.
Rav Moshe Feinstein (*Iggeros Moshe*, Y.D. 214) writes that the situation faced by King David posed only a remote risk to life, and he therefore did not wish to use his royal authority to order razing the field.
Rav Asher Weiss (*Minchas Asher*, *Vayikra*, 50) explains Rashi's comments to mean simply that אסור להציל עצמו בממון חבירו allows one to rescue himself with his fellow's property only if no other options are available, and in King David's situation, the field did not have to be destroyed to avert the threat posed by the Philistines.
Others interpret Rashi's comments as referring to the *Binyan Tziyon*'s position cited below.

Apparently, even according to the accepted view that one may seize another person's property to save his life, this license is not absolute. Under certain circumstances, one is required to surrender his life to avoid stealing.

This theory is developed by Rav Shmuel Rozovsky (*Zichron Shmuel*, 83), who explains the right to take a person's money to save himself based on the Torah obligation to rescue a fellow Jew in danger. Rav Rozovsky asserts that even according to the Rosh, it is fundamentally forbidden to save oneself by seizing another person's property. In practice, this is generally permitted only because of the Torah obligation to save a fellow Jew from danger. The risk to life does not override the prohibition of theft, but rather imposes an obligation upon those capable of helping to rescue the endangered individual. As such, if he is able to rescue himself by seizing another person's property, he is allowed to do so, since that person in any event bears an obligation to spend this money if this is necessary to rescue his fellow from danger. Accordingly, Rav Rozovsky writes that if a situation arises in which a person, for whatever reason, would not be obligated to pay money to rescue a fellow Jew in danger, then the endangered individual would be required to surrender his life rather than take the person's property to save himself. Since the license to save oneself with another person's property is granted only by the force of that person's obligation to rescue his fellow in danger, one is allowed to take that person's property only in situations in which he bears an obligation to give it.

This theory — that one may not, in principle, steal to save his life — is likely predicated upon the premise that the rule of פקוח נפש, that Torah law is suspended for the sake of protecting human life, applies only to מצוות בין אדם למקום — our obligations to God, as opposed to our obligations to our fellow man. There is no halachic mandate allowing us to violate the Torah's code of interpersonal conduct to save our lives. Rav Ettlinger advances this notion in explaining Rashi's position that one may not steal to save his life — a position that Rav Ettlinger claims is accepted, fundamentally, as the *halacha*.[36]

A practical application would be stealing an organ that one needs to save his life. For example, if a surgeon is in a position to secretly take and harvest a patient's kidney for the purpose of a life-saving transplant, this is clearly forbidden, even if the procedure poses no health risks to the patient. Since the patient

---

36. Rav Ettlinger raises the question of why, according to his theory, the Gemara (*Yoma* 82b) needs to explain the reason that one may not kill to save his life. Seemingly, this law is self-evident, in light of the fact that פקוח נפש does not override the Torah's interpersonal code. Rav Ettlinger answers that although interpersonal laws may not be violated to save oneself, one is certainly allowed to save himself with his fellow's property with his permission, and thus one may have thought that he may likewise kill to save his life if the other person agrees to be killed for this purpose.

bears no obligation to give his kidney to rescue another person, it may not be taken from him against his will.

Possibly, we might explain the surprising ruling of the *Halachos Ketanos* that one may not read someone else's letter, even if he is concerned about it containing a threat to his life, along these lines. He perhaps maintains that a person has legal ownership over material he sends by mail, and reading his mail without his permission thus constitutes theft. However, unlike the theft of tangible possessions, the "theft" of private information can never be returned; the violator of one's privacy can never "repay" the privacy he has taken from him. As such, the *Halachos Ketanos* ruled that one may not save his life by accessing someone's private, confidential information. He may destroy another person's physical property with the intent to repay, but he may not "rob" his personal information. Therefore, the *Halachos Ketanos* permits destroying the letter, but forbids reading it.[37]

A possible precedent to this ruling is the aforementioned passage in the Midrash (*Bamidbar Rabba, Masei* 23) claiming that Yoav was punished for showing his officers the letter sent by King David instructing him to position Uriya in a place in which he would be killed in battle. As the Midrash describes, Yoav showed his men the letter after they threatened to kill him for what he did to Uriya: נתקבצו כל ראשי החיילים על יואב להרגו...הראה להם את הכתב ("All the heads of the troops assembled against Yoav to kill him…he showed them the letter"). Nevertheless, the Midrash condemns Yoav's decision, stating that he was severely punished for this offense. The Midrash's comments may be understood in light of the ruling of the *Halachos Ketanos* that divulging private information is forbidden even for the purpose of saving one's life.[38]

As a practical matter, it is unlikely that this ruling should be accepted as

---

37. The *Halachos Ketanos* speaks in this responsum specifically of a letter upon which the writer wrote חדר"ג — applying the חרם דרבנו גרשום to the content of the letter — seemingly suggesting that otherwise, the deliverer would be allowed to read the letter for the purpose of protecting himself. The reason, it would seem, is that this declaration is needed to affirm the writer's insistence on confidentiality. If the letter did not bear this sign, then the deliverer may rely on the possibility that the writer did not intend the letter to be confidential, and he may therefore read the letter for the sake of protecting himself.

38. There may, however, be other reasons for why Yoav should have refused to show the letter. Since David was the king, showing the letter against David's presumed wishes constituted מרד במלכות — betrayal of the king — which is punishable by death. The *Meshech Chochma* (*Vayelech, haftara*) explains that in this case, revealing the letter created a grave חילול ה', and was therefore forbidden even for the sake of protection. Others have suggested that revealing the letter caused David humiliation, and the Gemara (*Sota* 10b) states that one should surrender his life to avoid publicly humiliating his fellow,

authoritative *halacha*. Rav Moshe Feinstein rejects out of hand the possibility that one should surrender his life to avoid theft.[39] Certainly, then, we would presumably permit invading someone's privacy when this is necessary to protect human life.[40] Nevertheless, this analysis, and the sources cited, underscore the gravity with which *halacha* treats the violation of people's privacy and accessing of their personal information.

Violating Privacy for Public Safety

We should note that numerous sources state explicitly that revealing someone's secrets is allowed in order to protect other people. Commenting on the sixth of the Ten Commandments, לא תרצח (*Shemos* 20:12), Ibn Ezra writes that the Torah prohibition against murder applies even to certain forms of indirect murder, including withholding secret information that is needed to save lives:

> או שנגלה לך סוד שתוכל להצילו מן המות אם תגלהו לו, ואם לא גלית אתה כמו רוצח.

> Or, if a secret was revealed to you and you can save someone from death by revealing it to him — if you do not reveal it, you are like a murderer.

Additionally, several commentators note that the Torah (*Vayikra* 19:16) juxtaposes the prohibition against gossip (לא תלך רכיל בעמך) with that of לא תעמוד על דם רעך — sitting idly while one's fellow faces danger — to teach that the former is suspended for the sake of the latter.[41] If a person has confidential information that could save a life, he is required to divulge it.

Accordingly, Rav Moshe Sternbuch (*Teshuvos Ve-Hanhagos* 1:869) rules that if a doctor determined that his patient is physically unfit to drive — such as in the case of an ophthalmologist who diagnoses his patient with a visual impairment that compromises his ability to drive safely — he can and must inform the relevant government authorities. Although medical information is confidential, the doctor must break his trust of confidentiality for the sake of public safety. Rav Ovadia Yosef (*Yechaveh Da'as* 4:60) issued a similar ruling

---

though this assumes that the Gemara's statement is to be taken literally, a matter that is subject to considerable debate.

39. In the responsum referenced above, note 35.
40. Rav Asher Weiss, in a letter to Professor Rakover (p. 249), dismisses the possibility that the concern for human life would not override the prohibition of theft. He writes that the prohibition against invading privacy is less severe than theft, and certainly would be waived to save a life or even to save oneself from a large financial loss or great distress. Even he, however, cautions against flippant and irresponsible breaches of this law: אין להקל ראש באיסור זה משום תועלת מועטה.
41. See *Moshav Zekeinim*, *Or Ha-Chayim*, Netziv (*Ha'amek Davar*), and others.

concerning a patient with epilepsy. If the doctor determines that this condition makes it unsafe for the patient to drive, he must notify the authorities.

It stands to reason that this would also apply to the case with which we began — the FBI's demand that Apple unlock Syed Farook's mobile phone. Given the international threat of Islamic terrorism and the vital importance of intelligence information in identifying and capturing potential attackers and their accomplices, accessing the information on a terrorist's device would certainly appear to fall under the category of public safety, which, as noted, overrides the prohibition against invading privacy.

Advancing Justice Through DNA Technology: Using DNA To Solve Crimes

September 9, 2014

The past decade has seen great advances in a powerful criminal justice tool: deoxyribonucleic acid, or DNA. DNA can be used to identify criminals with incredible accuracy when biological evidence exists. By the same token, DNA can be used to clear suspects and exonerate persons mistakenly accused or convicted of crimes. In all, DNA technology is increasingly vital to ensuring accuracy and fairness in the criminal justice system.

News stories extolling the successful use of DNA to solve crimes abound. For example, in 1999, New York authorities linked a man through DNA evidence to at least 22 sexual assaults and robberies that had terrorized the city. In 2002, authorities in Philadelphia, Pennsylvania, and Fort Collins, Colorado, used DNA evidence to link and solve a series of crimes (rapes and a murder) perpetrated by the same individual. In the 2001 "Green River" killings, DNA evidence provided a major breakthrough in a series of crimes that had remained unsolved for years despite a large law enforcement task force and a $15 million investigation.

DNA is generally used to solve crimes in one of two ways. In cases where a suspect is identified, a sample of that person's DNA can be compared to evidence from the crime scene. The results of this comparison may help establish whether the suspect committed the crime. In cases where a suspect has not yet been identified, biological evidence from the crime scene can be analyzed and compared to offender profiles in DNA databases to help identify the perpetrator. Crime scene evidence can also be linked to other crime scenes through the use of DNA databases.

For example, assume that a man was convicted of sexual assault. At the time of his conviction, he was required to provide a sample of his DNA, and the resulting DNA profile was entered into a DNA database. Several years later, another sexual assault was committed. A Sexual Assault Nurse Examiner worked with the victim and was able to obtain biological evidence from the rape. This evidence was analyzed, the resulting profile was run against a DNA database, and a match was made to the man's DNA profile. He was apprehended, tried, and sentenced for his second crime. In this hypothetical case, he was also prevented from committing other crimes during the period of his incarceration.

DNA evidence is generally linked to DNA offender profiles through DNA databases. In the late 1980s, the federal government laid the groundwork for a system of national, state, and local DNA databases for the storage and exchange of DNA profiles. This system, called the Combined DNA Index System (CODIS), maintains DNA profiles obtained under the federal, state, and local systems in a set of databases that are available to law enforcement agencies across the country for law enforcement purposes. CODIS can compare crime scene evidence to a database of DNA profiles obtained from convicted offenders. CODIS can also link DNA evidence obtained from different crime scenes, thereby identifying serial criminals.

In order to take advantage of the investigative potential of CODIS, in the late 1980s and early 1990s, states began passing laws requiring offenders convicted of certain offenses to provide DNA samples. Currently all 50 states and the federal government have laws requiring that DNA samples be collected from some categories of offenders.

Copyright © justice.gov

DNA as Halachic Evidence

DNA (deoxyribonucleic acid) has become a mainstay of legal and criminal investigation, and an invaluable tool for forensic experts and others seeking evidence of identity. Strands of DNA are found in every cell of the human body, and they contain all the information about a person's physical makeup. All it takes is a single thread of hair, a piece of a fingernail, a drop of saliva, or even a used tissue to determine the person's identity. Thus, DNA can be taken from these samples and matched against samples provided by the person in question to conclusively resolve many questions. DNA samples of alleged family members can also be compared to one another to determine whether they are indeed related. This method is used in a wide range of circumstances, such as in criminal investigations, to affirm biological relationships, and so on.

The question as to the status of DNA evidence in *halacha* came to the fore after the 9/11 terror attacks, when fifteen cases involving wives of presumed victims were presented to *batei din* in the New York area. The deadly inferno that consumed and destroyed the Twin Towers on that tragic day consumed scores of people without leaving behind discernible remains. Forensic teams were forced to collect DNA samples and match them up with reference samples provided by the bereaved families (such as hair from a brush). The question arose as to whether such evidence of death was sufficient to halachically prove that the husband had perished, and thus allow the widows to remarry.

The Beth Din of America, under the leadership of Rav Gedalia Dov Schwartz, handled ten of these cases, and permitted all ten women to remarry based on DNA evidence.[1] This policy was in line with the decision of the *beis din* of Rav Shmuel Wosner in Bnei-Brak, which issued a formal statement on the topic that was later published in the journal *Techumin*[2] and reproduced by Rabbi Dr. Avraham Sofer Abraham in *Nishmas Avraham*.[3] The statement determined that a match between DNA remnants found at the scene of the attack and a reference sample may be considered קרוב לסימן מובהק — nearly a clear-cut sign of identity, which is a sufficient level of evidence to allow a woman to remarry. The *dayanim* added, however, that a wife should not remarry on the basis of DNA samples

---

1. See Rav Schwartz's responsum on the subject in *Hadarom* (5763/2003) and Rav Chaim Jachter's essays on the topic in *Kol Torah* (vol. 12, no. 28), available online at http://koltorah.org/ravj/Agunot%201.htm.
2. *Techumin*, vol. 21, p. 121.
3. Vol. 3, p. 70.

alone, but rather when there is also good reason to assume that the husband had died. Since this was certainly the case with the victims of 9/11 who were in their offices at the time of the attack, the wives were declared widows and thus permitted to remarry.

Rav Zalman Nechemia Goldberg, in an article published in a later volume of *Techumin*,[4] went further, asserting that DNA evidence of death qualifies as an actual סימן מובהק. He noted that DNA evidence cannot be treated as less then טביעת עין — recognition of a dead man's appearance. *Halacha* permits a woman to remarry if someone who knew her husband's appearance identified a cadaver as her husband.[5] Rav Goldberg argued that DNA identification via a professional laboratory cannot be regarded as less proof than general recognition, and thus suffices to permit the woman to remarry. Rav Yosef Shalom Elyashiv similarly ruled that DNA evidence of identity qualifies as a סימן מובהק.[6]

The question remains, however, as to whether DNA evidence would suffice in areas of *halacha* requiring higher levels of proof. When it comes to cases involving a potential *aguna*, in which a husband is presumed dead and the wife is unable to remarry without confirmation of the husband's death, there are longstanding *halachic* precedents to relax standards of evidence. Quite reasonably, then, DNA evidence is generally accepted as valid proof in this regard, especially in the presence of other strong indications of death. There are, however, other contexts in which stronger proof is required. For example, the famous halachic axiom of המוציא מחבירו עליו הראיה establishes that *beis din* will not rule in favor of a plaintiff, awarding him money from the defendant, without the formal testimony of two valid witnesses. If DNA testing can somehow prove that money is owed, would this be sufficient grounds for *beis din* to award money to the plaintiff? This question becomes relevant in cases in which someone claims to be a child of a deceased person and demands a share of the estate, or when a woman demands alimony payments from her ex-husband for her child whom the husband claims to be the product of an adulterous affair. Would a DNA test's results suffice to determine — or disprove — the child's relationship to the father in such cases?

Scientific Data and Halacha

Before examining specific areas of *halacha* to determine whether DNA evidence would suffice, let us first address the more general question as to the status of

---

4. Vol. 23, p. 116. A segment of this article was also reproduced in *Nishmas Avraham*.
5. See *Yevamos* 120a; *Shulchan Aruch*, E.H. 17.
6. Cited in *Nishmas Avraham*, p. 75.

scientifically-obtained information in *halacha*. In light of the fact that DNA testing did not exist in the times of *Chazal*, does such data carry any halachic weight at all? Does information obtained through modern scientific methods affect *halacha*, or should it be disregarded?

A precedent for relying on such data in the process of halachic decision-making is a fascinating story told by Rabbeinu Yehuda Ha-Chasid about Rav Saadia Gaon (*Sefer Ha-Chasidim* 232). A wealthy man traveled far from home with his servant, leaving behind his wife, who was pregnant with their only child. The man died, whereupon his servant seized control over his assets, claiming to be the man's son. Years later, the man's true son heard about what happened, and he wanted to claim his fortune. The case came before Rav Saadia Gaon, who devised a "scientific" solution to the problem. He had blood drawn from both men who claimed to be the son of the deceased, and each one's blood was placed in a separate container. He then had a bone taken from the father's remains, and the bone was placed in one jar and then the other. The bone absorbed the blood of the man's son, but not the blood of the servant. Rav Saadia Gaon awarded the estate to the real son, claiming that the bone absorbed his blood because of their biological relationship.

Clearly, Rav Saadia felt that this method was reliable; he considered this "blood test" sufficient proof to extract a large fortune from its presumed owner and award it to someone else.

Many have noted, however, that Rav Saadia Gaon's ruling runs in opposition to the view expressed by the Rivash (447), who denies the validity of scientific and medical findings with respect to *halacha*. The Rivash writes:

אין לנו לדון בדיני תורתנו ומצוותיה על פי חכמי הטבע והרפואה, שאם נאמין לדבריהם, אין תורה מן השמיים, חלילה... כי לא מפי הטבע והרפואה, אנו חיין, ואנחנו על חכמינו ז"ל, נסמוך, אפילו יאמרו לנו על ימין שהוא שמאל, שהם קבלו האמת ופירושי המצוה איש מפי איש, עד משה רבינו, ע"ה.

> We should not reach decisions regarding the laws of our Torah and its commands based on the scholars of science and medicine, because if we trust their words, then there is no Torah from heaven, God forbid… For we do not rely upon science and medicine, and we instead rely on our Sages, *z"l*, even if they say that right is left, for they have received the truth and the interpretations of the law, one person from the next, back to Moshe Rabbeinu *a"h*.

In truth, however, it is far from clear that the Rivash would be in disagreement with Rav Saadia Gaon in this regard. The Rivash speaks here of situations in which scientific conclusions clash with accepted halachic axioms and would alter the practical conclusion. For example, he mentions the issue of טריפות — fatal medical conditions in an animal that render it forbidden for consumption. As the Rivash notes, the conditions outlined by *Chazal* for determining a fatal illness differ from those noted by the scientific experts of his time, and yet we classify an animal as permissible or forbidden based on the guidelines presented by our Sages.⁷ It is thus quite possible that the Rivash would accept Rav Saadia Gaon's view that scientifically-obtained data can be used as factual evidence when no such evidence is available in Rabbinic sources.⁸

Indeed, Rav Yitzchak Herzog, in a responsum printed in the journal *Assia*, emphatically supported the use of scientifically-obtained data as factual evidence in halachic decision-making, and sharply condemned those who disapprove of such use:

מה שייך לדבר על נאמנות הרופאים בדבר שנתקבל לברור מכל גדולי המדע הרפואי בכל העולם כולו...ואיזה הבדל גדול בין המדע הרפואי שבימיהם ושבימינו...חבל שבעוד שהמדע הולך וכובש עולמות ומגלה סודי סודות, אם כי גם הוא טועה לפרקים, אנו בקשר לעניני מדע הנוגעים לתורה הקדושה משקיעים ראשינו בחול...

> How is it relevant to speak of the reliability of physicians when it comes to something that is definitively accepted by all the greatest medical scholars throughout the world? ... And what a vast difference there is between the medical science in their [*Chazal*'s] time and in our times... It is a shame that while science is continually breaking new ground and revealing deep secrets, even if it is occasionally mistaken, we, in regard to scientific matters that are relevant to the sacred Torah, bury our heads in the sand...⁹

By contrast, Rav Eliezer Waldenberg (*Tzitz Eliezer* 13:104) dismisses the precedent of Rav Saadia Gaon's "blood test." He writes that to the contrary, the Gemara in *Maseches Nidda* (31a) establishes which parts of an infant are formed from the father's sperm and which from the mother's body, and states that the

---

7. The context of the Rivash's discussion is a complicated case concerning a widow who gave birth to a baby during the eighth month after her husband's passing, and the child died less than thirty days after birth. The doctors determined that the baby was fully formed at the time of birth, in opposition to the view of *Chazal* that a child born during the eighth month of pregnancy is not fully formed. The question thus arose as to whether this widow required *chalitza*. In this instance, the medical professionals' view yielded the opposite halachic ruling to that of *Chazal*.
8. This point is made by Rav Avraham Price in his *Mishnas Avraham* commentary to the *Sefer Chasidim* (1:291).
9. *Assia*, vol. 35, p. 49.

blood is received from the mother. As such, Rav Waldenberg contends, the nature of a person's blood can confirm his relationship to his mother, but not to his father. Rav Waldenberg opines that Rav Saadia Gaon's method cannot set a halachic precedent, because it is not mentioned anywhere in the Talmud or in a halachic source, and because we do not have more details about how exactly this procedure was done.[10] Accordingly, Rav Waldenberg rules that one may not rely upon blood tests to ascertain biological relationships for halachic purposes. He cites this ruling — along with the proof from the Gemara in *Maseches Nidda* — from Rav Bentzion Meir Chai Uziel (*Sha'arei Uziel* 40:1:18).[11]

However, as the aforementioned ruling of numerous leading contemporary and recent *poskim* after the World Trade Center tragedy would seem to indicate, it has become accepted to rely on scientifically-obtained data as evidence with respect to halachic matters.[12] What remains to be seen, then, is whether and to what extent DNA evidence suffices as proof in different situations in which proof of identity is needed.

Determining *Mamzerus*

Can DNA testing be used in cases of suspected or confirmed infidelity, to determine whether one's presumed child is indeed his child or a *mamzer*, the product of his wife's adulterous relationship?

The Gemara in *Maseches Bava Basra* (58a) tells of a man who, before his death, overheard his wife say that only one of their ten sons was his biological child, as the others resulted from her adulterous relationships. The man bequeathed his entire estate to his single biological son, but it was unknown which son this was. After his death, the case came before Rabbi Bena'a, who instructed the sons to go to the father's grave and strike it until his soul revealed

---

10. Rav Waldenberg adds that the *Gemara* lists bones among the body parts received from the father, and this may have been the reason why Rav Saadia Gaon's method was reliable, as it involved the bones. See also *Ben Yehoyada*, *Makkos* 23b ד"ה ברם.
11. This was also the position taken by Rav Yehoshua Ehrenberg (*Devar Yehoshua*, E.H. 5). We might question the assumption implicitly made by Rav Waldenberg that the Gemara in *Nidda* truly intended to establish the biological fact that a person's blood is formed solely by the mother's body and is not affected by the father. As with many aggadic passages in the Talmud, we cannot necessarily apply the Gemara's comment to determine the practical *halacha*. (Admittedly, however, this particular passage has been noted and applied in a halachic context; see *Bei'ur Ha-Gra*, Y.D. 263:2.) Moreover, even if we do accept the literal reading of the Gemara's remark, it does not negate the possibility that the nature and composition of a person's blood is affected by the father, even if it was initially formed by the mother.
12. See also the sources cited in the article in *Assia* mentioned above, note 9.

to them the answer. Nine of the men went to the grave and began striking it, but the tenth could not bring himself to disrespect his father in this fashion. Rabbi Bena'a determined that the son who refused to violate the grave was the biological son. The Rashbam comments that this ruling was issued as a שודא דדייני — a discretionary judgment issued in the absence of true evidence. In other words, the fact that this tenth son did not participate in the desecration of the grave did not prove that he was the biological son, but it gave Rabbi Bena'a a reason to choose one son over the others.

The Rashash raises the question of why Rabbi Bena'a did not utilize Rav Saadia Gaon's method and see which of the brothers' blood was absorbed into the father's bone.[13] He suggests that Rav Saadia Gaon's method would have constituted real evidence, to the extent that the other brothers would then be considered *mamzerim*. Rabbi Bena'a's solution did not provide actual evidence that could establish a status of *mamzerus*, but simply gave him reason to award the estate to one brother over the others. He did not want clear-cut proof of the true son's identity, as this would result in assigning the others the status of *mamzerim*.

Two important practical conclusions emerge from the Rashash's comments. First, he clearly maintains that scientific experimentation suffices as evidence even to establish a child's illegitimate status. Second, the Rashash's comments indicate that we should avoid such experimentation when it would yield this result, forcing us to declare a child illegitimate. (Indeed, Rav Yosef Shalom Elyashiv ruled against performing a DNA test to determine if one's presumed daughter was not in fact his biological daughter, citing these comments of the Rashash.[14])

The Rashash's implicit assumption that evidence obtained through scientific experimentation suffices to render a child a *mamzer* is difficult to accept in light of the fact that *halacha* goes very far to avoid assigning the status of *mamzerus*. The Gemara in *Maseches Yevamos* (80b) addresses the case of a woman who delivered a child twelve months after her husband had gone overseas. Rava Tosfa'a ruled that the child may be presumed to be legitimate, in light of the far-fetched possibility that the wife had conceived before her husband left and the pregnancy endured for twelve months. Although it was highly unlikely that this is what happened, *halacha* allows us to consider even the remotest possibility for the sake of maintaining a person's status of legitimacy. The *Or Zarua* (vol. 1, *Yibum*, 657) comments that a twelve-month gestation period falls under the

---

13. See also *Elya Rabba* 568:15.
14. *Kovetz Teshuvos*, E.H. 1:135.

category of מיעוט שאינו מצוי כלל — a statistically negligible possibility[15] — and yet it may be considered to avoid declaring a child a *mamzer*. The Rivash (446) similarly writes:

אף על פי שהוא בתכלית הזרות, כל שאפשר לתלות את הולד בבעל, אין תולין אותו בזנות אלא בבעל.

> Even if [the possibility] is exceedingly rare, anytime it is possible to attribute the child to the husband, we attribute him not to adultery, but to the husband.

The only exception to this rule, as noted by the Rama (E.H. 4:14), is when the wife is guilty of a דבר מכוער — unbecoming conduct that gives us reason to suspect her of an adulterous relationship — in which case we cannot consider remote, far-fetched possibilities to avoid labeling her child a *mamzer*. But generally, we may entertain even the unlikeliest possibilities to maintain a child's presumed status of legitimacy.

Rav Moshe Feinstein (*Iggeros Moshe*, E.H. 4:17:6) explains that the halachic principle of רוב, which mandates that we assume the statistical majority, applies only in situations of ספק — when an actual halachic uncertainty arises. Until we are faced with a ספק, we assume the status quo has not changed unless we are forced to believe otherwise. As long as there is even a minuscule statistical chance that the status quo remains, we assume as such. Thus, a child maintains his presumed status of legitimacy even when this requires assuming a far-fetched possibility, unless the woman has acted in a manner that gives rise to a ספק concerning her fidelity.

It stands to reason, then, that even if scientific experimentation determined that a child could not possibly be his or her father's biological offspring, the child would not be declared a *mamzer*, as we can consider the remote possibility that the child is the product of artificial insemination, or some other unlikely explanation. The Rashash, surprisingly, seems to have felt otherwise, as he maintained that Rav Saadia Gaon's "blood test" would suffice to establish *mamzerus*.

Practically speaking, the consensus among the *poskim* is that neither a blood test nor a DNA test suffices to prove that a child was born out of wedlock and is thus a *mamzer*, as documented in *Nishmas Avraham*.[16] Indeed, this is the view expressed in the ruling issued by Rav Wosner's *beis din* in the wake of the 9/11 tragedy. However, in situations of valid grounds for suspicion of infidelity,

---

15. I have heard that the chances of a woman gestating for twelve months are one in 2.5 million.
16. Vol. 3, p. 69, notes 18–19.

DNA confirmation of out-of-wedlock conception would seemingly suffice to determine the child's status of *mamzerus*, as in such a case we cannot rely on far-fetched possibilities such as artificial insemination.

A Wife's Presumption of Innocence

This principle applies as well to חזקת היתר אשה לבעלה — a wife's presumed status of permissibility to her husband.

The *Behag*, cited by the Rosh (*Yevamos* 2:8), asserts that the standards of evidence required to prove a wife's infidelity, for the purpose of determining that relations with her husband are forbidden, are higher than those required to sentence adulterers to capital punishment. *Halacha* follows the view of Shmuel (*Makkos* 7a) that witnesses to a forbidden sexual relationship do not have to testify to having seen the actual insertion of the male organ into the woman's body. If they testify that the couple acted כדרך המנאפים — the way a man and woman act when engaging in intimacy — then this suffices for *beis din* to sentence the couple to capital punishment. The Rambam (*Hilchos Issurei Bi'ah* 1:19) explains that the witnesses need to testify to having seen the alleged violators together in a position of intercourse. However, the *Behag* maintains that such testimony does not suffice to declare a woman an adulteress, such that relations with her husband are forbidden. A woman is considered an adulteress in this respect only if witnesses can testify that penetration occurred.

The Rosh questions this ruling, noting the rule of והצילו העדה,[17] which requires a *beis din* to search for a basis to acquit a defendant accused of a capital offense (*Rosh Hashana* 26a). If, in spite of this requirement, *beis din* is authorized to sentence a defendant to execution based on testimony of כדרך המנאפים, the Rosh argues, then certainly this testimony should suffice to declare a woman forbidden to her husband. How, the Rosh asks, could the standard of testimony to declare a wife forbidden be stricter than the standard needed to sentence her and her alleged partner to capital punishment?

Several approaches have been advanced to explain the *Behag*'s ruling. The *Noda Be-Yehuda* (*Mahadura Tinyana*, E.H. 11) suggests that testimony of כדרך המנאפים suffices for a conviction because *beis din* can convict alleged transgressors only if the witnesses testify to having warned them of the consequences of their act. If witnesses see a couple engage in an illicit relationship, their testimony can lead to capital punishment only if they had first warned the couple that they would be liable to death for the sinful act that they were about to commit and the couple had explicitly acknowledged the warning. Once such a warning has been

---

17. *Bamidbar* 35:25.

issued and verbally acknowledged, the *Noda Be-Yehuda* explains, observing the couple acting כדרך המנאפים is sufficient evidence for a conviction. However, when it comes to declaring a wife forbidden to her husband, no prior warning is necessary. Hence, the bar of evidence is raised, and the witnesses must testify to having seen the actual penetration.[18]

In any event, it is clear that just as we may rely on a remote possibility to avoid declaring *mamzerus*, we may similarly consider far-fetched scenarios to maintain a woman's status of permissibility. Even if witnesses testify to having seen a married woman in bed, unclothed, with a man other than her husband, she remains permissible to her husband, as we consider the unlikely possibility that penetration never occurred. Accordingly, Rav Avraham Yisrael Zeevi (*Urim Gedolim* 18:108) writes based on earlier sources:

> אף בדבר הרחוק מן השכל וחוץ מדרך הטבע תלינן להעמיד אשה בחזקת כשרות.
>
> We rely even on something that is far from conceivable and outside the natural order in order to maintain a woman's presumption of validity.

Presumably, then, even if a DNA test confirms that a married woman cohabited with another man, such as if the DNA of semen taken from her body was found to match his DNA, she would not be declared forbidden to her husband, as we may rely on the remote possibility that she underwent artificial insemination, or that the test results were tampered with. As mentioned earlier, however, this would depend on the circumstances; if the wife had conducted herself in a manner that undermines her presumption of innocence, a DNA test could very well be considered compelling evidence to forbid relations with her husband.

DNA as Evidence in Civil Suits

Finally, let us turn our attention to the question of whether DNA evidence suffices for a *beis din* to award money to a plaintiff. As noted above, the famous rule of המוציא מחבירו עליו הראיה establishes that *beis din* will not rule against the presumed owner of money or property that has come under dispute without outright proof, generally defined as the testimony of two valid witnesses who have been cross-examined. Would DNA evidence suffice as proof for this purpose? If a person shows up claiming to be the long-lost son of a deceased person, and DNA testing proves this to be the case, would *beis din* compel his siblings

---

18. The *Noda Be-Yehuda*'s son advanced a different explanation, as cited in a note to the aforementioned responsum. Yet another theory was proposed by the *Avnei Nezer*, E.H. 31.

to pay him his due share of their father's estate, which they had inherited in the interim? And could a woman prove the identity of her child's father through DNA testing in order to demand alimony payments?

These cases would certainly appear to resemble the aforementioned story involving Rav Saadia Gaon, who ruled that a large fortune be taken out of the possession of its presumed owner due to "scientific" evidence that it rightfully belonged to someone else. Rav Saadia Gaon clearly maintained that such evidence suffices even להוציא ממון — to compel a defendant to pay a plaintiff.[19]

Rav Avraham Price, in his *Mishnas Avraham* commentary to the *Sefer Chasidim*, offers the following explanation for this view of Rav Saadia Gaon:

...נראה, דהא דהצריכה תורה שני עדים לענין ממון הוא מטעם בירור... אבל במקום שיש בירור גמור, אז אין הדבר צריך לעדים. לכן אם מתברר בבירור גמור שלא ע"י עדים, גם כן אנו יכולים לחייב ממון. והבחינה הלזו של רבנו סעדיה הוא בירור גמור, כי מה שמתברר ע"י חכמת הטבע אמת היא.

> ...It would appear that when the Torah requires two witnesses in financial matters, this is for the purpose of confirmation [of what happened]... But in a case in which there is definitive confirmation, the matter does not require witnesses. Therefore, if [the matter] is determined with definitive confirmation without witnesses, we can also obligate [the defendant to pay] money. And this test of Rabbeinu Saadia provides definitive confirmation because that which is confirmed by scientific knowledge is true.

Beis din requires the testimony of two valid witnesses only when there is a question surrounding the facts that needs to be resolved. But if the facts can be definitively determined through other means, then witnesses are not necessary. Therefore, since Rav Saadia Gaon believed that his method definitively determined the identity of the biological son, he extracted money from the other man.

---

19. Earlier, we noted the incident told in the Gemara involving Rabbi Bena'a, who determined the true inheritor by seeing which son refused to defile the father's grave. This might, at first glance, prove that financial conflicts can be resolved even without compelling evidence, based on even psychological analysis. However, as we saw, the Rashbam explains Rabbi Bena'a's ruling as an instance of שודא דדייני, where the judge uses his discretion given the lack of clear-cut evidence. His "experiment," then, was not sufficient for an actual legal ruling; it was conducted merely as a last resort method to choose one child to whom to award the estate.

The Talmudic source for this concept is the Gemara's famous ruling in *Maseches Bava Kama* (74b) concerning בא הרוג ברגליו — a case in which an alleged murder victim showed up alive and well. The witnesses who had testified to the murder are rejected as false witnesses and punished for their crime. Although *halacha* generally follows the rule of תרי כמאה — the testimony of two valid witnesses who have undergone cross-examination is regarded as established fact — this applies only when they provide information that would otherwise be unknown. If they testify against a clearly evident fact, their testimony is determined as false, because definitively established fact is stronger than the testimony of any number of witnesses. As *Tosfos* comment (in *Yevamos* 88), witnesses' testimony is meaningless when they contradict דבר הנראה וידוע לכל — a clearly and unmistakably recognizable fact.[20]

Accordingly, the result of a DNA test result should also suffice as evidence to extract money from a defendant. Certainly, a DNA test provides no less definitive evidence than Rav Saadia Gaon's blood test — and, in light of scientific research, it is unquestionably far more definitive — and thus it should be relied upon as clear-cut evidence of a biological relationship in civil suits. Hence, for example, a DNA test should suffice to prove that someone is an inheritor worthy of a share in the deceased's estate, or to prove that a divorced man is a child's father with respect to alimony payments. Despite the fact that, as we have shown, DNA testing is not sufficient to determine *mamzerus* or to prove that a woman had an adulterous affair, it would be sufficient in monetary civil suits.

---

20. This point is developed in numerous other sources as well. See, for example, *Shevus Yaakov* 1:125; *Hagahos Imrei Baruch* C.M. 46 (commenting on the *Nesivos* 46:7); and *Dibros Moshe, Pesachim* 2:3.

The Gemara in *Bava Kama* establishes that in a case of בא הרוג ברגליו, the witnesses who falsely testified to the murder are liable to corporal punishment (*malkos*) for giving false testimony, indicating that definitively confirmed facts can override testimony to the point of warranting court-administered punishment. Conceivably, this might also be true with regard to capital punishment. Although the Rambam emphatically writes that capital punishment cannot be administered unless two witnesses actually saw the forbidden act (*Sefer Ha-Mitzvos, lo sa'aseh* 290; *Hilchos Sanhedrin* 20:1), nevertheless, if established fact is stronger than testimony, then perhaps *beis din* could administer capital punishment even in the absence of witnesses if the facts can be definitively established through other means. However, Rav Meir Dan Plotzky, in his *Keli Chemda* (*Parshas Shoftim*), asserts that testimony is a prerequisite for capital punishment by force of a גזירת הכתוב — the decree of the Torah — and is thus necessary even if the facts are established without it.

DNA Versus Witnesses

The fact that DNA constitutes a בירור גמור — conclusive and definitive evidence — challenges us to consider the question of whether it should even override the testimony of two witnesses.

As noted above, testimony is not accepted when it contradicts a דבר הנראה וידוע לכל — an undisputed, verified fact. In the opinion of this author, a DNA test result constitutes a דבר הנראה וידוע לכל and is halachically equivalent to בא הרוג ברגליו. If, for example, two witnesses identify a deceased person as a certain individual, and a DNA test conclusively determines that the deceased person could not be that individual, it seems inconceivable that we should accept the witnesses' testimony. The margin of error of a DNA test is infinitesimally low — in the neighborhood of one in a trillion — to the point that it can be considered negligible, and hence the results can be considered definitive and a דבר הנראה וידוע לכל.

It must be emphasized that DNA testing is not "experimentation." This is not a system with a high success rate. Scientists examining strands of DNA under a microscope can definitively determine the complete genetic makeup of the organism from which it was taken, and the method has been proven beyond any shred of doubt. If a DNA test determines that a deceased person is not the person witnesses identified him as, there is no question in anyone's mind that the witnesses were mistaken, and we make a mockery of *halacha* by suggesting that the witnesses' testimony should be accepted in such a situation.

While this might not be the view taken by leading contemporary *poskim*,[21] this conclusion is clear in the mind of this writer.

INTERVIEWS

Rav Asher Weiss on Headlines with Dovid Lichtenstein*

Establishing paternity through DNA — this is a very relevant question which affects *Yoreh Dei'a*, *Even Ha-Ezer*, and *Choshen Mishpat* — many different areas. There are common questions of *yerusha* (inheritance), when we want to determine whether so-and-so is so-and-so's son; claims for *mezonos* (alimony),

---

21. See the citations below from the interviews conducted with Rav Asher Weiss *shlit"a* and Rav Moshe Sternbuch *shlit"a*.

mamzerus, *kehuna*, and in Israel, questions regarding the burial of soldiers killed in combat who, to our dismay, cannot be identified by facial features and the only way to identify them is with DNA. And *agunos* — I wrote a number of *teshuvos* regarding *agunos* after 9/11, and I was asked questions also after the Tsunami in the Far East.

I think the first source of a scientific method to determine whether a person is the son of another person is *Sefer Chasidim*, which tells an interesting story of a person who went overseas with his slave, and his son was born after he left. The slave said he was the son, and the *Sefer Chasidim* said that when the father passed away, they should take blood from both parties and place a bone from the father into the blood. The *Elya Rabba* (568) asks from *Bava Basra* (58a), where we find a story of Rav Bena'a. A person heard his wife saying that of her ten children, only one is from her husband. Before his demise, he wrote in his will that he leaves all his estate to this one son. Then his ten sons argued, each saying that he was the chosen son. Rav Bena'a said they should all go to the grave and bang on the grave until the father gets up and says who the real son is. One of the sons said he would not disgrace his father's memory, and Rav Bena'a said that he should receive the entire inheritance. The *Elya Rabba* asks, why didn't they do the method of the *Sefer Chasidim*? The Rashash, in his *hagahos*, answered that they were afraid, as they did not want to determine *mamzerus*. Some present-day *gedolim* prove from the Rashash that scientific experimentation would be sufficient to determine *mamzerus*.

As a general comment, I do not think this is the *derech* in *halacha*. The *Sefer Chasidim*'s comment, like almost everything in the *Sefer Chasidim*, is a *chiddush*. The *Elya Rabba*'s question is not a question at all; who said Rav Bena'a was aware of the *Sefer Chasidim*? And I don't think the Rashash intended to determine the *halacha*. All he meant to say was that some people might think that this proves *mamzerus*, and so Rav Bena'a preferred not to use this method.

The *Tzitz Eliezer* and some other *gedolim* — going back to before the time when DNA testing was available, but when there were blood tests — argued that proving the father's identity with blood tests is in opposition to *Chazal*. The Gemara in *Nidda* (31a) says that the father contributes the לובן (whiteness), and the mother contributes אודם (redness). So, according to *Chazal*, blood comes from the mother. How, then, could a blood test determine who the father is?

I tremendously admire the *Tzitz Eliezer*, but I think this is off-mark. I don't think we can use a statement of *Chazal* which does not refer to halachic criteria to determine *halacha*. אין למדין מן האגדות. There is a big *machlokes* between the *Shevus Yaakov* and the *Noda Be-Yehuda* whether this applies even when the *aggada* does not contradict the *halacha*. But in any event, we don't really know what *Chazal* mean when they say that the father provides the לובן. *Chazal* say this includes the bones, the sinews, the nails, and the white of the eyes, and that the mother gives the "red" — the skin, flesh, hair, and black of the eye. *Chazal* were definitely aware of the fact that every living creature has blood. Yet, they don't mention blood here. Obviously, blood was excluded from this Gemara, and therefore, it is not relevant to our question.

As to defining DNA testing — DNA is definitely not *eidus*. The Rambam twice in *Hilchos Yesodei Ha-Torah* (7:7, 8:2) says that we do not believe *eidim* because we know they are correct. We are fully aware that they might be false witnesses; otherwise, the prohibition would not appear in the *Aseres Ha-Dibros*. Some misunderstand the Rambam to mean that *eidus* is not בירור (confirmation of the facts). In truth, it is the ultimate בירור, but it is a בירור because the Torah gives witnesses נאמנות (reliability). The Rambam means that this is not a סברא (logical deduction) or a reality. We can never be fully confident that they testify truthfully. But this is the Torah's law.

DNA could, perhaps, fit into the category of אומדנא, though I don't think it does. אומדנא is what we call today circumstantial evidence. The two most important sources of אומדנא are *Bava Basra* 93a, regarding when we have to determine which animal killed a camel, and it was most likely the camel that had been standing next to it, and the famous story in *Shevuos* 34a of Shimon ben Shetach, who saw a person with a sword running after his fellow who ran into a building. By the time Shimon ben Shetach got to the building, the person was breathing his last breaths of life, and the pursuer was holding his sword with blood dripping from it. Shimon ben Shetach said to him, "You *rasha*, I know you killed him, but I have no witnesses" — obviously proving that אומדנא is not sufficient for דיני נפשות (capital cases). However, *Tosfos* in *Shevuos* says — and this is a minority position — that אומדנא דמוכח is relevant in דיני נפשות. According to *Tosfos*, there is the theoretical possibility that the dying person had snatched the sword from the hands of his assailant and killed himself, and then the assailant picked up the sword. This is very unlikely, but it is a theoretical possibility. But if a person chases another into a room, and he has signs of a bite on his back — since a person cannot bite his own back, it is not only unreasonable that he bit himself, it is impossible, and that אומדנא would be sufficient for דיני נפשות. But this is against the Rambam, who says there is a גזירת הכתוב (scriptural decree) that we do not judge דיני נפשות based on אומדנא.

I do not think DNA testing is an אומדנא, which refers to circumstantial evidence. It is a סימן מובהק — a clear sign. The principle of סימנים is that it is totally unreasonable that two objects would have precisely the same features. And *Chazal* say that this works even מדאורייתא (on the level of Torah law). There is a *machlokes* between the *Shach* and the *Ketzos* (297) whether a סימן is sufficient against a חזקת ממון (presumption of ownership). The *Shach* says that money can be extracted based on a סימן, but the *Ketzos* doesn't think so. There is one *Tosfos* in *Chullin* (96a) which says that a סימן מובהק would be sufficient for דיני נפשות, but the *halacha* does not follow this view.

I think *eidim* would override a סימן מובהק because *eidim* are sufficient for everything. The only thing that overrides *eidim* is mentioned in *Yevamos* (88) — בא הרוג ברגליו. (Incidentally, the Yerushalmi argues on the Bavli in this regard.) *Tosfos* asks the question, if the testimony of two witnesses is as good as the testimony of one hundred witnesses, then why does בא הרוג ברגליו override testimony? *Tosfos* says that the consent of the entire *tzibur* is beyond *eidus*, and this is the rule of בא הרוג ברגליו. It means ידיעה בלתי אמצעית — something that everybody sees with their own eyes.

My *psak* is that DNA does not suffice to declare a status of *mamzerus*, for several reasons. First, there is only one source that a סימן מובהק would be sufficient for דיני נפשות — the aforementioned *Tosfos* in *Chullin* (96a) — and the *halacha* does not follow that view. Rabbi Akiva Eiger ruled in one of his *teshuvos* (100) that ממזרות כדיני נפשות דמיין — *mamzerus* is treated like capital cases — and so DNA is insufficient. We find many sources in the *Acharonim* of the kinds of extremes to which we should go not to declare *mamzerus* upon a person. And according to Rabbi Akiva Eiger, what's not sufficient for דיני נפשות would not be sufficient for *mamzerus*. The Gemara in *Kiddushin* (73a) learns from a *pasuk* that ממזר ודאי אסרה תורה ולא ממזר ספק — only someone who is certainly a *mamzer* is forbidden. The *Shev Shemaitsa* (1:1) has a lengthy discussion and says… even a רוב (statistical majority) is not sufficient to declare *mamzerus* upon a person. The only thing that is a ודאי regarding *mamzerus* is either *eidus* or בא הרוג ברגליו.

Also — and I know to some people this might seem strange, but to me it is not strange at all — the nature of science is such that many assumptions are indisputable, but then a later generation understands the scientific reality in a completely different way. I know this seems very unlikely concerning DNA testing, but at the time it seemed very unlikely that the world is round… We could give many other examples of how basic scientific knowledge and scientific assumptions were considered iron-clad at the time, but then a later generation came along and understood more than previous generations did. Scientific truth is shifting sands. Does that mean we will not rely on science? No, we definitely would. We find in *Nidda* (22b) that *Chazal* consulted with doctors regarding *hilchos nidda* and relied on them, and in *Shabbos* (85a) regarding *kil'ayim* and the understanding of agriculture, they consulted with experts. And so according to *halacha*, we definitely rely on science and doctors. However, I think we should differentiate between questions that are relevant here and now, such as whether a woman is a *nidda* and whether something is *kil'ayim*, regarding which we rely on scientific knowledge, and issues of *mamzerus*, where our *psak* today affects future generations, and so we would not rely on pure scientific criteria, as they may change. Although it is very unlikely that they will change, you never know. In science, everything can change. In my view, then, *mamzerus* is different than any other kind of question, as it invalidates future generations, and so we cannot do that based on scientific criteria.

Also, we know that human error is always a possibility. Regarding testimony, there is a גזירת הכתוב that it is accepted as fact. But anyone who has dealt with doctors and laboratories knows that there is a margin of human error that needs to be taken account. Therefore, we cannot declare a person *pasul*.

Furthermore, you can only declare a person *pasul* with proper *eidim*. The laboratory technicians are not valid witnesses, and the clerk who hands over the information is not a valid witness. Even if we assume the actual testing is foolproof, there are different stages, and we have no עדות כשרה.

Finally — and although it's *aggedeta*, it's interesting, and it might have significance — there is an amazing Midrash Rabba in *Parshas Naso* (9). The Midrash says that when a woman betrays her husband and has a baby, but the baby is from her husband, and not from the other person, צר הקב"ה פניו כפני הבועל להודיע קלונו ברבים ("the Almighty forms his face like the face of the adulterer, to publicize his shame"). We learn from the Midrash that sometimes HKB"H tosses away nature and genetics, להודיע קלונו ברבים. As unlikely as it might seem, the baby's face could be the same as the person from whom he did not come. If HKB"H plays around with genetics, then He might be playing around with DNA, as well. This Midrash, then, is an additional reason why we would not declare a person a *mamzer* based on DNA.

[Addressing the question of why a DNA test would not qualify as בא הרוג ברגליו:] בא הרוג ברגליו is something natural, that is seen with the eyes, not scientific knowledge. Scientific knowledge is not the same as seeing with one's eyes. They don't see the person's face under a microscope. In my opinion, there is scientific knowledge that is not בא הרוג ברגליו. I think the Rambam makes this point very clear. If we would have to rate *eidus* against a סימן מובהק, then we would say that a סימן מובהק overrides *eidus*. If we did statistical screening, then perhaps one out of 100 or 200 *eidim* is dishonest. So a סימן מובהק should override *eidim*. But a סימן מובהק is not sufficient for דיני נפשות, while *eidim* are. By halachic criteria, it's not the numbers. The only thing that overrides *eidus* is ידיעה בלתי אמצעית, such as בא הרוג ברגליו. It's what you see. Scientific testing is not ידיעה בלתי אמצעית; it is based on scientific equations and mathematics. This is not בא הרוג ברגליו.

I would permit an *aguna* to remarry based on DNA testing.

I think this does disqualify them from the *kehuna* [if DNA indicates that the father is not a *Kohen*]. The *Shev Shemaitsa* (6:15) writes that two *eidim* are needed to disqualify a person, and therefore you need two witnesses to declare somebody a *chalal* (invalid *Kohen*). I argue that you need two *eidim* only because a *Kohen*'s presumed status gives him rights of *kehuna* — to *duchen*, for *pidyon ha-ben*, etc. — and this is no less than a חזקת ממון. Once he is disqualified from the *kehuna*, you do not then need two *eidim* to permit him to marry a divorcee or a convert. And so once we say that DNA testing suffices to disqualify him from the *kehuna*, then you no longer need two *eidim* to permit him to marry a convert. And therefore, since I think that DNA proves this man is not his father's son, and so he can no longer *duchen*, this would also be sufficient to enable him to marry a divorcee, and this was my *psak* in this case.

I would rely on DNA regarding *agunos*, inheritance, monetary matters, but not *mamzerus*, for the many reasons I've explained.

It is a great challenge to *pasken shaylos* in our changing world, and we need to begin and end every day with a *tefilla* to HKB"H שלא נכשל בדבר הלכה, and we should always be *zocheh* להגדיל תורה ולהאדירה and to be מקדש שם שמים.

* Broadcast on 18 Tammuz, 5776 (July 23, 2016).

Rav Moshe Sternbuch on *Headlines with Dovid Lichtenstein**

It seems that *beis din* can rely on DNA testing, and I do; I think it's right to rely on it… In my opinion, you can rely on it. But if witnesses say the opposite, then we don't rely on it. There is a גזירת הכתוב, as the Rambam writes in *Hilchos Yesodei Ha-Torah*, that we do not question the testimony of witnesses. [If the chances of error are] one in ten billion — it doesn't matter. I would not allow it. When two frummer witnesses testify against this evidence — once the witnesses are here, we rely on them. The Rambam writes that this is a גזירת הכתוב; this is how HKB"H wanted it — if two witnesses who are שומרי תורה ומצוות and presumed reliable come — we accept them.

* Broadcast on 18 Tammuz, 5776 (July 23, 2016).

REUTERS

Kentucky Clerk Still in Contempt of Gay Marriage Order: Plaintiffs

September 22, 2015
Reporting by Steve Bittenbender; Writing by David Bailey; Editing by Miral Fahmy

A county clerk from Kentucky who went to jail rather than issue marriage licenses to gay couples made material changes to the forms upon her return and is not in compliance with a federal court order, lawyers for couples suing her said on Monday.

Rowan County Clerk Kim Davis should be ordered to allow the licenses to be issued under the earlier format or the clerk's office should be put in receivership and fines imposed, the attorneys from the American Civil Liberties Union of Kentucky said in a federal court filing.

The issuance of marriage licenses to same-sex couples in Kentucky and other states has become the latest focal point in a long-running debate over gay marriage in the United States.

Davis, 50, has said her beliefs as an Apostolic Christian prevent her from issuing marriage licenses to same-sex couples. U.S. District Judge David Bunning ordered her jailed for failing to issue licenses in line with a Supreme Court ruling in June that made gay marriage legal across the United States.

Kim Davis addresses the media just before the doors are opened to the Rowan County Clerk's Office in Morehead, Kentucky, September 14, 2015. REUTERS/Chris Tilley

Davis, who was jailed five days, was released on the condition that she not interfere directly or indirectly with the issuance of marriage licenses. She returned to work on Sept. 14.

Mat Staver, an attorney for Davis, said on Monday she has made a good faith effort to comply with Bunning's order.

"The ACLU's motion to again hold Kim Davis in contempt reveals that their interest is not the license but rather a marriage license bearing the name of Kim Davis. They want her scalp to hang on the wall as a trophy," Staver said.

On Friday, the lawyer for Deputy Clerk Brian Mason, who has been issuing licenses since Davis was jailed, told the court Davis confiscated the licenses upon her return and gave him a document that removed references to Rowan County and Davis' office and required him to list his title as a notary public.

The changes run afoul of Bunning's order, the filing by the lawyers for the plaintiffs said. At the minimum, she has created considerable uncertainty for marriage applicants about their licenses and subsequent marriages, the filing said.

Bunning should direct that licenses be issued under the former format and the office reissue the licenses issued in the past week that could be open to legal challenges, it said.

While Davis has said she does not believe the licenses issued are valid, their legality has not been challenged in court. Bunning has said licenses issues while Davis was jailed are valid and the governor has said he had no problem with altered licenses, if the judge considered them valid.

Copyright © reuters.com

What if Kim Davis Were an Orthodox Jew? Issuing Marriage Licenses to Same-Sex Couples

In September 2015, a county clerk in Kentucky named Kim Davis earned international renown when she was imprisoned for refusing to issue marriage certificates to engaged homosexual and lesbian couples. After spending five days in jail, Ms. Davis was released, and she returned to work when an arrangement was made such that all marriage licenses issued by her office would not bear her name or official authorization.

Explaining her position, Ms. Davis said that even a license that she did not directly issue, but which bears her name, effectively "authorizes marriage that conflicts with God's definition of marriage as a union between one man and one woman [and] violates my deeply-held religious convictions and conscience. For me, this would be an act of disobedience to my God… Whether I personally issue the license or whether one of my deputies issues it, the result is the same. The license is issued under the authority of Kim Davis, County Clerk of Rowan County."

In the wake of the U.S. Supreme Court's decision (*Obergefell v. Hodges*) on June 26, 2015, holding that the right to legal marriage cannot be denied to same-sex couples, and as opposition to homosexuality becomes increasingly taboo, many have expressed concern that the rights of those opposing same-sex marriage, including Orthodox Jews, may be threatened. The story of Kim Davis could, potentially, portend similar problems for Jews refusing to participate in activities that tacitly affirm the legitimacy of a homosexual union. In fact, already several months before the Supreme Court's landmark decision, the owners of a small bakery near Portland, Oregon, were fined $135,000 for refusing to prepare a wedding cake for a same-sex wedding.

These incidents underscore the urgent need for *poskim* to determine whether, and to what extent, it would be permissible for a Jew to take part in a same-sex couple's marriage, including registration, wedding arrangements, and so on.

Unlike the vast majority of Torah laws, homosexuality is forbidden even for gentiles, and taking part in a process that lends official approval to such relationships could therefore potentially violate several halachic prohibitions related to abetting or sanctioning sinful behavior. Specifically, we must consider the possible violation of three prohibitions:

1. לפני עור לא תתן מכשול — "placing a stumbling block before a blind man" (*Vayikra* 19:14), which refers to causing people to sin.
2. מסייע לדבר עבירה — lending assistance to help facilitate a sin. Even in situations in which לפני עור does not apply, because the sinner can commit the offense independently without any assistance, one is nevertheless forbidden to assist him in committing the prohibited act.
3. חנופה לרשעים — "flattering" the wicked in a manner that suggests approval of their wrongdoing.

Officiating at Weddings of Non-Observant Couples

We might compare this question to one that has already been addressed by several halachic authorities, as to whether a rabbi may serve as מסדר קידושין at the wedding of a non-observant couple who clearly have no intention of obeying the laws of family purity, but who would not live together without getting married. Would the rabbi's participation in such a wedding be forbidden on the grounds that it facilitates sinful behavior?

Rav Mordechai Yaakov Breisch addressed this question in *Chelkas Yaakov* (E.H. 75), and ruled that a rabbi may officiate at such a wedding. He notes that since the couple in any event will get married, whether or not the rabbi officiates, this is comparable to a case of handing someone forbidden food to eat when he could have accessed it through other means (חד עיברא דנהרא).

Rav Breisch at first questions this viewpoint, in light of the fact that if the rabbi were to refuse to officiate, the couple would find a different rabbi to officiate, and that rabbi would be in violation of לפני עור. The *Mishneh Le-Melech* (*Hilchos Malveh Ve-Loveh* 4, cited in *Pischei Teshuva*, Y.D. 160) advances the theory that one transgresses לפני עור by facilitating a sin even if the individual could commit the offense without his assistance, if the individual needs someone else's assistance. In other words, even if several people could potentially abet the sinner, and thus no single individual is indispensable to the act, nevertheless, whichever one of them facilitates the sin transgresses לפני עור. The context of the *Mishneh Le-Melech*'s discussion is the case of a money lender who lends on interest. The *Mishneh Le-Melech* asserts that the borrower transgresses לפני עור by accepting such a loan, even though the lender would have certainly found other Jewish borrowers. Since the sinner requires another person's assistance to commit the forbidden act, any person who facilitates the act violates לפני עור,

even though the sinner would have found someone else to help him commit his sin.

Seemingly, Rav Breisch notes, we should apply that same logic to the case of the non-observant couple seeking an officiating rabbi. Whichever rabbi agrees to officiate would appear to violate לפני עור, despite the fact that another rabbi would have been found to officiate if he refused.

Rav Breisch dismisses this argument, however, for several reasons. First, he writes, we might distinguish between the case of a money lender, who might not find a Jew willing to pay interest in violation of Torah law, and the case of a non-observant couple, who would get married even if they could not find a rabbi to officiate. The *Mishneh Le-Melech* might limit his ruling to a situation similar to that of the money lender, where it is possible, albeit unlikely, that the lender would be unable to find an abettor for his sin, and thus one who abets his sin by borrowing on interest violates לפני עור. In the case of a couple wishing to get married, however, they would get married with or without an officiating rabbi, and thus a rabbi who agrees to officiate is not considered to have "placed a stumbling block" before them.

Additionally, Rav Breisch notes, several *poskim* dispute the *Mishneh Le-Melech*'s view, and maintain that the prohibition of לפני עור does not apply if the transgressor can find other people to facilitate his violation. One example is a responsum of the Maharsham (2:184), in which he permits a Jew in Cracow to lease a storefront property to a Jewish barber who would work on Shabbos. The Maharsham does not even cite the *Mishneh Le-Melech*'s position, and rules that since the barber will find another Jew to lease him property, לפני עור does not apply. Moreover, Rav Breisch contends that in the case of a non-observant couple seeking an officiating rabbi, a rabbi might agree to perform the ceremony because he regards this as a *mitzva*, enabling a Jewish man and woman to marry in a halachic manner. Thus, even if we were to conclude, in principle, that officiating is forbidden, nevertheless, the couple would in all likelihood find a rabbi who considers it permissible and even laudable. Rav Breisch argues that the *Mishneh Le-Melech*'s position only applies to facilitating something which is obviously prohibited, such as lending with interest. But in this case, where other rabbis will reach the conclusion that officiating at the wedding is not prohibited at all, there is no problem serving as the officiating rabbi since the transgression of לפני עור is not inevitable.

This line of reasoning would likely apply to our discussion as well. Even if the Orthodox Jewish clerk refuses to grant the homosexual couple their marriage license, they will undoubtedly complete the registration process through a different office, or they will live together without a marriage license. Therefore, it stands to reason that processing the registration request would not constitute a violation of לפני עור.

A *Shadchan*'s Quandary

We still need to determine, however, whether this would violate the prohibition of מסייע לדבר עבירה. A possible precedent may be found in a responsum of the Netziv (*Meishiv Davar* 2:32) which discusses the question of whether a *shadchan* (matchmaker) may make a match between a man and woman knowing that they will not observe the family purity laws. The Netziv cites earlier sources that limit the prohibition of מסייע לדבר עבירה to assistance lent to the sinner at the time of the forbidden act, as opposed to lending assistance that helps facilitate a sin at a later time. In light of this distinction, the Netziv asserts that suggesting a match does not transgress this prohibition, since the couple will not violate the family purity laws until much later. Moreover, the Netziv adds, lending assistance to sinners is permitted for the purpose of earning a livelihood, and therefore one who earns money from matchmaking is allowed to make matches that would result in Torah violations.

Rav Moshe Feinstein cites the Netziv's ruling in *Iggeros Moshe* (E.H. 4:87), in discussing the question of officiating at a wedding of a couple who will not observe the family purity laws. He notes that a distinction might be drawn between matchmaking and officiating at the wedding, as the latter situation should perhaps be regarded as assistance lent at the time of the sinful act. Nevertheless, Rav Moshe adds, the Netziv's ruling that מסייע is permitted for the sake of earning a livelihood would apply to a rabbi whose formal duties to his congregation require him to officiate at weddings regardless of the couple's level of observance. Moreover, Rav Moshe points to the ruling of the *Shach* (Y.D. 151:6) that the prohibition of מסייע does not pertain to the case of a מומר — a person who rejects the authority of Torah law. The *Dagul Mei-Revava* (Y.D. ad loc.) extends this position even further, claiming that מסייע does not apply any time one seeks to intentionally commit a sin. According to the *Dagul Mei-Revava*, the prohibition of מסייע לדבר עבירה applies only to helping someone unwittingly violate the Torah. Rav Moshe writes that this view can certainly be taken into account to permit rabbis to officiate at the wedding of a non-observant couple, especially when this is necessary for a rabbi's livelihood.

It would certainly appear that this ruling would also apply to a clerk whose job requires issuing marriage licenses even to homosexual couples. Since the couple knowingly commits the violation, and since the clerk needs to issue the license for his or her livelihood, the prohibition of מסייע does not apply.

Life-Saving Flattery

As mentioned, however, in addition to the prohibitions of לפני עור and מסייע, we must also consider the possibility that issuing such a license might fall under the prohibition of חנופה — flattering sinners. In order to determine whether this is indeed the case, we must briefly explore the definition and parameters of this prohibition.[1]

The Talmudic source of this prohibition is the Mishna in *Maseches Sota* (41a) which recounts that the sages who had assembled in the *Beis Ha-Mikdash* once complimented the sinful King Agrippas. The Gemara (41b) relates that a decree of annihilation was issued against the Jewish People at that time, because they flattered a wicked man.

The *Sefer Ha-Yerei'im* includes the prohibition of חנופה in his listing of the Torah's commands (248), citing as the Biblical source the verse toward the end of *Sefer Bamidbar* (35:33), ולא תחניפו את הארץ. He defines the prohibition as follows:

כל השומע דבר עולה ושאינו הגון או רואה דבר רע ואמר טוב הוא, או שותק, ואינו מתוך יראה לא מגופו ולא מממונו, אלא מתוך רשע לבבו, או חושב בלבבו פן יחרה אפו עלי ויתקוטט עמי ואיני מפסיד בקטיטתו כי אם חסדו ואהבתו, נקרא חנף.

> Whoever hears something sinful and improper, or sees something evil and says that it is good, or remains silent, and this is not because of fear for his body or property, but rather because of his evil-hearted nature, or because he thinks to himself, "He might become angry with me and fight with me, and all I will lose if he fights with me is his favor and affection" — he is considered a flatterer.

According to the *Yerei'im*, the prohibition of חנופה, by definition, does not apply to flattering for the sake of saving oneself from physical or financial harm. The prohibition forbids engaging in flattery due to genuine approval of the individual's sinful conduct or to earn that individual's favor and affection. It is entirely permissible to flatter a sinner when this is necessary to protect oneself.

Similarly, *Tosfos* (*Sota* 41b, ד"ה כל המחניף) write that flattery is permissible in situations of danger, noting the incident recounted in *Maseches Nedarim* (22a) in which Ula complimented a murderer on the way he killed somebody, in order to protect himself from the killer, who would have otherwise killed him, too. After the incident, Rabbi Yochanan assured Ula that he acted appropriately in light of the life-threatening situation he faced.

---

1. The reader is referred to the first volume of *Headlines*, chapter 14, where the definition of חנופה is discussed at length in reference to the permissibility of voting for a political candidate running on a platform that conflicts with Torah values.

Surprisingly, however, Rabbeinu Yona takes a different view in his *Sha'arei Teshuva* (3:187–188). Rabbeinu Yona delineates nine different forms of forbidden חנופה, the first of which is forbidden even in the face of life-threatening danger:

החלק הראשון – החנף אשר הכיר או ראה או ידע כי יש עול בכף חבירו וכי החזיק בתרמית או כי יחטא איש בלשון הרע או באונאת דברים, ויחליק לו לשון הרע לאמר לא פעלת און... וחייב האדם למסור עצמו לסכנה ואל ישיא את נפשו עון אשמה כזאת.

> The first category — the flatterer who discerns, sees, or knows that his fellow has perpetrated evil, acted with deceit, or sinned through negative speech or through abusive speech, and he flatters [the wrongdoer] with an evil tongue, saying, "You did no wrong"... A person must expose himself to danger rather than bear this guilt upon his soul.

Rabbeinu Yona proceeds to note the people's flattery of Agrippas, which the Gemara condemns despite the fact that they presumably complimented him in order to protect themselves. Additionally, Rabbeinu Yona cites Moshe Rabbeinu's admonition to the newly-appointed judges in the wilderness, לא תגורו מפני איש (*Devarim* 1:17) — that they should judge fairly and accurately even in the face of threats.

The question obviously arises as to why one would be required to risk his life to avoid violating חנופה. It is generally assumed that the concern for human life overrides all Torah prohibitions with the exception of idolatry, murder, and sexual immorality. On what basis does Rabbeinu Yona forbid flattery even for the sake of protecting one's life?

The answer likely emerges from the comments of the Maharshal in his *Yam Shel Shlomo* (*Bava Kama* 4:9), where he writes, אסור לשנות דברי תורה אף כי הסכנה וחייב למסור עצמו עליה — "It is forbidden to distort the words of Torah, even in the face of danger, and one must surrender himself for it." The Maharshal makes this comment in reference to the story told in the Gemara (*Bava Kama* 38a) of two Roman officials who were sent by the Roman government to study the Jews' Torah. After these two officials studied with the Jews, they accepted everything except for the law that absolves a Jew from liability if his ox kills a gentile's ox, but imposes liability upon a gentile whose ox gores a Jew's ox. The Maharshal notes that the Jews who taught these two officials informed them of these laws despite the grave danger to which they would be exposed. Rather than alter the content in order to protect the Jews from the hostility of the Roman authorities, the scholars taught the Roman officials the truth. The reason, the Maharshal explains, is because it is forbidden to distort the Torah even to protect against life-threatening danger. He writes:

> לומר על הפטור חייב או להיפך היה ככופר בתורת משה – מה לי דבור אחד, מה לי כל התורה.
>
> Saying that one who is exempt is really obligated, or vice versa, would be akin to denying the Torah of Moshe. What difference does it make if it is one precept or the entire Torah?

Distorting even a single law of the Torah amounts to rejecting the Torah's authenticity, and thus constitutes heresy. As such, one is required to surrender his life rather than falsify any part of the Torah.

This premise perhaps underlies Rabbeinu Yona's ruling that חנופה is forbidden even in the face of danger. In emphasizing the particular gravity of flattery, Rabbeinu Yona writes:

> והנה זה ביד החנף האויל עון פלילי כי לא יקנא לאמת, אבל יעזור אחרי השקר ויאמר לרע טוב וישם חושך לאור.
>
> This nefarious flatterer is guilty of a grievous offense because he is not zealous for truth, and instead resorts to falsehood, saying that evil is good and turning darkness into light.

Flattery is a "grievous offense" because it distorts God's law, misrepresenting good as evil and evil as good. For this reason, in line with the Maharshal's ruling, Rabbeinu Yona maintains that flattery is forbidden even in situations of life-threatening danger. Thus, Rabbeinu Yona cites as proof Moshe's admonition to judges not to fear the consequences of a truthful sentence. They must speak the truth and issue accurate rulings that correctly reflect Torah law, even in the face of danger.[2]

However, as noted earlier, *Tosfos* do not follow this view, but instead maintain that one is not obligated to surrender his life to avoid חנופה, drawing proof from Ula's flattery of a murderer. The question we need to address is whether *Tosfos*' ruling indicates that they do not accept the Maharshal's view that one must risk his life to avoid distorting Torah law, or if some distinction may be drawn between the Maharshal's discussion and the situation faced by Ula.

Honoring a Sinner in the Synagogue

Rav Moshe Feinstein discusses *Tosfos*' view at length in the context of the situation faced by a synagogue that wished to give honor to a prominent member

---

2. The source of Rabbeinu Yona's comments is the *Sifrei*, cited by the *Sefer Ha-Chinuch* (415):

   שמא תאמר ירא אני מאיש פלוני **שמא יהרגני או יהרוג אחד מבני ביתי**, שמא ידליק את גדישי או שמא יקצוץ את נטיעותי, תלמוד לומר לא תגורו מפני איש.

who had married a non-Jewish woman (*Iggeros Moshe*, O.C. 2:51). This member, a wealthy physician, was exceedingly generous and actively involved in the community, whose members turned to him and relied upon him for assistance and support. The congregation's leaders were concerned that if they did not show him honor in the synagogue, such as by inviting him to open the ark, he might leave, denying the members access to this vital source of support.

Based on his analysis of *Tosfos*' position, Rav Moshe permitted the congregation to give the man honor. Although one must generally surrender his life to avoid distorting the Torah, as the Maharshal writes, Rav Moshe draws a subtle distinction between explicit distortion of Torah and expressing approval of sin. Ula did not explicitly say that murder is permissible; he complimented the murderer for the "impressive" manner in which he slit the victim's throat.[3] This could be understood to mean that the killer acted in accordance with appropriate protocols for people like him. Under normal circumstances, expressing approval of sin in this manner is forbidden, but it is permissible for the purpose of saving one's life. It is only the explicit distortion of Torah — such as stating clearly that the Torah sanctions murder — that is forbidden even in the face of danger.

On this basis, Rav Moshe asserts that the entire prohibition of חנופה refers to approving of sinful behavior. If this is done in a manner that explicitly distorts Torah law, then it is forbidden even for the sake of saving one's life, whereas expressing approval without explicitly misrepresenting the law is allowed in situations of danger. However, giving honor and complimenting a sinner for his favorable qualities, when it is clear that he is not being commended for his sinful conduct, is entirely permissible, and does not fall under the category of חנופה at all.[4]

Clearly, Rav Moshe forbids lending tacit approval to sinful behavior except when this is necessary to avoid danger. Thus, in the situation of a clerk processing marriage licenses, it would seem that issuing a license to a homosexual couple would be forbidden on the grounds of חנופה. Even though the clerk issues the license simply as part of his or her job, nevertheless, doing so implies approval of the marriage, and would therefore seemingly fall under the strict prohibition of חנופה. Especially when we consider the public and permanent nature of this expression of approval — a certificate that will be kept forever in

---

3. The Gemara relates that the killer turned to Ula and asked, יאות עבדי ("Did I do this well?"), and Ula answered in the affirmative.
4. Rav Moshe does not discuss in this responsum Rabbeinu Yona's ruling and how it may be reconciled with the story of Ula. See *Yad Ketana* to *Hilchos Dei'os* (10:14), who suggests a number of possible answers.

the local government's records — it seems clear that one would not be allowed to participate in the issuance of such a document.

INTERVIEW

Rav Dovid Cohen on *Headlines with Dovid Lichtenstein**

To my mind, what she [Kim Davis] did was a great קידוש ה׳. If a Jew would ask me what to do [in that situation], I would say that according to *halacha*, you are required to do what she did, because of a Rabbeinu Yona…Rabbeinu Yona says a person is obligated to give his life not to violate this sin [of חנופה]. He maintained that it's a חילול ה׳, and for חילול ה׳, it's יהרג ואל יעבור [one must give his life when necessary to avoid violating this sin]. For a person to say, "It's OK. There's such a thing as marriage between identical sexes" — it's a חילול ה׳, because the Torah says it's a *to'eiva* [abomination]… I believe that halachically, if you're obligated to let yourselves be killed, then certainly you're obligated to lose *parnasa*.

* Broadcast on 29 Elul, 5775 (September 12, 2015).

aeon

Undercover Atheists

February 11, 2015
by Batya Ungar-Sargon

The moment Solomon lost his faith, he was standing on the D train, swaying back and forth with its movement as if in prayer. But it wasn't a prayer book that the young law student was reading — he had already been to synagogue, where he had wrapped himself in the leather thongs that bound him to Orthodox Judaism, laying phylacteries and reciting the prayers three times daily.

The tome in his hands now was Alan Dershowitz's *The Genesis of Justice* (2000), which used Talmudic and Hasidic interpretations of the Bible to argue that stories in the book of Genesis, from Adam and Eve eating the apple to Noah and his ark, constituted God's learning curve — a means of establishing a moral code and the rules of justice that prevail today.

What struck him about the book was its depth, and a complexity of thought that he had been raised to believe was the exclusive domain of the rabbis whose authority commanded his community of ultra-Orthodox Jews. The book's brilliance, coupled with its unabashed heresy, created the first of many cracks in Solomon's faith. Seeing the scriptures interpreted in methods so compelling and yet entirely inconsistent with the dogmas of his youth caused Solomon to question everything he believed to be true.

From Dershowitz, Solomon moved on to evolutionary biology, and then to Stephen Hawking and cosmology, and then biblical criticism, until finally, he was unable to deny the conclusion his newly developed capacity for critical thinking had led him to: he no longer believed in the existence of God.

'It was the most devastating moment of my life,' he told me. 'I wish to this day that I could find the holy grail that proves that I'm wrong, that it's all true.'

And yet 15 years later, Solomon's life looks exactly the way it did the day of that fateful train ride, give or take a few infractions. Solomon is still leading the life of an Orthodox Jew. He is married to an Orthodox Jew. His children are Orthodox Jews who go to study the Torah at yeshiva. His parents are ultra-Orthodox Jews. And so, with his new-found atheism, Solomon did nothing.

Solomon is one of hundreds, perhaps thousands, of men and women whose encounters with evolution, science, new atheism and biblical criticism have led them to the conclusion that there is no God, and yet whose social, economic and familial connections to the ultra-Orthodox and Hasidic communities prevent them from giving up the rituals of faith. Those I spoke to could not bring themselves to upend their families and their children's lives. With too much integrity to believe, they also have too much to leave behind, and so they remain closeted atheists within ultra-Orthodox communities. Names and some places have been changed — every person spoke to me for this story on condition of anonymity. Part of a secret, underground intellectual elite, these people live in fear of being discovered and penalised by an increasingly insular society...

But they are also proof of the increasing challenges fundamentalist religious groups face in the age of the internet and a globalised world. With so much information so readily available, such groups can no longer rely on physical and intellectual isolation to maintain their boundaries. In addition to exposing religious adherents to information that challenges the hegemony of their belief systems, the internet gives individuals living in restrictive environments an alternative community...

They call themselves 'Orthoprax' — those of correct practice — to distinguish themselves from the Orthodox — those of correct belief. Every time I met one, they would introduce me to a few of their friends, though many refused to speak for fear of being discovered. There are far fewer women in this situation than men, and the women were even harder to draw out. They risk losing their children, especially in New York State, where custody is often given to the more religious parent.

Yet things have changed: once so isolated in their atheism, double-lifers passing for Orthodox, ultra-Orthodox and Yeshivish (known for devouring the Talmud) all gather online in chat rooms. I met undercover atheists from many different Hasidic sects — Satmar, Skver, Bobov — where the focus is mystical. They live in Williamsburg, Long Island, New Skver, Jerusalem. Wherever there is an insular Jewish enclave, there are individuals who have come to the conclusion that God does not exist, and yet they maintain their religious cover for social, familial and economic reasons. Many are well-established in their communities, even leaders. Many are financially successful, family men and women, moral people. 'I am your neighbour with kids in your children's class,' wrote one undercover atheist anonymously on a blog. 'I am one of the weekly sponsors of the Kiddush club... I was your counselor in camp... I do not believe in God.'...

Copyright © aeon.co

Who is a Believer?

Faith, like many things in our rapidly-changing world, is a far more complex matter than it was in the past.

Several factors have combined to rattle the intellectual and emotional foundations of faith among Orthodox Jews. For one thing, the internet connects people from vastly different backgrounds, allowing them to share their ideas and their worlds, and exposing people to the full range of opinions, beliefs, and arguments on any subject — including those that go against everything they are taught in home or school. Whereas in the past parents could generally control their children's range of exposure, today, children go "out into the world" at a much younger age via the internet and social media.

Moreover, the last two decades or so have seen a growing trend of passionate atheism, emerging from several different sources. The barbarism of radical Islam and the threat it poses to the Western world has bred an attitude of cynicism towards religion, a feeling that has been exacerbated by the revelation of scandals in the Roman Catholic Church and other religious bodies. Closer to home, Orthodox Jewry has been mercilessly rocked by scores of scandals involving rabbis found to have engaged in inappropriate behavior, leading to widespread disillusionment and cynicism. People today are perhaps more suspicious of religion than ever before, and prone to easily dismissing faith and practice as a fabrication or a cruel way to manipulate and prey on people's fears and insecurities. This suspicion is abetted by the ongoing intellectual assault on religion, led by acclaimed writers such as physicist Stephen Hawking, who has declared, "No one created the universe and no one directs our fate," and has dismissed the belief in God and the afterlife as "a fairy tale for people afraid of the dark."

Much has been written and spoken about two disturbing effects of the strong secular influences that surround the modern Jew: the phenomenon of youngsters leaving the fold of Orthodox Jewish practice ("off the *derech*"), and the phenomenon of so-called "Orthoprax" Jews — those who follow the Orthodox Jewish lifestyle but do not truly believe in God's existence, the authority of Torah, or the authority of rabbinic tradition.

Much less attention, however, has been paid to a third result of this exposure: many sincerely devoted Orthodox Jews who struggle and grapple with questions surrounding the tenets of our belief.[1] These are the Jews who want to

---

1. By "tenets" we refer to the thirteen principles set forth by the Rambam, which have been

believe, and for the most part do believe, but who find it difficult to silence the nagging voice within them that poses questions regarding the existence of God, the Divine authorship of the Torah, the truth of the Biblical narrative, and the authority of the Talmud and halachic codes. Many Jews who proudly consider themselves "believers" nevertheless entertain serious doubts about some or all of the basic tenets of faith. They pray with emotion and sincerity, and they seek to observe *Halacha* to the best of their ability, but they remain uncertain about the fundamental axioms upon which the Jewish religion stands.

The potential halachic implications of this phenomenon are immense. A person defined by *halacha* as a heretic is disqualified from basic synagogue functions such as leading the services, reading the Torah, and receiving an *aliya*, and cannot even be counted for a *minyan*. He also may not serve as a witness at weddings or before a *beis din*. These restrictions call upon us to carefully define the term "heretic." The Rambam in *Hilchos Teshuva* (3:6–8), and in greater detail in his commentary to the Mishna (*Sanhedrin*, introduction to *Chelek*), lists the core tenets that a Jew must accept to be considered a believing Jew. But the ambiguity lies in the question of what degree of "acceptance" is required. If a person avows belief but is plagued by gnawing doubts, must he be treated as a halachic heretic? Does "belief" require firm, absolute conviction, and leave no room for struggle and doubt?

In truth, this question can be asked even about self-described atheists and "Orthoprax" Jews. Many of them do not outright reject core beliefs such as the belief in a Creator, or even the belief in the Revelation at Sinai. Their attitude is one of skepticism, not firm refutation. How does *halacha* regard these "atheists"? Are they considered "believers" as long as they stop short of definitive rejection, or are they branded heretics as long as they stop short of definitive acceptance of Jewish faith?

We must also consider the possibility of distinguishing between different articles of faith. Does *halacha* equate a person who questions God's existence with one who, for example, questions the Divine authorship of the Torah? Both tenets are included in the Rambam's thirteen principles, but does this necessarily mean that they are on equal halachic footing?

קטני אמנה

As an introduction to this topic, it is important to establish that faith is not an "all or nothing" enterprise. Our tradition recognizes that people have different levels of belief. Rashi, in his Torah commentary (*Bereishis* 6:7), describes Noach

---

generally accepted throughout the ages as the defining parameters of Jewish belief.

WHO IS A BELIEVER?

as מקטני אמנה — "among those with little faith" — and writes that Noach "believed but did not believe" (מאמין ואינו מאמין) that the flood would occur. He therefore did not enter the ark until he was forced to escape from the rising floodwaters. Although the Torah glowingly describes Noach as an איש צדיק ("righteous man"), his faith was nevertheless imperfect. This clearly demonstrates that as with all areas of religion, there exist different levels, and even those who have yet to achieve perfection can be called "righteous."

This point is made explicitly by the *Chazon Ish* in his *Sefer Emuna U-Bitachon* (chapter 2). He writes:

> כן מדת האמונה – יש בה מדרגות זה למעלה מזה, **וקטני אמנה ג"כ בכלל מאמינים, כיון שאינם בכלל הכופרים והמינים**, אבל אמונתם חלושה, ואין פעולת אמונה שולטת עליהם, רק נגד עבירות היותר מפורסמות ואשר כל הצבור נזהרים בהן...

> The same is true regarding the attribute of faith — there are different levels, one higher than the next. Those of little faith are also considered believers, because they are not among the heretics and apostates. Rather, their faith is weak, and the effects of faith exert control upon them only against the more famous sins which everyone avoids…

Clearly, then, imperfect faith does not render a person a halachic "heretic." The question then becomes whether this can be said also of an agnostic, who is undecided about the basic tenets of Jewish faith.

ונתברר בה אמונתו בהם

As mentioned above, the Rambam lists the various forms of heresy in *Hilchos Teshuva*, where he speaks of those who reject certain beliefs. We present here several examples:

האומר שאין שם אלו-ה ואין לעולם מנהיג — One who says there is no God and the world has no ruler;

האומר שיש שם מנהיג אבל הוא שניים או יותר — One who says there is a Ruler, but there are two or more;

האומר...שהוא גוף ובעל תמונה — One who says that He…is a body and has an image;

האומר שאינו לבדו הראשון — One who says that He is not the only first [cause];

האומר שאין שם נבואה כלל — One who says there is no prophecy whatsoever;

האומר שאין התורה מעם ה' — One who says the Torah does not come from God.

In all these examples, the Rambam speaks of האומר — "one who says" that a tenet of Jewish faith is incorrect. This terminology is borrowed from the Mishna in *Maseches Sanhedrin* (90a), which lists among those who have no share in the afterlife, האומר אין תחיית המתים מן התורה ואין תורה מן השמיים — **"One who says** there is no Torah source for resurrection, and the Torah does not come from the heavens." The simple reading of this phrase is that it refers to someone who definitively rejects the given tenet of faith, and not someone who entertains doubts.

The precise opposite conclusion, however, appears to emerge from the Rambam's comments in his commentary to the Mishna. After enumerating the famous thirteen עיקרי אמונה ("principles of faith"), the Rambam writes:

וכאשר יאמין האדם אלה היסודות כולם ונתברר בה אמונתו בהם, הוא נכנס בכלל ישראל ומצוה לאהבו... וכשנתקלקל לאדם יסוד מאלה היסודות הרי יצא מן הכלל וכפר בעיקר... ומצוה לשונאו...

> If a person believes all these principles, and his faith in them is affirmed, he is included among Israel and it is a *mitzva* to love him... But if any one of these principles is shaken within a person, then he has left the fold and become a heretic...and it is a *mitzva* to despise him...

The Rambam here requires that נתברר...אמונתו — a person's faith must be strongly affirmed — and he considers someone heretic when נתקלקל לאדם יסוד מאלה היסודות — the foundations of his belief is shaken. This point becomes clearer in light of Rav Yosef Kapach's translation of this passage:[2]

כאשר יהיו קיימים לאדם כל היסודות הללו ואמונתו בהם אמיתית, הרי הוא נכנס בכלל ישראל... וכאשר יפקפק אדם ביסוד מאלו היסודות, הרי זה יצא מן הכלל וכפר בעיקר...

> If all these principles are established for a person, and his belief in them is genuine, then he is included among Israel... But if a person questions any of these principles, he has left the fold and is a heretic...

The clear implication of this passage is that even questioning or entertaining doubts about any of the articles of faith renders one a כופר בעיקר (heretic). Seemingly, then, we must explain that when the Rambam speaks in *Hilchos Teshuva* of האומר — one who holds heretical beliefs — he refers not only to the

---

2. The Rambam wrote his commentary to the Mishna in Arabic. The standard Hebrew translation of the introduction to *Chelek*, which appears in the Vilna edition of the Talmud, dates back to medieval Spain. Rav Kapach's translation of the Rambam's commentary to the Mishna, which was published during the 1960s, is regarded by many as more accurate.

definitive rejection of the tenets of faith, but also to doubting or questioning these tenets, as even entertaining doubts falls under the category of heresy.

This also appears to be the position of the Ramban, who, in his critique of the Rambam's *Sefer Ha-Mitzvos* (omitted *lavin*, 1), writes that it is forbidden to question or deny the belief in God:

...שלא נשכח עיקר האלקות ונכפור או נסתפק בו לומר שאין אלו-ה ושהעולם קדמון...

[We are commanded] not to forget the principle of divinity, or deny or entertain doubts about it, thinking that there is no God and the world always existed…

The Ramban explicitly includes נסתפק בו — entertaining doubts about God's existence — under the Torah prohibition against heresy.

התרים אחר מחשבות לבם

In contradistinction to the Rambam's remarks in his commentary to the Mishna, a different passage in his writings strongly suggests that he did not equate agnosticism with outright heresy. In *Hilchos Avoda Zara* (2:3), the Rambam discusses the prohibition of ולא תתורו אחרי לבבכם (*Bamidbar* 15:39), which he understands as forbidding engaging in thoughts that can lead to heresy. He writes:

כל מחשבה שהוא גורם לו לאדם לעקור עיקר מעיקרי התורה מוזהרין אנו שלא להעלותה על לבנו ולא נסיח דעתנו לכך ונחשוב ונמשך אחר הרהורי הלב... כיצד? פעמים יתור אחר עבודת כוכבים ופעמים יחשוב ביחוד הבורא שמא הוא שמא אינו...ופעמים בנבואה, שמא היא אמת שמא היא אינה, ופעמים בתורה, שמא היא מן השמיים, שמא אינה...ונמצא יוצא לידי מינות...

Any thought which causes a person to uproot one of the principles of Torah — it is forbidden for us to bring it to mind, or to turn our minds to it, contemplate [it] and be drawn after such thoughts of the heart… How? Sometimes one inquires about idolatry, and sometimes one thinks about the Oneness of the Creator, perhaps it is so, and perhaps it isn't; sometimes about prophecy — perhaps it is true, and perhaps it isn't; and sometimes about Torah — perhaps it is from the heavens, and perhaps it isn't…and he will then end up becoming a heretic.

According to the Rambam, it appears, inquiring about the basic tenets of Jewish belief is forbidden because it **can lead to heresy**, not because it constitutes heresy. Contemplating and questioning basic tenets such as the existence of a single Creator, the truth of prophecy, and the Divine origin of the Torah is forbidden by force of the Biblical command of ולא תתורו, but does not result in a person's classification as a heretic. This implication stands in direct contrast to the Rambam's aforementioned remarks in his commentary to the Mishna, where he seems to require definitive affirmation of the tenets of faith, and considers it heretical to even question or entertain doubts about them.

The confusion surrounding the Rambam's view is compounded by his comments later in this same chapter in *Hilchos Avodas Kochavim* (2:5), where he defines the term אפיקורסים:

> האפיקורסים הם התרים אחר מחשבות לבם בסכלות דברים שאמרנו עד שנמצאו עוברים על גופי תורה להכעיס...ואומרים שאין בזה עוון.

> Heretics are those who stray after the thoughts of their heart with the foolishness of the aforementioned matters, until they violate the fundamentals of Torah to anger [God]...and say this entails no sin.

Here, the Rambam classifies התרים — those who "search" and questioningly explore the principles of faith — as actual heretics, not as people who are on the road that will lead to heresy.

Doubting God's Existence

The question surrounding the Rambam's position is addressed at length by Rav Yechezkel Sarna in his *Daliyos Yechezkel* (vol. 5, p. 169). He answers by distinguishing between God's existence and the other principles of faith. In describing the prohibition of ולא תתורו, the Rambam gives three examples — questioning the belief in God's unity, the belief in prophecy, and the belief in the Divine origin of the Torah. Significantly, the Rambam does not discuss in this context the belief in God's existence. When it comes to this tenet of faith, questioning constitutes outright heresy, not merely a violation of ולא תתורו. Rav Sarna writes:

> המאמין הוא השלם באמונתו והמסתפק הוא הכופר ונקרא אפיקורוס. במה דברים אמורים, בעיקר מציאות ה' שאין בו מקום לשמא, וכל שמא בו היא כפירה ודאית ונקרא אפיקורוס. אבל בשאר העיקרים, אף כי אין רשות לכל אדם לחקור ולהסתפק בהם, ועל זה נאמר הלאו של לא תתורו...מכל מקום אינו קרוי אפיקורוס על חקירתו בלבד...

> A believer is one who is firm in his faith, and one who entertains doubt is a heretic and is called an אפיקורס. But this applies only with regard to the tenet of God's existence, which does not allow room for doubt, and any doubt constitutes definitive heresy, and he is called an אפיקורוס. But when it comes to the other tenets, even though not every person[3] is allowed to inquire about them and question them, and regarding this

---

3. As Rav Sarna later discusses, the Rambam applies this prohibition to ordinary laymen,

the prohibition of ולא תתורו was said…nevertheless, one is not considered an אפיקורוס solely because of his inquiry…

We may apply this distinction also to the aforementioned comments of the Ramban, who wrote that it is forbidden to entertain doubts about God's existence. This position does not necessarily extend to the other tenets of Jewish faith, and very likely was said only in reference to the belief in the existence of a Supreme Being.[4]

We should note, however, that Rav Sarna's distinction does not resolve the Rambam's remarks in his commentary to the Mishna, where he considers it heresy כאשר יפקפק אדם ביסוד מאלו היסודות — to question **any** of the articles of faith, without distinguishing between the belief in God's existence and the other tenets.

Faith and אונס

This question concerning the status of agnosticism might hinge on the precise reason why rejection of the articles of faith renders one a heretic.

This issue arises amid the discussion surrounding the Ra'avad's controversial stance concerning the tenet of Divine incorporeality. In *Hilchos Teshuva* (3:7), the Rambam rules unequivocally that one who believes that God has a physical body or image is considered a heretic. The Ra'avad comments:

ולמה קרא לזה מין? וכמה גדולים וטובים ממנו הלכו בזו המחשבה לפי מה שראו במקראות ויותר ממה שראו דברי האגדות המשבשות את הדעות.

> Why did he call such a person a heretic? Several people greater and better than him[5] followed this view based on what they saw in the Scriptures and — more so — what they saw in the words of the *aggados*, which confuse the minds.[6]

---

whereas יחידי סגולה — uniquely gifted individuals — are allowed to inquire about the articles of faith.

4. At first glance, we might also explain on this basis the term האומר used by the Mishna in reference to those who deny resurrection and the Divine origin of the Torah. As we noted, this term appears to describe definitive rejection, not skepticism. It is perhaps significant that the Mishna speaks of belief in resurrection and the Divine origin of the Torah, and not of the belief in God's existence, perhaps because even questioning this belief constitutes heresy. However, the Rambam in *Hilchos Teshuva*, as cited earlier, speaks also of אלו-ה האומר שאין שם — "one who says there is no God."
5. The *Or Sameiach* claims that the word ממנו ("than him") is a mistake, and the word should be מעמנו ("from among us").
6. The *Kesef Mishneh* cites from the *Sefer Ha-Ikarim* (1:2) a different version of the Ra'avad's

The Ra'avad observes that many people were misled by the numerous anthropomorphic references to God that appear both in *Tanach* and in the writings of *Chazal*. Many verses and Midrashic sources seem to ascribe physical properties to God, leading some people to believe that God has a body. Such people, the Ra'avad writes, should not be regarded as heretics, despite their following incorrect views about God.

Rav Chayim of Brisk[7] explained that the Rambam did not agree with the Ra'avad because the familiar rule of אונס, which absolves a sinner of culpability if he transgresses due to circumstances entirely beyond his control, does not apply to belief in the thirteen articles of faith. A person who does not accept the basic tenets of Jewish belief cannot be part of *Klal Yisrael*, and it does not matter whether or not he is to be blamed for his failure to accept these beliefs. Rav Chayim drew proof to this theory from the Rambam's comment in his commentary to the Mishna, which we noted earlier: וכשנתקלקל...הרי יצא מן הכלל. This implies that once a person's belief is corrupted, regardless of how or why this occurred, the person is no longer regarded as a believer.[8]

---

comment: אע"פ שעיקר האמונה כן הוא, המאמין היותו גוף מצד תפיסתו לשונות הפסוקים והמדרשות כפשטן, אין ראוי לקרותו מין — "Although this is, indeed, the correct belief, one who believes He is a body because of his understanding the text of the verses and *midrashim* according to their plain meaning, should not be called a heretic."

7. Cited by his disciple, Rav Elchanan Wasserman, in *Kovetz Ma'amarim* (מאמר שיבוש הדעת), and at the end of *Kovetz He'aros* (דוגמאות לביאור אגדות, 12:8). In *Kovetz Ma'amarim*, Rav Elchanan comments that Rav Chayim would say, דער וואס איז נעביך אאפיקורוס, איז אויך אאפיקורוס — "One who is *nebach* an *apikorus* is still an *apikorus*."

8. See *Haggadas Mi-Beis Levi*, p. 190. Rav Elchanan Wasserman, in *Kovetz Ma'amarim*, asserts that the Ra'avad, who disputes the Rambam's position, accepts this premise, but makes an exception for those who accept incorrect beliefs thinking they are espoused by the Torah. The Ra'avad speaks here specifically of those who reach the wrong conclusions about God based on the Torah and rabbinic literature. Such people cannot be considered heretics because they are misled by the Torah itself. But in general, those who deny articles of faith due to some mistake are regarded as heretics, even according to the Ra'avad. Rav Elchanan draws proof to the Ra'avad's position from the Gemara's comment in *Maseches Sanhedrin* (98b) that Rabbi Hillel did not believe *Mashiach* would come, as he felt that the opportunity for the Messianic Era was forfeited during the time of King Chizkiyahu. It is hardly conceivable that one of the Talmudic Sages had the status of heretic (and, indeed, the *Sefer Ha-Ikarim* drew proof from the Gemara's comment that belief in *Mashiach*'s arrival does not constitute an article of faith). Presumably, Rabbi Hillel was not a heretic, because he reached this conclusion based on an incorrect interpretation of Torah texts. This point was made much earlier, by the Radbaz (4:187): ממי שטועה באחד מעיקרי הדת מחמת עיונו הנפסד שלא נקרא בשביל זה כופר, והרי [רבי] הלל היה אדם גדול וטעה באחד מעיקרי הדת שאמר אין להם משיח לישראל שכבר אכלוהו בימי חזקיהו. ומפני זה הטעות לא חשבוהו כופר ח"ו דאם לא כן איך היו אומרים שמועה משמו. והטעם מבואר כיון שאין כפירתו אלא מפני שחשב שמה שעלה בעיונו אמת, ואם כן אנוס הוא ופטור.

Oxygen and Poison

Abarbanel, in his *Rosh Amana* (12), formulates this concept somewhat differently. In rejecting the Ra'avad's argument that those who mistakenly believe in a corporeal God are not heretics, Abarbanel likens incorrect beliefs to poison, as they have a corrosive effect upon a person's soul:

> הדעת הכוזב, כשיהיה בעיקר מעיקרי האמונה, כבר יסיר הנפש מהצלחתו האמיתית ולא יביאהו לחיי העולם הבא, אע"פ שלא יעשה אותה בכוונה למרוד, כי כמו שהסם המות כשיאכל האדם אותו יכלה רוחו, ונשמתו אליו יאסוף, אף על פי שנאמר שאכל אותו בחשבו שהיה מאכל בריא ונאות, כן הכפירה והאמונה הכוזבת בענין עיקרי הדת יגרשו נפש האדם וימנעהו מירושת העולם הבא בלא ספק.

A false idea relevant to any of the principles of faith will already deny the soul its true success, and will cause it not to reach life in the next world, even if this was not done with the intention of rebelling. For just as when a person eats poison his spirit will perish and his soul will depart even though we know that he ate it thinking it was healthy, proper food, similarly, heresy and false beliefs relevant to the principles of religion banish the person's soul and undoubtedly prevent him from inheriting the next world.

Like Rav Chayim, Abarbanel asserts that intent is not a factor when it comes to the principles of Jewish faith. However, there is a subtle but crucial difference between their approaches. Rav Chayim claimed that correct beliefs are necessary for one to earn inclusion in the faith community of *Klal Yisrael*, whereas Abarbanel wrote that false beliefs corrupt the soul. The difference between these two formulations is whether we need to embrace the correct beliefs (Rav Chayim), or whether we must avoid incorrect beliefs (Abarbanel). In Rav Chayim's view, accepting the articles of faith is a necessity for the Jewish soul like oxygen is a necessity for the body, whereas according to Abarbanel, accepting beliefs that run counter the articles of faith destroys the Jewish soul like poison destroys the body.[9]

Seemingly, the status of agnostics, who neither definitively accept nor definitively reject the tenets of Jewish faith, hinges on this very question. If we must actively embrace the articles of faith, as Rav Chayim maintained, then agnostics

---

9. An interesting expression of this difference is the question posed by Rav Elchanan Wasserman in *Kovetz Ma'amarim* as to why, according to Rav Chayim, a young child is considered part of the faith community. If these beliefs are requisites for inclusion, then even those who are intellectually incapable of embracing them should be excluded. Clearly, this question does not arise according to Abarbanel.

are no different from heretics, as both groups fail to affirm the required beliefs. If, however, we need only not to embrace opposing beliefs, than an agnostic, who has not fully embraced any belief, would not be considered a heretic.

We might, at first glance, consider distinguishing in this regard between the different articles of faith, along the lines of Rav Yechezkel Sarna's aforementioned discussion. Perhaps, belief in God's existence is the "oxygen" for the soul, and thus even innocently denying this belief as a result of mistaken information or logic constitutes heresy. By contrast, when it comes to the other articles of faith, the requirement is that we do not embrace false beliefs, and thus innocent intellectual errors and skepticism would not be regarded as heresy. According to this distinction, the Ra'avad might agree with the Rambam that those who do not accept God's existence due to an innocent mistake would be considered heretics, as innocence is a factor only with respect to the other twelve principles of faith, such as Divine incorporeality, the context of the Ra'avad's remark.[10]

In truth, however, neither Abarbanel nor the Rambam draw any distinction in this regard between the different articles of faith. And, as cited above, the Rambam in his commentary to the Mishna clearly indicates that uncertainty surrounding any of the thirteen articles of faith amounts to heresy: וכשנתקלקל לאדם יסוד מאלה היסודות הרי יצא מן הכלל...

הוי ליה למידק

An entirely different approach is taken by Rav Shlomo Ashkenazi Rappaport of Chelm, in his *Mirkeves Ha-Mishneh* (*Hilchos Teshuva* 3:7). In responding to the Ra'avad's objection to the Rambam's ruling, Rav Rappaport writes, חמיר שגגת אמונה זרה דהוה ליה למידק — "A mistake regarding a foreign belief is more stringent [than mistakes involving other violations], because he should have studied more carefully."

In his view, there is no such thing as "innocent mistakes" when it comes to the thirteen articles of faith, because one is required to arrive at the correct beliefs. According to this view, agnostics, too, would be classified as heretics, for the same reason of הוה ליה למידק — they are expected to overcome their doubts and reach the correct conclusions. This comment was made with regard to the belief in Divine incorporeality, and it would therefore certainly apply to the belief in God's existence.

---

10. According to Rav Elchanan Wasserman's analysis of the Ra'avad's position discussed in n.8 above, the Ra'avad in any event would consider such a person a heretic, as one cannot possibly reject God's existence based on a faulty reading of the Torah or rabbinic writings.

Summary

The simple reading of the Rambam suggests that one must definitively accept all thirteen articles of faith, and entertaining doubts qualifies as heresy. However, it is possible that this applies only to the belief in God's existence, but not to the other tenets of faith, regarding which uncertainty would not be akin to heresy. The Ra'avad maintains that innocently failing to accept a tenet of Jewish faith as a result of a mistake does not qualify as heresy. It is possible, however, that even in his view, when it comes to the belief in God's existence, there is no difference between intentional rejection and an innocent intellectual mistake.

THE JERUSALEM POST

Prominent Rabbi and Educator Accused of Sexual Abuse

June 21, 2016
by Jeremy Sharon

A prominent rabbi and educator living in Beit Shemesh has been accused of misusing his authority and position for his sexual gratification.

An ad hoc rabbinical court of senior rabbis in Israel and the US issued a warning instructing women to avoid all contact with Rabbi P, the founder of a website and study program called Master Torah, designed to aid the study of religious texts and retain the knowledge acquired.

According to the Master Torah website, P has rabbinical ordination from several authorities, including from the Chief Rabbinate, and is qualified as a rabbinical judge.

He has taught at Yeshiva University High Schools of Los Angeles, the Michlala seminary in Jerusalem, and was head of the Kollel (program for married yeshiva students) of Aish HaTorah in Jerusalem and Austin, Texas.

Following the publication of the rabbinical court ruling, Tamara Schoor, P's former student, welcomed the decision but said the ruling had been "a long-time coming" and that the rabbinical court "should have addressed this a long time ago, but better late than never."

Schoor told the press she met P at the age of 15 when "the process of grooming and manipulation began."

She was introduced by a camp counselor who had been in contact with P while she was at Michlala, and was told the rabbi would be able to help her regarding questions about Judaism and religious faith.

Schoor would meet with P in New York at his mother's house and he built up a mentor relationship with her over several years.

When Schoor came to Israel to study at Michlala at the age of 18, she made contact with P again, and would often meet with him at his home in Beit Shemesh, where she was also a frequent guest for Shabbat.

"Over the course of my year of religious study in Israel, he carefully broke down my personal boundaries, creating a high level of dependence and isolation, ensuring I was fully reliant on him for spiritual guidance, love and support," she said. "Alone in a foreign country, he became my mentor, role model and family. A brilliant manipulator, he was able to convince me that his sole intention was to care for and empower me and my every action."

Schoor said it took years for her to recognize and accept the insidious mind games, betrayal of trust and carefully orchestrated destruction of her innocence.

"It was only when I became aware of the existence of other victims that I was determined to take action and prevent additional abuse. I began a campaign of phone calls and emails, reaching out to anyone I could identify in the hopes of finding additional victims to speak out with and a safe and reliable method of publicizing it anonymously.

"But at every turn a door closed: victims afraid to be exposed, rabbis finding excuses not to address it, organizations lying to protect themselves and much more."

When contacted by The Jerusalem Post, P said he would not comment on the allegations themselves.

He said however that "I was never presented with any specific allegations when I visited the rabbinical court," and added that he was never contacted by the rabbinical court after his one and only meeting with the rabbis concerned.

Schoor has provided a statement to Israeli police.

In the ruling issued by the ad hoc rabbinical court on June 14, Rabbis Menachem Mendel Hacohen Shafran, Gershon Bass and Haim Malinowitz said several rabbis and community figures had reported P's "deviant" behavior.

Having spoken with P, the rabbis issued a ruling prohibiting him from associating with women in any way and for any reason, including married and unmarried women of any age.

The rabbis also warned all women against meeting with P for any reason publicly or privately, and from contacting him in any way including by phone or email and any other form of electronic correspondence...

...

Schoor herself issued concerns she had with the process of the rabbinical court in dealing with such issues, including that the system is reliant on the victim to bring additional victims forward as a part of the investigative process, and that the victim has to deal with rabbis and other officials who have no training in this field and don't always have the qualities of empathy and sensitivity that are crucial in dealing with victims.

"While I wish the process hadn't taken so long I want to thank the Beit Din for their leadership on this issue in making a strong statement about the danger P poses," said Schoor.

"Rabbis have an undeniable role to play in these cases and can effect tremendous change. In light of the impact the Rabbinic statement has had, I implore community leaders and rabbis to follow the precedence that has been set for exposing dangerous predators. I know that the downfall of a well-respected and admired rabbi or community member causes confusion, fear and turmoil but the community relies on their leaders to protect them."

Copyright © jpost.com

The Disgraced Rabbi

One of the most tragic and harmful ills of contemporary Jewish life is the seemingly endless stream of scandals involving prominent rabbis and Torah educators. Shamefully, hardly a month goes by without the media reporting salacious allegations of corruption, abuse, or sexual impropriety involving clergy. These damning reports have caused and continue to cause a great deal of shame and embarrassment to Orthodox Jewry worldwide, as erstwhile role models and educators are exposed as criminals or sexual deviants.

As the Orthodox community engages in much-needed soul-searching and explores ways to purge this dreadful phenomenon from its midst, among the questions that have arisen relates to the status of Torah material produced by rabbis accused of inappropriate conduct. This question became relevant in February 2010 after the news broke of allegations of sexual misconduct perpetrated by a prominent figure in Israel's religious community, "Rabbi A". Rabbi A had been a highly popular lecturer, and recordings and transcriptions of his discourses were widely disseminated and recognized for their ingenuity and depth. Many of Rabbi A's former students and admirers were left wondering whether or not they may continue reading and listening to this material. More recently, in the summer of 2015, the esteemed "Rabbi B," Rosh Yeshiva and author of an acclaimed series of books, was arrested on serious charges of rape and molestation. News outlets reported that after the news broke, students in Rabbi B's yeshiva discarded all copies of his books on the premises.

Less than a year later, in June 2016, two letters were signed by prominent rabbis and *dayanim* in Israel and the United States warning women to keep a distance from "Rabbi C," an accomplished Torah scholar and educator. The signatories affirmed that they received credible testimonies from numerous girls and women of his sexual misconduct, and urged all women to avoid any sort of contact with Rabbi C. Rabbi C had previously launched and maintained a popular Torah website, which features thousands of Torah classes on a variety of subjects, delivered with exceptional clarity and breadth. Given the immense scholarly value of this material, many wondered whether they may still access and benefit from the resources on the rabbi's website, even after he was discovered to be guilty of some of the most severe Torah violations.

This essay will deal with three questions relevant to the unfortunate situation of a disgraced rabbi: 1) Is it permissible to continue studying Torah from him, despite the grave misconduct of which he is allegedly guilty? 2) Even if *halacha* forbids studying from him in the present, may one learn material produced before the allegations surfaced? 3) May a disgraced rabbi resume his Torah educational activities after repenting?

Unsubstantiated Rumors

Before addressing the permissibility of learning Torah from a disgraced rabbi, we must first emphasize that this entire discussion refers to a rabbi whose misconduct has been confirmed. Unfortunately, in today's age of digital communication, unsubstantiated rumors contrived and disseminated by agenda-driven parties fly through the news, and especially social media, before the facts are sorted out and verified. Knowing the impatience of media consumers, many of whom do not generally read past article titles, some news websites run irresponsible, sensationalist headlines that misrepresent the facts and can lead to baseless suspicions. The "juicy" nature of rabbinic scandals, along with the anti-Orthodox agenda of many media outlets, make rabbis prime targets of unverified rumors and allegations. Common sense, common decency, and the obligation to respect Torah scholars all dictate that we avoid reaching conclusions based on hearsay or melodramatic headlines, and reserve judgment until allegations brought against Torah scholars are confirmed.

This warning was issued already by the Rambam in one of his published responsa (*Teshuvos Ha-Rambam*, 111), where he addresses the situation of a well-respected scholar who served as his congregation's cantor, and about whom rumors spread of serious misdeeds. The Rambam devotes the bulk of his responsum to emphasizing that no one should be demoted from his post based on rumors, particularly if that individual has adversaries with a motive to sully his reputation. Drawing upon the Gemara's discussion in *Maseches Moed Katan* (17a), the Rambam writes that a Torah scholar who is suspected of wrongdoing should be privately reprimanded, and if he mends his ways, then he may retain his post. It is only if the wrongdoing is committed publicly that he must be demoted.

Similarly, the *Chasam Sofer* (*Teshuvos*, O.C. 1:175) addresses the case of a גבאי צדקה — a director of a charity fund — about whom rumors spread of an inappropriate relationship with a certain non-Jewish woman. In the wake of these rumors, community members pressured the rabbi to remove him from his post, but the rabbi refused. The *Chasam Sofer* emphatically supported the rabbi's decision, asserting that no one should be deposed based on rumors and hearsay:

אין לפסול איש על רינון וקול בעלמא, ואין להחזיק הקול אלא בעדים ברורים.

One should not disqualify a person based on murmurings and mere rumors, and the rumors should be verified only with reliable witnesses.

The *Chasam Sofer* writes that in the end, the person confessed to his wrongdoing, and he was promptly dismissed from his position.

Another example appears in a responsum of Rav Meir Simcha of Dvinsk (13), who was asked about a certain *shochet* who was imprisoned by a non-Jewish court for an alleged crime. Rav Meir Simcha ruled that the court's guilty verdict did not suffice as grounds for removing this *shochet* from his post, as the courts at that time could not be trusted.

Of particular relevance to our discussion is a responsum by Rav Aharon Walkin of Pinsk in his *Zekan Aharon* (30), addressing the question posed to him by Rav Zalman Sorotzkin concerning a *shochet* who was rumored to have had occasionally visited the home of a woman suspected of prostitution. Rav Walkin writes that sexual impropriety does not, strictly speaking, disqualify someone from serving as *shochet*, but additionally, the *shochet* in question should not be dismissed solely on the basis of rumors. Writing with particular passion and vehemence, Rav Walkin says that as disturbing as these rumors were, and notwithstanding the fact that a person filling such a distinguished role must have an unimpeachable record, it is forbidden to remove a person from a post based on mere hearsay:

> גם אני מרחוק הנני נרעש ונפחד לשמוע כזה על משרת בקודש שנצרך להיות מצויין ביר"ש שכם אחד יותר על סתם בני אדם, אבל בכ"ז בבואי לחתוך עליו דין תורה, את האלקים אני ירא לשפוך עליו כל חמתי ולירד לחייו לקפח פרנסתו דההוא גברא דתלי ביה טפלי. וכל גופא מרתע בי להיות שוחט ולשחוט אב לבנים ובעל לאשה על יסוד שמועות קלושות כאלה... השתא שו"ב ששוחט בהמות אם ידיו מרתתות בו שחיטתו פסולה, כ"ש אני שבאתי לשחוט נפשות אדם, ולא רק ידי אלא כל גופי מרתת, היאך אוכל לשחטו בשעה שעפ"י דין תורה אין יסוד לזה? האם אפשר להתחסד יותר מהתורה עצמה?

> I, too, even from afar, am shaken and horrified to hear such things about someone serving in a sacred post, who is supposed to be outstanding in fear of God, on a level above most people. But nevertheless, as I come to decide Torah law with regard to him, I am too fearful of God to pour my wrath upon him, to disrupt the livelihood and deny the sustenance of that person accused of wrongdoing. My entire body shudders [at the thought of] being a slaughterer and slaughtering a father of children and husband of a woman on the basis of weak rumors such as these… A *shochet* who slaughters animals — if his hands tremble, his slaughtering is invalid; all the more so, then, as I come to slaughter human lives, not only my hands, but my entire body trembles. How can I slaughter him when I know that according to Torah law there is no basis for this? Is it possible to be more pious than the Torah itself?

Rav Walkin advised Rav Sorotzkin to have the *shochet* make a formal promise to avoid going anywhere near the house in question, and, as a precaution, to inspect his knife twice each week for a year.

This responsum underscores the extreme caution that is needed before acting upon rumors of misconduct, even as it points to the need for prudent and discreet measures in response to such rumors to ensure that the alleged misconduct does not continue.

Moreover, we must bear in mind the Gemara's instruction in *Maseches Berachos* (19a), "If you saw a Torah scholar who committed a transgression at night, do not suspect him the next day because…he definitely repented." In other words, not every wrongful act committed by a religious leader warrants public condemnation and a public outcry. Rabbis, like all people, may be flawed and plagued by weaknesses and occasional lapses in judgment. A person with a reputation of piety who is seen acting wrongly on one occasion must be given the benefit of the doubt that he has acknowledged his wrongdoing and has repented. Accordingly, the *Chafetz Chayim* writes (*Hilchos Lashon Ha-Ra* 4:14):

> וכל שכן אם הוא איש תלמיד חכם וירא חטא, אך עתה גבר יצרו עליו, בודאי עון גדול הוא לפרסם חטאו ואסור אפילו להרהר אחריו כי בודאי עשה תשובה, ואף אם יצרו נתחזק עליו פעם אחת, נפשו מרה לו אחר כך על זה ולבבו ירא וחרד מאד על אשמתו...

> All the more so, if the person is a Torah scholar and God-fearing, but now his evil inclination overcame him, it is definitely a grievous sin to publicize his wrongdoing, and it is forbidden even to suspect him, because he definitely repented, and although his evil inclination overpowered him on one occasion, his soul is distressed over this afterward, and his heart fears and trembles greatly out of guilt…

Our discussion, then, relates to the unfortunate situations of Torah scholars who have been determined to regularly engage in improper behavior, and the question then arises as to whether people may continue learning from them or making use of their inherently valuable Torah resources.

Rabbi Meir and Elisha ben Avuya

The most famous example of a student learning Torah from a disgraced rabbi is Rabbi Meir, who continued studying under his teacher, Elisha ben Avuya, even after Elisha abandoned Jewish faith and become a heretic, whereupon the rabbis began derisively calling Elisha ben Avuyah *Acher* ("The Other"). The Gemara in *Maseches Chagiga* (15b) questions Rabbi Meir's practice to learn from *Acher*, on the basis of a verse in *Sefer Malachi* (2:7): כי שפתי כהן ישמרו דעת ותורה יבקשו מפיהו כי

מלאך ה' צבאות הוא — "For the lips of a *Kohen* shall preserve knowledge, and they shall seek Torah from his mouth, because he is an angel of the Lord of Hosts." The verse here urges us to "seek Torah" from a teacher who can be described as "an angel of the Lord of Hosts," and thus Rabbi Yochanan, as the Gemara cites, established that one may not study Torah from a teacher who conducts himself improperly and therefore does not resemble an "angel." How, then, was Rabbi Meir permitted to learn Torah from an apostate?

The Gemara answers that Rabbi Meir based himself on other verses, which indicate that one may learn Torah wisdom even from sinful people.[1] To reconcile the seeming contradiction between these verses and Malachi's admonition to study only from rabbis who resemble an "angel," the Gemara distinguishes between a גדול and a קטן — meaning, between great scholars, like Rabbi Meir, and people of lesser stature. Exceptional scholars, who are capable of absorbing the valuable wisdom of a wayward rabbi without coming under his negative influence, may do so, but others must avoid such rabbis and not learn from them.[2]

The Gemara then proceeds to cite an aphorism that was reportedly spoken by the Jews of *Eretz Yisrael*: "Rabbi Meir ate the fig and discarded the peel." He had the ability to distinguish between the "fig" — the genius of Elisha ben Avuya's Torah wisdom — and the "peel" — his heretical beliefs. This statement is likely brought to explain the distinction drawn between קטן and גדול, noting that only those who reached a level where they are capable of discarding the "peel" may study under a Torah scholar who acts improperly.

Does Halacha Accept Rabbi Meir's View?

Tosfos apply this distinction in reference to the Gemara's comment (*Maseches Ta'anis* 7a) permitting studying only from a תלמיד חכם הגון — an upstanding Torah scholar. Noting the Gemara's discussion in *Chagiga* regarding Rabbi Meir and Elisha ben Avuya, *Tosfos* explain that Rabbi Meir was exceptional due to his special stature, and thus he was permitted to study under Elisha ben Avuya despite the general prohibition against learning under sinful scholars.

Among later *poskim*, however, we find different views as to whether this

---

1. The verses are שמעי בת וראי והטי אזנך ושמע דברי חכמים ולבך תשית לדעתי (*Mishlei* 22:17), and אזנך ושכחי עמך ובית אביך (*Tehillim* 45:11), both of which are interpreted by the Gemara as referring to studying Torah from one who conducts himself improperly (see Rashi).
2. This is how Rashi explained the rationale underlying the Gemara's distinction between a גדול and a קטן. For a different explanation, see Maharal, *Nesivos Olam* (*Nesiv Ha-Torah*, chapter 8).

distinction is accepted as normative *halacha*. The Rambam (*Hilchos Talmud Torah* 4:1) codifies the prohibition against learning from a rabbi who acts improperly, without making an exception for people of special stature:

> הרב שאינו הולך בדרך טובה אף על פי שחכם גדול הוא וכל העם צריכים לו, אין מתלמדים ממנו עד שובו למוטב.

> A rabbi who does not follow the proper path, even if he is a great scholar and everyone needs him — people should not learn from him until he returns to proper conduct.

The Rambam's ruling is cited by the *Shulchan Aruch* (Y.D. 246:8).

The *Shach* raises the question of why the Rambam and *Shulchan Aruch* do not make an exception for a גדול, and instead appear to forbid all students from studying under a sinful rabbi. He suggests that the Rambam perhaps felt that in his time, all people were considered קטנים and should not be permitted to study under a wayward teacher. In a somewhat similar vein, the Chida (*Birkei Yosef*, Y.D. 246:9) suggests that the Rambam viewed the exception made for a גדול as applicable only in the very rare case of an extraordinary and unique scholar, such as a Rabbi Meir. For this reason, the Rambam did not codify this exception in presenting the prohibition against studying from a sinner, even though, as some have speculated, the Rambam relied on this distinction as the basis for his study of the works of Aristotle and other non-Jewish philosophers.[3] Although in principle a גדול is permitted to study from a wayward rabbi, the Rambam chose not to codify this provision, because, in the Chida's words, לא רבים יחכמו כרבי מאיר, — ואם כה יאמר דגדול שרי, כל אחד ידמה בדעתו כי גדול הוא וילכד בפח "Not everyone is as wise as Rabbi Meir, and if he [the Rambam] would say that it is permissible for a גדול, everyone would consider himself a גדול in his mind, and then fall into the trap." The Chida similarly writes in his *Sha'ar Yosef* (*Horiyos* 12a):

> כל אחד מחזיק עצמו לגדול הדור שניתנה לו בינה יתירה ואין באחיו גדול ממנו, ומשום הכי לא רצה לכתוב חילוק זה.

> Everyone considers himself the leading sage of the generation to whom

---

3. See also the Chida's comments in *Devarim Achadim*, p. 174, and *Or Ha-Chayim* to *Devarim* 12:28.
Several *Acharonim* noted that the Rambam, at the beginning of his *Guide for the Perplexed*, cites one of the two verses that were suggested as bases for Rabbi Meir's decision to continue studying from Elisha ben Avuya (הט אזנך ושמע דברי חכמים ולבך תשית לדעתי). The reason, some have conjectured, is that the Rambam sought to justify his intensive engagement in the works of gentile philosophers, whom he cites extensively in the *Guide*. See *Yad Shaul*, Y.D. 246:5.

special wisdom has been granted, and [thinks] there is none greater than him among his peers. Therefore, [the Rambam] did not wish to write this distinction.

On the basis of this approach, several authorities concluded that as a practical matter, it is forbidden nowadays to learn Torah from a sinner. This is the view adopted by the *Sha'arei Dei'a* (Y.D. 246:3), and, more recently, by Rav Ovadia Yosef (*Yabia Omer*, Y.D. 7:19).

The *Shach* also cites a second possibility in the name of his father, suggesting that although the Gemara justified Rabbi Meir's practice by distinguishing between a קטן and a גדול, this represents a minority view that is not accepted as the *halacha*. The accepted position is that studying under an iniquitous rabbi is forbidden across the board, without any exceptions. This answer is also given by the *Lechem Mishneh*. Similarly, the *Ein Yaakov* cites those who observe that in *Maseches Moed Katan* (17a), the Gemara forbids learning from a rabbi who is suspected of inappropriate conduct, without distinguishing between different kinds of students. Apparently, the Gemara in *Moed Katan* does not accept the distinction drawn by the Gemara in *Chagiga*, and maintains that it is never permissible to learn from a wayward rabbi. Moreover, as some writers have noted,[4] the Gemara in *Moed Katan* forbids studying from a sinful teacher even if צריכין ליה רבנן — "the rabbis need him" for Torah knowledge and instruction. The Gemara appears to refer to a rabbi who is needed even by the scholarly elite, and yet it forbids even these outstanding students to learn from him, indicating that the distinction between גדול and קטן is not accepted as normative *halacha*.[5]

If, indeed, this question of whether an exceptional student may study under a sinful rabbi is subject to debate, it might depend upon the general question as to the reason that *halacha* forbids learning Torah from a sinner. The distinction

---

4. See for example, Rav Menachem Krakowski's *Avodas Ha-Melech* (*Hilchos Talmud Torah*).
5. One might question this approach, however, in light of the Gemara's comments in *Maseches Makkos* (10a) concerning the case of a rabbi or student who accidentally kills and must therefore relocate in an עיר מקלט (city of refuge). The Gemara cites a ruling that in the case of a student, his rabbi must go with him to the עיר מקלט, so that he may continue learning. Commenting on this *halacha*, the Gemara warns that a rabbi should not teach a תלמיד שאינו הגון — a student who does not act properly — as such a student is prone to accidentally killing, and this would require the rabbi to relocate in an עיר מקלט. The Gemara also instructs that when a rabbi relocates to an עיר מקלט, his students must join him, but we do not find any parallel comment warning against learning from a רב שאינו הגון. The Maharsha explains that the Gemara could not issue this kind of blanket warning, because a גדול is allowed to learn from a teacher who acts improperly. Clearly, the Maharsha assumes that the distinction between a קטן and a גדול is accepted as authoritative, as perhaps implied by the Gemara there in *Makkos*.

between a קטן and a גדול is likely predicated on the assumption that the prohibition stems from the concern that the teacher will negatively influence the student, and it therefore allows for exceptions for those unique individuals who can be assured to withstand such influence. One could suggest, however, that studying from a sinner is inherently problematic, and not merely because of the potential repercussions. Rav Simcha Zissel Ziv Broida (the "Alter of Kelm") writes in his *Chochma U-Mussar,* based on the teachings of Rav Yisrael Salanter, that if a rabbi with an unrefined character teaches Torah, אין תורתו תורה כלל — his words of Torah do not qualify as valuable Torah at all. A sinful rabbi, Rav Broida writes, is incapable of arriving at the truth of Torah, and for this reason the Gemara requires studying only from a rabbi who "resembles an angel," as only such a rabbi's Torah knowledge and wisdom can be regarded as "Torah."[6] According to this approach, it is unlikely that exceptions should be made for anyone, since irrespective of any concerns of negative influence, the material that is taught has no value. This outlook perhaps underlies the position taken by the aforementioned *poskim* that studying from sinners is forbidden for all people, regardless of their stature of scholarship and piety.[7]

Public and Private Study

A different approach to explaining the Rambam's view is suggested by Rav Nachum Eliezer Rabinovitch in his *Yad Peshuta* commentary to *Mishneh Torah*. Rav Rabinovitch observes that the Rambam links this prohibition with the prohibition against teaching a תלמיד שאינו הגון — a student who conducts himself improperly. The Rambam establishes that one should not teach Torah to a student who "follows an improper path," but should rather guide such a student towards appropriate behavior, after which מכניסין אותו לבית המדרש ומלמדין

---

6. In a similar vein, Rav Yaakov Dovid Wilovsky (the "Ridbaz"), in *Nimukei Ridbaz* (*Parshas Teruma*), cites Rav Chaim of Volozhin as commenting that a person with heretical ideas is incapable of arriving at correct Torah conclusions: מי שיש בו מינות לא יזכה לכוון לאמיתה של תורה. Rav Wilovsky explains that correct understanding of Torah must be received from the Almighty, and thus only those who fully believe in God are capable of grasping the truth of any Torah concept.
7. Interestingly, Rav Chaim Steinberg (*Mishnas Chayim, Parshas Toldos,* 96), suggests that this might be the reason why the Rambam needed to mention that one may not learn from a sinful rabbi עד שובו למוטב — until he returns to the proper mode of conduct. One might have thought that since a rabbi's Torah loses all validity if he acts improperly, one may not study his Torah even after he repents and abandons the path of sin. The Rambam therefore noted that once the rabbi has repented, students may again learn from him and gain from his knowledge and wisdom.

אותו — "he is brought into the study hall and then taught." In other words, a wayward student should be taught privately until his behavior improves, at which point he may be allowed to join the *beis midrash* and learn with the other students. The Rambam then writes, וכן הרב שאינו הולך בדרך טובה...אין מתלמדין ממנו — "**Similarly**, a rabbi who does not follow the proper path…people should not learn from him." The word וכן suggests a degree of parity between these two *halachos* — the prohibition against teaching a wayward student and the prohibition against learning from a wayward teacher. Accordingly, Rav Rabinovitch suggests, the second prohibition parallels the first, and thus we must distinguish between public lecturing and private study. Just as a wayward student is not allowed into the *beis midrash* to study with other students, a wayward teacher is not permitted to serve in any sort of public capacity, and this is the Rambam's intent when he writes, אין מתלמדין ממנו — he may not be allowed to teach groups of students. Exceptional individuals, however, the likes of Rabbi Meir, are permitted to study from a wayward rabbi, just as a wayward student should be taught privately until he is deemed worthy of joining the *beis midrash* to participate in public Torah study.

According to this approach, the Rambam accepts Rabbi Meir's position that a גדול may study from a wayward teacher, but this is permissible only on an individual basis, as the teacher may not be allowed to fill any sort of public educational role.

In any event, it is clear that studying Torah from a confirmed sinner is, as a general rule, forbidden, even if different views exist as to whether an exception may be made for especially pious and talented students.

Who is a "Wayward Teacher"?

The Rambam and *Shulchan Aruch* define the prohibition as forbidding studying from a teacher שאינו הולך בדרך טובה — "who does not follow the proper path." To whom exactly does this refer? After all, even the greatest rabbis and *tzadikim* are far from perfect, and the *Tanach* tells of the mistakes made even by Moshe Rabbeinu and King David. Undoubtedly, then, when the Gemara requires studying only from a teacher who "resembles an angel," it does not refer to a person of moral and spiritual perfection, as such people do not exist. Who, then, is considered to fail to "follow the proper path," and thus loses his halachic eligibility to teach Torah?

The answer may perhaps be found in the commentaries of the *Rishonim* to *Maseches Moed Katan* (17a), in reference to the story told there of a Torah scholar דהוו סנו שומעניה — whose reputation was disgraced. Rav Yehuda, the Gemara relates, debated as to whether he should act upon the damning reports, until he was told of Rabbi Yochanan's statement that one must not learn from a rabbi who does not "resemble an angel." At that point, he excommunicated the disgraced rabbi. The Gemara does not specify the precise nature of the rabbi's misconduct, informing us only that he traveled to a remote place, where no one knew him, to commit his wrongdoing, so as to avoid public disgrace. We are not told in what kind of wayward behavior he engaged.

Several different explanations appear in the *Rishonim*. The *Talmid Rabbeinu Yechiel* (cited in *Kovetz Shitos Kamai*) explains that the rabbi committed adultery. According to this interpretation, we might be compelled to limit the prohibition against learning from a wayward rabbi to cases of a rabbi who committed a grave capital offense, such as adultery. The Ritva, however, writes that the scholar in this story was פרוץ קצת בזימה — "somewhat licentious" — in that היה מתייחד עם הפנויות והיה כיעור גדול לצורבא מרבנן — "he would seclude himself with single women, which is a great disgrace for a Torah scholar." According to this reading, we should seemingly apply this law to any rabbi who commits an act which constitutes כיעור גדול לצורבא מרבנן — a disgrace for a Torah scholar. Even if the act did not violate a capital Biblical offense, it nevertheless renders the rabbi ineligible to teach Torah if it is deemed grossly inappropriate for a person serving this lofty role.

A different formulation appears in the commentary of Rabbeinu Chananel, who interprets דהוו סני שומעניה to mean שהיה שם שמיים מתחלל על ידו — his conduct resulted in a חילול ה׳ (defamation of God's Name). Rabbeinu Chananel elaborates further by citing the Gemara's discussion in *Maseches Yoma* (86a) concerning the definition of חילול ה׳. One of the definitions given is כל שחביריו מתביישין מחמת שמועתו — "anyone whose colleagues are ashamed because of what is told about him." According to Rabbeinu Chananel, this is the kind of Torah scholar from whom the Gemara in *Moed Katan* forbids learning, and who deserves excommunication. As examples of this kind of behavior, Rabbeinu Chananel mentions the case of a Torah scholar who engages in the study of heresy or in frivolous drinking. This definition is accepted by the Rosh and the *Tur* (Y.D. 334), and based on these sources, the *Shulchan Aruch* (Y.D. 334:42) rules:

אי סני שומעניה, כגון שמתעסק בספרי אפיקורוס ושותה במיני זמר או שחביריו מתביישין ממנו ושם שמיים מתחלל על ידו – משמתינן ליה.

> If [a scholar's] reputation is disgraced, such as if he engages in books of heresy or drinks amid all kinds of song, or if his colleagues are ashamed of him, and he causes the Name of God to be defamed — he is excommunicated.

As mentioned, Rav Yehuda reached the conclusion that the scholar in question deserved excommunication because of the prohibition against studying Torah from a teacher who acts inappropriately. We might thus infer that this prohibition applies to any rabbi whose "colleagues are ashamed of him" and who "causes the Name of God to be defamed."

If so, then the category of סנו שומעניה is quite broad, and may also depend on time and place. Conceivably, any kind of behavior that brings shame to the rabbinate and to Torah, even if it does not entail any specific halachic violation, would fall under this category and render a rabbi unfit for Torah education and leadership. Therefore, even if a rabbi engages in conduct which was deemed acceptable in the past but is now considered inappropriate, such that he embarrasses his colleagues and arouses contempt for Torah, it would seemingly be forbidden to learn Torah from him.[8]

Studying a Disgraced Scholar's Works

Until now, we have discussed the question of learning directly from a disgraced rabbi. We will now turn our attention to the question of whether one may access his materials, such as his books or recordings.

As mentioned earlier, the requirement to study only from an "angelic" rabbi is inferred from the verse in *Sefer Malachi* (2:7), "They shall seek Torah from his mouth, because he is an angel of the Lord of Hosts." Rav Yirmiyahu Löw, in his *Divrei Yirmiyahu* commentary to the Rambam's *Mishneh Torah* (*Hilchos Talmud Torah* 4:1), boldly asserts (citing his father) that this *halacha* refers only to studying Torah from the "mouth" of a wayward scholar, meaning through direct communication, as opposed to through the written word. Direct study from an evildoer exposes the student to the teacher's sinful qualities and conduct, which could negatively impact the student. However, Rav Löw posits, when one

---

8. One example might be reports that appeared several years ago of a prominent New York rabbi who would bring teenagers from his congregation, as well as young interns, with him to the sauna, where they would sit together without clothing. Although it seems clear that no crimes or technical halachic violations were committed, such activity might very likely fall under the category of חביריו מתביישין ממנו ושם שמים מתחלל על ידו, which disqualifies a rabbi from teaching Torah.

    We might also wonder how this *halacha* might apply to a rabbi who expresses his views in an especially harsh and offensive tone. In today's media culture, there is great sensitivity to the way opinions are formulated, and an especially high standard of dignity and courtesy is expected from religious leaders. Possibly, then, a rabbi or teacher who expresses himself in a manner deemed by today's standards inappropriately coarse and unbecoming, which brings disgrace to the rabbinate, would fall under the category of חביריו מתביישין ממנו ושם שמים מתחלל על ידו.

reads the writings of a wayward scholar, he can access the valuable wisdom and knowledge from the material without exposing himself to the author's sinful character. As such, there is no prohibition against reading material authored by a sinful scholar.[9] On this basis, Rav Löw sought to reconcile this *halacha* with the fact that the Rambam studied the works of non-Jewish scholars.

This was also the view of Rav Yosef Zecharya Stern, as articulated in a letter defending his occasional citation of Moses Mendelssohn's works, in which he approvingly mentions this passage from *Divrei Yirmiyahu*.[10]

It stands to reason that the exception made by Rav Löw for written material would apply to recordings as well. Rav Löw explains the prohibition as based on the negative influence that would result from the relationship between the student and the wayward teacher: שחיבור עם רשע רע וגורם רעה והשחתה לאדם — "for the connection with an evil person is bad and causes a person harm and [spiritual] destruction." One who listens to or views a recording of a rabbi's lecture does not, seemingly, forge the kind of חיבור ("connection") that could yield a deleterious spiritual effect. As such, Rav Löw would likely permit using recorded material of a sinful teacher.

However, other *poskim* dispute this position. Rav Shmuel Wosner (*Shevet Ha-Levi* 3:145) writes explicitly that one may not read the works of a wayward scholar:

כמו דאז"ל דאסור ללמוד תורה מרב שאינו הגון כך אסור ללמוד תורה שנכתב או נדפס ממי שאינו הגון, שבלי ספק פוגם.

> Just as the Sages said that it is forbidden to study Torah from a wayward rabbi, it is likewise forbidden to study Torah that was written or printed by someone who is wayward, as this undoubtedly causes harm.

In Rav Wosner's view, reading material written by a sinner — and even material authored by an upstanding scholar, but printed by a sinner — can cause a person harm, and is thus forbidden. This is also the ruling of Rav Avraham Yaffe Shlesinger (*Be'er Sarim, Likutim* 39:3).[11]

We should add that according to the comments of the Alter of Kelm cited

---

9. It should also be noted that when the Gemara initially questioned the legitimacy of Rabbi Meir's studying under Elisha ben Avuya, it asked, ורבי מאיר היכא למד **מפומא** דאחר — "How did Rabbi Meir learn **from the mouth** of *Acher*," perhaps suggesting that the prohibition relates specifically to study through direct, verbal communication.
10. The letter was written to Rav Chaim Chizkiya Medini (author of *Sedei Chemed*), and appears in *Pakuos Sadeh*, a booklet published by Rav Medini in Jerusalem in 1900, and in *Sedei Chemed* (*Ma'areches Alef*, p. 188).
11. See also Rav Menachem Giat, *Toras Chacham*, vol. 1, p. 371.

earlier, that the Torah taught by an evildoer cannot actually be considered "Torah," there is certainly no reason to distinguish between direct contact and studying from an evildoer's written or recorded materials.[12]

Thus, different views exist as to whether one may study from written or recorded Torah materials produced by a sinner.

Studying Torah Produced Before the Scholar's Misconduct

If indeed this prohibition includes studying from a disgraced scholar's printed or recorded material, the question becomes whether this applies even to material produced before the scholar turned sinful. Does this material become illegitimate once the author or speaker sins, or does it retain its validity despite his subsequent fall into the abyss of sinful conduct?

The answer to this question appears to emerge from a responsum of Rav Moshe Feinstein (*Iggeros Moshe*, E.H. 1:96) concerning the case of a composer of popular religious songs who became known as a sinner.[13] The question arose whether it was permissible to sing the songs he composed while he was still reputed to be a God-fearing, upstanding Jew, and, if so, whether it was permissible to also sing the songs composed after he was determined to act sinfully. Rav Moshe ruled that singing any of this musician's songs is permissible, for several reasons, some of which are relevant also to the case of a wayward Torah scholar.

The basis for considering forbidding the use of these songs, Rav Moshe writes, is the Rambam's ruling (*Hilchos Yesodei Ha-Torah* 6:8) that a *sefer Torah* written by a heretic should be burned, כדי שלא להניח שם למינים ולא למעשיהם — "in order not to make a name for the heretics or their deeds." One might have thought to extend this *halacha* and forbid making use of anything produced

---

12. The Gemara in *Maseches Sanhedrin* (106b) recounts that God acceded to David's request that the words of Torah taught by Doeg and Achisofel — two Torah scholars who became evil and betrayed David — should not be shared in study halls. This would seem to indicate that the Torah taught by a wayward scholar should not even be cited, let alone read and studied. In truth, however, it is likely that this measure was taken as a special penalty against Doeg and Achisofel for their especially grievous crimes. Indeed, the Gemara states that God initially thought that their words of Torah should be shared among scholars, until David requested that they should never be cited. It thus appears that this was an extraordinary provision that cannot necessarily be applied in cases of other sinners. Moreover, the Maharal (*Nesivos Olam*, *Nesiv Ha-Torah*, chapter 8) cites this comment of the Gemara as proof that one should not study Torah that was taught by a heretic. As such, this comment does not necessarily indicate that one must avoid the Torah of other sinners, who do not hold heretical beliefs.
13. Rav Moshe writes that this musician "brings unmarried men and unmarried women together and plays before them."

by a sinner, as one thereby publicizes him and his work. Rav Moshe dismisses this conclusion, noting that, for one thing, the Rambam's ruling applies only to Torah scrolls written after the person became a heretic; there is no indication that a *sefer Torah* written by a pious scribe is rendered invalid once he becomes a heretic.[14] Second, Rav Moshe asserts that the rule of שלא להניח שם applies only to heretics, those who deny the basic tenets of Jewish faith. It does not apply to those who are believers but act inappropriately, such as the composer in question. Therefore, Rav Moshe writes, as long as there is no indication that this composer embraced heresy, his songs may be sung without any concern.[15]

Both of these arguments directly apply to the case of a disgraced scholar. Even though *halacha* forbids studying from such a rabbi after he has been determined to be sinful, the material he produced before then is permissible for use, particularly if there is no indication of heresy, such as cases of rabbis who succumbed to greed, lust, and other vices.

Learning from a Disgraced Rabbi who Repents

In conclusion, let us turn our attention to the situation of a disgraced rabbi who appears to sincerely regret his misconduct and to have undergone a process of genuine *teshuva*. The Rambam and *Shulchan Aruch* forbid learning

---

14. Rav Moshe cites as his source the *Pischei Teshuva*, Y.D. 281:2.
    Interestingly, Rav Yaakov Sasportas (1610–1698), one of the first outspoken opponents of Shabtai Tzvi, writes in his *Ohalei Yaakov* (68) that communities should not adopt the practice championed by Shabtai Tzvi to recite *Birkas Kohanim* every day, despite the sound halachic basis for this practice, so that this evil person would not receive credit for a worthwhile practice. He cites as his source the Rambam's remark in *Hilchos Ma'aser* (9:1) identifying Yochanan Kohen Gadol, who is credited with instituting the requirement to tithe produce purchased from an עם הארץ ("ignoramus"), as the high priest who succeeded Simon the Just. The *Kessef Mishneh* explains that the Rambam made this comment to clarify that he does not refer to the other Yochanan Kohen Gadol, who lived later and who became a heretic at the end of his life. Rav Sasportas understood that if this had been the later Yochanan Kohen Gadol, the Sages would not have memorialized his enactment, since he subsequently became a heretic. This would appear to suggest that according to Rav Sasportas, if a rabbi becomes a heretic, it is forbidden to cite even the scholarship he produced while he was still a scholar in good standing, in contradistinction to Rav Moshe's ruling. (Rav Moshe also cites the Rambam's comment, but explains it differently.)
15. Rav Moshe also contends that the law of שלא להניח שם applies only to matters of sanctity, such as a *sefer Torah*, but not to other products, such as music.

from a wayward rabbi עד שובו למוטב — "until he returns to proper conduct."[16] Significantly, the *halacha* does not require distancing oneself from a disgraced scholar forever; it takes into account the possibility of *teshuva*, the opportunity given to all sinners to repent and regain their good standing before God and before their peers.

The question, however, becomes how we determine that the rabbi has repented. In many cases, the rabbi had successfully projected an image of genuine piety even as he committed the most unspeakable crimes. A rabbi who was initially able to convince nearly everyone of his spiritual greatness as he perpetrated grave religious and ethical wrongs is likewise capable, after he is caught, of convincing the public that he has since repented. What measures are required to trust that such a rabbi has truly "returned to proper conduct," such that he may once again be turned to as a source of Torah scholarship and guidance?

The *poskim* discuss the issue of verifying a sinner's *teshuva* with regard to eligibility for *eidus* (giving testimony). *Halacha* disqualifies various categories of sinners for *eidus*, but allows these sinners to regain their eligibility through repentance. The case of a disgraced rabbi most likely resembles that of a מומר — a person who is known to be a habitual and unabashed sinner. Regarding such a person, the Rama (C.M. 34:22) writes, citing the Maharik:

מומר שחזר בו וקיבל עליו תשובה כשר מיד אע"פ שלא עשאה עדיין.

A מומר who had a change of heart and took it upon himself to repent is eligible immediately, even though he did not yet perform [repentance].

According to the Maharik, the moment a מומר affirms his commitment to repent, he regains his eligibility to testify, even before he actually takes concrete measures of *teshuva*. The Maharik draws proof to his view from the Gemara's ruling in *Maseches Gittin* (35b) concerning a *Kohen* who marries a woman whom he is forbidden to marry, such as a divorcee. The Gemara rules that although such a *Kohen* may not perform the *avoda* in the *Beis Ha-Mikdash*, he regains his eligibility to perform the *avoda* the moment he vows to divorce the woman, even before he actually grants the divorce. Just as a verbal commitment of repentance suffices to allow this *Kohen* to again perform the *avoda*, similarly, the Maharik maintains, a habitual sinner's verbal commitment to repent suffices for him to regain his eligibility to testify.

However, the scope of this *halacha* is subject to debate among the *Acharonim*. The *Shach* asserts that this rule may be applied broadly to all cases of habitual sinners. Once they verbally commit to repent, they regain their eligibility. Rav

---

16. The *Shulchan Aruch*'s formulation is עד שיחזור למוטב.

Yehonasan Eibushitz, however, disagrees (*Tumim* 34:21). In his view, in order for a sinner to regain his eligibility, we require דבר מוכיח וניכר לכל שחזר — "something that proves and makes it clear to all that he has repented." In the case of the מומר discussed by the Maharik, the very fact that he withdrew from the non-Jewish crowd with whom he had been associating suffices as proof of his sincere resolve to change, and thus he regains his eligibility even before we see him follow up on his commitment. For this same reason, Rav Eibushitz explains, a *Kohen* who had married a divorcee must formally vow to divorce her before regaining his eligibility, and a mere proclamation does not suffice. Only a formal vow provides the clear evidence that is needed for a sinner to demonstrate his resolve to repent.

One may, at first glance, draw proof to the *Tumim*'s view from the *Shulchan Aruch*'s later ruling (34:30–31) concerning מפריחי יונים — people who train birds to capture other birds — and משחקי בקוביא — gamblers. Such people are disqualified for *eidus*, as the *Shulchan Aruch* states earlier (34:16), because these activities either resemble or generally entail theft, and they remain disqualified even after they repent, until they disassemble the tools used for these undignified activities. This requirement would seem to prove that, as the *Tumim* claims, a verbal commitment to change does not suffice, and that we demand a דבר מוכיח וניכר לכל — some clear indication of a genuine change of heart.

This point was noted by the *Nesivos* (*Bi'urim* 34:13), who follows the *Shach*'s lenient ruling that it suffices for a sinner to avow his commitment to repent. In defense of this position, the *Nesivos* writes that an exception is made for עבירה דחימוד ממון — sins involving material lust, such as gambling. Habitual sinners of this kind are especially prone to recidivism, and thus a mere declaration of a desire to change is insufficient to affirm repentance and restore their status of presumed eligibility.

Although the *Nesivos* specifies the exception of חימוד ממון, we might wonder whether it may apply to other categories of sin as well. Withdrawing from habitual sexual indiscretion, including child molestation, would seem to be no less difficult than withdrawing from habitual financial misdemeanors. Logically, and in consideration of human nature, we have no more reason to rely upon a verbal proclamation of repentance in the case of a sexual offender than in the case of a gambler. Possibly, then, even the *Shach* and *Nesivos* would concede that when dealing with a rabbi found guilty of frequent sexual misconduct, a mere declaration of a change of heart would be insufficient, and a more compelling demonstration of *teshuva* would be required before he could be allowed to resume teaching Torah.

It emerges that according to Rav Yehonasan Eibushitz, a sinner does not regain his presumed status of eligibility until he has demonstratively repented and made it clear that he has firmly resolved to never repeat his offenses.

According to the *Shach*, even a verbal declaration of *teshuva* suffices, but when it comes to certain types of sin, even the *Shach* might concede that the sinner must prove that he has repented.[17]

Reinstatement to a Rabbinic or Educational Post

While it is clear that a rabbi who sinned may resume teaching Torah after repenting — notwithstanding the practical question of how to ascertain the sincerity of his *teshuva* — it is questionable whether he may return to his previous formal rabbinic position, even after demonstrable repentance. The basis for this distinction is the contrast between the Rambam's aforementioned ruling, allowing studying from a wayward rabbi once he "returns to proper conduct," and his ruling elsewhere, in *Hilchos Sanhedrin* (17:9): אבל ראש הישיבה שחטא מלקין אותו ואינו חוזר לשררותו. The Rambam here establishes that a ראש הישיבה who sins may not be reinstated to his prior post, even after enduring court-administered corporal punishment. No mention is made of the possibility of his reinstatement after repenting, implying that even though, as the Rambam indicates in *Hilchos Talmud Torah*, a wayward rabbi may resume teaching Torah once he repents, a ראש הישיבה may not return to his position even after performing *teshuva*.

The question then becomes to whom exactly the Rambam refers in this *halacha*, and to which kind of rabbinic posts this rule applies.

Both the *Kessef Mishneh* and the Radbaz, in their respective commentaries to *Hilchos Sanhedrin*, explain that the Rambam refers here to the post of נשיא — the head of the *Sanhedrin*. The Rambam's ruling, according to these commentators, is drawn from the Talmud Yerushalmi, which, in *Maseches Horiyos* (3:1), establishes that a נשיא who commits a sin is not reinstated to his post. If so, then we must address the question of why a נשיא may not return to his position after repenting, and whether this *halacha* may be applicable to other positions of Torah education and leadership.[18]

The *Kessef Mishneh* and Radbaz explain that a נשיא may not return to his position of leadership because he may seek revenge against the court that had sentenced him to corporal punishment.[19] According to this explanation, this

---

17. See also the comments of Rav Mordechai Willig, cited below in the transcription of an interview he gave, where he states that a disgraced rabbi may not be allowed to resume teaching Torah until he undergoes the process of *teshuva* outlined by the Rambam in the second chapter of *Hilchos Teshuva*.
18. For a thorough presentation of the various sources relevant to the Rambam's ruling, see Professor Nachum Rakover's article, "*Oved Tzibur She-Sarach Ve-Ritza Es Onsho*," at http://www.daat.ac.il/mishpat-ivri/skirot/180-2.htm.
19. This explanation is based on the aforementioned passage in the Yerushalmi, which states

halacha is very limited in scope, and applies only to positions of authority that may be abused for the sake of revenge. In virtually all cases of a disgraced rabbi, then, he may return to his prior position after repenting.

However, the *Kessef Mishneh* then adds a second explanation, namely, that even after repenting, the disgraced נשיא cannot ever earn the respect and esteem that the position deserves, and for this reason he is not reinstated. It is unclear, according to this approach, whether this concern for respect is relevant specifically when dealing with the lofty position of head of the *Sanhedrin*, or to any distinguished rabbinic post. Hence, no definitive conclusion can be reached on the basis of this comment of the *Kessef Mishneh*.

The Radbaz, in one of his responsa (6:2078), advances a different explanation of the Rambam's ruling. He writes:

מפני שכל חטאות הנשיא חשבינן להו כאילו עבר בפרהסיא, ואיכא חילול השם טובא.

…because all the sins of a נשיא are considered as though they were committed publicly, and there is thus an especially grave defamation of God's Name.

Generally, when a person serving in a religious post sins privately, the matter can be resolved in a discreet fashion, by privately meeting with the rabbi to reprimand him, quietly imposing whatever punitive measures are appropriate, and ensuring that he has sincerely repented and is committed to never repeating the sinful act. Hence, the Radbaz writes, such a person, in most cases, should not be demoted. The Rambam makes an exception in the case of a נשיא, however, because even his private misdeeds are considered public, due to the uniquely prominent stature of his position. Therefore, reinstating a נשיא who committed even a private offense is akin to reinstating a person who had filled a different public religious role and publicly sinned. His reinstatement would create a grave חילול ה׳, and is thus forbidden.[20]

According to the Radbaz, it would seem, the yardstick by which we determine whether a disgraced rabbi may resume his position after repentance is חילול ה׳. If his crime became public knowledge, such that his reinstatement would bring dishonor to Torah and the rabbinate, as the public associates him with the

---

that a נשיא who sinned is not reinstated because מוטב דינון מחזירין ליה דו קטלון ליה, which the *Kessef Mishneh* understood to mean that the reinstated נשיא may seek to kill those who had demoted him.

20. The Radbaz offered this explanation to reconcile the Rambam's ruling in *Hilchos Sanhedrin* with his comments in the responsum noted earlier, which states that no holder of a religious post is demoted after committing a sin, as long as the sin was committed privately.

sin he had committed, then he may never return to his post even after sincere *teshuva*. If so, then the Radbaz's approach may yield important ramifications for most modern-day rabbinic scandals, which, due to the swift flow of information and news, enter the public sphere very quickly. Any serious offense of which a rabbi is found guilty in our day and age *ipso facto* becomes an עבירה בפרהסיא — a public offense — and therefore, according to the Radbaz, it should perhaps be equated with the case of a sin committed by a נשיא, and render the perpetrator permanently disqualified for a rabbinic post.[21]

Rav Moshe Feinstein (*Dibberos Moshe, Gittin*, vol. 1, p. 355) explains the Rambam's ruling much differently, claiming that the term ראש הישיבה in this context refers to one who teaches advanced Torah scholars. A person who fills such a post and is found to have sinned may not return to his position even after repentance, and he is deemed forever unsuitable for this lofty role. According to Rav Moshe, then, ordinary rabbis and teachers may resume their posts after repenting, but those who teach advanced *talmidei chachamim* become permanently disqualified for this job once they have been disgraced.[22]

Thus, although a disgraced rabbi may once again teach Torah once he had demonstrably repented and mended his ways, he might still be disqualified for a formal post if this would create a חילול ה' (Radbaz) or if he teaches advanced students (Rav Moshe Feinstein).

Conclusion

In light of what we have seen, the following guidelines apply when a rabbi or educator is alleged to have engaged in inappropriate conduct:

1. One must not reach any definitive conclusions based on hearsay, and judgment must be reserved until rumors of misconduct have been substantiated.

---

21. Conceivably, however, if the prohibition against reinstatement stems from the consideration of חילול ה', then at least in principle, if the rabbi's sincere repentance is also done publicly and he succeeds in projecting a public image of genuine penitence, then perhaps he should be allowed to return to his prior position. This point was made by Professor Rakover (above, n. 18).
22. Curiously, Rav Moshe cites as the basis for this disqualification the rule mentioned earlier, that a rabbi must resemble a מלאך ה'. It is difficult to understand, then, how Rav Moshe distinguishes in this regard between different kinds of Torah educators, as the rule of דומה למלאך ה' clearly refers to all teachers of Torah. Moreover, the Rambam cites this requirement of דומה למלאך ה' in *Hilchos Talmud Torah*, where he clearly indicates that a disgraced teacher is allowed to teach after he repents. Rav Moshe's distinction therefore requires explanation.

2. If it is confirmed that the rabbi in question engaged in behavior that brings shame to Torah, one may not learn Torah from him.
3. It is questionable whether one may read a sinful rabbi's written works or use his recorded material.
4. Written or recorded material that the rabbi produced before he became a sinner may be used.
5. If a disgraced rabbi has sincerely repented, he may once again teach Torah, though it would appear that according to some views, there must be compelling evidence of true, genuine *teshuva*.
6. At least according to some opinions, even after a disgraced rabbi has genuinely and demonstrably repented, he may not resume his official rabbinic post or educational position if his reinstatement will create a חילול ה׳, or if the position is an especially distinguished post, such as in the case of a Rosh Yeshiva.

INTERVIEWS

Rav Mordechai Willig
on *Headlines with Dovid Lichtenstein**

We are not blessed with רוח הקדש, and therefore it's not always possible to predict [when an upstanding rabbi will be exposed as a sinner]. But the truth is that when some of these scandals break, I hear a refrain, "I'm surprised, but not shocked." That means there was a certain suspicion of irregularity in the person's conduct, but we didn't know for sure; we had a little suspicion which we tucked away and went on. Perhaps we ought to be more careful when these warning signs appear, and be more proactive. If a rabbi conducts himself inappropriately with respect to women, and certainly if he violates the specific prohibitions of יחוד (seclusion)… if he creates a situation of excessive dependence, where a young lady is dependent upon this charismatic leader for her spirituality, or he spends an inordinate amount of time talking to women, or sees to it to find out many personal details about her life — these are all warning signs that he may be grooming the young lady for something sinful and horrific. If one sees this kind of behavior, I believe this is a strong enough warning sign to see to it to put a stop to it immediately. And if the person ignores the warnings, I believe this is sufficient cause to terminate such a person's employment in a school for women. I do not believe it is possible to terminate somebody immediately without warning. We're afraid of something which he may do, and therefore it may be illegal to terminate somebody without prior warning. He's just talking. But, talking is the first stage. There are major organizations — I believe Torah Umesorah is one of them — that have specific guidelines in terms of a man talking to a female on the job, on-site, off-site, etc. These are guidelines which should be formulated appropriately, and if somebody steps over that line, he should be warned of termination if he repeats the violation…

The fact that somebody "rubs you the wrong way," to my mind, is not enough of a reason to take action against that person. I think that would be inappropriate. At the same time, as *Chazal* put it, למיחש מיבעי — we have to worry that something is there. And if you look in the *Sefer Chafetz Chayim*, [it says] you can warn people not to get close to him. But to destroy his reputation through public exposure — I believe this requires a higher level of evidence… To warn an individual to watch out and not to hire somebody — it is sufficient even if he "rubs you the wrong way," but as for a public statement that would ruin his reputation, I believe this requires a higher level of proof.

You have to watch out for certain charismatic individuals, especially charismatic rabbis dealing with young ladies. Excessive charisma can be damaging even when rabbis deal with boys and female teachers with girls, as they try recreating people in their image. This can be dangerous. You do need some charisma to influence youngsters to go higher in their spiritual growth, which is the essence of the job of a *rebbe* or *morah* [female teacher]. But you have to set limits, and the more charismatic a person is, the greater the limits that he needs… Even without halachic seclusion, there can be inappropriate conversations which are a warning sign of danger of גילוי עריות.

We should encourage individuals who speak out, [and let them know] that we are going to listen to them very carefully. It is not always possible to believe an unsubstantiated report by one individual and destroy a rabbi who was previously in good standing, because sometimes these things are inaccurate, either intentionally or by mistake. Nonetheless, if there are repeated complaints — we have to learn from our collective mistakes that when there are repeated mistakes, the time to act is now, and we should not wait for worse things to occur.

Any indiscretion with respect to עריות [sexual misconduct] is an absolute disqualification [from serving a role in Torah education]. When it comes to monetary matters, there are so many different levels of monetary violations. It seems to me that a significant monetary violation is enough to disqualify a person, though it is hard to define "significant" precisely. As far as גאוה [arrogance] is concerned, it should certainly disqualify an individual, but it is hard to define the term בעל גאוה [an arrogant person]. Unfortunately, there are people with גאוה who sit comfortably in their seats in the world of Torah education and the rabbinate, and have not been fired for the sin of גאוה… Not every instance of גאוה translates into malfeasance. Hubris often leads to misconduct, but not always. If you ask me, such an individual should not be a rabbi, but once he is a rabbi, it's hard to terminate him. The reality is that גאוה can lead to sins involving גילוי עריות [sexual immorality] and also sins involving money. I know of somebody who was suspected of lying in monetary matters, and one of the *gedolim* said that he can very well end up lying also in terms of עריות, and this proved to be prophetic — this is exactly what happened. Somebody who is honest in all areas of life, he is a דומה למלאך ה' צב-אות. Once there's dishonesty, especially when it's combined with hubris — this is a recipe for disaster, and can lead to גילוי עריות as well. But if a person is a sitting rabbi in a shul or in a yeshiva, and he does a good job, but his deficiency is גאוה, I don't know if that is grounds for termination.

Can students continue learning from a rabbi's sefarim after he is exposed as a sinner?

No, no, no. *Chazal* tell us, אם דומה הרב למלאך ה' צבאות, תורה יבקשו מפיהו; ואם לאו, אל יבקשו תורה מפיהו ["If the rabbi resembles an 'angel of the Lord of Hosts,' then seek Torah from his mouth, but if not, then do not seek Torah from his mouth"]… This kind of sinful behavior is so far from the proper standard, that I believe his *sefarim*, his Torah, his websites, his *derashos* — should all be discarded. We should not be learning his Torah at all.

Rabbi Meir was unique; *Chazal* tell us that he was able to separate the inner Torah from the *kelipa* (shell). This, I believe, is something a man of Rabbi Meir's stature can do, but would not be recommended for others. Moreover, the sin of Acher was more philosophical. It's hard to compare a philosophical sin, as bad as it is, to a sin that is anything but victimless — a sin that has victims who were terribly damaged, some with permanent damage. If others continue having a warm and cordial relationship with the offender, without his having a change of heart, this can inflict additional damage, even if he is no longer actually victimizing people.

Should former students maintain their sense of gratitude for what the rabbi had done for them, and try to help him?

Hakaras ha-tov [gratitude] is certainly appropriate. If somebody did something for me, then no matter how bad the person is, I should have *hakaras ha-tov*. The Rambam says that a person should have *hakaras ha-tov* for a parent no matter how bad the parent is. He gives the example of a *mamzer*, when the parent conceived the child in sin. There is still an obligation of כיבוד אב ואם [honoring parents], and the *Sefer Ha-Chinuch* explains that this is because of the obligation of *hakaras ha-tov*, to be grateful. In the case of a scandal with a rabbi, I believe that the *hakaras ha-tov* should not be pervasive, and should be limited to those individuals who received specific benefit from this person and were not victimized by him. They may show *hakaras ha-tov*.

With regard to giving the person *tzedaka* [in the case of a rabbi who is convicted of a crime and after being released has no way to support himself], the greatest form of *tzedaka*, as the Rambam teaches, is giving somebody a job. If the person in such a case cannot find a job, the greatest charity is to find him a job in the private sector where there are no women, where he can earn a livelihood. Nowhere is it written that he should starve to death. So if somebody had learned and gained from this individual way back when, and he wants to repay him, the best thing he can do is to find him employment somewhere where there are no women. This would be the appropriate way to do things, as opposed to giving him regular charity, which is not so appropriate, because he is not deserving. We can't let him starve, but he should be allowed to support himself through good, old-fashioned hard work, even manual labor if need be. Given the fact that he has disqualified himself from anything in the rabbinic world, he might have to work with his hands and through other activities where these particular *yetzer haras* cannot lead him to sin…

I've come to learn that victims feel upset when the perpetrator receives honor, even after he his dead. I'm not an expert in victim psychology, but people have taught me things. We cannot judge others who have gone through difficult situations such as this.

Teshuva is possible, but who said he did *teshuva*? There was once a situation of a major *kashrus* scandal, and there was a debate in Jerusalem whether the man should be allowed into a shul. Somebody noted that *teshuva* is always possible, but somebody else responded, "Yes, but he didn't do *teshuva*." *Teshuva* means that he is contrite, asked forgiveness, is sincere, and is not just bluffing, accepts upon himself סייגים and גדרים ["fences" and safeguards against repeating the sin], and is broken, and there is no longer any trace of the original גאוה. The Rambam writes in *Hilchos Teshuva* (2:4) that a person who does *teshuva* cries out to Hashem בבכי ובתחנונים [with weeping and supplication], and he distances himself from that in which he had stumbled. If the sin is interpersonal, he must also ask forgiveness from those whom he had harmed. And, he must be an ענו ושפל רוח [humble and lowly of spirit]. Unfortunately, I know too many of these individuals who were caught in scandalous behavior who, incredibly, still seem arrogant. They haven't lost that aspect of their personalities. So, sure, they can do *teshuva*, but many haven't. And even once a perpetrator did *teshuva*, we need to balance the needs of the *ba'al teshuva*, which is significant, with the needs of the victims. And it's impossible to give a "one size fits all" answer [to the question of whether a penitent perpetrator should be welcomed into a community]. It depends on the nature of the sin, the nature of the perpetrator, the nature of the victims, and the place where the *ba'al teshuva*'s activities are taking place as compared to where the victim is. All this needs to be taken into consideration.

I do not think it is enough [for such a person to perform the kind of repentance needed for a sinner to regain his eligibility for *eidus*]. He needs, as the Rambam writes, to cry and be humbled. This is not a prerequisite for becoming qualified for *eidus*, but I believe it is a prerequisite to accept such a person [a disgraced rabbi] in some way, especially given the down side in terms of the effect on the victims, in the case of abuse. This is not the same as a scandal where the victims bought non-kosher chicken. Great sensitivity and careful evaluation is required...

Once a person is caught in illicit behavior with respect to women, I don't think he should be trusted on anything. I would say that nothing he said is reliable, and so I recommend to those who had learned information from him that they should study the material again from a reliable individual.

It is very important for a person whose trust in a rav was broken, whether it is a man or a woman, to try to find a new rav whom they can really trust. Going through life without any rav, with the feeling that every rav is suspect, is also a disaster. There are rotten apples in every barrel — too many, unfortunately — but we cannot throw all the rabbis out because of the unsavory, illicit, illegal, and horrific behavior exhibited by some. These individuals should find someone whom they feel they can trust, and any questions they have about things they learned from a scandal-ridden rabbi should be reviewed. They should find a good rabbi whom they feel they can trust, as otherwise their only rabbi is someone who has been exposed [as a sinner].

* Broadcast on 20 Sivan, 5776 (June 25, 2016).

Rav Moshe Sternbuch on *Headlines with Dovid Lichtenstein**

Talmidim [of a rabbi who is found to be a sinner] should be told not to have any connection with him, because he is מחלל ה'...

Aveiros that cause a חילול ה' should be publicized, and the public should be warned that this man does not represent religious Jews...

Such a man needs to do *teshuva* very strongly and go to extremes. Normally we're not so happy with extremists, but he must be an extremist... His *teshuva* is different from other people's *teshuva*. He was מכשיל את הרבים, and so he must show [his repentance] very strongly...

* Broadcast on 18 Tammuz, 5776 (July 23, 2016).

Druze Religious Leader Commits to Noachide "Seven Laws"

The spiritual leader of the Druze community in Israel, Sheikh Mowafak Tarif, this weekend signed a declaration calling on non-Jews in Israel to observe the Seven Noachide Commandments, as laid down in the Bible and expounded upon in Jewish tradition.

January 18, 2004

Several weeks ago, the mayor of the primarily Druze city of Shfaram, in the Galilee, also signed the document.

The declaration includes the commitment to make a better "humane world based on the Seven Noachide Commandments and the values they represent commanded by the Creator to all mankind through Moses on Mount Sinai."

Behind the efforts to spread awareness of the Torah's Seven Universal Laws is Rabbi Boaz Kelly, of the directors of Chabad-Lubavitch institutions in the Krayot area of Haifa and the chairman of the Worldwide Committee for the Seven Noachide Commandments. The recent signature by Sheikh Tarif is part of Rabbi Kelly's ongoing efforts among Israel's non-Jewish community. In the past few years, Rabbi Kelly's organization has placed roadside ads in Arabic calling for observance of the Noachide laws, as well as distributing Arabic-language pamphlets on the subject among Arabs in Israel and the Palestinian Authority.

According to the Torah, all humankind (the offspring of Noah, or *Bnei Noach*) is subject to seven Divine commandments. They are: to refrain from idolatry; to refrain from sexual immorality; to refrain from blasphemy; to refrain from murder; to refrain from theft; to refrain from eating the limb of a living animal; and to establish courts of law.

Support for the spread of the Seven Noachide Commandments by the Druze spiritual leader contains within it echoes of the Biblical narrative itself. The Druze community reveres as a prophet the non-Jewish father-in-law of Moses, Jethro (Yitro), whom they call Shu'eib. According to the Biblical narrative, Jethro joined and assisted the Jewish people in the desert during the Exodus, accepted monotheism, but ultimately rejoined his own people. The Tiberias tomb of Jethro is the most important religious site for the Druze community.

Copyright © israelnationalnews.com

Light Unto the Nations, or None of Our Business? Influencing Gentiles to Observe the Noachide Laws

Throughout the centuries, Jewish activism and diplomacy focused on the effort to secure the Jews' right to observe our traditions without fear or intimidation. The goal, in short, was to be left alone so that we could practice our religion without disturbance from our gentile hosts. Whatever influence and leverage Jews had was used to help enable their communities to live Jewish lives. Few Jews, if any, considered the possibility of influencing the surrounding gentiles' personal religious beliefs or practices.

With the blossoming of the American Jewish community in the latter part of the 20th century, when religious freedom was self-understood and Jews rose to positions of prominence and influence, the opportunity arose for a much different kind of activism: inspiring the gentile world to embrace Judaism's universal code. The liberties guaranteed by the U.S. Constitution, as well as the culture of tolerance and freedom that characterizes the United States, has given American Jews a level of comfort and confidence that offers the prospect of influencing our gentile neighbors to adopt the beliefs and lifestyle that we believe to be obligatory upon all mankind.

Beginning in the 1980s, the Lubavitcher Rebbe energetically called upon his followers to not only spread the teachings of Torah and *chassidus* throughout the Jewish world, but to also spread the שבע מצוות בני נח — the Seven Noachide Laws — among the gentile world. Jewish tradition teaches that whereas only Jews are bound by the Torah's laws, all of mankind is expected to abide by the Seven Noachide Laws.[1] The Lubavitcher Rebbe felt very strongly that Jews who are in a position to encourage non-Jews to embrace and follow these laws are obligated to do so. Thus, for example, in an address delivered on 19 Kislev, 5743 (December 5, 1982), the Rebbe issued the following emphatic statements:[2]

---

1. The Seven Noachide Laws are the prohibitions of murder, idolatry, sexual immorality, blasphemy, theft, and the consumption of meat taken from a live animal, and the obligation to maintain a fair justice system. See *Sanhedrin* 56a.
2. The transcript, in English translation, is available online at http://hebrewbooks.org/

...The purpose of the giving of the Torah was to create peace within the world. Similarly, the Rambam writes that every Jew is obligated to try to influence the gentiles to fulfill the Seven Noachide Laws.[3] Furthermore, one of the achievements of *Moshiach* will be, as the Rambam writes, to refine and elevate the gentiles until they also become aware of G-d, to the point where G-dliness will be revealed "to all flesh," even to gentiles. Since the rewards of Torah come measure for measure, it follows that among the efforts to bring the Messianic age must be the efforts to spread the Seven Noachide Laws, including the wellsprings associated with them, outward to the gentiles. Indeed, the prophets tell us, "Nations shall walk following your light."[4] Though Torah was given to the Jews, it will also serve as a light to gentiles...

Today, each one of us, whether his major occupation is Torah study or business affairs, has some contact with the secular world and with gentiles. Since everything G-d creates has a specific purpose, it follows that the fact that G-d brought a person into contact with the secular world also has a purpose — namely, that the person should try to influence the gentiles to fulfill their Seven Noachide Laws, and by doing so, he prepares the world for the Messianic age...

Every Jew who has a connection with gentiles or could establish such a connection should use them for the benefit of the Jewish people and the benefit of the world at large by stressing the observance of the Noachide laws. Surely if a person is willing to make an effort to establish connections with a gentile in order to benefit financially, he should use those same connections to spread the Noachide laws.

The Rebbe himself pushed for recognition of the Seven Noachide Laws in his correspondence with President Reagan. On April 3, 1982, in celebration of the Rebbe's 80th birthday, the President proclaimed the following day, April 4th, a "National Day of Reflection," explaining that "it is appropriate that Americans pause to reflect upon the ancient ethical principles and moral values which are the foundation of our character as a nation." In this proclamation, the President noted in particular the Lubavitcher Rebbe's call for observing the Seven Noachide Laws:

> One shining example for people of all faiths of what education ought to be is that provided by the Lubavitch movement, headed by Rabbi

---

pdfpager.aspx?req=15515&st=&pgnum=30&hilite=.
3. *Hilchos Melachim* 8:10. We will discuss the Rambam's view below.
4. והלכו גויים לאורך (*Yeshayahu* 60:3).

Menachem Schneerson, a worldwide spiritual leader who will celebrate his 80th birthday on April 4, 1982. The Lubavitcher Rebbe's work stands as a reminder that knowledge is an unworthy goal unless it is accompanied by moral and spiritual wisdom and understanding. He has provided a vivid example of the eternal validity of the Seven Noahide Laws, a moral code for all of us regardless of religious faith. May he go from strength to strength.[5]

President Reagan's successor, President George H.W. Bush, issued a similar proclamation on April 14, 1989, declaring the observance of "Education Day, U.S.A." on April 16, 1989 and April 6, 1990.[6]

In the pages that follow, we will explore the Rebbe's assumption that Jews bear a religious obligation to inspire gentiles' observance of the Noachide laws, in light of halachic sources. Are we, in fact, halachically required to influence our gentile neighbors and associates to abide by these obligations? For example, if a non-Jew informs his Jewish associate that he is having an adulterous affair, is the Jew required to use his influence to try to persuade him to stop engaging in this sinful conduct? Should the Orthodox Jewish community be joining Catholic and Evangelical Americans in protesting the recognition of homosexual marriages, given that homosexual relations violate one of the Noachide laws?

אור גויים

We will begin by addressing the commonly accepted axiom that the Jewish nation is assigned the role of אור גויים, to serve as "a light unto the nations" and guide them towards proper beliefs and conduct.

The source for this concept is two verses in *Sefer Yeshayahu*:

> אני ה' קראתיך בצדק ואחזק בידך ואצרך ואתנך לברית עם לאור גויים.

> I, God, have summoned you with righteousness and have strengthened your hand; I have formed you and made you into a covenant for the nation, a light for the nations (42:6).

> נקל מהיותך לי עבד...ונתתיך לאור גויים להיות ישועתי עד קצה הארץ.

> It is not enough for you to be My servant... I have made you a light for the nations, to be My salvation until the end of the earth (49:6).

---

5. The full text of the proclamation can be found at http://www.chabad.org/therebbe/article_cdo/aid/142535/jewish/The-Rebbe-and-President-Reagan.htm.
6. The text of the proclamation is available at http://www.presidency.ucsb.edu/ws/index.php?pid=23514.

It is commonly understood that in these verses, God charges the Jewish nation with the role of אור גויים, to "illuminate" — to guide, influence, and inspire — the other nations of the world. Rashi, however, commenting on the first of these two verses, writes explicitly that God here speaks to the prophet, Yeshayahu, and explains that He has assigned him the task of illuminating the path of the tribes of Israel, who are referred to here as גויים. According to Rashi, then, this verse clearly cannot provide any source for an obligation to influence and inspire the other nations.

The Radak explains the verse differently, writing that God here indeed speaks of the Jewish people as serving the role of אור גויים. However, the Radak writes clearly that this role will be fulfilled only in the future, after the final redemption:

אני ה'...יכול להוציאך מהגלות, ואני הוא שקראתיך...כשהגיע זמנך לצאת שתצא ולא תירא בצאתך כי אני אחזיק בידך...וכן תהיה גם כן לאור גויים...והאור הוא התורה שתצא להם מציון...

> I, God...am able to take you out of exile, and I am the One who has summoned you...when the time for you to leave has arrived, you shall leave, and not be afraid, because I will hold your hand... And you will also be a light for the nations... And the light is the Torah, which shall go forth to them from Zion.

The Radak proceeds to explain that in the Messianic Era, the Jewish nation will sustain the other peoples of the world:

וישראל יהיו קיום האומות על שני פנים: האחד, שיהיה שלום בעבורם בכל הגויים...השנית, כי בסבת ישראל יהיו הגויים שומרים שבע מצוות וילכו בדרך טובה.

> And Israel will sustain the nations in two ways. First, there will be peace among all nations because of them... Second, the nations will observe the Seven [Noachide] Laws and follow the path of goodness because of Israel.[7]

The Radak cites in this context the verse later in *Yeshayahu* (60:3), והלכו גויים לאורך — "Nations shall walk in your light" — as another expression of this concept of ונתתיך לאור גויים. That verse appears in a prophecy that quite clearly speaks of the final redemption, as the Radak himself writes in explaining that prophecy's opening verse: הגיע זמן ישועתך שהוא לך אורה גדולה — "The time for your salvation has arrived, which is a great light for you."

The Netziv, however, explained the concept of אור גויים differently, in a manner

---

7. See also *Metzudos David* and Malbim.

consistent with the popular understanding. In his *Haamek Davar* commentary (*Bereishis* 9:27), the Netziv writes:

"ואצרך ואתנך לברית עם לאור גויים" – משמעו שישראל נוצרו להיטיב אמונת כל עם...
ולהקים דרך ארץ שלהם.

> "I have formed you and made you into a covenant for the nation, a light for the nations" — this means that Israel was created to improve the faith of every nation...and to enhance their conduct.

Later in his commentary (*Herchev Davar*, *Bereishis* 17:5), the Netziv writes explicitly that the Jewish Nation bears this responsibility even during their exile, and, in fact, the purpose of the Jews' dispersion is to disseminate the awareness and recognition of the Almighty.[8]

Thus, it is unclear whether the Jewish people is charged with the role of "light unto the nations" during our current state of exile, as this matter depends on the different interpretations of the verses in question.

עמד והתירן להן

The *Rishonim* address the question of teaching gentiles the Seven Noachide Laws in the context of the Gemara's ruling in *Maseches Chagiga* (13a), אין מוסרים דברי תורה לעובד כוכבים — it is forbidden to transmit words of Torah to gentiles.[9] The question arises as to whether this prohibition includes the Seven Noachide Laws, or refers only to Torah material that is not relevant to non-Jews. *Tosfos* (*Chagiga* ad loc.) write explicitly that this prohibition does not include the Noachide laws, and go so far as to say that there is a *mitzva* to teach gentiles the Noachide laws: מצוה איכא למוסרם להם.

However, *Tosfos* elsewhere (in the commentaries that appear in the *Ein Yaakov* and cited by *Hagahos Ha-Bach* in *Chagiga*, ad loc.) disagree, and claim that it is forbidden to teach gentiles even the Seven Noachide Laws. The basis for this view is the Gemara's discussion in *Maseches Bava Kama* (38a), where it establishes that the gentiles are, at least in some sense, no longer bound by the Seven Noachide Laws:

---

8. The Midrash (*Vayikra Rabba* 6) writes explicitly, אם לא תגידו אלקותי לאומות העולם הרי אני פורע מכם — "If you do not tell of My Divinity to the nations of the world, I will hereby exact retribution from you." It is unclear, however, whether the Midrash applies only to the Messianic Era, or even in exile.
9. The Gemara infers this prohibition from the verse in *Tehillim* (147:20), לא עשה כן לכל גוי ומשפטים בל ידעום.

ראה שבע מצוות שקיבלו עליהם בני נח ולא קיימום, עמד והתירן להם.

> He [the Almighty] saw the seven commandments that the children of Noach accepted, that they did not observe them, and so He arose and made them permissible for them...

The Gemara recounts that at the time of *Matan Torah*, God took away the privilege of being bound by the שבע מצוות. Seeing that mankind neglected their seven basic obligations for so long, God voided these obligations, thus denying the gentiles the opportunity to earn reward though the observance of these laws. The Gemara proceeds to clarify that even after God absolved the gentiles of the Noachide laws, a gentile receives reward for studying and observing the Seven Noachide Laws, but only on the level of אינו מצווה ועושה — as one who fulfills a *mitzva* regarding which he is not obligated. The laws are no longer binding in the sense that a gentile does not receive the exalted rewards earned by a מצווה ועושה — one who observes obligatory commands — and earns only the lower-level reward for fulfilling that which he is not strictly required to perform.

On the basis of the Gemara's comment regarding the status of the Seven Laws today, *Tosfos* understood that there is no reason to teach the שבע מצוות to non-Jews. Since they are no longer strictly bound by these laws, there is no need to inform them of these laws, and, as such, even the Noachide laws fall under the prohibition against teaching Torah to gentiles.

This view was embraced by a number of *Acharonim*, including Rav Yaakov Yehoshua Falk, in one of his published responsa (*Penei Yehoshua*, Y.D. 3), who writes that although it is forbidden to cause a gentile to transgress one of the Noachide laws,[10] there is no obligation to instruct gentiles to observe these laws.[11]

By contrast, numerous *poskim*, including Rav Moshe Feinstein (*Iggeros Moshe*, Y.D. 3:89) and Rav Yosef Shalom Elyashiv (*Kovetz Teshuvos* 3:142, ד"ה לפי האמור), accepted the view of *Tosfos* in *Chagiga* that it is permissible to teach the שבע מצוות to gentiles. Rav Eliyahu of Lublin (*Yad Eliyahu* 48) drew proof to this view from the Rambam's ruling at the end of *Hilchos Ma'aseh Ha-Korbanos* (19:16) that one may advise a non-Jew how to offer sacrifices in a permissible manner. This would certainly seem to indicate that one is allowed to teach non-Jews the laws that are relevant to them.

---

10. The *Penei Yehoshua* asserts that even this prohibition applies only on the level of Rabbinic enactment. The *Chasam Sofer* (responsa, C.M. 185) questions this claim, noting that although gentiles do not receive the rewards of a מצווה ועושה, they are nevertheless subject to punishment for violating the Noachide laws, as stated explicitly by Rashi in his commentary to the Gemara in *Bava Kama* (אבל מעונשין לא פטרן). Therefore, facilitating such violations should transgress the Biblical prohibition of לפני עור.
11. See also *Yafeh La-Lev* 5:240:9.

The *Shulchan Aruch Ha-Rav* (composed by the *Ba'al Ha-Tanya*, the first Lubavitcher Rebbe), in *Hilchos Talmud Torah* (1:14), also adopts *Tosfos'* view, and explicitly rules that one is not only permitted to teach the Noachide laws to gentiles, but fulfills a *mitzva* by doing so.

The rationale underlying this view is seemingly that since gentiles receive some reward for their observance of the Noachide laws, clearly indicating that God wants them to observe these laws, we should assist them in this endeavor by informing them about their obligations.[12]

Indeed, the Rambam writes in *Hilchos Melachim* (8:10) that when conditions allow, we are required to compel the gentiles living under Jewish rule to observe the Noachide laws:

וכן צוה משה רבנו מפי הגבורה לכוף את כל באי העולם לקבל מצות שנצטוו בני נח.

Similarly, Moshe Rabbeinu commanded by the word of God to coerce all people to accept the commands issued to the descendants of Noach.

It stands to reason that if we are enjoined to compel non-Jews to commit to the observance of the Noachide laws, then, necessarily, we are required to inform them of these laws.[13] Although some recent scholars limited the Rambam's ruling to very specific contexts,[14] nevertheless, the Rambam clearly assumed that the

---

12. See Rav Avraham Erlanger, *Birkas Avraham, Sanhedrin* 59a. Those who disagree and maintain that there is no room to allow teaching the שבע מצוות to gentiles perhaps understand the Gemara to mean that gentiles are fully absolved from these laws, even though they receive some reward for their observance. See Ritva, *Makkos* 9a, and the responsa of Rav Menachem Azarya of Fano, 123.
13. Rav Moshe Sternbuch (*Teshuvos Ve-Hanhagos* 3:317) writes that some interpret the Rambam to mean only that we are obligated to compel gentiles to accept the Noachide laws, but not to enforce their observance. Clearly, this reading is difficult to sustain.
   Elsewhere, in his *Chochma Va-Daas*, Rav Sternbuch raises the question of why, in the Rambam's view, we are required to compel non-Jews to observe the Noachide laws, a requirement that appears to have no source. This question was addressed by the Lubavitcher Rebbe in an article published in the journal *Ha-Pardes* (May 1985, available online at http://hebrewbooks.org/pdfpager.aspx?req=12398&st=&pgnum=9&hilite=). The Rebbe writes that the very fact that the שבע מצוות are mentioned by the Torah dictates that we are charged with the responsibility of enforcing them. Since the Torah was given exclusively to the Jewish people, there is no purpose served by the Torah's introducing laws relevant to the gentiles unless they are to be enforced by *Am Yisrael*.
14. Rav Menachem Kasher (*Torah Sheleima*, vol. 17, p. 220) asserts that it is only in the Messianic Era that we will bear an obligation to compel the gentiles to observe the Noachide laws. Rav Shaul Yisraeli (*Amud Ha-Yemini*, p. 83) writes that the Rambam refers to periods of Jewish sovereignty in *Eretz Yisrael*, when there is an obligation to enforce compliance with the Divine law.

Noachide laws are binding upon gentiles, and it thus stands to reason that it is important to inform them of their obligations.

Additionally, the Rambam writes later in *Hilchos Melachim* (10:9) that it is forbidden for gentiles to learn Torah or observe Shabbos, and if a non-Jew transgresses these prohibitions, he should be told that this is strictly forbidden. This, too, suggests that we are required to inform non-Jews of their obligations under Torah law.[15]

It emerges that whereas the *Penei Yehoshua* maintains that there is no obligation whatsoever to try to influence non-Jews to observe the שבע מצוות, other authorities clearly maintain that this constitutes a *mitzva*.

אהבת ה'

Influencing the gentile world to embrace the Noachide laws may also fall under the command of אהבת ה' — love of God — as defined by the Rambam. In *Sefer Ha-Mitzvos* (*asei* 3), the Rambam enumerates several different requirements that are included in this command, among them the requirement to work towards bringing others into the service of the Almighty. The Rambam writes:

> וכבר אמרו שמצוה זו כוללת גם כן שנדרוש ונקרא האנשים כולם לעבודתו יתעלה ולהאמין בו. וזה כי כשתאהב אדם תשים לבך עליו ותשבחהו ותבקש האנשים לאהוב אותו. וזה על צד המשל כן כשתאהב האל באמת...הנה אתה בלא ספק תדרוש ותקרא הכופרים והסכלים לידיעת האמת אשר ידעת אותה.

> This command also includes our teaching and summoning all people to His service, may He be exalted, and to believe in Him. This is because when you love a person, you place your heart upon him and praise him, and ask people to love him… Similarly, when you truly love the Almighty…then you will, without doubt, teach and summon the heretics and fools to the knowledge of the truth that you know.

The Rambam proceeds to cite as his source a passage in the *Sifrei* (*Va'eschanan* 32), which explains the command of ואהבת את ה' אלקיך — "You shall love the Lord your God" — to mean, אהבהו על הבריות כאברהם אביך — "Make Him beloved to people, like your patriarch Avraham." The *Sifrei* cites the Torah's famous description of how Avraham and Sara "made souls" — ואת הנפש אשר עשו בחרן (*Bereishis* 12:5) — and explains that Avraham inspired people to believe in God. In the *Sifrei*'s words: היה אברהם אבינו מגיירם ומכניסם תחת כנפי השכינה — "Our patriarch

---

15. See *Chasam Sofer*, cited above, n. 10.

Avraham would have them convert and bring them under the wings of the Divine Presence."

Significantly, neither the *Sifrei* nor the Rambam speak in this context of influencing specifically fellow Jews; rather, they speak of leading "all people" to faith. Seemingly, then, the obligation of אהבת ה' requires us to try to inspire all people to recognize God and do His will.

However, this conclusion depends on the precise type of influence that the Rambam refers to in this passage. Rav Yerucham Perlow, in his work on Rav Saadia Gaon's listing of the *mitzvos* (end of *mitzva* 19), explains the Rambam's comments to mean that the *mitzva* of אהבת ה' includes קבלת גרים — the obligation upon *batei din* to accept and welcome converts to Judaism. Rav Perlow answers on this basis the question raised by the Tashbatz, in *Zohar Ha-Rakia*, of how to classify the *mitzva* of קבלת גרים. In light of the Rambam's discussion of אהבת ה', Rav Perlow suggests, the answer is clear, as this *mitzva* includes bringing gentiles "under the wings of the Divine Presence" by accepting them as converts.[16]

However, we may question this reading of the Rambam's comments. For one thing, the fact that the Tashbatz did not suggest classifying קבלת הגרים under the *mitzva* of אהבת ה' would seem to prove that to the contrary, he did not view the Rambam's understanding of אהבת ה' as referring to accepting converts. Moreover, while the *Sifrei* indeed speaks in this context of Avraham "converting" idolaters, the Rambam writes that Avraham "called people to faith." The Rambam describes at length Avraham's efforts to spread monotheism in *Hilchos Avodas Kochavim* (1:3), where he writes that Avraham would debate the pagans of his time and speak to people עד שיחזירהו לדרך האמת — in order to bring them "to the true path." The clear implication is that Avraham did not work to "convert" the people of his time, but rather to spread the knowledge of God.[17]

Moreover, it is difficult to speak of "conversion" before *Matan Torah*, when there was not yet a nation of Israel that a person could join through a formal conversion process. Indeed, the Netziv, in his *Ha'amek Davar* (*Bereishis* 9:27), writes explicitly that God's charge to Avraham to serve as an אב המון גויים ("father

---

16. This reading of the Rambam's comments is also advanced by Rav Yitzchak Hurewitz in his *Yad Ha-Levi* commentary to *Sefer Ha-Mitzvos*.
17. In one of his published responsa (50; 149 in the Blau edition), the Rambam discusses the question of teaching Torah to gentiles and writes, מותר ללמד המצוות לנוצרים ולמשכם אל דתנו — "It is permissible to teach the commandments to Christians and draw them to our faith." This remark may suggest that we are encouraged to proselytize and try to inspire gentiles to convert. However, since the focus of the Rambam's discussion was the permissibility of teaching, and not the possibility of an obligation to influence non-Jews, it is difficult to reach any sort of definitive conclusion from this passage regarding our topic.

of a multitude of nations" — *Bereishis* 17:5) meant not that he should have all people become part of *Am Yisrael*, but rather that he should disseminate monotheistic faith among all mankind.[18]

Rav Moshe Sternbuch's Ruling

Rav Moshe Sternbuch, in a responsum published in his work *Teshuvos Ve-Hanhagos* (3:317), addresses the question of teaching the שבע מצוות to gentiles, and strongly disapproves of such efforts for various reasons, each of which can be questioned.

a. The Trinity and שיתוף

First, Rav Sternbuch writes that teaching Christians the Noachide laws is strictly forbidden because this results in implicit approval of their belief in the Trinity. The Christian conception of monotheism differs from ours in that they believe that God embodies three entities. Thus, even if a Christian proclaims his commitment to the Noachide laws, his commitment is deficient, as he does not accept true monotheistic belief as defined by the Jewish religion. Hence, if we express support for a Christian who proclaims his acceptance of the Noachide laws, we are implicitly approving of his belief in the Trinity.

However, we may question this rationale in light of the Rama's famous ruling (Y.D. 151:1) distinguishing between Christian belief and classic paganism. Whereas the Rambam famously classified Christianity as outright idolatry, the Rama placed Christianity under the category of שיתוף — including the worship of another being together with the belief in a single Creator. Although such a belief is forbidden for Jews, the Rama writes, it is not forbidden for gentiles. The Rama thus rules that the laws restricting engagement with pagans would not apply to our relationships with Christians. Accordingly, it would be perfectly acceptable to recognize a Christian's acceptance of the Noachide laws, as the belief in the Trinity does not undermine a gentile's status as a monotheist.

---

18. The Ra'avad (*Ba'alei Ha-Nefesh*, *Sha'ar Ha-Tevila*, 3) indeed claims that the *mitzva* of accepting converts is derived from the precedent of Avraham, who had people "convert." However, as discussed, this does not appear to be the view of the Rambam, whose comments indicate that Avraham's example requires disseminating monotheistic faith, and not the effort to have non-Jews convert to Judaism.

b. ביבש קצירה תשברנה

Rav Sternbuch also points to the Gemara's ruling in *Maseches Bava Basra* (10b) that charity donations from gentiles should not be accepted, because the merit of their good deeds has the effect of prolonging their dominion over the Jewish nation.[19] The Gemara cites the verse in *Yeshayahu* (27:11), ביבש קצירה תשברנה (literally, "When the harvest dries — it is broken"), and explains this to mean that the enemy nations' subjugation of the Jewish people will end when their merits are depleted. Hence, we should not allow the gentiles the opportunity to accrue merit through charitable donations, as this prolongs our exile.

By the same token, Rav Sternbuch writes, we should not be working to encourage the gentiles to observe the Noachide laws, through which they would earn merit that would prolong our exile. Although the Rambam writes that we are required to compel gentiles to observe the Noachide laws when they live under our rule, Rav Sternbuch contends that this is not the case when we live in exile. He points to the precedent of Yona, the prophet who refused to encourage the people of Nineveh to repent, knowing that this would give them an advantage over *Am Yisrael*, which was steeped in sin at that time. Although Yona was wrong for refusing to deliver prophecy, Rav Sternbuch writes that this is only because he received an explicit command from God to urge the people of Nineveh to repent. Absent an explicit command from God, we should not be trying to influence other nations to repent and follow the Noachide laws.

This argument seems flawed, for several reasons. First, the *Sefer Chasidim* (1124) reaches the precise opposite conclusion from the precedent of Yona:

> אם רואה אדם נכרי עושה עבירה, אם יכול למחות ימחה, שהרי שלח הקדוש ברוך הוא את יונה לנינוה להשיבם...

> If a person sees a non-Jew committing a transgression — if he can protest, he should protest, for the Almighty sent Yona to Nineveh to have them repent...

Additionally, we may distinguish between charity, which is not a strict obligation for non-Jews,[20] and the Seven Noachide Laws, which constitute a gentile's basic religious requirements. Although the Gemara forbids accepting charity from gentiles so as not to increase their merit, it stands to reason that we ought to be assisting them to meet their minimum obligations to God, as clearly indicated by the *Sefer Chasidim*. Moreover, the *Shulchan Aruch* (Y.D. 254:2) rules that if

---

19. We discussed this prohibition at length in the first volume of *Headlines*, pp. 167–180.
20. See *Kovetz Shiurim*, *Bava Basra* 4a (#24).

a non-Jew wishes to make a donation to a synagogue, the congregation may accept it. The *Shach* (254:4) explains that a donation to a synagogue resembles a sacrifice, and it thus may be accepted, just as in the times of a *Beis Ha-Mikdash* sacrifices were accepted from non-Jews. Furthermore, the *Shach* writes, the rule that we do not accept charity from gentiles is limited to charity for the poor, but does not apply to other donations. Accordingly, there is no basis for comparing the שבע מצוות — a gentile's basic obligations — to charity. Although charity is not accepted, we should be assisting gentiles to fulfill the Noachide laws.

We might also question why, according to Rav Sternbuch's ruling, the prohibition of לפני עור לא תתן מכשול — causing others to sin — forbids causing gentiles to violate the laws that apply to them. If we do not wish for the gentiles to earn merit through the observance of the שבע מצוות, then there should be nothing wrong with causing them to transgress these laws. The fact that *halacha* forbids doing so demonstrates that a distinction exists between charity and the Noachide laws in this regard. Whereas the gentiles' voluntary charitable donations give them an edge, so-to-speak, over the Jews, this is not the case with regard to the Noachide laws, as the gentiles' observance of these laws is something that we should encourage.

Additionally, it seems inconceivable that effectively leading gentiles to do the right thing is detrimental to us and the world and delays the redemption. Undoubtedly, God wants all people — Jews and non-Jews alike — to acknowledge His existence, to avoid theft, murder, and immorality, and to abide by the other Noachide laws. Can we really be seen as hurting ourselves by promoting these laws throughout the world? It is hard to imagine that we become less worthy of redemption by influencing the non-Jews around us to do what God expects mankind to do!

c. ערבות

More generally, Rav Sternbuch contends in this responsum that Jews bear no obligation whatsoever to help non-Jews fulfill their religious obligations. We Jews bear an obligation towards one another, to help ensure our fellow Jews' observance of *mitzvos*, because of the concept of ערבות — the mutual responsibility that we accepted for one another. Since we never accepted such responsibility towards non-Jews, we bear no obligation to try to ensure their compliance with the Noachide laws.

This view is also cited in the name of Rav Moshe Feinstein. In *Mesoras Moshe* (vol. 1, pp. 504–505), it is recorded that Rav Moshe strongly opposed efforts to influence non-Jews to embrace the Noachide laws, and maintained that we bear no obligation in this regard. Rav Moshe reportedly ruled:

לדינא אין לנו שום התחייבות של תוכחה וכדומה על גויים.

> Halachically, we have no obligation of reproof and the like towards the gentiles.[21]

This assertion, however, appears to be contradicted by several sources that we have encountered, including the *Sefer Chasidim*'s explicit ruling that we must, when possible, protest sinful conduct of non-Jews, *Tosofos*' comment that there is a *mitzva* to teach the Seven Noachide laws to gentiles, and the Rambam's comments in *Sefer Ha-Mitzvos* that the *mitzva* of אהבת ה' includes working to bring all people to the recognition and service of God.[22]

Rav Sternbuch concludes by noting the serious risks entailed in our involvement in the religious beliefs and practices of our non-Jewish neighbors. These efforts could easily trigger suspicion and hostility, and the non-Jewish world might respond by reinforcing their own missionizing work. This is certainly a legitimate concern, and extreme caution is needed both to avoid arousing hostility and to refrain from participation in forums that give the impression that we are on equal footing with adherents of other faiths.[23]

In conclusion, although Rav Moshe Feinstein and Rav Moshe Sternbuch strongly opposed efforts to encourage gentiles to observe the Noachide laws, there appears to be legitimate basis in the halachic sources for such activities. As a practical matter, however, it is debatable, to say the least, whether in today's day and age and under current circumstances, these efforts can be made without evoking the hostility and resentment of the non-Jewish world. Rav Sternbuch is undoubtedly correct that our first priority must be peaceful relations with the non-Jewish world and ensuring our freedom to observe the Torah without fear or intimidation. If efforts to spread the שבע מצוות will in any way compromise this freedom — which they likely will — then they must definitely be avoided.

---

21. Rav Moshe also points to the potential dangers that could arise from religious engagement with gentiles, also noting that it is preferable not to provide gentiles with the merit of observing the Noachide laws.
22. Rav Sternbuch also raises the argument that gentiles are no longer bound by the שבע מצוות, as we noted above. However, we saw that most *poskim* maintain that although the gentiles are rewarded only on the level of אינו מצווה ועושה, it is clearly God's will that they should observe the Noachide laws, and thus this is something we should be encouraging.
23. See *Iggeros Moshe*, Y.D. 3:43.

INTERVIEW

Rav Yaakov Feitman
on *Headlines with David Lichtenstein**

This is an interesting question, which is a *machlokes* between two *gedolim* who continue the *mesora* of their ancestors. The Lubavitcher Rebbe continues the *mesora* of *Chassidus*, that we have obligations to gentiles in terms of שבע מצות בני נח. Rav Sternbuch, להבדיל בין חיים לחיים, who is a direct descendant of the Vilna Gaon, holds it is none of our business and we should leave them alone…

Rav Sternbuch refers to Jewish history and says we don't find in history that we went out and enhanced [the gentiles' observance of the Noachide laws]. There were never Jewish missionaries…

Another point Rav Sternbuch makes is that…if rabbis, outreach people, and others start negating Christianity, this will cause a potential danger to *Klal Yisrael*. This is all we need. We're fragile enough in this exile, so let's leave it alone. This is not something that our ancestors got involved in…

To some extent, this *machlokes* is that of the insular, "Litvishe" approach and the outreach approach of *Chassidus*. It is fascinating to look at the larger *machlokes* between the two.

* broadcast on April 18, 2015 (30 Nissan, 5775).

Maryland — Mr. "A" Moves to Baltimore*

Dec 31 2009

Well, Mr. "A" is now ordering pizza at the local kosher pizza shops in Baltimore, according to a report in Baltimore Jewish Times. Indeed, he was seen at Tov Pizza on Reisterstown Road.

He is here in Baltimore apparently with the knowledge of the rabbinical Vaad. They knew he was coming, but we, the community they supposedly serve, were supposed to find out when he showed up in public.

Is it possible that his very presence poses a risk to the Jewish community? Is it over the top to even think that?

But Mr. A is bringing the baggage of his fraud conviction and even his informant status to Baltimore.

It just seems as if our rabbinic "leadership," has acted on this community's behalf without checking the pulse of the very people they serve. Or maybe the leadership doesn't care what you think or what I think.

It doesn't take much imagination to see how a person with Mr. A's status could cause collateral damage in terms of pure personal safety to the members of our community.

* This article originally appeared in a Baltimore Jewish Times blog. This post was not online as of January 2, 2017. Vosizneias re-published this post on December 31, 2009. The name of the alleged criminal has been omitted.

Copyright © vosizneias.com

Criminals in Shul: Should Convicted Felons be Welcomed in Our Communities?

One of the most tragic phenomena plaguing contemporary Orthodox Jewry, without question, is that of highly publicized crimes committed by members of our communities. Tragically, and shamefully, we are no longer shocked to see news broadcasts showing *yarmulke*-clad men in handcuffs or on the defendant's stand in court. To our disgrace, Orthodox Jewry has produced in recent years a significant number of high-profile criminals convicted of molestation, rape, drug trafficking, money laundering, bank fraud, Ponzi schemes, and all kinds of other serious offenses. Each and every incident on its own, not to mention their cumulative effect in the aggregate, has created a grave חילול ה' that must concern all of us.

As part of our community's effort to properly and effectively respond and put an end to the disturbing trend, we need to address the difficult question of how to treat convicted criminals after their prison terms are completed. Should they be accepted and granted the opportunity to prove themselves again worthy of respect and the benefits of communal membership, or should they be shunned? On the one hand, we might assume that once a prison sentence has been served, and the offender has received his due punishment as deemed appropriate by our country's justice system, there is no longer any need or justification for imposing additional suffering upon the criminal and his family. On the other hand, it could be argued that the Orthodox community has the responsibility to send a loud, clear and unequivocal message rejecting criminal behavior, and accepting former convicts as congregation members could easily be interpreted as accepting their misdeeds, as well.

This question can also be asked with regard to non-prosecutable moral failings, such as instances of a consensual extramarital affair and the like. If a prominent figure has been disgraced by revelations of illicit behavior, should he be reaccepted to his congregation and community, or should he be banished as a statement of condemnation of his wayward conduct?

It must be emphasized that this entire discussion relates specifically to situations where the convict can be assumed not to pose any sort of public threat. Violent criminals may reasonably be considered dangerous even after serving prison sentences, and thus communities would do well to contact their local law enforcement officials for guidance and direction when these offenders move back into the community after serving their sentences. This essay will address the status of wrongdoers whose past offenses do not give us any reason to fear that associating with them compromises our safety, such as violators of white collar crimes, or those who had engaged in illicit but consensual sexual relationships, regarding whom the sole concern is the vital communal need to take a strong, unrelenting stance of rejection of such behavior.

One example is the widely-reported case of a prominent Orthodox Jewish businessman who was arrested on serious charges of bank fraud, and reached an agreement whereby his sentence would be lightened in exchange for his services as a government informant. This man proceeded to ensnare numerous fellow Jews, including prominent figures, by pressuring them to commit white collar crimes and then producing evidence to incriminate them. After his release from prison, this felon was not welcome in the synagogue where he wished to pray, and his daughter was not accepted into the local Beis Yaakov school. Was this rejection appropriate? And even if it is proper to deny the criminal synagogue membership, is it justifiable to punish his children by denying them entry into community schools?

We must also address the concern that failing to welcome a felon back into the community could push him away from observance altogether. Even if we conclude that rejection is warranted for the sake of broadcasting a vehement repudiation of the offender's criminal conduct, would this apply even if the result would be his complete estrangement from Jewish practice?

I. Excommunication That Will Lead to Defection

This final question was already debated centuries ago by leading halachic authorities. The Rama, in his glosses to the *Shulchan Aruch* (Y.D. 334:1), cites the ruling of the *Terumas Ha-Deshen* that a person deserving of excommunication should be handed this punishment even if this would result in his estrangement from Jewish practice.[1] The *Terumas Ha-Deshen* drew proof from the story told in *Maseches Kiddushin* (72a) of Rabbi Yehuda Ha-Nasi, who made several pronouncements before his death about certain developments taking place in the Jewish communities of Babylonia. One incident he noted is that Jews in a certain Babylonian town were found fishing on Shabbos, for which they were excommunicated by Rabbi Achi ben Rabbi Yoshiya. As a result of the

---

1. The Rama's formulation is: מנדין למי שהוא חייב נדוי ואפילו יש לחוש שעל ידי כן יצא לתרבות רעה, אין לחוש בכך.

excommunication, the violators abandoned Judaism. Presumably, Rabbi Achi had reason to anticipate this outcome, yet he decided upon excommunication in order to make a public statement about the severity of Shabbos desecration. Accordingly, the *Terumas Ha-Deshen* ruled that excommunication is declared regardless of legitimate concerns of the offender's consequent estrangement.

The *Taz* (Y.D. 334:1) strongly objects to this ruling, arguing that this incident told by Rabbi Yehuda Ha'nasi was not intended as a halachic prescription authorizing the excommunication of an offender who will likely abandon Jewish practice as a result. As counterproof, the *Taz* notes a passage earlier in *Maseches Kiddushin* (20b), where Rabbi Yishmael establishes that when a Jew sells himself as a servant to an idolater due to financial straits, knowingly putting himself in a position where he would have to work on behalf of idol-worship, there is an obligation to redeem him. Based on the Torah's command in *Sefer Vayikra* (25:48 — אחרי נמכר גאולה תהיה לו), Rabbi Yishmael asserts that we do not allow the slave to suffer the consequences of his wrong decision and remain in the service of pagans for the rest of his life. Rather, we must spend the money needed to redeem him from his master so he can rejoin the Jewish community and return to a religiously observant lifestyle. The *Taz* reasons that if the Torah commands us to redeem a fellow Jew who knowingly brought himself into the service of idol-worship, then certainly we must avoid any action that would lead a fellow Jew to defect.

The *Shach*, commenting briefly in his *Nekudos Ha-Kesef*, dismisses the *Taz*'s rationale, noting that a formal decision by *beis din* to excommunicate is legitimate regardless of the result. Otherwise, the *Shach* contends, בטלה דין ישראל — *beis din* has no real authority at all. The *Shach* appears to distinguish between the general responsibility to help ensure that our fellow Jew does not abandon Judaism even if he has knowingly begun heading in that direction, and the official responsibilities of *beis din*, which include taking strong action against certain violators.

Rav Yair Bachrach, in *Chavos Yair* (141), likewise refutes the *Taz*'s argument. He contends that the concern of the offender's defection cannot possibly override the need to make a strong public statement condemning wayward behavior. The concern of קלקול הדור — widespread abandonment of Torah — outweighs the concern of a particular's Jew disaffection, and thus when excommunication is warranted, it should be issued even if it will lead the violator to distance himself further from observance. Rav Bachrach advances this position in reference to the case of a person who was found neglecting the prohibitions against drinking non-Jewish wine. The community demanded that the man be fined and excommunicated until he repented, but the local rabbi refused, out of concern that harsh measures would only push the violator further away from halachic observance. Rav Bachrach opposed the rabbi's decision, insisting that punitive measures should be taken against the violator.

This is also the view of the *Chasam Sofer* (responsa, vol. 2, Y.D. 322), who refutes the *Taz*'s proof from the case of one who sold himself into the service of idolatry, noting that the Gemara there in Kiddushin deals with a person facing dire financial straits who felt compelled to undertake this drastic measure. Although he acted incorrectly, his guilt is mitigated by his circumstances, as he did not intend to distance himself from Torah observance, and thus there is an obligation to redeem him. This provides no proof, the *Chasam Sofer* writes, with regard to a violator deserving of excommunication. The *Chasam Sofer* further notes that to the contrary, the Gemara in *Maseches Gittin* (46b) establishes that if a person sold himself into the service of gentiles several times, the community is no longer required to ransom him, and he is left to continue the process of spiritual deterioration which he knowingly triggered. By the same token, somebody who is guilty of a violation that warrants excommunication should be excommunicated even if this leads to his estrangement from Judaism.

The *Taz* suggests drawing proof also from a different source. The Mahari Mintz wrote a responsum (5) in which he permitted a couple to marry despite the fact that the woman was at the time nursing a baby from a different man. Although *halacha* generally forbids a woman to marry while she has a child under the age of two from a different man (E.H. 13:11), the Mahari Mintz permitted this particular couple to marry because they would have otherwise lived together without halachic marriage and abandoned Jewish practice. The *Taz* argued that if the Mahari Mintz allowed suspending a rabbinic enactment to prevent Jews from slipping away from observance, then we should certainly not proactively undertake measures that will have the effect of distancing a Jew from observance.

The *Chasam Sofer* dismisses this proof, noting that *Chazal* enacted the prohibition of מינקת חבירו (marrying a woman with an infant from another man) for the benefit of the infant, as a means of guaranteeing that the woman could continue nursing and caring for him or her. If, however, the woman threatens to abandon Jewish practice if she is not permitted to halachically marry at that point, then it is to the child's benefit for the woman to remarry, so that he or she will be raised in an observant Jewish home. This ruling, then, has no bearing whatsoever on the case of a violator who will be led to abandon observance if he is excommunicated.[2]

---

2. In a letter addressed to Rav Azriel Hildesheimer (published in his responsa, 252), the writer refuted this proof differently, noting that in the case addressed by the Mahari Mintz, the woman would not only have lived with the man without marrying him, but

This view is also accepted by the *Chasam Sofer*'s son, the *Kesav Sofer* (responsa, Y.D. 168).

This question was addressed already much earlier, by the Radbaz (1:187), in reference to a situation where an offender openly threatened to convert to a different religion if he was reprimanded by the Jewish community. The Radbaz writes, כל ימי אני מצטער על זה — that he was troubled by this question his entire life, torn between the threat of losing a Jewish soul and the need to strictly uphold Torah law. After briefly considering the possibility of refraining from punishing sinners in such cases, the Radbaz concludes that to the contrary, religious authorities have the responsibility to enforce Torah law even at the expense of a violator's defection from Judaism. He writes:

> אם באנו לחוש לזה, תתבטל התורה לגמרי, כיון שיתפרסם הדבר שבשביל חששא זו אנו מעלימים עינינו מהרשעים, בני עולה יוסיפו לחטוא, וירבה הגזל והחמס והניאוף וכיוצא בזה, ולא מתקיים התורה אלא בשרידים.

> Once we concern ourselves with this [the prospect of the violator's defection], the Torah will be annulled altogether, because once it becomes known that out of this concern we turn our eyes away from the wicked, evildoers will continue sinning, and theft, violence, adultery and the like will abound, and Torah will be fulfilled only by a remnant.[3]

The Radbaz adds, however, that a great deal of thought and consideration must be invested before reaching a decision in such cases:

> ואע"ג שכתבתי כל זה להלכה, מ"מ יש למנהיג הדור להיות מתון בדברים כאלה, לפי שאין כל האנשים שוין ולא כל העבירות שוות... אדם שהוא רגיל בעבירות ובוטח בעצמו בטענתו, אין חוששין לו, ויהיה מה שיהיה, ונעמיד התורה. ואם אינו רגיל, וקרוב הדבר שישמע, ממשיכין אותו בדברים עד שישוב מעט, ואין ממהרין להענישו, מפני התקלה...והכל לפי ראות עיני הדיין המנהיג, ובלבד שיהיו כל מעשיו לשם שמים.

But although I've written all this as *halacha*, nevertheless, the leader of

---

would have likely engaged in illicit relations with other men, as well. This situation thus posed a spiritual danger to the public at large, and for this reason the Mahari Mintz felt that she should be allowed to marry the man. That case is quite different, then, from a situation where shunning the offender is necessary to maintain appropriate standards of conduct in the community.

3. The Radbaz proceeds to draw proof from the story told in the Gemara about the fishermen in Babylonia, as noted by the *Terumas Ha-Deshen*. He also adds that in most cases, a person who has already committed grievous sins and threatens to abandon Judaism altogether will likely follow through on his threat regardless of whether his demands are met.

the generation must be very cautious in regard to such matters, because not everybody is the same, and not all sins are the same… A person who is accustomed to sinning and feels confident with himself in his claim, we do not concern ourselves with him, and we uphold the Torah, come what may. But if he is not accustomed, and he will likely listen, we draw him close with words until he returns somewhat, and we do not rush to punish him, because [this can lead to] negative outcomes… Everything must be done as the judge and leader sees fit, provided that all his actions are done for the sake of Heaven.

The consensus[4] among the *poskim* seems to be that a violator may be shunned when this is deemed necessary for the sake of upholding Torah law and values, even if this will cause that violator to abandon Judaism. However, as the Radbaz warns, this decision must be made only after careful and cautious consideration, to ensure that the situation indeed warrants shunning the offender. When such situations arise, then, the community leaders must very carefully consider whether the criminal's actions are severe enough to necessitate barring him from our communities as a statement of condemnation of his crimes.

II. Expelling an Offender's Children From School

The right to expel a criminal's children from school is explicitly codified by the Rama (Y.D. 334:6), who writes the following regarding a person placed into excommunication:

יש רשות לבית דין להחמיר עליו שלא ימולו בניו ושלא יקבר אם ימות ולגרש את בניו מבית הספר ואשתו מבית הכנסת עד שיקבל עליו את הדין.

> *Beis din* has the authority to enact that his sons not be circumcised and he not be buried if he dies, and to expel his children from school and his wife from the synagogue, until he accepts the judgment upon himself.

The source of the Rama's ruling is the *Nimukei Yosef* (Bava Kama 39b in the Rif), where this ruling is cited in the name of Rav Paltoy Gaon.

The Maharshal, in *Yam Shel Shlomo* (Bava Kama 10:13), strongly objects to this ruling, and expresses astonishment over the prospect of denying innocent children a Torah education on account of their parent's misdeeds. He is likewise baffled by the notion that the offender's wife, who committed no wrongdoing, should be barred from the synagogue. In his amazement, the Maharshal writes,

---

4. See *Sdei Chemed* (*Ma'areches Hei*, 37), who shows that the consensus among the *poskim* follows the Rama's view.

לא אאמין שיצאו ב' דברים אלו מפי הגאון — "I cannot believe that these two things left the mouth of the Gaon."[5] How, he asks, can we deny an evildoer's wife and children the opportunity to pray in the synagogue and receive a Torah education on account of his sinful conduct?

We find among the *poskim* three approaches to defend Rav Paltoy Gaon's ruling. The first is suggested by the *Taz*, who distinguishes between older and younger children. The Torah learning of younger children, the *Taz* writes, is credited solely to the father, and they have no merit of their own. Therefore, it is legitimate and appropriate to deny them the opportunity to learn on account of their father's wrongdoing. Older children, however, who have already reached the age of *mitzva* obligation, earn their own merit for Torah study, and they may not be denied this opportunity simply because their father deserves excommunication. The *Taz* does not defend Rav Paltoy's position permitting barring the offender's wife from the synagogue, and accepts the Maharshal's view forbidding such a measure.[6]

A second, particularly creative, approach is taken by the *Chasam Sofer* (Y.D. 2:322). He asserts that when a sinner commits a grave offense warranting excommunication, he should be denied the opportunity to earn merits through which he could continue living his wayward life. Therefore, the community should bar members of the violator's household from communal prayer and Torah study, as their involvement in *mitzvos* is a source of merit for the offender. And while this might seem unjust to the family members, who forfeit the benefits of these *mitzvos* for no fault of their own, the *Chasam Sofer* invokes the rule that a person who genuinely aspires to perform a *mitzva* earns the merits of that *mitzva* even if circumstances prevent him from fulfilling his wish (אפילו חשב אדם לעשות מצוה, ונאנס ולא עשאה מעלה עליו הכתוב כאילו עשאה — Shabbos 63a). The excommunicated violator's family members do not forfeit the merits of the *mitzvos* they are barred from performing on his account, because their inability to perform these deeds results from circumstances entirely beyond their control. Thus, the violator loses the merits of his family members' *mitzvos*, which they are prevented from performing due to his sinfulness, but they forfeit nothing, because they desire to perform these *mitzvot* but are prevented from doing by external factors.[7]

---

5. The Maharshal accepts Rav Paltoy Gaon's ruling regarding circumcising the offender's sons, noting that these are obligations cast upon the offender himself, and thus refusing to perform these rituals is a valid punishment.
6. This distinction drawn by the *Taz* between older and younger children is made as well by the Maharal, in *Gur Aryeh* (*Vayikra* 20:20), in reference to the punishment of *kareis*: דכרת הוא ובנין נכרתין ר"ל בבנים קטנים, דאין להם זכות עצמן, אבל בבנים גדולים לא איירי.
7. The *Chasam Sofer*'s approach reflects a literal understanding of the rule of מעלה עליו הכתוב כאלו עשאה, such that one who is prevented by circumstances from performing a *mitzva*

A much simpler approach is taken by Rav Yechiel Epstein, in his *Aruch Ha-Shulchan* (Y.D. 334:6). Rav Epstein cites the Rama's ruling and then adds the words, אם יראו שבזה יכוף ראשו — "if they see that he will thereby submit." In other words, punitive measures against the wife and children are acceptable only as threats that will likely achieve the desired result of coercing the violator into submission. Rav Epstein continues:

אבל בלאו הכי אין להעניש בנים בשביל אביהם ואשה בשביל בעלה, ואפילו בנים קטנים.

> Otherwise, however, children should not be punished on account of their father, nor a wife on account of her husband, even young children.

Rav Epstein rejects the distinction drawn by the *Taz* between older and younger children, and maintains that children of any age may be banned from school as part of their father's punishment only if the community leaders have reason to believe that this will force the father into submission. Indeed, the Rama permitted barring an offender's children from school עד שיקבל עליו את הדין — "until he accepts the judgment," suggesting that this may be done to force the delinquent parent into compliance, but not as a *post facto* punitive measure.

This approach was also taken by the *Chasam Sofer*'s son, the *Kesav Sofer*, in a responsum (Y.D. 168) addressing the situation of a man who married his aunt (his mother's brother's wife), and they refused to separate.[8] The concern arose that punitive measures against the couple would cause them to abandon Jewish practice entirely, together with their children. The *Kesav Sofer* wrote that although the prospect of their defection from Judaism is not a factor, in light of the generally accepted ruling of the Rama noted above, the community must take into account the impact that sanctions will have upon the couple's children. After referencing his father's explanation of the Rama's ruling permitting banishing an offender's children from school, the *Kesav Sofer* appears to reach a different conclusion, significantly limiting the scope of this ruling:

---

receives all the rewards and benefits of that *mitzva*. This premise can be found elsewhere in the *Chasam Sofer*'s writings, as well. In his commentary to *Maseches Sukka* (31b), for example, the *Chasam Sofer* explains the principle of מצוות לאו ליהנות ניתנו by asserting that one receives no benefits from the actual performance of a *mitzva*, since all benefits offered by a *mitzva* can be gained simply by genuinely desiring to perform it. See also the *Chasam Sofer*'s responsa, C.M. 1. For a comprehensive treatment of this topic, see Rav Chaim Eisenstein, *Peninim Mi'bei Midrasha, Vayikra*, pp. 157–161.

8. Marrying the wife of one's biological uncle is forbidden by force of rabbinic enactment. In the case addressed by the *Kesav Sofer*, the couple cohabited while the woman was still married to the man's uncle, and thus they were forbidden to marry due to the law that those who committed an adulterous act may not engage in relations subsequently.

ולא דמי למש"ש ברמ"א סי' רל"ד סעי' ו' וי"ו דיש רשות לב"ד לגרש בניו מבית הספר ולגרש אשתו מבה"כ עד שיקבל עליו הדין...דאין לדמותו לנידון דידן כי שם אשרי לבנים כשהאב יקבל הדין ושב ורפא לו...ויש תקוה שע"י שמגרשין הבנים מבית הספר ישוב כי גדול בושתו, ומוטב שיהיו בטלים מדברי תורה על זמן מה כדי שיזכה האב וישוב והבן ג"כ זוכה, משא"כ בנידן שלפנינו שע"י הכפיה יש לחוש ששניהם האבות והבנים יצאו לתרבות רעה ח"ו, בודאי טוב לנו למשוך ידינו...

This is not similar to what the Rama writes (334:6), that a *beis din* has the authority to expel his children from school and his wife from the synagogue until he accepts the law... because in that case, fortunate are the children whose father accepts the law and returns and is [spiritually] healed...and there is hope that by banishing the children from school he will return due to his great embarrassment. It is thus preferable that they miss Torah learning for a period of time so that the father will have the privilege of returning, which is beneficial also for the child. In the case before us, by contrast, where there is concern that coercion will lead both the parents and the children to a wayward lifestyle, Heaven forbid, it is definitely preferable for us to abstain...

Like Rav Epstein, the *Kesav Sofer* understood that the Rama permits expelling the children from school only as a means of effecting a change of heart in the parent. Such measures are not legitimate, however, as a *post facto* response intended to send a strong message of condemnation. As the *Kesav Sofer* explains, there is no reason to be more concerned with the religious commitment of the greater community than with that of the offender's children. It is wholly illogical, he argues, to risk religiously alienating the children for the purpose of conveying a message and seeking to prevent violations by others. Although it is legitimate to risk alienating the offenders themselves through strong condemnation for the sake of maintaining our religious and moral standards, there is no sense in risking the alienation of their children for this purpose.

The *Kesav Sofer* draws proof from the Gemara's ruling in *Maseches Kiddushin* (81a) that no punitive measures are taken against a married woman who goes into seclusion with a man other than her husband. Punishing a woman for such conduct might lead people to question her children's status, and to suspect that they were not fathered by her husband, suspicions which must be avoided. The *Kesav Sofer* reasons that if punishment is withheld out of concern for the reputation of the offender's children, it goes without saying that punishment is withheld if the children's spiritual future is at stake.

We thus find three views among the *Acharonim* regarding the permissibility of expelling a student from school as a punitive measure against a parent:

1. According to the *Taz*, younger children may be expelled, but older students may not.
2. The *Chasam Sofer* permits expelling children of any age in order to deny the offender the merit of his children's Torah education.
3. The *Kesav Sofer* and *Aruch Ha-Shulchan* allow expelling a sinner's children from school only in the rare case when this drastic measure will be effective in causing the sinner to submit to authority. This may not be done as a statement of condemnation.

An important distinction is drawn in this regard by Rav Menashe Klein, in *Mishneh Halachos* (17:96), in reference to the unfortunate case of a bitter conflict that arose between a parent and his child's school. The school summoned the father to *beis din*, and the father refused and proceeded to report the school to the government authorities, causing the school a great deal of damage. Rav Klein permitted the school to expel the child as a means of censuring his father, noting that since other suitable institutions were available, all opinions would approve of such a measure in this case. The aforementioned debate revolves around the question of denying the offender's child a Jewish education altogether. However, if a school sees fit to expel a student because of his or her parent's crimes, and the student can be enrolled in a different institution, this measure is acceptable according to all opinions.

III. Collective Punishment

We might suggest a different perspective on the issue of barring children from schools on account of a parent's crimes, by examining the broader question of collective punishment in Jewish law. Let us first step back and ask, does *halacha* recognize the legitimacy of punishing innocent people due to their association or relationship with an evildoer? Is it ever acceptable to punish one person for another person's wrongdoing, and, if so, when?[9]

The Torah explicitly warns against punishing children for their parents' wrongdoing (*Devarim* 24:16):

לא יומתו אבות על בנים ובנים לא יומתו על אבות, איש בחטאו יומתו.

> Fathers shall not be put to death on account of sons, and sons shall not be put to death on account of fathers; a person shall be put to death [only] for his sin.

---

9. For an extensive discussion of the Torah's approach to collective punishment, see Rav Meir Batist's article published in *Techumin* (vol. 12).

This prohibition is emphatically reiterated by the prophet Yechezkel (18:2):

הנפש החטאת היא תמות, בן לא ישא בעון האב ואב לא ישא בעון הבן, צדקת הצדיק עליו תהיה רשעת הרשע עליו תהיה.

> The soul that sins — it shall die; a son shall not bear the iniquity of the father, and a father shall not bear the iniquity of the son; the righteousness of the righteous shall be upon him, and the evil of the evildoer shall be upon him.

These verses make it clear that the Torah's justice system, as a rule, precludes the possibility of punishing one person for the crimes of another.

This fundamental axiom was expressed by Moshe and Aharon in response to God's declaration of His intent to annihilate *Am Yisrael* in the wake of Korach's revolt. Moshe and Aharon exclaimed, האיש אחד יחטא ועל כל העדה תקצוף — "Shall one man sin, and Your wrath shall be upon the entire congregation?!" (*Bamidbar* 16:22). Rashi, citing the *Midrash Tanchuma*, writes that God agreed with Moshe and Aharon's claim, and informed them that He would punish only the guilty parties.[10]

We do, however, find in the Torah several instances of punishments endured by people associated with the perpetrator or perpetrators of an offense, who do not seem to have been guilty of any wrongdoing themselves. One striking example is the law of עיר הנדחת, which the Torah introduces in *Sefer Devarim* (13:13–19). This law refers to the case of a city whose inhabitants were lured to worship idols, and requires killing all the town's residents and destroying their property. The Rambam, in *Hilchos Avodas Kochavim* (4:6), explains that a city becomes an עיר הנדחת when the majority of its men worship idols, and once the city has been declared an עיר הנדחת, all those who worshipped idols are put to death, along with their wives and children. The same Torah that strictly forbids killing innocent people for offenses committed by their family members requires killing innocent women and children for the pagan worship of their husbands and fathers. How do we explain this law?

This question is discussed in the *Migdal Oz* commentary to the Rambam's *Mishneh Torah*, which relates that the Ramah (Rabbi Meir Abulafia of Toledo) questioned this ruling in his letters to the rabbis of Lunel protesting portions of the Rambam's writings. How, the Ramah asked, could the Rambam require the execution of innocent women and children for the idol-worship of their husbands and fathers?[11]

---

10. אמר הקב"ה יפה אמרתם, אני יודע ומודיע מי חטא ומי לא חטא.
11. In the next passage, the Rambam writes that when a city is declared an עיר הנדחת, all

The rabbis of Lunel, as cited in *Migdal Oz*, gave two explanations for the Rambam's ruling:

חדא שהם סבה וגורמים לישיבת הגדולים, ועוד לרדות הגדולים בהריגתן שהן חביבין עליהן.

> First, they are the reason and cause for the adults' residence [in the city], and also, [this is done] in order to threaten the adults with their execution, for they cherish them.

The first explanation attempts to assign a degree of culpability to the children, by claiming that they are somehow to blame for the adults' decision to reside in the sinful city. Clearly, this explanation seems very difficult to accept, as there appears to be no reason to hold young children accountable — to the point of being worthy of execution — for their parents' choice of a place of residence.

In their second answer, the scholars of Lunel seem to suggest that the execution of the wives and children is legislated only as a warning and threat. Perhaps drawing upon the well-known tradition that the law of עיר הנדחת is introduced in the Torah as a hypothetical model, and can never be actually implemented,[12] the rabbis of Lunel assert that the Torah does not wish for the wives and children to die, and this punishment is prescribed purely for deterrent purposes, to discourage the men from worshipping idols.[13]

---

the town's property, including the possessions of those who did not worship idols, is destroyed. Once again, the innocent minority is, seemingly, being punished for the crimes of the majority. However, the Rambam himself briefly explains the reason for the destruction of these residents' property, writing, הואיל וישבו שם ממונם אבד — they lose their property as punishment for choosing to live in a wicked city. The Rambam's remark is likely based upon Rabbi Shimon's comment in the Tosefta (Sanhedrin 14:1) that the innocent residents of an עיר הנדחת lose their possessions "because they caused the righteous to reside with the wicked." The decision to live among evildoers was likely made out of financial considerations, and thus the innocent townspeople are punished by losing their possessions.

12. The Gemara in *Maseches Sanhedrin* (71a) cites the Tosefta which notes that there never was or will ever be a situation of עיר הנדחת. *Halacha* imposes so many conditions upon the applicability of this law that it is all but impossible for such a situation to ever arise.

13. In their response, the scholars of Lunel note two precedents to wives and children being punished for the crimes of the husbands and fathers: the deaths of the family members of Korach, Dasan and Aviram (*Bamidbar* 16:32), and the execution of all residents of Yaveish Gilad, who ignored the order to arrive in Mitzpa following the civil war between Binyamin and the other tribes (*Shoftim* 21). Curiously, however, neither answer suggested by the sages of Lunel to explain the Rambam's ruling concerning עיר הנדחת is applicable to these incidents, and thus it is difficult to understand why they invoked these examples. Moreover, the story of Korach can easily be discounted in light of the fact that the punishment was brought by God, and it therefore cannot serve as

A different explanation was offered by Rav Aharon of Lunel, who wrote a response to the Ramah's objection to the Rambam's ruling. He writes:

חומר הוא שהחמיר הקב"ה בעבודה זרה ושבועה וחילול ה' להחרים ולהשמיד הכל למען ישמעו ויראו הנשארים...

> This is a measure of stringency enacted by the Almighty with regard to idolatry, [false] oaths and defamation of God's Name — to eradicate and destroy all so that those who remain will listen and see…[14]

Rav Aharon of Lunel here asserts that there are rare instances where the Torah calls for punishing innocent people affiliated with wrongdoers for the purpose of underscoring the severity of the offense.

Another example might be the Gemara's discussion at the end of *Maseches Sukka* (56b) regarding the story told of Miriam bas Bilga, a Jewish woman who married a Greek official and joined the Greeks in defiling the *Beis Ha-Mikdash* during the period of Greek oppression. Miriam belonged to one of the twenty-four families of *kohanim*, and the Sages penalized her entire family by imposing special restrictions upon the *kohanim* from that family serving in the *Mikdash*. This was done, presumably, as a reminder of Miriam's betrayal and a warning to those who might seek to repeat her actions. The Gemara justifies these measures, which penalized Miriam's family for her act of treason, by invoking the rabbinic adage, אוי לרשע אוי לשכנו ("Woe unto the wicked, woe unto his neighbor"). In other words, people affiliated with a wrongdoer — even for no fault of their own — will sometimes suffer the consequences of this association, and will

---

a precedent for protocols followed by human authorities. As for the execution of the women and children of Yaveish Gilad, we might note that the stories told at the end of *Sefer Shoftim* are intended to demonstrate the state of dysfunction and anarchy that existed during this period, when *Bnei Yisrael* had no centralized authority. Therefore, policies implemented and followed during this period do not necessarily reflect the halachic ideal that we are to embrace.

Rav David Tzvi Hoffman, in his commentary to *Sefer Devarim*, offers a much different explanation for why the wives and children in an עיר הנדחת are killed, claiming that the city's destruction is ordained as a Divine punishment, much like the destruction of the world in the time of Noach, and the destruction of Sedom and Amora during the time of Avraham. The situation of עיר הנדחת is extraordinary in that *Bnei Yisrael* are commanded to carry out the Divine retribution. This execution, unlike all other instances of punishments administered by *beis din*, is carried out in the capacity of God's messengers, and not by the authority invested by the Torah in the court. God, in His infinite wisdom and justice, can determine who lives and who dies, and we cannot question His decisions. As such, we cannot question the justice of the requirement to kill the women and children of an עיר הנדחת.

14. *Iggeros Ha-Ramah*, letters 26–27.

need to be penalized as part of the collective effort to forcefully denounce the wrongdoer's actions.

Indeed, the Gemara in *Maseches Bava Kama* (92a) records the ancient proverb בהדי הוצא לקי כרבא — "The cabbage is ruined together with the thorns." In the process of eliminating the "thorns" from our communities, it may occasionally be necessary to harm even the "cabbage" — the innocent affiliates of the offender.

A modern example of this concept appears in a responsum of Rav Avraham Yitzchak Kook (*Da'as Kohen*, 193) addressing the case of a synagogue that honored a prominent member who had heartily eaten on Yom Kippur by calling him for the coveted *aliya* of *maftir Yona* that same afternoon. The congregation's rabbi instructed the leadership to deny this individual the rights to receive an *aliya* for the next several years, and he threatened to never again speak or teach in the synagogue if they failed to comply. Rav Kook approved of this measure, despite the fact that it punished the entire congregation for the disobedience of one or several of its leaders. In light of the grave חילול ה' that transpired, Rav Kook felt that an especially strong response was warranted even if this meant punishing innocent congregants. Among the sources cited by Rav Kook to support his ruling is the Gemara's discussion in *Maseches Yevamos* (79a) of the story of King David, who acceded to the demand of the Givoni tribe to hand over members of King Shaul's family. Shaul had unlawfully executed seven members of this tribe, and the *Givonim* demanded revenge. The Gemara explains that although the Torah forbids punishing children for their parents' crimes, King David nevertheless granted the *Givonim*'s request to avoid the grave חילול ה' that would result from allowing King Shaul's crime to go unpunished. This discussion demonstrates that in situations of a grave חילול ה', a harsh response is warranted even if this requires punishing innocent people affiliated with the offender.

All this hearkens back to the extraordinary law of עיר הנדחת, where even innocent women and children are killed along with the idolaters, a requirement which Rav Aharon of Lunel attributes to the especially grievous nature of idol worship.

Declaration of War

It would seem, however, that there is also a different explanation for the extraordinary provision requiring the execution of innocent residents of an עיר הנדחת.

One of the most shocking instances of collective punishment found in the *Tanach* is the massacre perpetrated by Shimon and Levi on the city of Shechem after the city's prince abducted and defiled their sister (*Bereishis* 34). Although Yaakov vehemently censured his sons' violent actions (*Bereishis* 34:30, 49:5-7), many commentators and *poskim* presumed that Shimon and Levi must have felt — albeit perhaps incorrectly — that their assault was halachically appropriate. The Rambam (*Hilchos Melachim* 9:14) famously asserted that the townspeople deserved execution for failing to maintain a proper justice system whereby Shechem would be tried and punished for his grievous crime. Rav Pinchas Horowitz, in his *Panim Yafos* commentary, suggests that Shimon and Levi's objective was to rescue their sister from Shechem's home. It was clear to them, however, that Shechem and his father would kill them if they tried to take Dina, and that if they killed Shechem and his father, the townspeople would all arise to avenge their leaders' deaths. Shimon and Levi thus had no choice but to kill all the men of Shechem as part of their just and noble effort to rescue Dina from the clutches of her abductor. As such, the deadly assault was necessary as a means of self-defense.

According to these approaches, the townspeople of Shechem deserved to be killed, either for their own crimes, or because of the threat they posed to Shimon and Levi, and thus they were not killed as a form of collective punishment.

A different approach is taken by the Maharal of Prague, in his *Gur Aryeh* (*Bereishis* 34:13), where he writes that collective punishment is acceptable in the context of warfare, when a battle is waged between nations, as opposed to individuals. The Maharal postulates that Yaakov's family and Shechem were essentially two "nations," and Dina's abduction legitimately warranted a strong military response. This was a conflict between two nations, not between individuals, and thus Shimon and Levi felt authorized to assault not only the perpetrator, but also the entire city. This approach is also taken by Rav Zalman Sorotzkin, in his *Oznayim La-Torah* commentary.

Indeed, warfare, almost by definition, entails a degree of collective punishment. In war, the parties to the conflict are large, diverse groups of people, not all of whom are necessarily culpable in the wrongs or perceived wrongs that precipitated the hostilities, and yet they all suffer the effects of the war. If a legitimate war is being fought against an aggressor nation, some sort of pain will be inflicted upon the general population. Even if civilians are not intentionally targeted, it is all but inevitable for the civilian population to suffer, either as a result of blockades and sanctions, or as collateral casualties of combat. In World War II, of course, thousands of civilians in places like Dresden, Hiroshima and Nagasaki were targeted in an effort to force the Axis powers to surrender. More recently, Israel has been compelled on numerous occasions to attack Hamas military assets and installations in densely-populated areas in the Gaza Strip during wars waged to protect against rocket fire on Israeli civilians. And while Israel has come under relentless criticism for these measures, the legality of exacting civilian casualties in the course of pursuing a legitimate military objective during war — provided that the civilian casualties are not the objective — has never before been questioned. Likewise, economic sanctions against rogue regimes are standard in the modern world, despite the "collective punishment" imposed on the country's entire populace for the crimes committed by its government, which may even be ruling them against their will.

The context of warfare, then, marks a significant exception to the rule forbidding inflicting punishment on somebody for a different person's crime.

This concept may help explain the other contexts in which we find collective punishment being sanctioned. The situation of an עיר הנדחת is unique in that the majority of a city, and not merely a random assortment of individuals, embrace idolatry. When a city becomes pagan, it essentially declares war against the Jewish nation. We view the city not as a place where many people have abandoned Jewish belief, but rather as an entity that has arisen against the collective of Israel. The עיר הנדחת seeks to secede, in a sense, from *Am Yisrael*, and thus the Torah requires waging a fierce and relentless battle against the town. This is why even innocent inhabitants are killed. Since this response falls under the category of warfare — a military operation against a rogue regime, as opposed to the execution of a group of violators — it is legitimate to punish even innocent townspeople.

This theory can be applied also to other situations of collective punishment. In *Sefer Bamidbar* (16:32), we read that although God heeded Moshe and Aharon's plea on behalf of the people during Korach's revolt, He nevertheless killed the revolt's leaders as well as their family members. Korach's followers were spared, but his wife and children — and those of his primary cohorts, Dasan and Aviram — were killed. The explanation, perhaps, is that Korach launched an all-out "war" against Moshe and Aharon. This was not a case of several people acting wrongly, but rather a rebellion against the establishment, and thus even innocent lives were not spared.

Another example is the story of Yaveish Gilad, a community that ignored the call to convene with the rest of the nation after the civil war waged between Binyamin and the other tribes (*Shoftim* 21). The entire town — including the women and children — were killed (21:10). It would seem that this refusal constituted an act of secession, a declaration by the people of Yaveish Gilad that they did not see themselves as part of the Jewish nation. Once the townspeople declared war against the nation, an extraordinary circumstance arose whereby even innocents were allowed to be killed.

In light of this theory, we may perhaps explain the Rama's ruling permitting the exclusion of an offender's children from Torah educational frameworks. The circumstances that warrant excommunication are those involving a sinner who poses a direct threat to the Jewish community. It does not apply to a person who failed in a moment of weakness, or who makes an occasional mistake. Excommunication was declared when somebody showed disdain or disregard for the community, such as by flagrantly and unabashedly violating basic communal norms, by brazenly opposing its leadership, or by tainting its reputation. In essence, *cherem* is a response to a declaration of "war" against the Jewish community. It is the way a community or the establishment fights back when it comes under assault, and returns fire to those who threaten it. Therefore, as in the cases of Korach and עיר הנדחת, innocent affiliates may be harmed in the process. As part of the community's efforts to defend itself against those who wage war against it, causing harm to the offender's family becomes a legitimate option to consider.

In the view of this author, this perspective ought to inform our response to perpetrators of heinous crimes who arise from our community. When dealing with a serial pedophile, a financier who for years ran a fraudulent Ponzi scheme, or other high-profile criminals, it could legitimately be argued that such people have declared war on our community. If an Orthodox Jew is discovered to have molested dozens of children, cheated dozens of clients, or evaded millions of dollars' worth of taxes, and his crime is widely reported throughout the world, bringing shame and humiliation upon the entire Orthodox Jewish community, he causes irreparable damage to us all. Therefore, it is entirely reasonable, and appropriate, to respond by shunning that individual along with his family members. When somebody declares war against the Jewish people, his innocent family members may, tragically, need to be harmed as part of our response.

If a Jew was discovered working in support of Hamas or the Islamic Jihad, and he wished to enroll his children in one of our community schools, the community would, in all likelihood, unanimously demand that the school reject the application. If this individual was planning his son's bar-mitzva, it is hardly conceivable that any Orthodox synagogue would open its doors to host this celebration. Serial and high profile criminals should not be treated any differently. They place a nearly indelible a stain upon us all, and need to be openly and forcefully opposed. While their spouses and children certainly cannot be blamed for their nefarious acts of treason against the Orthodox community, the war we are compelled to wage against criminals produced by our communities will sometimes result in unfortunate "collateral damage," affecting the innocent family members.

IV. Accepting a Penitent Criminal

Let us now turn our attention to the case of an observant Jew who, after having been found guilty of grave crimes or moral indiscretions, expresses what appears to be genuine remorse and a sincere desire to make amends and return to the Orthodox Jewish community. What sort of penitence would suffice for us to welcome him back? (As mentioned earlier, we raise this question only in regard to criminals who cannot be assumed to pose any sort of risk.)

The *Shulchan Aruch* (C.M. 34:22) rules that apostates and מוסרים — those who betray their fellow Jews by disclosing information about them to hostile gentiles — are not accepted as witnesses until they repent. The Rama clarifies that a מוסר regains his eligibility after his victims grant him forgiveness and he formally repents. Importantly, the Maharam of Rotenberg (4:1022) ruled that a מוסר must also compensate all those who lost money because of the information he disclosed.

Similarly, with regard to social sanctions against a wrongdoer, the Ramban writes in his *Mishpat Ha-Cherem* that a writ of excommunication is annulled when the offender repents:

אם עשה תשובה...ובא לב"ד או לפני טובי העיר במעמד אנשי העיר, יכולים הם בעצמם להתיר לו...

> If...[he] repented and came to *beis din* or before the town's leaders in the presence of the townspeople, they themselves can annul it for him.

We might add, however, that when it comes to the particular sin of מסירה, the bar of *teshuva* is raised especially high. *Chazal* teach in *Maseches Kalla Rabasi* (3:18), כל המלשין אין לו רפואה — whoever disseminates negative information about his fellow cannot be "cured" of his sin. Once the negative reports — whether true of false — have been disseminated, their effects are no longer under the disseminator's control, and their impact cannot possibly be measured in any sort of quantitative terms. As such, rectifying such a sin is all but impossible. Accordingly, Rabbi Elazar of Worms, in his *Sefer Ha-Rokei'ach* (*Hilchos Teshuva*, 27), prescribes the following "program" for repenting for this sin:

יהא לו כעבד עולם, ויבקש ממנו מחילה בפני כל העולם, וילקה ויתענה ויתודה כאלו הרג כל בניו ובנותיו וכל בני ביתו...יהיו חטאיו נגדו, וישוב וישבור רוחו בכל כחו...ואם אין לו לשלם ירבה עליו ריעים ויבקש מחילה למי שהפסיד טרם ימות, וכאשר ירויח, יצמצם ויפרע למי שנת-חייב או ליורשו, כי למלשין אין לו רפואה, אם לא יסור חלאה, ויתודה חובו וישוב בכל לבבו.

> He shall be like an eternal servant to him [his victim], and publicly request his forgiveness. He should be whipped and should fast and confess as though he killed all [of the victim's] sons, daughters and household members... His sins should be in front of him, and he should repent and break his spirit with all his might... If he does not have with what to repay, then he should bring many friends and ask forgiveness

from the one to whom he caused a loss, before he dies. And when he earns money, he should limit [his own expenditures] and repay the one he owes or his inheritors, for the informant has no "cure" unless he removes the illness, confesses his guilt, and repents with all his heart.

In cases where a person's actions result in the incarceration of fellow Jews, it is all but impossible to speak of any kind of compensation for the pain and humiliation caused to the victim and his family. As such, one could argue that such an offender has no possibility of regaining his eligibility to rejoin the Orthodox Jewish community.

It seems reasonable to assume that the same basic principle would apply to other forms of criminal activity that caused harm to a great number of people, such as large-scale Ponzi schemes, or the highly-publicized case of a respected rabbi who was found secretly video recording prospective converts in his synagogue's *mikveh*. Although these kinds of violators can, in principle, regain acceptance into the community through repentance, their repentance must include reparations and a sincere apology accepted by their victims, something which seems all but impossible.

Thus, while in principle a sincerely penitent offender deserves the right to resume communal life, it is very difficult to determine what kind of penitence would suffice in the case of a person who caused a great deal of pain and suffering to many fellow Jews.

Erasing a Lifetime of Piety

In discussions regarding the handling of high-profile Orthodox Jewish criminals, advocates for welcoming such figures back into the community often point to the fact that they are, when all is said and done, not much different from the rest of us. Just as we all have our share of faults, we sometimes hear, these convicted offenders, too, are generally decent, hard-working, God-fearing Jews with flaws that landed them in trouble with the law. If a person is a devoted, loving, hard-working spouse and parent, a devoutly observant Jew, and an active community member who has made meaningful contributions — financial or otherwise — to the Jewish nation, then why, some people ask, should he be ostracized because of one grave mistake, severe as it may be?

The answer can be found in a famous story told by the Gemara (*Berachos* 28b) about the final moments of the life of Rabban Yochanan ben Zakai. As his students gathered around, they noticed their revered rabbi crying, and they asked him why he wept. He explained:

יש לפני שני דרכים, אחת של גן עדן ואחת של גיהנם, ואיני יודע באיזו מוליכים אותי, ולא אבכה?

> I have before me two paths — one to *Gan Eden*, and one to *Gehinnom*, and I know not in which I will be led. Shall I not cry?

Remarkably, Rabban Yochanan ben Zakai, the great sage who led the Jewish people during one of the most tumultuous periods in our history — before, during and following the fall of the Second Commonwealth — and who established the academy in Yavneh which ensured the renewed flourishing of Torah scholarship following the destruction, feared that he might be condemned to *Gehinnom*. We can only wonder, what could he have possibly done that would have sentenced him to eternal suffering? While we understand that no human is perfect and free of spiritual blemish, and that even the most righteous among us have stains on their record for which a reckoning will be made, what could have made Rabban Yochanan fear that he would be led away from *Gan Eden* and towards the suffering of *Gehinnom*?

Rav Yosef Dov Soloveitchik boldly suggested that Rabban Yochanan was plagued by a fateful decision he had made years earlier, on the eve of the fall of Jerusalem.

The Talmud in *Maseches Gittin* (56b) tells of the dramatic events that unfolded as the Roman army besieged Jerusalem and the Jewish zealots persisted unrelentingly in their ill-conceived and ill-fated revolt. Rabban Yochanan's disciples secretly brought him outside the city, and he managed to secure a meeting with the Roman general and future emperor, Vespasian. During this meeting, Rabban Yochanan earned the general's trust and affection, and Vespasian invited him to make a request. Rabban Yochanan asked that the general spare the academy in Yavneh, as well as the scholarly family of Rabban Gamliel, and arrange for medical care for Rabbi Tzadok who was gravely ill. Generations later, the Gemara tells, there were those who wondered why Rabban Yochanan stopped there, and did not request that the general leave Jerusalem and the Temple intact. Once Vespasian offered to grant a request, why did Rabban Yochanan not plead on behalf of the city and the *Beis Ha-Mikdash*? The Gemara explains that Rabban Yochanan feared that such a bold request would be denied, and the Jews would then be left with nothing after the failed revolt. A modest request, he figured, would be granted, but requesting that Jerusalem be spared would be met with fierce rejection.

We can only imagine, Rav Soloveitchik noted, how this controversial decision weighed on Rabban Yochanan's mind after Jerusalem and the Temple were set ablaze and thousands of Jews were slaughtered by the marauding Roman legions. He must have been haunted for the rest of his life by the nagging voice in his mind asking the excruciating question of "what if?" There was no way of knowing for certain that the tragedy of the *churban* was unavoidable. Maybe he was wrong? Perhaps at that moment, when Rabban Yochanan earned Vespasian's favor, he could have prevented the destruction, if he just had a bit more courage. These were the questions that tormented Rabban Yochanan for the rest of his life, even as he breathed his final breaths.

And thus he told his students with overwhelming dread, "I know not in which direction I will be led." Rav Soloveitchik explained that when a leader makes a wrong, fateful decision that yields especially grave consequences, his mistake could potentially outweigh on the heavenly scales a lifetime of religious devotion. Rabban Yochanan recognized that if his decision was, in fact, incorrect, then his life of Torah, *mitzvos* and invaluable leadership would not necessarily suffice to save him from *Gehinnom*. Even if this were his only mistake, it was a mistake with such devastating consequences that it could not be cancelled by his life of unequaled piety and Torah scholarship.

When we hear the question, "Should one serious crime erase a lifetime of religious devotion," the answer, in many instances, must be an unequivocal and resounding "Yes." When a clearly identifiable Orthodox Jew commits a crime that brings shame upon our entire community, lending credence to the cruelest stereotypes about our people, this crime cannot just fade away into the background of this person's otherwise noble life. Rabban Yochanan made a controversial decision using his best judgment, and was still worried until his dying day. When far lesser people than Rabban Yochanan make the inexcusable decision to commit a crime, and their decision causes irreparable harm to the entire Orthodox Jewish world, this mistake cannot simply be overshadowed by the upstanding life they otherwise lead. And thus a strong, harsh communal response is not only appropriate, but a matter of vital importance for us all.

INTERVIEWS

Rav Ron Eisenman
*on Headlines with Dovid Lichtenstein**

There was a Reform rabbi in the Washington, DC area who spent time in prison for — I think — allegedly trying to prey on a minor via the internet. When he came back to his Reform congregation, they actually had a vote, and they voted to deny him access — even though he claimed to be a *"ba'al teshuva"* already.

They voted about such a person, ובערת הרע מקרבך. I think this is something we should consider. Obviously, we should speak to the person, and he could make a public plea explaining that he is totally repentant and following *hilchos teshuva*, regretting everything he did. When we are dealing with sexual molestation, you have the idea of recidivism of crime, which involves a mental health issue. As Rabbi Abraham J. Twerski would say, "How do you know when an addict is lying? When his lips are moving." I think you would find that despite their promises to the contrary, they are people we can no longer trust. But if it's a financial issue, and he's totally repentant, and he says he will do whatever it takes to allow him back into shul, then maybe there is room [to accept him]. But if he comes defiantly, with his head up, saying, "I never did anything wrong," of course I would never allow such a person to be part of the *kehilla*. I've asked people to leave for less.

* Broadcast on 5 Marcheshvan, 5776 (November 5, 2016).

Rabbi Zvi Weiss
on *Headlines with Dovid Lichtenstein**

This is a complicated and sensitive issue, and not a *shayla* from today, or even from the last fifty or one hundred years. It's come up throughout history. *Baruch Hashem*, *Klal Yisrael* from its inception until today has had multitudes — רובא דרובא — of *Yidden* who are *ehrlich*, who did the right thing, and who created קידוש ה', both as individuals and as part of a community. But unfortunately, in the world we live in, people have free will and face all kinds of challenges, and there have been individuals who have behaved in horrific, harmful ways both to themselves, spiritually, to their families, or to their communities. There have been people who are חוטא ומחטיא (who sin and lead others to sin), who pose danger to society. These *shaylos* came up regarding the followers of Shabtai Tzvi who went out recruiting and pulling Yidden away from doing the right thing, and it's a complicated *shayla*.

A single cookie-cutter answer will not work, so we are talking theoretically. Every individual and every case must be judged on its own and examined with all kinds of emotions — compassion for the individual who went off the path, compassion for the people around him, and compassion for the *tzibur*...

Unfortunately, for a community rabbi, these kinds of issues are going to present themselves, and our responsibility, the way I understand it, is not to run away from these situations, and to instead address them head-on.

In cases of a sexual predator, in my opinion and in the opinion of experts

I've spoken to, it's almost impossible to say he's been cured and is no longer a danger to society. And therefore, those cases have to be looked at that from that standpoint. And though the question comes up about the innocent children of the perpetrator, we have to look at it from the standpoint of protecting our children, the innocent children who are unrelated to the story.

The *Shulchan Aruch* (Y.D. 334) talks about a case where a fellow was put into *nidui* because he was an *avaryan* [sinner] — he didn't behave properly. He did not necessarily entice others, or cause harm, he didn't pose a threat and he wasn't a predator. Within his own ד' אמות, in the privacy of his home, he was not following halacha. Back then people understood that just like we have a responsibility for each other's wellbeing…there is also a concept of being responsible for their spiritual wellbeing. *Chazal* understood that sometimes, when other means don't work, when מקרבת ימין ["the right hand drawing close"] does not bear fruit, then unfortunately, for the benefit of the *avaryan* to motivate him, we need to… [declare] *nidui*, which *beis din* is empowered and obligated to do. It means he cannot come to shul, one cannot be within his ד' אמות or have anything to do with him, he cannot be incorporated into a minyan, and there's even a *shayla* if you can have a *minyan* while he's there… Right there in the first *se'if* of 334, the Rama quotes that we put into *cherem* somebody who deserves *cherem*…even if he will go off the *derech*. The preponderance of *poskim* hold like the Rama. The *Taz* argues very strongly, but the *Shach* in *Nekudos Ha-Kesef*, after a whole litany of proofs from the *Taz*, simply says we don't have to worry about what the *Taz* is saying, because if so, then בטלה דין ישראל [there would be no possibility of judgment in the Jewish community].

The *nidui* is not only to stop the *avaryan* from his behavior, but it's also למען ישמעו ולמען יראו — people need to know that you have to behave and do the right thing. We try to do it by exciting people, and by giving them the beauty and sweetness of Yiddishkeit, and showing them the privilege of being able to have an intimate relationship with the *Ribono Shel Olam* based on Torah and *mitzvos*. But if this doesn't work, we have to start thinking about the people he might be influencing, even if he is not trying to influence anybody. We have to protect the people.

The *Chasam Sofer* says a fascinating thing… This fellow whom we put into *cherem* — what's keeping him around is that he has some merits, perhaps that his children are having a Jewish education. Perhaps this is why he is not gone and off the scene. Therefore, as part of our obligation to take away his merits, we do not let him have children in school so they do not receive a Jewish education and thus do not bring him merits. As for their souls — we don't have to worry about it, the *Chasam Sofer* says, because they are innocent. The *Ribono Shel Olam* will look upon them as אנוסים. They would have done the right thing, but they were not given the opportunity, so their souls are protected. This is an unbelievable *teshuva* of the *Chasam Sofer*.

However, the *Chasam Sofer* says at the end that we have to be very patient and look through the situation carefully. It has to be done with trepidation and fear, he writes, "and Hashem will protect us" so we should know what the right thing is.

So as for the question of the criminal's children, if it's an outsider coming into the community, we can tell him before he comes that he should not come, because his children will not be allowed into the school…

* Broadcast on 12 Marcheshvan, 5776 (November 12, 2016).

Money

Amazon Lawsuit Shows That Fake Online Reviews Are a Big Problem

October 19, 2015
by Brad Tuttle

So much for the "wisdom" of the crowds.

Last week, Amazon filed a lawsuit against more than 1,114 individuals who allegedly have posted fake product reviews on the site. Amazon claims many of the defendants have operated mostly out in the open, listing their services and answering ads via the "gig site" Fiverr.com to write glowing five-star reviews for $5 a pop.

"Unfortunately, a very small minority of sellers and manufacturers sometimes try to gain unfair competitive advantages for their products on Amazon.com. One such method is creating false, misleading, and inauthentic customer reviews," the lawsuit states. "Amazon has conducted an extensive investigation of the defendants' activities on Fiverr, including purchasing 'reviews' for products and communicating directly with some of the defendants."

The suit states that even though fake reviews are "small in number," they "significantly undermine the trust that consumers and the vast majority of sellers and manufacturers place in Amazon."

But is the rate of "false, misleading, and inauthentic customer reviews" truly small? Previous research estimates that 30% of product reviews are fake. That seems pretty big — enough to have real influence in a product's overall ratings, and higher than the projected rate of fake online reviews for other things like hotels and restaurants (10% to 20%).

The Amazon crackdown is hardly the first investigation focused on outing fake online reviews. In 2013 the auto research site Edmunds.com sued an "online reputation company" for promising to flood sites such as Yelp, Cars.com, and Google+ with fake online reviews of car dealerships. Yelp has likewise unearthed conspiracies of local businesses agreeing to rub each other's backs, in the form of swapping five-star reviews all around. For years, software engineers have been working on algorithms to detect fake online reviews and put a stop to them. But based on Amazon's lawsuit — which is the first to target individuals rather than websites where short-term freelancers can be hired — apparently there's still a market for them.

Many of the listings at Fiverr.com are for jobs in which the reviews are blatantly fake, based on no experience whatsoever with the product or service. One freelancer named as a defendant wasn't even promising to make up the review, instead offering to companies in need of ratings assistance: "Please write a review then I will post it." As of Monday afternoon, there were still plenty of listings at Fiverr from freelancers who will happily write five-star reviews for any business paying $5.

Others have grown more careful about how to generate positive reviews. The gig site Freelancer.com used to have a category of jobs titled simply "Fake Review Writer," but now its "Reviews Writing" section tells businesses that the "the best marketing ploy" is to pay reviewers "after you have let them try out your product." Judging how little these sites pay, however, it's hard to believe the reviewer spends much time with each product, if indeed reviewers ever get their hands on them.

Copyright © time.com

Fraud and Deceit in the Contemporary Marketplace

In the opening chapter of *Sefer Yeshayahu*, which we read every year on the Shabbos preceding Tisha Be-Av, the prophet describes a society overrun by corruption and deceit, where people used counterfeit money and knowingly sold corrupted merchandise: כספך היה לסגים סבאך מהול במים — "Your money has become counterfeit; your wine is diluted with water" (*Yeshayahu* 1:22). The people at this time were fervently devoted to the rituals of the *Beis Ha-Mikdash*, regularly offering sacrifices, but God rejected these offerings due to the people's unethical behavior (למה לי רב זבחיכם...שבעתי עולות אילים וחלב מריאים — ibid. 1:11).

In this prophecy, Yeshayahu also describes how the city of Jerusalem remained alone among all the cities of the Judean Kingdom, as the others had all been destroyed: ארצכם שממה עריכם שרופות אש...ונותרה בת ציון כסכה בכרם (ibid. 1:7). The Radak explains that this refers to the period of King Chizkiyahu, during whose reign the Assyrian Empire overran the Judean Kingdom, captured its major cities, and nearly seized Jerusalem.[1]

Chizkiyahu was a righteous king who rid the kingdom of idolatry and eliminated the *bamos* (private altars), such that the people would bring their sacrifices exclusively to the *Beis Ha-Mikdash*, as *halacha* requires.[2] Moreover, the Gemara (*Sanhedrin* 94b) records that during the period of Chizkiyahu's reign, there was not a child in the kingdom who was not proficient in the intricate laws of ritual impurity. This was a period of national spiritual renewal, as Chizkiyahu inspired and motivated the people to reject the idolatrous beliefs and practices introduced by his father, the wicked King Achaz, and to embrace the service of God in the *Beis Ha-Mikdash* and in the nation's study halls. Remarkably, it was specifically during this period that the prophet Yeshayahu arose to excoriate the people, calling them a גוי חוטא עם כבד עוון זרע מרעים בנים משחיתים — "a sinful people; a nation laden with sin; evil seed; corrupt children" (*Yeshayahu* 1:4). Although they devotedly offered sacrifices to God in the *Mikdash*, He rejected these offerings because of their dishonesty and corruption, and warned of devastating calamity if they failed to mend their crooked ways.

---

1. See *Melachim* II, chapters 18–19.
2. הוא הסיר את הבמות — ibid. 18:4.

Several decades later, on the eve of the fall of the First Commonwealth, the prophet Yirmiyahu foresaw the imminent destruction and bemoaned the widespread deceit and fraud that characterized the Jewish kingdom. In a prophecy that is read, appropriately enough, as the *haftara* on Tisha Be-Av, Yirmiyahu cries:

וידרכו את לשונם קשתם שקר...איש מרעהו השמרו ועל כל אח אל תבטחו, כי כל אח עקוב יעקב וכל רע רכיל יהלוך. ואיש ברעהו יהתלו ואמת לא ידברו, למדו לשונם דבר שקר...חץ שחוט לשונם מרמה דבר, בפיו שלום את רעהו ידבר ובקרבו ישים ארבו.

> They drew their tongues like a bow of falsehood… Beware each person of his fellow, and do not trust any brother, for every brother deceives and every friend goes about tale-bearing. And each person fools his friend, they do not speak the truth; they have trained their tongues to speak falsely… Their tongues are a sharpened arrow, speaking fraudulently. With his mouth one speaks peacefully to his fellow, while planning his ambush inside. (*Yirmiyahu* 9:2–7)

In response to this culture of dishonesty, the prophet says, God declares, העל אלה לא אפקד בם...אם בגוי אשר כזה לא תתנקם נפשי — "Shall I not make a reckoning for them over these… Shall My soul not exact revenge from such a people?!" (ibid. 9:8). God is willing to tolerate and forgive many different forms of wrongdoing, but crimes of dishonesty and deceit are deemed unforgivable.

Disgracefully, many Jews today strictly follow a halachic lifestyle and devote time and energy to Torah study and observance of *mitzvos*, but feel no compunction about lying and deceiving other people to save or make money. To our utter shame and horror, many such crimes have been reported in the media, giving ammunition to those who wish to perpetuate the anti-Semitic stereotype of Jews as conniving and dishonest. Many of today's Jewish communities frighteningly resemble the condition lamented by Yeshayahu, a condition of faithful ritual devotion amid rampant corruption and deceit. There can be no more urgent matter for contemporary Jewry than returning to the basics, to the ABCs of Jewish ethics, reinforcing our commitment to the highest and strictest ethical standards in all of our financial dealings, and reminding ourselves that this forms the foundation and cornerstone of a religious life.

This essay will examine the nature and scope of the prohibition against deceiving or lying to one's fellow, and explore some of the contemporary applications of this prohibition.

אסור לגנוב דעת הבריות

The Gemara establishes in *Maseches Chullin* (94a), אסור לגנוב דעת הבריות — "It is forbidden to deceive people," and it proceeds to present several examples of this law. Specifically, the Gemara speaks of situations in which one deceives his fellow into thinking he did a favor for him, when in truth he did not. For example, one may not sell to a gentile non-kosher meat that the gentile presumes to be kosher, as the gentile will mistakenly think that the Jew is doing him a favor by selling him meat that the Jew could have eaten himself. Another example is inviting one's fellow to eat with him, knowing that he will be unable to accept the invitation. One who extends an invitation to his fellow under these circumstances gives the false impression of sincerely wishing to host him, and this constitutes גניבת דעת. Likewise, the Gemara notes the case of a host who opens a new bottle of wine for a guest, giving the impression that he is opening it especially for him, when in truth he needs to open it anyway. All these gestures are forbidden because they give a false impression of generosity and mislead the other person to owe an unwarranted debt of gratitude.

Another form of גניבת דעת, discussed by the Mishna and Gemara in *Maseches Bava Metzia* (59b-60a), forbids the deception of prospective customers. On the basis of the Gemara's discussion, the *Shulchan Aruch* (C.M. 228:6) rules:

> אסור לרמות בני אדם במקח וממכר או לגנוב דעתן, כגון אם יש מום במקחו צריך להודיעו.
>
> It is forbidden to trick people when transacting, or to deceive them; for example, if there is a defect in one's merchandise, he must inform [the buyer].

Later (228:9), the *Shulchan Aruch* codifies the prohibition against polishing merchandise to make it appear newer than it is,[3] or taking measures to make an animal appear younger than its actual age. Another example noted by the *Shulchan Aruch* (228:10), based on the Mishna, is mixing low-quality fruits among high-quality fruits so they can be sold together for the price of high-quality produce. All these cases involve an attempt to make merchandise appear more valuable than it actually is, thus deceiving the consumer, and they all violate the prohibition of גניבת דעת.

Different views exist among the *Rishonim* as to the source and nature of this prohibition. The Ritva, commenting on the Gemara's discussion in *Chullin*, cites those who claim that גניבת דעת falls under the Torah prohibition of theft and is

---

3. The *Sema*, citing the *Tur*, comments that one who sells brand new merchandise may polish it to make it appear shiny and appealing, since this does not involve deception of the consumer.

included in the command, לא תגנובו (*Vayikra* 19:11). Proof to this view, as the Ritva notes, may be drawn from the Tosefta (*Bava Kama* 7:3), which lists several types of theft, and writes, גדול שבכולם גונב דעת הבריות — the worst of all forms of theft is גניבת דעת. This would certainly suggest that deceiving someone falls under the Torah prohibition of theft. According to the Ritva, it seems, deception causes or can potentially cause the victim to spend money that he would not have wanted to spend, and it therefore constitutes a form of theft. For example, if one is deceived into thinking that another person wished to do him a favor, he will likely feel indebted and seek to repay the perceived favor, thereby incurring an expense that he would not have otherwise incurred. Obviously, deceptively misrepresenting merchandise as high-quality will cause a customer to decide to purchase something he would not have bought otherwise. The fraudster thus improperly obtains another person's money or favors, in violation of the prohibition of לא תגנובו.

Others, however, classify גניבת דעת not under the category of theft, but rather under the category of שקר — speaking falsely. Rabbeinu Yona writes in *Sha'arei Teshuva* (3:184), in reference to גניבת דעת:

> הנה החטא הזה חמור אצל חכמי ישראל יותר מגזל יען וביען כי שפת שקר אשמה רבה. ונתחייבנו על גדרי האמת כי הוא מיסודי הנפש.
>
> Now the Sages of Israel regarded this sin as more grievous than theft, because false speech is a great misdeed, and we are obligated to maintain truthfulness because it is among the fundamentals of the soul.

According to Rabbeinu Yona, the prohibition of גניבת דעת is rooted not in the unlawful appropriation of another person's property or goodwill, but rather in the falsehood itself. Giving a false and misleading impression is, in itself, forbidden, irrespective of the harm caused to the other person.[4]

These different perspectives may likely yield a number of interesting practical ramifications. If we view גניבת דעת as a form of theft, then it stands to reason that one who violates this prohibition and causes financial harm would be required to compensate the victim. Just as *halacha* requires a thief to return the stolen goods to the victim, similarly, one who caused a customer to make a purchase through deceptive misrepresentation of the product would, at least in principle, be required to return the money. On the other hand, if we view this prohibition as a violation of מדבר שקר תרחק, no compensation should be required. According

---

4. This perspective on גניבת דעת also seems to emerge from the comments of the *Chazon Ish* in *Emuna U-Bitachon* (4:13), where he discusses the severity of deception in the context of his discussion of the severity of falsehood: אם שנוא הוא השקר הקל, שאינו פוגע בחבירו בשיקרו משנה תועבה היא המירמה...שכונן כזביו כדי להוליך את רעהו שולל. וקראו חז"ל לחולי זה "גניבת דעת".

to this perspective, the violator committed a halachic offense by deceiving his fellow, but he is not considered as having unlawfully obtained his fellow's money or property. As such, he does not have in his possession another person's assets that must be returned.[5]

By the same token, if we view גניבת דעת as a form of theft, then the violator must seek the victim's forgiveness in order to achieve atonement. The Mishna in *Maseches Yoma* (8:9) famously establishes that one who causes harm to his fellow must ask the victim for forgiveness, beyond paying the compensation required by *halacha*, and this law is codified in the *Shulchan Aruch* (O.C. 606:1).[6] If deception constitutes theft, it must be treated as an interpersonal offense that cannot be atoned without the victim's forgiveness. If, however, גניבת דעת falls under the prohibition of שקר, then we might classify it as a sin committed against the Almighty, as opposed to an interpersonal violation. Accordingly, repentance would suffice to obtain atonement, without the need to ask the deceived party for his forgiveness. Rav David Ariav (*Le-Rei'acha Kamocha* 1:1:21) rules that one who violates the prohibition of גניבת דעת must, in fact, ask his victim for forgiveness.

גניבת דעת as a Biblical Prohibition

It seems clear from the comments of both the Ritva and Rabbeinu Yona that they regarded גניבת דעת as a Biblical prohibition, falling under the category of either מדבר שקר תרחק or לא תגנובו. This view is found in the writings of other *Rishonim* as well, specifically the *Yerei'im* (124) and *Semag* (*lo sa'aseh* 155). Several *Acharonim*, including the Mabit (*Kiryas Sefer, Hilchos Mechira* 18) and *Shulchan Aruch Ha-Rav* (*Hilchos Ona'ah* 11), follow this view. By contrast, the *Semak* (260) writes that the prohibition of גניבת דעת was enacted by *Chazal* and is not included under any Biblical prohibition. This is the view accepted by the *Sefer Chareidim* in his list of prohibitions enacted by *Chazal* (chapter 4), as well as by the *Bach* (C.M. 288).

Rav Menachem Krakowski, in his *Avodas Ha-Melech* commentary on the Rambam's *Mishneh Torah* (*Hilchos Dei'os* 2:6), suggests distinguishing in this regard between fraudulent practices that result in financial harm, and other forms of deceit. If one deceptively extracts money from his fellow, Rav Krakowski avers, then he has violated the Torah prohibition of theft, whereas deception that does not cause any expenditure, such as misleading someone into thinking one has done him a favor, would not constitute theft and is forbidden only by

---

5. See Rav David Ariav's *Le-Rei'acha Kamocha* 1:1:21, note 30, where he cites several sources indicating that one must indeed return money obtained through a violation of גניבת דעת.
6. עבירות שבין אדם לחבירו אין יום הכפורים מכפר עד שיפייסנו.

force of Rabbinic enactment. It is possible that the *Semak*, *Sefer Chareidim*, and *Bach* agree to this distinction and view גניבת דעת as a Rabbinic prohibition only in cases that do not involve financial harm. They might agree that in a case in which one misleads a customer to purchase a product or to offer a higher price for a product, he has in fact transgressed a Torah violation.

Jew and Gentile

As mentioned above, the Gemara in *Maseches Chullin* (94a) establishes that one may not sell non-kosher meat to a gentile if the gentile assumes the meat is kosher, and the gentile is fooled into believing that the Jew is doing him the favor of selling meat that he could have eaten himself. This clearly indicates that the prohibition of גניבת דעת forbids deceiving either a Jew or a gentile, and indeed, the Gemara cites Shmuel's explicit ruling, אסור לגנוב דעת הבריות ואפילו דעתו של עובד כוכבים — deceiving any person, whether a Jew or a gentile, is prohibited.

Accordingly, the Rambam writes in *Hilchos Mechira* (18:1):

אסור לרמות את בני אדם במקח וממכר או לגנוב את דעתם, ואחד גוים ואחד ישראל בדבר זה.

It is forbidden to fool people in commerce, or to deceive them, and this applies to both gentiles and Jews.

He likewise writes in *Hilchos Dei'os* (2:6):

ואסור לגנוב דעת הבריות אפילו דעת הגוי.

And it is forbidden to deceive people, even a gentile.

Similarly, in *Hilchos Gezeila* (11:4), the Rambam writes that it is forbidden to knowingly deceive a gentile. The Rambam draws proof from the Torah's discussion in *Sefer Vayikra* (25:50) of the procedure for redeeming a Jew whose poverty had forced him to sell himself as a servant to a gentile. The Torah instructs, וחשב עם קונהו, indicating that a precise calculation must be made to accurately determine the price for redeeming the Jewish servant. The term וחשב would seem to negate the permissibility of intentionally miscalculating in order to deceive the non-Jewish master. The Rambam also cites in this context the verse in *Sefer Devarim* (25:16) referring to deceit and fraud as תועבת ה' — "an abomination to God" — which would certainly suggest that this is forbidden under all circumstances, regardless of whether or not the victim is Jewish.

The Ritva, in the passage referenced above, similarly writes that it is forbidden to deceive both Jews and gentiles. This is mentioned also by the Mordechai (*Bava Kama* 158), whose view is cited by the Rama (C.M. 348:2). The *Shulchan Aruch Ha-Rav* (*Hilchos Ona'ah* 11) rules accordingly.

This point is also made by the Rashash in his notes to *Maseches Bechoros* (13b). The Rashash explains that since the prohibition of גניבת דעת forbids deceiving either a Jew or a gentile, it is forbidden to mislead a gentile to pay an exorbitantly high price or to accept a price drastically lower than market value, which clearly falls under the category of גניבת דעת.[7]

Surprisingly, however, despite the Gemara's explicit ruling that the prohibition of גניבת דעת forbids deceiving both Jews and gentiles, the *Tur* (C.M. 348), cited by the Rama (348:2), limits the prohibition of deceiving a gentile to a case in which this would result in a חילול ה' (defamation of God and the Jewish people).[8] It is difficult to understand how those holding this view reconciled their position with the Gemara's unequivocal ruling in *Chullin* forbidding גניבת דעת in one's dealings with both Jews and gentiles.[9]

Although the Rama cites both of these divergent views, it seems clear that we should follow the stringent ruling of the Rambam and Mordechai, for several reasons. First, this view appears to have been accepted by the consensus of later authorities. As noted above, this is the ruling of the *Shulchan Aruch Ha-Rav*, and, moreover, the *Shach* (348:3), commenting on the Rama's statements, refers us to the Maharshal's discussion in *Yam Shel Shlomo* (*Bava Kama* 10:20), where he rules stringently in this regard. Furthermore, both the Ritva and the *Shulchan Aruch Ha-Rav* state explicitly that deceiving a gentile violates a Torah prohibition, and since a Torah violation is at stake, it seems reasonable to follow the stringent view.[10]

Indeed, Rav Moshe Feinstein, in his responsum on the subject of cheating

---

7. The Rashash raises the question of why the Rambam (*Hilchos Mechira* 13:7) and *Shulchan Aruch* (C.M. 227:26) write clearly that the law of אונאה (overcharging or underpaying) does not apply when dealing with gentiles, suggesting that this is entirely permissible. The likely answer is that the Rambam and *Shulchan Aruch* indeed maintain that the specific prohibition of אונאה does not apply to commerce with gentiles, but unfairly overcharging or underpaying is nevertheless prohibited on the grounds of גניבת דעת, which applies to dealings with all people.
8. See also the *Bach* and the Vilna Gaon's discussion in *Bei'ur Ha-Gra* (348:13).
9. The *Bach*, in an earlier context (228), addresses a similar question regarding אונאה. (We noted this question in n. 7 above.) We may be able to apply the *Bach*'s distinction there to explain the *Tur*'s ruling, although it is clearly far-fetched and very difficult to accept.
10. Additionally, the *Aruch Ha-Shulchan* (348:2) writes that this entire debate among the *Rishonim* refers only to the אנסים הקדמונים — the gentiles who, in earlier generations, tried to seize Jews' property through violent and unlawful means. According to the *Aruch Ha-Shulchan*, then, there is no question that *halacha* forbids deceiving generally decent, law-abiding gentiles. It is possible, however, that the *Aruch Ha-Shulchan* made this qualification only to pacify the Russian censors. See the article by Rav Eitam Henkin hy"d in *Chitzei Giborim*, vol. 7, pp. 520–524.

on New York State Regents exams (*Iggeros Moshe*, C.M. 2:30), writes that this is strictly forbidden on the grounds of גניבת דעת, which forbids deceiving Jews or gentiles.[11] This is also the view of Rav Moshe Sternbuch in his *Teshuvos Ve-Hanhagos* (4:216), where he writes that a seller may not falsely claim to a prospective buyer that others are interested in the item, in order to raise the price, as this constitutes גניבת דעת. Rav Sternbuch emphasizes that this is forbidden regardless of whether or not the prospective buyer is a Jew.[12]

Rav Eliezer Waldenberg (*Tzitz Eliezer* 15:12) likewise rules unequivocally that it is forbidden to deceive a Jew or gentile, noting the aforementioned rulings of the Rambam, as well as the explicit comments of the *Sefer Yerei'im* (255). He also cites the aforementioned passage from Rabbeinu Yona's *Sha'arei Teshuva*, indicating that dishonesty must be avoided not only because of the harm inflicted on the victim, but also because of its corrosive effects on the character of the deceiver.

Furthermore, Rav Moshe Rivkis, author of the *Be'er Ha-Gola* annotation to the *Shulchan Aruch*, writes in the context of the prohibition of *mesira* — reporting one's fellow Jew to the gentile authorities (C.M. 388:11) — that it has become accepted to strictly forbid dishonest conduct of any kind with gentiles:

> כבר פשט התיקון והמנהג שמנהיגי הקהילה...עומדים על המשמר שלא לעשות שקר ועולה לאומות, ומכריזים ונותנים רשות לפרסם ולגלות להם על האנשים אשר לוקחים בהקפה או לווים בהלואה ואין דעתם לשלם, והכל מדעת המנהיגים.

> The enactment and custom has already spread that the community leaders...stand guard against falsehood or deceit towards the other nations, and they announce and grant permission to publicize and expose those people who purchase on credit or borrow on loan without any intention to pay, and all this is done with the leaders' knowledge.

Earlier, in discussing the different views pertaining to misleading a gentile (C.M. 348:2), Rav Rivkis makes a remarkable statement emphasizing the importance of honest conduct in one's dealings with gentiles:

> ואני כותב זאת לדורות – שראיתי רבים גדלו והעשירו מן טעות שהטעו העכו"ם ולא הצליחו וירדו נכסיהם לטמיון ולא הניחו אחריהם ברכה...רבים אשר קדשו ה' והחזירו טעות העכו"ם בדבר חשוב גדלו והעשירו והצליחו והניחו יתרם לעולליהם.

> I am writing this for future generations: I have seen many who have

---

11. Rav Moshe gives several other reasons for why cheating is forbidden. See also Rav Shmuel Wosner, *Shevet Ha-Levi* 10:163.
12. זהו גניבת דעת שאסור אפילו לעכו"ם.

become great and rich due to a mistake that they caused a gentile to make, but they were not successful, and their assets were permanently lost… Many who glorified God by returning a significant sum of money obtained as a result of a gentile's mistake became great and wealthy, and left their excess to their children.

חילול ה'

Moreover, even those who permit such conduct in certain circumstances limit this provision to situations in which there is no possibility of causing a חילול ה'. As we know, all too well, however, in many cases in which Jews have dealt less than honestly with gentiles, their misconduct was ultimately exposed. Particularly in our day and age, it is nearly impossible to ascertain with any sort of confidence that a scheme will remain undiscovered. The Mishna in *Avos* (4:4) famously warns, אחד שוגג ואחד מזיד בחילול השם — a person is held liable for חילול ה', the gravest of all sins, even if he defamed God's Name unintentionally. When it comes to the Orthodox Jewish community's reputation, the stakes are very high. Thus, even if we could come up with a technical halachic basis for a degree of dishonesty, there is no justification at all for risking our community's reputation by engaging in ethically questionable conduct.

The Rambam in *Sefer Ha-Mitzvos* (*lo sa'aseh* 63) lists the three categories of חילול ה', and describes the third category as follows:

> הוא שיעשה האדם ידוע במעלה והטוב פעולה אחת תיראה בעיני ההמון שהוא עבירה ושאין דמיון הפועל ההוא ראוי לנכבד כמוהו לעשות אף על פי שיהיה הפועל מותר הנה הוא חילל את השם.

> [The third category] is when a person known for his stature and piety performs an act that is perceived by the masses as a sin, and the act as it is perceived is something that is inappropriate for a person of stature like him to do. Even though the act itself is permissible, he has profaned the Name [of God].

The Rambam likewise writes in *Hilchos Yesodei Ha-Torah* (5:11):

> ויש דברים אחרים שהן בכלל חילול השם, והוא שיעשה אותם אדם גדול בתורה ומפורסם בחסידות דברים שהבריות מרננים אחריו בשבילם, ואף על פי שאינן עבירות הרי זה חילל את השם.

> There are other things included under חילול השם and that is when a person who is accomplished in Torah and known for his piety does things that

make people suspicious of him. Even though they [the actions] are not sins, he has profaned the Name [of God].¹³

Even if a certain practice is technically legal and halachically permissible, it constitutes a חילול השם if it appears dishonest and gives the impression of unethical conduct.

Finally, we must remember Rabbeinu Yona's strong and far-reaching remark cited earlier: ונתחייבנו על גדרי האמת כי הוא מיסודי הנפש. Honesty is among the most fundamental of all Torah values. If we would have to choose one specific area of religious life upon which to focus our attention and regarding which to maintain the strictest standards, we would be hard-pressed to find a reason to choose anything other than integrity. Even if we could ignore the concern of חילול השם (which we of course cannot, and must not), our own development as moral and religious people, and as worthy representatives of the Almighty in this world, demands, first and foremost, scrupulously honest and ethical conduct. No amount of profit could possibly be large enough to compensate for what we lose by compromising our integrity.

With this in mind, let us proceed to address several unfortunately common examples of unethical conduct in the contemporary marketplace.

Fake Customer Reviews and "Shill Bidding"

People with online businesses, or those who market their goods and services online using sites such as eBay and Amazon, often rely on positive customer reviews as an important and effective method of attracting new customers. It has become standard in the virtual marketplace for companies to run a "customer reviews" section on their websites, featuring enthusiastic praise for the goods or services being offered. It is known, however, that not all of these compliments are authentic. Some companies have their own marketing teams write this material, disguising themselves as satisfied customers, or even offer discounts to customers who write exaggeratedly glowing reviews. Similarly, rookie entrepreneurs looking to launch a business might be tempted to write their own "customer reviews" to make it appear as though their enterprise has already been successfully running. The problem became sufficiently widespread to lead Amazon to file a lawsuit in the fall of 2015 against over 1,000 people who allegedly posed fake reviews on its website.¹⁴

---

13. See also the first volume of *Headlines* (chapter 9), where we discuss the parameters of חילול השם in greater detail.
14. Reported by *Fortune*, October 19, 2015.

This practice is, quite clearly, forbidden. It certainly falls under the prohibition of גניבת דעת which, as we saw earlier, includes misleading customers. The *Shulchan Aruch* (C.M. 228) rules explicitly that one may not undertake measures to make the quality of his merchandise appear higher than its true quality. Publishing false praise for goods would certainly fall under this category, and is strictly forbidden.

This would apply as well to fraudulent bidding on auction sales sites. "Shill bidders," as they are called, are people who place a high bid on their own product, or their friend's product, in order to raise the bidding so that actual customers will agree to pay a high sum for the item. Already in 2004, the New York State Attorney General's office announced that criminal charges were filed against three individuals who fraudulently raised the bidding on each other's products, which were posted for sale on eBay.[15] Besides being illegal, shill bidding undoubtedly constitutes fraudulent misrepresentation of merchandise, and thus falls under the prohibition of גניבת דעת.

Schemes to Lower an Asking Price

Another example of forbidden fraudulent activity is soliciting friends to convince a seller that his product is overpriced. For instance, if a person is interested in a certain home that has gone on the market, he might ask his friends to see the home under the guise of prospective buyers, and then inform the seller that they do not accept the asking price. This will likely lead the seller to lower his price, thus enabling the one who truly wishes to purchase the home to do so cheaply.

This scheme not only constitutes גניבת דעת, as the friends give a false, misleading impression, but also violates the Torah prohibition of אונאת דברים — verbally causing people distress. The Gemara in *Maseches Bava Metzia* (58b) presents several different examples of אונאת דברים, including לא יתלה עיניו על המקח בשעה שאין לו דמים — expressing interest in merchandise that one has no intention of buying. The Meiri explains that this constitutes אונאת דברים for two reasons. First, when people express interest in a product and then decline to make the purchase, the proprietor might feel compelled to lower the price in order to attract buyers. Disingenuous inquiry about a piece of merchandise can thus cause a merchant considerable financial harm. Second, the Meiri explains, showing interest in a product without purchasing it causes the seller emotional distress, as his hopes of a sale are aroused and then shattered.

Both these reasons apply in the case described above. When a prospective

---

15. The press release is available online, at http://www.ag.ny.gov/press-release/shill-bidding-exposed-online-auctions.

buyer's friends falsely express interest in a home that they have no intention of buying, they unnecessarily inconvenience and disappoint the seller, while also causing him to lose money by making him feel compelled to lower the price. As such, these schemes are prohibited on the grounds of both גניבת דעת and אונאת דברים.

A third prohibition is violated if the friends not only falsely express interest, but also advise the seller to lower his price, deceptively presenting themselves as pricing experts familiar with the market. Commenting on the famous verse, לפני עוור לא תתן מכשול ("You shall not place a stumbling block before a blind man"), Rashi explains (citing *Toras Kohanim*) that this refers to knowingly giving imprudent advice to mislead somebody. This prohibition is codified by the Rambam in *Hilchos Rotzei'ach* (12:14):

> כל המכשיל עיוור בדבר, והשיאו עצה שאינה הוגנת, או שחיזק ידי עוברי עבירה שהוא עיוור ואינו רואה את דרך האמת מפני תאוות ליבו, הרי זה עובר בלא תעשה, שנאמר ולפני עיוור לא תיתן מכשול.

> Whoever causes a person who is "blind" about something to stumble, by offering him imprudent advice, or by encouraging sinners — one who is "blind" and does not see the true path because of his heart's desire — he has transgressed a prohibition, as it says, "You shall not place a stumbling block before a blind man."[16]

Clearly, then, convincing a seller to lower his price for the benefit of a prospective buyer, when in truth the asking price is reasonable, would transgress the Torah prohibition of לפני עוור לא תתן מכשול.

"Wardrobing" and Return Policies

Many stores — both online and retail — offer generous return policies on sales, allowing customers to return purchased products for either a cash refund or store credit. While there is certainly no reason not to take advantage of such policies when one is legitimately dissatisfied with a purchased product, one must avoid the various ethical pitfalls that return policies present.

"Wardrobing" is the term used to describe customers who abuse a store's return policy to "rent" a piece of merchandise for free. They purchase the product with the intention of using it just once, and then return it the next day for a full refund. For example, a woman may want to purchase an expensive gown or piece of fine jewelry for a banquet, intending from the outset to return it the

---

16. See also *Sefer Ha-Mitzvos, lo sa'aseh* 299.

next day. A job applicant may decide to purchase a suit for his or her interview and then return it. People going boating or fishing may try to save themselves rental costs by purchasing equipment and then returning it.

"Wardrobing" — which is also known as "retail renting" — affects some 65% of retail businesses, according to a 2012 survey by the National Retail Federation,[17] and causes them considerable harm. Used products often need to be sold for lower prices, or taken off the shelves entirely, and so the retailer loses money. And even if the product is returned in pristine condition and can be sold at the original sale price, the staff must go through the trouble of repackaging the item and returning it to the shelf, work that salaried workers need to do without any profit for the business. The problem became so significant that in 2013, Bloomingdales began attaching to certain products special tags that were visible when worn, and needed to be presented intact with the garment in order for a refund to be granted. This precluded the possibility of worn products being returned.

There is no question that this practice is forbidden outright by *halacha*. Even if one can somehow ascertain that the returned product can be sold at the original price, this would still constitute גניבת דעת, as the customer falsely gives the impression of making a purchase. The store would certainly not allow the customer to rent the item for free, and therefore wardrobing, by definition, entails deception, and is thus forbidden.

In general, one should make sure to understand the store or business's return policy to ensure that he is not returning merchandise under circumstances that the store would not allow, as returning under such circumstances by withholding relevant information would constitute גניבת דעת.[18]

Of course, if a customer purchased an item fully intending to keep it permanently, but found himself genuinely dissatisfied, he may return it to the store for a full refund, even if he knows that the store will then be compelled to lower its sale price. Retailers take this specter into account when offering return policies, figuring that the loss incurred is more than offset by the business they generate through consumer-friendly policies. It stands to reason that the customer may even purchase the item again at its now discounted price, if he changes his mind and decides he wants the product. As long as he had truly been dissatisfied at the time he returned the product, he is entitled to take advantage of the discounted price after it is returned if he reconsiders his decision, and he is not required to inform the store that he had previously purchased the item at a higher price.

A somewhat similar case sparked a degree of controversy in Israel during

---

17. Reported on Bloomberg News, September 27, 2013.
18. See the interview with Rav Doniel Neustadt, below.

the summer of 2011.[19] The story circulated of a family of five married siblings who rented a vacation complex consisting of five residential units, where the families would spend several days together during summer break. The contract allowed for cancellations up to one month before the rental period. As it turned out, one of the siblings needed to schedule a trip abroad for that period, and was thus forced to cancel his reservation, for which he received a full refund. In the end, however, he did not need to travel, and so he decided to rent the vacation apartment after all. He phoned the owner, and, without identifying himself as the fifth sibling, inquired into the availability of a vacation unit for that period. The owner explained that there was one unit remaining, but it was part of a complex of other apartments that would all be rented during that period by members of one family, and he was therefore offering that unit for half its usual price. The man was thus able to rent the vacation apartment for half the amount he would have paid had he not cancelled his initial reservation.

Unsure whether or not he acted appropriately, the man approached Rav Yitzchak Zilberstein and explained to him the situation. Rav Zilberstein ruled that since the man truly planned to travel abroad, and thus cancelled his reservation honestly, without any intention to cheat the property owner, it was perfectly acceptable to rent the property at the discounted rate. Due to the circumstances, the discounted rate represented the true value of the apartment in the rental market, and so he was entitled to rent the property at that rate.

This incident generated a great deal of discussion and debate, as many *poskim* disputed Rav Zilberstein's ruling. It would seem, however, that since the man had no intention to deceive the property owner, and he cancelled the reservation and then made it anew due to an actual change in plans, he was allowed to rent at the discounted price.

It goes without saying, however, that if the customer might be recognized as having purchased the item originally for the higher price, and would thus be suspected of scheming to purchase the product at a discounted price, this is certainly forbidden. As cited above from the Rambam, one violates the grave prohibition of חילול ה׳ even by doing something inherently permissible if it appears unethical. Therefore, if the purchase is made in a small store, or in any other situation in which the customer could easily be identified as having made the original purchase, he should not purchase the item at the discounted price, in order to avoid suspicion.

---

19. This story was reported in an article on the *Bechadrei Chareidim* website (August 15, 2011), which noted that it created quite a stir among the yeshiva communities in Bnei-Brak.

Frequent and High Volume Returns

Additionally, customers must exercise sensitivity and common sense in deciding when to return items. In September 2016, during the back-to-school season, it was reported that the Shan and Toad online children's attire store singled out five specific geographic areas for a special restrictive return policy. The website said that customers in Brooklyn, Lakewood, Passaic, Monsey, and Monroe would be allowed to return merchandise only for store credit or exchanges — but not for a cash refund — and would be required to pay a $5 restocking fee. The store's owner later explained that residents of these areas — all of which, of course, are heavily populated by Orthodox Jews with large families — were abusing the return policy by frequently purchasing large quantities of merchandise and then returning it all, long after the purchase, occasionally when the products were in poor condition. The owner explained that the damaged clothing could not be resold, and, moreover, the large orders depleted the company's stock in the interim, which made it difficult to process other orders. It therefore became unprofitable to offer full-refund returns to customers in those areas.[20]

This unfortunate incident highlights the importance of looking beyond the strict letter of the law and respecting the right of merchants to keep their enterprise profitable. Abusing full-refund return policies by regularly purchasing and returning in high volume is unfair and insensitive, and makes it difficult for businesses — particularly small businesses — to sustain themselves and continue serving the public.

Broker Schemes

Another example of גניבת דעת involves real estate agents who secretly convince the seller to accept a lower price than the offer made by a prospective buyer, and then pocket the difference. For instance, if a buyer approaches a broker and offers $1 million for a certain home, the agent might persuade the owner to accept $800,000, so he can keep the extra $200,000.

Agents might not see anything immoral in this practice, since, after all, the buyer pays precisely according to the terms he initiated, without having been misled or deceived, and the seller likewise receives the amount to which he agreed. Nevertheless, it seems clear that this practice constitutes outright גניבת דעת, as the buyer is misled into thinking he is paying the complete sum for a house, when in truth a sizable portion is being spent on the broker's "fee."

---

20. The Times of Israel, September 8, 2016.

Motivating Prospective Donors with an Insincere Pledge

A number of *poskim* addressed the question of whether an influential figure may announce a pledge of a considerably higher amount than he plans to donate in order to motivate others to donate. If people hear that a person of stature is committing such a large sum, they will likely appreciate the importance of the cause, and thus be more likely to make generous donations. Some charities therefore ask prominent figures to announce a pledge they have no intention of fulfilling, and to which they will not be held, for the sake of eliciting a generous response to a fundraising campaign. Seemingly, although this ruse might result in greater sums for charity, it violates גבינת דעת, as it misleads people to think that the donor feels more strongly about the cause than he actually does.[21]

This is indeed the ruling of Rav Yitzchak Weiss in *Minchas Yitzchak* (3:97). Rav Weiss draws proof from the comments of the Maharsha in *Maseches Sukka* (29a) explaining the Gemara's remark condemning those who publicly pledge money to charity and fail to follow through on their commitments. The Maharsha explains that the Gemara speaks of those who excuse themselves from fulfilling their pledges by claiming that their intent was only to encourage others to donate. According to the Maharsha's understanding of the Gemara's comment, it seems, the Gemara strongly condemns the practice of making insincere pledges as a means of motivating others to give charity.

In truth, however, the Maharsha explains the Gemara as condemning those who claim after the fact that their pledge was insincere, in order to excuse themselves from paying the pledged sum. This does not necessarily mean that it is forbidden to announce a pledge to which from the outset one does not truly intend to commit.[22]

Rav Weiss also suggests drawing proof from the story told in the Talmud Yerushalmi (*Berachos* 7:2) of Rabbi Shimon ben Shetach, who devised a scheme to assist three hundred nazirites who could not afford the sacrifices that the Torah requires a *nazir* to bring upon completing the period of his vow. Rabbi Shimon reached an agreement with his brother-in-law, King Yannai, that they would each pay for half the sacrifices. Yannai fulfilled his pledge and paid the stipulated sum, whereas Rabbi Shimon annulled the vows of half the nazirites, thereby absolving them of their sacrificial requirements. When Yannai later

---

21. Rav Moshe Sternbuch (*Teshuvos Ve-Hanhagos* 4:216) notes that a donor in such a situation is not considered in violation of a vow by failing to fulfill his pledge, since from the outset the pledge was not sincere. He adds that even if we would consider his pledge a bona fide vow, the treasurer has the authority to waive his rights to the money.
22. This point is made by Rav Yisrael Yaakov Fisher in his letter of approbation to Rav Yaakov Fisch's *Titein Emes Le-Yaakov*, and by Rav Moshe Sternbuch (see previous note).

complained to Rabbi Shimon that he failed to meet his commitment, Rabbi Shimon replied that whereas Yannai fulfilled his pledge with money, he fulfilled his pledge through his Torah knowledge. Rabbi Shimon justified his scheme by noting that he did not renege on his commitment, but rather met his commitment in an unusual manner. The implication, Rav Weiss writes, is that it would have been forbidden to make an insincere pledge as a means of soliciting a donation from the king.

Seemingly, however, the story of Rabbi Shimon ben Shetach proves just the opposite — that גניבת דעת is allowed for the purpose of soliciting a charitable donation. The story concludes with Yannai asking Rabbi Shimon why he hadn't informed him from the outset of his plan, to which Rabbi Shimon replied that the king would have refused to participate if he had been told that Rabbi Shimon had no intention of funding any sacrifices. Rabbi Shimon clearly deceived the king into pledging a donation, seemingly proving that deception is permissible for the sake of convincing someone to donate to charity.[23] While it is unclear why a special dispensation would be given to permit dishonesty for the sake of soliciting charity, Rabbi Shimon ben Shetach apparently felt this was permissible.

We might, at first glance, also draw proof to this effect from a story told in *Maseches Kalla* (1:21). Rabbi Tarfon, who was very wealthy, did not donate as much charity as was expected of him, and Rabbi Akiva therefore approached him and offered to invest his money for him by purchasing a city. Rabbi Tarfon promptly gave Rabbi Akiva 4,000 gold coins, which Rabbi Akiva then gave to the poor. Later, when Rabbi Tarfon discovered what Rabbi Akiva had done, he kissed him and thanked him for teaching him proper character traits. Rabbi Akiva clearly deceived Rabbi Tarfon for the sake of raising money for the needy, and his ruse was deemed acceptable and even praiseworthy.

However, Rav Yitzchak Zilberstein (*Chashukei Chemed*, Sukka, pp. 229–230) refutes this proof, claiming that Rabbi Akiva was confident that Rabbi Tarfon would agree to his decision to distribute the money to the poor. He knew this with certainty, and thus this case resembles the situation discussed by the *Shach* (C.M. 358:1) of a person who gives someone his friend's food, fully confident

---

23. However, Rav David Pinto (*Otzros David, Parshas Miketz*) suggests a novel reading of this story, proposing that it should be understood in light of the fierce struggles that raged at that time between the rabbis and Sadducees, who rejected the authority of the Rabbinic oral tradition. King Yannai himself would have fully accepted this arrangement, whereby Rabbi Shimon fulfilled his obligation by annulling the half the nazirites' vows, but his Sadducee advisors rejected the notion of *hataras nedarim* (annulling vows) and therefore convinced Yannai to condemn Rabbi Shimon's actions. According to this reading, Rabbi Shimon did not, in fact, deceive King Yannai, and thus this episode cannot provide a precedent for allowing deceit for the purpose of soliciting charity.

that his friend would not object. The *Shach* rules that the recipient may eat the food on the basis of the giver's trust in the friend's consent. By the same token, Rabbi Akiva was entitled to distribute Rabbi Tarfon's money in a manner that he knew Rabbi Tarfon would find acceptable.[24]

Rav Zilberstein made this point in reference to a case of a man who was given money to invest in an enterprise, but instead distributed the money to needy kollel students. The investor was enraged, and the man justified his actions on the basis of the story of Rabbi Akiva and Rabbi Tarfon. Rav Zilberstein ruled unequivocally that the money received by the kollel students is considered stolen and must be returned to the investor. The case of Rabbi Akiva marked an exception due to his unique relationship with Rabbi Tarfon, and it thus cannot serve as a precedent for allowing deceit for charitable purposes.

A similar ruling was issued by the Chida (*Yosef Ometz* 57) concerning a *gabbai* who conspired with a congregant to raise the bidding price of certain honors that were auctioned in their synagogue. The plan was for this congregant to bid an unusually high sum for the honors, in order to encourage others to bid even higher. The *gabbai* agreed that if no one outbid this congregant, he would be required to pay no more than half the sum. The Chida ruled that such a scheme constitutes גניבת דעת and is strictly forbidden, noting that this is no different than misrepresenting a piece of merchandise to make it appear more valuable than it is. This ruling would seemingly apply as well to making a fraudulent pledge to encourage other potential donors.

Rav Moshe Sternbuch likewise rules that it is forbidden to make a false pledge in an effort to motivate others to donate.[25] He adds that in principle, this would be permissible if there are people capable of donating but have refused to do so. The Gemara in *Maseches Bava Basra* (8b) rules that *beis din* has the authority to confiscate property from those who refuse to donate what they should to charity, and it therefore would presumably be permissible to announce a fraudulent pledge as a means of soliciting from someone the amount that he ought to be donating. However, Rav Sternbuch writes that in practice, we cannot know with certainty the sum that any given prospective donor is obligated to give, and thus we cannot permit such a scheme on this basis. This is also the ruling of Rav Eliyahu David Rabinowitz-Teomim (the "Aderes"), cited by Rav Shmuel Eliezer Stern in *Shevivei Eish* (vol. 2, *Parshas Behar*).

Although the Brisker Rav (Rav Yitzchak Zev Soloveitchik) reportedly

---

24. This point is also made by Rav Pinto, referenced in the previous note.
25. See n. 21 above.

permitted the practice of making fraudulent pledges,[26] the consensus among the *poskim* appears to forbid this practice.

INTERVIEW

Rav Doniel Neustadt on *Headlines with Dovid Lichtenstein**

If someone purchases clothes in the beginning of the season from places like Lands' End or Nordstrom's, which offer unlimited return policies, may he return all the clothing after the season, when the clothing is worn out, and ask for a refund?

I think in this case it should be permissible, because the store can clearly see that you bought the clothes at the beginning of the season and are now coming to them several months later saying they're torn. If they have a policy that they accept anything that tears, no questions asked, and they take it back, then you're allowed to take advantage of that. For some business-related reason, they have a policy to take back anything that tears, so I see no reason not to take advantage of that.

What if someone buys his three-year-old clothes at the beginning of the season with the full intention of returning them after the season and then using the refund to buy four-year-old clothes?

If the store has such a policy, and you are not lying to them, you tell them, "I bought it, I used it, and I want to return it," and store says, "Yes, we accept it," then there's nothing wrong with that. If this is the store's policy, then it is based on the fact that most of the people are going to keep it and won't return it. They know [customer tendencies] better than us. So I think you can take advantage of it. The only problem I see is if a store is clearly against this and says they don't take it back if it was used. Then you can't from the outset buy it in order to return it. This costs the company money in terms of restocking, labor, and so on, and so you're causing them a loss. For example, if somebody is going on a trip and needs a GPS, and he wants to buy one and return it after the trip — that's wrong. There's a fine line here, and one needs to know the company's policy. If they say they have no problem with you returning the clothes after the season, then this is not forbidden. If they would not allow it if they knew about it — then it

---

26. Rav Yaakov Fisch (*Titein Emes Le-Yaakov* 5:3) writes that he heard this ruling from the Brisker Rav's son, Rav Raphael Soloveitchik.

would be problematic. It would be at least גניבת דעת, and maybe even גניבת ממון (actual theft).

What if someone buys something on his credit card to build up miles, and then returns the item in a way that he can still keep the miles, having never intended to keep the item — is this permissible?

This would certainly be problematic, because this is not the intent of the company.

* Broadcast on 25 Tammuz, 5776 (July 30, 2016).

THE TIMES OF ISRAEL

'The hardest thing in the world is to lose a child'

Israeli Couple Wins Right to Produce and Raise Grandchild from Fallen Soldier Son's Sperm

November 16, 2016
by Renee Ghert-Zand

Kfar Saba — Like many couples in their early 50s with grown children, Irit and Asher Shahar look forward to becoming grandparents in the near future. The Shahars, however, plan on welcoming their first grandchild in a highly unconventional way.

Ever since their son Omri, a captain in the Israeli Navy on active duty, was killed in a June 2012 car crash at the age of 25, the couple has fought the state to gain the legal right to produce a child from their son's posthumously-retrieved sperm. The Shahars plan to raise that child themselves.

Irit and Asher's hard-fought battle ended this past September in a precedent-setting ruling. The Petah Tikvah Family Court granted permission for them to raise a child created from their deceased son's sperm and a purchased female egg. The embryo would be carried by a gestational surrogate.

The court's decision is believed to not only be a first for Israel, but also for the world. Since 2003, Israeli regulations have allowed for posthumous sperm retrieval for the purpose of later insemination or IVF by a surviving female partner. In the last decade there have also been numerous instances of parents legally providing their sons' posthumously retrieved sperm to single women wishing to become pregnant. In those cases, the women were the biological mothers of the children. They raised the children, and the parents of the posthumous sperm donors remained in the picture as engaged grandparents.

Despite the September ruling, however, the state is currently preparing an appeal linked to the unusual circumstance of the Shahars' desire to be, in effect, both grandparents and parents to Omri's offspring. In the meantime the court has issued an injunction preventing Irit and Asher from accessing and using Omer's stored gametes.

"As soon as the injunction is lifted, we are going to move on things right away," Irit told The Times of Israel in an interview at the spacious Kfar Saba home she shares with Asher and their youngest daughter, 16-year-old Lotem. A second daughter, Inbar, 26, was recently married.

Confident the state will not succeed in its possible appeal, Irit believes it is not unrealistic for her and her husband to hold Omri's biological son or daughter in their arms within a year or two...

The Shahars, who have already spent hundreds of thousands of shekels in their quest to continue their son's biological line, remain undaunted. Cost, including surrogacy fees reaching as high as $130,000 in the US, is no object.

"I am ready to sacrifice so that Omri will have a continuation here in Israel," Irit insisted.

...

Irit said she understood people's opposition, but that she can't understand the cruelty with which some critics have expressed their disapproval. She is especially hurt by erroneous assumptions that she and Asher are just doing this so they can collect from the state. (The Defense Ministry does not make regular allowance payments to orphans of fallen IDF soldiers.)

"It angers me that people respond this way to someone who has experienced such a terrible fate," Irit shared.

Asher put the legal battle's hardships into perspective.

"The legal process and its pressure are nothing compared to the depths of our grief. The hardest thing in the world is to lose a child. All the other things that people complain about in life are tiny and inconsequential in comparison," he said.

An unprecedented court decision, but not a legal precedent.

While all professional experts the Shahars approached were sympathetic to their plight, only some were willing to support their case. One of them was philosopher Asa Kasher, who related to the bereaved parents' pain on a personal level. Co-author of the IDF Code of Ethics and himself the father of a fallen soldier, he provided a key opinion that helped sway Judge Yocheved Greenwald-Rand to rule against the state's claims, as reported in Ha'aretz, that the child would be subject to a "planned orphanhood," and would be "fragile in relation to children from normative families."

The judge wrote in her opinion that "there is nothing unacceptable about the way [the Shahars] chose to deal with their bereavement and their request to give their late son descendants and raise them as their own."

The opinion further stated that whereas many children are brought into the world in less than favorable circumstances and suffer for it, this child would be born into a loving, supportive family deemed by the court to be more than fit enough to raise it.

...

The world looks on

As the court's decision in favor of the Shahars pushes the bioethical envelope here in Israel, the world looks on with interest. Some countries permit posthumous sperm retrieval when the deceased has left a written directive. Others such as France, Germany and Sweden ban it outright.

In the US, the law in this regard has varied from state to state, and key legal cases have centered more on the inheritance and social security consequences of the use of such sperm, rather than on permission for its use.

According to Harvard University law professor I. Glenn Cohen, a leading expert on the intersection of bioethics and law, there are many issues to be considered in cases such as the Shahars'. These include the invasion of the body, the right not to procreate or be a parent, harm to the children (as well as to other children in the family), rights claims of grandparents, and intent of the deceased.

While Cohen preferred not to comment in detail on the Shahar case, he did tell The Times of Israel that he was not taken aback by the Israel court's decision.

Irit Shahar at her son Omri's grave in Kfar Saba. (Courtesy)

"I will say that Israel is well known in terms of policy, culture, and court decisions as one of the most pro-natalist countries in the world — think about the funding for IVF in Israel which is about as robust as any country I know of," said Cohen.

"The whole effect of the halachic [Jewish religious law] view of be fruitful and multiply no doubt has an impact here too, so it doesn't surprise me if Israel authorizes posthumous reproduction in these cases where many other countries would not," he said.

Irit and Asher recalled their son speaking many times about wanting to marry and have a large family. Therefore, they are certain they are doing not only what is right for them and their daughters, but also what their son would have wanted.

According to Asher, they are doing it not only for their own family, but also for parents the world over.

"It is important for everyone to know that if you lose your child, it doesn't mean that you lose the chance for his children to be born," Asher said.

Copyright © timesofisrael.com

Fathering a Child After Death

In June 2012, Omri Shahar, a Captain in the Israeli Navy, was tragically killed in a car accident near Rishon Letzion, along with First Lieutenant Rafael Bublil. After the tragedy, Omri's parents, Irit and Asher Shahar of Kfar-Saba, decided to have sperm removed from his body and stored for later use in the production of a child, whom they would then adopt and raise. A tense and costly legal battle ensued, and it was only four years later, in September 2016, that a court in Petach-Tikva granted Irit and Asher the right to produce a child from their fallen son's reproductive material and raise that child.

According to a Times of Israel report covering the story,[1] posthumous retrieval of sperm has been allowed in Israel since 2003 for the purpose of impregnating a surviving partner, and more recently, Israeli courts have permitted parents to have sperm removed from their deceased sons and used to impregnate single women desiring to conceive through artificial insemination. The Shahars' case marks the first time a deceased man's parents were given the right to have the sperm conceive a child whom they would adopt and raise as their own.

Would *halacha* approve of such a practice? Is it permissible, from a halachic standpoint, to extract a man's reproductive material after death and to then use it to artificially inseminate a woman?[2]

A second halachic question relates to the possible implications of this procedure vis-à-vis the obligation of יבום. The Torah (*Devarim* 25:5–10) requires that when a married man dies without children, his widow must either marry his brother (יבום), or be "released" from the levirate bond through the חליצה

---

1. See media article above.
2. This essay will deal exclusively with the question of extracting sperm from a deceased male's body, without addressing the issue of artificial insemination for a married couple that is incapable of producing children through cohabitation. The consensus among the halachic authorities permits the extraction of sperm from a husband for the sake of artificially inseminating his wife (see Maharsham 3:268; *Zekan Aharon, Tinyana* 97; *Iggeros Moshe*, E.H. 2:18). The notable exception is Rav Malkiel Tzvi Tannenbaum of Lomza (*Divrei Malkiel* 4:107), who forbade this practice, arguing that given the possibility that the doctor may not in the end use the sperm for insemination purposes and the chance that the sperm may be ineffective in fertilizing the ovum, producing sperm for this purpose constitutes "wasting seed" (הוצאת זרע לבטלה). For a discussion of other halachic aspects of artificial insemination, see the next chapter, "Is Artificial Insemination an Option for Unmarried Women?"

ritual performed by the deceased's brother. Nowadays, חליצה is always performed instead of יבום. If a man's only child is produced from sperm extracted from that man's body after his death, would that child suffice to absolve the widow of the need to undergo חליצה?

I. מת אסור בהנאה — Deriving Benefit From a Human Corpse

The Gemara in *Maseches Avoda Zara* (29b) establishes that it is forbidden to derive benefit from a human corpse. This prohibition is derived from a textual parallel between the Torah's brief account of Miriam's death (ותמת שם מרים — *Bamidbar* 20:1) and the command of עגלה ערופה, the special ritual performed when a murder victim is found between cities, in which a calf is killed for atonement (וערפו שם את העגלה — *Devarim* 21:4). The Gemara infers that just as it is forbidden to use the עגלה ערופה for personal benefit, as it has the status of a quasi-sacrifice, it is similarly forbidden to use a human body after death. The consensus among the *poskim* follows the straightforward reading of the Gemara, which indicates that benefitting from a human corpse constitutes an outright Biblical violation.[3] Seemingly, using sperm taken from a human corpse to produce a child would violate this prohibition, as the inseminated woman is clearly deriving practical benefit from part of the deceased's body.

Using Body Parts for the Deceased's Honor

One might argue that the Torah prohibition against deriving benefit from a human corpse is intended for the sake of כבוד המת — preserving the deceased's honor — and that this prohibition would thus not forbid making use of someone's body after his death for the sake of his honor. In the case under discussion, particularly if the deceased had not fathered any children during his lifetime,

---

3. Shach, Y.D. 79:3; *Mishneh Le-Melech*, *Hilchos Avel* 14:21; *Sedei Chemed* 9:51. The *Mishneh Le-Melech* there asserts that the Rambam considered this a Rabbinic prohibition, but the Chida (*Birkei Yosef*, Y.D. 349) rejects this claim and insisted that benefiting from a corpse constitutes a Torah prohibition even according to the Rambam. Some draw proof to this conclusion from the Rambam's ruling in *Hilchos Ma'achalos Asuros* (11:1) that drinking wine that had been used in pagan worship is forbidden for consumption by force of the comparison drawn in the Torah between such wine and pagan sacrifices (אשר חלב זבחימו יאכלו ישתו יין נסיכים — *Devarim* 32:38). This inference is based on the Gemara (*Avoda Zara* 29b), which establishes the prohibition against benefiting from pagan sacrifices on the basis of the fact that such sacrifices are considered like human corpses (ויאכלו זבחי מתים — *Tehillim* 106:28). Since the Rambam bases the prohibited status of ritual wine on this inference, he must, *ipso facto*, recognize the Biblical prohibition against deriving benefit from a human corpse.

producing children from his reproductive material ensures a biological legacy that he would otherwise not leave behind. Far from being a cause of disgrace, extracting sperm for the sake of producing offspring would certainly appear to be in the posthumous interest of the deceased. Perhaps, then, the prohibition against deriving benefit from a human corpse, which the Torah introduced to preserve the dignity of the deceased, would not forbid the extraction of sperm to produce a child and thereby perpetuate the man's memory and legacy.

Several sources, however, indicate that to the contrary, the prohibition against making use of a human corpse stands independently of the concern to preserve the deceased's dignity. Rav Yosef Engel (*Beis Ha-Otzar*, kelal 8, 2) writes that a living human being is endowed with sanctity, and the loss of this special sanctity with a person's death results in what Rav Engel calls תיעוב (contamination). This תיעוב, he writes, is the basis and source of the prohibition against making use of the body. According to this approach, we certainly have no reason to distinguish between benefit that brings disgrace to the deceased and benefit that brings him honor. Therefore, preserving the deceased's legacy would not offer us any grounds for an exception to this prohibition.

Similarly, Rav Moshe Feinstein rules (*Iggeros Moshe*, Y.D. 3:140, 4:59) that a deceased person's remains may not be taken for the purpose of medical research, even if this was his explicitly stated wish during his lifetime. A person does not enjoy ownership over his body, Rav Moshe explains, as the human body is given to him on loan, as it were, to use during his lifetime. After death, the body in its entirety must be interred, regardless of the deceased's wishes to the contrary.[4] Clearly, then, honoring a deceased person by producing offspring would not permit the use of his reproductive material after death.

It is important to distinguish in this regard between two distinct prohibitions: benefiting from a corpse and disgracing a corpse (ניוול המת). The Rashba (Responsa 1:369) writes that although it is generally forbidden to tamper with a human corpse out of concern for the deceased's dignity, postmortem procedures are allowed when this serves the purpose of preserving the deceased's dignity. The question addressed by the Rashba relates to a procedure to hasten the body's decomposition so that it can be transported for interment in the deceased's specifically chosen burial site. Such a procedure, the Rashba rules, is permissible, since the prohibition of ניוול המת is defined as disgracing the deceased; thus, postmortem tampering intended for his honor is allowed. This is quite different from the prohibition against deriving benefit from a corpse, which, as we have seen, does not relate to the concern for preserving the deceased's dignity.

---

4. We do not discuss here the question of harvesting organs from a brain-dead patient to save a gravely ill patient, which is an entirely separate issue.

A "Resurrected" Body Part

Nevertheless, according to one prominent 20th century *posek*, we might be able to permit the posthumous extraction and use of sperm by viewing the material as "resurrected" in the woman's body.

Rav Isser Yehuda Unterman, in a responsum cited and discussed by Rav Shlomo Zalman Auerbach (*Minchas Shlomo, Tinyana* 97), permitted transplanting a cornea taken from a deceased person into the eye of a live patient. This does not violate the prohibition against benefiting from a human corpse, Rav Unterman averred, because this prohibition applies only to a "dead" body part. Once the cornea is implanted within the living patient's eye, it is "resurrected," as it were, in the sense that it again becomes functional. Rav Shlomo Zalman suggests an analogy to the case addressed by the Mishna (*Terumos* 9:7) of a sapling designated as תרומה (a gift for the *Kohen*) that became טמא, but was then planted in the ground. The planting has the effect of divesting the tree of its status of impurity, as it is, in effect, "born" anew. In a similar vein, the cornea regains its "living" status by being implanted in the eye of a living human being, and is thus no longer subject to the prohibition against deriving benefit from a dead body.

Conceivably, this rationale could apply to insemination as well. Even though the sperm is taken from a corpse, and is thus forbidden for benefit, the moment it is injected into the woman's uterus, it becomes a functional part of a living human organism. As such, it becomes permissible for use, as it is no longer deemed part of a deceased person.

However, while it is indeed likely that Rav Unterman would approve of this posthumous procedure, Rav Shlomo Zalman Auerbach did not accept his view. He argued that if benefit from something is halachically forbidden, then transforming it into something that is no longer forbidden is prohibited as well, since in the end, one derives benefit from the forbidden entity. Rav Shlomo Zalman notes the case of מבטלין איסור לכתחילה — intentionally mixing a small amount of prohibited food with a much larger amount of permissible food so that the entire mixture will be permissible. While the intentional creation of such a mixture is clearly forbidden, some authorities maintain that this prohibition applies only on the level of Rabbinic enactment. Rav Shlomo Zalman notes, however, that according to all views, this would be forbidden on the level of Torah law when dealing with a food for which not only consumption, but also all other kinds of benefit, are forbidden. Making forbidden food permissible through the process of ביטול ("nullification" by a majority) effectively amounts to benefit. Therefore, if benefit from the food is forbidden, knowingly triggering ביטול is forbidden. By the same token, Rav Shlomo Zalman reasons, "resurrecting" a body part taken from a human corpse through transplantation would violate the prohibition against deriving benefit from a corpse. In his view, then, it would likely be forbidden to extract sperm from a deceased man for insemination, even though the sperm is "resurrected" inside the woman's body.

Hair and Skin from a Human Corpse

Another possible argument that could perhaps be advanced for permitting posthumous fathering is that sperm may be viewed as extraneous matter, and not as an actual part of the deceased person's body.

Such a possibility might hinge on a debate among the *Rishonim* concerning the status of hair taken from a deceased person — an issue that was debated already by the *Amoraim*, as discussed by the Gemara (*Arachin* 7b). While the Rambam (*Hilchos Avel* 14:21) permits the use of a deceased person's hair, the *Shulchan Aruch* (Y.D. 350:2) follows the stringent position, forbidding the use of even hair taken from a corpse. We may reasonably assume that the sperm found inside a deceased person's body is no less "extraneous" than his hair. Thus, if the *Shulchan Aruch* forbids benefiting from the hair, it would likewise be forbidden to use sperm taken from the body.

One might, however, suggest comparing sperm taken from a deceased man to skin taken from a deceased person, which some *Rishonim* permit for use. *Tosfos* (*Nidda* 55a) raise the possibility that since the prohibition against benefiting from a human corpse is, as mentioned above, rooted in the implied association between a corpse and sacrifices, it does not apply to skin, since the hide of sacrificial animals is permissible for use (once the sacrificial blood has been sprinkled). Just as the skin of sacrifices is permissible, *Tosfos* contend, the skin of a human corpse should likewise be permitted for use. This theory is also proposed by the Rashba in one of his responsa (1:365).

The halachic status of skin taken from a corpse is addressed by the *Rishonim* in the context of a perplexing comment made by the Gemara in *Maseches Chullin* (122a). The Gemara establishes that although the skin of a deceased person is not, strictly speaking, considered טמא (ritually impure), the Sages legislated that it be treated as such, in order to prevent people from using their deceased parents' skin as carpets. The implication of the Gemara's remark is that using a deceased parent's skin as floor carpeting is technically permissible, but as this would be inappropriate, the Sages proclaimed the skin טמא, which would prevent people from making practical use of them. The Rashba, in the aforementioned responsum, cites those who drew proof from the Gemara's comment that skin taken from a deceased person is, indeed, permissible for use.

The Rashba refutes this proof, however, noting that *Chazal* were perhaps concerned about foolish people who are more deterred by the status of טומאה

assigned to the skin of their deceased parents than by the strict prohibition against deriving benefit from a human corpse. The designation of skin as טמא was made specifically to prevent against violations of the halacha forbidding benefit from the skins, a prohibition that some people would likely otherwise ignore. The Rashba concludes that he prefers this understanding of the Gemara, according to which skin from a deceased person is forbidden for use.[5]

The Ramban and Ran add a different explanation, suggesting that the Gemara speaks of people who would spread the skins of deceased loved ones and eulogize them in front of the skins. The concern was that with time, people might forget the origins of these skins and then use them as carpets. According to this approach as well, the Gemara never considered the permissibility of making use of skin from a deceased person.

This also appears to be the position taken by the Rambam, who writes (*Hilchos Avel* 14:21), המת אסור בהנאה כולו חוץ משערו — "The entire corpse is forbidden for benefit, except its hair." This clear-cut ruling would certainly indicate that every part of the corpse is forbidden with the exception of the hair.[6]

To this we might add the fact that, as we have seen, the *Shulchan Aruch* forbids the use of even hair taken from a human corpse. It stands to reason that if the hair is forbidden for use, then certainly the skin, which is more integral to the body than the hair, is forbidden.[7]

---

5. Several *Rishonim* — including the Rashba himself — offer this explanation of the Gemara's remark in their commentaries to *Maseches Chullin*. See Ramban and *Tosfos Ha-Rosh*.

6. Interestingly, however, Rav Shlomo Eiger (*Gilyon Maharsha, Avoda Zara* 29b) asserts that the Rambam permits benefiting from the skin of a deceased person, based on the Rambam's ruling (*Hilchos Avodas Kochavim* 7:3) that the skin of pagan animal sacrifices are permissible for benefit. The Gemara infers the prohibition against benefiting from pagan sacrifices from the comparison made by a verse between such sacrifices and human corpses. Thus, if the Rambam permits the use of skins of pagan sacrifices, he must also permit the use of skin of a human corpse. It is unclear how Rav Shlomo Eiger would reconcile this inference with the Rambam's categorical ruling in *Hilchos Avel* forbidden the use of the entire corpse with the exception of its hair.

7. Indeed, the *Chasam Sofer*, in his commentary to *Chullin*, notes that according to the view that hair taken from a corpse is forbidden for use, it is clear that the skin is likewise forbidden, *a fortiori*.
Elsewhere (*Avoda Zara* 29b), the *Chasam Sofer* writes that just as a deceased person's shrouds are forbidden for use, since they were placed on the body for it be buried in them, the deceased person's skin is likewise forbidden for use, according to all opinions, since the intention is to bury the body in the skin. Those *Rishonim* who permit deriving benefit from the skin of a human corpse, the *Chasam Sofer* contends, refer only to the rare case in which the intention before the person's death was for his skin to be removed from his body before burial.

In conclusion, it would seem that there is no room to permit using sperm taken from a corpse on the basis of its being considered extraneous matter and not an actual part of the body.

שלא כדרך הנאתו

Another factor to consider in determining the permissibility of extracting sperm from a deceased person is the rule established by the Gemara in *Maseches Pesachim* (24b), כל איסורין שבתורה אין לוקין עליהם אלא דרך הנאתן — "All Torah prohibitions are violated only in the normal manner of benefit." When the Torah forbids deriving benefit from a particular object, the prohibition applies only to the standard uses of that object. It is permissible on the level of Torah law to derive benefit from a forbidden object in an unusual manner, i.e., for a purpose for which it is not ordinarily used.

Later, the Gemara qualifies this rule, stating that it was stated only in regard to prohibitions that the Torah formulates by forbidding consumption. When the Torah introduces a prohibition against eating a certain food — which is understood as referring to other forms of benefit as well, and not merely consumption — we apply the prohibition only to standard types of benefit. However, when the Torah introduces a prohibition without specifying consumption, then all forms of benefit are included in the prohibition, even unusual ways of using the object in question.[8]

How would this rule apply with regard to the prohibition against deriving benefit from a human corpse? This prohibition, as noted, is based upon an association indicated by the Torah between a human corpse and עגלה ערופה, which is forbidden for benefit by virtue of its being a quasi-sacrifice. It would seem, then, that if sacrifices are forbidden only כדרך הנאתן — for standard forms of use — then a human corpse should similarly be forbidden only for ordinary uses, and not for unusual forms of benefit.

The issue of whether sacrifices are forbidden for all uses or only כדרך הנאתן is a matter of debate among the *Rishonim*. The debate revolves around the Gemara's remark in *Maseches Pesachim* (26a) that one may sit just outside the wall of the *Beis Ha-Mikdash* and benefit from the shade it produces. Rashi and *Tosfos* explain that although one may not derive personal benefit from the structure of the Temple, sitting outside the wall to benefit from its shade is permissible because it falls under the category of שלא כדרך הנאתן. Walls of buildings are constructed to provide shelter for those inside, not for people situated outside the

---

8. The Gemara makes this point in reference to *kilayim*, from which any kind of benefit is forbidden since the Torah does not formulate this prohibition as a prohibition against consumption (*Devarim* 22:9).

building. Therefore, sitting outside the Temple's wall and benefiting from its shade is considered an abnormal form of benefit, and is thus permitted.⁹ By contrast, the Rambam (*Hilchos Me'ila* 5:5) writes that one may benefit from the shade of sacred structures only because this prohibition does not apply to hallowed objects attached to the ground. The implication, as noted and discussed by Rav Moshe Feinstein (*Iggeros Moshe*, Y.D. 1:229), is that כדרך הנאתן is not a factor when it comes to the prohibition against benefiting from sacred objects. As such, it would seem that according to the Rambam, the prohibition against benefiting from a human corpse, which is rooted in the prohibition against benefiting from sacrifices, would apply even to unusual forms of benefit.

This debate does not appear to have been conclusively resolved. The Radbaz wrote a responsum about the permissibility of the use of mummies for medicinal purposes (3:548), concluding that this form of benefit constitutes שלא כדרך הנאתו and is thus permissible. This view is adopted by several *Acharonim*.¹⁰ By contrast, Rabbi Akiva Eiger, in his commentary to the *Shulchan Aruch* (Y.D. 349), citing the *Ginas Veradim*, disputes this position and maintains that all uses of a human corpse are forbidden, even non-standard forms of benefit.

The question then becomes whether extracting sperm from the body of a deceased male for insemination qualifies as "unusual" benefit from the corpse. On the one hand, one might argue that sperm found inside a dead body has no other useful function than fertilization through artificial insemination, and thus such utilization of sperm is precisely its "ordinary" form of benefit. However, one might counter that to the contrary, after a person's death, the sperm in his body is no longer considered to be reproductive material designated for the purpose of fertilization. We might even go further and contend that the "normal" use of sperm is fertilization through intercourse, and not via artificial insemination, even during a man's lifetime. Accordingly, we should perhaps deem the posthumous extraction of semen for fertilization שלא כדרך הנאתו, such that it would be permissible according to the view of the Radbaz, assuming that allowing the widow to bear offspring from her late husband offers the same grounds for leniency as treating an illness.

This question likely hinges on another question inconclusively addressed by Rav Tzvi Pesach Frank (*Har Tzvi*, Y.D. 277) concerning corneal transplants.¹¹

---

9. Tosfos comment that although the Torah does not formulate the prohibition of מעילה (benefiting from hallowed property) as a prohibition against consumption, nevertheless, the Gemara elsewhere associates this prohibition with the prohibition against benefiting from תרומה, which is indeed introduced as a prohibition against eating תרומה.
10. Rav Shmuel Landau, *Shivas Tziyon* (62); Rav Shlomo Kluger, *Mei Nidda* (p. 52); *Mishneh Le-Melech*, *Hilchos Avel* 14.
11. See the appended notes to this responsum published at the end of the volume (p. 258),

Rav Frank raises the possibility of considering transplanting a cornea into a live patient שלא כדרך הנאתו, since once a person dies, his cornea is no longer slated to serve the function of facilitating vision. On the other hand, one might insist that facilitating vision is precisely the cornea's purpose, and thus implanting it into a live patient so that he can see is actually its "standard" use.

Rav Moshe Feinstein addresses a similar question regarding the transplantation of organs from a human cadaver to a live patient (*Iggeros Moshe*, Y.D. 1:229). He writes that although nowadays it is not customary to use human corpses for any purpose other than organ transplantation, nevertheless, this form of benefit qualifies as שלא כדרך הנאתו, since this is not the normal function of a person's organs. However, Rav Moshe firmly sides with the stringent view of Rabbi Akiva Eiger, forbidding even unusual benefit from a human corpse, and thus he concludes that it is forbidden to benefit from a deceased person's organs through transplantation. According to Rav Moshe, then, we certainly cannot permit the use of a deceased's posthumously extracted sperm on the grounds of שלא כדרך הנאתו.

Moreover, it is possible that even Rav Moshe would view the posthumous extraction of sperm for fertilization as "normal" use, and thus consider it forbidden according to all *poskim*. Body parts are intended to sustain the individual's own body, and thus utilizing them to sustain someone else's body would be deemed abnormal use. Sperm, however, is specifically intended to exit the body and fertilize an ovum. Conceivably, then, extracting sperm from a deceased man for insemination would qualify as "normal" use of the sperm, and would thus be forbidden even according to the Radbaz.

Regardless, as noted, Rav Moshe ruled in accordance with Rabbi Akiva Eiger's view, and thus he would not permit extracting sperm posthumously on the basis of the rule of שלא כדרך הנאתו.

כזית

Another argument that may be advanced to permit this posthumous procedure is that the volume of sperm taken from the deceased for fertilization amounts to less than the minimum volume required for the prohibition to be applicable.

The *Acharonim* debate the question as to the minimum size required for an object or substance to be considered forbidden for use. Generally, when the Torah forbids a certain food for consumption, one must consume at least a כזית (the volume of an olive) in order to be liable for a Biblical violation. Does this rule apply as well to objects forbidden for other forms of benefit, or are

---

where the point of uncertainty is clarified.

such prohibitions subject to different guidelines, and thus require a different minimum size?

The *Mishneh Le-Melech* (*Hilchos Me'ila* 1:3) establishes that if the prohibition is formulated by the Torah as a prohibition against eating, then the minimum size is a כזית even with respect to other forms of forbidden benefit. When it comes to such prohibitions, one is not liable for a Biblical violation unless he derives benefit from a כזית of the forbidden food, regardless of the monetary value of the benefit he enjoyed. However, with regard to prohibitions that are not formulated in the Torah as prohibitions against consumption, one is guilty of a violation by deriving benefit the value of a פרוטה (the smallest unit of currency in Talmudic times), regardless of the size of the forbidden object. Since the Torah forbade the use of the object in question without any reference to consumption, there is no reason for the violation to depend on any particular physical size. The only relevant factor is the benefit enjoyed, and thus any significant benefit — defined as a פרוטה's worth — suffices for the prohibition to take effect, irrespective of the object's physical properties. This is also the view taken by the *Peri Megadim* (introduction to *Hilchos Pesach* 2:3).

Rabbi Akiva Eiger, in one of his published responsa (190), disagrees, and maintains that physical size is never a factor with respect to forbidden benefit. Even if the Torah formulates the given prohibition by forbidding eating the product in question, one violates the prohibition by deriving a פרוטה's worth of benefit from the product, regardless of its size. Even if one made use of a tiny morsel of forbidden food, he has transgressed the Biblical prohibition if the value of the benefit equals or exceeds one פרוטה.

Applying this debate to the question surrounding the use of a cadaver, we must seemingly return to the earlier discussion concerning שלא כדרך הנאתו. As noted, Rashi and *Tosfos* would treat the prohibition against the use of a human corpse as a prohibition formulated in terms of consumption. According to this view, the permissibility of using a small piece of a cadaver would appear to hinge on the debate between the *Mishneh Le-Melech* and Rabbi Akiva Eiger. The *Mishneh Le-Melech* would permit the use of a substance amounting to less than a כזית,[12] whereas Rabbi Akiva Eiger would forbid using such a substance if the

---

12. At first glance, one might argue that even according to the view of the *Mishneh Le-Melech*, benefiting from a small morsel of human remains would be forbidden by force of the rule of חצי שיעור — the notion that although one is liable to punishment only if his violation involved the minimum requisite amount, one nevertheless commits a sinful act with even a small quantity. Thus, for example, although one is liable to punishment for breaking the Yom Kippur fast only if he consumes the volume of a large date, nevertheless, it is forbidden to consume any amount (*Yoma* 74a). Seemingly, then, benefiting from even a minuscule portion of a corpse would be forbidden, irrespective of the debate between

benefit is valued at a פרוטה or more. However, as we saw, the Rambam seems to forbid benefiting from a human corpse even in an unusual manner, since this prohibition is not treated as a law associated with consumption, and this is the position accepted by Rav Moshe Feinstein. In his view, then, benefit from any quantity of human remains would be forbidden, even according to the *Mishneh Le-Melech*.

In truth, however, it is possible that this question hinges on an entirely separate issue. The Ran, in his commentary to *Maseches Chullin* (122a), cites a view that the prohibition against using human remains is dependent upon the status of טומאה assigned to human remains. In other words, only parts of a cadaver that are deemed ritually impure are forbidden for use. This theory was advanced to explain the aforementioned passage in the Gemara that indicates that skins taken from a deceased person may, in principle, be used as carpeting. The Gemara elsewhere (*Nidda* 55a) establishes that body parts that regenerate — such as hair, nails, and skin — are not considered טמא after a person's death. The view cited by the Ran asserts that since skin does not — on the level of Torah law — become impure after death, there is no prohibition against benefiting from it.[13]

According to this view, it would seem that a portion from a corpse comprising less than a כזית would be permissible for use, since a body part detached from a corpse is deemed טמא only if it comprises a כזית or more. This position is cited by the *Sedei Chemed* (*Ma'areches Mem*, 103) in the name of other *poskim*. Likewise, the *Chasam Sofer* (Y.D. 336) suggests that the Torah imposes an especially stringent status of טומאה upon a corpse specifically to prevent people from deriving personal benefit from human remains. This would seem to imply that body parts that are not considered impure are not included in the prohibition against deriving benefit from a corpse. By extension, then, a portion of human

---

the *Mishneh Le-Melech* and Rabbi Akiva Eiger. However, as noted by Rav Tzvi Pesach Frank (in the aforementioned responsum), the rule of חצי שיעור is not applicable to the case of a small piece of human remains implanted in a live patient. The prohibition of חצי שיעור, as the Gemara explains, is rooted in the factor of חזי לאצטרופי — the possibility of this small portion of forbidden matter combining with other small portions to reach the requisite quantity. For example, if one eats a small portion of forbidden food, he might then eat another small portion, and then another, until he eventually reaches the volume of a כזית, and thus each small portion is deemed independently forbidden. In the case of a transplant, there is no possibility of deriving additional benefit to reach the minimum required quantity. (See the notes to this responsum in *Har Tzvi*, p. 158.)

13. The Ran writes that those who advance this view draw proof from the Gemara's account in *Maseches Berachos* (5b) of Rabbi Yochanan, who lost all of his children and would carry around a tooth taken from his tenth son in order to comfort bereaved parents. Rabbi Yochanan was permitted to make use of this tooth, these *Rishonim* contend, because a deceased person's teeth are not deemed טמא.

remains that it is too small for טומאה is not forbidden for use. Indeed, Rav Tzvi Pesach Frank permitted the use a cornea taken from a cadaver because, among other reasons, its size is smaller than a כזית.

Accordingly, we might similarly permit the use of sperm taken from a deceased person for the purpose of fertilization. Since only a very small quantity of sperm is used — certainly less than a כזית — this procedure does not fall under the prohibition against deriving benefit from human remains. Furthermore, it stands to reason that since sperm is regenerated by the body, like hair and nails, sperm extracted from a deceased person does not have the status of impurity assigned to other parts of a cadaver. Hence, if we assume that the prohibition against benefit hinges upon the status of impurity, a deceased person's sperm is entirely permissible for use.

We might, however, question Rav Frank's ruling in light of the fact that the Ran disputes the claim that the prohibition against using human remains is linked to a corpse's status of טומאה. He notes that hair taken from a corpse is unquestionably excluded from the cadaver's status of impurity, and yet its status vis-à-vis the prohibition against benefit is subject to debate among the *Amoraim* (as we noted above). This would seem to indicate that the prohibition against using a corpse and the status of impurity assigned to a corpse are not interdependent.

One could defend the view cited by the Ran by suggesting that the debate among the *Amoraim* regarding the use of hair taken from a corpse hinges on this very question of whether the prohibition against benefiting from a corpse is linked to its status of טומאה. As we saw earlier, the *Shulchan Aruch* codifies the position that hair taken from a corpse is forbidden for benefit, which might prove that according to the accepted *halacha*, the prohibition against benefiting from human remains applies independently of the status of טומאה. As such, we should perhaps conclude that one may not make use of even a tiny morsel of matter taken from a corpse.

Interim Summary

We have seen that the consensus view among the *poskim* would likely forbid making use of posthumously extracted semen, although this would be permissible according to those authorities who permitted corneal transplants. Rav Unterman maintains that "resurrecting" a dead organ in the body of a live patient is permitted, and Rav Frank asserts that a small organ such as a cornea does not fall under the prohibition of benefiting from human remains, and a transplant may constitute an abnormal form of benefit. It would appear that in the case of a man who died childless and whose wife very much wishes to perpetuate his biological legacy, especially if it is known that this was the man's desire, we may rely on these rulings of Rav Unterman and Rav Frank to allow inseminating the wife from the husband's posthumously retrieved sperm.[14]

II. Absolving the Widow from יבום and חליצה

Let us now turn our attention to the question of whether a man's posthumously conceived child suffices to absolve the widow of the obligation of יבום or חליצה. As noted in the introduction, the Torah requires the widow of a childless man to either marry his brother or to perform the חליצה ceremony, which releases her from this responsibility and allows her to marry any man she wishes. The fascinating question thus arises as to the status of a widow who was impregnated with sperm extracted from her husband's body after his death. Whether or not this procedure is halachically permissible, if it is performed and the widow conceives and delivers a child, is she now absolved of the obligation of יבום and חליצה, since her husband had fathered a child? Or does the obligation take effect the moment the husband dies without children, irrespective of his wife's subsequent conception?

Conception between Intercourse and the Husband's Death

A similar question was addressed in a famous and controversial responsum of Rav Yechezkel Landau (*Noda Be-Yehuda, Mahadura Kama*, E.H. 69). He notes that, as the Mishna and Gemara in *Maseches Yevamos* (35b) unequivocally establish, if a woman is pregnant with her husband's only child when the husband dies, she does not require יבום or חליצה (on condition that the pregnancy reaches full-term and the infant survives). The question he addresses is whether this also applies if the husband died immediately after intercourse, before conception occurs. On the one hand, since the woman was not pregnant at the time of her husband's death, perhaps she is subject to the requirement of יבום. On the other hand, one could argue that since the husband had already ejaculated his sperm inside the wife's body before his death, and it was only a matter of time before the sperm would fertilize her ovum, she may be considered halachically pregnant at the time of the husband's death.

---

14. Rav Yitzchak Herzog (*Pesakim U'Ksavim*, vol. 5, Y.D. 157) permitted corneal transplants for a different reason, asserting that this kind of benefit is not direct, and is thus forbidden only on the level of Rabbinic enactment. This prohibition is therefore overridden by the concern to restore a visually-impaired patient's eyesight. It is unlikely that this rationale would apply to posthumously retrieved sperm. See *Be-Mareh Ha-Bazak*, vol. 5, pp. 165–166.

The *Noda Be-Yehuda* advances the theory that a woman is not halachically considered "pregnant" before conception. Thus, if a husband died before the wife conceived with his only child, she is obligated to perform either יבום or חליצה. This theory is proposed to answer the question posed by a contemporary of the *Noda Be-Yehuda* ("the elderly sage of Tartakow") as to how the *halacha* permits יבום ninety days after the husband's death. *Chazal* assumed that pregnancy can be detected within ninety days after conception, and they therefore required a widow to wait this period before marrying her brother-in-law, in order to ascertain that she had not been impregnated by her first husband, and thus that יבום is warranted.[15] However, the sage of Tartakow wonders why the Sages did not require waiting an additional several days, to account for the delay between intercourse and conception. Even if the woman does not appear pregnant ninety days after the husband's death, it is possible that she will appear pregnant several days later, when ninety days will have passed since the moment of conception. Seemingly, then, *Chazal* should have ordained an additional several days of waiting.[16]

To answer this question, the *Noda Be-Yehuda* proposes that conception that occurs between intercourse and the husband's death does not absolve the woman of the יבום obligation. If the woman was not pregnant at the moment her childless husband died, the Biblical command of יבום applies even if she conceives immediately thereafter from sperm ejaculated from her husband during intercourse before his passing. Therefore, she needs to wait only ninety days before marrying the deceased's brother, for even if she conceived several days after her husband's death, this has no effect on the יבום obligation.

The *Noda Be-Yehuda* concludes by expressing his ambivalence regarding his theory, which he openly acknowledges appears nowhere in earlier halachic literature. He goes so far as to say that this novel theory should not inform normative halachic practice. Thus, a woman whose pregnancy is discerned ninety-two days after her husband's death does not require חליצה. Although it is possible that she conceived with his only child only after his death, nevertheless, the *Noda Be-Yehuda* was not prepared to introduce a new measure of stringency that does not appear in earlier sources.

Notwithstanding the *Noda Be-Yehuda*'s ambivalence, we might draw proof

---

15. Normally, it is forbidden for a woman to marry her husband's brother, even after her husband's death. It is only when the husband dies without children that the Torah sanctions a woman's marriage to her brother-in-law. *Chazal* therefore required waiting ninety days before performing יבום to ascertain that the deceased had not fathered a child, and thus that the widow's marriage to his brother is legitimate.
16. The *Noda Be-Yehuda* speaks of a three-day delay, in light of the assumption made by *Chazal* that a woman can conceive up to three days after intercourse.

to his theory from the Gemara's discussion in *Maseches Yevamos* (87a) regarding the case of an only child who died after his father's passing. The Gemara establishes that the widow does not require יבום, despite the fact that her deceased husband now has no children. The reason cited by the Gemara is the famous verse in *Mishlei* (3:17), דרכיה דרכי נעם ("Its ways are ways of pleasantness"), which conveys the message that Torah law must apply in a "pleasant" manner. In the case in which a man died and left behind a child, whereupon the widow remarried, if *halacha* would retroactively require יבום after the death of the first husband's child, this would create a gravely disagreeable situation, whereby the woman would now have to divorce, as she is retroactively required to marry her brother-in-law. Such a scenario, the Gemara instructs, is inconceivable in light of the principle of דרכיה דרכי נעם. Thus, necessarily, *halacha* does not require יבום in such a case.

The Gemara's application of דרכיה דרכי נעם would seemingly be relevant also in the case of conception after the husband's death, in the converse. The widow in such a case has no children at the time of her husband's death, and is thus required to marry the deceased's brother. If we then retroactively revoke the יבום obligation upon her conception, this would certainly cause a most undesirable situation. Thus, in this instance, too, we should determine a widow's status vis-à-vis יבום based only upon the circumstances at the time of the husband's death; if she was not pregnant at that time, she requires יבום even if she subsequently conceives her husband's child.[17]

One might refute this argument, however, by claiming that we do not have the authority to expand the halachic application of דרכיה דרכי נעם beyond the scenario to which the Gemara applies it. The Gemara invokes this factor to explain the specific rule that a child's death does not retroactively trigger a יבום obligation upon the mother, but this does not necessarily give us license to assume that this would apply in the reverse case as well.

Returning to the case of a widow inseminated with her husband's sperm after his death, her status vis-à-vis יבום would seemingly hinge on this theory postulated by the *Noda Be-Yehuda*. According to this theory, the determining factor is the presence of biological offspring — either living or in utero — at the moment of the husband's death. Therefore, since the widow was not pregnant at the time the husband died, she requires יבום or חליצה before remarrying, even though her husband will later have a child. However, as the *Noda Be-Yehuda* was reluctant to apply his theory as normative halachic practice, perhaps we

---

17. This point is made by Rav Shaul Yisraeli in an article published in *Torah She-Be'al Peh*, vol. 33 (5752).

should not require a woman to perform חליצה in such a case, since her husband ultimately produced a child.

Objections to the *Noda Be-Yehuda*'s Position

Rav Yitzchak Minkovsky of Karlin (*Keren Ora*, *Yevamos* 87a) dismisses the *Noda Be-Yehuda*'s theory. He notes the Gemara's discussion (*Yevamos* 87b) comparing the rules that apply to יבום to those that that apply to תרומה (hallowed portions of food given to a *Kohen*). A *Kohen*'s daughter is permitted to eat תרומה until she marries a non-*Kohen*, whereupon she loses this privilege. Even after she is widowed, she is forbidden to eat תרומה if she has children from her husband. The Gemara indicates that this woman's disqualification from תרומה after her husband's death is subject to the same guidelines as a widow's exclusion from יבום by virtue of having borne her husband's children. The only difference between the two cases, the Gemara establishes, is that in the case of תרומה, the widow regains her right to eat תרומה if her child dies, as the child's death breaks her connection to her husband. Although the widow's status vis-à-vis יבום is not affected by her child's death, her status vis-à-vis תרומה indeed changes. In every other respect, however, these two issues are identical. Clearly, Rav Minkovsky writes, if the woman conceives after her husband's death, she remains disqualified from eating תרומה, since she carries her husband's child. Necessarily, then, this conception also disqualifies her from יבום.

We can easily refute this argument, however, in light of the point made earlier regarding the possibility of applying the concept of דרכיה דרכי נעם to the case addressed by the *Noda Be-Yehuda*. The Gemara's distinction between the cases of יבום and תרומה is the situation of a child who dies subsequent to the father's death, which does not change the widow's status vis-à-vis יבום due to the consideration of דרכיה דרכי נעם. This same consideration, as noted, could perhaps apply in the converse, so that the woman would be obligated in יבום even when she conceives from the husband after the husband's death. If so, we can argue that this case, too, is subsumed under the exception noted by the Gemara.

Rav Minkovsky further argues that the *Noda Be-Yehuda*'s position yields the inherently paradoxical situation of a son inheriting the estate of his father whose widow was obligated to perform יבום. If a father has a son eligible to inherit his possessions, then by definition, his wife is excluded from יבום. This point is also made by Rav Tzvi Pesach Frank (*Har Tzvi*, E.H. 8), who notes the Gemara's remark (*Yevamos* 17b, 24a), יבום בנחלה תלה רחמנא — the יבום obligation is directly linked to the inheritance of the deceased's estate. If a deceased man has a son who inherits his estate, then by definition, his widow is not eligible for יבום.[18]

Rav Mordechai Halperin,[19] however, questions this argument, noting a precedent for יבום without inheritance. The Mishna (4:7) addresses the case of a childless man who dies during his father's lifetime, and cites the view of Rabbi Yehuda that the father inherits the deceased's estate, despite the fact that the deceased's brother performs יבום and marries the widow. The Gemara (40a) explicitly states that the obligation of יבום can be fulfilled without inheriting the deceased's estate, and thus Rabbi Yehuda awards the deceased's estate to the father even though the deceased's brother marries his widow to perpetuate his memory. Although the majority view disputes Rabbi Yehuda's ruling, Rav Halperin contends that the majority view accepts the premise that יבום can occur independently of inheritance rights, but simply maintains that the Torah grants precedence to the brother-in-law who performs יבום over the deceased's father.[20]

However, one could argue that to the contrary, herein precisely lies the point of debate between Rabbi Yehuda and the majority view. The other *Tanna'im* may have disputed Rabbi Yehuda's view specifically because they maintained that inheritance rights are inherent to the יבום process, and thus there can be no possibility of a man marrying his sister-in-law in fulfillment of the יבום obligation without also inheriting the deceased's estate. Hence, since the *halacha* follows the majority opinion,[21] we should perhaps conclude that יבום cannot occur in the absence of inheritance rights, in support of Rav Minkovsky's objection to the *Noda Be-Yehuda*'s theory.[22]

Rav Shlomo Zalman Auerbach (*Minchas Shlomo, Tinyana* 124) raises a different question concerning the *Noda Be-Yehuda*'s theory. He argues that if, with regard to יבום, halachic pregnancy does not begin immediately following intercourse, this should conceivably be true with regard to other areas of *halacha*

---

18. Interestingly, however, Rav Frank is reluctant to reach a definitive conclusion, and thus rules that if a widow is inseminated from her husband's sperm after his death, she should perform חליצה in deference to the *Noda Be-Yehuda*'s position.
19. In an article published in the compendium *Devarim She-Yesh Lahem Shiur* (pp. 159–180), available online at http://www.medethics.org.il/website/index.php/he/homepage/101-2012-02-20-09-46-54/assia/2012-03-05-10-02-56/1000-2012-03-22-17-04-184.
20. As for the Gemara's comment יבום בנחלה תלה רחמנא, Rav Halperin cites a number of *Rishonim* who clarify that this does not mean that יבום necessarily includes inheritance rights. See *Tosfos Yeshanim* to 40a, and the Rashba to 108a.
21. Rambam, *Hilchos Nachalos* 3:7; *Shulchan Aruch*, E.H. 163:1.
22. This point was made by Rav Aryeh Katz of the Puah Institute, in an article published online at http://www.puah.org.il/page.aspx?id=260.

as well. Thus, for example, if a married woman had an extramarital relationship, and in the period between intercourse and conception she was widowed or divorced, the child should not be assigned the status of *mamzer*. Since the child was conceived after the dissolution of the mother's marriage, the child should not be considered the product of infidelity. Conversely, if an unmarried woman has intimate relations with one man and then gets married to another before conception, the child should, according to the *Noda Be-Yehuda*, be considered a *mamzer*, as he was conceived in the womb of a married woman from another man's sperm.[23] Such a theory appears nowhere in the Talmud or later halachic sources, seemingly indicating that the father-child relationship is established at the time of intercourse, regardless of any developments that occur between the intercourse and conception.[24]

Rav Shlomo Zalman therefore dismisses the *Noda Be-Yehuda*'s view and maintains that if intercourse leads to pregnancy, the woman is halachically deemed pregnant from the moment of intercourse, even though the conception occurs sometime later. Since the process of conception takes place inside the woman's body and is not visible, *halacha* ignores the time lapse between intercourse and conception, and treats the pregnancy as beginning from the time of the union between the father and mother.[25]

In light of this analysis, Rav Shlomo Zalman distinguishes between the issue addressed by the *Noda Be-Yehuda* and the case of posthumous fertilization. Since conception occurs naturally and indiscernibly after intercourse, *halacha* overlooks the time lapse between the two, and treats the pregnancy as though it commences at the time of intercourse. As such, a woman who is widowed after

---

23. Rav Shlomo Zalman raises this point in reference to the theory he seeks to prove in this responsum that the status of *mamzer* is defined not by the act of infidelity, but rather by the biological merging of two halachically incompatible people. Thus, the fact that the child owes his existence to an illicit relationship does not, in itself, render him a *mamzer*.
24. Interestingly, Rav Shlomo Zalman does not entertain the possibility of distinguishing between different areas of *halacha* with respect to the lapse between intercourse and conception. It was obvious to him that since a child's status of *mamzeirus* is determined at the moment of intercourse, this is true as well with regard to יבום in a case of an only child conceived after the father's death. The *Noda Be-Yehuda* presumably maintained that these different areas of *halacha* follow separate guidelines in this respect, and thus even though a child's status of *mamzeirus* is determined at the time of intercourse, his status vis-à-vis יבום is determined by whether he was conceived before his father's passing.
25. Regarding the question raised by the *Noda Be-Yehuda* as to why *halacha* allows a widow to perform יבום immediately after the passage of ninety days from her husband's death, Rav Halperin references several other approaches taken to resolve this difficulty that appear in the Talmudic commentaries.

intercourse with her husband does not require יבום or חליצה if their final union produces a child, even if conception occurs after the husband's death. Artificial insemination, by contrast, is the result of human intervention, a separate step that needs to be taken in order for conception to take place. Therefore, a woman whose husband died without a child, and who is then artificially impregnated with his semen after his passing, requires יבום or חליצה even though her husband ended up begetting a child. Rav Shlomo Zalman applied this conclusion to the case of a husband who produced sperm during his lifetime that was stored and then used to inseminate his wife after his death. Even though Rav Shlomo Zalman rejects the position of the *Noda Be-Yehuda*, he concludes that in the case of posthumous insemination, the woman requires יבום or חליצה despite subsequently delivering her husband's child, since at the time of his death she was not in a position to naturally conceive from him.[26]

This is also the view taken by Rav Moshe Sternbuch (*Teshuvos Ve-Hanhagos* 6:244). However, Rav Sternbuch extends his ruling even further than Rav Shlomo Zalman, postulating that a child produced from a man's sperm after his death is not considered his father's halachic son in any respect. The halachic concept of "fathering," Rav Sternbuch writes, is likely inapplicable after a man dies. Although a man who dies immediately after intercourse is considered the child's father even if his death precedes conception, this does not apply when his sperm is posthumously injected into his wife's uterus. In the former case, the man has, for all intents and purpose, fathered a child before leaving this world, as he had completely performed the male role in reproduction. In the latter case,

---

26. Based on this distinction, Rav Shlomo Zalman addresses the interesting case of a married woman with an intrauterine contraceptive device (IUD) who betrayed her husband shortly before his death, and just after his death the device was removed and she conceived from her adulterer. Rav Shlomo Zalman notes that the child might not be considered a *mamzer*, because he was conceived after the husband's death and only as a result of medical intervention (i.e., the removal of the IUD). However, Rav Shlomo Zalman adds that he is uncomfortable with this conclusion, and he leaves the question unresolved.

Dr. Yossi Green, in an article published in *Techumin* (vol. 30, p. 145), contends that Rav Shlomo Zalman would not apply this conclusion to a case in which conception occurred via in vitro fertilization before the husband's death. Since the woman's egg was already fertilized — albeit outside her body — at the time her husband passed away, she is considered "pregnant" at the moment of the husband's death, thus absolving her of the need to undergo יבום or חליצה. Rav Katz (in the article referenced above, note 22) dismisses this claim, noting that since the fertilized egg must still be implanted in the woman's uterus, Rav Shlomo Zalman would not consider the woman pregnant at the time she is widowed, and she would thus require יבום or חליצה. See Rav Tzvi Ryzman's discussion in *Ratz Ka-Tzvi — Even Ha-Ezer, Poriyus*, pp. 120–123.

however, the process of "fathering" had not begun before the man's death, and thus he can no longer be considered a father. Rav Sternbuch therefore concludes that with respect to all *halachos*, a child produced from a man's sperm after his death is not considered his father's child. This means that he does not inherit his father's estate, and he is permitted to marry his father's family members. In light of this theory, Rav Sternbuch writes that fathering a child after death is forbidden, as it is improper to knowingly produce a child that has no halachic father.

Rav Shlomo Zalman, however, clearly did not take this view; he recognized a posthumously fathered child as the man's child, despite the fact that the mother requires יבום or חליצה.

Conclusion

According to the *poskim* who permit removing a cornea from a human corpse for transplantation in a live patient, it is likely that fathering a child from sperm taken from a deceased man would be permissible, whereas those who forbid the use of a deceased person's cornea would likewise forbid the use of posthumously retrieved sperm.

According to Rav Moshe Sternbuch, a child produced after the biological father's death is not halachically regarded as the father's child, and this procedure is thus forbidden due to the impropriety of knowingly producing a child who has no halachic father.

The consensus among the *poskim* is that a child produced from a man's sperm after his death does not absolve the widow of the obligation of חליצה.

Dina Pinner of KayamaMoms Talks Motherhood for Single Orthodox Women

May 2, 2016
by Rebecca Schischa

"I'm 41, religious and single. I'm not prepared to give up on motherhood and I'm also not prepared to give up on my halakhic devotion. If I can't have a partner, at least I should have a child."

With this impassioned plea, Aviva Harbater opened up the 2011 inaugural conference of KayamaMoms, a Jerusalem-based organization set up to support religious women anywhere on "the single mother by choice journey."

Five years later, KayamaMoms can take credit for some 48 babies born to single mothers, and for creating a unique supportive community for these alternative families. The organization provides information on pregnancy and adoption, advice on financial planning and parenting, and runs seminars and regular support groups.

The Sisterhood recently interviewed KayamaMoms co-founder and co-director Dina Pinner, originally from the U.K. and living in Jerusalem for many years now.

Rebecca Schischa: How did KayamaMoms come about?

Dina Pinner: I was 37 and a friend sent an informal email round saying: "We're all single and none of us is getting any younger — let's have children and form a community." I thought: "Why not?" We met at the home of one woman — who already had children on her own — and sat around the table discussing it. But it was completely

Kate with Amichai and Akiva

non-committal. We met again a few months later and this time we said: "OK, let's organize a conference."

Together with my co-founders/co-directors, Yael Ukeles and Dvora Ross (and another woman who since left the group and got married), we spent a year planning, and our inaugural conference took place in November 2011.

And during this time, I met my partner! I was meant to be setting up this thing with single women and I felt kind of bad. Finally, about three months after we met, I emailed the others and said: "I've met someone, can I still be involved?"

How does KayamaMoms support single women to become moms?

We run two separate monthly meetings. One is for anyone on the journey to becoming a single mother by choice — to talk, ask questions, think out loud.

The other is for moms and kids. It's important for the kids to meet up and realize that although their family does not look like other families, there are others just like theirs. It's also important for our moms to have a safe space to talk. Single mothers by choice have particular challenges. One mom said when she was pregnant with her second child, her doctor told her not to carry anything heavy. She laughed and asked the doctor: "Can you carry my child and my shopping for me?"

Merav with Yoav and Eitan

We're an international organization and have two secret Facebook groups, one in Hebrew and one English. We have women from the U.S., England, Europe, all over the place. I'll be in New York and London in the next few months and hope to organize meetings in both places.

Have attitudes changed towards single mothers by choice in the religious community in Israel?

We knew we had become mainstream when my friend — who always tells me about Yossi, the janitor at the big organization where she works, who's been saying to her for years: "Nu, when are you getting married?" — called me up and said: "You cannot believe what just happened to me! Yossi said to me: 'What are you waiting for? Go have a baby! Haven't you heard — religious women are having babies on their own now!'" We knew we had arrived then.

What kind of issues do single moms by choice describe?

The single mother by choice story is a beautiful story, which our moms pass on to their kids: "I was willing to do absolutely everything to have you." All the kids know their stories. But situations do come up. One member described a conversation with her son. They were in the car and he said out of the blue:

"Yuval's got an abba [dad], Can I have an abba?" At first she panicked...but then she remembered how to approach the subject: "Yes, Yuval's got an abba — what did you notice about his abba that made you think you wanted one?" "Well, Yuval's abba helped him learn to ride a bike. Who's going to help me learn to ride a bike?" "OK, no problem, we're going to speak to Saba [grandpa] tomorrow and he's going to teach you how to ride a bike too."

Are there any halakhic issues involved in single women becoming mothers?

There are rabbis who have said we are "destroying the Jewish family." But there is no halakhic prohibition. Our rabbi-advisor, Rabbi Yuval Cherlow, says that a woman shouldn't really go into this before she's around 34, as she should make "a gallant effort" to get married first. He says that ideally women should use non-Jewish sperm to prevent any issues later on of *yichus* [when someone could inadvertently marry a sibling]. But some women prefer to use Jewish sperm. It's a personal choice.

Any final thought?

Alternative families are not going away anywhere, and either we can embrace them or we can make them and their children feel rejected. It's the choice of the rabbi of each community as to what message they want to send out: that the unmarried and the childless should be ignored or that they should be embraced.

Copyright © forward.com

Is Artificial Insemination an Option for Unmarried Women?

The so-called "*shidduch* crisis" — the term used to describe the difficulties faced by many Orthodox men and women in finding suitable marriage partners — has triggered a great deal of discussion, aimed primarily at identifying the root cause of the problem and possible effective solutions. Traditional Judaism, of course, has always placed great emphasis on the importance of marriage, not only as a means of producing children, but also as a value unto itself, as God Himself proclaimed immediately after Adam's creation: לא טוב היות האדם לבדו אעשה לו עזר כנגדו — "It is not good for man to be alone; I shall make for him a helpmate alongside him" (*Bereishis* 2:18). Unfortunately, however, there are many who, for any one of a large variety of reasons, have been unable to find their "helpmate," and thus live alone, without a spouse and without children.

While living unmarried is difficult and agonizing for both men and women, it is especially disheartening, and even frightening, for single women, who face the prospect of entering menopause childless. Women naturally wish to bear children, and no one wishes to spend their elderly years alone, without any family around to offer affection, love, and practical support. The fear of finding themselves alone in old age has prompted a growing number of unmarried Orthodox Jewish women to turn to artificial insemination as a means of conceiving and begetting children. Most of these women have reached their upper 30s or 40s without marrying, and have begun to realize that the window of opportunity to produce children — and to raise them while still young, healthy, and energetic — would soon close. They thus decided to bear and raise children alone, preferring single motherhood over the risk of never experiencing the joy and satisfaction of raising a child.

In 2011, two such women — Dvora Ross and Yael Ukeles — as well as a third woman, Dina Pinner, started an organization in Israel called Kayama Moms, which provides information and assistance to single women aged 35 and over seeking to conceive. It is reported that Rabbi Yuval Charlow, Rosh Yeshiva of the Orot Shaul hesder yeshiva in Raanana, serves as the organization's rabbinic advisor.[1]

---

1. Jennifer Richler, "In Israel, Religious Single Moms Gain Greater Acceptance," http://www.jta.org/2017/01/12/life-religion/in-israel-religious-single-moms-gain-greater-acceptance.

Many other rabbis, however, have expressed strong opposition to the practice. This essay will examine the possible halachic barriers to this practice, and will seek to determine whether these concerns suffice to deny unmarried women the possibility of producing children.

Distinguishing Between Insemination and Intimacy

The first question that arises when considering this option is whether the introduction of a man's previously-ejaculated sperm into a woman's body through the vaginal tract is considered a sexual act that would be forbidden if the man is not her husband. When the Torah forbids sexual relationships outside the framework of marriage, does it forbid specifically the act of intercourse, or the introduction of a man's sperm into a woman's body?

Numerous sources indicate that it is the physical union, rather than the introduction of sperm, that the Torah forbids. The Rambam, for example, writes in his commentary to the Mishna (*Sanhedrin* 7:4):

> ואין להוצאת שכבת זרע בענין חיוב העונשין סרך בשום פנים אלא כיון שהכניס האבר יתחייב העונש עליה ואפי' פירש מיד.

> The ejaculation of sperm is of no consequence whatsoever with regard to liability to punishment; rather, once he inserted his organ, he is liable to punishment for it, even if he withdraws immediately [before ejaculation].

One transgresses the Torah's sexual code not by ejaculating inside the body of a woman to whom he is not married, but rather by performing the act of intercourse, irrespective of whether ejaculation occurs during the act. The clear implication of the Rambam's remarks is that the sole defining component of a forbidden sexual act is the physical union, not the introduction of the man's sperm into the woman's body.

Similarly, the Gemara in *Maseches Chagiga* (14b-15a) addresses the case of נתעברה באמבטי, whereby a woman who bathed conceived from sperm that was ejaculated by a man who had used the bath previously. It was believed that sperm in a tub could potentially enter a bathing woman's body and impregnate her, and the halachic literature surrounding this scenario provides us with a test case of conception without intercourse. The Gemara in *Chagiga* establishes that a virgin woman who conceived in this fashion does not lose her halachic status as בתולה (virgin), and thus remains eligible to marry a *Kohen Gadol*.[2] A

---

2. The Torah in *Sefer Vayikra* (21:13) requires a *Kohen Gadol* to marry specifically a virgin:

number of writers suggested drawing proof from this ruling that *halacha* does not equate the introduction of sperm into the woman's body with intercourse. The fact that a woman who conceived without intercourse retains her status of בתולה, as she has never experienced an intimate encounter with a man, indicates that the insertion of sperm is not halachically equivalent to a sexual act.

Rav Eliezer Waldenberg (*Tzitz Eliezer*, vol. 9, p.241), however, refutes this proof, asserting that the status of בתולה vis-à-vis eligibility to marry a *Kohen Gadol* hinges on the physical presence of the hymen, and not on the woman's sexual history. In other words, even if *halacha* regards the body's absorption of sperm as a sexual act, a woman who conceived without intercourse is nevertheless permitted to marry a *Kohen Gadol* because her hymen is still intact.[3] Therefore, a woman's status with respect to her marriage to a *Kohen Gadol* provides no proof of the halachic status of inserting sperm without physical intimacy.

Others draw proof from the Gemara's ruling in *Maseches Yevamos* (76a) regarding the status of homosexual intimacy between two females. The Gemara establishes that such activity is deemed פריצותא — inappropriately promiscuous — but does not fall under the category of forbidden sexual relations. As such, a woman who engages in such activity is permitted to marry a *Kohen,* even though women who are guilty of a forbidden sexual act may not marry *Kohanim*. Rashi comments that the Gemara speaks of an encounter involving direct contact between the partners' genitals, and the Rivan adds that this results in each woman's husband's sperm entering the other woman's body. The Gemara does not regard such an act as forbidden sexual relations, despite the introduction of sperm into a married woman's body, seemingly proving that the introduction of sperm into the body does not independently constitute an illicit act.[4]

Yet another source that has been cited in reference to this question is the Gemara's comment in *Maseches Bava Kama* (32a) in explaining the warning in *Sefer Vayikra* (18:29) of punishment for forbidden sexual acts: ונכרתו הנפשות העושות — literally, "The souls who perform [this] shall be excised." The Gemara notes that both partners are described with the term עושות ("perform"), despite the fact that the female is passive during the act of intercourse. The reason, the Gemara explains, is that both the male and the female derive enjoyment from

---

והוא אשה בבתוליה יקח.

3. Rav Waldenberg notes that this is how the *Mishneh Le-Melech* (*Hilchos Issurei Bi'a* 17:13) understood the Gemara's ruling, although the *Mishneh Le-Melech* maintained that the *halacha* does not follow this view regarding the definition of בתולה vis-à-vis eligibility to marry a *Kohen Gadol*.
4. This proof is brought by Rav Dov Krauser, citing earlier writers, in an article published in the first volume of *Noam* (p. 119).

intercourse, and it is to this aspect of intercourse — the enjoyment, as opposed to the performance of the act — to which the Torah here refers. It has been suggested on the basis of this Talmudic passage that the prohibitions against illicit relations are defined as prohibitions of הנאה — enjoyment.[5] By definition, a violation of the Torah's sexual code requires הנאה, and absent the experience of enjoyment, no violation has occurred.

Others, however, refute this proof,[6] suggesting that the Gemara introduced the factor of הנאה only to explain why both partners are liable to court-administered punishment. Normally, *beis din* does not administer punishment to violators who commit a transgression that entails no concrete action. When it comes to sexual offenses, however, the experience of הנאה obviates the need for an action to warrant punishment, and thus even the passive partner of a sexual union is punishable.[7] Hence, the Gemara's comment cannot be enlisted as proof that the introduction of sperm without intercourse does not qualify as a halachically-defined sexual act.

Rabbeinu Peretz

Another source cited by numerous *poskim* is a ruling of Rabbeinu Peretz, cited by the *Bach* (Y.D. 195) and his son-in-law, the *Taz* (Y.D. 195:7). Rabbeinu Peretz noted the practice of married woman to avoid sleeping on bedding on which a man other than their husbands had slept. This practice stems from the concern that the man may have experienced a seminal emission, and his sperm may enter the woman's body if she sleeps on the bedding. The woman would then conceive a child that is presumed to be her husband's son or daughter, while in truth that child was fathered by a different man. This confusion could give rise to numerous halachic concerns, and so such a situation should be avoided.

Rabbeinu Peretz states explicitly that the reason this situation must be avoided is because of the need to identify the child's father. There is no mention at all of this conception constituting an inadvertent adulterous act. To the contrary, Rabbeinu Peretz observes that common practice allows women to sleep on their husbands' bedding during their period of *nidda*, despite the possibility that they might conceive. Although relations with a *nidda* are strictly forbidden, and a child conceived from such a union — even in the case of a married couple

---

5. Rav Chaim Mednick, writing in *HaPardes* (Nissan, 5713).
6. See Rav Eliyahu Meir Bloch's response in *HaPardes* (Sivan, 5713).
7. Rav Bloch adds that *Tosfos* (*Yoma* 82b) write explicitly that one is liable to punishment for a forbidden sexual act even if no enjoyment is experienced.

— is considered "defective,"⁸ nevertheless, there is no need for a wife to avoid her husband's bedding while she is a *nidda*. Rabbeinu Peretz notes the legend of Ben Sira, author of a famous ancient work of ethics, who is said to have been conceived by the daughter of the prophet Yirmiyahu while she bathed in a tub that contained semen from her father. Ben Sira was not considered a *mamzer* or in any way "defective," and thus a child conceived when his mother was a *nidda* and slept on her husband's bedding is likely not to be deemed "defective." This would seem to prove that conception without intercourse is not halachically akin to intercourse from the man who produced the sperm.

This inference was made already by the *Mishneh Le-Melech* (*Hilchos Ishus* 15:4), who proved from Rabbeinu Peretz's comments that a married woman who conceived from another man's sperm while bathing is not considered an adulteress and may continue living with her husband. Numerous recent *poskim*, including Rav Yechiel Yaakov Weinberg,⁹ Rav Moshe Feinstein,¹⁰ and Rav Ovadia Yosef,¹¹ likewise draw proof from this source that the entrance of sperm into a woman's body does not qualify as an act of intercourse.

On this basis, Rav Moshe Feinstein, in a responsum that elicited a great deal of fierce opposition, ruled that a woman married to an infertile man, who endures a great deal of grief due to her inability to have children, may be artificially inseminated with the sperm of a non-Jewish man. As cited from Rabbeinu Peretz, the only reason to forbid allowing another man's sperm into a woman's body is the concern that her child will be mistakenly identified as her husband's offspring. This concern does not arise when the sperm is taken from a non-Jew, as *halacha* does not recognize any familial relationship between a Jew and his or her non-Jewish father.¹² In a letter published years later,¹³ Rav Moshe emphasized that he issued this ruling only in exceptional cases, when the physicians

---

8. *Shulchan Aruch* (E.H. 4:13). The *Beis Shmuel* comments that it is proper not to marry a child born from a couple that did not observe the laws of *nidda*, although recent *poskim* have generally ruled that this does not apply if the child is an upstanding and God-fearing individual. See Rav Shimon Eider's *Halachos of Niddah*, vol. 1, p. 3, note 15, and the letter by Rav Moshe Feinstein published at the end of that volume, section 19.
9. In *HaPardes* (October, 1950), pp. 7–8.
10. *Iggeros Moshe*, E.H. 71.
11. *Yabia Omer*, vol. 2, E.H. 1.
12. That is to say, in the case of a Jewish woman who cohabited with a non-Jewish man, the child is Jewish and is not considered the halachic offspring of the father. This would apply also in the case of a child fathered by a gentile through artificial insemination.
13. The letter appeared in Rav Tzvi Hersh Friedman's *Tzvi Chemed*, and is cited by Rav Ovadia Yosef in *Yabia Omer*, vol. 8, E.H. 21:5.

are certain that the couple is unable to produce a child because of the husband's infertility, and the couple is in great anguish over their state of childlessness.

Rav Yoel Teitelbaum — the first Satmar Rebbe — penned a lengthy letter condemning Rav Moshe Feinstein's ruling permitting artificial insemination, which was published in the journal *HaMa'or*.[14] He dismissed the proof drawn from Rabbeinu Peretz's ruling, for two reasons. First, the Chida (*Birkei Yosef*, E.H. 1:14) suggests an alternate reading of Rabbeinu Peretz's responsum, arguing that when a woman conceives while sleeping on a bed that was used previously by a man, the child is not considered to have a father. Since the child was not produced through intercourse, *halacha* does not treat him as the offspring of the father whose sperm had entered the mother's body. Rabbeinu Peretz nevertheless forbids a woman to sleep on bedding that had been used previously by a man other than her husband because the entry of another man's sperm into her body is itself problematic. Even though the child is not halachically related to that man in any way, the "mixing" of sperm inside a woman's body is prohibited.[15] According to this reading of Rabbeinu Peretz's ruling, the introduction of sperm from someone other than a woman's husband into her body is forbidden.

It should be noted, however, that the Chida proposed this reading only to establish that Rabbeinu Peretz's ruling does not provide definitive proof that a child conceived without intercourse is halachically considered the son of the man whose sperm impregnated the mother. The Chida concedes that according to the simple reading of the responsum, a woman should not sleep on bedding that might contain another man's sperm only because of the confusion that will arise if she conceives with another man's child, which could lead to a brother marring his sister. The novel, strained reading[16] suggested by the Chida was intended only to leave open the possibility that a child conceived without intercourse is not halachically related to the biological father.

The Satmar Rebbe also asserts that Rabbeinu Peretz considers the child produced in this manner a legitimate child only because the woman did not knowingly inject the sperm into her body. True, Rabbeinu Peretz writes, כיון דאין כאן ביאת איסור הולד כשר לגמרי — "Since there was no forbidden intercourse here, the child is entirely legitimate" — implying that it is forbidden intercourse that determines a child's illegitimate status. However, the Satmar Rebbe claims that Rabbeinu Peretz's intent is that in the case of a woman lying on a bed, there was

---

14. *HaMa'or*, Av, 5724.
15. The Chida's formulation is, הגם דלא שייכא גזרה שמא ישא אחותו מאביו ואין אב, מ"מ יש להקפיד בדין עירובא זרע הבא ממקום אחר.
16. Rav Waldenberg (p. 247) questions the validity of the Chida's reading of Rabbeinu Peretz's responsum, noting that it is very difficult to sustain.

no forbidden act. As Rabbeinu Peretz was entirely unaware of the possibility of artificial insemination, he mentioned specifically intercourse, which in his time was the only way to knowingly inject sperm into a woman's body. In truth, however, even other methods are forbidden.

However, this interpretation of Rabbeinu Peretz's formulation is highly speculative, as the simple reading suggests that a child's status of illegitimacy stems from a forbidden intimate encounter, and not from the entry of semen into the woman's body.

Rav Waldenberg[17] presents a different argument for why we cannot permit artificial insemination on the basis of Rabbeinu Peretz's responsum. He notes that the Chida, in the passage noted earlier, writes that he found a manuscript of ancient responsa that included a ruling by Rav Shlomo of London forbidding a wife who is a *nidda* to bathe in the same water in which her husband had bathed. The wife might conceive from the husband's semen in the water, and the child would then have been conceived during the wife's period of impurity. This ruling would certainly appear to reflect the view that insemination without intercourse is halachically equivalent to intercourse, in contradistinction to Rabbeinu Peretz's position.

Rav Waldenberg goes even further, suggesting that Rabbeinu Peretz might accept this ruling of Rav Shlomo of London. The Chida, after noting that Rav Shlomo of London appears to dispute Rabbeinu Peretz's position, writes ambiguously that there might be room to distinguish between the two cases such that these rulings do not conflict. Although the Chida does not specify any distinction, Rav Waldenberg suggests that the Chida refers to the possibility of distinguishing between conception while sleeping on bedding with semen, which happens passively, and conception while bathing, which occurs as the woman bathes and inadvertently brings the semen into her body. Even Rabbeinu Peretz, who permits a wife to sleep on her husband's bedding while she is a *nidda*, might forbid her to bathe in water in which her husband had bathed previously, as she would then actively bring his sperm into her body over the course of bathing.[18]

If so, Rav Waldenberg writes, then even Rabbeinu Peretz would concede

---

17. *Tzitz Eliezer*, vol. 9, pp. 244–245.
18. As mentioned, Rabbeinu Peretz also notes the example of Ben-Sira, who, according to legend, was conceived while his mother bathed and Yirmiyahu's sperm entered her body. This would seem to negate the theory that Rabbeinu Peretz distinguished between bathing and sleeping. However, Rav Waldenberg notes that the legend surrounding Ben-Sira's conception recounts that Yirmiyahu and his daughter were coerced into this situation, and so the action that brought Yirmiyahu's sperm into his daughter's body was performed against her will. Ordinarily, however, Rabbeinu Peretz would not permit a woman to bathe in water in which a man other than her husband had previously bathed.

that knowingly injecting a man's sperm into a married woman's body would be forbidden, and the child would be considered a *mamzer*.

Rav Waldenberg proceeds to draw our attention to the *Shiltei Ha-Gibborim* commentary to the Rif (*Shevuos* 2a), which cites a responsum of the Maharam on the very same topic addressed by Rabbeinu Peretz. Asked why women do not avoid sleeping on their husbands' bedding while in a state of *nidda*, the Maharam replied that the "deficiency" ascribed to a child conceived while his mother was a *nidda* is not a significant enough concern to warrant measures to avoid a remote risk of conception. In essence, the Maharam claims that a child conceived without intercourse while the mother was a *nidda* is, indeed, considered to have been conceived by a *nidda*, but since the consequences of this status are not terribly significant, women need not go to such great lengths to avoid it. Rav Waldenberg speculates that this responsum cited by the *Shiltei Ha-Gibborim* was in fact authored by Rabbeinu Peretz, but a copyist mistakenly wrote the name מהר״פ (referring to Rabbeinu Peretz) as מהר״ם. According to this theory, two different versions of Rabbeinu Peretz's responsum exist, such that no definitive conclusion can be reached on the basis of the responsum cited by the *Bach* and the *Taz*.[19]

We might respond, however, that since the *Bach* and the *Taz* cite Rabbeinu Peretz's ruling that a child conceived without intercourse is perfectly legitimate, this is the accepted position. Indeed, Rav Ovadia Yosef comments that Rabbeinu Peretz is a more widely accepted halachic authority than Rav Shlomo of London, and thus one may rely upon the lenient ruling of Rabbeinu Peretz.[20]

Seemingly, then, we should conclude, as Rav Feinstein ruled, that a woman may undergo artificial insemination with sperm produced by a non-Jewish man. Since artificial insemination is not halachically equivalent to an intimate relationship, and the only potential concern is the halachic pitfalls one could face if he cannot identify his father — a concern that does not arise when the sperm donor is a gentile — there appears to be no halachic barrier to this procedure.

Artificial Insemination as an Intimate Relationship

However, many *poskim* disputed Rav Feinstein's ruling and forbade artificial insemination, for a variety of reasons.

---

19. Rav Waldenberg (*Tzitz Eliezer*, vol. 9, p. 246) adds that several sources question the authenticity of the legend of Ben-Sira's conception, and so it cannot serve as a reliable source for permitting artificial insemination.
20. *Yabia Omer*, vol. 8, p. 450. However, Rav Ovadia Yosef nevertheless forbids artificial insemination, for other reasons.

One of the earliest responsa on the subject was penned by Rav Yehuda Leib Tsirelson and published in 1932 in his work *Ma'archei Lev* (73). Rav Tsirelson strictly forbids women from undergoing artificial insemination with another man's sperm, arguing that such a procedure constitutes a forbidden sexual act. He claims that this "union" between a man and woman would fall under the category of שלא כדרך הנאתן — deriving benefit from something forbidden by the Torah in the unusual manner. Injecting another man's sperm into a married woman's body is, in Rav Tsirelson's view, an unusual form of intercourse, and it thus constitutes שלא כדרך הנאתן. Since even such forms of benefit are forbidden by the Torah,[21] the prohibition against illicit sexual relations includes even this abnormal form of intercourse.

This contention, however, is very difficult to understand. The rule of שלא כדרך הנאתן applies to prohibitions against utilizing a certain item, extending that prohibition to include even unusual forms of use. When it comes to illicit sexual relations, the Torah forbids the act of intercourse. Injecting sperm with a tube into a woman's body is not an unusual form of that which the Torah forbids, but rather an entirely different act, which the Torah never prohibits.

Rav Tsirelson then proceeds to note the Torah's formulation in introducing the prohibition against adulterous relations with a married woman: ואל אשת עמיתך לא תתן שכבתך לזרע (*Vayikra* 18:20). The Torah here does not simply forbid intimate relations with another man's wife, but rather forbids inserting one's semen into another man's wife. The implication of this wording, Rav Tsirelson claims, is that any manner of inseminating another man's wife is prohibited, and not only through intercourse.

This inference was proposed already by Rav Yehonatan Eybeschutz in his *Benei Ahuva* (*Hilchos Ishus*, chapter 15), amidst his discussion of the case of a woman who conceives from another man's sperm in the bath. Rav Eybeschutz suggested that since the Torah describes adultery as the entry of another man's sperm into a married woman's body, a woman who inadvertently absorbs another man's sperm should perhaps be considered an adulteress and may therefore no longer engage in relations with her husband. However, Rav Eybeschutz immediately dismisses this contention, noting the Gemara's ruling noted earlier that such a woman retains her status of בתולה and may marry a *Kohen Gadol*.

This theory is embraced, however, by the Satmar Rebbe, in the aforementioned letter, where he draws support from the Ramban's discussion of this verse in his Torah commentary. The Ramban observes the Torah's formulation of the

---

21. *Pesachim* 24b. The exception to this rule is food items that the Torah forbids specifically for consumption; unusual forms of benefit from such products are forbidden only by force of rabbinic enactment (See previous chapter).

prohibition of adultery, and explains that the reason underlying the Torah's ban on adultery is the fact that the woman's offspring will be unable to identify their father. As this is the basic reason behind the prohibition, the Torah formulated this law as a prohibition against the introduction of another man's reproductive material in the body of another man's wife. And although one transgresses the Torah prohibition at the moment of penetration, irrespective of the ejaculation of sperm, the Satmar Rebbe explains that the Torah imposed an outright prohibition against all intercourse, even that which cannot lead to fertilization, but the core reason and essence of this prohibition is the need to ensure that all of a woman's children were fathered by her husband. As such, it applies even to the introduction of sperm in a woman's body without intercourse.[22] The Satmar Rebbe thus ruled that if a married woman is artificially inseminated with the sperm of a man other than her husband, she is guilty of an adulterous relationship. She must therefore divorce her husband, and the child she conceives is considered a *mamzer*.

Other *poskim*, however, rejected this argument. Rav Yechiel Yaakov Weinberg noted that we find no such inference in Talmudic literature from the verse לא תתן שכבתך לזרע, and we do not have the authority to determine practical *halacha* on the basis of our own exegesis.[23] Rav Moshe Feinstein addresses this verse in a later responsum,[24] where he denies outright the claim that the prohibition of adultery is linked to the interest in avoiding illegitimate children. He notes that Ibn Ezra, in his commentary to this verse, makes reference to those who suggested such an interpretation in order to justify intimate relations with women in situations in which conception is impossible, and Ibn Ezra strongly condemns this theory. The Torah formulates the prohibition with a reference to the offspring, Ibn Ezra explains, in order to clarify that an adulterous relationship is forbidden even if one's intent is strictly for the noble purpose of procreation, as opposed to simply satisfying lust. As for the Ramban's comments regarding the reason underlying the prohibition of adultery, Rav Feinstein counters that the Ramban noted the concern of illegitimate children as a factor that makes an adulterous relationship an especially severe offense, and not as the exclusive

---

22. The Satmar Rebbe concedes that we generally do not invoke the reasons and rational underpinnings of the Torah's laws as proofs in halachic discourse. However, he contends that when the Torah explicitly states the reason of a given law, that reason can and must be used to inform halachic decision-making. The Rebbe further states that according to some *poskim*, the reasons behind the Torah's laws must be taken into consideration when they yield stringencies; it is only when they imply a lenient conclusion that they cannot be invoked.
23. In the article referenced above, n. 9.
24. *Iggeros Moshe*, E.H. 2:11.

or even primary reason for this law. Moreover, Rav Feinstein adds, the Ramban introduces this interpretation of the verse with the word "*Ve'efshar*" — "Possibly," indicating that he does not definitively accept this reading. And he concludes his remarks by noting that he prefers a different interpretation, that the Torah makes specific reference to sperm in this context to clarify that the capital offense of adultery is violated only through full intercourse, and not through other forms of intimate physical contact. In other words, those who seek to draw proof from the Ramban's commentary that the prohibition of adultery refers even to the introduction of sperm without intercourse rely on a reading that the Ramban proposes with considerable skepticism.

Rav Feinstein also points to the fact that relations with another man's wife are forbidden even when there is no possibility of conception — such as if one of the parties is infertile or in a case of anal penetration. This fact, Rav Feinstein argues, demonstrates that it is the sexual act, and not the married woman's conception, that lies at the heart of this prohibition.

אין השכינה שרויה אלא על הודאים

Both the Satmar Rebbe[25] and Rav Waldenberg[26] forbid artificial insemination from a sperm bank for an additional reason, namely, on the basis of the requirement of הבחנה — ascertaining that a child's father can be definitively identified.

The Mishna in *Maseches Yevamos* (41a) establishes that a divorced or widowed woman may not remarry until three months have passed since her divorce or her first husband's passing, in order to avoid uncertainty regarding the biological origins of her next child. In earlier times, pregnancy could generally be detected only after three months from conception, but not earlier.[27] Therefore, if a woman remarries within three months of being widowed or divorced, and then immediately conceives, it will be unknown whether that child was fathered by the first husband or the new husband. In order to avoid such uncertainty, *halacha* requires the woman to wait three months after her divorce or her husband's death before remarrying.

The Gemara (*Yevamos* 42a) brings several different reasons for why this uncertainty must be avoided. The first is God's promise to Avraham, להיות לך

---

25. In the aforementioned article in *HaMa'or* (Av, 5724), p. 4.
26. *Tzitz Eliezer*, vol. 9, p. 252.
27. Nowadays, of course, pregnancy tests can determine if a woman is pregnant before the three-month period. The results of pregnancy tests, however, do not usually eliminate the halachically mandated need to wait a three-month period before a woman can get remarried.

לאלוקים ולזרעך אחריך — that He would establish a special relationship with him and "with your offspring after you" (*Bereishis* 17:7). This phrase implies that God's blessing depends upon a definitive connection between parents and their offspring, and thus instructs that children should not be produced in a manner that makes the identity of their biological father uncertain. Rashi explains by commenting, אין השכינה שורה אלא על הוודאים שזרעו מיוחס אחריו — "The Divine presence rests only on the 'certain' ones — a person whose offspring is attributed to him." The source of Rashi's comment is the Talmudic teaching presented in *Maseches Kiddushin* (70b), כשהקב"ה משרה שכינתו אין משרה אלא על משפחות מיוחסות שבישראל — "When the Almighty rests His presence, He rests it only upon the families in Israel with clear pedigree." The ability to definitively identify one's father and one's children is a *sine qua non* of Jewish life, without which we cannot merit the Divine presence in our midst.

Second, the Gemara notes, the situation of a child who cannot definitively identify his biological father can result in catastrophic halachic consequences. For example, if a person thinks his father is his mother's second husband, but he was really fathered by her first husband, he might marry the daughter of the first husband, thereby inadvertently marrying his sister — in violation of the Torah's prohibition against incest. Furthermore, the Gemara adds, if the child was conceived by the first husband, but is presumed to have been fathered by the second husband, he will naturally be considered the full brother of the second husband's other children. If the second husband's other son gets married and then dies childless, such that his widow is subject to the obligation of *yibum*, requiring her to marry her deceased husband's brother, his half-brother, who is mistakenly presumed to be his full brother, might marry her to fulfill this obligation. However, as *yibum* applies only to brothers who share the same father, the marriage in this case is not required, and as such, it is forbidden.[28]

Another concern noted by the Gemara is that the second husband might die without children, and since he was mistakenly assumed to have fathered a child, his wife will be unaware that she is bound by the *yibum* obligation. She might then remarry without being released by her brother-in-law through the *chalitza* ritual, in violation of a Biblical command. Likewise, if the first husband had one other son, and that son marries and then dies childless, his widow will assume that as her husband had no brothers, she is not subject to the obligation of *yibum*, when in reality, her husband had a brother, who must first perform *chalitza* before she may remarry.

The Satmar Rebbe and Rav Waldenberg note that nearly all these concerns

---

28. The Torah forbids marrying one's brother's wife, even after the brother's passing, except when this is required by force of the command of *yibum*.

apply as well to a woman who is artificially inseminated with a non-Jewish man's sperm. The exception is the concern of an incestuous marriage; as noted earlier, since *halacha* does not recognize familial relationships between a Jew and a non-Jew, a Jew fathered by a gentile is not halachically related to his father's other children. (Of course, there is also no concern regarding the possibility of the biological father having another child who will mistakenly assume that he has no brothers and whose widow will thus not realize she is bound by the *yibum* obligation, as this obviously does not apply to gentiles.) The other concerns, however, seem to apply. Artificial insemination with a non-Jew's sperm creates a child without a Jewish father, and the *yibum*-related concerns involving his mother and half-brothers are relevant in such a case. Rav Waldenberg argues that if *Chazal* were concerned about the remote possibility that a woman who remarried less than three months after being widowed or divorced might have conceived from her first husband, then *a fortiori* they would forbid actively and knowingly impregnating a woman with another man's sperm.[29]

Rav Moshe Feinstein addresses this argument in one of his responsa on the subject,[30] and he convincingly refutes the claim. Regarding the principle that אין השכינה שורה אלא על הוודאין, Rav Feinstein notes that there is no uncertainty at all when a child is conceived by sperm produced by a gentile. Halachically speaking, this child simply has no father. The rule established by the Gemara requires ascertaining the identity of every Jew's father; if a person has no father, then quite obviously this requirement is entirely irrelevant. As for the practical halachic consequences of a child who is mistakenly attributed to his mother's husband, Rav Feinstein writes that this concern applies only when no one knows who fathered the child. The Gemara requires a divorced or widowed woman to wait three months before remarrying because otherwise, no one — not even she — will know whether her child was fathered by the first or second husband. Likewise, as we saw earlier, Rabbeinu Peretz ruled that a married woman should not sleep on bedding used by a man other than her husband due to the concern

---

29. Intuitively, we might respond that we do not have the authority to extend *Chazal*'s decrees beyond the specific contexts for which they were enacted. Thus, although *Chazal* required a divorced or widowed woman to wait three months before remarrying to avoid uncertainty about her child's pedigree, we cannot forbid artificial insemination despite the fact that it poses the same concerns. However, as discussed earlier, Rabbeinu Peretz forbade married women to sleep on bedding that had been used by a man other than her husband due to the possibility that she might conceive with that man's sperm, and the child will be mistakenly identified as her husband's son. Rabbeinu Peretz clearly works off the assumption that *Chazal*'s enactment requires avoiding all situations of uncertain pedigree.
30. Referenced above, note 24.

that she might conceive from his sperm and the child will be misidentified. In that case as well, no one will know that the child presumed to have been fathered by the mother's husband is actually a different man's child.

In the case of a child conceived through artificial insemination with donor sperm, by contrast, the parents know full well that this is not their biological child. The requirement of הבחנה was not instituted for situations in which the parents know the child's biological origins but others might not. If הבחנה would, in fact, apply in such cases, Rav Feinstein argues, then *halacha* would have forbidden adoption, since people might mistakenly assume that a couple's adopted child is their biological child. The concept of הבחנה was introduced to prevent situations in which no one, including the mother, knows who fathered a child. Therefore, Rav Feinstein contends, the Gemara's discussion of הבחנה has no bearing whatsoever on the question surrounding the permissibility of artificial insemination.[31]

We might add another reason to discount this challenge to Rav Feinstein's ruling. The Gemara addresses the case of a widow or divorcee who wishes to remarry, and in order to avoid misidentification of the child's father, it requires her to wait three months. In such a situation, there is a very reasonable measure that can be taken to avoid the risk of attributing the child to the wrong father — a three-month waiting period. There is no reason to assume that *Chazal* would apply this measure in the situation of a woman who has no other possibility of bearing children. For a woman married to an infertile man, artificial insemination with donor sperm represents the only opportunity to become a mother. Thus, even if *halacha* prefers producing children with a definitively-identified Jewish father, we cannot presume, without compelling evidence, that this preference suffices to deny a woman the possibility of bearing children.

לא תהיה קדשה

A later edition of *HaMa'or* featured an essay by Rav Yosef Eliyahu Henkin strongly condemning artificial insemination with donor sperm.[32] Among the arguments he advances is that although this procedure does not halachically constitute a sexual act, it might nevertheless fall under the Torah prohibition of לא תהיה קדשה מבנות ישראל (*Devarim* 23:18) — the prohibition against harlotry. As opposed to other prohibitions in the Torah's sexual code, Rav Henkin observes, this law is not formulated as a prohibition against intercourse. Rather, it forbids being a קדשה (prostitute), and not the act per se. Perhaps, then, it refers to what

---

31. This point is also made by Rav Shlomo Zalman Aurbach, *Minchas Shlomo*, vol. 3, p. 10.
32. *HaMa'or*, Tishrei, 5725.

Rav Henkin terms בלבול הזרע — a woman's absorbing into her body sperm from different men. Conceivably, this could apply even to artificial insemination, when no sexual act is performed.

Rav Henkin adds that *Targum Onkelos* famously translates this verse as a prohibition against marrying a slave or maidservant. The reason for this prohibition, it could be argued, is that, as the Gemara (*Kiddushin* 69a) establishes, עבד אין לו חייס — a servant has no familial connections. Halachically, his children are not regarded as his offspring. Accordingly, Rav Henkin suggests understanding the command לא תהיה קדשה as a prohibition against creating a situation in which a woman may conceive a child who is not halachically related to his father. If so, then undergoing artificial insemination with a non-Jewish man's sperm would transgress this prohibition.

One could easily argue, however, that this is a far-fetched application of the prohibition of קדשה. Stronger evidence is needed to establish that this transgression can be violated without sexual intercourse.

ודבק באשתו

Rav Shmuel Wosner, in his treatment of the topic,[33] boldly asserts that although artificial insemination with donor sperm does not qualify as a sinful intimate act, it is nevertheless forbidden by force of the Torah's earliest description of marriage (*Bereishis* 2:24): על כן יעזב איש את אביו ואת אמו ודבק באשתו והיו לבשר אחד — "Therefore, a man leaves his father and mother and attaches to his wife, and they become one flesh." The Gemara (*Sanhedrin* 58a) cites this verse as the source for the prohibition of adultery as it applies to non-Jews. This verse establishes already from the time of Adam and Chava's creation, before the Torah was given, that a man "clings to his wife," implying that he must avoid physical relationships with the wives of other men.[34] *Tosfos* (*Kiddushin* 13b) comment that although a separate Torah prohibition forbids adultery for Jews, this verse from the time of man's creation is relevant even to us, adding a *mitzvas asei* (affirmative command) to avoid physical unions with other men's wives, alongside the *lo sa'aseh* (prohibition) forbidding adulterous acts.

Rav Wosner claims that the command of ודבק באשתו, unlike the *lo sa'aseh* of adultery, refers to the production of offspring, and not to the act of sexual intimacy. He bases this contention on Rashi's interpretation of this verse in his Torah commentary: הולד נוצר על ידי שניהם ושם נעשה בשרם אחד — "The child is created by them both, and there their flesh becomes one." Accordingly, this

---

33. *Shevet Ha-Levi* 3:175.
34. In the Gemara's words, ודבק באשתו ולא באשת חבירו.

verse introduces a prohibition not against sexual intercourse with another man's wife, but against creating a child with another man's wife. Hence, impregnating a woman with another man's sperm is forbidden, even if no sexual act occurs.

It seems highly questionable, however, whether we can reach such a far-reaching practical halachic conclusion based on this inference from Rashi's Torah commentary.[35]

Other Concerns

Numerous *poskim* forbade the practice of artificial insemination with donor sperm due to the deleterious spiritual effects of conceiving children from members of foreign nations. These *poskim* note the comment of the *Sefer Ha-Chinuch* (560), ואין ספק כי טבע האב צפון בבן — "There is no doubt that the father's nature is embedded within the son." Therefore, in order to preserve our nation's singularity and purity, it is argued, we must not allow creating Jewish children from non-Jewish fathers.

This is the theme of a lengthy and strident letter by the Bobover Rebbe printed in 1964,[36] and it is a point emphasized by Rav Waldenberg in the beginning of his treatment of the topic.[37] Rav Waldenberg emphatically states that halachic arguments are unnecessary to establish the prohibition of such a practice, given its harmful spiritual effects. He writes that he was compelled to present technical halachic reasons for prohibiting artificial insemination with a gentile's sperm only because there were those who permitted the procedure — referring, quite obviously, to Rav Moshe Feinstein.

We must wonder, however, whether these "mystical" concerns suffice to compel a woman to lifelong childlessness. While we would of course ideally prefer producing Jewish children naturally, through the union between a lawfully wedded husband and wife, it seems difficult to understand why, when a woman cannot conceive from her husband, we would deny her the joy and satisfaction of raising children due to mystical concerns that do not appear to have any halachic basis.[38]

---

35. We might also add that Rabbeinu Peretz, as discussed, forbids a married woman to put herself in a situation where her body might absorb another man's sperm only because the child will be mistakenly attributed to her husband. According to Rav Wosner's theory, this should be forbidden also due to the concern of accidentally violating the prohibition of ודבק באשתו.
36. *HaMa'or*, Tishrei, 5725.
37. *Tzitz Eliezer*, vol. 9, p. 251.
38. Rav Henkin (in the essay referenced above, note 31) wrote that if the husband is biologically incapable of producing children, the couple should adopt orphans in lieu of bearing

This consideration is noted by Rav Shlomo Zalman Auerbach at the outset of his discussion of the topic.³⁹ After noting the adverse spiritual effects of conceiving through artificial insemination with a gentile's sperm, Rav Auerbach writes:

אך היות ובשביל רוב הנשים הבאות לשאול על כך והנכונות לפעולה זו ה"ז ממש שאילת חיים, כיון שאי אפשר לעשות ההזרעה מישראל...חושבני דכל זמן שחכמי הדור לא גזרו איסור ברור על כך שומה עלינו לברר מצד ההלכה אם מותר או אסור.

> However, since for most of the women who come to ask about this, and who are prepared to undergo this procedure, this is an actual question about life, as the insemination cannot be done from a Jew…I think that as long as the sages of the generation have not decreed a clear-cut prohibition against it, it behooves us to determine halachically whether this is permissible or forbidden.

Rav Auerbach then proceeds to show that there is no clear halachic prohibition against such a procedure. Nevertheless, his close disciple, Rav Yehoshua Neuwirth, reported that despite this conclusion, Rav Auerbach did not permit artificial insemination as a matter of practice.⁴⁰

Another consideration that has been raised is that of צניעות ("modesty"). The aforementioned *poskim*, as well as others,⁴¹ contended that it is simply inappropriate for a married woman to receive in her body the sperm produced by another man. Even Rav Moshe Feinstein, who permitted artificial insemination in principle, writes that it should generally be discouraged, as it could create tension in the marriage.⁴²

Once again, however, we must ask whether a couple that sincerely wishes to have and raise a child should be denied this opportunity due to this concern. While we can certainly understand discouraging this option if the husband has misgivings about the injection of another man's reproductive material into his wife's body, it is hard to forbid this practice if the husband is fully on board.

Unmarried Women

All of the essays and responsa referenced until now dealt with the situation of a woman married to an infertile husband, who desires to conceive by receiving

---

children. While this solution might be satisfactory to some childless couples, we cannot overlook or discount the natural desire of a woman to produce children of her own.
39. *Minchas Shlomo*, vol. 3, pp. 8–9.
40. Cited in *Nishmas Avraham*, vol. 3, p. 44.
41. See, for example, Rav Yechiel Yaakov Weinberg's responsum referenced above, note 9.
42. שייך שיצא מזה קנאה גדולה לבעלה ולכן אין זה עצה טובה (*Iggeros Moshe*, E.H. 4:32:5).

the sperm of another man. Most of the reasons given for forbidding the practice would apply also to unmarried women seeking to conceive through artificial insemination.[43] As we saw, however, these reasons are either based on tenuous theories, or do not appear to outweigh the legitimate and noble desire of women to bear children. The question then becomes whether Rav Moshe Feinstein's ruling that artificial insemination could, in some circumstances, be an option for a married woman, would apply also to single women who fear that they will not find their soulmate before they become biologically incapable of conceiving.

Rav Shlomo Zalman Auerbach — who, as we saw earlier, ruled that artificial insemination is, in principle, permitted for married women — opposed artificial insemination for unmarried women. As cited in *Nishmas Avraham* (vol. 3, p. 49), Rav Auerbach expressed the concern that as the child grows up and is raised by a mother who had never married, false rumors will spread that he is the product of an illicit union. The halachic basis of this consideration is the ruling of the Rama (E.H. 1:13) that a woman should endeavor to get married in order to avoid suspicions that she engages in illicit relationships. It has been argued that if a woman should not remain unmarried by choice due to the concern of disparaging rumors, then she should certainly not choose to become pregnant without marrying, which would appear even more suspicious.

One could easily argue, however, that this concern would not apply nowadays, when artificial insemination has become a standard reproductive procedure, and when the phenomenon of unmarried women conceiving through this method is becoming increasingly common. When a religiously observant single woman chooses to undergo artificial insemination, and openly speaks about having conceived her child in this manner, it is difficult to imagine anyone seriously raising allegations about sexual misconduct.

Rav Auerbach also raised the concern that since the process of artificial insemination requires a man to ejaculate outside of the context of intercourse, something that *halacha* strictly forbids, conception through this method could result in a spiritual defect in the child.[44] Since this child was created through an inappropriate autoerotic act, he may be spiritually "tainted," and this is therefore a situation that ought to be avoided.

However, as noted by Rav Mordechai Halperin,[45] the consensus among the

---

43. The two exceptions are the theory that the specific prohibition of adultery relates to the introduction of another man's sperm into the body (based on the verse לא תתן שכבתך לזרע) and the concern of creating tension in the marriage.
44. Rav Auerbach's formulation, as cited in *Nishmas Avraham*, is: יש לחשוש שזרע פגום שנולד בעבירה של מוציא שכבת זרע לבטלה, יתכן שיש לזה השפעה גם על הנוצר מזה.
45. In an article published in *Assia*, vol. 20, pp. 113–123, available online at http://www.

poskim permits a man to produce sperm without intercourse for the purpose of reproduction. Therefore, even if we accept the premise that fertilization with sperm ejaculated through a forbidden autoerotic act would result in a spiritual deficiency that overrides the value of producing a child, this is entirely irrelevant in the case of sperm that was produced specifically for the purpose of insemination. Moreover, this assumption itself seems highly questionable. If a woman's choice is either to beget a child with sperm that had already been produced through halachically illegitimate means, or to never have children, there is little reason to assume that Torah law and ethics would encourage her to choose the latter option.

Indeed, Rav Yechiel Yaakov Weinberg, in the aforementioned essay, writes that as long as the sperm is taken from a non-Jewish man, there should seemingly be no halachic barrier to artificial insemination for an unmarried woman. However, Rav Weinberg stopped short of permitting this as a practical matter, emphasizing that his comments were intended only for the purpose of theoretical halachic discussion.[46]

A number of contemporary *poskim* discourage this practice out of practical and societal concerns, such as the difficulties the child will experience as he or she grows up without a father, and the potential long-term consequences of formally authorizing reproduction without marriage.[47] However, while these concerns are certainly valid, it is doubtful whether they suffice to forever deny a woman the joy and privilege of having a child.

כך עונים את המעיקות?

In conclusion, it is worth taking a moment to reflect upon the way our Sages taught us to view the plight of childless women.

The Torah tells of how Rachel expressed to her husband, Yaakov, her anguish over her inability to conceive: הבה לי בנים ואם אין מתה אנכי — "Give me children, and if not, I will die!" (*Bereishis* 30:1). Yaakov responded angrily, rhetorically asking his wife, התחת אלוקים אנכי אשר מנע ממך פרי בטן — "Am I in the place of God, who has withheld from you fruit of the belly?" (30:2).

The Midrash (*Bereishis Rabba* 71:7) sharply criticizes Yaakov for his angry

---

medethics.org.il/website/index.php/he/research/2012-02-29-11-36-06/2012-03-05-10-08-21/101-2012-03-05-10-02-56/1008-2012-03-22-17-04-192.

46. Referenced above, note 9. The essay was later printed in *Seridei Eish* 3:5.
47. See the letters of several leading sages cited by Rav Tzvi Ryzman in *Ratz KaTzvi — Even HaEzer, Poriyus*, pp. 108–111, and the transcriptions of interviews with leading contemporary *poskim* printed below.

response: אמר לו הקב"ה: כך עונים את המעיקות? — "The Almighty said to him [Yaakov]: This is how one responds to women in distress?"

Rachel's cry to Yaakov was, fundamentally, inappropriate, as she appeared to cast upon him the blame for her infertility. Nevertheless, it was wrong for Yaakov for react harshly. What Rachel needed at that time was sensitivity and compassion, not a cold, rational response to her outburst of raw emotion. The inability to bear children naturally causes a woman a great deal of anguish and distress, and we are bidden to show them support and sensitivity.

In our day and age, *Chazal*'s proclamation, כך עונים את המעיקות?, must inform our attitude not only to married women struggling with infertility, but also to the large number of God-fearing women who have been unable to find a suitable marriage partner. As these women grow older, they endure not only the anguish of loneliness and the absence of a soulmate, but also the anguish of childlessness. They deserve our support, encouragement, and assistance.

While sensitivity for מעיקות certainly does not override *halacha*, and there is no justification whatsoever for suspending or overturning clear-cut halachic dictates in order to help a woman conceive, our concern for their plight must certainly be taken into consideration and introduced into the discussion as a significant factor. As the trend towards artificial insemination as an option for unmarried women continues to gain traction, this issue will become an increasingly important one for modern-day *poskim*, who will need to delicately balance the relevant halachic and practical concerns with the natural and noble desire of women to bear and raise children. The sensitivity owed to the מעיקות requires us to seriously consider legitimate grounds for leniency — which, as we have seen, indeed exist — as part of our effort to give all women who so desire the ability to raise Jewish children.

INTERVIEWS

Rav Herschel Schachter
on *Headlines with Dovid Lichtenstein**

Yes, it's permissible, but you're creating a *yasom* (orphan). The child is going to wonder who the father is. The woman feels terrible, she has no family, but now she's going to create a child who is going to be a *yasom*, and the child is going to wonder, maybe the mother had an affair with somebody. It's not at all recommended. The *gedolim* said it's not recommended. I know in Dr.

Abraham's *sefer* about *halacha* and medicine…he says it doesn't make sense that a single girl should have artificial insemination in order to have children. It's not right.

* Broadcast on 2 Shevat, 5777 (January 28, 2017).

Rav Dovid Cohen
on *Headlines with Dovid Lichtenstein**

Unfortunately, as a *rav* who deals with human beings, [I know that]…there are many women who have this situation. I maintain that there is an איסור גמור. It is an act of selfishness, really, to create a *yasom*. Let's forget about other problems. This person, because she does not want to be alone, which is very understandable, is creating an individual [in a condition] that the Torah says is the most pitiful — the widow, the foreigner, and the orphan are really lonely people. The *yasom* is a very lonely person… It's one of the biggest *aveiros* that I can conceive of, and I say it's איסור גמור to do it. This is besides the fact that it borders on ומלאה הארץ זמה — the whole concept of becoming pregnant with the sperm of somebody who is totally unknown. That [concern] can perhaps be handled, because it could be the sperm of an אדם כשר, though you're getting into great debates among the *poskim*.

In any event, I feel it's איסור גמור to do this. The Torah says that a *yasom* is unhappy, and this child is almost guaranteed to be an unhappy child… A *yasom* is a *yasom* is a *yasom*.

* Broadcast on 9 Shevat, 5777 (February 4, 2017).

Rav Mendel Shafran
on *Headlines with Dovid Lichtenstein**

According to *halacha*, בן הפנויה כשר לבא בקהל [the son of an unmarried Jewish woman who was impregnated by a non-Jewish man is allowed to marry into the Jewish nation]. As for whether she should do it or not — it's not simple to do it. He will be the child of a single parent. I don't know if she'll have a lot of *nachas* from him… This is not the way to solve a problem. It will just make bigger problems. She will have to tell the whole city that she had a child like this… And how will she bring up this child? The child is going to have a lot of problems…

* Broadcast on 9 Shevat, 5777 (February 4, 2017).

Dr. David Pelcovitz
on *Headlines with Dovid Lichtenstein**

There is a series of studies that were done in London that looked at single mothers by choice — most of whom got married later in life, who could not find the right person, women who would have loved to get married but just couldn't find anybody. These are women in their late 30s and early 40s who decided to conceive by donor insemination. The researchers compared a group of these women and their children with a group of women who were married and conceived by donor insemination because of medical reasons. They looked at it in an interesting way — the quality of the mother-child relationship, and how the kid does.

In every study done that I've seen, both here and in *Eretz Yisrael* — though these are not large-scale studies, around 50 or 60 people in each comparison group — the kids of single mothers seemed for the most part to be doing just as well, if not better, than the others. For example, when they compared in London those who are single mothers by choice and their children, with kids of regular marriages conceived by donor insemination, they found no differences in parenting quality, or in the kids' adjustment. The reason is because of everything we know about the problems in cases of single mothers. These are largely due to the fact that children of divorce are at risk for obvious reasons — because they were exposed to conflict, and there are often financial problems afterward. Here [with single women having children through donor insemination], you don't have it. Here's a kid who is very much loved, who is, in many cases, brought into the world by a more mature mother. Most of these mothers are financially able to care for their child, are settled, and the child is incredibly loved.

Of course, I certainly understand what the various *poskim* are saying. It makes a lot of sense — how can you bring a child into the world who is not going to have a father actively involved? But when you look at it more empirically... it seems there is no obvious kind of difference in any findings. Everything they have found thus far has been positive.

However, here's the problem: This hasn't been going on long enough for us to have permanent answers. Right now, the studies are of kids who are, let's say, six years old. We don't know what it's going to look like when these kids are fifteen years old and much more aware of who they are and the differences between them and kids who have fathers actively involved. But in terms of main measures, there is a wonderful relationship between the kid and his or her mother, and there tends to be great functioning all around, in any way they could measure it.

When a child grew up with a father and then lost the father — that's the *yasom*. Here, we're dealing with a child who never knew anything else. There's no loss of any kind. They're born to a mother who wanted them more than anything in the world. They are born to a mother who, in the studies, is as psychologically healthy as any other women. The reason they are single has nothing at all to do with psychological health. It's a whole different psychological process.

The reality is that we don't know. As these kids get older, and many of them will know how they came into this world — because the tendency of women in these situations is to share the story of how the children came into being — we don't know how this will look as their kids become old enough to be self-aware and aware of how they are alike and different. But in the short term — the first five or six years of life — I am not aware of any studies that show anything other than significant evidence of good functioning in every area that has been looked at.

* Broadcast on 9 Shevat, 5777 (February 4, 2017).

Nepal's Organ Trail: How Traffickers Steal Kidneys

July 15, 2015
Sugam Pokharel

Kathmandu, Nepal (CNN)

On the streets of Kathmandu, the sight of people begging for kidney treatment has become common.

The capital of Nepal is no different from many places in the world where aging populations, poor diets and no health insurance systems mean increased organ disease.

The organ in highest demand is the kidney and black market traffickers are meeting that demand. Up to 7,000 kidneys are obtained illegally every year, according to a report by Global Financial Integrity.

Organ trafficking is an illegal, yet thriving trade around the globe.

That same report shows the illegal organ trade generates profits between $514 million to $1 billion a year...

Two brothers who were duped by kidney traffickers show their scars

Nepal's 'kidney bank'

We traveled to Kavre, a tiny district close to Kathmandu, and what activists and authorities say is a ground zero for the black market organ trade in Nepal.

Here, kidney trafficking rackets — well organized and well funded — dupe the poor and uneducated into giving away a piece of themselves.

The district has developed an unfortunate reputation as the "kidney bank of Nepal."

For more than 20 years, activists say, people from villages in Kavre have been the primary source of kidneys for sick and desperate patients throughout Nepal. But now the numbers are being tracked.

In the last five years more than 300 people have been reported to be victims of kidney traffickers in this district alone, according to Forum for Protection of People's

Rights, a Kathmandu-based non-profit human rights organization. Some activists say the number is much higher.

"Social stigma and threats from traffickers keep many victims from coming forward," said Rajendra Ghimire, a human rights lawyer, and director of Forum for Protection of People's Rights.

'The meat will grow back'

Nawaraj Pariyar is one of the many victims of kidney traffickers.

Like many in Kavre, Pariyar makes a living from selling cattle milk and doing seasonal labor jobs on nearby farms. Poor and uneducated, all he has is two cows, a house and a tiny plot of land.

Pariyar used to visit Kathmandu to find construction work. He was on a site in 2000 when the foreman approached him with a dubious offer: if he let doctors cut out a "hunk of meat" from his body, he would be given 30 lakhs — about $30,000. What he wasn't told: the piece of "meat" was actually his kidney.

"The foreman told me that the meat will grow back," Pariyar said.

"Then I thought, 'If the meat will regrow again, and I get about $30,000, why not?'"

"What if I die?" Pariyar remembers asking the foreman.

The foreman assured Pariyar that nothing would happen. He was given good food and clothes, and was even taken to see a movie.

Then he was escorted to a hospital in Chennai, a southern state of India. Traffickers assigned a fake name to Pariyar and told the hospital he was a relative of the recipient. The traffickers, Pariyar says, had all the fake documents ready to prove his false identity.

"At the hospital, the doctor asked me if the recipient was my sister. I was told by the traffickers to say yes. So I did," Pariyar said.

"I heard them repeatedly saying 'kidney'. But I had no idea what 'kidney' meant. I only knew Mirgaula (the Nepali term for kidney.)

"Since I didn't know the local language, I couldn't understand any conversation between the trafficker and the hospital staff."

Pariyar was discharged and sent home with about 20,000 Nepali rupees — less than one percent of the agreed amount — and a promise he would have the rest shortly.

He never received any more money and never found the trafficker.

"After I came back to Nepal, I had a doubt. So, I went to the doctor. That's when I found out I am missing a kidney," Pariyar said.

Pariyar is now sick and getting worse by the day. He has a urinary problem and constant severe back pain.

But he cannot afford a trip to the doctor and is afraid he will die. "If I die I can only hope for the government to take care of my two children. I don't know if I will die today or tomorrow. I'm just counting my days," Pariyar said.

Pariyar's experience is one of many similar stories we heard in Kavre.

Understanding the economic situation in this district is the key to understanding why so many people here easily fall prey to kidney traffickers.

There are hardly any other economic opportunities other than subsistence farming and rearing livestock. One bad harvest or a big medical bill can easily ruin families.

"The main reason is poverty and lack of awareness. It is very easy for the traffickers to brainwash the villagers. Also, the villages in Kavre are close to the capital and are easily accessible," Ghimire said...

The attention to this problem is growing in Kavre. Kidney trafficking stories are making headlines on the local and national newspapers.

But for victims like Pariyar and others, the media attention is too late.

Copyright © edition.cnn.com

Why is it Forbidden to Steal a Kidney?

The crime of organ trafficking has a storied history — including both truth and fiction. Already in 1994, the organization Human Rights Watch published a report confirming allegations that the Chinese government killed political dissidents for the purpose of harvesting their organs for the benefit of patients in need of transplants. Since then, urban legends have abounded of nefarious conspiracies to steal organs. In 1997, for example, rumors circulated that a crime gang in New Orleans was planning to drug visitors to the city's annual Mardi Gras festivities in order to steal their kidneys — a rumor that had no basis in reality. However, while many of the stories that have made their rounds were discovered to be hoaxes, credible investigative reports have been published drawing attention to the unfortunate phenomenon of illicit organ trafficking. In 2012, the British newspaper *The Guardian* reported that worldwide, an organ is sold illegally every hour.[1] More recently, in the summer of 2015, CNN featured on its webpage an investigative report about organ trafficking in Nepal, with fraudsters luring desperate, illiterate peasants into agreeing to have a kidney removed for a handsome amount of money, only a small fraction of which is actually paid.[2]

Law of Necessity

While we intuitively and rightly react to such schemes with revulsion and contempt, the question arises, from a technical, halachic viewpoint, as to why illegal organ trafficking would be forbidden. A fundamental halachic principle establishes that the concern for saving a human life overrides virtually all Torah precepts, the only exceptions being the prohibitions of idolatry, murder and sexual immorality. Seemingly, then, prohibitions such as theft, inflicting bodily harm and other criminal activities should be waived when this is needed for a life-saving purpose. It would thus stand to reason, at first glance, that when a kidney patient's life is at stake, strict ethical violations such as theft, fraud and even unwanted organ removal would be allowed. Clearly, however, the prospect of taking advantage of the needy by promising them money for a kidney, not

---

1. "Illegal Kidney Trade Booms as New Organ is 'Sold Every Hour,'" *The Guardian*, May 27, 2012.
2. See media article above.

to mention forcefully removing a kidney, as a halachically-sanctioned means of saving a life seems morally unthinkable.

This tension between legal flexibility under dire circumstances and the need to maintain law and order parallels the unresolved question regarding the "law of necessity," which exempts or exculpates offenders who committed crimes due to an emergency situation. A classic case would be a driver exceeding the speed limit or driving through a red light to bring a patient to the emergency room. New York State, for example, states that an action which would normally constitute a criminal offense is considered legally justifiable if "such conduct is necessary as an emergency measure to avoid an imminent public or private injury which is about to occur by reason of a situation occasioned or developed through no fault of the actor, and which is of such gravity that, according to ordinary standards of intelligence and morality, the desirability and urgency of avoiding such injury clearly outweigh the desirability of avoiding the injury sought to be prevented by the statute defining the offense in issue."

Interestingly, the law of necessity was not always recognized in English law as a legitimate legal defense. In 1975, Lord Alfred Denning ruled that a driver of a fire engine would be punishable for running through a red light even if he saw a man by a window in a burning house down the block crying desperately for help. Four years earlier, Lord Denning rejected the law of necessity as a defense for people who desperately needed housing and entered empty homes owned by the local authority. He explained, "...if hunger was once allowed to be an excuse for stealing, it would open a door through which all kinds of lawlessness and disorder would pass... If homelessness were once admitted as a defense to trespass, no one's house could be safe. Necessity would open a door which no man could shut. It would not only be those in extreme need who would enter. There would be others who would imagine that they were in need, or would invent a need, so as to gain entry."

Halacha, of course, recognizes the law of necessity and thus permits Torah violations for the purpose of saving lives. Far less clear, however, is how *halacha* balances this intuitively just legal provision with the need to avoid "lawlessness and disorder." In other words, what are the limits on the degree of "lawlessness" permitted in situations of mortal danger? Which crimes would be allowed for the purpose of saving a life, and which crimes must be avoided even at the expense of human life?

Destroying Property to Save One's Life

The Gemara in *Maseches Bava Kama* (60b) addresses this question in the context of the story told of King David, who was threatened by Philistine soldiers hiding in a barley field. David posed the question of whether it was permissible to set the field ablaze in order to protect himself, and the answer was given that this was allowed only because of his royal authority, which permits blazing a trail when necessary. Ordinarily, however, אסור להציל עצמו בממון חבירו — it is forbidden for a person to save himself by destroying somebody else's property.

Rashi, as many *Acharonim* noted,[3] appears to follow the straightforward reading of the Gemara, according to which *halacha* requires one to surrender his life rather than destroy property that belongs to another person. Rashi writes, איכא איסורא לאיניש בעלמא — it is prohibited for people other than kings to destroy property for a life-saving purpose.

Tosfos and the Rosh, however, explain the Gemara differently, claiming that it is unquestionably permissible to cause somebody a financial loss for a life-saving purpose, and the Gemara speaks only of the requirement to compensate the property owner afterward. According to this view, as the *Tosfos Ha-Rosh* explains, the question posed by King David was whether he was permitted to set the field ablaze without any intention to repay the owner, or whether he needed to commit to repay. He was certain that *halacha* allowed him to destroy the field, but he wondered whether he needed to destroy the property with the intention of fully compensating the owner. This view of *Tosfos* and the Rosh is supported by the parallel account in the Talmud Yerushalmi (*Sanhedrin* 2:5), which states explicitly that King David's question related only to the responsibility to compensate the owner for the damage.[4]

The *Tur* (C.M. 359) follows the position of his father, the Rosh, and writes that one may seize another person's property in order to save his life, and the *Shulchan Aruch* (C.M. 359:4) rules accordingly.

Interestingly, Rav Moshe Feinstein, in *Iggeros Moshe* (Y.D. 1:214) dismisses the conventional understanding of Rashi's view, according to which seizing or destroying another's property is forbidden even for a life-saving purpose. Rav Moshe insists that such a position is untenable, in light of the universally accepted axiom permitting all Torah violations for the sake of preserving human life, except for only the three cardinal sins of murder, idolatry and sexual immorality. In Rav Moshe's view, Rashi understood that the ambushed Philistines posed only a very slight risk to King David's life, and thus it would have been forbidden to destroy the field if not for the special privileges granted to kings. Alternatively, Rav Moshe suggests, King David perhaps trusted with full confidence that God would save him, and thus it was not vitally necessary to burn

---

3. See Rav Yehuda Rosanes, *Parshas Derachim*, 19; Rav Yaakov Ettlinger, *Binyan Tziyon*, 167.
4. פשיטא ליה לאביד וליתן דמים.

down the field. If so, the Gemara's discussion relates to King David's unique circumstances, and does not establish any kind of precedent that can inform normative halachic practice.

Likewise, Rav Asher Weiss (*Minchas Asher, Vayikra*, 50) outright rejected the possibility that *halacha* would forbid theft or property damage for the sake of saving one's life. He contended that according to Rashi's understanding, King David had other options available for averting the threat posed by the Philistines, such as stationing guards around the site or erecting a makeshift fence. The question he posed was whether or not he was required to pursue those other options, just as *halacha* requires avoiding Torah violations to whatever extent possible in situations of life-threatening danger. One might have thought that utilizing somebody's property to save a life does not constitute formal, halachic "theft" at all, and thus it would be allowed even when one has other options. The conclusion, however, was that theft resembles other Torah prohibitions in this regard, and must be avoided even in situations of life-threatening danger unless one sees no other options for rescuing his life.

Surrendering One's Life to Avoid Theft

The precise opposite view is taken by Rav Yaakov Ettlinger, in a series of responsa published in his *Binyan Tziyon* (1:167–171). Rav Ettlinger discusses Rashi's view at length, and insists that the straightforward reading of the Gemara supports the position that the concern for human life does not override the prohibition against theft. He proceeds to demonstrate on the basis of other Talmudic passages that this issue is subject to a debate among the *Tannaim*. One such source is the story told in *Maseches Yoma* (83b) of Rabbi Yehuda, who forcefully seized food from a shepherd when he desperately needed food due to a dire medical condition. Rabbi Yossi, who had accompanied Rabbi Yehuda during this incident, expressed disapproval of Rabbi Yehuda's action. Rav Ettlinger understands from this account that the question of whether the concern for human life permits theft is subject to a debate between Rabbi Yehuda and Rabbi Yossi. Rashi followed Rabbi Yossi's stringent ruling, Rav Ettlinger suggests, because the Gemara elsewhere (*Eiruvin* 46b) establishes that *halacha* sides with Rabbi Yossi in his debates with Rabbi Yehuda.

Rav Ettlinger goes even further, qualifying the lenient ruling of the *Shulchan Aruch*. He notes that the *Shulchan Aruch* permits stealing or destroying property to save one's life only if he intends to compensate the property's owner:

אפילו הוא בסכנת מות וצריך לגזול את חבירו כדי להציל נפשו, צריך שלא יקחנו אלא על דעת לשלם.

> Even if one is in mortal danger and must steal from his fellow in order to save his life, he must take it only with the intent to repay.

The implication is that if one has no intention to repay, or if he knows that he will be unable to repay, then he must surrender his life to avoid stealing or damaging property. Rav Ettlinger thus asserts that *Tosfos* and the Rosh fundamentally agree with Rashi, that one may not steal to save a life. However, they maintain that if one seizes or destroys property with the intention of repaying, the temporary loss of property does not qualify as "theft" that overrides the concern for human life, and it is thus permissible.

On the basis of this inference, Rav Ettlinger ruled that it is forbidden to perform an autopsy for a life-saving purpose, such as to study the effects of a fatal illness on a deceased patient's body in order to determine how to effectively treat another patient stricken with the same illness. Since one cannot ever "repay" a deceased person for the dishonor of opening his corpse, this is forbidden even at the expense of human life.

Rav Ettlinger's ruling gives rise to the question of why theft or property damage differs from other Torah violations which are overridden by the concern for human life. If we routinely permit patients, caregivers, ambulance drivers and physicians to violate Shabbos — a prohibition that ordinarily constitutes a capital offense — why would we tell a patient that he must die rather than steal medication?

Rav Ettlinger himself addresses this question (in *siman* 171), and explains that God relieves us of our duties to Him for the sake of saving a life, but not of our elementary responsibilities to our fellow man. One of the sources establishing the rule of פקוח נפש, which allows violating the Torah to save a life, is the verse in *Sefer Vayikra* (18:5), ושמרתם את חקותי ואת משפטי אשר יעשה אותם האדם וחי בהם — "You shall observe My statutes and My laws which a person shall perform and live by them." The Gemara (*Yoma* 85b) famously comments that the purpose of God's laws is that וחי בהם — we should live, and not lose our lives. Rav Ettlinger notes, however, that this rule is said only in regard to חוקותי ואת משפטי — "**My** statutes and **My** laws" — our obligations to the Almighty, but not our obligations to other people. These laws are not subject to the condition of וחי בהם, and must be observed even at the risk of one's life.

A different approach is taken by Rav Shlomo Kluger, in *Ha-Elef Lecha Shlomo* (Y.D. 200), where he considers the possibility that theft is forbidden even for the sake of saving a life (though he leaves this issue unresolved). Rav Kluger notes a different reason mentioned by the Gemara for the rule of פקוח נפש, namely, the rationale of חלל עליו שבת אחת כדי שישמור שבתות הרבה — "Desecrate one Shabbos on his behalf so he can observe many Shabbosos." God prefers that the

Torah's laws be temporarily suspended, and His honor thereby compromised, so that the endangered individual can be saved and thereby continue living, performing *mitzvos*, and bringing honor to the Almighty. But when it comes to interpersonal offenses, it does not help the victim that the endangered person survives and continues living a life of Torah devotion. For the Almighty, it is worth compromising His honor for a brief period for the benefit, so-to-speak, of a lifetime of religious observance, but for people, there is no such calculus. Therefore, interpersonal offenses that cannot be reversed through monetary compensation are not allowed even for the sake of preserving life.

Rav Ettlinger also alludes to a different explanation. In his first responsum on the subject (167), he addresses a question posed by many writers, regarding the source of the requirement to surrender one's life to avoid murder. The Gemara (*Yoma* 82b) cites Rava's famous axiom, מאי חזית דדמא דידך סומק טפי — "Why do you think that your blood is redder?" The reason why murder is forbidden even at the expense of one's life, Rava explains, is because nobody can ever assume that his life is more valuable than any other person's life. Seemingly, the need for such a rationale to forbid murder to preserve one's life proves that other interpersonal offenses are suspended for the sake of human life. After all, if even theft is forbidden for life-saving purposes, then clearly this is true of murder, as well. Rava's remark seems to suggest that murder is unique, as all other interpersonal offenses, like virtually all Torah laws, are suspended when human life is at risk. Rav Ettlinger responds, יש לומר דרבא קושטא קאמר, דהא הוי נפש חבירו. This seems to mean that Rava's remark regarding murder in truth applies even to theft. A person's material assets are part of his "soul," in that they sustain his life. Seizing somebody's property is, to some degree, akin to taking part of his "life," and thus the rationale of מאי חזית דדמא דידך סומק טפי establishes that both murder and theft are forbidden even in the face of life-threatening danger.[5] (Rav Ettlinger also offers a second answer, suggesting that Rava's rationale is necessary to establish that one may not volunteer to surrender his life for the sake of rescuing his fellow. The principle of מאי חזית דדמא דידך סומק טפי expresses that one may not kill to save his life even if the other fellow is prepared to be killed for this purpose.[6])

---

5. The Maharsham (5:54) advances this theory in presenting the view that although one may steal to save his life, especially pious people are entitled to surrender their lives to avoid theft. He writes that stealing is a degree of "murder," in that it diminishes from the victim's sustenance, and thus the rule of פקוח נפש does not apply to theft just as it does not apply to murder.

6. We might also suggest a different answer to this question, distinguishing between cases where one's life is endangered by another person, who forces him to commit a transgression at the threat of death, and cases where one needs to commit a violation to save himself from an illness or some similar situation. When a person commits a violation

Numerous other *poskim*, however, disagree with this ruling. As mentioned earlier, Rav Moshe Feinstein and Rav Asher Weiss claimed that even Rashi accepts the view permitting seizing another person's property to save one's life. Likewise, the Maharsham (5:54) rules explicitly that a person dying of starvation may steal food even though he will be unable to repay the owner.[7] This is also the position taken by Rav Yehuda Ayash, in his *Beis Yehuda* (Y.D. 47). The Maharsham explains that when the *Shulchan Aruch* forbids seizing somebody's property for a life-saving purpose without the intention of repaying, it refers only to one who has the means of repaying afterward but from the outset refuses to do so. If, however, one is in a situation where he needs to steal to save his life and does not have the means of repaying, he is allowed to steal, in direct contradistinction to Rav Ettlinger's position.[8]

---

    under coercion, we can legally divorce the action from the individual, such that the offense is not attributable to him at all. He is not merely exempt from culpability, but rather altogether dissociated from the act. (The basis for such a theory is the Rambam's famous ruling in *Hilchos Yesodei Ha-Torah* 5:4 that one who violates one of the three cardinal sins due to religious coercion is not liable to punishment, despite the fact that he was obligated to surrender his life to avoid the transgression. This contrasts with the Rambam's ruling in *Hilchos Yesodei Ha-Torah* 5:6, where the Rambam rules that one is liable to punishment if he violated one of the three cardinal sins in order to heal himself.) Therefore, one might have considered permitting murder when it is performed under duress, since such an act does not legally constitute a formal act of murder. The rationale of מאי חזית instructs that killing must be avoided even in situations of coercion, given our inability to consider one person's life more valuable that another person's. For this reason, Rava found it necessary to resort to the argument of מאי חזית, as one might have otherwise assumed that a person being forced to kill by an oppressor would be allowed to kill to save his life.

7. However, as mentioned in note 5, the Maharsham allows surrendering one's life to avoid theft as a measure of special piety.
8. It is worth reflecting on the broader implications of this discussion. The fact that a recognized halachic authority ruled as a matter of practical *halacha* that one may not commit an interpersonal offense even for the sake of saving his life underscores the primary importance that Judaism accords to the Torah's code of interpersonal conduct, which exceeds that of other fundamental components of Jewish life such as Shabbos and *kashrus*. The all-too-common phenomenon of ostensibly observant Jews who meticulously follow ritualistic *halacha* but allow themselves to lie, cheat, steal, gossip and offend people is unfortunate not only because of the defamation it causes to the Jewish people and the Jewish faith, but also because it reflects a grotesquely distorted perception of how God wants us to live. Our interpersonal obligations form the basis and foundation upon which our ritual obligations rest, and thus, according to one view, compromising ethics and integrity is no less severe a breach than idolatry, as it undermines the core essence of the Jewish religion.

Inflicting Bodily Harm to Save a Life

Both these positions give rise to difficult questions. According to the view of the Maharsham, that *halacha* allows stealing for the sake of saving a life, we must ask whether this would apply also to inflicting bodily harm. It hardly seems plausible, for example, that if the only eligible kidney donor for a certain patient refuses to donate his kidney, the patient (or anybody else) is permitted to drug the person and remove the kidney against his will. Even if this could be done in a manner that guarantees no danger to his life, we would intuitively recoil at such a possibility. Indeed, while there is some discussion among the *poskim* as to whether one is required to subject himself to bodily harm for the sake of saving another person's life,[9] it seems clear that one may not cause another person bodily harm against his will to save a life. The question, then, arises, if the principle of פקוח נפש applies to interpersonal offenses, then why would we not allow inflicting non-life-threatening bodily harm to save a life? While we certainly understand that one may not endanger somebody's life to save another person's life, why would it not be permissible to inflict physical harm that does not endanger the victim's life when this is necessary to save another person? Seemingly, this intuitive law is acceptable only if we accept Rav Ettlinger's premise that one may steal for a life-saving purpose only if he is able and willing to repay. Bodily harm can never be fully compensated, and so understandably, according to Rav Ettlinger, one may not save his life by physically injuring another person. According to the other *poskim*, however, this intuition seems difficult to defend.

On the other hand, Rav Ettlinger's position also appears to suffer from a significant flaw, one which is reflected in a comment made by a different scholar, some five centuries earlier. The Rashba, in one of his responsa (4:17), advances a simple logical argument to prove the permissibility of stealing to save one's life. If a dehydrated desert traveler on the brink of death suddenly meets another traveler with water to spare, the second traveler would be halachically required to share his water with the first to save his life, as mandated by the Torah prohibition of לא תעמוד על דם רעך — "Do not stand idly by your fellow's blood" (*Vayikra* 19:16). As the Gemara (*Sanhedrin* 73a) notes, this verse introduces the obligation to rescue one's fellow from life-threatening danger, an obligation which applies even when this entails financial sacrifice. In light of this obligation, one would certainly be required to share his water with somebody dying of dehydration. In fact, according to the view of Ben Petura — which is not accepted as *halacha* — even if one has only enough water to sustain his own life, he must share his small remaining portion of water with his fellow traveler (*Bava Metzia* 62a).

---

9. For a summary of the various opinions, see *Nishmas Avraham*, vol. 2, pp. 112–113.

It is inconceivable, the Rashba contends, that one would be required to share his water with a dying wayfarer, but if that dying wayfarer sees somebody's water and the owner is not present, he would be forbidden from taking it. The dehydrated traveler is not stealing water at all; rather, he takes that which the Torah commands his fellow to give him. How could this possibly be forbidden?

We might sharpen the Rashba's argument in light of the Gemara's discussion in *Maseches Kiddushin* (8b) concerning the possibility of effecting *kiddushin* (betrothal) by saving a woman's life. The case addressed by the Gemara is where a dangerous dog runs after a woman, and a man throws food at the dog to rescue her. The question becomes whether the man could betroth the woman with the value of the favor he performs at that moment. The Gemara dismisses this possibility, noting, "She can say to him: 'You are obligated by the Torah to save me!'" In other words, this method of betrothal is ineffective because the man gives the woman something she already deserved by force of Torah law. As the man was in a position to feed the dog and thereby rescue the woman, Torah law required doing so, despite the financial expense entailed. The money and effort he expended was already hers, in a sense, and thus he did not give her anything of value for the purpose of betrothal. The Gemara's ruling would certainly suggest that life-saving assistance is something that is owed to an endangered individual by somebody capable of helping him. As such, as the Rashba argued, it seems difficult to imagine that the individual would be forbidden from seizing the means of assistance on his own accord.

This anomaly noted by the Rashba seems to be a fatal flaw in Rav Ettlinger's position. In his view, a pauper dying of starvation may not steal food if he would be unable to repay — even though the person from whom he wishes to steal is obligated by Torah law to feed him.

We might therefore suggest a third, more nuanced, position.[10] Namely, Rav Ettlinger is fundamentally correct, that interpersonal offenses are not overridden by the concern for human life, and the Maharsham is also correct that it is permissible for one to steal to save his life. The reason one may take another person's property to save his life — even if he will be unable to repay — is because that other person bears the obligation to save him and even to spend money for this purpose. This law is based not upon the principle of פקוח נפש, which suspends Torah law for the sake of preserving human life, but rather upon the command of לא תעמוד על דם רעך, which requires helping people in danger when one is in a position to do so.[11]

---

10. The basic thrust of the theory developed here is based upon Rav Shmuel Rozovsky's analysis in *Zichron Shmuel*, 83.
11. This approach is taken by the Ra'avad (cited in *Shita Mekubetzes, Bava Kama* 117b). He

On this basis, we can explain the intuitive distinction between financial and physical harm. While the Gemara explicitly requires spending money when necessary to rescue somebody from danger, it is questionable whether one must endure physical harm for the sake of rescuing his fellow. As briefly noted earlier, this issue is subject to debate. The consensus, however, appears to follow the view of the Radbaz, who wrote a responsum (3:627) expressing the view that *halacha* does not require subjecting oneself to physical harm to save another person's life. He writes that although one may not violate Shabbos to avoid physical danger that is not life threatening, one is not required to knowingly place himself in such danger for the sake of saving somebody from death. The Radbaz gives several reasons for his ruling, primarily the fact that causing oneself physical harm can, in many instances, expose him to some degree of life-threatening risk. Additionally, he writes:

דכתיב דרכיה דרכי נועם, וצריך שמשפטי תורתינו יהיו מסכימים אל השכל והסברא. ואיך יעלה על דעתנו שיניח אדם לסמא את עינו או לחתוך את ידו או רגלו כדי שלא ימיתו את חבירו?

It is written (*Mishlei* 3:17), "Its ways are ways of pleasantness" — and the Torah's laws must be agreeable to intellect and logic. How can we imagine that a person should allow his eye to be blinded, or his arm or leg to be severed, so that his fellow not be killed?

The Radbaz asserts that our intuitive sense of morality and logic precludes the possibility of a requirement to cause oneself physical harm — even harm that does not threaten his life — for the sake of saving another person. (He concedes, however, that one may expose himself to such harm as a measure of exceptional piety.)

Accordingly, it would seem, whereas *halacha* would allow theft for the sake of saving one's life, it would be forbidden to cause another person bodily harm even for a life-saving purpose. Since we are not required to sacrifice our physical wellbeing for the sake of rescuing a fellow Jew, an endangered individual is not entitled to rescue himself by physically injuring another person.

---

writes that one is allowed to save himself by seizing another person's property because of the other person's obligation to rescue him, and for this reason, one may seize the property only once the other person is aware of the life-threatening situation. The Ra'avad argues that the obligation to rescue a person in danger takes effect only when one learns of the person's situation, and thus one may save himself with another person's property only if that other person knows of his predicament and thus bears the obligation to rescue him.

How Much May One Steal?

This perspective, viewing the right to steal property to save one's life as a product of the owner's obligation to rescue the other person, would, presumably, affect the question of how much an endangered person is entitled to steal. Let us imagine a case of a gravely ill patient who cannot afford to pay for the medical procedure he needs to cure his fatal disease, and who happens to work in a bank. Armed with a key to the vaults and the codes of all the various alarms, he could easily steal the valuables of any of the bank's clients without getting caught. Would it be permissible for him to steal a customer's assets, leaving that customer broke and financially ruined?

In light of what we have seen, this would depend on a difficult question with which many *poskim* have grappled: how much money is one obligated to spend for the sake of saving a fellow Jew's life? Is a person required to part with all his assets and subject himself to poverty for the sake of rescuing a fellow Jew from danger? Or is there some limit to the extent of our financial responsibility to help those facing life-threatening situations?[12]

The basic rule that applies regarding expenditures for *mitzvos* is that one must spend up to one-fifth of his assets for the sake of fulfilling a *mitzvas asei* (affirmative Biblical command), and to spend all the money he has to avoid transgressing a *mitzvas lo sa'aseh* (Biblical prohibition). This rule is explicitly codified by the *Shulchan Aruch* (O.C. 656:1), and noted as well by the Rama (Y.D. 157:1). Accordingly, at first glance, one should be required to sacrifice all his possessions for the sake of saving somebody in danger, in order to avoid transgressing the prohibition of לא תעמוד על דם רעך.

Several *poskim*,[13] however, dispute this conclusion, arguing that a *mitzvas lo sa'aseh* which requires performing an action, as opposed to avoiding an action, is treated as a *mitzvas asei* in this regard. Meaning, if the Torah formulates an affirmative command as a prohibition, then this command is classified as a *mitzvas asei*, and thus requires an expenditure of no more than one-fifth of one's assets. As the command of לא תעמוד על דם רעך is observed through action, by intervening to rescue one's fellow, it falls under the category of *mitzvos asei* with respect to the issue of maximum expenditure. Hence, according to this view, one does not need to spend more than one-fifth of his assets to rescue a person in danger.

---

12. This question is addressed at length in the first volume of *Headlines* (pp. 24–28), in the context of our discussion of the halachic considerations applicable to the rationing of healthcare. We present here just a brief overview of the sources relevant to this question.
13. See *Pischei Teshuva*, Y.D. 157:4, 357:1.

This question has not been conclusively resolved, as several different opinions exist among the later *poskim*. The *Chafetz Chayim*, in *Ahavas Chesed* (vol. 2, 20:2), ruled that one must spend all his money for the sake of saving a life, drawing proof from the famous rule of חייך קודמין לחיי חברך — "your life takes precedence over your fellow's life" (*Bava Metzia* 62a). This rabbinic adage suggests that one is not required to sacrifice his life to save another person, but every other sacrifice — including sacrificing all his property — is required for this purpose. This position was also taken by Rav Yisrael Salanter, in *Even Yisrael* (*Derush* 4, p. 16). By contrast, it is told that Rav Yosef Shalom Elyashiv ruled that the *mitzva* of saving people from danger does not require spending more than one-fifth of one's assets.[14]

Rav Shlomo Zalman Auerbach, in his *Minchas Shlomo* (vol. 2, 7:4), draws an important distinction in this regard between different situations of mortal danger. He suggests that when a person is the only one capable of rescuing somebody, then he must spend everything he has to save the endangered individual. For example, if kidnappers threaten to kill their hostage if a certain person does not immediately hand over all his savings, he must comply, despite the financial ruin he will endure. In most cases, however, such as when an ill patient cannot afford a desperately-needed procedure, no single individual can be viewed as the sole prospective savior. Under such circumstances, Rav Shlomo Zalman asserts, the obligation falls upon the Jewish community collectively, and each person must contribute in accordance with his financial situation and ability to assist.

Accordingly, it would seem that when only one particular person is capable of rescuing somebody in danger, one may steal all of that person's assets if this is necessary to help the endangered individual. If, however, somebody simply needs a sum of money to rescue his life, he would not be entitled to steal at all, since no single individual bears the obligation to save him.

Conclusion

Let us now turn our attention to several specific examples of life-threatening situations, and try to determine which crimes would be allowed under these different circumstances in light of what we have seen:

- A patient facing immediate danger who urgently requires food or medication may steal what he needs, provided that he does not thereby endanger somebody else. For example, an asthma patient suffering an attack and has no money with him would be permitted, if he has no alternative, to steal

---

14. *Avnei Zikaron*, p. 286.

an inhaler from a nearby store, as the store's owner is in a unique position to rescue the patient's life and therefore bears the obligation to do so. The patient would not be allowed to steal another patient's inhaler, unless he can immediately return it, as this would pose a risk to that other patient who might need the inhaler at any moment.

- A patient in need of a large sum of money for a life-saving medical procedure may not steal money to pay for the procedure. Since no individual person bears the obligation to single-handedly rescue the patient, the patient is not entitled to take money from any given person.
- One may not inflict physical harm to rescue his own life, as the generally accepted view is that one is not required to endure bodily harm to save another person. As such, it would be forbidden to secretly remove an organ from somebody's body, no matter how urgently a patient requires a transplant, and even if it can be ascertained that the other person's life will not be endangered by the loss of that organ.
- Stealing organs from an organ bank is forbidden because one thereby endangers the lives of other patients in need of transplants, given the limited supply of harvested organs. When there is a limited supply of blood for transfusions, it would likewise be forbidden to steal blood from a blood bank.
- Rav Yitzchak Zilberstein (*Shiurei Torah Le-Rof'im*, 2:129) addressed the question of whether a surgeon may secretly take blood while performing surgery on a patient whose blood type matched that of a different patient in desperate need of a life-saving transfusion. The case involved a patient who was undergoing surgery and had refused to give blood to save a fellow patient despite the doctor's assurances that donating blood posed no health risk whatsoever. Rav Zilberstein ruled that the surgeon may secretly take the patient's blood, as long as the patient had been informed that a different patient needed his blood to survive.[15] It appears that taking a person's blood — assuming, of course, that this poses no risk at all of any sort of physical harm — is akin to stealing money, as opposed to causing physical injury, since the body's blood supply replenishes itself and thus the loss of blood has no effect at all on the person's body. As such, it is permissible to "steal" blood from a patient during surgery. However, one would not be allowed to forcefully inject a needle into a person's body to take blood for a life-saving purpose, as he thereby creates a wound in the body which the person would otherwise not have to suffer.
- Falsely promising large sums of money to a needy person in exchange

---

15. This condition is based on the view of the Ra'avad referenced above, note 12.

for his organ, even when it is desperately needed to save a dying patient, would certainly be forbidden. Since the pauper agreed to donate his organ only for the stipulated sum, taking the organ without the intention of paying constitutes theft, and stealing a part of a person's body to save a life is not permitted, because, as we have seen, one bears no obligation to compromise his physical wellbeing to save a life.

- If armed traffickers force a physician to remove an organ from a coerced donor, he must surrender his life to avoid performing the procedure, as one is not allowed to inflict bodily harm on another person in order to save his life.

Is Orthodoxy Unhealthy?

August 1, 2015
by Rabbi Reuven Spolter

About a decade ago, a short time after I arrived in Oak Park, Michigan, I visited a doctor for a checkup. I already knew the drill. He'd come in, examine me, draw blood and adjust my medications based on the results. The examination began, and everything was going well — until the doctor started talking.

"If you don't lose weight, in ten years you'll have type-2 diabetes."

Then the doctor, a secular Jew, added, "You Orthodox eat too much."

"Why's he picking on us?" I thought.

But upon further reflection, I realized that he was right. Consider a typical Shabbat. Friday night begins with a big meal: wine, challah, appetizer, soup, main course and dessert. Then we might attend a *Shalom Zachar*: some beer, a couple pieces of cake. Drag yourself home and conk out. We wake up on Shabbat morning with a piece of cake and cup of coffee before *davening*. (For now, I'll ignore the halachic issues of eating before *davening*.) After *davening*, we head for the *kiddush*, a mainstay at shuls looking to attract and retain members. At best, we sample a few pieces of cake and some chips. At worst, we've loaded up on cholent, kugel, maybe some herring — without a doubt a full meal on any other day of the week. And then we head home and do what? Eat another meal-and a large one at that. Again with wine, challah, maybe some chicken, cholent, cold cuts, and dessert. After *minchah-seudah shelishit*. At most shuls this is a simple affair, but it's still a meal; maybe a roll, some tuna fish, and a piece of now stale cake left over from the *kiddush*. Often we were not even hungry for *seudah shelishit*, but it's a social thing; everyone's eating, and hey, it's a mitzvah! And whether we call it a *melaveh malkah* or not, what's Saturday night without a slice of pizza (or two or three), a movie, some popcorn too, perhaps?

Orthodoxy, of course, does not demand overeating and unhealthy living. Yet, especially in America, the Orthodox lifestyle has led many into a dangerous cycle of overeating and indulgence.

A rabbi I know once lost a great deal of weight. When I asked him how he did it, he said simply, "I decided that at *simchas* I was only going to eat one meal, either at the *shmorg* or at the sit-down dinner." Think about it: How many functions do we attend at which we eat more than one meal? How many Bar Mitzvahs, school dinners, weddings?

I started thinking about our unhealthy lifestyle after reading a recent issue of *Jewish Action* that featured an article about the challenges of eating healthfully at a *kiddush* (Shira Isenberg, "A Kiddush Conundrum," [winter, 2010]). Soon after reading it, I received, via e-mail, a number of photos of a *frum* wedding. The people in the photographs were total strangers. Yet, looking at them, I was struck by the fact that they were all overweight — significantly so.

I remember when the *frum* community of Oak Park waged a battle to open a kosher Dunkin' Donuts in the area (for reasons I cannot fathom, the parent company was giving the franchise a hard time about going kosher). After the battle had been won and the store opened, I got a call from a local columnist. When he asked me how I felt about the victory I said, "I'm not sure that we've struck a blow for the waistlines of Orthodox Jews, but it's a great win for our community. I only hope we can bring the same energy to more important issues down the road."

I call upon Jewish organizations to undertake a study of the collective health of Orthodox people. I worry about the long-term health of Orthodox Jews, especially in America. I fear an epidemic of heart disease, diabetes, and of course, unnecessary deaths resulting from complications of obesity.

Our community rightly protects the value of life. We'll fight for the right to cling to every last second of life, devoted to the notion that every moment is precious and holy. And yet, at the very same time, under the banner of *frumkeit*, we've adopted a lifestyle that's literally going to cut years and perhaps decades from our lives.

Copyright © ou.org

Maintaining Good Health as a Halachic Imperative

The consistent, well-documented rise in obesity rates in the United States and throughout the Western world has not skipped over the Orthodox Jewish community, as a casual glance at waistlines in a typical synagogue will show. In fact, there are some indications that Orthodox Jews are even more likely to be dangerously overweight. Already in 2011, Israel's Ministry of Health issued a report stating that obesity rates were seven times higher among the country's ultra-Orthodox population than among secular Israelis. The report cast the blame on the prominent place occupied by food in religious observance, as well as the tendency among ultra-Orthodox Jews not to engage in serious physical activity.[1]

In light of the well-known risks associated with overeating and obesity — most notably, type-2 diabetes and heart disease — the widespread unhealthful habits in the Orthodox Jewish world, such as overeating and lack of physical activity, are troubling. *Halacha* very clearly and emphatically requires us to avoid activities and habits that endanger our physical wellbeing, and to implement reasonable measures to ensure our personal safety and health. This essay will present just a small sampling of the halachic literature on this critically important topic, and show the severity with which *halacha* approaches the religious imperative to care for one's physical wellbeing, in the hope of spurring discussion and generating greater awareness of this *mitzva*.

ונשמרתם מאד לנפשותיכם

Numerous *poskim* famously cite as the source of this obligation the verse in *Sefer Devarim* (4:15), ונשמרתם מאד לנפשותיכם. For example, the *Peri Megadim* (O.C. 328:6) writes that a seriously ill patient may not refuse to take his medication, due to the command of ונשמרתם מאד לנפשותיכם. It should be noted that the Rambam (*Hilchos Rotzeiach* 11:4) and the *Shulchan Aruch* (C.M. 427:8) cite as the source of this requirement an earlier verse from that same chapter in *Devarim* (verse 9): רק השמר לך ושמור נפשך מאד. The Gemara in *Maseches Berachos* (32b) cites both

---

1. The findings were reported by Ynet on September 1, 2011.

verses in the context of the obligation to care for one's physical wellbeing and to avoid danger.

The *Chasam Sofer*, in one of his responsa (Y.D. 241), indicates that this requirement constitutes an outright Biblical obligation and that the entire institution of נזיקין — liability for damage caused to people — was established as a safeguard to the obligation of ונשמרתם. By imposing financial liability for damage, the *Chasam Sofer* explains, the Torah incentivizes responsible and safe conduct. It therefore appears that at least in the *Chasam Sofer*'s view, maintaining one's physical wellbeing constitutes a Torah obligation.[2]

The *Levush* (116:1), by contrast, writes that this requirement was enacted by *Chazal*, and the Biblical source was noted merely as an אסמכתא (an allusion in the Biblical text to a law enacted later).[3]

Regardless, the halachic obligation to refrain from dangerous activities is codified in the conclusion of the *Choshen Mishpat* section of the *Shulchan Aruch*. After noting the example of drinking unprocessed water without first inspecting it for insects, the *Shulchan Aruch* writes:

> כל העובר על דברים אלו וכיוצא בהם ואומר הריני מסכן בעצמי, ומה לאחרים עלי בכך, או איני מקפיד בכך, מכין אותו מכת מרדות, והנזהר מהם עליו תבא ברכת טוב.
>
> Whoever violates these and similar matters, saying, "I will endanger myself — why does anyone else's opinion about this matter to me?" or "I am not careful about this," he should be given lashes for his betrayal. And one who is careful in this regard — a blessing of goodness shall come upon him.

Elsewhere (O.C. 613:5), the *Shulchan Aruch* rules that walking through מים רודפים — a gushing river — is forbidden due to the danger entailed, even if the water does not extend any higher than one's waist. The contemporary application of this ruling would be going into the water at a beach where no lifeguard is present.

Another vitally important contemporary application of the requirement to avoid danger is road safety. In a published collection of Rav Yosef Shalom Elyashiv's letters (*Kisvuni Le-Doros*, p. 315), a letter appears bearing his and other leading sages' signatures,[4] lamenting the sore lack of awareness of this halachic imperative and urging greater caution in this area:

---

2. The *Chasam Sofer* here mentions not only ונשמרתם, but also the prohibition of לא תעמוד על דם רעך — ignoring the life-threatening danger facing others (*Vayikra* 19:16) — and לא תשים דמים בביתיך — having hazardous items in one's possession (*Devarim* 22:8).
3. See Rav Asher Weiss, *Minchas Asher, Devarim* 7:1.
4. The other rabbis who signed the letter were Rav Simcha Kook, Rav Shmuel Eliezer Stern, and Rav Naftali Nussbaum, who were members of the ועדת הרבנים לזהירות ובטיחות בדרכים

הנה חובת שמירת הגוף והנפש היא מהחובות הגדולים שהאדם מחויב בהם בחובה גמורה על פי דין תורתנו הקדושה, וכן אמרו חז"ל חמירא סכנתא מאיסורא. לדאבוננו ישנו רפיון נורא בעניין הזה גם בקרב מחננו וגם בני התורה הזהירים בדקדוק ההלכה מתרשלים בחובת הזהירות בדרכים ונכנסים לסכנה או לספק סכנה הי"ו ובחלקו הגדול מחוסר ידיעה וחינוך לדבר זה בפרט רבה העזובה בקרב ילדי ובני נוער אשר מחוסר חינוך מספיק לחומרת הדבר וגודל החובה להישמר לנפשותם לפעמים מסכנים עצמם בסכנת נפשות ממש וכמה וכמה אסונות נגרמו בעקבות כך... ויהי רצון שבזכות ההתעוררות בציבור להיזהר ולהישמר כדין נזכה כולנו להישמר ולהינצל מכל פגע...

The obligation to protect one's body and life is among the great obligations to which a person is bound as an outright requirement according to the law of the sacred Torah. Indeed, our Sages said, "Matters of danger are stricter than matters of prohibition." To our dismay, there is grave disregard of this matter even among our camp, and even Torah students, who are careful about halachic details, are negligent with regard to road safety and enter situations of danger or possible danger — may Hashem guard and protect them! This is mostly due to a lack of knowledge and education about this matter. The problem is especially pronounced among children and youth, who, due to a lack of adequate education about the severity of this matter and the great obligation to guard their lives, sometimes place themselves in real life-threatening danger. Numerous tragedies have been caused as a result... May it be His will that in the merit of the awakening of the public to exercise care and caution as required, we will all earn protection and safety from all harm...

The sources cited thus far have all dealt with the obligation to avoid hazardous activities and situations. The Rambam, in a famous passage in *Hilchos Dei'os* (4:1), speaks of the need to also lead a healthy lifestyle by accustoming oneself to habits that promote health and avoiding habits that threaten one's wellbeing:

הואיל והיות הגוף בריא ושלם מדרכי השם הוא שהרי אי אפשר שיבין או ידע דבר מידיעת הבורא והוא חולה לפיכך צריך להרחיק אדם עצמו מדברים המאבדין את הגוף ולהנהיג עצמו בדברים המבריין והמחלימים.

Since having a healthy, complete body is among the ways of God, as it is impossible to understand or know anything about the Creator if one

---

— "The Rabbinic Council for Road Caution and Safety." Before appending his signature, Rav Elyashiv wrote, ב' ברכות לב עי' ,לנפשותיכם מאד ונשמרתם לקיים אחד כל על — referencing the Gemara's interpretation of the command לנפשותיכם מאד ונשמרתם as an obligation to care for one's personal safety.

is ill — a person must therefore distance himself from things that harm the body and accustom himself to things that strengthen [the body] and maintain health.

The Rambam proceeds to delineate numerous measures that ought to be taken, and those which should be avoided, in order to maintain good health, based on the medical knowledge of his time.

Similarly, the *Shulchan Aruch* (Y.D. 116) sets forth laws forbidding the consumption of potentially hazardous foods. He begins with the prohibition of מים מגולין — drinking water that was left exposed and may have thus been contaminated by a snake's venom. (The *Shulchan Aruch* then adds that this law does not apply in societies in which snakes are uncommon.) In the next passage, the *Shulchan Aruch* codifies the prohibition against eating meat together with fish, which was thought to cause leprosy. Later (116:4), the *Shulchan Aruch* warns against ingesting human perspiration, which was considered toxic. He also forbids placing in one's mouth objects that may be infected by germs, as well as consuming foods or beverages that had been kept under a bed overnight, as such foods were believed to be contaminated (116:5).

It clearly emerges from the *Shulchan Aruch*'s rulings that one may not ingest foods or beverages that are deemed harmful to one's health. Presumably, then, the *Shulchan Aruch* would forbid nowadays the regular consumption of foods and drinks deemed harmful by the mainstream medical community, such as those with high sugar and salt content, excessive quantities of carbohydrates, or foods with high levels of fat and cholesterol. If *halacha* forbids the consumption of meat with fish due to the belief that it could potentially cause leprosy, then it would certainly forbid excessive consumption of sugar, or overeating in general, which today's medical experts have universally and unequivocally deemed dangerous.

חמירא סכנתא מאיסורא

The Gemara in *Maseches Chullin* (9a-10a) establishes the famous rule of חמירא סכנתא מאיסורא — *halacha* treats matters of physical danger with greater stringency than it treats matters of ritual law. The practical implication of this rule is that although *halacha* allows relying on statistical probability in matters pertaining general ritual prohibitions (*issurim*), with respect to physical harm, even small risks of physical danger must be avoided.

The Gemara there discusses a case in which a kosher animal was slaughtered, whereupon a beast of prey took the slaughtered animal's intestines. When the intestines were retrieved, they contained perforations. If these perforations were caused by the beast that preyed on the slaughtered carcass, then the animal would be kosher, but if the perforations were present before the slaughtering, then the animal would be a טריפה (stricken with a terminal illness), and its meat may not be consumed. The Gemara rules that one may rely on the statistical probability that the perforations were caused by the beast, and had not been present before שחיטה. However, the Gemara rules differently in the case of a fruit that was pecked at by a bird, and in which one later saw holes. Although the holes were most likely caused by the bird's pecking, the fruit may not be eaten, given the remote possibility that the hole resulted from the bite of a snake whose venom may now be present in the fruit. The Gemara explains that when the issue at stake is a possible violation of the Torah's dietary code, one may rely on the statistical probability that the food is kosher. When, however, the concern is one of physical safety, then a heightened level of caution is required. Even though the holes in the fruit are most likely benign, *halacha* forbids consumption of the fruit because of the minute risk that the holes signify the presence of venom.

The Gemara proceeds to note the aforementioned example of מים מגולין — the prohibition against drinking water that had been left exposed overnight, which may have been contaminated by a poisonous snake. This prohibition applies even to cases of ספק מים מגולין, where it is uncertain whether the water had been left uncovered. In parallel cases involving ritual laws, the Gemara observes, we would certainly allow relying on the statistical probability that the water is permissible. However, since the concern pertains to physical danger, we are required to avoid water if there is any doubt regarding its safety.

Accordingly, the Rama (C.M. 116:5) rules, יש לחוש יותר לספק סכנה מלספק איסור — one must be stricter in situations of uncertainty involving danger than in situations of uncertainty involving ritual prohibitions.

What is the rationale underlying this distinction between סכנתא and איסורא? Why does *halacha* require us to avoid even slight possibilities of risk to our physical wellbeing, while allowing us to rely on statistical probability with regard to ritual prohibitions?

The answer to this question appears, albeit somewhat ambiguously, in the comments of the *Chasam Sofer* (*Chiddushim* on *Chullin*):

> החילוק קל להבין – באיסורא אפי' יזדמן לו ממיעוט טריפות אין לו עון אשר חטא דכתורה עשה לסמוך על הרוב, ומי שהזהיר על הטריפה הוא התיר לסמוך על רובא, משא"כ בסכנת נפשות אם יזדמן לו מהמיעוט ויסתכן א"א להשיב נפש, ופשוט.

The distinction is easy to understand: With regard to prohibitions, even if he ends up with the minority, which is non-kosher, he is not guilty of any violation, for he acted appropriately by relying on the majority, and the One who forbade טריפה allowed him to rely on the majority. By contrast, when it comes to risk to life, if he ends up with the minority and endangers himself, his life cannot be retrieved. This is obvious.[5]

The *Chasam Sofer* explains that God Himself, who introduced the Torah's prohibitions, stipulated that one need not avoid slight risks of violation in certain situations of uncertainty. The loss of human life, however, is permanent, and so God indeed expects us to exercise great caution to maintain our physical wellbeing. The Torah forbade certain activities, but also allowed performing those very activities in certain doubtful situations. When it comes to maintaining our physical wellbeing, however, not only is suicide forbidden, but, given the high value the Torah assigns to human life, it mandates exercising special caution to protect it even in situations that entail only a slight risk of harm.[6]

The Status of "Mystical" Dangers

Several *poskim* distinguish between two different types of hazards: activities that are scientifically established as dangerous, and those which are considered harmful due solely to mystical theories and beliefs. This distinction was proposed by Rav Meir Eisenstadter (*Imrei Eish* Y.D. 60) in response to a question posed by a man who was considering selecting as a match for his daughter someone whose name was the same as his. Rabbeinu Yehuda Ha-Chasid, in his famous *tzava'a*, or ethical will (#23), warned that a girl's marriage to a man with the same name as her father could pose danger. This man was therefore wary of such a match, despite the fact that the young man was otherwise a perfectly suitable mate for his daughter. Although the *Noda Be-Yehuda* (*Mahadura Tinyana*, E.H. 79) claimed that Rabbeinu Yehuda Ha-Chasid issued these warnings only to his descendants, the man wrote to Rav Eisenstadter that he has heard that his family descends from Rabbeinu Yehuda Ha-Chasid. Therefore, in light of the rule of חמירא סכנתא מאיסורא, he felt that perhaps he should not pursue this match.

In his response, Rav Eisenstadter dismisses the factor of חמירא סכנתא מאיסורא, claiming that this principle applies only with respect to natural dangers. The dangers of which Rabbeinu Yehuda Ha-Chasid warned are mystical by nature, and not grounded in natural science. When it comes to mystical risks, Rav Eisenstadter writes, we need not be concerned in situations of uncertainty, as

---

5. See also the *Chasam Sofer*'s comments in *Maseches Avoda Zara* (30a).
6. We should also note the comments of Rav Moshe Rivkis in *Be'er Ha-Gola* (end of *Choshen Mishpat*): המסכן את עצמו כאלו מואס ברצון בוראו ואינו רוצה לא בעבודתו ולא במתן שכרו ואין לך זלזול אפיקורתא יותר מזה — one who endangers himself demonstrates a disregard for the life given to him by God in order for him to serve his Creator and thereby earn reward.

we are in situations of potential natural danger. Rav Eisenstadter conceded, however, that he had no source supporting this distinction.

Rav Amram Blum (*Beis She'arim*, Y.D. 196) suggests proving this theory from a passage in the Rambam's commentary to the Mishna (*Yoma* 83a), where he writes that a gravely ill patient may not eat on Yom Kippur food to which people ascribe mystical healing powers. The Rambam asserts that eating on Yom Kippur is permitted only if the food will naturally sustain the person so that he can survive, but not if it is considered therapeutic only according to mystical teaching, because such remedies are not scientifically verified and their benefit is therefore questionable.[7] Therefore, if a seriously ill patient's only remedy on Yom Kippur is eating food that is perceived to have mystical healing powers, the patient may not eat that food.[8] Rav Blum reasons that if the Rambam discounts the effectiveness of mystical remedies and does not permit violating Yom Kippur to employ an allegedly life-saving mystical remedy even when one is already in a state of danger, he would certainly not require one to avoid an action that would potentially be harmful according to mystical belief. These comments seem to support Rav Eisenstadter's hypothesis that the rule of חמירא סכנתא מאיסורא does not apply to mystical dangers.[9]

Rav David Sperber (*Afarkasta De-Anya* 1:169) draws proof from elsewhere in the Rambam's writings: a responsum (*Pe'er Ha-Dor* 146) regarding the status of a קטלנית — a woman who was twice widowed. *Chazal* appear to forbid marrying such a woman, but the Rambam insists that this was intended as a suggestion for those concerned about the possibility that the woman possesses some dangerous mystical powers. The Rambam thus ridiculed those who questioned whether the obligation of יבום (marrying one's deceased brother's wife if the brother had no children) applies if the widow is a קטלנית. Clearly, according to the Rambam, one may be lenient with regard to potential mystical dangers in situations of uncertainty, as such dangers need not be taken so seriously to begin with.[10]

---

7. The Rambam's formulation is כי כוחם חלוש, אינו מצד הדעת ונסיונו רחוק.
8. Below, we will show that others disputed this position of the Rambam concerning mystical remedies.
9. We should note, however, that one could distinguish between actively taking mystical remedial measures on Yom Kippur, which the Rambam maintains is not permitted, and knowingly performing an action mystically associated with dangers, which even he might forbid. As such, the Rambam's comments regarding the situation of an ill patient on Yom Kippur do not necessarily prove that one may run the risk of violating Rabbeinu Yehuda Ha-Chasid's warnings in situations of uncertainty. (See also next note.)
10. In truth, however, it seems very difficult to prove from the Rambam's comments that Rabbeinu Yehuda Ha-Chasid's warnings need not be observed in situations of uncertainty. The Rambam denied, or at least doubted, the veracity of mystical, non-scientific

Similarly, Rav Sperber elsewhere (3:264) cites the comments of Rav Avraham David of Buchach, in his *Mili De-Chasidusa* commentary to Rabbeinu Yehuda Ha-Chasid's *tzava'a*, who writes that one may be lenient in regard to Rabbeinu Yehuda Ha-Chasid's warnings if there is any kind of question or doubt.[11]

Numerous other *poskim* also follow this view that one may disregard mystical dangers in situations of uncertainty.[12]

Others, however, disagree. Rav Eliezer Deutsch (*Chelkas Ha-Sadeh* 25) cites the comments of the Chida (*Birkei Yosef*, Y.D. 339:8) regarding the practice to discard water that was drawn from a well in the vicinity of a deceased person. This practice is codified by the *Shulchan Aruch* (Y.D. 339:5), and one of the reasons given (as noted by the *Shach*) is that the Angel of Death places a drop of the deceased's blood in this water, and drinking it is thus considered dangerous. The Chida raises the question of whether this custom applies even to water drawn in the vicinity of a deceased gentile, and he concludes that there is no conclusive answer. One should therefore discard this water, because חמירא סכנתא מאיסורא. This clearly indicates that in his view, mystical dangers are no different from natural danger with respect to the rule of חמירא סכנתא מאיסורא even in doubtful situations.

The Chida here is consistent with the view he expresses elsewhere in *Birkei Yosef* (O.C. 301:6). The case under discussion is writing an amulet on Shabbos to cure a patient who had ingested poison. The Chida rules that it is permissible to violate Shabbos in order to save a gravely ill patient through a mystical remedy. In direct contrast to the Rambam, who, as we saw, forbade breaking the Yom Kippur fast for the sake of utilizing a mystical life-saving cure, the Chida permits Shabbos desecration to save someone's life through a mystical remedy. The Chida clearly accepted the position that mystical medical guidelines and procedures are halachically equivalent to natural ones, and thus, Shabbos may be violated for a life-saving mystical procedure just as it may be violated to save a person's life through natural means. By the same token, according to the Chida,

---

safety measures and precautions altogether, and he would not have afforded any legitimacy to Rabbeinu Yehuda Ha-Chasid's warnings to begin with. Those who accept the validity of Rabbeinu Yehuda Ha-Chasid's warnings clearly do not accept the Rambam's rejection of mystical theories, and so the Rambam's views on the subject are of no practical relevance in determining the extent to which these warnings must be heeded.

11. See על ידי אמתלא כל דהוא מקילין ואין חשש עוד בכך, והלכה כדברי כל המקיל בכך ואינו סגנון קבוע היזיקא. See also *Even Yekara*, E.H. 15; *Kenesses Yaakov*, p. 121.

12. Rav Shlomo Kluger, *Tuv Ta'am Va-Da'as*, *Mahadura Telisa'a* 2:198; Rav Menachem Mendel Schneersohn, *Tzemach Tzedek*, E.H. 27:6; Rav Schneur Zalman Fradkin, *Toras Chesed*, E.H. 5:5; Rav Shimon Greenfeld, *Shu"t Maharshag* 2:240.

one must exercise as much caution to avoid mystical risks as one must to avoid dangers posed by natural forces.

Similarly, Rav Chaim Palagi (*Ruach Chayim*, E.H. 62:15) writes that one must heed Rabbeinu Yehuda Ha-Chasid's warnings even in cases of uncertainty, given that they involve risks of danger. Rav Palagi rules that this applies even in situations of ספק ספיקא — where there are two different uncertainties involved. Since the person's physical wellbeing is at stake, he must avoid even a slight possibility of risk.[13] A contemporary *posek*, Rav Yaakov Chaim Sofer, follows this view in his *Borchi Nafshi* (pp. 136–147), citing many authorities who require avoiding mystical dangers even in situations of uncertainty.

In concluding this section, we should note the significance of the fact that such a debate exists. Several *poskim* discount the effectiveness of mystically-based safety and health measures. Certainly, then, it would be wholly irrational to turn the tables and treat mystical risks with greater severity and concern than natural risks. Hence, if we are careful — as we should be — not to eat meat with fish and to eat them with separate utensils, due to the belief that eating them together can cause leprosy, we cannot be any less strict when it comes to the scientifically confirmed risks of an unhealthful diet. It is simply inconsistent to regularly consume hamburgers, French fries, and soda while making sure to keep the burger separate from fish! Our strict compliance with the guidelines of contemporary health professionals is as halachically mandated as complying with the *Shulchan Aruch*'s warning against eating meat with fish, and perhaps even more so.

Endangering Oneself for a *Mitzva*

Some have argued that indulging on Shabbos and Yom Tov is acceptable, and perhaps even to be encouraged, given the *mitzva* to enjoy oneself through food and drink on these occasions. Even if a person's cardiologist warns against excessive consumption of red meat and fried foods, for example, he might

---

13. Rav Shlomo Kluger issues a similar ruling in his *Ha-Elef Lecha Shlomo* (E.H. 46) regarding the situation of a קטלנית. Even in a case in which a woman's קטלנית status hinges on two uncertainties, he writes, one should not marry her, given the risk entailed. This ruling, at first glance, appears to contradict Rav Kluger's position expressed elsewhere (see above, n. 12) that the rule of חמירא סכנתא מאיסורא does not apply to the custom to discard water drawn near a deceased person, as the risk of danger is mystical by nature. The likely explanation is that Rav Kluger viewed marriage to a קטלנית as posing natural, rather than mystical, danger, as the deaths of her previous husbands may likely testify to an illness that she transmits to her mates. This theory was, in fact, suggested by Rav Sperber (*Afarkasta De-Anya* 3:263).

nevertheless insist on enjoying hefty portions of *cholent* and fried chicken at his synagogue's *kiddush*, at the Shabbos table, or at his grandson's bar-mitzva, since he is, after all, fulfilling a *mitzva*. Assuming the food poses no immediate, life-threatening risk, and the concern relates to the potential adverse long-term effects of these foods, is such an argument valid?

A similar question is raised by Rav Yom Tov Lipman Halperin (*Oneg Yom Tov* 41), who addresses the case of someone for whom eating *matza* poses danger, but who insists on eating *matza* despite the risk entailed. Rav Halperin cites Rashi's comment in *Maseches Yevamos* (64b) that if someone circumcises an infant on Shabbos who is exempt from the *bris mila* obligation, he is guilty of Shabbos desecration. The case under discussion pertains to an infant whose two older brothers had died after being circumcised and is thus presumed to suffer from hemophilia, and hence exempt from *bris mila*. Since there is no *mitzva* to circumcise this child due to a health concern, this circumcision does not justify Shabbos desecration. Rav Halperin applies this principle to other *mitzvos* as well, concluding that whenever one is absolved of a *mitzva* due to the risk it poses to his physical wellbeing, there is no value whatsoever in performing the *mitzva*. He receives no credit for the *mitzva*; he actually violates *halacha* by unnecessarily exposing himself to danger.

Rav Moshe Sternbuch cites Rav Halperin's comments in his *Teshuvos Ve-Hanhagos* (2:241) and suggests a distinction between different levels of risk. In the case of a child whose two older brothers died as a result of *bris mila*, the child can be presumed to be genetically incapable of surviving a circumcision. Therefore, given the high risk, there is no *mitzva* whatsoever to circumcise this infant. However, in situations in which doctors warn a patient that eating *matza* or drinking wine poses a small risk of danger, it is possible that one fulfills a *mitzva* if he partakes of the *matza* or wine against the doctor's advice. Rav Sternbuch asserts that under such circumstances, where the *mitzva* entails just a small risk of danger, people of spiritual stature may apply the principle, שומר מצוה לא ידע דבר רע — "He who observes a command will know no evil" (*Koheles* 8:5). Indeed, Rav Sternbuch observes, there are accounts of great *tzaddikim* who exposed themselves to a degree of danger for the sake of performing *mitzvos*.

Rav Sternbuch refers to the comments of the *Tiferes Yisrael* commentary to the Mishna (*Berachos* 1:3) allowing one to expose himself to a small degree of risk for the sake of a *mitzva*. The *Tiferes Yisrael* notes the precedent of Rabbi Akiva, who risked his life while he was in prison to fulfill the *mitzva* of *netilas yadayim* (*Eiruvin* 21b). Thus, as long as the level of danger is low, one may expose himself to such risk for the sake of fulfilling a *mitzva*.

Nevertheless, Rav Sternbuch concludes that it is preferable for a person not to fulfill a *mitzva* under such circumstances, when it poses a small risk, as such allowances are reserved for spiritual giants like Rabbi Akiva.[14]

Of course, this would depend on the level of risk involved. Rav Yitzchak Zilberstein (*Chashukei Chemed*, *Yoma* 84b) addresses the question of whether one should travel on dangerous roads in Israel for the sake of a *mitzva*. He mentions the example of a doctor who is asked to come and treat a patient or a *mohel* who is asked to perform a *bris* in communities in the West Bank when the roads to these areas are being targeted by terrorist sniper fire. Rav Zilberstein concludes that if these roads are safely traveled by thousands of motorists every day, and shootings take place on very rare occasions, one should not refuse to perform the *mitzva* due to the danger involved. As long as the risk of danger is very slight, one should be prepared to expose himself to such a risk for the sake of a *mitzva*.

Returning to the question concerning eating heartily on Shabbos and Yom Tov despite health concerns, the *halacha* would likely depend on the level of risk involved. If occasionally breaking one's diet does not pose any significant health risk, then it would seem perfectly acceptable to indulge for the sake of enhancing one's Shabbos and Yom Tov observance. If, however, the doctor warns that even occasional indulgence can be harmful, the *mitzva* of enjoying Shabbos and Yom Tov would not be legitimate grounds for risking one's health.

---

14. The *Menoras Ha-Maor* (3:18) writes that an especially pious person who is exceedingly meticulous with regard a particular *mitzva* may perform that *mitzva* even in situations of grave danger, and rely on God's protection. Rav Yitzchak Zilberstein cites this source in his *Chashukei Chemed* (*Sukka* 23a) amidst his discussion of the story told of Rav Chaim Yaakov Rotenberg, who erected a makeshift *sukka* in a Nazi labor camp during the Holocaust in order to fulfill the *mitzva* of *sukka*, despite the obvious danger involved. Rav Zilberstein suggests that either Rav Rotenberg felt that he would not likely be discovered in the short time it took him to build the *sukka*, eat a portion of bread, and dismantle the *sukka*, or he relied upon this view of the *Menoras Ha-Maor*. He also raises the possibility of making an exception during שעת השמד — periods of religious persecution against Jews, when it would be deemed admirable to risk one's life for the sake of fulfilling *mitzvos*.

Doctor Contracts Ebola in Sierra Leone, Will be Flown to Nebraska for Treatment

November 13, 2014

A surgeon from Sierra Leone and a permanent resident of the United States who contracted Ebola while working in West Africa will be flown to the United States to receive treatment for the deadly virus, according to a government official.

Dr. Martin Salia is expected to arrive in the United States on Saturday and will receive treatment at Nebraska Medical Center, the official told ABC News.

It is unclear how he contracted Ebola, but the official said he was in Sierra Leone at the time.

A hospital spokesman would only say that he would soon be evaluated for possible treatment. He would not give any other details.

In a statement, Jen Psaki, a spokeswoman for the State Department, said they were working "in consultation with the Centers for Disease Control and Prevention" and were "in touch with the family of a U.S. legal permanent resident working in Sierra Leone who has contracted Ebola.

Dr. Craig Spencer is seen in this undated LinkedIn profile photo.

"His wife, who resides in Maryland, has asked the State Department to investigate whether he is well enough to be transported back to the University of Nebraska Medical Center for treatment," the statement added.

This comes two days after Dr. Craig Spencer, who contracted Ebola treating patients in West Africa, was discharged from a New York City hospital Ebola-free. Spencer, 33, who treated Ebola patients in Guinea for Doctors Without Borders, spent 20 days in isolation at Bellevue Hospital in Manhattan after testing positive for Ebola there on Oct. 23.

Spencer was the fourth person to be diagnosed with Ebola in the United States and the ninth Ebola patient to be treated in this country. Only Thomas Eric Duncan, the Liberian national who was diagnosed in Dallas, Texas, in late September, has died of the virus in the United States.

More than 5,000 people have died in the Ebola outbreak that is ravaging parts of West Africa, the World Health Organization reported on Wednesday.

This is the largest Ebola outbreak ever recorded — the vast majority in the West African countries of Liberia, Guinea and Sierra Leone.

Copyright © abcnews.go.com

Ebola: May a Doctor Endanger Himself by Treating Patients?

The 2014 Ebola outbreak in West Africa was the largest such epidemic in history, with over 28,000 cases of the disease reported and over 11,000 deaths confirmed, mainly in Guinea, Liberia, and Sierra Leone. The Ebola virus causes internal and external hemorrhaging, resulting in the death of an estimated 50% of patients. It is very contagious, transmitted through virtually all bodily fluids, including saliva, sweat, urine, vomit, and blood. As bleeding and vomiting are common symptoms of the disease, it can spread rapidly. There is currently no vaccine to immunize against the Ebola virus, or specific medication to cure patients. However, Ebola mortality rates can be significantly reduced through intensive treatment of the symptoms and rehydration therapy to compensate for lost fluids.

Several humanitarian organizations, such as Doctors Without Borders, sent healthcare professionals to West Africa to treat patients and help curb the spread of the deadly disease. Unfortunately, several professionals contracted the disease over the course of their work. New York resident Dr. Craig Spencer, a physician at New York Presbyterian Hospital who worked in Guinea as part of Doctors Without Borders, returned to the United States on October 17, 2014. Several days later, on October 23, he was rushed to Bellevue Hospital Center after developing a high fever. After testing positive for Ebola, he was placed in isolation. Thankfully, Dr. Spencer was discharged from the hospital twenty days later, on November 11, with a clean bill of health.

The humanitarian disaster wrought by the Ebola epidemic, and the sense of duty felt by many in the international healthcare community who wanted to help, raises the difficult question of whether one should expose himself to risk for the sake of saving lives. Treating Ebola patients was an urgent necessity both for the patients and for the world at large, which could have otherwise faced an international epidemic. Thus, the professionals who endangered themselves for the sake of treating patients were, rightfully, hailed as courageous heroes. From a halachic standpoint, however, the question arises as to whether one is permitted to put his life at risk in order to save others. Would it have been permissible for a physician to travel to West Africa to treat patients, or would it have been forbidden for him to risk his life for this purpose?

השמר לך ושמור נפשך מאד

The prohibition against exposing oneself to danger is explicitly codified by the Rambam in *Hilchos Rotzei'ach* (11:4), where he writes that one is required to remove all life-threatening hazards from his property and protect himself from them:

כל מכשול שיש בו סכנת נפשות מצות עשה להסירו ולהשמר ממנו ולהזהר בדבר יפה יפה...

> Any hazard that poses a risk to life — there is an affirmative command to eliminate it, to protect oneself from it, and to exercise extreme care with regard to it...

The Rambam writes that one who has in his possession something dangerous violates the command of השמר לך ושמור נפשך מאד — "Guard yourself, and protect your life vigilantly" (*Devarim* 4:9) — as well as the prohibition of ולא תשים דמים בביתך — "Do not place bloodguilt upon your home" (*Devarim* 22:8). The source for this interpretation of the first of these verses as referring to protecting oneself from harm is a story told by the Gemara in *Maseches Berachos* (32b) about a certain pious man who refused to interrupt his prayer to respond to the greeting of a government official. The official questioned the man's refusal to return his greeting, as he thereby endangered his life, in violation of השמר לך ושמור נפשך מאד.

In the next paragraph (11:5), the Rambam writes that "the Sages forbade" various kinds of dangerous activities. The Rambam proceeds to list such activities, including drinking water that may have been contaminated with toxins. Later (12:6), the Rambam lists other forbidden dangerous activities, such as walking on an unstable bridge or next to an unstable wall. Both passages are cited by the *Shulchan Aruch* (C.M. 427:8–9).

Several *Acharonim* noted the apparent contradiction in the Rambam's comments, as he cites a Biblical source for this prohibition, while also establishing that "the Sages forbade" engaging in dangerous activities, suggesting that this prohibition applies only on the level of Rabbinic enactment, as opposed to Torah law.[1] The *Be'er Ha-Gola* (C.M. 427:70) suggests that this prohibition is in fact Rabbinic in origin; the verse cited by the Gemara — and the Rambam — was intended merely as an אסמכתא (an allusion in the Biblical text to a law enacted later by *Chazal*). By contrast, Rav Alexander Sender Shor (*Tevuos Shor* 13) writes that the prohibition against engaging in dangerous activities clearly applies on the level of Torah law, as evidenced by the common Rabbinic dictum חמירא סכנתא מאיסורא — matters of safety and health are treated more seriously than halachic

---

1. See *Minchas Chinuch*, mitzva 547; *Kiryas Sefer* in *Hilchos Rotzei'ach*; *Sema*, C.M. 427:12; and *Chasam Sofer, Avoda Zara* 30a.

violations. The Rambam writes אסרו חכמים — that these activities were proscribed by the Sages — only because these prohibitions are not stated explicitly by the Torah, but are rather established on the basis of *Chazal*'s exegesis of the imperative רק השמר לך ושמור נפשך מאד. The Rambam did not mean that these prohibitions were introduced by the Sages, but rather that the Sages interpreted the Biblical text as forbidding such activities.[2]

ספק סכנה

Regardless, it is clear that *halacha* forbids knowingly entering into a dangerous situation, either on the level of Torah law or by force of Rabbinic enactment, and the question thus becomes whether this prohibition is overridden by the concern for human life. Certainly, one is not required — or even allowed — to surrender his life to save another (unless he is ordered to kill or be killed). But in the case of an infectious disease, the doctors are asked not to surrender their lives, but to expose themselves to risk. Is this exposure permissible for the sake of saving patients who would otherwise die, or does the halachic obligation to care for one's own physical wellbeing override the obligation to save human life?

At first glance, this question hinges on the well-known debate among the *poskim* as to whether one may or should place himself in a situation in which he might lose his life in order to rescue someone who would otherwise definitely lose his life. The *Beis Yosef* (C.M. 426), citing the *Hagahos Maimoniyos*, rules that *halacha* requires rescuing someone who would otherwise certainly die, even if this entails endangering oneself. As long as the rescuer needs to place himself in a situation of only ספק סכנה — in which he is exposed to the risk of death, as opposed to a situation in which he would certainly die — he is required to act to rescue a person who would otherwise definitely die. The *Sema* (426:2), however, notes that other *poskim* seem to disagree, and do not require a person to endanger himself in order to rescue somebody from death. The Radbaz, in one of his responsa (3:627), writes that it is forbidden to endanger oneself to rescue another person, and one who does so falls under the category of חסיד שוטה (a "pious fool").

---

2. The context of the *Tevuos Shor*'s discussion is the prohibition of בל תשקצו (*Vayikra* 11:43), which *Chazal* understood as forbidding activities that are deemed revolting. In reference to this prohibition as well, the Rambam speaks of *Chazal* proscribing these activities: אסרו חכמים מאכלות ומשקין שנפש רוב בני אדם קיהה מהן. This led several *Acharonim* to conclude that the Rambam considered this a Rabbinic prohibition. The *Tevuos Shor* contends, however, that the Rambam in fact speaks here of a Torah prohibition; the Rambam writes that the Sages forbade these activities only because they are established on the basis of *Chazal*'s interpretation of the verse.

Elsewhere (*Shu"t Le-Leshonos Ha-Rambam*, *Hilchos Rotzei'ach* 1:14), the Radbaz concedes that if the risk is slight, then one must expose himself to the danger for the sake of rescuing his fellow. The Radbaz adds that for this reason *Chazal* establish the obligation to rescue one's fellow from danger with the example of הרואה חבירו טובע בנהר — where someone is drowning. Jumping into a river to save someone from drowning entails a small degree of risk, and *Chazal* therefore noted this example in order to instruct that the obligation to rescue someone from danger applies even when this entails exposing oneself to slight danger.

Seemingly, the permissibility of a healthcare professional traveling to areas ravaged by the Ebola epidemic to treat patients would depend upon this debate. Ebola patients who do not receive adequate medical care would all but certainly die, whereas the doctors who treat them only face the possibility of contracting the virus. At first glance, this situation is a classic example of exposing oneself to danger for the sake of rescuing people from certain death, and the *halacha* would thus depend on the different views cited above.

Upon further consideration, however, it would appear that even the *Sema* and Radbaz would concede that treating contagious patients is permissible, and perhaps even obligatory. To explain why, we need to explore the precise parameters of the prohibition against exposing oneself to danger.

Why is Overseas Travel Permitted?

It is clear from the examples of dangerous activity given by the Rambam that this prohibition applies even to situations in which the risk of danger is remote. The Rambam mentions in his list drinking from natural bodies of water in the dark of night, when one cannot check to see if leeches are present in the water; drinking water that had been left uncovered, and thus may have been poisoned with a snake's venom; placing coins in one's mouth, which is deemed hazardous because they may have been infected with germs; and keeping a knife thrust into a fruit or vegetable such that its blade is concealed, which could endanger somebody who leans on the fruit or vegetable. In all these examples, there is only a remote possibility of life-threatening danger, and yet the Rambam forbids these actions because they expose one (or others) to danger.[3]

---

3. Rav Zevulun Graz, former Chief Rabbi of Rechovot, offered a clever insight to explain why in virtually all areas of *halacha* we may rely on a statistical majority (רוב) to permit that which might perhaps be forbidden, yet when it comes to matters involving personal safety, we must avoid even remote chances of harm. The Ramban (*Chullin* 2b) writes that hallowed food — *teruma* and sacrifices — is not subject to the rule of ספק טומאה ברשות

How can we reconcile this prohibition with the fact that since time immemorial, people have engaged in potentially dangerous activities that were deemed perfectly acceptable? The *Shulchan Aruch* (O.C. 219:1), based on the Gemara (*Berachos* 54b), lists the four types of people who must recite ברכת הגומל to thank God for protecting them from harm, two of which are those who traveled through a desert and those who traveled overseas. The clear assumption, of course, is that these are considered dangerous situations in which one depends upon the Almighty's special protection. Thus, upon emerging safely from these situations, one is required to offer a special blessing of thanksgiving. Yet, nowhere in halachic literature do we find any mention of a prohibition against traveling due to the dangers involved! Indeed, the *Shulchan Aruch* (O.C. 248) addresses the prohibition against embarking on a sea voyage close to Shabbos, clearly indicating that traveling at other times is perfectly acceptable.[4] Why is one allowed to travel, if this is considered dangerous?[5]

This question was already raised by Rav Malkiel Tzvi Tannenbaum of Lomza (*Divrei Malkiel* 5:35), and he concedes that it is unclear where the line is drawn between permissible and forbidden exposure to danger:

> הרי מצינו שיורדי הים צריכים להודות...משום דשכיחא סכנתא, ומ"מ ודאי מותר לירד בים ולא מיקרי מאבד עצמו לדעת. ואם צריך לירד לים כדי לקיים איזה מצוה בודאי מחויב לירד ואסור לו למנוע משום חשש סכנה. הרי חזינן שמותר להכניס א"ע בחשש סכנה היכא שאינו רק חשש בעלמא. ויש להאריך בזה ולבאר הגבול לזה, אך אין העת מסכמת.

> We find, after all, that sea travelers are required to thank [God upon the safe completion of their voyage]…because danger is common [when traveling by sea], yet it is certainly permissible to sail at sea, and this

---

הרבים טהור. Normally, when uncertainty arises concerning a person or object's status of purity, we may consider it pure if this occurred in a public location. When it comes to *teruma* and sacrifices, the Ramban asserted, this rule does not suffice, because the Torah (*Bamidbar* 18:8) commands משמרת תרומותי — that we must safeguard hallowed food. Whenever the Torah requires "guarding" something, we must avoid even situations of uncertainty. By the same token, then, when the Torah commands us to safeguard our personal wellbeing — השמר לך ושמור נפשך מאד — it means that we must avoid even potential hazards.

4. This point is made by the *Shem Aryeh*, in the passage cited below.
5. The Talmud Yerushalmi (*Pesachim* 4:1) cites the view of Rabbi Yehuda, who forbids traveling overseas, and the commentators explain this ruling as based upon the risk of danger. However, the *Ohel Moshe* (1) asserts that Rabbi Yehuda speaks of very specific instances, when sea voyages are especially dangerous. Regardless, the commentators to *Maseches Moed Katan* (14a) note that the Talmud Bavli understood Rabbi Yehuda as forbidding not sea travel per se, but rather leaving *Eretz Yisrael*. In any event, common practice clearly permits overseas travel.

is not considered knowingly killing oneself. And if one must travel by sea to fulfill a certain *mitzva*, he is certainly obligated to travel, and it is forbidden for him to refrain because of the possible danger. We thus see that it is permissible to place oneself in a situation of possible danger, as long as there is only a remote risk. Elaboration is needed to explain the limits in this regard, but time does not allow.

Traveling overseas is not dangerous enough to be forbidden, but it remains unclear just how dangerous something must be to be prohibited by force of the command of רק השמר לך.

Other sources also indicate that *halacha* permits placing oneself in situations that present a very slight risk. The *Magen Avraham* (316:23) condemns those who allowed killing a certain type of lizard on Shabbos, noting the very low level of risk posed by this creature. Similarly, Rav Aryeh Leibush Lifshitz, in a responsum published in his *Shem Aryeh* (Y.D. 28), notes that in *Sefer Chasidim* Rabbeinu Yehuda Ha-Chasid lists numerous activities from which one should refrain due to safety concerns, yet these are not mentioned in later halachic works. The *Shem Aryeh* suggests that since the risk presented by these activities is very slight, they are not strictly prohibited.

However, in contradistinction to the *Divrei Malkiel*, the *Elya Rabba* (O.C. 219) asserts that sea travel is actually **more** dangerous than activities that *halacha* forbids due to danger. The *Elya Rabba* notes that *halacha* does not require reciting ברכת הגומל after safely emerging from other dangerous situations, such as passing underneath an unsteady wall or walking over an unsteady bridge. The *Elya Rabba* explains that the level of risk in these situations is not high enough to warrant an obligation to give praise upon emerging safely. According to the *Elya Rabba*, then, passing under an unstable wall, which *halacha* clearly forbids, is less dangerous than traveling overseas, which *halacha* clearly permits. How can we explain this anomaly?

מנהגו של עולם

The answer to this question is expressed by the *Shem Aryeh* in the aforementioned responsum:

> ודע דאף בדברים שיש בהם סכנה, מ"מ בדבר שהוא מנהגו של עולם ודרך הכרח אין לחוש, דהרי ארבעה צריכים להודות, וב' מהם הולכי מדברות והולכי ימים. הרי דאיכא בהם סכנה, ומ"מ מותר לפרוש בספינה ולילך במדבר... ולמה לא נאסור משום סכנה... אלא ודאי דבדברים כאלו אשר הם לצורך העולם אין איסור כלל.

You should know that when it comes to things that entail danger

> — nevertheless, if it is something that is the way of the world and a necessity, there is no concern. After all, "four people are required to give thanks," and two of them are desert travelers and travelers at sea. Thus, they entail danger, and yet it is permissible to voyage out to sea and to travel in the desert… Why do we not forbid [this] due to danger?… Rather, it is clear that when it comes to things such as these, which are necessary for the world, there is no prohibition whatsoever.

Although traveling overseas and through deserts is considered dangerous, it is nevertheless permissible because it falls under the category of מנהגו של עולם — common and conventional human activity. Societies establish which behaviors and activities are acceptable despite their posing certain risks, and *halacha* does not forbid such activities.

One simple example might be highway driving, which clearly entails some degree of danger due to the possibility of fatal accidents, yet has been accepted by modern society as an essential part of day-to-day living. Since travel is regarded as a vital part of life, it is permissible, even though it poses greater danger than other activities that *halacha* forbids, since they can be avoided without disrupting one's normal mode of living.

This approach was similarly formulated by Rav Elchanan Wasserman (*Kovetz Shiurim, Kesubos* #136) in explaining the Gemara's remark in several contexts that שומר פתאים ה' — certain potentially dangerous practices are permissible because "God protects the fool-hearted."[6] Rav Elchanan writes:

> צ"ל דאין האדם חייב להמנע ממנהג דרך ארץ, וממילא הוי כאילו אין בידו לשמור את עצמו, ואז נשמר מן השמיים. אבל היכא שבידו להזהר אינו בכלל פתאים, ואם לא ישמור את עצמו הוא מתחייב בנפשו ולא יהא משומר מן השמיים.

> We must explain that a person is not required to refrain from ordinary conduct, and hence one is considered unable to protect himself, and he is then protected by God. But when one is able to be careful, he is not in the category of the "fool-hearted," and if he does not protect himself, he puts his life at risk and will not be protected by God.

When we engage in dangerous activities that are accepted as part of daily living, we are not considered to be acting recklessly. Rather, we are considered as having been placed in a potentially dangerous situation against our will, and we may thus rely on God's protection.[7]

---

6. The source of the phrase שומר פתאים ה' is *Tehillim* 116:6.
7. This approach is also developed at length by Rav Yehuda Unterman, *Shevet Mi-Yehuda*, vol. 1, *Mahadura Kama*, p. 50. Additionally, it is cited in the name of the *Chazon Ish* by

Applying this principle to the area of professional healthcare, it would certainly appear that treating contagious patients would be permissible — and perhaps even obligatory — in light of the fact that this falls under the category of מנהגו של עולם — conventional practice. Despite the risk entailed, it is accepted that healthcare professionals treat contagious patients, obviously taking reasonable precautions, and it is thus permissible, if not obligatory, for the sake of saving lives.

אליו הוא נושא את נפשו

Another reason to permit physicians to treat infected patients arises from the Gemara's comment in *Maseches Bava Metzia* (112a) that appears to permit one to risk his life for the sake of earning a livelihood. The Torah in *Sefer Devarim* (24:15) issues the command to pay one's workers on time, and explains, כי עני הוא ואליו הוא נשא את נפשו — literally, "for he is poor, and he makes his life dependent on it [his salary]." The Gemara explains the phrase אליו הוא נושא את נפשו to mean that an employee, in many instances, is forced to risk his life in order to satisfy his responsibilities to his employer and earn his wages:

מפני מה עלה זה בכבש ונתלה באילן ומסר עצמו למיתה – לא על שכרו?

For what did this [worker] climb up a ramp and hang onto a tree, subjecting himself to [the risk of] death — was it not for his wages?

As Rashi explains, certain jobs — such as harvesting fruits from trees — require climbing to high places and risking one's life, and thus an employer who fails to pay his workers commits a grave offense. The clear implication of the Gemara's comment is that it is acceptable for an employee to put himself at risk when this is necessary to earn his wages.

This point is made by Rav Eliezer Waldenberg (*Tzitz Eliezer* 9:17, *Kuntres Refua Be-Shabbos* 5:9), who concludes that one may place himself in a potentially

---

Rav Avraham Farbstein. Rav Yehoshua Neuwirth (*Shemiras Shabbos Ke-Hilchasa*, ch. 32, n. 2) also advances this theory, noting that this was the view of Rav Shlomo Zalman Auerbach. It should be noted, however, that the formulation in *Shemiras Shabbos Ke-Hilchasa* differs somewhat from the way it is presented in the aforementioned sources. Rav Neuwirth asserts that the determining factor is whether people commonly consider the given activity dangerous, rather than whether the activity is regarded as part of ordinary life. This subtle but significant distinction could yield important ramifications, particularly with regard to the question at hand concerning treating contagious patients, which on the one hand is considered part and parcel of the medical profession and a physician's responsibility, but yet is regarded as a dangerous activity.

hazardous situation when this is required for his profession, as in the case of a doctor treating contagious patients. Rav Waldenberg writes:

> נלפע"ד דבהיות דהרופא עושה כן ליטפל בחולים עבור פרנסתו א"כ מותר לו משום כך ליכנס גם בספק סכנה, ובדומה למה שהתירה תורה לפועל ליכנס למקומות סכנה עבור פרנסתו כדכתיב ואליו הוא נושא את נפשו...הרי דמותר לאדם למסור את עצמו למיתה דהיינו ליכנס למקומות מסוכנים שיתכן שיהרג שם לשם פרנסתו...וא"כ ה"ה גם ברופא העובד לשם פרנסה, ובפרט כשחוק המדינה הוא שאם לא יתנהג בכזאת ויתרשל ליטפל בחולים כאלה ישללו ממנו רשיונו ותישלל פרנסתו ממנו.

> It seems, in my humble opinion, that since a physician treats patients for the sake of his livelihood, he is allowed to expose himself to potential risk for this purpose, similar to the Torah's allowing a worker to enter dangerous places for his livelihood, as it says, ואליו הוא נושא את נפשו... indicating that it is permissible for a person to expose himself to the risk of death — meaning, to enter dangerous places, where he might be killed — for the sake of his livelihood... Therefore, the same would apply to a physician who works for his livelihood, especially when the country's laws are such that if he does not conduct himself this way, but rather neglects the treatment of these patients, his license will be revoked and he will lose his livelihood.

This point is also made by Rav Moshe Feinstein (*Iggeros Moshe*, C.M. 1:104), who permits earning a livelihood from an athletic career, even if one plays a sport that entails a small risk to one's life or to the lives of other players. Citing the Gemara's comments concerning an employee's exposing himself to risk for his job, Rav Moshe asserts that for the sake of earning a living, one may expose himself to a level of risk, and even expose others to risk, as long as they chose to place themselves in that situation, as is the case when playing professional sports.

Rav Moshe makes reference in this context to a responsum of the *Noda Be-Yehuda* (*Mahadura Tinyana*, Y.D. 10), who forbids hunting for sport, both because of its unbecoming nature and due to the life-threatening dangers entailed, but then adds that hunting is allowed for the sake of earning a living:

> מי שהוא עני ועושה זו למחייתו, לזה התורה התירה כמו כל סוחרי ימים מעבר לים שכל מה שהוא לצורך מחייתו ופרנסתו אין ברירה, והתורה אמרה ואליו הוא נושא את נפשו.

> Someone who is poor and does this for his sustenance — this the Torah allowed, as is the case regarding all merchants who sail overseas, because

regarding all that is required for one's sustenance and livelihood, there is no alternative, and the Torah said, ואליו הוא נושא את נפשו.

The reason for this exception likely relates to the aforementioned principle — namely, that one is permitted to expose himself to risks that have been societally accepted as part of normal life. Certain occupations that are necessary for the greater good entail a degree of risk, and society has accepted these risks for the benefit of both the employers and employees, as well as for the benefit of people generally. Therefore, for example, *halacha* allows roofers to install rooftops and construction workers to work on scaffoldings near the top of skyscrapers, and homeowners and contractors are allowed to commission this kind of labor, despite the hazards involved. Since such jobs are integral to modern living and are deemed acceptable by society, they are halachically permissible.

By the same token, society looks to and relies upon doctors to treat infectious diseases and contain deadly outbreaks of illness. Exposure to infected patients is, of course, an unavoidable component of this process, and so the risk of infection is one that has been accepted as part of normal life. It would thus stand to reason that a doctor may, and in fact should, treat infected patients even if this entails exposing himself to the risk of contracting the disease.

Rav Asher Weiss[8]

I am writing to you quickly, due to the urgency of the matter.

A Jewish doctor who specializes in microbiology was offered to join a medical delegation that is going to Africa to treat patients infected with the Ebola virus. Is it permissible for him to join, and is he commanded to do so, or is it perhaps forbidden for him to join because he is not allowed to endanger himself to save others? He says that the risk of contracting the disease is about 8%. This virus is especially dangerous, and thus far, about half the people who were infected by the disease have died.

I have already addressed at length in several contexts the important question of whether a person is allowed to expose himself to a certain degree of risk in order to save his fellow from grave danger. I explained, based on the responsa of the Radbaz, that three different categories exist in this regard:

1) When dealing with a remote, negligible risk, whereas one's fellow faces grave danger, it is certainly permissible to endanger oneself, and this constitutes a מדת חסידות (measure of piety). It may possibly even be obligatory.

---

8. In a letter written to this author; translated from Hebrew.

2) When dealing with a real danger, but where it is more likely that he will be safe, then it is permissible to endanger oneself, but this is certainly not obligatory.

3) When dealing with an actual risk, then even if one's fellow is in greater danger, it is forbidden to put himself at risk.

As I have elaborated on this subject in several places in my books, I will not elaborate here; you can access the information there (*Shu"t Minchas Asher* 1:115; *Minchas Asher, Bamidbar*, 73).

Regarding that which you wrote, that perhaps he is allowed to endanger himself in order to earn a livelihood, as written in the *Noda Be-Yehuda* (*Tinyana*, Y.D. 10) — I have already expressed my view in several places (*Minchas Asher, Devarim* 7; *Minchas Asher, Shabbos* 87:2; *Haggadas Minchas Asher, Sha'arei Teshuva* 19:3) that in truth, there is no specific dispensation allowing one to endanger himself for his livelihood. After all, nowhere do we find that earning a living overrides the concern for human life. Rather, there is a general rule that one is permitted to expose himself to a certain degree of risk in order to improve his quality of life, and one is therefore permitted to climb a tree and set sail in the ocean for the purpose of his livelihood. Indeed, this happens every day, as people engage in all kinds of activities that entail some small degree of risk for enjoyment, such as riding motorcycles, parachuting from planes, skiing, and many other such activities that certainly expose one to greater risk than staying at home or walking. Since this entails only a remote risk, there is no prohibition.

However, I do not believe this is relevant to our issue, as anything that poses a risk of several percentages is a discernible risk and is forbidden.

Therefore, it would seem, at first glance, that the man should not join this delegation.

I wonder, however, if there is truly an 8% chance of infection. Seemingly, the main risk factor is people's negligence in taking the protective measures necessary to avoid infection, and if a person strictly and carefully abides by appropriate safeguards, I would imagine that the danger is very remote. If, indeed, it can be determined that he can take safety measures that would lower the risk of infection to a minimum, it would seem that there is room to allow him to join the delegation in order to save human life and be מקדש שם שמיים.

יה"ר שלא ניכשל בדבר הלכה
With much admiration and with blessings for a good, sweet year,

Asher Weiss

Exchange with Rav Yitzchak Zilberstein *shlit"a*[9]

I was approached with a question by a physician who lives in our area and has great expertise in the field of infectious diseases (microbiology), and who was asked by his hospital's administration to travel together with a delegation of doctors to an African country to treat patients infected with the Ebola disease, as the country [the United States] has taken upon itself, together with several other countries, to send doctors to treat this dreadful disease in order to prevent it from spreading and to treat and cure the patients who have already been infected. Based on what he told me, someone who is infected with this disease faces grave danger, as so far approximately 50% of the infected patients have died. This physician, who is religiously observant, asked whether it is forbidden for him to expose himself to possible danger due to the chance that he will be at risk (in his view, the chance of a doctor contracting the disease from patients under his care is approximately 8%), and he would be in violation of אך את דמכם וכו'. While there are those (*Beis Yosef*, citing the *Hagahos Maimoniyos*) who maintain that one is even required to place himself in a situation of possible danger to save a fellow Jew — and even among those who disagree, some consider such a person "pious" for doing so — nevertheless, we are dealing here with rescuing non-Jews (who are not idol-worshippers), and so perhaps it is halachically forbidden for him to get involved in this.

When he came to me, I noted that his refusal to travel with the delegation might cause a חילול ה' and possibly arouse enmity. He responded, however, that in his view, there is no reason why it would be known that his reason is because he is a religiously observant Jew.

It also occurred to me that perhaps this should be allowed because this is his livelihood, and we might apply to this case that which *Chazal* said in *Bava Metzia* (112), מפני מה עלה זה בכבש וכו', as discussed by the *Noda Be-Yehuda*, *Mahadura Tinyana*, Y.D. 10.

I have therefore brought this question before the Rav *shlit"a* to receive his guidance and דעת תורה. And even if his conclusion is that this is forbidden, nevertheless, perhaps we must be concerned about the possibility of arousing enmity, though I am uncertain if this concern is grounds for allowing him to endanger himself.

Respectfully,
Dovid Lichtenstein

---

9. Elul 5764 (2014). Translated from Hebrew.

Rav Zilberstein's response:

An 8% risk that the doctor will become ill is considered a possible danger. Although the risk is not great, nevertheless, one must be concerned and one cannot belittle such a risk. The *Mishkenos Yaakov* (Y.D. 17, in the context of the risk of abrasions and *tarfus*) writes that a 10% chance qualifies as מיעוט המצוי (a minority occurrence that is common) [meaning, if ten of a group of 100 animals are found to be *tereifos*, this is considered a מיעוט המצוי and all the animals must be examined]. I heard from my teacher and father-in-law, Rav Yosef Shalom Elyashiv zt"l, that a 5% chance would likely be considered a מיעוט שאינו מצוי (uncommon minority) [and less than that would be a minority that is not common at all].

Although the *poskim* disagree as to whether it is permissible for a person to place himself in a situation of possible danger to save another person facing certain danger, and the *Mishna Berura* (329:19) rules that one is not obligated to place himself in a situation of possible danger to save his fellow from certain danger, nevertheless, he added, citing poskim (*Pischei Teshuva*, C.M. 426), that the situation must be carefully assessed to determine whether there is truly a possible risk, but one should not be too exacting, as the saying goes, המדקדק עצמו בכך בא לידי כך (if a person is too concerned about something, it will happen).

In this case, where the risk is 8%, which is a risk of danger but not a great risk, a person should expose himself to this amount of risk for the sake of saving a fellow Jew from certain danger.

Similarly, the *Noda Be-Yehuda* (*Tinyana*, Y.D. 10) allowed hunting animals for the purposes of livelihood, despite the dangers entailed. For no one was greater and more proficient in hunting than Esav, of whom the verse testifies, "Esav was a man who knew hunting, a man of the field" (*Bereishis* 25:27), and yet he said about himself, "Behold, I am going to die" (25:32), and the Ramban explained the plain meaning of this to be that Esav endangered himself every day among the legions of animals. This is because the Torah allows endangering oneself for the sake of livelihood, just as it is permissible for merchants to cross oceans for their livelihood. The Torah (*Devarim* 24:15) says, ואליו הוא נושא את נפשו, and *Chazal* explain in *Bava Metzia* (112a), "For what did this [worker] climb up a ramp and hang onto a tree, subjecting himself to death — was it not for his wages?"

A similar question was posed to my teacher and father-in-law, Rav Yosef Shalom Elyashiv zt"l — as mentioned in *Chashukei Chemed* on *Bava Metzia* (112b) — as to whether a Rosh Yeshiva was allowed to travel on a road that was targeted by shooting attacks in order to teach students, which was necessary for his livelihood. He replied that since it says in *Bava Metzia* (112a) about an employee, ואליו הוא נושא את נפשו, we see that the Torah permits a worker to endanger himself somewhat for the purpose of his livelihood, for this is the decree of the King of the world. In a similar vein, it is explained in *Iggeros Moshe* (C.M. 1:104) that it is permissible to earn a living through ball-playing, as they said, ואליו הוא נושא את נפשו.

In our case, however, the question concerns a doctor who has a livelihood, and he wants to endanger himself in order to earn extra money. May a person put himself in danger even under such circumstances?

The answer is that it is permissible, because even extra livelihood is considered a *mitzva*, just as a person is permitted to leave *Eretz Yisrael* for the purposes of his livelihood, and it is permissible to leave even to earn extra money. As explained in *Mo'ed Katan* (14), one who goes on a trip abroad and returns on *Chol Ha-Mo'ed* may not cut his hair, even if he was unable to do so on Erev Yom Tov, since he was not allowed to leave. If, however, he had left for the purposes of his livelihood, even just to earn extra money, then he is allowed to cut his hair.

Similarly, the *Shulchan Aruch* (O.C. 248:4) draws halachic distinctions between one who leaves by boat or in a caravan on Erev Shabbos for the purpose of a *mitzva*, and one who leaves to tend to optional matters. The Rama writes that leaving for business is considered leaving for the sake of a *mitzva*, and the *Mishna Berura* (248:34) adds that this includes traveling to earn extra money.

Conclusion: If the risk is only 8%, then strictly speaking, it is permissible for the physician to travel with a medical delegation to try to stop the plague. However, if he would ask for our advice, we would advise him not to go, because 8% is not a small risk.

theguardian

Abortion Demand Soars in Countries Hit by Zika outbreak, Study Finds

June 23, 2016
by Sarah Boseley. Health Editor

Women in Latin America, where abortion is often illegal, are seeking online help in unprecedented numbers in response to the virus linked to birth defects.

Demand for abortions has soared among women living in countries hit by the spread of the Zika virus who fear having a baby with severe birth defects, new data shows.

In unprecedented numbers, women in Latin America are accessing the website Women on Web, which has a long history of helping those in countries where abortion is illegal to obtain pills which will terminate an early pregnancy. In Brazil, Venezuela and Ecuador the requests for help have doubled, while in other Latin American countries they have risen by a third.

Revelations about the scale of abortion demand published in the New England Journal of Medicine come as the golfer Rory McIlroy pulled out of the Olympics in Rio, citing anxiety over potential Zika infection. "I've come to realise that my health and my family's health comes before anything else," he said in a statement.

"Even though the risk of infection from the Zika virus is considered low, it is a risk nonetheless and a risk I am unwilling to take."

The World Health Organisation is advising travellers to the Olympics to practise safe sex using condoms or abstain for eight weeks after their return, to avoid the risk of sexual transmission of the virus to a woman who is pregnant or planning to become so.

Many women living in Latin America, however, find it hard to protect themselves against the virus spread by mosquitoes and do not have the option of termination in the event of an unwanted pregnancy. It is particularly hard for those in poorer communities, living in difficult conditions where mosquitoes readily breed.

"One of the reasons for doing this study is to give a voice to women trapped in this epidemic," said Dr Catherine Aiken, academic clinical lecturer in the department of obstetrics and gynaecology of the University of Cambridge, "and to bring to light that with all the virology, the vaccination and containment strategy and all the great things that people are doing, there is no voice for those women on the ground."

In a supplement to the study, the researchers have published some of the emails to Women on Web which reveal their fears. "I need to do an abortion because of the great risk of infection with Zika here ... Please help me. My economic situation is extremely difficult," said one woman in Brazil.

Another in Colombia wrote: "Here Zika is a major problem and the health authorities do not help with it ... I have no resources at this time and want to ask for your help because fear overwhelms me. What if the baby is born sick?" An email from a woman in Venezuela said: "We are going through a really serious situation for the economic and humanitarian crisis unleashed by Zika. There are no treatments, contraceptives nor pills to abort. I want to terminate my pregnancy but I cannot."

Women on Web is a longstanding and well-used website which had its origins in a boat that used to moor off the shores of countries where abortion was illegal and offer help to women who arrived in dinghies. The researchers analysed data from January 2010 to March 2016 for 19 Latin American countries, comparing the numbers of requests with three countries — Chile, Poland and Uruguay — where there have been no health warnings about the dangers of Zika virus in pregnancy.

"There is a huge surge," said Aiken. "It's over 100% increase in demand in some of the countries we looked at — almost 110% increase in Brazil." In those countries with no Zika outbreak, there was no such rise in demand.

The study, funded by the National Institutes of Health and the National Science Foundation, was carried out by researchers in the US and the UK. Abigail Aiken, an assistant professor at the University of Texas at Austin, said the numbers inevitably underrepresented the demand. "Accurate data on the choices pregnant women make in Latin America is hard to obtain. If anything, our approach may underestimate the impact of health warnings on requests for abortion, as many women may have used an unsafe method or visited local underground providers," she said.

Aiken spoke of "a much, much wider problem with women who don't have access [to the internet] and live in very poor rural areas and are in very dire straits and will be driven to less safe methods of illegal and underground abortion. We think we are looking at the tip of the iceberg."

Copyright © theguardian.com

Aborting a Fetus Infected With the Zika Virus

The outbreak of the mosquito-borne Zika virus in 2015–2016, first in Brazil and then throughout the Americas, has produced heartbreaking images of sickly infants suffering from microcephaly — an underdeveloped brain that results in a small head — and other malformations. Although people who contract the disease generally show either no or mild symptoms, in the case of a pregnant woman Zika can cause severe defects in the fetus, which translate into devastating disabilities throughout the child's life. The underdevelopment of a fetus's brain due to the mother's infection can lead to premature death, in the most extreme cases, and in others, to significant lifelong disabilities and impairments.

In June 2016, the Center for Disease Control and Prevention reported that 234 pregnant women in the United States — including both U.S. residents and visitors — had been diagnosed with Zika since the beginning of that year, three of whom had delivered babies with Zika-related defects. Three others chose to terminate their pregnancies after deformities were found in the fetuses they were carrying.

Abortion has indeed emerged as a strong preference among pregnant women diagnosed with Zika. On June 22, 2016, the *New England Journal of Medicine* reported a surge in the demand for abortions in Latin America, the region worst hit by the epidemic. In Brazil, Venezuela, and Ecuador, abortion requests doubled after warnings were issued of the disease's devastating effects on developing fetuses.

Jewish law and tradition, of course, regards the creation and maintenance of human life as the most sacred of a person's duties, and has thus always opposed the termination of pregnancies. But might there be halachic justification for permitting abortions in the case of an unborn child diagnosed with Zika? If so, at which stage of gestation would this be permitted?[1]

In an attempt to answer this question, we will explore the basis and nature of the halachic prohibition of killing an unborn child.

---

1. Of course, this question is not limited to cases of Zika infection, and applies also to fetuses diagnosed with Tay-Sachs and other severe conditions, as we will see below.

ליכא מידעם דלישראל שרי ולבני נח אסור

The Mishna in *Maseches Nidda* (44a) establishes that a killer is liable to capital punishment regardless of the victim's age, even if the victim was an infant who had just been born (תינוק בן יום אחד). The clear implication is that killing an unborn child does not render one liable to capital punishment. This is noted explicitly by the *Mechilta*, cited by Rashi in his Torah commentary (*Shemos* 21:12), in reference to the verse, מכה איש ומת מות יומת ("One who strikes a man and he dies shall be put to death"). The Torah considers killing an איש — a "man" — a capital offense, and the *Mechilta* interprets the term איש in this context as referring to a human being that has been born.[2]

Interestingly, *halacha* distinguishes in this regard between Jews and gentiles. In *Maseches Sanhedrin* (57b), the Gemara rules that for gentiles, killing even an unborn fetus constitutes a capital offense, punishable by execution. The Gemara infers this rule from God's command to Noach after the flood forbidding murder, which applies to all humankind: שופך דם האדם באדם דמו ישפך (*Bereishis* 9:6). The phrase שופך דם האדם באדם could be interpreted as a reference to killing a "person in a person" — namely, a fetus — and since the Torah declares this crime a capital offense (דמו ישפך), the Gemara concludes that killing an unborn child, like ordinary murder, is punishable by execution. However, once the Torah was given, *Am Yisrael* became subject to the Torah's laws, not the universal code presented to Noach after the flood, and according to Torah law, as noted earlier, killing a fetus does not constitute a capital offense. This distinction between Jews and gentiles is codified by the Rambam (*Hilchos Melachim* 9:4).

Nevertheless, while it is clear that for a Jew, killing a fetus is not equivalent to actual murder with respect to liability to capital punishment, the question remains whether it is still forbidden by Torah law.

Tosfos, later in *Maseches Sanhedrin* (59a), indicate that killing a fetus is forbidden due to the rule of ליכא מידעם דלישראל שרי ולבני נח אסור — "There is nothing that is permissible for a Jew and forbidden for gentiles."[3] The Gemara there establishes this rule to explain why laws that were given to mankind before the Revelation at Sinai, but were not subsequently repeated to *Am Yisrael* after they received the Torah, are binding for Jews. Although the Jewish nation transitioned at Mount Sinai from the universal code applicable to all humanity to the system of Torah law, nevertheless, there cannot be an obligation or prohibition by which gentiles are bound but Jews are not. As Rashi explains, *Am Yisrael* was set apart at Mount Sinai for a special stature of sanctity — להתקדש — and not

---

2. אינו חייב עד שיכה בן קיימא הראוי להיות איש.
3. Henceforth, we will refer to this rule with the abbreviated phrase ליכא מידעם.

to be relieved of obligations charged to all humankind. Therefore, even if a law that preceded the Revelation was not later repeated to the Jewish people, it can be assumed to be binding upon them. *Tosfos* apply this rule to the prohibition of killing fetuses, noting that although Jews are not liable to the same severe punishment for this offense as gentiles, it is nevertheless forbidden for Jews just as it is for gentiles. This comment is also made by *Tosfos* in *Maseches Chullin* (33a).

Abortion as Murder

The implications of *Tosfos*' view are expressed by Rav Meir Simcha of Dvinsk in *Or Samei'ach* (*Hilchos Issurei Bi'ah* 3:2):

> גבי קדושת המצוות ודאי דמצווין אחר מתן תורה מה שהיו מצווים קודם. רק לעניין עונשין, אם עבר ועשה, טפי חסה רחמנא על דם ישראל...

> With regard to the sanctity of the *mitzvos* — certainly, [Jews] after the giving of the Torah are bound by all the commands by which they were bound beforehand. But with regard to punishments, if one transgressed and committed [the forbidden act], the Torah showed greater compassion for the blood of a Jew...

According to Rav Meir Simcha, the rule of ליכא מידעם means that Jews are bound by precisely the same prohibitions that applied before they received the Torah. Even when the Torah treats Jewish violators more leniently, as in the case of killing an unborn child, the initial prohibition remains fully in force for both gentiles and Jews alike. According to this perspective, killing a fetus is strictly forbidden on the level of Torah law and constitutes outright murder, notwithstanding the exceptional provision absolving Jewish offenders from capital punishment.

Rav Meir Simcha follows this approach in his *Meshech Chochma* (*Shemos* 35:2) as well, where he writes about a Jew who kills a fetus, נמסר מיתתו לדיני שמיים — meaning, he is liable to death, but the punishment will be brought upon him by God, and not by the human court.[4] In his view, it appears, killing an unborn

---

4. The *Chemdas Yisrael* (*Kuntres Ner Mitzvah*, pp. 175–176) cites this theory from the work *Zechusa De-Avraham*, and raises the question of how to reconcile this view with the explicit Torah law requiring one to pay reparations if he kills a fetus by beating its mother (*Shemos* 21:22). The famous rule of קים ליה בדרבה מיניה absolves one of restitution payments for damages if he incurred a capital punishment at the same time he caused the damage, and Rabbi Nechunya ben Ha-Kaneh (*Kesubos* 30a) famously applies this rule even if the capital offense is punishable only by God. Accordingly, if killing a fetus

child qualifies as murder in every respect, the lone exception being that *beis din* will not sentence the offender to execution.

This is also the implication of the Maharal in his *Gur Aryeh* (*Shemos* 21:12), where he raises the question of why the difference between Jews and gentiles with respect to the punishment for killing a fetus does not violate the rule of ליכא מידעם. Even once *Tosfos* establish that this is forbidden for both Jews and gentiles, gentiles are still held to a stricter halachic standard by being liable to capital punishment. How can this be reconciled with the axiom of ליכא מידעם, which precludes the possibility of applying a stricter standard to gentiles than to Jews? The Maharal answers that in the case of a Jew who kills a fetus, the Torah does not treat the offender more leniently, but rather applies a stricter standard to *beis din*, preventing them from executing the perpetrator. Thus, this provision reflects not a looser standard for Jews, but rather a stricter standard. It emerges from the Maharal's comments that even for Jews, killing an unborn infant constitutes outright murder, but the Torah restrains *beis din* from executing the perpetrator.

According to these sources, and the straightforward reading of *Tosfos*, killing a fetus is strictly forbidden and constitutes murder.

At first glance, we might question this conclusion in light of the Mishna's ruling in *Maseches Ohalos* (7:6) concerning the case of a woman experiencing life-endangering complications during childbirth. The Mishna instructs that the fetus should be killed for the purpose of saving the mother's life, מפני שחייה קודמין לחייו — "because her life takes precedence over his." If, however, the woman's life is threatened after the infant's head exited her body, then the baby may not be killed to save the mother, שאין דוחין נפש מפני נפש — "we do not discard one life for the sake of another."

The Mishna here explicitly distinguishes between killing an unborn child and killing a newborn, permitting the former for the sake of rescuing a life, while forbidding the latter in such a case. This would appear to suggest that killing a fetus is fundamentally different from standard murder. A famous halachic principle forbids killing to save one's life (except when one comes under attack, in which case he is permitted to kill the pursuer in self-defense). As such, if killing an unborn child constitutes murder, there should be no basis for permitting killing such a child in order to save the mother — just as there is no basis for permitting killing the child to save the mother after he or she has begun exiting the womb.

The answer may lie in the reason that *halacha* forbids killing to save one's

---

renders one liable to death at the hands of God, then according to Rabbi Nechunya ben Ha-Kaneh, one should not be required to compensate the parents after killing a fetus.

life. The Gemara (*Sanhedrin* 74a) explains this rule as based on our inability to determine the relative value of different people's lives. In the Gemara's words, מאי חזית דדמא דידך סומק טפי — "How do you know that your blood is redder?" Only God can determine which life is more valuable than another, and thus a person has no right to take another life to save his own. The *Minchas Chinuch* (296:24) posits that in the case of a fetus, however, we are indeed authorized to choose one life over another. Since the fetus has not yet been born, and is thus not considered a complete human organism, we may grant preference to the life of a human being who has already been born. Thus, even if we assume that killing a fetus constitutes outright murder, we can easily explain why *halacha* permits killing a fetus to save its mother's life, as murder is permitted to save a life in the very rare situations in which we are authorized to grant preference to one person's life over another.[5]

A Fetus as a רודף

Another way of reconciling the Mishna's ruling with the assumption that abortion constitutes murder emerges from the surprising comments of the Rambam in *Hilchos Rotzei'ach* (1:9). The Rambam writes that in a case in which labor places a woman in a life-threatening situation, the infant is killed מפני שהוא כרודף אחריה להורגה — "because it is as though it pursues her to kill her." In the case in which the infant's head had already exited, the Rambam rules that the baby may not be killed because זהו טבעו של עולם — "this is the natural way of the world," in which the law of *rodef* cannot be applied. Surprisingly, the Rambam felt it necessary to resort to the law of רודף, which permits (and even requires) killing someone who seeks to kill another, to explain why a fetus may be killed to save its mother during childbirth. Many writers struggled to explain this comment and the distinction between the two cases in the Rambam's view.[6] Regardless, the Rambam clearly implies that before the fetus begins exiting the womb, it would be forbidden to take its life even for the sake of saving another life, except in the case in which the fetus itself threatens the mother.[7] Thus, for example, if a person is ordered at the threat of death to perform an abortion, the Rambam

---

5. See also Rav Shmuel Rozovsky's discussion in *Zichron Shmuel* 83:14–16. Rav Yechiel Yaakov Weinberg, however, rejects this approach in his *Seridei Eish* (3:127).
6. Rav Moshe Tzuriel, in an article on this topic published in *Techumin* (vol. 25), cites fourteen different explanations of the Rambam's view. Rav Tzuriel's essay can be accessed online, at http://www.zomet.org.il/?CategoryID=260&ArticleID=277.
7. The *Sema* (C.M. 425:8) surprisingly understood the Rambam to mean that the fetus may be killed in this case because it is not considered a full-fledged life, as it had not yet exited the womb. It is difficult to reconcile this reading with the Rambam's formulation,

would seemingly require him to surrender his life to avoid this transgression.[8] The Rambam understood the Mishna as permitted killing a fetus only in the unique case in which the fetus is regarded as a "pursuer" because it directly threatens the mother's life. Under all other circumstances, however, it would be forbidden to kill a fetus even to save a life, just as one may not kill anyone else to save a life. This is, in fact, the ruling of Rav Moshe Feinstein in his famous responsum on the subject (*Iggeros Moshe*, C.M. 2:69).

One might, however, distinguish between the case discussed by the Rambam and other situations of abortion. The Rambam speaks here of a fetus during childbirth, who has already entered the birth canal and is poised to enter into the world. It is perhaps for this reason that the infant is already considered a full-fledged human organism. Quite possibly, however, the Rambam would concede that at earlier stages, before childbirth, a fetus is not considered a full-fledged human organism with respect to which we can apply the prohibition of murder. Hence, the Rambam's ruling does not necessarily lead us to the conclusion that all abortions constitute outright murder. This point is made by Rav Chaim Ozer Grodzinsky (*Achiezer* 3:72:3).

Moreover, Rav Yechiel Yaakov Weinberg (*Seridei Eish* 3:127) explains the Rambam's comments differently, asserting that the Rambam does not, in fact, consider killing a fetus equivalent to murder. In Rav Weinberg's view, the Rambam utilizes the term רודף here the way he uses it in *Hilchos Chovel U-Mazik* (8:15), where he writes that one who throws a fellow passenger's belongings off a sinking ship to save the vessel does not have to compensate that passenger. The Rambam explains, שהמשא...כמו רודף אחריהם להרגם ומצוה רבה עשה שהשליך והושיעם — "because the cargo…is like someone chasing them to kill them, and he performed a great *mitzva* by discarding it and saving them." In other words, property that causes a threat to life may be destroyed without incurring liability for damages. Rav Weinberg boldly asserts that this is the Rambam's intent in formulating the provision permitting killing a fetus that endangers the mother. He means to say that although the fetus is the "property" of the father, it nevertheless may be killed because it poses a threat to the mother.[9] According to

---

however, as the Rambam clearly attributes this provision to the fact that the fetus "pursues" the mother.

8. Another example (noted by Rav Shmuel Auerbach in his *Darchei Shmuel* commentary to *Maseches Ohalos*) would be the case of a pregnant woman who requires life-saving surgery that would cause fatal harm to the fetus. According to the Rambam, it would presumably be forbidden to perform such an operation, as the fetus is not the cause of the mother's condition and is thus not a רודף.

9. This reading of the Rambam's comments is also suggested by Rav David Metzger in his annotation to the Rashba's commentary to *Maseches Nidda* (54a, note 184).

this reading, the Rambam does not consider killing a fetus akin to murder, but rather views it as an act of "damage" to the parents, which is permissible in cases of dire need.

It emerges, then, that *Tosfos* view the termination of a pregnancy as a Torah violation, and presumably an act of murder, and this may also be the view of the Rambam, depending on how one interprets his ruling.

Abortion as an איסור מדרבנן

The Ran (*Chullin* 19a in the Rif), commenting on a difficult passage in *Maseches Arachin* (7a), appears to take the view that killing a fetus as an איסור דרבנן (a prohibition enacted by *Chazal*).

The Mishna in *Arachin* establishes that if a pregnant woman is convicted of a capital offense, the sentence is carried out immediately, without waiting until she delivers her baby. The only exception is when the woman had already begun labor, in which case the execution is suspended until after the child's delivery. The Gemara reacts to the Mishna's ruling by wondering why such an obvious point needed explication: פשיטא, גופה היא — "This is obvious; it is part of her body!" As the fetus is part of the woman's body, the Gemara felt it obvious that the fetus should be killed along with the mother. To explain why the Mishna found it necessary to articulate this *halacha*, the Gemara comments that one might have thought otherwise due to the husband's stake. Since the infant inside the convicted mother's womb belongs to the father, one might have assumed that the sentence should be delayed to save his child. The Gemara concludes that the infant is not saved because the Torah indicates that a fetus inside a convicted pregnant woman dies along with the mother.[10]

Several *Rishonim* address the question of why the Gemara found it obvious that the fetus should perish along with the convicted mother, and what precisely the Gemara means by describing the fetus as גופה — part of the woman's body. *Tosfos* (*Sanhedrin* 80b), citing Rabbeinu Tam, explain that since the fetus is connected to and dependent upon the woman's body, the death sentence issued against the mother *ipso facto* applies to the fetus as well. This explanation of the Gemara's comment is noted by Rav Yair Bachrach (*Chavos Yair* 31), who draws proof from this passage that killing a fetus constitutes a Torah violation. The Gemara explained that the fetus is killed along with the mother only because the fetus is included in the mother's death sentence, indicating that otherwise, the court would be required to delay the execution in order to avoid killing

---

10. The Gemara infers this *halacha* from the phrase ומתו גם שניהם (*Devarim* 22:22).

the fetus. This would appear to prove that killing the fetus is, under ordinary circumstances, forbidden.[11]

The Ran, however, explains the Gemara's comment differently. He dismisses the aforementioned reading, noting that if the death sentence applies to the fetus, then in a case in which the infant is born after the court's ruling but before the woman's execution, the newborn infant should be executed, since it has been sentenced to death. This conclusion is clearly untenable, and the Ran therefore rejects the notion that the court's sentence incorporates the fetus.[12] To explain the Gemara's comment, the Ran writes, ולולד, כיון שלא יצא לאויר העולם, לא חיישינן — "As for the fetus, since it has not yet entered into the air of the world, we pay no concern." According to the Ran, it seems, the Gemara found it obvious and self-evident that the fetus is killed along with the mother because it is not considered a full-fledged human being, and thus it does not have to be taken into consideration. The Ran apparently understood the phrase גופה היא to mean that since the infant is part of the woman's body, it does not constitute an independent life, and thus killing it does not constitute murder. Accordingly, Rav Chaim Ozer Grodzinsky (*Achiezer* 3:65) notes that in the Ran's view, killing a fetus is not forbidden on the level of Torah law, and is rather prohibited only מדרבנן (by force of Rabbinic enactment). The only exception, as indicated by the Gemara, is after the onset the labor, when the fetus attains the status of a human being and thus comes under the Torah prohibition of murder.[13] (As we saw above, Rav Chaim Ozer applied this distinction to the issue of killing a fetus to save the mother from life-threatening labor.)

This view was taken later by the Maharit (1:99), who draws proof from the

---

11. Interestingly, however, the *Chavos Yair* contends that killing a fetus does not constitute murder, but rather falls under the category of הוצאת זרע לבטלה — "wasting seed," which is commonly used in reference to male masturbation. Just as it is forbidden for a man to purposely discharge from his body the "seed" that can be used to create life, it is similarly forbidden to purposely remove a fetus — a potential life — from a woman's body.
12. Rabbeinu Tam would likely respond to this argument that once the infant exits the mother's body, he assumes an entirely new identity, and is thus no longer subject to the mother's death sentence. See *Shiurei Rabbeinu Meshulam David Ha-Levi, Arachin* 7a.
13. Rav Moshe Feinstein, in the aforementioned responsum, insists that even the Ran considered killing a fetus a Torah violation. He understands the Ran to mean that once the Torah requires executing the pregnant woman without waiting for the baby to be delivered, as the Gemara infers from a verse in the Torah (cited above, note 10), we disregard the fetus in accordance with this extraordinary provision. In general, however, a fetus must be regarded as a full-fledged human being who may not be killed. This reading, however, is very difficult to accept, as the Ran made these comments in explaining the Gemara's initial reaction to the Mishna's ruling, whereas the Scriptural source for killing the fetus is mentioned later in the Gemara's discussion.

Gemara's discussion that the fetus's life is not a consideration in such a case, as it is only because of the husband's stake that one might have thought to delay the execution until after the child's birth. The Maharit thus rules that killing a fetus does not constitute murder at all.[14] This is also the ruling of former Sephardic Chief Rabbi Bentzion Meir Chai Uziel (*Mishpetei Uziel* 3:46), who explains the phrase פשיטא גופה היא to mean that since the fetus is considered part of the mother's body, there is no need to delay the execution in order to spare the infant.

The notion that killing a fetus is forbidden מדרבנן appears as well in a responsum of the Radbaz (2:695), who writes that although this does not constitute murder, it is forbidden משום דמיחזי כעין רציחה — it outwardly appears like murder. The clear implication is that this prohibition was enacted by *Chazal*, and does not fall under the Torah prohibition of murder.

Violating Shabbos to Save a Fetus

One of the arguments advanced against this position is the Gemara's explicit ruling in *Maseches Arachin* (7a) that one may violate Shabbos in order to save the life of a fetus, even in a situation in which the mother's life is not in danger. The Gemara there addresses the case of a pregnant woman who died during labor on Shabbos, and it states that baby should be surgically removed from the mother's body so that it can be saved, despite the Shabbos violation this entails. This ruling is codified in the *Shulchan Aruch* (O.C. 330:5). It emerges, then, that *halacha* permits desecrating Shabbos to save a fetus, even if the mother cannot be saved. Rav Moshe Feinstein contends that it is simply inconceivable that

---

14. Many later *poskim* noted that the Maharit appears here to contradict his own ruling just two responsa earlier (97), where he forbids killing a fetus and cites numerous sources indicating that a fetus is regarded as a full-fledged human being. Rav Moshe Feinstein boldly asserts that the second responsum was forged and was not actually authored by the Maharit. However, Rav Eliezer Waldenberg, in his response to Rav Moshe's stern rejection of his lenient ruling (*Tzitz Eliezer* 14:100), notes that the Maharit's own disciple, Rav Chaim Benveniste, cites this responsum of the Maharit in his *Shiyurei Kenesses Ha-Gedola* (Y.D. 154). In an earlier responsum (*Tzitz Eliezer*, vol. 9, pp. 233–234), Rav Waldenberg contends that the two seemingly conflicting responsa are, in fact, two segments of a single responsum, which were erroneously divided into two separate responsa, and the Maharit's conclusion is that killing a fetus does not constitute murder and is permitted when this is necessary for the mother's health.
Rav Shaul Yisraeli (*Amud Ha-Yemini*, 32) resolved the contradiction differently, noting that in the second responsum, the Maharit permits taking a fetus's life when this is necessary for the mother's health, whereas in the earlier responsum, he establishes that killing a fetus unnecessarily is forbidden.

Shabbos could be violated for an organism that the Torah permits killing. If a fetus is considered a living organism to which we apply the rule of פקוח נפש and suspend virtually all Torah laws to rescue, then how is it possible that killing this organism would not constitute murder?

However, as Rav Moshe himself acknowledges, this question appears to have already been addressed by the Ramban in his commentary to *Maseches Nidda* (54b). The Ramban there writes that killing a fetus does not constitute a capital offense, דלא קרינא ביה נפש אדם — because it is not considered a human life. The Ramban draws proof to his view from the fact that the Torah in *Sefer Shemos* (21:22) imposes a financial penalty upon one who causes a fetus to die by striking a pregnant woman. This *halacha* would seem to prove that the Torah classifies such a crime under the category of torts, as opposed to murder.[15] The Ramban then proceeds to pose the aforementioned question of why, if a fetus is not regarded as a human life, the Gemara permits violating Shabbos to rescue a fetus's life, even when there is no risk posed to the mother. The Ramban answers this question by invoking the concept of חלל עליו שבת אחת כדי שישמור שבתות הרבה — we allow a one-time act of Shabbos desecration to facilitate the birth of an infant who will grow to observe Shabbos each week throughout his life. Although the fetus is not halachically defined as a full-fledged human being, facilitating a fetus's birth nevertheless overrides the Shabbos prohibitions because the Torah's laws may be overridden for the sake of enabling a human being to be born and grow to observe the Torah's laws.

The explanation of the Ramban's comments appears to be that he distinguishes between two halachic concepts: פקוח נפש and חלל עליו שבת אחת כדי שישמור שבתות הרבה. The law of פקוח נפש establishes that Torah law, in virtually all circumstances, is overridden for the sake of preserving a human life. This law applies only to an organism that is currently defined by *halacha* as a human life, and therefore, according to the Ramban, it does not apply to a fetus, which is not considered a נפש אדם. The law of חלל עליו שבת אחת, by contrast, authorizes the violation of *mitzvos* for the sake of facilitating a lifetime of *mitzva* observance. As such, it applies not only with regard to full-fledged human beings, but also with regard to organisms that have the potential to become a full-fledged human life. Since a fetus has the potential to become a נפש אדם, Shabbos is violated for its sake, even though it is not yet considered a life and thus killing it would not fall under the Biblical prohibition of murder.

This analysis emerges from the Ramban's comments in *Toras Ha-Adam*, where he cites the *Behag*'s ruling that even in a situation in which an embryo is

---

15. Rav Waldenberg discusses this proof at length in *Tzitz Eliezer*, vol. 9, pp. 226–227.

endangered within forty days of conception, one may violate Shabbos to save its life. The Ramban writes:

אפילו בהצלת עובר פחות מבן ארבעים יום שאין לו חיות כלל מחללין עליו.

> Even to save a fetus less than forty days old [since conception], when it has no life at all, Shabbos is desecrated for its sake.

The Ramban clearly allows desecrating Shabbos for an organism שאין לו חיות כלל — that is not considered a life at all. Numerous sources (as we will see below) indicate that within forty days of conception, an embryo is not even considered a halachic "fetus." Yet according to the Ramban, one may desecrate Shabbos for the sake of protecting this embryo. In light of what we have seen, the reason for this ruling is clear. Since Torah law may be suspended even for a potential life, Shabbos is violated even to save an embryo within forty days of fertilization, which is not yet considered a life but has the potential to become a life.

This is the approach taken by Rav Eliezer Waldenberg in his controversial responsum permitting aborting a fetus determined to be afflicted with Tay-Sachs (*Tzitz Eliezer* 13:102). Citing the aforementioned comments of the Ramban, Rav Waldenberg writes that the status of a fetus with regard to abortion does not depend at all on its status with respect to the violation of Shabbos to save its life.

Rav Moshe Feinstein, however, resoundingly dismisses such a possibility. He could not countenance permitting Shabbos violation to save an organism that the Torah permits killing. In his view, once the Ramban permits violating Shabbos to save even an embryo within forty days of conception, killing an embryo even at that early stage, not to mention at later stages of pregnancy, constitutes an act of murder on the level of Torah law. As for the Ramban's comment that a fetus does not quality as נפש אדם, Rav Moshe explains this to mean that a fetus is not considered a full-fledged life in relation to others, who have already been born, and for this reason the fetus may be killed in order to save the mother. This does not mean, however, that killing the fetus does not ordinarily constitute a Torah violation.[16]

It should be noted that *Tosfos* in *Maseches Nidda* (54b) explicitly raise the

---

16. Support for Rav Moshe's reading may perhaps be drawn from the Ritva's discussion in his commentary to *Maseches Nidda*. After citing the Ramban's explanation for why one may violate Shabbos to save a fetus (although without mentioning the Ramban by name), the Ritva adds a brief elaboration: אע"ג דלאו נפש הוא, היינו לחייב ההורגו או לדחות נפש אמו...אבל לענין הצלתו בשבת דינו כנפש — "Although it is not a life, this is only with respect to sentencing one who kills it, or to override its mother's life… But with regard to saving it on Shabbos, it is considered a life." The Ritva clearly understood the Ramban to mean that although one who kills a fetus is not liable for murder, the fetus is nevertheless

possibility that killing a fetus is permissible, even though one may violate Shabbos to save a fetus, apparently seeing no contradiction at all between these two provisions. Rav Moshe dismisses this proof, however, asserting that although *Tosfos* use the term מותר — "permissible" — the intent must be that one is not liable to receive the death penalty, but not that it is actually permissible.[17]

Disputing ליכא מידעם

If we acknowledge that at least according to some *Rishonim*, killing a fetus does not constitute a Torah violation and is forbidden only מדרבנן, we must contend with *Tosfos*' comment applying to this issue the principle of ליכא מידעם דלישראל שרי ולבני נח מותר. How is it possible that the Torah would forbid gentiles from killing fetuses, but would permit Jews to commit such an act?

The answer lies in the claim made by a number of *Acharonim* that the rule of ליכא מידעם is subject to debate. As mentioned above, the Gemara invokes this rule in *Maseches Sanhedrin* (59a) to explain Rabbi Yossi ben Rabbi Chanina's remark that any command issued before *Matan Torah* is binding upon Jews even if it was not repeated after the Torah was given. Seemingly, the Gemara notes, the omission of such a law from the body of laws transmitted at Sinai implicitly suggests that it is no longer binding upon Jews. The Gemara explains, however, that since it is inconceivable that the Torah would permit for Jews that which is forbidden for gentiles, the omission of such a law at the time of *Matan Torah* cannot mean that Jews are absolved. Rabbi Yossi ben Rabbi Chanina himself notes that there is only one law in this category, which was issued before *Matan Torah* and not then repeated afterward — namely, the prohibition of גיד הנשה (eating the sciatic nerve). This prohibition appears in the Torah as the conclusion of the account of Yaakov's wrestling with an angel (*Bereishis* 32:33) and does not appear later in the Torah. Rabbi Yossi ben Rabbi Chanina observes that this

---

considered a human life in certain respects, and it would thus be forbidden to take its life.

17. This point is also made by the *Chavos Yair* (in his aforementioned responsum) and by Rav Yaakov Emden in his notes on *Maseches Nidda*.
Support for Rav Moshe's reading of *Tosfos* may perhaps be drawn from the fact that *Tosfos* bring as an analogy the case of a גוסס — a person who is about to die — noting that one may violate the Shabbos prohibitions for the purpose of attempting to save his life, even though one who kills him is not liable for murder. In reference to the case of one who kills a גוסס, *Tosfos* use the term פטור — the killer is not liable to receive the death penalty — not מותר ("permissible"). The fact that this case is used as an analogy for the case of killing a fetus would seem to indicate that in this case, too, the act is not permissible, even if it does not constitute a capital offense punishable by execution.

is the only instance of such a command. However, he adds, the status of גיד הנשה in this regard is subject to debate. Rabbi Yehuda, as cited by the Mishna (*Chullin* 100b), indeed maintains that the law of גיד הנשה was introduced in the times of Yaakov Avinu and was not repeated at the time the Torah was given.[18] However, the other *Tanna'im* (also cited in the Mishna in *Chullin*) dispute Rabbi Yehuda's view and maintain that the law of גיד הנשה was, in fact, introduced only at Sinai, despite the fact that it is mentioned already in *Sefer Bereishis*. According to the majority view, then, there is no law that was binding before *Matan Torah* which was not then reiterated at the time of *Matan Torah*.

As such, a number of *Acharonim*, including Rav Yaakov Ettlinger (*Aruch La-Ner*, Sanhedrin 59a) and the *Chasam Sofer* (Y.D. 19), assert that the rule of ליכא מידעם is not accepted as authoritative *halacha*. This rule was introduced by the Gemara to explain why we are bound by a law that was introduced before *Matan Torah* but not later reiterated — an explanation that is relevant only according to the minority view of Rabbi Yehuda. Since we follow the majority view, according to which this discussion is entirely unnecessary, there is no reason to assume that the notion of ליכא מידעם is accepted.

The aforementioned *Acharonim* explain on this basis the Rambam's surprising ruling in *Hilchos Melachim* (9:12–13) that gentiles may not partake of meat taken from a בהמה המפרכסת — an animal that has been slaughtered but is still convulsing — but a Jew may partake of such meat. This ruling seems to contradict the rule of ליכא מידעם. It thus seems reasonable to assume that the Rambam did not accept this rule as authoritative *halacha*, as it was introduced only to explain the minority view of Rabbi Yehuda.

If, indeed, we do not accept the rule of ליכא מידעם, then the entire basis of *Tosfos'* view is undermined. The whole reason why *Tosfos* concluded that Jews may not kill a fetus is because *halacha* cannot permit that which is forbidden for gentiles. But once we have determined that there may be restrictions that apply to gentiles but not to Jews, there is no reason to assume that the prohibition for gentiles to kill a fetus translates into a prohibition for Jews to kill a fetus.

On the basis of this argument, Rav Shmuel Engel concludes in one of his responsa (5:89) that at least according to the Rambam — who, as mentioned, likely does not accept the rule of ליכא מידעם — killing a fetus does not constitute a Torah violation. Rav Engel's comments are cited by Rav Waldenberg in a letter written to Rav Ovadia Yosef and published in *Tzitz Eliezer* (8:36), where he references several *Acharonim* who maintain that killing an unborn child is

---

18. The practical result of this view is that the prohibition applies even to the sciatic nerve of non-kosher animals, since it was introduced before the Torah forbade partaking of the meat of non-kosher animals, and thus it was stated in regard to all animals.

forbidden only on the level of Rabbinic enactment and does not constitute a Torah violation.

The *Tzitz Eliezer* and the *Iggeros Moshe*

The halachic controversy surrounding abortion erupted after Rav Waldenberg wrote a responsum to the director of Shaarei Zedek hospital in 1974 permitting aborting a fetus that has been determined to suffer from Tay-Sachs disease. He ruled that this would be permissible through the seventh month of pregnancy, after which point the fetus might already be ready for birth, such that abortion would constitute murder.

Rav Waldenberg based his position mainly on the rulings of earlier authorities who permitted terminating a pregnancy when this is necessary for the mother's wellbeing, even if her life is not at stake. Specifically, he noted the aforementioned responsum of the Maharit (97), as well as a responsum of Rav Yaakov Emden (1:43)[19] and of the Ben Ish Chai (*Rav Pe'alim*, E.H. 1:4).[20] Rav Waldenberg's responsum was later published in the thirteenth volume of his *Tzitz Eliezer* (102).

This lenient position is shared by a number of other 20th-century *poskim*, including Rav Yechiel Yaakov Weinberg and Rav Bentzion Meir Chai Uziel, in their respective responsa cited above, as well as Rav Shaul Yisraeli.[21]

Soon after Rav Waldenberg's responsum was publicized, in the fall of 1976, Rav Moshe Feinstein wrote a letter strongly condemning this ruling, rejecting out of hand the arguments of the Maharit, Rav Yaakov Emden, the Ben Ish Chai, and Rav Weinberg. He contended that the generally accepted view is that killing a fetus constitutes outright murder and is thus forbidden on the level of Torah law. As such, he maintained, it is permissible only when the fetus poses a direct, life-threatening risk to the mother, but not under other circumstances,

---

19. It should be noted that Rav Yaakov Emden definitively permits terminating a pregnancy only in the case of a married woman carrying a child conceived through an adulterous affair, because she — and, by extension, her fetus — are liable to execution (an argument that Rav Moshe Feinstein sharply rejects in his responsum). In other cases in which an abortion is necessary for the mother's wellbeing, Rav Yaakov Emden raises the possibility of permitting the abortion, but leaves the issue as an unresolved question.
20. While the Ben Ish Chai clearly indicates that there is room to allow aborting a fetus conceived out of wedlock to avoid disgrace, he stops sort of issuing a definitive ruling, writing that he did not feel confident enough to reach such a conclusion.
21. In the responsum mentioned above, n. 14. Rav Ovadia Yosef (*Yabia Omer*, E.H. 4:1) permits aborting the fetus in the case of a serious illness or defect only during the woman's first trimester.

even when the baby will suffer from a serious disease. This is also the view taken by Rav Isser Yehuda Unterman in an article published in *Noam* (vol. 6), where he forbids aborting a fetus whose mother suffered from the measles, which threatened to cause severe defects in the child.

This debate is directly relevant to Zika infection as well. Rav Moshe would forbid aborting the fetus, as the pregnancy poses no threat to the mother, whereas Rav Waldenberg would permit an abortion in light of the grave defects from which the infant will suffer throughout his life.

Aborting Before Forty Days and Post-Coital Contraception

Even if we accept the premise that abortion is forbidden in such cases, the possibility exists, in principle, of allowing an abortion if the condition is detected soon after conception, as several sources suggest that the fertilized egg is not even considered a fetus until forty days after fertilization.

The Torah in *Sefer Vayikra* (22:12–13) establishes that a *Kohen*'s daughter loses the right to partake of her father's *teruma* if she marries a non-*Kohen*, but if she is divorced or widowed, and she has no children from her husband, she regains this privilege. The Mishna in *Maseches Yevamos* (69b) adds that even if the *Kohen*'s daughter did not marry a non-*Kohen*, but she conceived by being raped or seduced by a non-*Kohen*, she may not eat *teruma*, since she carries a non-*Kohen*'s child in her womb. The Gemara clarifies that for forty days after the incident of rape or seduction, the *Kohen*'s daughter may eat *teruma*, because even if she had conceived, the fertilized egg does not yet halachically qualify as a fetus, as it is מיא בעלמא ("mere liquid"). After forty days, however, she must abstain from *teruma*, given the possibility that she had conceived. Rashi explains that the fetus is formed only forty days after conception, and thus until that point, the embryo is not halachically treated as an unborn child.

The *Shach* (C.M. 210:2) applies this concept also to the case of a father who wishes to legally transfer property to his child who is still in utero. *Halacha* recognizes the transfer of property from a father to his child in utero (*Bava Basra* 142b; *Shulchan Aruch*, C.M. 210:1), but the *Shach*, citing the Ritva (in *Bava Basra*), claims that this applies only if forty days have passed since conception. Within forty days, there is only מיא בעלמא, and not a fetus, and thus property cannot be transferred.[22]

---

22. Interestingly, however, Meiri (in *Yevamos*) dismisses this distinction. He understood that the only reason why one would think to distinguish between these two stages is because within forty days of conception there is no קורבת דעת — feeling of closeness — between the father and the child. Meiri then rejects this distinction, arguing that there is little

Similarly, the Mishna in *Maseches Nidda* (40a) rules that if a woman miscarries and knows with certainty that the conception had occurred less than forty days earlier (such as if she had only immersed and resumed marital relations with her husband within the last forty days), she is not considered to have delivered a child. She does not assume the status of טומאת לידה — the status of impurity assigned to a woman after childbirth — because the fetus she delivered is not halachically considered a fetus. Likewise, if a woman miscarried her first pregnancy within forty days of conception, and at some later point conceives again and gives birth to a boy, he is considered a firstborn and requires a *pidyon ha-ben* (Mishna, *Bechoros* 47b). Since the first pregnancy ended within forty days of conception, it does not halachically qualify as a pregnancy, and thus the child born from her second conception is regarded as a firstborn.

Another expression of this concept appears in the *Mishneh Le-Melech* (*Hilchos Tum'as Meis* 2:1), who writes that a stillborn delivered within forty days of conception is not considered a corpse with respect to the laws of *tum'a*. Although one who comes in contact with a stillborn is considered *tamei*, this is not the case if the fetus was delivered within forty days of conception, as the fetus at that point is considered מיא בעלמא, and not an actual human organism.

This concept likely underlies the Gemara's comment in *Maseches Berachos* (60a) that one may pray for his child to be a certain gender within forty days of conception. It is after forty days when the child's gender is determined, and thus from that point, a prayer for the gender constitutes a תפילת שוא (prayer recited in vain). Until forty days, however, such a prayer is legitimate. The explanation, seemingly, is that the fertilized egg becomes a "fetus" only at forty days, and so before then, as the fetus is still forming, one may pray that it should develop into either a male or a female.

Indeed, the *Toras Chayim* (*Sanhedrin* 91b) writes that within forty days of conception, the fetus is merely כחתיכת בשר בלא איברים וגידין ועצמות — "like a piece of flesh, without organs, veins or bones."

Accordingly, Rav Shlomo Dreimer (*Beis Shlomo*, C.M. 132) writes that although gentiles are liable to execution for killing a fetus, this applies only from forty days after conception. This is noted as well by Rav Chaim Ozer Grodzinsky (*Achiezer*, 3:65:14). Significantly, however, Rav Chaim Ozer indicates that for a Jew, killing a fetus within forty days of conception would still be forbidden, at least on the level of Rabbinic enactment. He writes, בישראל אפשר דאין איסור מן התורה — meaning, it is possible that this would be permitted on the level of Torah law

---

קורבת הדעת even at later stages, and yet *halacha* recognizes the fetus's ability to legally acquire property from his father.

for a Jew. Rav Chaim Ozer clearly considers this forbidden, and even considers the possibility that this would constitute a Torah violation.

Rav Moshe Feinstein, as noted above, applies his stringent ruling even at the earliest stages of pregnancy, noting the aforementioned ruling of the Ramban in *Toras Ha-Adam* allowing Shabbos violation to save a fetus's life even within forty days of conception. As discussed earlier, Rav Moshe refuses to accept the possibility that Shabbos may be violated to save a life that is not included in the Torah prohibition of murder. He thus concludes that if Shabbos desecration is mandated to rescue a fetus even within forty days of conception, then necessarily, the Torah prohibition of murder applies to such a fetus.

Even within Rav Moshe's position, we might raise the question of how soon after conception the prohibition takes effect. Rabbeinu Tam, cited by *Tosfos* (*Yevamos* 12b), rules that it is permissible for a woman to empty her body of semen after intercourse to ensure that she does not conceive. Rav Meir Dan Plotzky (*Chemdas Yisrael, Kuntres Ner Mitzva*, p. 176) raises the question of how this is permitted, in light of the fact that this process might have the effect of killing an egg that was fertilized during intercourse. Seemingly, Rav Plotzky writes, this proves that at least in Rabbeinu Tam's view, there is no prohibition against killing a fetus within forty days of conception, when an embryo is regarded as מיא בעלמא.

We may, however, refute this proof, by suggesting that the prohibition against killing an embryo begins only once it implants itself in the uterus, which generally occurs around a week or so (6–10 days) after fertilization. If so, then even if we accept Rav Moshe's stringent ruling that killing a fetus is forbidden even within forty days of conception, we might nevertheless permit killing an embryo within the first several days after conception. This would have important ramifications regarding post-coital contraceptive methods, such as the controversial "morning after pill," which prevents a fertilized egg from entering the uterus, thereby avoiding pregnancy.[23]

In truth, however, this conclusion would be correct only according to the position of Rabbeinu Tam, since other *Rishonim* maintain that a woman may not utilize this method to avoid pregnancy, as it falls under the prohibition of השחתת זרע (wasting seed).[24] According to their view, post-coital contraception would be allowed only if the pregnancy would pose some kind of risk, but not in other situations.

---

23. This would also mean that it would be forbidden to violate Shabbos to save a fertilized egg during this period, in light of Rav Moshe's contention that Shabbos violation is allowed only to save a life included in the prohibition against murder.
24. See *Teshuvos Rabbi Akiva Eiger, Mahadura Kama*, 71–72.

INTERVIEWS

Rav Dovid Cohen
on *Headlines with Dovid Lichtenstein**

I don't think it's appropriate for me to give a psak when it's such a controversial topic. It's well known that this was a *machlokes* between two very great *gedolim*, both of whom were רבן של כל בני הגולה, Rav Moshe Feinstein zt"l and Rav Eliezer Yehuda Waldenberg zt"l. These were literally גדולי עולם who had mastery of the entire Torah…

Ideally, a person should have a מרא דאתרא who is his rabbi. Every frummer Yid should follow the rules of his מרא דאתרא and ask him his question, and not bring his questions to the one who is most "convenient," who will give him the lenient answer…

Rav Moshe was very *machmir* about aborting. I can't even say how far he went. He considered it אבק רציחה [quasi-murder]. Rav Waldenberg, on the other hand, held that any kind or any source of עגמת נפש [anguish] to the woman allows it, because it has nothing whatsoever to do with רציחה [murder]. עובר ירך אמו [a fetus is like its mother's thigh, part of her body]…and so like any other operation, you don't do it for nothing, and maybe there are איסורים דרבנן involved that are overridden for valid reasons. He thought that for צער גדול [great distress], even in a situation of Downs' Syndrome, it would be permissible to terminate the pregnancy even at seven months, because as long as the fetus has not moved from its place [in preparation for birth], it has the status of ירך אמו…

In Rav Waldenberg's *teshuva*, he is incredulous. He writes as though he couldn't believe it, he couldn't understand how Rav Moshe went against all the *Acharonim*, and he gives a list of *Acharonim* who learned the *sugyos* against the view of Rav Moshe. *Tosfos* in *Nidda* (44) is clearly not like Rav Moshe, and Rav Moshe says it's a mistake — in two places in *Tosfos*!

…I mentioned to Rav Moshe the Maharit, who brings a proof that abortion has nothing to do with רציחה. It says וכי ינצו אנשים ונגפו אשה הרה (*Shemos* 21:22), and [*Chazal* say] it's talking about מצות שבמיתה — people fighting to kill. And even though the fetuses come out, there's only payment. If this entails any kind of רציחה, the Maharit asks, then why don't you say קים ליה בדרבה מיניה, according to Tanna De-Bei Chizkiya that קים ליה בדרבה מיניה applies even when there is no prior warning? This proves it has nothing to do with אבק רציחה…

The *Tzitz Eliezer* quotes a whole list of *Acharonim*, and everyone holds like him. Of course, no one says you're allowed to kill a *mamzer*, but Rav Yaakov Emden says that in a case of *mamzerus*, you can abort. It seems from all the

Acharonim that no one held like Rav Moshe. It's not only the *Maharit* — it's dozens of גדולי אחרונים throughout the ages.

They deal with the *Tosfos* in *Sanhedrin* [that killing a fetus must be forbidden because of ליכא מידעם]. They say that once there's any kind of *issur* you don't say ליכא מידעם. It doesn't have to be the same *issur*. The *Seridei Eish* talks about this, and says there's an *issur* of חבלה [inflicting a wound], so you don't say ליכא מידעם. So just like an operation, when there's a necessity we do not consider it חבלה. The *Acharonim* deal with the question.

It's a פלא [something startling] that Rav Moshe [discounted all these *Acharonim*]. This is what the *Tzitz Eliezer* says — we never heard this kind of reasoning, that you tell me that *Tosfos* is a mistake, a printing error in two places. What kind of *derech* [approach] is this?

This is what I want to comment on. The *Tzitz Eliezer* didn't realize…if you make a study of Rav Moshe's *teshuvos*, you'll see he had a different *mesora* [tradition] in *hora'ah* [halachic decision-making]. We know there was such a *mesora* from the Vilna Gaon, and Rav Chaim Volozhiner followed that *mesora*, that paskening a *shayla* does not mean putting together what other *poskim* say. I heard that in Lita [Lithuania], the greatest insult you could give to a Litvishe *posek* is that he paskened from the *Pischei Teshuva* or from the *Sha'arei Teshuva*. They said about those *poskim* who used to bring other *poskim* in their responsa that they should get paid for being a porter, for bringing together *poskim*. Paskening a *shayla* meant going through the *sugya* yourself and working through it as though you're a *Rishon*, and then determining the *halacha* according to your understanding of the *sugya*. You have the right to argue on any *Rishon* you wish. This was a *mesora*. But since it's not respectful to do so, they would explain בדוחק [with a strained, forced answer] why you're not dealing with the *sugya* like this *Rishon* or that *Rishon*. Rav Chaim Volozhiner once argued with the *Beis Yosef* on the subject of מליח הרי הוא כרותח, and they challenged him based on the *Beis Yosef*. He said, "Don't ask me questions from the *Beis Yosef* — he had a different kind of salt." In *halacha*, this is not meaningful. But he was saying, "I'm not arguing with him; don't ask me questions."

There are many cases where Rav Moshe reached his *psak* and wrote, "What about this Ramban, who is not like me?" And he would be מפלפל. But Rav Moshe paskened *shaylos* according to this *mesora*. It's clear to me. So when he amends the text of *Tosfos*, this is his way of being respectful to the *Rishonim*. But he is arguing because this was his *mesora* for paskening *shaylos*. And this is why the *Tzitz Eliezer*, who had a totally different *mesora*, bringing all the *poskim* he could find, found it incredulous that Rav Moshe said what he said. People have to understand where Rav Moshe was coming from.

The bottom line is that a person has to ask a *shayla* from his מרא דאתרא, and not pick and choose.

* Broadcast on 21 Iyar, 5776 (May 28, 2016)

Rabbi Dr. Aaron Glatt
on *Headlines with Dovid Lichtenstein**

At this moment in time — the 32nd day of the *Omer*, 5776 — the number of native cases of Zika in the United States remains zero. Right now, all the cases identified as Zika in the United States have been brought in by people who had traveled to locations in Central America and South America, where Zika is prevalent, transmitted by mosquitoes. Whether or not that will change is a very big question. As the virus vector — the mosquitoes — travel up into the United States, which they have done in the past, and have the potential to transmit the Zika virus when they bite people, there is concern that the number I just told you could change. This would be a very big change in the way the disease is spread in the United States.

There are a number of tests that any woman who had potentially been exposed to Zika, either through herself or through her husband, should take. She should absolutely be seen by a knowledgeable physician, which could be an obstetrician-gynecologist, an internist, or an infectious diseases specialist, who would know the appropriate blood tests that can be done. There is now also a urine test that can be done, as well as other tests, to determine whether someone has been infected with Zika. If the woman has been infected, there is the potential of it being transmitted to the baby inside her, which can lead to terrible consequences רחמנא ליצלן…such as serious birth defects and microcephaly. In some situations it can cause miscarriages. It is very important for any pregnant woman who is at risk for Zika acquisition to be seen by a physician, who would hopefully know what test to do and what advice to give. And that's when *shaylos* will come to a *rav* regarding what he would allow or not allow in terms of the kinds of intervention that medicine would recommend, which could possibly be against *halacha*.

If the mother has been infected, and we know for certain that there's the potential of it being transmitted to the baby, we don't have a way to test whether the baby is definitely infected or not, but we can look for evidence in sonograms of damage to the baby and see if the baby is developing properly. If there are findings on the sonogram — which would be recommended serially for such women — and changes are seen that are suggestive of a serious Zika infection, this is how we would detect the impact of Zika on a baby.

There are differences in the stages of pregnancy in *halacha*. *Halacha* would never sanction an unnecessary abortion even in the first forty days [after conception], when we refer to the growing fetus inside the mother as מיא בעלמא — a euphemism used in the Gemara. This does not imply that it's just water; we can detect that the baby is beginning to be formed. (*Chazal* obviously had *ru'ach ha-kodesh* and knew that something magically transforms at forty days. We know today, scientifically, that all of a baby's organs are developed in miniature form at forty days, so the halachic concept is an accurate medical concept, as well. In fact, we no longer call it an embryo at that point, but a fetus. So *halacha* parallels science beautifully.) The suggestion that it is permitted in any way to perform an abortion without any reason before forty days is halachically incorrect. But where *halacha* does sanction intervention to cause the mother to lose the baby — all things being equal, it is preferable to do so before forty days. But we may not know this information [about effects of Zika infection in a fetus] before day forty, so that is not going to be an option...

In the secular world, some would recommend avoiding the potential problem of microcephaly by aborting every pregnancy or avoiding pregnancy [if there is concern of Zika infection], but this, of course, poses huge halachic questions that need to be individualized in every case and brought to a גדול בתורה, to a *rav* who understands the issues.

Baruch Hashem, the [rate of Zika infection that affects fetuses] is not as bad as one may have guessed. In fact, if the mother was asymptomatic...the likelihood of transmitting it to the baby is very low, compared to a woman who did have symptoms. If a woman did have symptoms after being in an endemic area...then the baby has some sort of chance, as well. We don't yet know what exactly the number is. Some studies suggest that it's one in hundred, others as high as one in five. So we do not know the right answer. And even within that we do not know how severe it will be. Not even every mother who transfers the virus to the baby will have the worst scenario.

For these *shaylos* you need גדולי תורה to pasken, and each case needs to be individualized. If you know for a fact that the mother was symptomatic, and she's pregnant right now, that's a *shayla* they need to discuss with their *rav*. Statistically speaking, without knowing anything else about the patient, there's a good chance that the baby will be born healthy. I can't state — nobody can state — what the chances are, so a *rav* will need to get involved. You would need to look at the mother's mental state as well as other factors. There are also different views among the *poskim*.

These are *shaylos* that are עומדים ברומו של עולם and which need to be brought to a great *gadol*, to a tremendous *posek*, and must not be taken lightly.

* Broadcast on 21 Iyar, 5776 (May 28, 2016).

Rav Moshe Sternbuch on *Headlines with Dovid Lichtenstein**

We pasken that until forty days, we allow [aborting a fetus if there's a probability of serious illness], but after forty day we do not allow. We should ask two doctors to make sure — we never ask just one doctor for such an important case — and if in most cases it would cause the baby to suffer, you go after the *rov* [majority]. If not, I would not be *matir*. So up to forty days, I would allow [aborting] if there's a majority [probability that the child will end up suffering]…

Even if you have such a child…there are private people and institutions to look out for him, so you have no right to kill him. You don't want him, but others do. There are institutions for these children who are born to families that don't want them… A person can do a great thing by taking them in, so why should we kill them?

* Broadcast on 18 Tammuz, 5776 (July 23, 2016).

The New York Jewish Week

Orthodox Compulsive Disorder?

February 15, 2010
by Sharon Udasin

"Mr. A" is a 43-year-old chasidic man who is so afraid to make mistakes in his daily prayers that he cannot bring himself to get out of bed until noon or 1 p.m. The reason? Obsessions he's faced since his days in yeshiva, when he was consistently the last person to finish praying each morning.

"He thought he was just more religious than everyone in the class," said Dr. Steven Friedman, a professor of clinical psychiatry at SUNY Downstate, who was addressing a group of fellow therapists. "Patients who have religious obsessions often don't recognize or admit that they have symptoms."

Friedman was speaking to a group of 30 therapists — at least 20 of them Orthodox Jews — who had gathered for a three-day conference this week at SUNY Downstate Medical Center in Brooklyn sponsored by the Behavior Therapy Training Institute of the International Obsessive Compulsive Disorder Foundation. While the Institute holds about three of these meetings annually, this was the first conference tailored specifically to the needs of Orthodox Jewish therapists, who had been unable to attend regular Saturday programming.

Sessions last weekend were largely the same as any other Behavior Therapy Training curriculum, aside from Friedman's Sunday afternoon lecture about "Religious Scrupulosity," which targeted obsessions and compulsions rooted in Jewish ritual. In addition to discussing these specific behaviors and treatment techniques, the doctors focused on the unwillingness of many Orthodox Jews to even seek treatment, in a community where mental health issues are somewhat taboo.

"You can speak Yiddish like I do and you'll still find that that won't get you access to certain populations," Friedman said. "Since the community is so small, most of them you know and it's one degree of separation. If you give me the name of an Orthodox person in the United States, I can find someone who knows something all about them."

"This is problematic when you do therapy," he added.

OCD is a genetic disorder that equally affects men, women and children of all backgrounds, typically appearing between the ages of 10 to 12 or in late adolescence or early adulthood, according to the Foundation. On average, OCD inflicts 1 in 100 adults and 1 in 200 kids and teens, amounting to about 2 to 3 million adult cases and 500,000 childhood cases in the United States alone. Because OCD runs in families, there is a 15 percent chance that a patient's child will also exhibit OCD, though not necessarily in exactly the same form, Friedman explained. For example, he said, a parent might be an incessant hand-washer, while the child might become a compulsive checker.

Be it contamination, relationships or religion, OCD "always attacks what's most important," according to Friedman, and for Orthodox Jews with OCD what's most important is their daily commitment to Judaism. And so much of Orthodox Judaism — or anything religion — is about prescribed ritual, like the particular order in which Jews put on and tie their shoes, adjust tefillin precisely on their heads or clean themselves before prayer.

Ironically, however, OCD patients may get so much anxiety from the religious practices that they don't even enjoy the rituals and beliefs that are so important to them. Prayers and religious behaviors will often be painful processes, punctuated by incessant questioning and reassurance seeking from rabbis and elders.

"You see a lot of compulsive behaviors with the intention of undoing something that has been done wrong," said Dr. Jeff Szymanski, the executive director of the International OCD Foundation. "I have to repeat it until it's done perfectly."

Friedman added, "People with OCD don't really get any joy out of their religious experience."

Instead, they may spend inordinate amounts of time doubting and checking — whether they prayed correctly, whether they greeted every single person in shul, whether they scrubbed their hands for long enough between handling milk and meat. One patient was so worried about clearing his house of chametz during Passover that he built his own extremely dangerous — not to mention illegal — matzah-baking oven in his basement. Intrusive thoughts may also extend to aggressive and sexual obsessions, such as momentarily perceiving the rabbi as a Nazi, thinking the Second Temple was for pagans or fearing homosexuality when one is not actually gay.

"A lot of Orthodox Jewish men seem to have this fear. It's not usually true. I usually just ask them one question, are you attracted to men?" Friedman said. "And the answer is usually no."

For Orthodox women, he says, the most problematic Jewish rituals for patients are properly adhering to kashrut and observing "family purity" laws, which Friedman calls a "torture" for some OCD patients, particularly due to the meticulous checking and counting required of them each month.

"The rituals will typically be offshoots of their current religious practices. Their faith-based practices will get co-opted by the OCD, so [a Jewish patient's] compulsive behavior will look a bit different from someone who is Protestant or Muslim," Szymanski said. "But the themes are pretty consistent — it's typically a fear of offending God or engaging in something blasphemous, a fear of hell, of Satan, of doing something imperfectly. The compulsive behaviors are typically things like praying a certain way and praying enough."

Among patients of other religions, Friedman found one Hindu man who was so afraid of stepping on God that he wouldn't get out of bed, as well as many Muslims who were so concerned with performing ablutions (washing) properly that they were unable to begin prayers. For Catholics, imagining Jesus sleeping with the Virgin Mary is a popular obsessive fear.

The best way to conquer — or at least subdue — obsessions and compulsions is to undergo cognitive behavioral therapy with exposure to the trigger, a technique that is all too often left out of medical school and doctorate curricula, according to Szymanski. At their triennial conferences, the OCD Foundation aims to compensate for this oversight and teach therapists the newest techniques in cognitive behavioral therapy. For any patient with moderate to severe levels of OCD, Friedman adds that an on-site home visit is also crucial when assessing behavioral patterns.

"I actually go to the bathroom with them and say, 'Show me how you wash,'" he said. "People are not in touch with many of their compulsions."

And he believes that for the most part, Orthodox patients will progress better with Orthodox therapists, despite the fear that they may have some of the same friends and acquaintances in their close-knit communities.

"Ultimately for OCD and [religious manifestations of it], probably most of our patients are better served by seeing someone within the community who knows the intricacies," Friedman said, noting that he'll often help people by labeling their obsessions in Jewish terms — "mishegas" (craziness) for adults and "nudniks" for kids.

Copyright © thejewishweek.com

Suspending *Mitzva* Observance to Treat OCD

The National Institute of Mental Health estimates that some 2.2 million adults in the United States suffer from obsessive compulsive disorder (OCD),[1] a debilitating condition that manifests itself through, among other symptoms, incessant uncertainty about the satisfactory completion of tasks. For example, OCD patients are prone to repeatedly wash their hands due to the concern of germs, check their doors to ensure they are locked, and make sure electrical appliances are turned off before leaving the house. They might also count things multiple times out of fear that they may have counted incorrectly.

For the halachically observant Jew, OCD can be especially severe. *Halacha*, by nature, is very demanding and detailed, and given the religious importance we afford to the meticulous observance of all its minutiae, it can create a great deal of anxiety and result in compulsive behavior among those suffering from this disorder. Observant Jews with OCD may, for example, be unable to complete *berachos* or prayers, as the uncertainty as to whether they pronounced all the words properly will drive them to recite the texts repeatedly. Married Orthodox women with OCD may find themselves spending many hours preparing for the *mikveh* on the night of immersion, overcome by anxiety over the possible presence of *chatzitzos* (dirt or other foreign substances on the skin or in their hair, which could invalidate the immersion). They might also feel the need to consult about every light discoloration found on their undergarments and *bedika* (inspection) cloths. Pesach preparations can be exceedingly stressful for OCD patients, who will feel the need to check the entire house numerous times to ensure the absence of all *chametz*.

One Orthodox Jewish therapist explained that OCD "always attacks what's most important" — meaning, it creates anxiety regarding that which is most vital to a person.[2] For most people, this is personal safety and health, but for the conscientious observant Jew, this also includes meeting halachic obligations. The obsession with halachic details, coupled with the more standard obsessions

---

1. http://www.nimh.nih.gov/health/topics/obsessive-compulsive-disorder-ocd/index.shtml. Retrieved November 12, 2015.
2. Dr. Steven Friedman, quoted by *The Jewish Week*, February 16, 2010.

with health and safety, can make the patient entirely dysfunctional and hamper his or her ability to find fulfillment in any area of life.

OCD is generally treated through cognitive behavior therapy (CBT), and at times with medication as well. Typically, the therapy used to treat OCD involves "exposure and response prevention," whereby the patient is trained not to respond compulsively to the situations that trigger obsessive thoughts. In the case of "halachic OCD," this might mean training the patient not to repeat the *beracha* or prayer text, even if he knows for certain that he recited it improperly.

This gives rise to the intriguing question of whether, from a halachic standpoint, such treatment is permissible. Is a therapist allowed to train his patient not to repeat *berachos* over food, for example, even in cases in which the patient is certain that he missed a word? Is it halachically acceptable for an OCD patient to continue his recitation of the *Shema* or *Amida* even after mispronouncing or omitting some of the text? In other words, is the interest of restoring mental health a sufficient reason to knowingly allow the patient to fail to observe *mitzvos*?

This question was already addressed by the Steipler Gaon in one of his published letters (*Karyana De-Igresa*, 373). Without elaborating, the Steipler Gaon rules that the patient in question should be instructed to pray from a *siddur* and not to go back to recite any text that he fears may have been recited incorrectly. More recently, Rav Asher Weiss dealt with this question in the second volume of his responsa (*Shu"t Minchas Asher* 134). Rav Weiss rules unequivocally that an OCD patient may and must follow his therapist's instructions for overcoming his disorder, even at the expense of *mitzva* observance. He writes:

> ראשית חובתו של איש זה לעשות את כל הנדרש על מנת למצוא מזור ומרפא למחלתו, ולשם כך מותר לו אף לעבור על מצוות התורה.
>
> This man's primary obligation is to do everything that is necessary for him to cure his illness, and to this end he is allowed even to violate the Torah's commandments.

In the pages that follow, we will discuss Rav Weiss' arguments and explore the various sources relevant to this issue.

יותר מחומש

Rav Weiss begins by positing that *halacha* absolves one from fulfilling a *mitzva* when this is necessary to avoid illness. Just as one is not required to pay יותר מחומש — more than one-fifth of his assets — in order to fulfill a *mitzva*, one is similarly not required to subject himself to physical harm or debilitation for the sake of a *mitzva*. Therefore, if a person suffers from a debilitating mental illness, and his mental health professional determines that his recovery requires suspending *mitzva* observance, then the patient should comply. As long as he is only suspending the observance of *mitzvos asei* (affirmative commands), and not transgressing prohibitions, this is permissible for the sake of restoring his mental health.[3]

A similar line of reasoning can be found in a responsum of Rav Moshe Feinstein (*Iggeros Moshe*, E.H. 4:32), where he permits a young divorced woman to leave her hair uncovered so that people would not discern that she had been previously married. Rav Moshe writes that just as *halacha* does not require one to incur a loss of more than one-fifth of his assets for the sake of a *mitzva*, a divorcee is not required to compromise her ability to find a new husband for the sake of a *mitzva*. Therefore, if she truly believes that covering her hair would lower her chances of remarriage, then she is absolved of the hair-covering requirement. Similarly, in an earlier reponsum (E.H. 1:57), Rav Moshe permits a widow to leave her hair uncovered because she needs to work to support her children and the job she was offered requires her to leave her hair uncovered. Rav Moshe maintains that hair covering is considered a halachic requirement, as opposed to avoiding a prohibition, and it is therefore suspended in situations of dire need, such as in order to secure a livelihood or to find a spouse.

Another precedent is a responsum of the *Avnei Nezer* (E.H. 1:8), who explains on the basis of this principle the reason why a husband is not required to divorce his wife who is found to be infertile. Although he bears the Torah obligation to procreate, nevertheless, losing one's beloved wife is considered a far more significant loss than the loss of a large amount of money, and he is therefore exempt from this *mitzva*, just as one is exempt from a *mitzva* requiring a sacrifice of one-fifth of his assets.

The *Chasam Sofer* and the Non-Jewish Mental Hospital

Rav Weiss proceeds to assert that even if the treatment for OCD requires transgressing Torah violations, this would also be permissible, in light of a ruling by the *Chasam Sofer* (1:83) concerning the case of a mentally ill seven-year-old child. The boy's family wanted to enroll him in a non-Jewish mental institute that was able to cure his condition, but he would be fed non-kosher food and would not be trained in any *mitzva* observances throughout his stay in the

---

3. Rav Weiss asserts that this applies to eating without a *beracha* as well. Although it may appear, at first glance, that there is a prohibition against eating without reciting a *beracha*, in truth, reciting *berachos* is an obligation, not the avoidance of a prohibition.

facility. Although a child below the age of *mitzva* obligation is not bound by Torah law, it is nevertheless forbidden for adults to feed him non-kosher food. As the *Chasam Sofer* acknowledges, it is possible that enrolling one's child in an institute that serves non-kosher food would be halachically equivalent to actively feeding him non-kosher food, and thus forbidden on the level of Torah law. The question thus arises as to whether this prohibition may be suspended for the sake of curing a child's mental illness.

The *Chasam Sofer* rules that the child may be brought to such an institute, writing, מוטב שיחלל תורה זמן מה כדי שישמור מצוות הרבה — "It is preferable for him to violate the Torah for some time so that he can [later] observe many *mitzvos*." In other words, if the child's condition was not cured, he would remain a שוטה (mentally disabled person) throughout his life and be exempt entirely from *mitzva* obligation. Therefore, it is permissible to have him violate *mitzvos* temporarily if this is necessary for his recovery and would then allow him to become fully obligated in all of the Torah's commands.

The *Chasam Sofer* draws an analogy to the situation of a person who finds himself in a remote, deserted location, and has lost track of the days of the week. Such a person is permitted to do the minimum needed to preserve his life, but no more, given that it may be Shabbos on any given day. Nevertheless, he is allowed to walk as much as he wants, despite the Shabbos prohibition of *techumin* (walking beyond 2,000 *amos* in an uninhabited area). As the *Chasam Sofer* notes (citing *Tosfos* in *Maseches Shabbos* 69b), the person may walk as far as he wishes even according to the opinion that considers *techumin* a Torah violation. The concept underlying this *halacha* is that if the person does not travel, then he will never reach an inhabited area where he can resume a proper halachic lifestyle. Somewhat similarly, it is permissible to allow a mentally ill child to violate the Torah for the purpose of enabling him to become mentally stable, and thus fully obligated in all *mitzvos*.

Rav Weiss applies the *Chasam Sofer*'s ruling to the situation of an OCD patient. Without recovering from his disorder, an OCD patient who cannot complete *berachos* or prayers will likely never have the ability to properly fulfill these requirements. It is therefore preferable to have him knowingly suspend his observance of these *mitzvos* for the purpose of treatment, which will enable him to fulfill them properly throughout the rest of his life.

It should be noted, however, that later in his responsum, the *Chasam Sofer* imposes a significant qualification on his ruling, one which seemingly renders it inapplicable to the case of an OCD patient:

ברם דא צריכא: כשהוא מחוייב במצוות ולא הגיע לכלל שוטה שדברו בו חכמים בכל מקום, ואיננו אלא משום צרכי עוה"ז ועסקיו וכדומה, לכאורה אין ספק שאין להתיר שום איסור

בשביל זה, ומוטב שיהיה שוטה כל ימיו ואל יהיה רשע שעה אחת לפני המקום ב"ה, ומכל שכן שלא נעשה אנחנו איסורא זוטא בשבילו...

> However, this needs to be said: If one is obligated in *mitzvos* and has not reached the point of being a שוטה of which the Sages always speak, and [the therapeutic intervention is needed] only for worldly needs, his commercial affairs and the like, then there appears to be no doubt that no prohibition should be suspended for this purpose, and it is preferable to be mentally ill his entire life rather than be evil for one moment before the Almighty, may He be blessed, not to mention that we should not commit even a slight transgression for him...[4]

According to the *Chasam Sofer*, violating the Torah for the sake of treating mental disorders is permissible only if the patient currently qualifies as a halachic שוטה, and is thus not bound by Torah law. However, if a person suffers from a mental disability but his condition is not severe enough for him to qualify as a שוטה, then "it is preferable to be mentally ill his entire life rather than be evil for one moment before the Almighty," and thus neither he nor others may transgress the Torah for the sake of treatment.

In truth, however, it is possible that even the *Chasam Sofer* would agree to allow an OCD patient violate the Torah as part of his treatment. Rav Yitzchak Yehuda Shmelkes (*Beis Yitzchak*, E.H. 39) cites the *Chasam Sofer*'s comments in the context of the question of whether a mentally ill adult woman may be committed to a non-kosher mental institute. He writes that undoubtedly, a mental patient may violate the Torah for the sake of improving his condition and thereby enabling him to fulfill the Torah henceforth. Amidst his discussion, Rav Shmelkes contends that when the *Chasam Sofer* wrote, מוטב שיהיה שוטה כל ימיו ואל יהיה רשע שעה אחת לפני המקום, he meant that one may not transgress the Torah for the sake of improving mental health so that he can function more effectively in worldly affairs. If, however, one's condition compromises his ability to perform *mitzvos*, then even the *Chasam Sofer* would allow violating the Torah for the sake of treatment.

The *Chasam Sofer*'s formulation does not support this reading, as the *Chasam Sofer* wrote explicitly that his lenient ruling applies only to those who fall into

---

4. The person to whom the *Chasam Sofer* addressed this responsum had proposed in his original letter that enrolling the child in the facility should be permitted for the sake of כבוד הבריות — the child's dignity — as in his state of mental illness, he acted in a humiliating manner. The *Chasam Sofer* rejected this argument, however, noting the Gemara's comment that a שוטה does not experience actual humiliation (*Bava Kama* 86b), and the family's embarrassment over their son's mental illness does not warrant suspending Torah law.

the halachic category of שוטה. Regardless, the *Beis Yitzchak* clearly maintains that even other mentally ill patients are allowed to seek treatment that entails Torah violations if this would enable them to observe *mitzvos* properly.

ספק סכנה

Another basis for suspending *mitzva* observance in the case of an OCD patient is the concern of suicide. Studies have shown that as many as 25% of OCD patients become suicidal due to the unbearable hardship the disorder causes. A well-established halachic principle mandates violating any Torah law that is necessary to save a life, even if the statistical probability of death is low. As long as there is a risk, the concern to save a life overrides any Torah law.[5] Seemingly, then, the risk of suicide should suffice to allow the patient to suspend *mitzva* observance as necessary for effective treatment.

A precedent for this line of reasoning appears in a responsum of the Rashba (*Teshuvot Ha-Meyuchasos La-Ramban*, 281), who addresses the intriguing case of a person who had taken a vow not to laugh. He subsequently developed a severe mental disorder, and it was discovered that when people laughed in his presence and made him laugh, his condition was alleviated. The question was asked whether it was permissible to have this patient violate his vow in order to restore his mental functioning. The Rashba asserts that there is room to allow laughing in this individual's presence, as this situation involves ספק סכנה — the risk of death. He writes: הכא...דאיכא רוח רעה תקפה, אפשר דאתי בה לידי סכנה ומשום יתובי דעתא שרינן ליה — "Here...where there is a strong evil spirit [mental dysfunction], he might possibly put himself in danger, and so to settle his mind we allow this for him."

Similarly, Rav Nissim Mizrachi (*Admas Kodesh*, Y.D. 6) addresses the case of a man who experienced periodic bouts of mental insanity for several days at a time, and it was suggested that he be fed a certain non-kosher food, which would cure him.[6] Rav Mizrachi rules unequivocally that this person's condition is considered life-threatening, and his treatment therefore overrides all Torah laws:

ודאי חולי זה הוא חולי שיש בו סכנת נפשות, ואף שאינו מסוכן מחולי זה, מ"מ מסוכן הוא שהוא בידו ימית עצמו, ולכן נזהרין בני אדם שאין מניחין אצלו שום כלי משחית, אפילו מחט קטנה, וגם מניחין בידיו ורגליו כבלי ברזל כדי שלא יחנוק עצמו בידיו ולא יפיל עצמו מאיגרא רמה לבירא עמיקתא.

---

5. See *Bei'ur Halacha* 329, ד"ה אלא.
6. Specifically, it was recommended that he be fed the meat of a chicken that died naturally, without *shechita*.

Certainly, this is an illness that involves a risk to life, for even if he is not endangered by this illness, nevertheless, he is in danger of killing himself with his own hands, and therefore people are careful not to leave with him any destructive instrument, even a small needle, and they also place iron chains around his hands and feet so he will not choke himself or jump from a high rooftop to a low ditch.

By the same token, it would seem, it would be permissible for an OCD patient to undergo treatment that entails suspending *mitzvos* in order to save him from the potential fatal effects of this disorder.

ספיקות החמורות אשר אין להן קץ וסוף

Rav Weiss emphasizes that all this applies specifically to the *mitzva* observance of the patient himself. Others, however, are not permitted to compromise their fulfillment of halachic requirements for the sake of his treatment. Thus, for example, if an OCD patient is unable to properly recite *kiddush*, and he has a family, someone else should recite *kiddush* for everyone at the table. They should not forfeit the *mitzva* of *kiddush* for the sake of the patient's exposure and response prevention therapy.

This distinction poses an especially difficult problem in the case of a married woman suffering from OCD, who must prepare for immersion in the *mikveh* each month. Quite obviously, a couple may not resume marital relations if the woman did not properly ensure the absence of *chatzitzos* in her hair and body, yet, at the same time, it is imperative for the woman to overcome her obsessive tendencies and avoid excessive anxiety over the preparations for immersing. Such cases must be discussed with a competent halachic authority, who will provide guidance for the *mikveh* attendant, informing her of the minimum requirements that the woman needs to meet for her immersion to be valid, and which customary measures can be waived out of consideration for the patient's condition.

It is worth noting in this context an enlightening passage written by the Ramban (end of *Hilchos Nidda*) warning against unnecessary stringency and obsession with regard to preparations for the *mikveh*:

ומדיני חציצה לא טוב היות האדם מחמיר יותר מדאי ומחפש אחר הספיקות לפסול טבילתה בדבר הקל, כי אם כן, אין לדבר סוף. אלא, אחר שחפפה ראשה וסרקה במסרק וחפפה ורחצה כל גופה בחמין ונזהרה לבלתי תגע בשום דבר חוצץ, ותעשה טבילתה בפשיטות איבריה וכל גופה, לא יכניס אדם ראשו בספיקות החמורות אשר אין להן קץ וסוף, כגון עצמה עיניה ביותר, קרצה שפתותיה ביותר ומשאר הספיקות, כי מי יוכל להבחין בין עצמה ביותר ובין לא עצמה ביותר.

With regard to the laws of *chatziza*, it is not advisable for a person to be excessively stringent and to look for uncertainties to disqualify the immersion over some trivial matter, for if so, there is no end. Rather, after she cleaned her hair, combed it with a comb, cleaned and washed her entire body with hot water, was careful not to touch anything that could make an obstruction, and performed her immersion while spreading out her limbs and her entire body, one should not then give thought to grave uncertainties that are endless, such as whether she closed her eyes too tightly, clenched her lips too tightly, and other questions, because who can distinguish between too tightly and not too tightly?

In general, and certainly when dealing with a patient suffering from obsessive-compulsive disorder, a common sense approach is needed to ensure that halachic requirements are satisfied without excessive worry. A fine line — or perhaps not such a fine line — separates between proper halachic vigilance and harmful anxiety. Particularly in the case of an OCD patient, one must ensure to distinguish between strict halachic requirements and unnecessary, stress-inducing stringency, so that halachic observance will bring joy and fulfillment, and not aggravation and anxiety.

INTERVIEWS

Rav Asher Weiss on *Headlines with Dovid Lichtenstein**

OCD is very common and very prevalent in our society. I am sometimes asked about people who are suffering from OCD and have difficulty *davening* properly, and sometimes people are tormented by the way they *daven* or *bentch*.

The *teshuva* in *Minchas Asher* deals with a *talmid chacham* who felt he could not even say Hashem's Name properly, and he spent many hours a day just trying to *bentch*, recite *Shema*, and *daven*. The *psak* I gave him, basically, was that he should try to daven once and do his best, but never go back to repeat a *Shem*, *beracha*, or *pasuk*.

The *Chasam Sofer* argued that when a child suffers from limited mental capacity, it is in our interest to bring him into the category of a בר חיובא and enable him to fulfill all the *mitzvos*, and this overrides [Torah law]…

The treatment of OCD necessitates letting these people get over the tension and stress. So even if he would not properly fulfill these *mitzvos*, our *psak* would be: do the best you can, and move on. This is the only chance of helping these people in their healing process and enabling them to fulfill all the *mitzvos* בשלימות in the future.

This person turned to me once again, and, persisting, asked, "Do I fulfill the *mitzva* of *tefilla* or not?" I wrote an additional *teshuva*, which is not printed in my *sefarim* but which I hope will be included in chelek 3 [of *Shu"t Minchas Asher*]. I argued — and it's a big *chiddush*, but I stand behind it — that when it comes to the *mitzva* of *tefilla*, we do the best we can. Not only is one not obligated to do more — besides the *psak* that one should do what he can and move on because our primary interest is that he is healed — but he also fulfills the *mitzva*. This concept is unique to *tefilla* and to one other *mitzva* — *teshuva*. With regard to these two *mitzvos*, if a person is unable to fulfill the *mitzva* fully — not because he does not want to, but because of רצון ה' — then he fulfills the *mitzva* by doing what he can.

This is based on various sources in *Chazal*. The *Midrash Tehillim* (45) says:

רחש לבי דבר טוב – להודיעך שלא יכלו להתוודות בפיהם, אלא כיון שרחש לבם בתשובה קבלם הקב"ה.

"My heart has thought a good word" (*Tehillim* 45:2) — this is to teach you that [the sons of Korach] were not able to confess with their mouths, but since their hearts were moved by repentance, God accepted them.

The Rambam writes in *Hilchos Teshuva* (1:1) that וידוי פה is מעכב — without verbal confession, one does not fulfill the *mitzva* of *teshuva* and one does not earn atonement. Even if one performed complete *teshuva* in his heart, it does not count if he did not verbally confess. Nevertheless, the Midrash says, קבלם הקב"ה — Hashem accepts the *teshuva* of those who are incapable of verbally confessing. As we know, we don't *pasken* from Midrash. But this is not only a Midrash. The Rosh in *Moed Katan* (3:76) deals with the obligation to say *vidui* before one's demise, and he says that if one cannot say *vidui*, then if he did his best, he fulfilled the *mitzva* and he earned atonement.

I think we find the same concept regarding *tefilla*. The *Midrash Rabba* (*Shir Ha-Shirim*) says something shocking:

אמר רבי אחא עם הארץ שקורא לאהבה איבה, כגון ואהבת ואיבת, אמר הקדוש ברוך הוא ודלגו עלי אהבה.

If a person who does not know better mispronounces ואהבת את ה' אלקיך as ואיבת את ה' אלקיך — which means, "You should despise Hashem your God" instead of "You should love Hashem your G-d" — *Ha-Kadosh Baruch Hu* nevertheless accepts his prayer. This is a Midrash, but I believe that this is a common denominator shared by *teshuva* and *tefilla*. These are two *mitzvos* which, more so than other *mitzvos*, are not only an obligation, but also a gift and privilege. The *mitzva* of *teshuva* offers us the opportunity to earn forgiveness for our sins, and Rabbeinu Yona says that this is the greatest gift which *Ha-Kadosh Baruch Hu* bestows upon us. The same is true of *tefilla*. The Gemara says in *Berachos* (20) that *tefilla* is defined as רחמים, and thus even though *davening* is a מצוות עשה שהזמן גרמא, women are obligated in *tefilla*, because they need רחמים no less than men. Like *teshuva*, *davening* is a precious gift, giving us the opportunity to receive *Ha-Kadosh Baruch Hu*'s compassion. To me it is obvious that there cannot be an אדם מישראל who, for reasons that do not depend on him, cannot have the opportunity to fulfill the *mitzva* of *tefilla* and earn רחמי שמיים, or fulfill the *mitzva* of *teshuva* and earn forgiveness.

So my response to those people tormented by OCD, who feel that they cannot *daven* or *bentch* properly, is that not only do I *pasken* that they should move on because they need to heal, but far beyond that — when they do their best, they fulfill the *mitzva* of *tefilla*.

Ha-Kadosh Baruch Hu is שומע תפילת כל פה. This includes people who cannot really pronounce the words as they should. Parents always understand their child. Sometimes I visit people and the babies are chattering away and I don't understand a single word, but the father and mother always understand. *Ha-Kadosh Baruch Hu* is our Father, and He understands our *tefillos*. I am aware there are halachic criteria, but nevertheless, if you can't do any better, you fulfill the *mitzva* of *tefilla*.

Regarding women and *tevila* — I cannot say that *chatzitza* is the same as *tefilla*. But when the *mikveh* attendant is aware that the woman is totally clean and nothing more needs to be done…we need to do our best to comfort her. I assume that after [washing] once there is no longer any *chatzitza*. The body of an OCD patent is no different than that of any other person.

[As for treating OCD as a life-threatening situation due to the risk of suicide,] I don't think we need to go to this extreme, because most of the issues we are dealing with involve at most a *mitzvas asei*… [But,] there is a famous *teshuva* of the *Chasam Sofer* about an epileptic, and he says that because the epileptic might fall on a rock and hurt himself seriously, even though this is quite remote, he can be considered a חולה שיש בו סכנה. So if the statistics [about the high rates of suicide among OCD patients] are relevant [to the Orthodox Jewish community], then there definitely would be a basis to utilize the concept of חולה שיש בן סכנה. But I don't think we need to go to that extreme.

* Broadcast on 2 Av, 5775 (July 18, 2015).

Rav Dovid Cohen
on *Headlines with Dovid Lichtenstein**

I don't think that some anxiety which is based on *mitzvos* has no value. I think that in *Ha-Kadosh Baruch Hu*'s eyes, the anxiety that a person has for *mitzvos* — as long as it's limited — is a positive thing. The *pasuk* says, אם בחוקותי תלכו ואת מצוותי תשמורו ועשיתם אותם. Rashi interprets אם בחוקותי תלכו to mean, שתהיו עמלים בתורה. But what is תשמורו and ועשיתם? [The word] עשייה means "doing," but what's שמירה? In my humble opinion, it refers to the concept we find in *Chazal* of דאיגי במצוות — anxiety because of *mitzvos*. "I didn't *daven Mincha* yet today — what time is *shki'a*?" It's a normal anxiety, and this anxiety, I believe, is שמירת המצוות. *Davening* is עשיית המצוות. So I don't want to belittle the concept of דאיגי במצוות.

However, this must be to a degree that does not make a person sick. I know from speaking to top psychologists and psychiatrists that we have a problem which we can even call the מחלת הדור — the illness of our generation, of people who are stressed to the point of requiring professional help. We cannot say that stress has positive value in the eyes of *Ha-Kadosh Baruch Hu* if it brings a person to the point that he needs professional help… The Arizal taught that *simcha* is one of the highest levels, and that through depression a person can reach שאול תחתית — even lower than by committing an *aveira*. So we have to be careful with these things. Depression can lead a person to the end of his spiritual life — and I'm not even talking now about his physical life. If as a result of a *mitzva* a person experiences anxiety to the point where it spreads and overwhelms him — we need to be very careful, as this could lead him to שאול תחתית.

We need to have a sense of priorities. When it comes to a *mitzva* such as Pesach, which lends itself to anxiety, we must be careful to maintain proper priorities. We have to become knowledgeable. There is nothing in *halacha* that does not have a *machlokes*, so a person has to follow the *psak* of his מרא דאתרא. If a person wants to be *machmir*, then he can go a step further, but he first needs to know what the *halacha* is.

Many years ago, I asked Rav Yisrael Zev Gustman, who was in Rav Chaim Ozer's *beis din* when he was 20, 21 years old, the following question. Why is it that there are *poskim*, גדולי ישראל, who say that human beings were twice as big and chickens were twice as big in yesteryear, such that a כזית and כביצה were twice as big as our [olives and eggs]? We know through archaeological digs of *mikvaos*…that men and women were smaller than today!" He said, "You are right." Period. A few years ago, it was reported on the first page of the *New York Times* that they found olives in Israel that were preserved, and they were smaller than our present-day olives. So people tell me that their doctor said they cannot eat *matza*, and sometimes it can lead to severe illness, and I tell them to ask the doctor to think of an olive — even a large olive — and consider whether they can handle one or two of these quantities on the night of Pesach. If the doctor says yes, then do it.

There's a *teshuva* by Rav Moshe that a חולה שאין בו סכנה (an ill patient whose condition is not life-threatening) is exempt from *mitzvos asei*. So if a person can get sick and become a חולה שאין בו סכנה by eating more than a *kezayis* of *matza*, he should be careful not to be *machmir*... It is wrong for a person to become sick as a result of something which is clearly a *chumra*. There's a Yerushalmi about washing walls [before Pesach], and it has value, and the *Mekubalim* say that the perspiration when baking *matzos* is a great source of atonement. These things have value. But if a person does not have the proper balance, then this could lead to terrible things. Depression could lead to terrible things, as can anxiety. They can lead to addictions.

People with OCD are suffering from this illness. So one must be careful and judge himself, and ensure that everything is done intelligently. If a person can handle the stress, then it's wonderful for him to be דאיגי במצוות. But some people cannot handle the stress. There are those who get a rupture lifting 50 pounds, and some if they lift 300 pounds. It's similar with emotion — some can handle more, some less.

Another example — we teach our girls to daven, which is wonderful, but they are not being taught that the main obligation is *Shemoneh Esrei*, and there's some discussion about *Birkos Ha-Shachar* and one hundred *berachos*. There are women who, because of the tremendous burden of being wives and mothers, and sometimes they also have to "bring home the bacon" — pardon the expression — literally have no time to *daven*, and so they don't daven at all, because they know they can't handle it. No one told them that the Chafetz Chayim's rebbetzin didn't *daven* — she just said the minimum, according to the Rambam, because of the burden she carried. If a woman knows that all she really needs is *Birkos Ha-Shachar* and *Shemoneh Esrei*, then she won't give up *davening*, because this is something she could handle. The overwhelming desire to do a *chumra* when *halacha* doesn't require it diminishes from עשיית המצוות. And there are those who become sick as a result of stress.

A woman has to know that dirt is not *chametz*... If you really want to clean everything in the house and do spring cleaning as a *chumra* — fine, but only if you can handle it...

---

* Broadcast on 24 Adar II, 5776 (April 2, 2016). The interview focused mainly on OCD as it relates to Pesach.

Rabbi Dr. Jonathan Schwartz
on *Headlines with Dovid Lichtenstein**

Very often, there are two different ways people approach Pesach and Yiddishkeit in general. They come in the door and look at a *mitzva*, and many of us look with a very wide open eye, with an appreciation for the beauty and for everything about the *mitzva*. But there is a segment of the population that looks at it with a heavy dose of fear. This is the dividing line between a successful experience with *mitzvos* and an experience that is based less on Yiddishkeit and more on psychological anxiety.

A person who comes into Yom Tov with an understanding that his goal is to focus upon the מצוות ה' and the concept of חדות ה' היא מעוזכם will see all the different responsibilities as steps along a higher purpose. This is the first thing we need to keep our eyes on.

In a shiur given quite a while ago, Rav Scheinberg *zt"l* spoke to women in Jerusalem about cleaning for Pesach, and he made it very clear how important it is to clean but not to go crazy… We have to keep in mind that there is a purpose to what we are doing, and we are guided by *halacha*, which has been handed down generation to generation and interpreted by our *poskim*. There is a higher goal. If people can keep their minds on that, then they can separate from crazy anxiety before Pesach and extremes, and focus on achieving what they need to achieve before and during Pesach.

There is a Harvard study of Judaism and mental health run by Dr. Dovid Rosmarin. He published a series of studies, and one really nailed it. He said that we need to understand that OCD anxiety has nothing to do with religion per se. The cause of OCD is a series of obsessions, recurring unwanted thoughts, that cause a person to do repetitive behaviors. It is not anxiety about religion or *halacha*.

Another *chaver* of mine, Dr. Jonathan Huppert of Jerusalem, published a study in 2007 teaching therapists to make it clear to their patients dealing with OCD that seems to lie in religion that religion is not really causing it. If the person wouldn't be concerned about religion, he would be concerned about something else. It [OCD] affects areas about which a person cares. The patient cares about certain thoughts more than others do, and places undue stress on himself, which in turn causes him to have doubts that he cannot shake. Our Torah tells us what we're supposed to do when we have doubts; the OCD patient gets so overwhelmed by doubts that he goes out of bounds. He just needs to learn where and how he is taking it further than he needs to.

One person is obsessed about cleaning, with not getting sick, so he goes out of his way to clean obsessively. Somebody else says to himself that he doesn't want the *Ribono Shel Olam* to be angry at him, and he cannot handle the fact that He will punish him. This would cause religion-based OCD.

From my perspective, this comes from a misunderstanding, from mistaken beliefs. A person walks around with a mistaken belief — either he heard something in a *shiur* but paid attention to only half of it, or something somehow developed in his mind. What's more relevant to me as a therapist is to help the person understand that he is thinking errant thoughts which are causing him to have doubts, which are causing him to be scared, which is causing him to go to unreasonable extremes. If it is religion-based, then he is turning it into a halachic matter. His goal is to resolve all doubts, to get rid of all concerns. This is caused by a major fear that he has. In most cases of religion-based OCD, it's some variation of, "I don't want the *Ribono Shel Olam* to get angry at me; I don't want to go to *Gehinnom*." None of us want to be punished, but it's not the totality of how we engage in what we do. As a result, we are able to put this into context and live in a healthy environment and within the boundaries of *halacha* that tell us what to do when we have doubts. Someone who is overwhelmed will wind up running to do whatever he or she can to get out of doubt and can end up distorting *halacha*.

Every single one of us has obsessional thoughts. But a person with OCD lives a disordered life. I want to make sure the person understands where he is obsessing, what's causing him to do this, and to help him learn ways to live a completely normal life and place these thoughts into a context, so he can say, "This is obsessive, and I don't have to pay attention to it. I have to pay attention to reality and to *halacha*."

* Broadcast on 24 Adar II, 5776 (April 2, 2016). The interview focused mainly on OCD as it relates to Pesach.

Dr. Meshulem Epstein on *Headlines with Dovid Lichtenstein**

The gold standard of treatment for OCD is exposure and response prevention. This basically means the person is guided to expose himself to whatever it is he is afraid of — in this case, the fear of *Gehinnom*, of violating *halacha* — and not doing what he normally would in response to the fear, which is repeating or asking a lot of questions...

People who suffer from OCD — the most painful element, what keeps them doing things compulsively, is the inability to tolerate uncertainty. "Maybe the *tefillin* are in the wrong place"; "Maybe I damaged somebody"; "Maybe it's *treif.*" Around 95% of the OCD patients I treat are people who suffer from "Halacha OCD." We have to be very careful when we go to a *rav*, because what happens is that they get reassurance from the *rav*, in which case we may be unwittingly reinforcing OCD by providing reassurance, and now every time they feel uncertain, they will have to go to a *rav* for reassurance. Sometimes, asking a *rav* could provide more certainty for the person, which is the worst thing for an OCD patient. We're trying to condition him through behavioral exercises to accept more uncertainties. I say to a patient: "Your reality is no different than anyone else's, but you suffer from anxiety that constantly reminds you of that small chance of something going wrong. But the reality is that we all live in the same world, and everyone lives with uncertainty — halachic uncertainty, uncertainty about physical health, etc. There are many decisions in life which we don't get to know how great they are until later on in life, or never at all."

The critical issue is — and many clients have told me this is what made the difference — the acceptance of uncertainty, which is ubiquitous. Everyone has to live with it; it's part of life. Uncertainty is part of our halachic life. There is no way to avoid it, and this is what we want our clients to learn — that their compulsions are a way of running away from uncertainty.

* Broadcast on 24 Adar II, 5776 (April 2, 2016).

… algemeiner

Hamas Warns Gazans: Beware of Female IDF Soldiers

December 6, 2012
by Zach Pontz

The Elder of Ziyon blog reports on a recent post to Hamas's Palestine Times that warns Gaza residents to be careful of female IDF soldiers. Here's the translation of the article provided by EOZ:

Security sources belonging to the Palestinian resistance in the Gaza Strip disclosed that the "Karakal" Israeli unit — predominantly female — intensified its work on the eastern border of the Gaza in order to blackmail the Palestinians.

The resistance sources pointed out that they observed many soldiers in this unit trying to draw the attention of the Palestinians who returned to work in the lands adjacent to the border by showing parts of their bodies and inviting young people to talk with them.

A young female IDF soldier. Photo: Screesnhot.

Sources reported that 33 soldiers serve in the "Desert Cats" battalion, two-thirds of them female. They operate openly on the border with the Gaza Strip and Egypt. The "Shabak" intelligence works in cooperation with the Israeli army to work on recruiting new spies from the Gaza to refresh the list of potential targets which were exhausted during the recent war on the Gaza Strip.

This cooperation with the predominantly female Desert Cats are a means of attracting young people and citizens to entice them sexually, where the girls intentionally show parts of their bodies and do things that are not moral in order to excite young people and get them to collaborate. The collaboration process with security devices of the enemy on the border works two ways, either by giving young people the phone numbers to contact them or invite them to cross-border entry and trap them after extortion.

Elder of Ziyon notes: "Hamas can brag about its imagined prowess at standing up (actually, hiding underground) to the IDF, but they turn to jelly at the thought of female soldiers."

The IDF illuminates the actual objectives of the Karakal battalion on its website:

> The Karakal Battalion was founded in the year 2000 conceding to public pressures for the creation of an intensive combat unit for girls. They are given the name of a desert feline whose gender is barely distinguishable, and the battalion number signifies the number of women soldiers who fell in the Palmach Era.
>
> The girls volunteer to become combat soldiers, and must go through two days of mental examinations and physical challenges before joining, since the course is strenuous and identical to that of any other exclusively male battalion.
>
> As part of the Southern Command, Karakal men and women secure the Egyptian border from smugglers, infiltrators, and terrorists.

Copyright © algemeiner.com

Seducing the Enemy

In December 2012, several media outlets reported that Hamas, the Palestinian terrorist organization that rules the Gaza Strip, issued a warning about a new tactic allegedly devised by the Israel Defense Force as part of its effort to combat Hamas' terror activities. The claim was that female soldiers belonging to the female Karakal combat unit had been attempting to seduce young Palestinian males along the Gaza border in order to lure them to collaborate with the IDF.

While there does not appear to be any evidence to support this claim, to which Israelis generally reacted with amusement, the tactic of seduction has been utilized in at least one documented case. In 1986, the Mossad sent Cheryl Bentov, a married Israeli native, to London for the purpose of developing a romantic relationship with Mordechai Vanunu, a former technician at Israel's nuclear plant in Dimona who betrayed Israel by disclosing sensitive information about the country's nuclear project. Bentov succeeded in luring Vanunu to Rome, claiming that her sister owned an apartment there where they could live together. Mossad agents were waiting at the apartment, and they captured Vanunu and brought him to Israel to stand trial. He was ultimately convicted of treason and espionage, and sentenced to eighteen years in prison.

What would *halacha* say about this kind of unconventional military tactic? Would it be halachically permissible for a female Jew to seduce and engage in relations with an enemy in an effort to obtain important information that the IDF needs for its ongoing defense efforts, or to enlist the man's assistance in identifying terrorists and other military targets?

קרקע עולם

The Gemara in *Maseches Sanhedrin* (74b) addresses the question of why Esther did not refuse to sleep with Achashverosh, in light of the fact that this act constituted a transgression that must be avoided even at the expense of one's life.[1] To explain Esther's conduct, the Gemara cites two reasons why she did not

---

1. The Gemara comments that Esther should have surrendered her life because her relationship with Achashverosh was public, and a public violation of Torah law must be avoided even at the expense of one's life. Many *Rishonim* note that since Esther was married to Mordechai, as the Gemara comments elsewhere (*Megilla* 13), her relationship with Achashverosh would have constituted a capital sexual offense even if it was not made public.

surrender her life. Abayei answered that אסתר קרקע עולם היא (literally, "Esther was the ground of the earth"), meaning that she was entirely passive in her encounters with Achashverosh. Rava suggested a different reason, namely, that Achashverosh forced her to engage in relations not for the purpose of religious persecution, but rather for his own personal pleasure, and so the requirement of martyrdom did not apply.[2] The Rif (*Sanhedrin* 17b) cites both explanations, indicating that the *halacha* follows both Abayei and Rava in this regard.[3] In other words, even in situations in which martyrdom would normally be required, this law does not apply in situations of קרקע עולם or if the motive is personal benefit, as opposed to religious oppression.

Two different approaches to the notion of קרקע עולם appear in the writings of the *Rishonim*. The Ran, the Ramban (in *Milchamos Hashem*), and others explain this phrase to mean that martyrdom was not an option. Since Esther was completely powerless, Achashverosh would have slept with her even if she had expressed her preference to die. According to this view, Esther was, in fact, required to surrender her life to avoid intimate relations with Achashverosh, but this was not possible, as Achashverosh would have forced himself upon her even if she had refused.

According to this view, a Jewish woman who is given the option of martyrdom to avoid a forbidden sexual act must choose this option. The fact that she is passive during intercourse is immaterial, as the requirement of יהרג ואל יעבור — to surrender one's life rather than commit a cardinal sin of immorality — applies regardless of the nature of the Jew's participation in the sin. Esther, according to this view, does not represent an exception to the rule of יהרג ואל יעבור, as Achashverosh would have taken her by force even if she had protested and expressed her preference to die.

Tosfos (*Sanhedrin* ad loc.),[4] however, cite a different approach in the name of the Rivam, who claims that *halacha* requires surrendering one's life to avoid certain transgressions only if the transgression entails some action. When the sin that one is being forced to transgress would be violated passively, one is not obligated to surrender his life to avoid this violation. Hence, in the case of a female forced into a forbidden sexual act, she is not required to surrender her life, since her participation in the sinful act is entirely passive.

To explain the rationale underlying this theory, the Rivam notes the

---

2. Rashi explains that since martyrdom is required in order to avoid חילול ה', this requirement does not apply if the enemy's motive is for personal enjoyment, as a violation under these circumstances does not constitute an assault on the Jewish religion.
3. This point is made by the *Shach*, Y.D. 157:9.
4. See also *Tosfos*' comments on *Yoma* 82b, *Kesubos* 3b, and *Yevamos* 103a.

association between sexual offenses and murder. The Gemara in *Sanhedrin* (74a) observes that the Torah compares intercourse with a betrothed girl to murder,[5] and thus concludes that just as one must surrender his life to avoid committing murder,[6] he must likewise surrender his life to avoid גילוי עריות (capital sexual offenses). It emerges, then, that murder forms the basis for the requirement of martyrdom in situations of גילוי עריות. As such, the Rivam reasons, this requirement presumably applies only in situations that would require martyrdom in a parallel case of murder. When it comes to murder, the Rivam asserts, it is clear that martyrdom is required only if one is forced to actively kill. The Rivam notes that if one is faced with the decision of whether to be thrown onto an infant, which would result in the infant's death, or to be killed, it is clear that he does not have to surrender his life. The entire reason that one must surrender his life to avoid murder is our inability to determine whether his life is more valuable than that of the person he is ordered to kill.[7] Since no human being can make this determination, a person in such a case must remain passive and allow himself to be killed. But in a case in which the murder he is asked to commit would occur through inaction, he has no obligation to elect martyrdom over being thrown onto the child, as he has no reason to assume that the child's life is worth more than his. By extension, when it comes to sexual offenses, martyrdom is required only when the Jew is ordered to commit a forbidden act, but not if the violation entails purely passive cooperation.[8]

Tosfos note in this context the Gemara's comment in *Maseches Pesachim* (25b), נערה המאורסה תהרג ולא תעבור — a betrothed woman must surrender her life rather than commit an act of adultery, seemingly contradicting the Rivam's position. To refute this proof, *Tosfos* assert that the correct text of the Gemara reads יהרג in the masculine form, and thus refers to a man who is forced to defile a betrothed woman at the threat of death. The man, as the active partner in intercourse, must surrender his life to avoid this violation, but a woman in such a situation does not have to opt for martyrdom, according to the Rivam.

It emerges that according to the Rivam, a woman threatened with death if she refuses to commit a capital sexual offense is not required to surrender her life. Since her involvement in the forbidden act is entirely passive, she may consent rather than choose martyrdom.

---

5. כי כאשר יקום איש על רעהו ורצחו נפש כן הדבר הזה (*Devarim* 22:26).
6. The obvious exception is a situation of רודף, when one is permitted to kill his pursuer in self-defense.
7. מי יימר דדמא דידך סומק טפי, דלמא דמא דההוא גברא סומק טפי (*Sanhedrin* 74a).
8. This also appears to be the view of Rashi, who writes in *Maseches Yoma* (82a) that a betrothed woman is not required to be martyred to avoid sleeping with another man, דהיא אינה עושה כלום, דקרקע עולם בעלמא היא.

The Rivam's view is codified by the Rama (Y.D. 157:1):

ודוקא כשאומרים לו לעשות מעשה, כגון שאומרים לאיש לגלות ערוה או שיהרג, אבל אם אונסים לאשה לבא עליה, או שרוצים להשליכו על התינוק להרגו, או שהוא כבר מוקשה ורוצים לאנס אותו לערוה, אין צריך ליהרג.

[Martyrdom is required] only if they tell him to commit an act, such as if they tell him to commit a forbidden sexual act or be killed. But if they forcibly come upon a woman, or if they want to throw him on an infant to kill [the infant], or if he already has an erection and they want to force him to commit a sexual act, one does not have to be killed.

Initiating an Intimate Encounter

Having established that passive involvement in a sexual offense is permissible to save one's life, let us now address the question of whether this includes actively initiating a sexual offense, such as through seduction. Is it sufficient for the woman to remain passive during the act of intercourse, or must the entire situation unfold without her active involvement?

The difference between these two perspectives is manifest in the case of a woman who seduces a man or offers sexual favors for the purpose of self-defense. For example, Rav Yaakov Reischer (*Shevus Yaakov* 2:117) addresses the case of a group of men who were traveling and encountered a violent group of bandits who were prepared to kill them and seize their money. One of the travelers was accompanied by his wife, and with his consent, she offered herself to the bandits for intercourse in exchange for their sparing her and her group's lives. The gang accepted the offer, and the people's lives were saved. The question arose whether this woman acted properly, and if so, whether she and her husband would then have to divorce, in light of the fact that she willingly slept with other men.[9]

This question highlights the two different definitions of קרקע עולם, as understood by the Rivam. Does this term refer to passivity during the sinful act, irrespective of the woman's active involvement in initiating the act, or must the entire sinful context be forced upon the woman in order for her cooperation to be permitted?

A possible precedent to such a case is the story of Yael, the woman who heroically killed the enemy general Sisera, who had fled to her tent seeking refuge

---

9. A married woman who is raped may remain with her husband (unless he is a *Kohen*), whereas a married woman who willfully engages in relations with another man becomes forbidden for her husband henceforth.

after being defeated in battle by *Bnei Yisrael* (*Shoftim* 4). The Gemara (*Nazir* 23b; *Yevamos* 103b) recounts that Yael engaged in intercourse multiple times with Sisera in order to make him weary so he would sleep, enabling her to easily kill him. *Tosfos*, amidst their aforementioned discussion in *Sanhedrin*, address the story of Yael, and note that Sisera did not force himself upon her; rather, she initiated the intimate encounter through seduction. Another seeming precedent is the story of Esther approaching Achashverosh to invite him to a feast at which she would plead on behalf of the Jews. The Gemara in *Maseches Megilla* (15a) writes that on this occasion, Esther, for the first time, initiated intimate relations with Achashverosh, and she thereby became forbidden for Mordechai, to whom she was married. As in the case of Yael and Sisera, Esther presumably remained passive during this act of intercourse, but she initiated the act for a life-saving purpose.[10] Seemingly, these two precedents prove that as long as the woman remains passive during the forbidden act, the union qualifies as קרקע עולם and is permissible for the sake of saving lives, even if the woman initiates the process.

Indeed, *Tosfos* (in *Sanhedrin*) write that Yael's seduction of Sisera was permissible on the grounds of קרקע עולם. As the passive participant in the act of intercourse, she was permitted to initiate the act for the purpose of saving human life.

This may have also been the view of the Maharik, who, in a famous responsum (167), addresses the question of why it was permissible for Esther and Yael to initiate intimacy with Achashverosh and Sisera, respectively. The Maharik writes:

הנה דבר פשוט הוא...כי אסתר לא עשתה שום איסור ולא היה בדבר אפי׳ נדנוד עבירה אלא מצוה רבה עשתה שהצילה כל ישראל...פשיטא ופשיטא שעשתה מצוה רבה מאד **ובפרט דקרקע עולם היתה.**

> Now it is obvious...that Esther did not commit any violation, and the act did not entail even the slightest transgression. Rather, she performed a great *mitzva*, in that she saved all of Israel... It is abundantly clear that she performed a great *mitzva*, **especially since she was "the ground of the earth."**

Rav Yechiel Yaakov Weinberg (*Seridei Eish* 2:36–37) notes that the Maharik here points to two reasons for why Esther was allowed to initiate relations with Achashverosh: the future of the Jewish People was at stake and the factor of קרקע

---

10. While it is not entirely clear why Yael's case involved a life-threatening situation, as Sisera had fled to her tent as a fugitive after suffering defeat, it seems that Sisera could have likely remobilized his army and continued his violent aggression against *Bnei Yisrael*.

עולם. Rav Weinberg thus understands the Maharik to mean that the rule of קרקע עולם permits a woman even to initiate forbidden intercourse for a life-saving purpose, since the forbidden act itself occurs without her active participation.[11]

It appears, however, that this issue is subject to dispute. The Ran (*Sanhedrin* 74b), amidst his discussion of the Rivam's position, notes the aforementioned comment in *Maseches Pesachim* that seems to disprove this view: נערה המאורסה תהרג ואל תעבור. He writes that this passage can in fact be reconciled with the Rivam's view, as it might refer to a case of a woman who is forced to bring a man upon her, or of a woman who falls dangerously ill as a result of lust for intercourse with a certain man. These situations do not qualify as קרקע עולם, as the woman actively commits the violation, and thus intercourse is forbidden despite the threat posed to her life. The clear implication of the Ran's comments is that in the second case, the woman may not save her life by approaching the man to request intercourse, even if she remains passive throughout the act. According to the Ran's understanding of the Rivam, then, an intimate encounter qualifies as קרקע עולם only if the woman played no active role whatsoever, even before the forbidden act.[12]

We find different views in this regard among the *Acharonim* as well. Rav Yaakov of Zhitomir, in his responsa, *Beis Yaakov* (39), addresses the case of a man who was ordered on the threat of death to have relations with a certain married Jewish woman, who consented for the sake of rescuing that man's life. The question arose as to whether the woman remained permitted to her husband, and the *Beis Yaakov* writes that according to the Rivam, who applies the rule of קרקע עולם to any situation of passive intercourse, the woman in this case

---

11. This is in contrast to the view of the *Noda Be-Yehuda*, discussed below, that Esther was allowed to initiate intercourse only because all of *Am Yisrael* was in danger.
12. Rabbi Akiva Eiger (*Derush Ve-Chiddush*, Kesubos 3b) raises this question as to whether a woman would be allowed to engage in forbidden relations if this is necessary to cure her from a life-threatening illness, and he writes that according to the Rivam's view, this would be permissible. Surprisingly, he makes no mention of the Ran's comment that even according to the Rivam this would be forbidden because the woman takes an active role in initiating the encounter.
Rav Moshe Feinstein (*Iggeros Moshe*, Y.D. 1:74) writes that this question perhaps underlies the debate between Abayei and Rava in explaining Esther's justification for sleeping with Achashverosh. It is inconceivable, Rav Moshe asserts, that Esther was entirely passive throughout the period she was married to Achashverosh, and that she had to be physically forced into intercourse each time the king wished to sleep with her. Undoubtedly, Esther fully cooperated in the entire process except during the act of intercourse, when she was passive. Rav Moshe suggests that it is for this reason that Rava could not accept Abayei's reasoning of קרקע עולם, for although she was passive during the forbidden act, she was an active participant throughout the preliminary stages.

may remain with her husband. The clear assumption of the *Beis Yaakov*, upon which his entire discussion is predicated, is that the woman acted correctly by passively engaging in intercourse for a life-saving purpose.¹³

Others, however, rule more stringently, limiting the applicability of the precedents set by Yael and Esther. Rav Reischer, in the aforementioned responsum, rules that the woman who initiated intercourse in order to save her group of travelers acted correctly, שעשתה להצלת הרבים — because she acted for the sake of saving many lives.¹⁴ The implication is that this is permitted only when the act is needed to rescue a large number of people — as in the cases of Yael and Esther — but not for the sake of saving one person's life. An earlier source for this view can be found in the comments of the Meiri (cited in *Shita Mekubetzes, Kesubos* 3b), who writes that Yael was permitted to seduce Sisera for the sake of הצלת רבים — "saving the many." According to this view, a woman may not initiate an illicit intimate encounter to save her life or another individual's life, but may do so for the sake of rescuing the lives of many people.

Saving the Jewish People

A third view is taken by the *Noda Be-Yehuda* (*Mahadura Tinyana*, Y.D. 161), who ruled that a woman may not offer herself for intercourse even for the sake of rescuing a large group of people. In his view, the principle of קרקע עולם applies only when היא אנוסה על גוף הביאה — the act is done forcibly, against her will. But if she actively invites the man to commit the act, then this does not qualify as קרקע עולם, and the act is thus forbidden even for the purpose of saving lives. Esther's situation was exceptional, the *Noda Be-Yehuda* writes, in that the survival of the entire Jewish nation was at stake:

> אסתר שאני שהיתה להצלת כלל ישראל מהודו ועד כוש ואין למדין הצלת יחידים מהצלת כלל ישראל מנער ועד זקן מהודו ועד כוש ושם היה בהוראת מרדכי ובית דינו ואולי ברוח הקודש.

> [The case of] Esther was different, because she [acted] to save the entire nation of Israel from India to Ethiopia, and we may not infer the rescue of individuals from the rescue of the entire nation of Israel, young and

---

13. Although the Gemara in *Megilla* (noted above) says that Esther became forbidden to Mordechai after she initiated intimate relations with Achashverosh, the *Beis Yaakov* claims (rather questionably) that after her efforts proved successful in rescuing the Jews, her initiative was retroactively justified and she was thus permitted to Mordechai.
14. In contradistinction to the ruling of the *Beis Yaakov*, however, Rav Reischer rules that the woman was then forbidden to have marital relations with her husband, since she willfully slept with another man, albeit for a legitimate life-saving purpose.

old, from India to Ethiopia. And this was done with the instruction of Mordechai and his court, and perhaps through prophetic insight.

According to the *Noda Be-Yehuda*, then, a woman may not initiate intercourse for a life-saving purpose, except when this is necessary for the Jewish nation's survival.

A reason for this exception is cited in the name of Rav Yitzchak Hutner,[15] who suggested that the destruction of all of *Am Yisrael* would constitute a חילול ה'. After the sin of the golden calf, and again after the sin of the spies, Moshe pleaded with God to spare *Bnei Yisrael* because of the defamation to His honor that their destruction would cause (*Shemos* 32:12; *Bamidbar* 14:13–16). As such, any transgression, including the three cardinal sins of idolatry, murder, and sexual immorality, is allowed to protect the Jewish nation and thereby avoid a grave חילול ה'. The premise that any Torah violation is allowed to prevent a grave חילול ה' was also established by the *Chazon Ish*,[16] who noted, among other sources,[17] the Gemara's comment (*Yevamos* 79a) that David handed over seven sons of Shaul to the Givonim in retaliation for King Shaul's murder of seven members of that tribe. Even though the Torah forbids executing sons in retribution for their fathers' crimes (*Devarim* 24:16), this was nevertheless done for the sake of avoiding the חילול ה' that would have resulted if Shaul's crimes against the Givonim had gone unpunished. By the same token, the aforementioned *poskim* maintained that although Esther and Yael would not have been allowed to initiate intimacy to save their own lives, it was permissible for the purpose of saving the Jewish nation.

We might extend this notion to explain also the view of the *Shevus Yaakov* and Meiri, who permit initiating intercourse for the sake of הצלת רבים. They perhaps maintained that even the death of large numbers of Jews, and not only the entire nation's destruction, constitutes a חילול ה', and thus the martyrdom requirement is waived when many Jewish lives are at risk.

---

15. *Mishnas Pikuach Nefesh*, 63.
16. *Pe'er Ha-Dor*, vol. 3, p. 185.
17. The *Chazon Ish* also cited the Gemara's comment in *Maseches Sanhedrin* (107a) that as David fled from Jerusalem to escape the revolt mounted by his son, Avshalom, he planned to worship an idol to prevent a חילול ה'. News of a righteous king fleeing from his son's rebellion would cause people to question God's justness, and so David figured he would worship an idol to lead people to think he deserved this dreadful fate. However, the *Mishnas Pikuach Nefesh* (referenced above, note 15) observes that according to some commentators, David did not plan on actually worshipping an idol. See Maharsha and *Beis Ha-Levi*, vol. 2, *derush* 13.

Conclusion

With this in mind, let us return to our original question regarding the tactic of seducing an enemy or a Jewish traitor for an important military purpose. It would seem that since human life is at stake, such a tactic would certainly be permissible according to the *Beis Yaakov*, who allows a Jewish woman to seduce a man to save a life as long as she remains passive during the act of intercourse. This would likely be allowed also according to the Meiri, who permits seduction for the purpose of הצלת רבים, as the operations of the Israeli security forces serve to protect the multitudes of Jews living in Israel.

We should add that this holds true even if the success or urgency of the mission is uncertain, such as, for example, if the seducer may not succeed in obtaining the desired information even after developing a romantic relationship, or if the information may ultimately prove unhelpful. After all, as we have seen, this halachic ruling is based on the precedents of Esther and Yael, both of whom could not have known for certain that the intimate encounter they initiated would have the effect of rescuing the Jewish nation. In Yael's case, it was uncertain to begin with whether Sisera indeed still posed a threat after his army was miraculously defeated by *Bnei Yisrael*, and, moreover, Yael could not have known for certain that Sisera would not have fallen sound asleep without engaging in intercourse. In fact, as mentioned, the Gemara recounts that Yael had intercourse with Sisera seven times, presumably to ensure that he would sleep soundly. It is difficult to imagine that Yael considered each union definitively necessary for her life-saving objective. Rather, as it was urgently necessary to have Sisera fall into a deep slumber, she was permitted to do whatever she could to ensure this result. Similarly, Esther did not know for certain that her appeal to Achashverosh would succeed in annulling Haman's edict, yet she nevertheless approached him as a desperate attempt to save her people. By the same token, it would seem that according to the opinions noted above, a woman would be allowed to seduce an enemy for an urgent military purpose even if its success or necessity cannot be definitively ascertained.

Seemingly, however, this would not be allowed according to the view of the *Noda Be-Yehuda*, who, as noted above, permitted seduction only when the existence of the entire Jewish nation is at stake. Since the majority of the world's Jewish population still lives in the Diaspora, our nation's existence cannot be said to depend upon the security of the State of Israel. As such, the *Noda Be-Yehuda* would, in all likelihood, forbid a Jewish woman from participating in a military mission of seduction, even if it is deemed vital for the security of the

Jewish State.¹⁸ Moreover, the *Noda Be-Yehuda* speculates that Esther approached Achashverosh based on an exceptional ruling of Mordechai's *beis din*, or through רוח הקדש. This seems to imply that a formal הוראת שעה — an extraordinary ruling issued by an authoritative halachic body temporarily suspending normative *halacha* — or even רוח הקדש is required to permit illicit relations for the sake of rescuing the Jewish nation, neither of which, of course, is possible nowadays.

It should be noted, however, that this would likely depend on the woman's marital status. The requirement of martyrdom to avoid illicit sexual relations, according to many *poskim*,¹⁹ applies only when the relationship in question constitutes a capital offense (punishable by execution or *kares*). If the violation is a standard Torah prohibition, then one may transgress to save his or someone else's life. Accordingly, even if we accept the *Noda Be-Yehuda*'s stringent ruling regarding the provision of קרקע עולם, this would apply only to married women, as adultery constitutes a capital sexual offense. An unmarried woman, however, would likely be allowed to initiate an illicit relationship with a man as part of a vital military mission, since such a relationship does not constitute a capital offense.

---

18. In an extensive article in *Techumin* (30), Rav Ari Shvat explores the possibility that rescuing the Jews of *Eretz Yisrael* could perhaps halachically qualify as rescuing the entire Jewish nation. He notes, for example, Rabbeinu Tam's position (cited in *Talmidei Rabbeinu Yona, Berachos* 8a in the Rif) that *Chazal* established the recitation of *Hallel* only for miracles that resulted in the salvation of the entire Jewish nation. Yet, *Hallel* was instituted even for the Chanukah miracle, which did not seem to affect the Jewish communities in the Diaspora. Evidently, the salvation of the Jews of *Eretz Yisrael* is halachically equivalent to the salvation of the entire Jewish nation. Rav Shvat also suggests drawing proof from the famous story of Papus and Loliyanus, who were lauded for surrendering their lives to save the Jews of Lod (Rashi, *Ta'anis* 18b). Rav Moshe Feinstein (*Iggeros Moshe*, Y.D. 2:174) explains that this was permissible for the sake of הצלת ישראל — saving the Jewish nation. Although it was only a single Jewish community that was threatened, it is possible that this constituted הצלת ישראל because this was a community of Jews in the Land of Israel. Clearly, however, it is highly questionable whether these sources suffice as proof that a mission to secure the Jewish State is halachically equivalent to Esther's efforts to save the entire Jewish nation.
19. See, for example, *Chiddushei Rabbi Akiva Eiger*, Y.D. 157 (commenting on the *Shach* 157:10).

THE JERUSALEM POST

Soldier Arrested for Shooting Subdued Terrorist after Hebron Attack

03/24/2016
by Tova Lazaroff, Yaakov Lappin, Gil Stern Stern Hoffman

"This is a grave incident which contradicts the spirit of the IDF and what is expected of IDF soldiers and commanders," the army said in a statement to the press.

The Military Police on Thursday arrested a soldier who was seen firing a shot to the head of an already wounded Palestinian terrorist, as he lay on his back in a Hebron street, near the Jewish Tel Rumeida neighborhood.

A volunteer for the NGO B'Tselem who lives near the scene of the incident filmed the shooting from the window of his home. It was posted online and immediately went viral, fueling condemnations from the left and right.

"The IDF expects its soldiers to behave with composure and in accordance with the rules of engagement," Prime Minister Benjamin Netanyahu said in a statement, adding that this incident does not "represent the values of the IDF."

Defense Minister Moshe Ya'alon said, "We must not allow, even at a time that our blood boils, this loss of control. This incident will be dealt with the utmost severity."

IDF soldiers killed both Abdel Fattah al-Sharif and Ramzi al-Kasrawi after they stabbed a soldier guarding the road that leads to the small Tel Rumeida neighborhood. The scene right after the attack was captured on a three-minute video that opens when Sharif, 21, is still alive.

Its first scenes show Magen David Adom paramedics pushing a gurney with the wounded soldier toward an ambulance.

Two other ambulances are waiting nearby. The body of Kasrawi, 21, can be seen on the pavement near that ambulance.

The lens then moves to Sharif's upper body and shows him lying almost lifeless on the ground. A pool of blood has formed under his head, which he moves from one side to the other at around second 17 of the video.

The lens moves back to the soldier, who is bare-chested and wounded. He sits up on the gurney for a moment and then lies back down as paramedics lift him into the ambulance.

He was later taken to Shaare Zedek Medical Center in Jerusalem to be treated for light to moderate wounds.

As the Magen David ambulance heads away from the scene, a second ambulance moves past Sharif's body, obscuring it for a moment and the viewer can hear that a shot is fired.

The ambulance continues a few paces up the road and Sharif returns to view. He is still lying on the pavement, but it appears as if he has been shot again, at point 1:55 of the video. His head is still and drawn back and fresh blood is flowing from it in three small streams down the pavement. The video then shows one of the ambulances repositioning itself near Sharif's body as soldiers and civilians walk nearby.

Everyone who was present at the scene will be questioned, IDF Spokesman Brig.-Gen. Moti Almoz told reporters about the investigation.

IDF Chief of Staff Lt.-Gen. Gadi Eisenkot and OC Central Command Maj.-Gen. Roni Numa both take a "severe view" of the shooting, Almoz said. The investigation will "not leave any fact unclear, as to why a soldier opened fire on a terrorist who is lying on the ground. We have to understand what happened in regard to orders. Soldiers, after neutralizing a threat, are supposed to provide medical treatment, even if they are terrorists. There is no room for interpretation here," he added.

Until the last shot was fired at the already downed assailant, Almoz said, the incident had been handled correctly and was under control.

The investigation will seek to understand why the additional shot was fired.

...

Meretz MK Esawi Frej also commented on the incident, saying, "The video of the soldier has proved that an IDF uniform does not guarantee human compassion." Frej called the soldier a "murderer who fired in cold blood at the head of the helpless wounded man." He added that if the soldier did not face a murder trial it would be undemocratic and improper.

His Meretz colleague, Tamar Zandberg, praised the organization B'Tselem for distributing the video. "Without B'Tselem and Breaking the Silence we would have never known or seen," Zandberg wrote on Twitter — despite the fact that military sources reported that the investigation had commenced before the video emerged.

On the right, Bayit Yehudi MK Moti Yogev said it was too soon to judge the incident, because there have been recent incidents where wounded terrorists that were thought to have been neutralized attacked soldiers.

"The goal of the terrorist is to die, and I would prefer a dead terrorist to a dead soldier," he told Army Radio.

Amnesty International said an international body would need to investigate the incident, not just the IDF.

Opposition leader Isaac Herzog said "a black flag has been raised by the incident," but he trusts that the IDF and its officers will probe the incident properly and ensure that justice is done.

Ya'alon said that the shooting did not impact Israel's overall war on terrorism in which the IDF has acted "with a steel hand against terrorists and those who send them, as soldiers on the ground did in real time today, neutralizing the terrorists in Hebron. Even then, we must not act in violation of our values and conscience.

"Even when we must strike our enemies and defeat them in war or any battle with them, our moral obligation is... to safeguard our humanity.

"We must remember the limitations of power after the enemy has been struck, and avoid immoral behavior. We must remember that our power does not only stem from our military capability, but first of all, from our moral strength.

"This is our duty, to win, and to remain human," Ya'alon said.

Herb Keinon contributed to this report.

Copyright © jpost.com

Killing a Neutralized Terrorist

The so-called "knife Intifada," which began in September 2015, introduced a new trend of deadly Arab terrorism against Israelis, consisting mainly of random stabbing attacks throughout Israel, mostly on streets and at bus stops. In the vast majority of cases, the attacker was promptly shot by police offers, soldiers, or armed civilians who were in the vicinity of the attack or who rushed to the scene to help. Many times, the terrorist was shot dead, whereas on some occasions, he or she was incapacitated and subsequently arrested by Israel's security forces.

This unfortunate trend precipitated a public debate concerning the appropriate protocols to follow once the terrorist has been disarmed, restrained, or incapacitated such that he no longer poses a threat. Assuming that the absence of an immediate threat is definite — for example, the terrorist's weapon has been seized and he is unable to move — it would seem, at first glance, that there is no longer any justification to kill him. Even if it can be assumed that he wishes to resume his violent activity, once he is no longer capable of doing so, the grave prohibition against murder should seemingly apply, just as it applies to killing any other person. After all, while *halacha* quite clearly permits and requires killing a רודף — a "pursuer," someone seeking to kill another person[1] — we might assume that once a terrorist is no longer capable of "pursuing," he should be arrested and prosecuted like other dangerous criminals, and there is thus no reason to permit killing him.

This was, indeed, the directive issued in the fall of 2015 by then Attorney General Yehuda Weinstein.[2] Several prominent rabbis likewise ruled against killing a neutralized terrorist, including Rav Yaakov Ariel (Chief Rabbi of Ramat Gan) and Rav David Stav (Chief Rabbi of Shoham). Others, however — most notably, Rav Shmuel Eliyahu (Chief Rabbi of Safed) and Rav Bentzion Mutzafi (Jerusalem) — ruled that a terrorist may, and should, be killed after the attack, even after he no longer poses a threat.

This controversy erupted into a full-blown firestorm in late March 2016, when a video surfaced of an Israeli soldier in Hebron approaching and shooting

---

1. The law of רודף is set forth in the Mishna in *Maseches Sanhedrin* (73a). The Gemara identifies as the source of this law the comparison drawn by the Torah (*Devarim* 22:26) between one who pursues to murder and one who pursues to rape a betrothed woman, who should be killed if this is necessary to protect the woman.
2. As reported by numerous media outlets on October 26, 2015.

dead a terrorist who was lying on the ground, apparently incapacitated.³ Two terrorists had stabbed an IDF soldier, and a different soldier shot them, killing one and wounding the other. Several minutes later, another soldier was seen arriving at the scene and shooting the incapacitated terrorist. After the video was publicized, the soldier was arrested and tried for manslaughter. Much of the ensuing controversy revolved around the facts of the case, specifically the question as to whether there was still a credible threat given the possibility that the attacker may have been wearing an explosive belt underneath his thick jacket, which he was suspiciously wearing on a warm spring day. Additionally, however, this incident reignited the larger question as to whether an incapacitated terrorist should be killed.

This essay will explore the possible halachic basis for killing a neutralized terrorist to determine whether this is indeed permissible.

גברא קטילא

A possible Talmudic precedent for such a question is the Gemara's brief discussion concerning the status of a criminal attempting a burglary through an underground tunnel, upon whom the tunnel collapses in the process. The law of הבא במחתרת, as established by the Torah (*Shemos* 22:1–2) and explained by the Gemara (*Sanhedrin* 72a), permits a homeowner to kill an intruder, unless it is clear that the intruder has no intention of killing (such as if he is the homeowner's father). Normally, it can be assumed that a burglar anticipates a confrontation with the homeowner and thus comes prepared to kill, and, as such, the homeowner is granted the right to kill in self-defense. Amid its discussion of this law, the Gemara states that if the tunnel collapses on the intruder, he is not rescued from the tunnel, and is instead left there to die.⁴

Many authorities raised the question of why the intruder should not be rescued at this point, when presumably he no longer poses a threat. Once the tunnel has collapsed, he is, quite obviously, incapable of burglarizing the home,

---

3. http://www.timesofisrael.com/idf-hebron-soldier-said-stabber-deserved-to-die-then-shot-him/.
4. It is uncertain whether the Gemara refers here specifically to the question of desecrating Shabbos to rescue the intruder, or to the issue of rescuing him generally, even on a weekday. The *Yad Ramah* in *Sanhedrin* writes explicitly that the intruder is not rescued even on a weekday, whereas the Meiri indicates that the Gemara made this comment only in reference to the issue of Shabbos violation. Later authorities struggled to explain why there should be a difference in this regard between Shabbos and weekdays, given that the Shabbos restrictions are waived for the sake of saving human life. See *Iggeros Moshe*, Y.D. 2:151.

and he is very likely injured. Why would the *halacha* not require saving his life once he no longer poses a threat?

The Meiri suggests that this *halacha* stems from the possibility that he will still seek to kill after being rescued:

שמא כיון שיש לומר עליו שהוא משתדל בעצמו בפקוחו ולבו על גנבתו אין מפקחין.

> Perhaps, since it is possible that he is trying to rescue himself and his heart is still set upon his burglary — we do not rescue.[5]

Similarly, Rav Chaim Ozer Grodzinsky writes (*Achiezer*, vol. 1, E.H. 18) that the burglar is not rescued because אפשר דאחרי פיקוח הגל יהפך לרודף — "it is possible that after the debris is removed he will turn [back] into a pursuer." Rav Chaim Ozer proceeds to note that in a situation in which no such possibility exists, as it is certain that the burglar would no longer pose any threat after being rescued, he should, in fact, be removed from the tunnel.[6]

A different approach is taken by Rav Yerucham Perlman in his *Or Gadol* (chapter 1), where he establishes that there is no obligation to rescue a person from a situation of danger into which he knowingly put himself. The intruder is not rescued, Rav Perlman explains, because he endangered his life by attempting a burglary, knowing full well that the homeowner would try to defend himself and his property.[7]

However, Rashi, in his commentary on the Gemara, seems to point to a much different approach, one that may have crucial implications for other situations of a neutralized רודף. He writes:

כיון דניתן להרגו בלא התראה, גברא קטילא הוא משעת חתירה.

---

5. Before offering this suggestion, the Meiri proposes a different approach, distinguishing between a situation in which the burglar is known to be alive under the debris and a case in which it is questionable whether he is alive. Only in the second case, the Meiri suggests, does the Gemara forbid rescuing the burglar on Shabbos, given the possibility that he has already died. The obvious question arises as to why the Gemara would draw such a distinction, as Shabbos is violated even in situations of ספק פקוח נפש — a possible threat to life. See *Shiyurei Kenesses Ha-Gedola*, O.C. 329.
6. משכח"ל דמפקחים עליו אם אין לנו לחוש שיהפך אח"כ לרודף.
7. We addressed this theory at length in the first volume of *Headlines* (chapter 2), in reference to the question of whether *halacha* requires rescuing people from self-imposed danger, such as residents who knowingly ignore evacuation orders before a hurricane. This issue may bear relevance to the case of a wounded terrorist as well, regarding the question of whether a Jewish paramedic or doctor is obligated to treat him, considering that he knowingly placed himself in a dangerous position by launching a terror attack.

> Since one may kill him without warning, he is a "dead man" from the moment of digging.

Rashi writes that the intruder is not rescued because he is a גברא קטילא — a "dead man" — since the *halacha* permits killing him. Once he entered the tunnel to burglarize the home, the homeowner is licensed to kill him, and thus his life no longer needs to be protected even after the tunnel's collapse.

Rashi's comments here are consistent with his remarks in his Torah commentary (*Shemos* 22:1), where he explains that when the Torah describes the intruder as אין לו דמים ("there is no bloodguilt"), it means, הרי הוא כמת מעיקרו — "he is like a dead person from the outset." According to Rashi, it appears, the intruder is regarded as "dead," and thus there is no prohibition against killing him. He retains this status as long as he remains in the tunnel, even after the tunnel has collapsed and he no longer poses a threat.

Would this concept of גברא קטילא apply to all cases of an incapacitated or restrained רודף at the scene of the crime? Should we assume that just as a burglar is regarded as a גברא קטילא even in a state of presumed incapacitation, a neutralized terrorist likewise has this status, despite no longer posing a threat?

The answer to this question becomes quite clear in light of the discussions of later *Acharonim* regarding Rashi's comments. Rav Isser Zalman Meltzer (*Even Ha-Azel, Hilchos Geneiva* 9:13) explains Rashi's remarks as expressing a view similar to that taken by the Meiri — namely, that the intruder still might pose a risk to the homeowner. Since the intruder had entered the tunnel with the intention to kill the homeowner, he has the presumed status of a רודף even if his capacity to kill is uncertain. According to Rav Meltzer, when Rashi describes the intruder as a גברא קטילא, he means not that no concern needs to be shown for the intruder's life, but rather that he does not lose his status as a presumed "pursuer" as long as the possibility exists that he is capable of killing. Accordingly, Rashi would concede that if a pursuer is unquestionably and fully incapacitated, one would be required to rescue him.[8]

Rav Avraham Erlanger (*Birkas Avraham, Sanhedrin* 72b) explains Rashi differently, suggesting that since the intruder is "sentenced" to death the moment he sets out to burglarize the home, we view the tunnel's collapse as an execution

---

8. In a similar vein, Rav Asher Nissan Levitan, writing in the journal *Ha-Pardes* (27:3, Kislev 5713), explains Rashi to mean that whereas one is ordinarily required to expose himself to possible danger in order to rescue someone from certain danger, this does not apply to an individual who is himself pursued. He is not obligated to risk his life by rescuing his pursuer if the pursuer might still pose a risk. Therefore, the homeowner is not required to try to rescue the intruder, given the risk entailed, whereas others indeed bear such an obligation.

of this sentence. The status of גברא קטילא does not mean that the intruder may be killed even after losing the ability to kill, but rather that he has been sentenced to death as long as he is capable of, and interested in, killing. As such, there is no obligation to rescue him after the tunnel's collapse, as this event is seen as his due punishment.[9] Clearly, according to this reading, one may not kill a רודף after he is incapacitated and no longer able to inflict harm.

It thus emerges that even according to Rashi's interpretation of the Gemara's ruling, it cannot be applied to permit killing a רודף who no longer poses a threat.

Moreover, it is unclear whether the rules that apply in the case of הבא במחתרת are relevant to other situations of רודף as well. We find several indications that the license granted to a homeowner when confronted by an intruder extends beyond the standard halachic right to self-defense. For example, whereas *halacha* forbids killing a רודף if he can be stopped through other means,[10] no such provision is mentioned in reference to a situation of הבא במחתרת. This and other distinctions have led several authorities to conclude that the authorization to kill an intruder stands separate and apart from the ordinary rule of רודף.[11] Therefore, even if we were to accept the notion that a homeowner may kill an intruder even after he is incapacitated, this would not necessarily apply in other situations of רודף.

ספק רודף

The most common argument advanced for allowing — and requiring — killing incapacitated terrorists is to ensure they do not commit further crimes. Arab terrorists aim to kill as many Israelis as often as they can, and they will seize every opportunity to commit their deadly crimes, without concern for the repercussions. As such, the standard measures used to deter criminals, such as the prospect of prosecution and imprisonment, or even death, do not deter many prospective terrorists; even after serving prison terms, they are likely to resume their violent activity. Advocates of killing incapacitated terrorists point to the fact that prosecution and incarceration do not, unfortunately, guarantee the prevention of future attacks, and terrorists therefore continue to pose a risk even after being restrained and taken into custody.

---

9. This reading of Rashi is also suggested by Rav Yisrael Grossman in *Sha'arei Teirutzin* (1).
10. רודף שהיה רודף אחר חבירו להורגו ויכול להצילו באחד מאבריו ולא הציל נהרג עליו (*Sanhedrin* 74a).
11. See Rav Asher Weiss' *Minchas Asher* (*Pesachim* 3 and *Shemos* 39), where he develops this distinction at length, noting that he disagrees in this regard with Rav Shlomo Zalman Auerbach, who equated הבא במחתרת with other situations of רודף (*Minchas Shlomo* 1:7). See also our discussion of the topic in the first volume of *Headlines*, pp. 55–57.

Indeed, various Israeli governments have released Palestinian prisoners, including avowed terrorists who proudly confessed to murdering Jews, as part of negotiation processes or in exchange for Israeli prisoners. For example, in October 2011, Israeli released 1,027 Palestinian prisoners in exchange for captured IDF soldier Gilad Shalit. Just two years later, in December 2013, Israeli intelligence agencies reported that a group of the released prisoners in Gaza formed a wing to conduct terrorist operations in the West Bank. Tragically, by the summer of 2015, six Israelis had been killed by murderous acts perpetrated or orchestrated by terrorists released as part of the Shalit deal.[12] The latter include Mahmoud Kwasmah, who was sentenced to twenty years in prison for his role in a 2004 bombing attack in Beer Sheva that killed sixteen Israelis and wounded over 100. He was released as part of the Shalit deal and sent to his home in Gaza. Two-and-half years later, in April 2014, his brother, Hussam, who lived in Hebron, sent him a request for money to fund a terrorist attack. Over the next two months, Mahmoud arranged for the transfer of 220,000 shekels to his brother. These funds paid for the kidnapping and murder of Naftali Frankel, Gilad Shaer, and Eyal Yifrach in June of that year.

In light of these tragic precedents, some have argued that every avowed Palestinian terrorist has the status of רודף even after being incapacitated or detained, given his passionate desire to kill and the real possibility that he will be given the opportunity to do so. As such, it is claimed, terrorists should be killed after perpetrating an attack even after they are restrained, disarmed, or incapacitated.[13]

The validity of this argument likely hinges on the question regarding the status of a ספק רודף — a person whose intent or ability to kill is uncertain. If we know of a person who might be inclined to commit a murder, but this is not certain, should he be killed, or does the law of רודף apply only if the individual is clearly intending and able to kill?

The *Minchas Chinuch* (296:33) writes that one may kill a ספק רודף, drawing proof from the Gemara's discussion in *Maseches Yoma* (85a) concerning the general principle of פקוח נפש, which allows transgressing the Torah's laws for the sake of saving a life. Rabbi Yishmael, cited in the Gemara, identifies as the source of this law the aforementioned provision of הבא במחתרת. The Torah allows a homeowner to kill an intruder, in violation of the prohibition of murder, due to the possible threat posed to his life, thus establishing that the Torah laws are waived when necessary to preserve a life. Although the Gemara does not accept

---

12. This information was reported by Israeli media outlets on July 20, 2015.
13. This was the reason given by Rav Shmuel Eliyahu for his ruling requiring killing neutralized terrorists, as reported by Arutz Sheva, October 9, 2015.

this argument, and finds a different source for the law of פקוח נפש, the *Minchas Chinuch* notes that Rabbi Yishmael's rationale is nevertheless significant and revealing. Rabbi Yishmael notes that the Torah permits killing the intruder despite the uncertainty surrounding his intentions, as it is possible that he does not plan on acting violently. This would certainly indicate that even a ספק רודף may be killed, given the risk he poses.

As noted above, however, the rules that apply in the case of הבא במחתרת do not necessarily apply to other situations of רודף, and thus we cannot necessarily draw any conclusions regarding the general law of רודף from Rabbi Yishmael's remarks.

Another possible source for allowing the killing of a ספק רודף is the startling story told in *Maseches Avoda Zara* (10b) of the Roman Emperor Antoninus. The Gemara relates that Antoninus would hold clandestine meetings with Rabbi Yehuda Ha-Nasi, during which he learned about Judaism, and in order to maintain secrecy, he would kill the servants who escorted him to each meeting. The likely reason, as *Tosfos* explain, is that Antoninus feared he would be assassinated by his officials if they learned of his close relationship with the Jewish sage. *Tosfos*' formulation is: היה ירא פן יודיעו הדבר אל השרים והיו גורמין להרגו — "He feared that perhaps they would inform the officials of this matter, and cause him to be killed." This formulation clearly suggests that the risk was uncertain, and yet Antoninus was nevertheless justified in killing these royal servants.

Tosfos' comments may perhaps serve as the basis for the ruling of the *Sefer Chasidim* (1017) concerning a case in which Jewish travelers were attacked by bandits, but managed to defend themselves and kill their assailants. The *Sefer Chasidim* writes that if there were witnesses to the incident who might report the Jews to the authorities, in which case the Jews would be executed, the Jews may kill those witnesses. As in the case discussed by *Tosfos*, the *Sefer Chasidim* permits killing witnesses to an incident who would pose a danger if they disclose the information.

We may, however, distinguish between the case of Antoninus and other situations of ספק רודף. Rav Yaakov Reischer, in his *Iyun Yaakov*, suggests that a king is given greater license to kill potential foes in order to maintain stable rule over his kingdom. According to this view, we certainly cannot reach any conclusions with regard to general situations on the basis of *Tosfos*' comments.

Rav Avraham Reinhold (*Minchas Avraham* 42) suggests that *Tosfos* follow the surprising view of the Maharash Yafeh (Rav Shmuel Yafeh Ashkenazi), cited disapprovingly by the *Mishneh Le-Melech* (*Hilchos Melachim* 10:2), that non-Jews are not required to surrender their lives to avoid committing murder. According to the Maharash Yafeh, the provision requiring refraining from murder even at the expense of one's own life was introduced specifically with regard to Jews, and does not apply to gentiles. Therefore, whereas a Jew would be required to disobey an order to murder even at the risk of his life, a gentile would be permitted to kill in such a case. As such, in *Tosfos*' view, Antoninus was permitted to kill his servants to protect himself even though the risk posed by his servants was uncertain.

Rav Yitzchak Zilberstein of Bnei-Brak (*Chashukei Chemed, Kesubos* 37b) relates that he asked his father-in-law, Rav Yosef Shalom Elyashiv, whether *Tosfos*' comments prove that a ספק רודף may be killed. Rav Elyashiv answered in the negative, noting that *Tosfos* also provide a second explanation for Antoninus' practice, suggesting that these servants in any event deserved execution for other offenses. Surprisingly, Rav Elyashiv posited that *Tosfos* do not offer two separate approaches, but rather make two complementary statements: since these servants were in any event guilty of certain offenses, Antoninus felt justified killing them in light of the possible risk that they posed.

While this reading of *Tosfos* certainly seems strained, it testifies to Rav Elyashiv's insistence that a potentially dangerous person may not be killed unless he poses a clear threat.

Rav Moshe Feinstein likewise ruled that a ספק רודף may not be killed (*Iggeros Moshe*, C.M. 2:69:2). He writes, צריך שיהיה כעין ודאי שהוא רודף — one must be nearly certain of the risk posed by the potential pursuer in order to be allowed to kill him.[14] Rav Shlomo Zalman Auerbach, however, in a letter printed in *Nishmas Avraham* (vol. 4, p. 150), disputes Rav Moshe's ruling, noting the precedent of the בא במחתרת, who may be killed despite the uncertainty surrounding the danger he poses. This ruling is consistent with Rav Shlomo Zalman's position elsewhere that the laws of הבא במחתרת serve as a model of the standard rules governing situations of רודף,[15] a premise that other halachic authorities did not accept, as we noted above.

In any event, Rav Zilberstein cites Rav Elyashiv's ruling that a ספק רודף may not be killed unless there is a real possibility of risk, writing:

אין להרוג רודף אלא אם כן יש חשש רציני שיהרוג אותו, ולא בחשש רחוק.

> One should not kill a pursuer unless there is a serious concern that he will kill him, but not if the chances are remote.

---

14. Rav Zilberstein (*Chashukei Chemed, Makkos*, 7a) speculates that Rav Moshe might concede that if a person clearly wishes to kill and it is uncertain whether he is capable of doing so, then he may be killed, even if the risk is slight. Regardless, however, Rav Zilberstein concludes that a potential pursuer may not be killed unless he clearly poses a risk.

15. See above, note 10.

In the case of an incapacitated or restrained terrorist who is or will soon be in custody, it seems clear that the risk of his one day murdering can be described as a חשש רחוק — a remote possibility. While there have tragically been cases of convicted terrorists who were released and subsequently resumed their acts of terror, as mentioned above, these exceptional cases do not suffice to classify the risk posed by a restrained terrorist as a חשש רציני — Rav Zilberstein's formulation — and certainly not as a כעין ודאי, the level of risk required by Rav Moshe. Therefore, as far as the laws of רודף are concerned, it would be difficult to permit killing a terrorist who no longer poses an immediate threat, in light of the position taken by several leading *poskim* that one may not kill a ספק רודף.

Even more compellingly, the argument that an incapacitated terrorist should be killed due to the future danger he poses is negated by an explicit *halacha* in the Gemara. In *Maseches Sanhedrin* (74a), the Gemara establishes that if a person is able to stop a רודף by incapacitating him — יכול להצילו באחד מאבריו — but he kills him instead, he is guilty of murder. This ruling is codified by the Rambam in *Hilchos Rotzei'ach* (1:13), albeit with the qualification that the killer is liable to death at the hands of God and is not sentenced to death by *beis din*. This *halacha* explicitly requires stopping a would-be killer through incapacitation when possible, and considers unnecessarily killing him an act of murder. Nowhere do we find that the concern of the pursuer's future recovery warrants killing him in his current state of incapacitation.

To illustrate this point, let us take the example of a person who attempts to murder someone who ruined his life, such as by destroying his business or luring his wife away from him. His attempt fails, and he is arrested. As he is led away by the police, he shouts loudly and clearly that he will one day kill the intended victim. He repeats his vow as he sits on the defendant's bench in court and hears the judge sentence him to twenty years in prison. Would anyone consider such a man a רודף due to his plans to commit murder twenty years down the road? If he is a רודף, then anyone in the courtroom would have a halachic obligation to kill him right there and then! This is clearly inconceivable. It is thus likewise inconceivable that a terrorist lying on the ground, incapacitated by a gunshot wound, would be considered a רודף because he might one day be released from prison and seek to resume his violent activities.

מאי חזית דדמא דידך סומק טפי

Some have suggested that the aforementioned discussion is irrelevant in the case of terrorists, as they are not subject to the ordinary rules that govern situations of a רודף.

Murder (along with idolatry and sexual immorality) marks an exception to the standard rule of פקוח נפש, which allows violating Torah law for the sake of protecting one's life, even in situations of a slight risk. If one needs to commit murder to save his life, he is required to surrender his life to avoid committing this act, except in the situation of רודף, where *halacha* permits killing in self-defense. The reason why פקוח נפש does not override the prohibition of murder, as the Gemara establishes in *Maseches Sanhedrin* (74a), is מאי חזית דדמא דידך סומק טפי — one has no right to assume that the value of his life exceeds that of the life he needs to take to protect it. As Rashi explains, פקוח נפש generally overrides Torah law because God values human life over observance of His laws, and thus this rule cannot apply to murder, when one life would need to be taken to save another. Since one life cannot be assumed to have more value than another, one cannot save his life through murder. The exception to this rule, of course, is a situation of רודף, as the Torah instructs that a pursuer must be prevented from killing his target, even if this entails taking the pursuer's life.[16]

Some have argued that since the only basis for forbidding murder to save a life is the rationale of מאי חזית דדמא דידך סומק טפי, it would be permissible in situations in which one's life may indeed be presumed to be more precious than someone else's. Ordinarily, we lack the authority to determine the comparative values of different people's lives, but it is conceivably possible that in certain extreme situations such assessments can be made. Thus, it has been argued that in the case of a terrorist seeking to kill innocent Jews, we may presume that the lives of his potential victims are worth more than his own. As such, the concern for human life allows — and perhaps requires — one to kill the terrorist, even though he does not pose an immediate threat, given the small chance that he might strike again in the future.

This argument is flawed on several levels. First, while emotionally we might harbor a great deal of resentment and disdain for terrorists, for very good reason, the decision of whose life is more precious than whose seems to be one that only the Almighty can make. We might apply to this argument the timeless exhortation of the prophet Yeshayahu to King Chizkiyahu, who decided not to marry after prophetically foreseeing that he would be beget a wicked son: בהדי כבשי דרחמנא למה לך — "What are you doing probing God's secrets?" (*Berachos* 10a). The question as to the comparative worth of different people's lives, even if one of them is an avowed terrorist, can be answered only by the Almighty Himself.

Moreover, there are several indications that martyrdom is required for the sake of avoiding murder even when the argument of מאי חזית does not seem to apply. The Rambam rules (*Hilchos Yesodei Ha-Torah* 5:6) that if an enemy ruler demands that the Jewish community hand over one member to be killed, or else

---

16. See above, note 1.

the entire community will be killed, they must all be killed rather than hand over a single Jew to the enemy. According to the Rambam, this applies regardless of whether the enemy asks the Jews to choose a person to be executed or if a specific person is named.[17] The Ramach, cited by the *Kesef Mishneh*, raises the question of why the people are not entitled to hand over the named individual for the sake of saving the entire group. After all, if murder is prohibited at the risk of life only because of our inability to weigh the value of one life against the other, it should be permissible in this case, when the choice is between one life and many lives. Seemingly, the Ramach argues, we may assume that the combined value of the lives of a large group exceeds that of a single person, thus warranting killing one to rescue the others.

The Rambam apparently rules that murder for פקוח נפש is forbidden even in cases in which the rationale of מאי חזית appears to be inapplicable, and it is thus forbidden to kill even for the sake of rescuing a large group of people.[18]

Further proof to this contention may be drawn from the Gemara's discussion (*Sanhedrin* 74a) concerning the obligation of martyrdom to avoid גילוי עריות (sins of sexual immorality). The Gemara establishes this requirement on the basis of the comparison drawn by the Torah (*Devarim* 22:26) between murder and adultery. Just as murder is forbidden even for the sake of saving a life, the Gemara deduces, גילוי עריות likewise remains forbidden even in situations of life-threatening danger (such as when a Jew is forced to commit a sexual offense at the threat of death). At first glance, this line of reasoning seems flawed. The rationale of מאי חזית is, quite obviously, irrelevant in the context of sexual immorality, when no lives are being taken. If the prohibition of murder overrides the concern for human life only because of the rationale of מאי חזית, then there is no reason to require martyrdom to avoid גילוי עריות, a requirement that is sourced in the comparison between גילוי עריות and murder. The fact that the prohibition of murder serves as a model for the prohibition of גילוי עריות in this regard would seem to prove that martyrdom is required to avoid murder even when the rationale of מאי חזית does not apply.

Indeed, the *Kesef Mishneh*, in the aforementioned passage, posits that the requirement to surrender one's life to avoid committing murder was known to *Chazal* through oral tradition, and is not dependent upon the rationale of מאי חזית. Although the Gemara points to this rationale as the reason underlying the requirement of martyrdom to avoid an act of murder, this requirement applies

---

17. The only exception, the Rambam rules, is when the person demanded by the enemy is guilty of a capital offense.
18. See our discussion in the first volume of *Headlines* (chapter 5) as to whether a hijacked aircraft may be shot down to prevent the hijacker from flying the plane into a building.

even when the reasoning of מאי חזית does not. On this basis, the *Kesef Mishneh* answers the question raised by the Ramach as to why one person should not be handed over to be killed in order to save a large group of people. Murder is forbidden even at the expense of one's life, regardless of whether the rationale of מאי חזית is applicable, and the group must therefore allow themselves to be killed to avoid killing a single individual.

A similar theory was posited by Rav Shimon Shkop, as cited by Rav Shmuel Rozovsky (*Zichron Shmuel*, p. 332). As mentioned, the Gemara infers from the comparison drawn by the Torah between murder and sexual immorality that the latter is also forbidden even at the threat of death. Rav Shimon suggested that once the requirement of יהרג ואל יעבור (martyrdom to avoid transgressing) is applied to גילוי עריות based on this comparison, the comparison is then made in the opposite direction as well, such that we learn about the prohibition of murder from that of גילוי עריות. In other words, once we have established that one must surrender his life to avoid גילוי עריות, despite the fact that the rationale of מאי חזית is inapplicable, we then deduce from the Torah's comparison that the prohibition of murder also overrides the concern for human life even when the argument of מאי חזית is not relevant.[19]

These sources clearly indicate that even when we feel we are authorized to determine that one individual's life is more valuable than another, we may not commit an act of murder on the basis of this assumption.

שעת מלחמה and Osama bin Laden

There is, however, one more factor to consider, one which may perhaps render everything we have seen until now irrelevant.

From a number of sources, it appears that the standard laws governing the permissibility of killing in self-defense or to protect others do not apply in a שעת מלחמה — a time of war. When an army wages a legitimate war against an enemy, the halachic rules of engagement do not conform to the ordinary guidelines for

---

19. This theory appears in other sources as well. See, for example, Rav Baruch Mordechai Ezrachi's *Birkas Mordechai, Kesubos*, p. 79.
    Later (p. 342), Rav Rozovsky draws proof from Rabbeinu Yona's *Sha'arei Teshuva* (3:139), where Rabbeinu Yona writes that the prohibition of מלבין פני חבירו ברבים — publicly humiliating one's fellow — falls under the category of quasi-murder (אביזרייהו דשפיכות דמים), as indicated by the Gemara (*Sota* 10b), and one must therefore surrender his life to avoid embarrassing his fellow. Clearly, the rationale of מאי חזית does not apply in such a case, where the choice is between one person's actual death and the other person's shame, yet Rabbeinu Yona requires martyrdom — thus proving that the requirement to surrender one's life to avoid an act of murder does not depend on the factor of מאי חזית.

killing; instead, they permit taking lives even in situations when this would be forbidden during peacetime.

The special status of שעת מלחמה is noted by *Tosfos* in *Maseches Avoda Zara* (26b), in explaining the surprising passage in *Maseches Sofrim* (15:10), טוב שבכנע־נים הרוג — "[Even] the best of the Canaanites should be killed." *Tosfos* explain that this refers to times of warfare, when it is permissible, and perhaps even obligatory, to kill even "the best of the Canaanites."[20] This is also the clear implication of the Rambam in *Hilchos Rotzei'ach* (4:11), where he writes:

אבל הגוים שאין בינינו ובינם מלחמה...אין מסבבים להן המיתה.

But the gentiles with whom we are not engaged in war...we do not cause them to die.

This suggests that when we are engaged in war against an enemy nation, killing is allowed. Indeed, the *Shach* (Y.D. 158:1) writes, בשעת מלחמה היו הורגין אותן בידיים — "In wartime, they would kill [gentiles] with their hands." The *Shach* cites as his source *Tosfos*' comments explaining the ruling of טוב שבכנענים הרוג.

It remains unclear, however, how far this rule extends. Do *Tosfos* authorize killing all members of nations at war with us, or only those who pose a threat?

While it is difficult to determine *Tosfos*' intent, other *Rishonim* clearly indicate that the authorization to kill טוב שבכנענים is limited to those engaged in hostilities against the Jewish nation. The Rambam writes in *Hilchos Avodas Kochavim* (10:1), in reference to the prohibition against killing non-Jews:

אבל לאבדו בידו או לדחפו לבור וכיוצא בזה אסור **מפני שאינו עושה עמנו מלחמה**.

But directly killing him, or pushing him into a pit and the like, is forbidden, **since he is not waging war against us**.

The Rambam here establishes that one is allowed to kill only those gentiles engaged in warfare against the Jewish people.

Similarly, Rabbeinu Yechiel of Paris, in the famous 1240 Paris Disputation, was asked about the declaration טוב שבכנענים הרוג, and he explained that it refers specifically to enemy combatants:

טוב שבגוים במלחמה הרוג, כי אין לך אדם כשר ונאמן בהם, **שכיון שבא להלחם עמך ובא להרגך השכם להרגו**, ואפילו בישראל מותר.

"The best among the gentiles — kill" because there is no good, upright person among them, as **once he comes to wage war against you and**

---

20. In contemporary editions of *Maseches Sofrim*, it explicitly mentions שעת מלחמה.

comes to kill you, arise and kill him. This is permissible even in a case of a Jew [who seeks to kill].[21]

This understanding of טוב שבכנענים הרוג appears also in Rabbeinu Bachayei's Torah commentary (*Shemos* 14:7):

ובאור הדבר כי בשעת מלחמה בלבד הוא שמותר להרגו כי מאחר שהוא נלחם עמך ובא כנגדך להרגך אף אתה השכם להרגו.

This means that it is permissible to kill him only in wartime, for since he wages war against you and comes against you to kill you, you must likewise arise to kill him.

According to these sources, the dictum of טוב שבכנענים הרוג means that even an otherwise upstanding and respectable gentile must be killed when he wages war against us. Indeed, this dictum appears in the *Mechilta* (to *Shemos* 14:7) in reference to the Egyptians who pursued *Bnei Yisrael* after the Exodus. The *Mechilta* observes that the only Egyptians who still had horses in their possession at that time were those who "feared the word of God" and brought their animals into shelters in advance of the plague of hail (*Shemos* 9:20). Even these, the most God-fearing among the Egyptians, were drowned at sea because they pursued *Bnei Yisrael*, thus demonstrating the need to fight resolutely against all who wage war against us, even if these are the "best of the Canaanites."[22]

Interestingly, this question underlies, to a large extent, the controversy that arose among legal scholars following the U.S. Navy's killing of Osama bin Laden on May 2, 2011. Accounts of the raid on bin Laden's compound in Islamabad, Pakistan, indicate that he was unarmed and posed no threat to the Navy Seals who had invaded his hideout. Nevertheless, then Attorney General Eric Holder told the Senate Judiciary Committee after the raid that killing bin Laden was legally justified because he was an enemy combatant: "If someone is an enemy combatant, it does not matter if he is unarmed or not, because lethal force is permitted against enemy fighters and commanders in the course of an ongoing armed conflict." Similarly, the *International Business Times* cited legal expert Walter E. Dellinger as saying, "Under international law, bin Laden is an enemy combatant. And one of the points of war is that you can kill enemy combatants."[23]

---

21. Cited by Rav Menachem Kasher in *Torah Sheleima*, vol. 10, appendix 19. The entire text of the disputation can be found online at http://www.daat.ac.il/daat/mahshevt/natsrut/yehiel-2.htm.
22. See Rav Yoel Amital, "*Ma'aseh Shechem*," at http://shaalvim.co.il/torah/view.asp?id=38.
23. *International Business Times*, May 7, 2011. Available at http://www.ibtimes.com/osama-bin-laden-killing-legal-international-law-experts-divided-282739.

By contrast, the BBC cited international law specialist Benjamin Ferencz as arguing, "Killing a captive who poses no immediate threat is a crime under military law as well as all other law."[24]

This controversy might serve as an intriguing test case of the question under discussion. *Tosfos*' formulation, as we saw, might suggest that killing an enemy is acceptable during wartime even if he poses no direct threat, whereas the other sources cited state explicitly that only combatants who presently pose a threat may be killed.

Killing to Achieve a Legitimate Military Objective

Even if killing enemies who pose no direct threat is fundamentally forbidden, there are numerous sources that allow killing even non-threatening enemies when this is necessary for the purpose of achieving a legitimate military goal.

One such source is a passage in *Divrei David Turei Zahav*, the *Taz*'s work on Rashi's Torah commentary. The Torah relates (*Bereishis* 14:18) that after Avraham went to war against the four kingdoms that had captured his nephew, he was met upon his triumphant return by Malkitzedek, who hosted a celebration in Avraham's honor. Rashi comments that Malkitzedek brought food and wine because it was customary to bring food provisions to יגיעי מלחמה — weary warriors returning from battle. The *Taz* explains that Malkitzedek wanted to show that although Avraham could have rescued Lot and his property without killing enemy soldiers, Avraham was nevertheless justified in killing them because this was a legitimate war waged against an invading army. Malitzedek publicly treated Avraham and his men as soldiers returning from war to express that the conflict they waged was an actual war, and thus the killing was justified. The *Taz* makes mention in this context of the aforementioned law of יכול להצילו באחד מאבריו, which requires stopping a רודף through means other than killing when this is possible. Since Avraham's operation was carried out in the context of formal warfare, the *Taz* writes, this requirement did not apply, and Avraham was thus allowed to kill the marauders, even though he could have rescued Lot through other means.

Similarly, the Maharal of Prague, in his *Gur Aryeh* (*Bereishis* 34:13), writes that when Jews come under attack by another nation and must wage war to defend themselves, the military objectives may justify the killing of innocent enemy civilians. The Maharal advances this theory to explain Shimon and Levi's deadly assault on the city of Shechem following the abduction and rape of their sister. Shimon and Levi regarded the crime committed against their sister as an

---

24. BBC, May 12, 2011. Available at http://www.bbc.com/news/world-south-asia-13318372.

act of aggression that warranted a military response, and in the context of formal warfare, it sometimes becomes necessary to kill innocent civilians.[25]

Another relevant source is the Radak's commentary to *Sefer Divrei Ha-Yamim I* (22:88), where the Radak explains the reason given by the prophet for why King David was not permitted to build the *Beis Ha-Mikdash*. The prophet informed David that he could not build the Temple because of the large amount of blood that he spilled waging war,[26] and the Radak explains that this refers to the killing of innocent civilians. This was justified as part of David's military operations, the Radak writes, but it nevertheless disqualified him from the exalted role of building the *Beis Ha-Mikdash*. In the Radak's words:

> בדמי הגויים אשר שפך אותם...אפשר שהיו בהם אנשים טובים וחסידים ואעפ"כ לא נענש עליהם כי כוונתו לכלות הרשעים שלא יפרצו בישראל ולהציל עצמו... אבל כיון שנזדמן לו שפיכות דמים לרוב מנעו מלבנות בית המקדש שהוא לשלום ולכפרת עון ולעטרת תפלה...

> Among the blood of the gentiles which he shed…it is possible that there were good, upstanding people. Nevertheless, he was not punished for them, because his intention was to eliminate the wicked so they would not invade Israel and to save himself… But since it happened that he spilled a large amount of blood, he was prevented from building the *Beis Ha-Mikdash*, which is for peace, atonement of sin, and a glorious place of prayer…[27]

The unique status of warfare is also expressed in *Sefer Shmuel I* (15:6), where we read that King Shaul urged the friendly Keini tribe to distance themselves from the Amalekites before Shaul led *Bnei Yisrael* to battle against Amalek. Shaul warned the Keini, פן אוסיפך עמו — that they might be killed together with Amalek if they remained in the vicinity. This, too, would appear to indicate that killing innocent civilians is permissible when this is necessary as part of a legitimate military conflict.[28]

---

25. Significantly, Yaakov strongly condemned Shimon and Levi's violent response. Even if we accept the Maharal's halachic explanation of Shimon and Levi's assault on Shechem, Yaakov's condemnation demonstrates the severity of the matter and the extreme caution that must be exercised during warfare to minimize casualties.
26. דם לרב שפכת ומלחמות גדולות עשית, לא תבנה בית לשמי כי דמים רבים שפכת ארצה לפני.
27. The Radak's comments serve as an important expression of the Jewish ethic of warfare, which, on the one hand, recognizes the harsh realities of military conflict that often necessitate the killing of innocents, while at the same time demanding that we feel uneasy and discomfited by this unfortunate outcome. According to the Radak, David was justified in shedding innocent blood, but since this falls far short of the ideal to which we are to strive, the bloodshed disqualified him from building the *Mikdash*.
28. This proof was brought by Rav Asher Weiss, *Minchas Asher*, *Parshas Shoftim* (chapter

By the same token, there would conceivably be room to allow killing enemy combatants even after they flee, surrender, or no longer pose an immediate threat, if this is deemed necessary for achieving a legitimate military objective. One possible source for this conclusion, as noted by Rav Yaakov Ariel,[29] is King David's testimony of how he pursued his enemies until they were eliminated: ארדוף אויבי ואשיגם ולא אשוב עד כלותם (*Shmuel II* 22:38). If it is determined that killing immobilized or otherwise non-threatening combatants is a necessary measure for defeating the enemy and ensuring victory, then this is permissible, even though the combatants do not pose an immediate threat to anyone's life.

This conclusion opens the possibility of permitting killing neutralized terrorists even after they no longer pose an immediate threat. While terrorism clearly differs from conventional, battlefield combat, nevertheless, it seems reasonable to view Arab terror against Israelis as part of the ongoing war that has been waged against the State of Israel since — and, in fact, well before — its establishment. The overwhelming military superiority of the Israel Defense Forces has compelled the Arab foes of the Jewish State to resort to random knife attacks, but these attacks constitute part of the violent conflict that has unfortunately been forced upon Israel ever since it declared statehood. If, indeed, we view these attacks as part of an ongoing military campaign against the Jewish State, then the standard laws of רודף do not apply. The question of whether a restrained or incapacitated terrorist should be killed then hinges on the difficult question of whether this would help Israel obtain its military objective, which is ensuring the peace and security of its citizens. To the extent to which eliminating terrorists even after incapacitation helps achieve this goal, it would be permissible.

However, since this possibility rests solely on the present state of war, the protocols for handling disabled terrorists must be made by the government, the body that is responsible for waging this war. Rav Ariel writes:

> אלא שמלחמה, דווקא משום שהיא נושאת אופי ציבורי, חייבת להתנהל ע"י המלכות, או ע"י סמכות ציבורית מרכזית אחת, ולא ע"י אנשים פרטים. יתירה מזאת, הצלחתה של המלחמה מותנית ראשית כל במשמעת הפרט למסגרת הכללית. פריקת המסגרת הציבורית מסכנת את הכלל ואת הפרט גם יחד.

> However, specifically because of the public nature of war, it must be waged by the government, or by a single public authority, and not by private individuals. Moreover, the war's success depends primarily upon the individual's obedience to the general framework. The breakdown

---

32).
29. "*Ha-Intifada Be-Halacha*," *Techumin*, vol. 10.

of the public framework endangers both the public and the private individual.

If we indeed view isolated, random terror attacks within the larger framework of the decades-old Arab war on Israel, then the elected government of the State of Israel is authorized to decide how to most effectively wage this war and respond to these attacks. Given the complex nature of the Arab-Israeli conflict, there is, of course, a lack of unanimity regarding the most morally and practically sound measures Israel should take to defend itself and achieve security. However, notwithstanding the ongoing and often fierce public debate in Israel as to how to best respond to Arab violence, the elected government has the right and responsibility to make these decisions and determine effective policy and protocol. This includes the protocol for handling a terrorist who no longer poses a direct threat. Numerous factors must be taken into account in reaching this decision, including the intelligence information that might be provided by a captured terrorist, diplomatic concerns, and the legitimate fear of the long-term repercussions of a law permitting killing a restrained offender. While there is certainly room for debate, the government authorized to wage this war is the body responsible for making these difficult decisions.

As such, it would seem that from a halachic standpoint, soldiers and citizens should obey the government's directives in this regard, and abide by the rules of engagement set forth by the State judiciary and military establishment.

INTERVIEW

Rav Yosef Viener on *Headlines with Dovid Lichtenstein**

If bin Laden had been captured alive, he would not be a רודף, because he would have been brought to America, and, in the natural sequence of events, he would not have posed a danger to anyone. Unfortunately, your average terrorist in the street [in Israel] is up for political maneuvering, and down the line, after hundreds of thousands of dollars [in medical costs] and an education in jail [that will cause him] to be even more fanatical, he will be let out and will be a clear and present danger to society.

In *Sefer Melachim II* (6) there is a fascinating miracle that Elisha does when the king of Aram sent an army to get him. He was surrounded by soldiers, and he asked Hashem to smite them all with temporary blindness. He then took them to Shomron, to the king, and he asked Hashem to open their eyes. The king of Yisrael then asked whether he should kill them, and Elisha said (6:22):

לא תכה. האשר שבית בחרבך ובקשתך אתה מכה? שים לחם ומים לפניהם ויאכלו וישתו וילכו אל אדוניהם.

> Do not strike them. Do you strike those whom you capture with your sword and your bow? Place bread and water before them, and they shall eat, drink, and go back to their master.

Elisha made a political decision to give the prisoners food and let them go, and he was right. They had a few decades of peace after that. But what was Elisha telling him? That he should never kill POWs? Or that here he did not [really] capture them, [as] it was a miracle, and so he should try a different method?

Rashi says, וכי דרכך להרוג אותם שאתה מביא שבייה. It sounds like he is saying, "Do you always kill POWs? What for?" This sounds like the fallback position is not to kill POWs. The Ralbag says this quite clearly:

למה תכה אותם? האם תכה האנשים אשר תנהג בשבי בחרבך ובקשתך? אין זה ראוי, וכל שכן שאין ראוי זה באשר שבה אותם הש"י.

> Why should you strike them? Would you strike the people whom you take prisoner with your sword and bow? This is improper, and it is certainly not proper in this instance, as God captured them.

But the *Metzudos David* and the Radak say the opposite — that he had no right to kill them because this was not his doing. If it were a regular battle, then he would have the right to eliminate them if he saw fit. According to this, the fallback position is that if you feel it is necessary and prudent, you can eliminate POWs. So, we have a dispute among the *mefarshim* what the fallback position is.

The Rambam in *Hilchos Melachim* (6:1) writes that before attacking, you have to tell them you're coming [and provide them with an opportunity for a peaceful resolution]: אין עושין מלחמה עם אדם בעולם עד שקוראין לו שלום. And if they surrender and do *teshuva*, you don't kill them… If they accept the terms, then everything is fine. But if they don't accept the agreement, you kill all the adult males (6:4): עושין עמהם מלחמה והורגין כל הזכרים הגדולים. It is not clear whether the males are killed during battle or even afterwards. The implication is that you kill them even after they surrender.

I believe that there is ample evidence, and there are *Rishonim* who hold, that you can eliminate them, because if they came to fight, then they are dangerous and will pose a danger next time. This is certainly true of a terrorist who is not coming on his own, and terrorists become more hardened in jail and are even more dangerous when they get out…

The practical issue here is that we are not fighting an army, people who would honor a truce. This is a person who is out להשמיד ולהרוג. There's very little chance of him doing *teshuva* in the process, and he's dangerous…

D.L.: *But is it true that "once a רודף, always a רודף"?*

If it's a crime of passion, a one-time thing by a nice guy, then of course not. But if it's a person who says his existence is to eliminate the enemy, then yes…

There is one very important caveat.. People cannot lose sight of the fact that we need to be concerned about what אומות העולם will say [and the repercussions of such actions]. If eliminating someone when he was already down will cost more lives — we need to look at the bigger picture. [If] international opinion would not support it, and if this would have a negative impact, then we can't do it. It's a חילול ה' and it's dangerous. There could be a serious backlash. We need to consider what would work to save the most lives.

* Broadcast on 19 Marcheshvan, 5776 (October 31, 2015).

Is Kosher Switch Really Kosher for Shabbat?

April 16, 2015
by Uriel Heilman

NEW YORK (JTA) — It promises a revolutionary innovation that could transform Jewish Sabbath observance.

By changing the way a light switch works, the patented Kosher Switch offers a novel — and, its backers say, kosher — way to turn light switches (and, perhaps, other electrical appliances) on and off during Shabbat, circumventing one of the Sabbath's central restrictions: the use of electricity.

In just three days, the product's backers have raised more than $45,000 toward a $50,000 fundraising goal on Indiegogo, the crowdsourced fundraising website, to start manufacturing the device.

Menashe Kalati, the device's inventor, calls it a "long overdue, techno-halachic breakthrough." (Halachah refers to traditional Jewish law.)

But critics say the Kosher Switch isn't really kosher for Shabbat at all — and that Kalati is misrepresenting rabbinic opinions on the matter to give the false impression that he has their endorsements.

At issue is whether the device's permissibility for Shabbat relies on a Jewish legal loophole that applies only to extraordinary circumstances like medical or security needs.

In its first three days, the crowdsourced fundraising campaign for the Kosher Switch nearly met its $50,000 goal. (Kosher Switch video)

The loophole, known as a "gramma," allows for indirect activation of electronic devices on Shabbat.

How does gramma work? If, for example, a non-life-threatening field fire is burning on Shabbat, jugs full of water may be placed around the fire to indirectly cause its eventual extinguishing. Dowsing the fire directly — a Sabbath prohibition — is permitted only in life-threatening circumstances.

Kalati, 43, says his switch does not rely on the gramma loophole. When the switch is in the off position, a piece of plastic blocks an electronic light pulse that, when received, turns on the light. Turning the switch on moves the piece of plastic, which is not connected to anything electrical, so that it no longer obstructs the pulse. Because the light pulse is subject to a "random degree of uncertainty" and won't instantaneously kindle the light when in Sabbath mode, it is kosher for use on Shabbat, according to the video.

This "adds several layers of Halachic uncertainty, randomness, and delays, such that according to Jewish law, a user's action is not considered to have caused a given reaction," the company says on its website. (Kalati's office did not respond to phone calls or emails from JTA).

In the Indiegogo video, Kalati says his team has spent years on research and development, during which "we've been privileged to meet with Torah giants who have analyzed, endorsed and blessed our technology and endeavors."

But Yisrael Rosen, head of the Zomet Institute, the leading designer of electronic devices for use on the Jewish Sabbath, says the Kosher Switch is unfit for Sabbath use.

"Today, Israeli media reported the invention of an electric 'Kosher switch' for Shabbat, with the approval of various rabbis. This item was recycled from 2010 and already then denials and renunciation by great rabbinic authorities were published regarding everyday use for this product," Rosen wrote Tuesday on Zomet's website. "No Orthodox rabbi, Ashkenazi or Sephardi, has permitted this 'Gramma' method for pure convenience."

Rosen appended a letter from Rabbi Yehoshua Neuwirth, the first rabbi whose endorsement appears in the Kosher Switch video — in a one-second pull quote reading "I, too, humbly agree to the invention" — suggesting that his endorsement was misrepresented.

"To allow one a priori to turn on electricity on Shabbat — impossible, and I never considered permitting except for the needs of a sick person or security," reads the letter, which bears Neuwirth's signature and letterhead and is addressed to the manager of Kosher Switch. "And please publicize this thing so no [Sabbath] violation will be prompted by me."

The son of another rabbi whose endorsement appears in the video, Rabbi Noach Oelbaum (who says it does not violate the prohibition on Sabbath-day labor), told JTA that his father's position was distorted.

"I regret that my father's position on kosher switch was misrepresented by stating that he endorses it l'maaseh," the son, Moshe Oelbaum, wrote in a statement, using the Jewish term for "regular use."

Oelbaum said his father's true position is that while the switch does not involve a technical violation of the Sabbath prohibition against labor (which forbids electricity use), it is a desecration of the Sabbath spirit. Oelbaum advises consumers to consult their own rabbis on the question of whether or not they may use it on Shabbat.

Kosher Switch is hardly the first technological innovation devised to ease Sabbath observance. For decades, Sabbath-observant Jews have used electronic timers set before Friday night to control lights and appliances like air conditioners or hot plates. Multistory buildings throughout Israel and some in the United States have Shabbat elevators that can run on autopilot. In 2004, Canadian rabbi and entrepreneur Shmuel Veffer invented a bedside-style lamp called Kosher Lamp that could be "turned off" by twisting a cylinder encasing a lit bulb so that the bulb was completely concealed.

The Zomet Institute, located in the Jerusalem suburb of Gush Etzion in the West Bank, has invented baby sensors, sump pump gadgets, hot water heater contraptions, and special switches that modify wheelchairs, hospital beds, electronic scooters and staircase elevators for use on Shabbat. However, many of these devices rely on the gramma loophole and are permitted only for medical or security use.

Many observant Jews also rely upon non-Jews for help circumventing Sabbath restrictions, though such requests for help are forbidden from being expressed explicitly. The Kosher Switch video parodies this problem of using "Shabbos goys" [non-Jews] with a staged scene in which a bearded Orthodox Jewish man wearing a black hat stands on the steps outside his house and flags down a young black woman passing by. They have this exchange:

Man: "Excuse me, ma'am? Hi. I need a big favor. My bedroom — the lights are on, so I was wondering if maybe you could come up to my bedroom and …"

Woman (in a West Indian accent): "Are you crazy!? I ain't coming up to your bedroom!"

Man (nodding suggestively toward his open door): "Yeah but, the lights are on …"

Woman (walking away): "You're crazy."

Rabbi Mordechai Hecht, a Chabad rabbi from Queens, New York, who appears in the Kosher Switch video saying "I was mesmerized to be blessed to see such an invention in my lifetime," says the controversy surrounding its permissibility isn't simply a fight over Jewish law.

"There's politics in halachah," he said. "The conversations they have are often money-related. Everyone has an agenda."

Hecht said he cannot endorse or reject the product because he is not a halachic authority.

"Is there one way in halachah? Of course not. That's why the sages say, 'Make yourself a rabbi,'" Hecht said. "I think the rabbis need to be brave. A conversation needs to be had, and maybe this is a good place to have it. If there's really a halachic issue, let's talk about it. This is an amazing invention. The question is, can it enhance the Shabbos?"

Copyright © jta.org

How Kosher is the Kosher Switch?

The Kosher Switch burst into Orthodox Jewish discourse when the invention went public in 2011, offering the prospect — or, for some, posing the threat — of a permissible way to activate or deactivate electric devices, particularly lighting, on Shabbos. A full-fledged firestorm erupted in April 2015, with the widespread publicity and wild success of the company's crowdsourcing campaign, which raised over $50,000 in just several days. The idea — to revolutionize Shabbos observance by harnessing technology to create a halachically permissible way to turn electric lights on and off on Shabbos — was met with both great enthusiasm and sharp condemnation. The invention received emphatic support and endorsements from several renowned rabbis, but was caustically rejected by others.

The Kosher Switch controversy is likely only the first in what we can anticipate to be a long series of difficult questions surrounding the effects of 21st-century technology on the universally-accepted prohibition against activating electricity on Shabbos. As digital and "smart" technology continues to expand and develop, we are fast approaching the time when we will be inadvertently activating electronic devices through the most ordinary actions, such as motion and speech, at any point during the day and everywhere, including our homes. Technologies for voice and face recognition, for example, are poised to revolutionize modern life. It is not at all difficult to imagine the time when full home automation will become the norm, when basic systems such as alarms, lighting, and climate control, and perhaps individual appliances, will operate automatically as we move about and talk. As such, rigorous halachic analysis of the Kosher Switch is vitally important not only to determine its status vis-à-vis Shabbos, but also as a precedential case study of indirect activation or deactivation of electric currents on Shabbos. This controversy challenges contemporary *poskim* to carefully examine models of indirect מלאכה on Shabbos to determine how they are treated by *halacha* — an enterprise that will lay the groundwork for the classification of future inventions and their status with respect to Shabbos.

The Kosher Switch company's website describes the product as follows:

> When you slide the on/off button, you're moving an isolated piece of plastic. It is purely mechanical and is not attached to anything electrical (electro-mechanically isolated). This is done at a time when you see a green Status Light, which provides 100% assurance that the relevant components within the switch are inactive. Subsequently, after a

random interval, the device will activate and determine the position of the plastic by flashing an internal light pulse. The attached light fixture will be triggered only after the switch overcomes two failure probability processes — one prior to this light pulse and one after it. Halachically, your action is simply the movement of an isolated piece of plastic with no implications of causation.[1]

The switch that the user turns does nothing other than move a piece of plastic into a certain position. When the user wishes to turn off the light, the switch moves the plastic piece such that it will block the electronic pulses that are sent at random intervals. The device will turn off around half a minute or a minute later, when it detects — through a random messaging system — that the pulses are not reaching the receptors. When one wishes to turn the light on, the switch moves the plastic piece out of the field, so that the random pulse will be received, and the device will be activated shortly thereafter, upon detecting successful reception. An external light signals to the user when no pulses are being sent, so he knows that he can turn the switch without triggering any immediate electronic activity.

The inventors and supporters of the Kosher Switch contend that since the user merely moves a piece of plastic and does not create or disrupt an electric current, no Shabbos violation is entailed whatsoever, despite the fact that this piece's position will affect the device's operation.

The Candle by the Window

One of the sources cited in support of the Kosher Switch is the Rama's ruling (O.C. 514:3), based on the Maharil, allowing one to move a candle on Yom Tov to a place where it will likely be extinguished by a gust of wind.[2] Although it is forbidden to directly expose the flame to wind, the Rama allows moving it to a place where one anticipates a gust, as long as the wind is not currently blowing there. The Rama permits this indirect method of extinguishing without any qualification, seemingly in contrast to his ruling earlier (334:22) permitting גרם כיבוי — indirect extinguishing of a flame — only in cases of פסידא, meaning, when one would otherwise suffer a financial loss. The earlier case involves placing earthenware jugs of water in the path of a fire, and the Rama permits extinguishing in this manner only if this is necessary to prevent the loss of property. In

---

1. http://www.kosherswitch.com/live/tech/how. Retrieved November 3, 2015.
2. This *halacha* is relevant only for Yom Tov because on Shabbos, one may not move a candle.

the case of moving a candle to a place where wind is expected to blow, however, the Rama allows this method without any conditions, even if no financial loss is at stake.

Rav Chaim Tzvi Shapiro *shlit"a* of Bnei-Brak concluded on the basis of these two rulings that placing a candle in the path of an anticipated gust of wind does not even constitute גרם כיבוי.[3] Since the wind is not currently blowing, one is not extinguishing the candle even indirectly; he is simply moving the candle from one place to another, and the anticipated outcome is of no consequence. This is far different from the situation of placing jugs of water in the path of a flame, where the fire is approaching and one is extinguishing it indirectly by placing water in front of it. By the same token, Rav Shapiro contended, moving the Kosher Switch does not constitute even indirect activation of electricity. As in the case of the candle by the window, there are no current conditions that could extinguish the flame; these conditions are anticipated, but not currently present. The random electronic pulses are expected just like the gust of wind, but are not occurring at the time the switch is turned. As such, this does not constitute even indirect activation.[4]

The flaw in this argument, as Rav Shapiro concedes, is that he is not the first scholar to address the seeming contradiction between the Rama's rulings. It was noted already by the *Magen Avraham*, as cited by the Chafetz Chayim in *Sha'ar Ha-Tziyun* (514:31). The Chafetz Chayim concludes his discussion of this issue by citing the *Ma'amar Mordechai*, who distinguishes between Shabbos and Yom Tov in this regard. With regard to Shabbos, the Rama allowed גרם כיבוי only when a financial loss is at stake, whereas on Yom Tov, he allows it under all circumstances.[5] According to the Chafetz Chayim, then, placing a candle in the path of an anticipated gust of wind indeed falls under the prohibition of גרם כיבוי, even though no wind currently blows in that location, and it is permitted

---

3. In a responsum dated 6 Nissan, 5770 (March 21, 2010). The responsum is available online at http://www.kosherswitch.com/live/?wpfb_dl=10.
4. This situation differs from the case of moving the pegs on a "Shabbos clock" so that the device will turn on or off earlier than it was originally set for. Rav Yosef Shalom Elyashiv (cited in *Orchos Shabbos*, chapter 29, note 26; and in *Shevus Yitzchak* 6:15) ruled that moving the pegs may constitute a Torah violation because this is the normal manner of activating or deactivating electricity. In that case, the clock of the timer is moving and the electricity is in place ready to activate the device. This is quite different from the situation of the candle by the door, where no wind is currently blowing, and from the Kosher Switch, where the pulses are not present at the time the switch is turned.
5. The Chafetz Chayim initially questions the Rama's ruling restricting the permissibility of גרם כיבוי to situations of פסידא, noting that there does not appear to be any source for such a qualification. In his conclusion, however, the Chafetz Chayim accepts the distinction drawn by the *Ma'amar Mordechai* between Shabbos and Yom Tov.

on Shabbos only to avoid a financial loss. Seemingly, then, it would be forbidden to turn the Kosher Switch on Shabbos, except in the very rare situation in which the light needs to be turned on or off to prevent a loss of property.

Rav Shapiro contends, however, that even according to the Chafetz Chayim's conclusion, a distinction may be drawn between the Kosher Switch and the cases of גרם כיבוי. In the cases addressed by the Rama, one directly handles either the flame or the extinguishing force. In one case, he places the water in the path of the fire, and in the other, he places the fire in the path of the anticipated gust of wind. Therefore, these actions qualify as גרם כיבוי and are forbidden unless a financial loss is at stake. When one turns the Kosher Switch, by contrast, he does not directly handle the electronic mechanism; he merely places or removes an obstruction. This action is comparable to the situation addressed by the *Mishna Berura* earlier (277:3) of opening a door or window in front of a candle when there is no wind currently blowing. Several *poskim*, as the *Mishna Berura* cites,[6] forbid opening the door or window in this case only because the motion of the door or window may extinguish the flame. In principle, however, such an action is permissible because one does not directly handle either the flame or the extinguishing force.[7] By the same token, Rav Shapiro argues, it should be entirely permissible to turn on the Kosher Switch, whereby one indirectly activates electricity without any direct handling of the mechanism.[8]

---

6. In his *Bei'ur Halacha*, the Chafetz Chayim identifies these *poskim* as the *Elya Rabba* and *Mateh Yehuda*.
7. The *Mishna Berura* cites the *Magen Avraham* as forbidding opening the window or door even when there is no wind blowing, because one never knows when a gust of wind will blow. The *Mishna Berura* therefore permits opening a door or window only במקום דחק — in situations of dire necessity. It seems clear, however, that if there were a way to know for certain that no wind would blow at the time one opens the window, this would be permissible.
8. One might, at first glance, question this theory in light of a responsum of the Maharil, cited by the *Magen Avraham* (265:3), concerning the prohibition of מבטל כלי מהיכנו — making a usable utensil *muktzeh* on Shabbos. It is forbidden to place a utensil on Shabbos underneath a dripping candle to catch the oil, because the oil is *muktzeh* and the utensil thus becomes *muktzeh* when the oil falls into it. However, the Maharil ruled that before Shabbos, one may position an oil lamp above a table with a utensil underneath the table, and then move the table on Shabbos so that the oil drips into the utensil. The Maharil writes that although this situation is comparable to one of גרם כיבוי, it is permitted to move the table (for several reasons noted in the responsum). The Maharil's comparison of this case to גרם כיבוי seems to suggest that an indirect activity qualifies as גרם כיבוי even if one does not directly handle the fire or the extinguishing force.
We may easily refute this contention, however, in light of the fact that in the case of the dripping oil lamp, the oil is dripping at the time one moves the table, as opposed to the Kosher Switch, where the pulses are not present at all at the time the switch is moved.

מלאכת מחשבת אסרה תורה

Rav Shlomo Miller, among the opponents of the Kosher Switch, notes that several *poskim* forbid indirect מלאכה on Shabbos anytime one specifically intends for the מלאכה to be performed.[9] The Gemara in *Maseches Bava Kama* (60a) addresses the case of רוח מסייעתו — in which one begins performing an action that is completed by the wind. If a person kindled a flame that would not ordinarily be sustained, but the wind enabled the flame to take hold, and it then caused damage, the person is not liable for the damage, since he did not play a dominant role in creating the fire. The Gemara distinguishes between this case and the situation of זורה — winnowing — in which one throws raw produce into the air and the wind separates the grain and the chaff. Such an act constitutes a Shabbos violation, the Gemara notes, despite the fact that the forbidden effect — separating the grain from the chaff — is caused mainly by the wind. The Gemara explains that when it comes to damage liability, one is liable to compensate the victim only if he caused the damage directly (גרמא בנזיקין פטור), but when it comes to the Shabbos prohibitions, מלאכת מחשבת אסרה תורה — the Torah forbids intentional acts of מלאכה, even when the result is produced indirectly.

On the basis of the Gemara's discussion, Rav Miller writes, several *poskim* forbid indirect מלאכה on Shabbos if one intends for the מלאכה to occur.[10] Therefore, since one turns the Kosher Switch with the clear intent of turning on or off the light, the act is forbidden even though the effect is caused indirectly.

We may, however, refute this argument in light of the question raised by several *Rishonim* as to how to reconcile the Gemara's discussion with the law of גרם כיבוי. Indirectly extinguishing a flame on Shabbos does not constitute a Torah violation; as we saw, the only question is whether it is permissible under all circumstances, or only to avoid financial loss. Why does winnowing — indirectly separating grain from chaff — transgress a Torah violation, while indirect extinguishing does not? One answer emerges from the comments of the Rosh (*Bava Kama* 6:11), who explains that in the case of winnowing, עיקר עשייתה על ידי הרוח — the normal way of performing this action is via the wind. Although the separation occurs indirectly, this is immaterial, since one produces this effect in the way this is ordinarily done. Extinguishing, however, is commonly achieved through a direct action — pouring water or blowing air directly onto the flame — and thus גרם כיבוי is permissible. Therefore, whereas indirectly separating

---

9. In a responsum dated 5 Iyar, 5775 (April 24, 2015), available online with an English translation at http://5tjt.com/translation-of-rav-shlomo-millers-responsa-on-kosher-switch/.
10. Rav Miller cites in particular *Yeshuos Yaakov* 334, where numerous sources are cited advancing this claim.

grain from chaff by throwing the wheat into the air violates a Torah prohibition, indirectly extinguishing by placing water in the path of the fire does not. This distinction is drawn explicitly by Rav Chayim Ozer Grodzinsky (*Achiezer* 3:60).[11]

There are several precedents to this theory that an indirect מלאכה on Shabbos constitutes a Torah violation if this is the standard manner of performing the מלאכה. The *Bei'ur Halacha* (252, ד"ה להשמעת קול) notes that according to the consensus among the *Acharonim*, placing wheat in a water-powered mill violates the Torah prohibition of grinding,[12] because this is the standard manner of grinding wheat. Similarly, the Rama (316:2) rules that sending a dog on Shabbos to capture an animal violates the Torah prohibition of צידה (hunting). The *Mishna Berura* explains that if one contributed to the dog catching the animal, even indirectly, this constitutes צידה because כן דרך הציידים — this is a standard manner of hunting. (In *Sha'ar Ha'tziyun*, the Chafetz Chayim compares this case to that of winnowing.)

A different distinction between winnowing and indirect extinguishing is suggested by the *Zera Emes* (O.C. 44), who notes that in the case of winnowing, the מלאכה effect begins at the moment that the person performs the act. As soon as one casts the unprocessed grain into the air, the wind begins separating the various components from one another. By contrast, when one places water in the path of a fire, the מלאכה effect — the extinguishing — occurs only later, once the fire reaches the water.

The rationale likely underlying this distinction is that in the case of winnowing, the wind is simply the means by which one performs the action. To take an extreme example, if one cuts down a tree on Shabbos with an axe, we would not consider this act a case of גרמא because the bulk of the work was done by an instrument. Clearly, the individual committed an act of detaching a tree; the tool is the means with which he performed this act. Likewise, when a person places raw food over a fire on Shabbos, he is liable for directly cooking on Shabbos, even though the cooking effect is caused by the fire, and not by his action. Since the effect begins immediately, we consider the fire simply a "tool" through which the מלאכה is performed. Similarly, when a farmer casts grain into the air and the wind immediately separates the grain from the chaff, he has performed an act of separation, using the wind as his "tool." This is not the case when one places

---

11. Rav Chayim Ozer formulates the principle as follows: באופן שהמלאכה היא תמיד על ידי גרמא זהו חשוב מלאכת מחשבת. See also *Chazon Ish*, O.C. 38:1 (ד"ה ונראה).
12. The *Magen Avraham* (252:20) ruled that this is forbidden only מדרבנן, but the *Bei'ur Halacha* notes that the consensus among the *poskim* follows the view of the *Even Ha-Ozer* (328) that this is forbidden on the level of a Torah prohibition.

water in the path of a flame, as there one arranges a situation whereby the מלאכה effect will occur, but he does not actually perform a מלאכה.

In light of this distinction, there is very good reason to permit use of the Kosher Switch on Shabbos. When one turns the switch, moving the plastic piece into or away from the field, he is not using the pulses as his "tools" to turn on or off the light. He performs an action that indirectly, and after the passage of a brief period of time, causes the light to turn on or off. This cannot be compared to the case of winnowing, where one performs the forbidden act using the wind.[13]

The Oil in the Eggshell

Rav Miller advanced yet another argument to forbid use of the Kosher Switch, namely, the Rosh's ruling in *Maseches Beitza* (2:17) concerning the case of an eggshell containing oil that drips into a lamp beneath it, thereby sustaining the flame. The Rosh rules, based on the Gemara in *Beitza* 22a and the Mishna in *Shabbos* 29b, that removing oil from the eggshell on Shabbos transgresses the Torah violation of מכבה (extinguishing), despite the fact that this only indirectly causes the flame to be extinguished. The question naturally arises as to why such an act would be forbidden, whereas other forms of גרם כיבוי are permissible.

The Rosh explains that גרם כיבוי is permissible when the action is external to the flame. In the case which the Gemara forbids, one hampers with the actual mechanism of the fire, diminishing from the oil supply, and such an action is therefore prohibited. The Rosh writes:

> דעד כאן לא פליגי התם אלא משום דאינו נוגע בדבר הדולק אלא עושה דבר חוצה לו הגורם את הכיבוי כשתגיע שמה הדליקה. אבל הכא השמן והפתילה שתיהן גורמים את הדליקה, והממעט מאחד מהן וממהר את הכיבוי חייב.

The Rabbis are lenient [regarding גרם כיבוי] only in a case which does not

---

13. One might challenge this theory in light of the *Magen Avraham*'s discussion (316:20) of the case of setting a trap on Shabbos, which is forbidden only מדרבנן and does not violate a Torah prohibition. Based on *Tosfos* (*Shabbos* 17b), the *Magen Avraham* explains that since there is no guarantee that an animal will be caught by the trap, setting the trap does not qualify as צידה. The implication is that in a situation in which the מלאכה is guaranteed to occur, a Torah prohibition is violated, even if the effect will occur sometime after the act — in direct contradiction to the *Zera Emes*'s theory. However, it is likely that the *Magen Avraham* made this comment only because this is the standard method of hunting — to set a trap for the animal. Specifically for this reason, the מלאכה would be violated on the level of Torah law if it were certain that the trap would achieve the desired result.

involve contact with the object that burns, but one rather does something external to it which causes it to extinguish when the fire reaches there. But here, the oil and wick both cause [the fire to burn], and one who diminishes either one of them so it will extinguish sooner is liable.

As such, indirectly extinguishing a flame is permissible only if one's actions remain external to the mechanism; actions performed to the mechanism itself are forbidden. Applying this ruling to the Kosher Switch, Rav Miller argued that when one disrupts the path of the electric pulses, he is directly tampering with the mechanism, similar to removing oil from a container that feeds a flame.

One may, however, challenge this line of reasoning. For one thing, several *Acharonim* noted that the Rama appears to have disputed the Rosh's ruling, and maintained — based on the view of *Tosfos* — that one may take oil from the eggshell as long as this does not diminish from the light produced by the candle at that moment. This is evidenced by the Rama's ruling (514:3) that one may cut a lit wax candle on Yom Tov if this has no effect on the strength of the flame, even though this will cause the fire to be extinguished sooner than it would have otherwise. This ruling seems to express *Tosfos'* view that one may accelerate a candle's extinguishing process by diminishing its fuel supply, as long as the act has no immediate effect on the flame.

It is true that the *Machatzis Ha-Shekel* (514:19) argues that the Rama in fact follows the stringent view of the Rosh, and the *Mishna Berura* (514:23; *Sha'ar Ha-Tziyun* 514:29) notes that several *Acharonim* rule in accordance with the Rosh's position. Nevertheless, there is reason to distinguish between the case addressed by the Rosh and that of the Kosher Switch. The *Magen Avraham* (514:7) notes that the *Shulchan Aruch* codifies the Rosh's ruling, but also permits placing water on the end of a garment that has caught fire in order to indirectly extinguish the flames. In order to reconcile these seemingly contradictory rulings concerning indirect extinguishing, the *Magen Avraham* writes:

נראה לי דלא אסר הרא"ש אלא ליקח מגוף דבר הדולק, אבל כשנותן דבר חוצה לה, שרי.

The *Magen Avraham* limits the Rosh's ruling, and distinguishes between removing fuel from the flame — which is forbidden — and introducing an extinguishing force, which is permissible. According to the *Magen Avraham's* understanding of the Rosh, it would seem, turning off a light with the Kosher Switch would be permissible, as one adds a piece of plastic to the apparatus, which has the effect of blocking the pulses so the light will be deactivated.

זילותא דשבת

Based on what we have seen, there appears to be sufficient basis to permit the Kosher Switch, which seems to resemble the models of permissible גרם כיבוי, and may perhaps even warrant greater leniency than those models.

However, many *poskim* have correctly noted the concern of זילותא דשבת — that permitting the activation and deactivation of lighting systems on Shabbos infringes upon the honor due to Shabbos and the atmosphere that should prevail in the home.

Along somewhat similar lines, there is reason for forbid the Kosher Switch in light of the comments of the *Tiferes Yisrael* (*Maseches Shabbos* 7, הלכתא גבירתא):

> ישנם עוד פעולות שאסור מדרבנן מחמת עובדין דחול, והם בדומה קצת לאיזה מט"ל מלאכות, כמזקק משקה מזוקק ע"י הסודר שעושה בו גומא ושופך המשקה לתוכה דומה לבורר, וכן המבקע עצים לחתיכות דקות דומה לטוחן, או אפילו דומה לדומה כמבקע עצים לחתיכות גדולות, או אפילו אינו דומה אבל מכל מקום שיערו חז"ל ברוח קדשם שבקל יכול לבא לאיסור דאורייתא...וכן אסור לשרות עשבים לרפואה דבקל יבא לשחיקת סממנים דהו"ל טוחן...

> There are other actions that are forbidden by force of Rabbinic enactment because they are weekday activities. These [are forbidden] because they resemble somewhat one of the thirty-nine *melachos*, such as distilling a beverage with a cloth by making an indentation and pouring the beverage into it, which resembles בורר [separating], and also chopping wood into thin pieces, which resembles טוחן [grinding]; and even if it only slightly resembles [a מלאכה], such as chopping wood into large pieces; and even if it does not resemble [a מלאכה] but our Sages nevertheless realized through their holy insight that it can easily lead to a Torah violation... Thus, it is forbidden to soak herbs to prepare medicine, which can easily lead to grinding ingredients, which constitutes טוחן.

The Kosher Switch falls under two of the categories mentioned by the *Tiferes Yisrael*: it resembles one of the Torah prohibitions, as it appears as though one directly activates or deactivates the light, and it can easily lead one to transgress Torah violations, as he might activate other lights and electronic appliances.[14] Therefore, even if the Kosher Switch does not technically violate Shabbos as far as the use of electricity and kindling lights are concerned, it should be prohibited due the fact that it resembles a מלאכה and its potential to lead to Shabbos violations.

---

14. See *Iggeros Moshe*, O.C. 4:74:2 (*Hilchos Tochein*, 4).

INTERVIEWS

Rav Moshe Heinemann *shlit"a* on *Headlines with Dovid Lichtenstein**

[The Kosher Switch] is nothing more than a גרמא and is אסור מדרבנן. We look at it the way it seems to us. We don't look at what is actually happening; that is not important. If you have two letters in a Sefer Torah that seem to be touching, but with a magnifying glass you can see that they are not actually touching, the Sefer Torah is not kosher. On the other hand, if two letters do not seem to be touching, but with a magnifying glass you see they are touching, it is kosher — because we go according to the way it seems, the way we can understand something with our five normal senses which the *Ribono Shel Olam* gave us. With this switch — if you move something, the light goes on a few seconds later...

There are three consecutive *teshuvos* from Rav Moshe Feinstein. In one, he discusses the question of whether one can fulfill the obligation of *havdala* or Megilla over the phone. If somebody is confined to the home and cannot go to a *minyan*, can you call him up and read the Megilla to him? Rav Moshe says it depends on the question of what the phone does. Does the phone "call" the voice into the receiver, or is the voice reconstituted in the receiver? Is this a new voice, or the old voice pulled through the wires? Rav Moshe says that it's easier to believe that the voice is pulled through the wires, and therefore, you can do it. In the next *teshuva*, he asks whether one can fulfill the obligation of Megilla over a microphone. [He writes] that of course one cannot, because it's considered making a new sound. On Shabbos it's *assur* — maybe מן התורה, maybe מדרבנן — because you're making a new sound; the speaker makes a new sound. The next *teshuva* asks whether you can speak to someone with a hearing aid on Shabbos, and he says that it depends on the same question, of whether you are making a new sound or the sound is pulled into the person's ear. He said that he spoke to various professionals, and they did not have a clear answer. He said that it's more reasonable that [the device] pulls the sound, because you hear the sound as if the person is talking. Therefore, it is permitted on Shabbos.

Rav Moshe understood that it's not what is happening [that matters]; it's the way we perceive it. We are allowed to eat cheese even though it is made with bacteria, and we do not have to *shecht* the bacteria. We don't see them, and so from a halachic standpoint, they're not there. So the question is how we understand on the basis of our five senses how a telephone works. He said that it does not sound like a new sound, but like the original sound being pulled, and so from the Torah, we can go with that. When it comes to a loudspeaker, the sound is much louder than that of the person talking, so it must be a new sound. When it comes to a hearing aid, he said he spoke to various professionals. He probably asked them whether one can actually tell that the sound heard through the hearing aid is not the sound of the person talking, and [it turned out that] this is not a "yes" or "no" question. It sounds pretty much the same, so we can assume that the sound is just pulled and we can consider it that one is not making a new sound.

Over here, you flip a piece of plastic, and the light goes on a few seconds later. The way it seems is that you caused something to move a few seconds later, and so it's a regular גרמא, and גרמא is forbidden מדרבנן; it is permissible only במקום פסידא, like in the case of a fire. But to use it regularly — this is definitely אסור מדרבנן.

On Yom Tov, when גרמא is allowed even in situations that are not מקום פסידא, I believe the Kosher Switch would be allowed, but this would be הלכה ואין מורין כן, because people are not accustomed to understanding [these distinctions].

For an ill patient, it would be permitted, but each case would have to be evaluated. When a patient is in the hospital for observation, this is not [necessarily] considered a חולה. I wouldn't give a "blank check."

* Broadcast on 13 Sivan, 5775 (May 30, 2015).

Rav Asher Weiss shlit"a on Headlines with Dovid Lichtenstein*

I am aware that many *gedolim* came out with very harsh language about the Kosher Switch. The *Divrei Chayim*, around 200 years ago, in a different context and regarding a different *shayla*, wrote that he received [a tradition] from his great father-in-law, the *Baruch Ta'am*, that when it comes to something like this, we should not get into the *pilpul*; we should reject it outright and say that it's *assur*. I think that in today's day and age, this approach is no longer a wise approach. When *gedolim* say that something is אסור מדאורייתא and איסור סקילה, many people question it and demand to know why. People today are more cynical and skeptical than they were in the past. I think it's important to state if this [the Kosher Switch] is a חשש איסור דאורייתא and why we think so, and this is why I wrote a lengthy *teshuva* about it.[15]

I really think this is a חשש איסור דאורייתא. According to all approaches [to understanding when גרמא on Shabbos is permissible], I believe, the Kosher

---

15. http://www.torahbase.org/kosher-switch-5775/.

Switch and all גרמא devices do not the pass the test. The time delay of [permissible] גרם כיבוי[16] is a process — a process that people could follow and understand. [In the classic case of גרם כיבוי,] the fire has to spread, the heat has to rise, the vessels have to break, the water rushes out. This is a process. But when you have it all in electronics and it's an artificial time delay, then in my opinion this [time delay] would not be relevant. When you're dealing with technology that was planned and worked out, and you turn on a switch and the electricity will go on in two or three minutes — I definitely think that this would be considered a מעשה [direct action].

מלאכת מחשבת is about perception, not scientific criteria. When you have a switch, and people know that when you turn the switch the light will go on, this is a מעשה of kindling the light. The fact that it is built such that the light will go on in 2–3 minutes is irrelevant. When you plan electronics, build the device, and invest a million dollars to put together a system so that when you push a switch the electricity will go on, in my opinion, it makes no difference what the electronic process is. That is totally irrelevant. These *halachos* are about perception, the eye of the beholder.

The common denominator between *Orach Chayim* 277:3 [where the *Mishna Berura* permits opening a window near a candle to extinguish it as long as no wind currently blows] and *Orach Chayim* 514:3 [where the Rama permits bringing a candle on Yom Tov to a place where no wind currently blows but it is expected to blow later] is that in terms of people's perception, the person's action has nothing to do with the fire. There are a million reasons to open or close a window that have nothing to do with putting out a fire. Therefore, this case is not defined as גרמא. Taking a candle outside [when no wind blows] is not כיבוי. In our case, where the device is manufactured and built with a single motive — to turn on the light — this is different. I think it would definitely be אסור מדרבנן because of גרמא, and also a ספק דאורייתא.

I recommend גרמא devices for three bodies in *Eretz Yisrael*: the IDF, the police, and hospitals. The common denominator of these three bodies is that they all deal with situations of potential פקוח נפש. Since it is impossible to precisely and definitively define ספק פקוח נפש, we need to enable the security mechanisms and hospitals to operate in a normal way. So for these bodies, which essentially deal with פקוח נפש, due to the inability to precisely define ספק פקוח נפש, I recommend using גרמא devices.

---

16. Rav Weiss speaks here of the position of the *Zera Emes*, cited above, who writes that indirect מלאכה is forbidden if the מלאכה occurs immediately, and permissible if there is a delay. He argues that even according to the *Zera Emes*, the delay in the activating of the light with the Kosher Switch would not suffice to make it permissible.

With every passing day, it is becoming more difficult to avoid activating sensors in our homes. Even today, it is almost impossible. You open the door — you activate the sensor in your air conditioning. We enable doctors on call to walk around with a cell phone, even though as they walk from one room to another, the reception signals are moving. We are not going to say that they cannot move. Even if one disables his alarm system, the sensors are working. It will eventually be impossible to move about and live without activating electronics. In my opinion, when there is no intent, this is not considered a מלאכה at all. When it comes to modern electronics, the distinction has to be the intent. If there is intent, this is a חשש איסור דאורייתא; if you have no interest, then it's not even a דרבנן.

I would like to make one final point. When the Rambam explains the prohibition of *muktzeh* (*Hilchos Shabbos* 22:13), he offers an amazing insight, which I think is very profound. Why did *Chazal* forbid handling *muktzeh*? The Rambam writes that there needs to be שבת ניכרת לכל — a unified code of Shabbos observance. The Rambam observes that most people aren't farmers, so זורע and דש are not relevant; not all people are builders, so בונה and סותר are not relevant. What would create a unified Shabbos observance by all *Klal Yisrael*? Refraining from handling *muktzeh*. In our day and age, we don't sow fields and we don't build. What unites all *shomrei Shabbos* throughout the world is refraining from the use of technology. If we go down this path [of the Kosher Switch], then one person will use a Kosher Switch and another guy a "non-kosher" switch; one person will use a "kosher" cellphone, and the other a "non-kosher" one; one person will use a "kosher" car, and another a regular car. The only thing that brings all *shomrei Shabbos* together is avoiding the use of technology. So, in accordance with the Rambam's approach concerning *muktzeh*, beyond the halachic criteria regarding גרמא, we should reject the Kosher Switch and all גרמא mechanisms, except when dealing with situations of ספק פקוח נפש.

---

* Headlines with Dovid Lichtenstein, broadcast on 1 Elul, 5775 (August 15, 2015).

NorthJersey.com
PART OF THE USA TODAY NETWORK

13 Are Treated for Carbon Monoxide Exposure in Teaneck After a Stove is Left on Over Jewish Holiday

June 9, 2011
by Erik Shilling and Andrea Alexander

TEANECK — Thirteen people were taken to area hospitals Thursday morning with symptoms of carbon monoxide poisoning after a gas oven was left on for at least two days in a house on Brinkerhoff Avenue, authorities said.

The injuries were not believed to be serious and most of the victims were treated and released from Holy Name Hospital and Englewood Hospital and Medical Center, said Battalion Chief Paul Browning of the Teaneck Fire Department. The occupants of the house were observing the annual Jewish holiday of Shavuot, which Browning said may have been the reason why the oven had been left on.

Firefighters first received a call from one of the occupants just before 8 a.m. after a carbon monoxide alarm sounded, Browning said. When firefighters responded, they found high levels of the gas in the house and evacuated the occupants, some of whom complained of nausea and headaches.

The 2½ story house was mostly sealed with the air conditioning running, Browning said. An ambulance was dispatched to administer oxygen while firefighters ventilated the building.

"If you leave your stove on for two days, this is bound to happen," Browning said.

He added that carbon monoxide calls are a fairly frequent occurrence in the township during Jewish holidays. The Fire Department received two reports on Wednesday of carbon monoxide detectors being set off by stoves that had been left on, and authorities receive similar calls almost every Friday night when Jewish families are observing the Sabbath, Browning said. Work that exercises control over a person's environment, including starting or putting out a fire, is prohibited on the Sabbath and many holidays under Jewish law.

"We are afraid one day there will be someone who doesn't have a carbon monoxide alarm in their house and we will have a very bad outcome," Browning said.

Copyright © northjersey.com

Adjusting "Sabbath Mode" Ovens on Yom Tov

Especially in the Diaspora, where an extra day of Yom Tom is observed and where Yom Tov can frequently fall on Thursday and Friday or Sunday and Monday, resulting in the mislabeled phenomenon of the "three-day Yom Tov," many people need to cook on Yom Tov. It is difficult to prepare all the meals for two or three days of Shabbos/Yom Tov in advance, and in homes with only one refrigerator and freezer, such a large quantity of food cannot be stored in any event. Moreover, freshly-prepared food is certainly recommended in the interest of עונג שבת and שמחת יום טוב.

Cooking, of course, is permitted on Yom Tov, but operating electrical appliances is not. In ancient times, ovens were heated with firewood, and thus the oven would be lit before Yom Tov, and, when necessary, firewood was added over the course of Yom Tov to maintain the fire. In modern times, when electrical appliances are used, this translates into leaving the oven and stove on throughout the two or three days of Yom Tov and Shabbos.

The problem with such an arrangement — beyond the financial expense of wasted electricity and gas — came to the fore in the spring of 2011, when thirteen people in Teaneck, NJ, were hospitalized on Shavuos due to carbon monoxide exposure, blamed on a faulty stove that had been left on for Yom Tov. It was reported that all the windows of the home were shut and sealed as the air conditioning was running, thus resulting in a high concentration of carbon monoxide in the home.[1] The report cited a Teaneck Fire Department official who remarked, "If you leave your stove on for two days, this is bound to happen." The incident prompted Teaneck officials to issue a warning to Jewish residents several months later, before Rosh Hashanah, not to leave their stoves on over the holiday. Teaneck Fire Chief Anthony Verley said in a statement reported by *The Bergen Record*, "With leaving the stove on, we certainly know that it puts the community at a greater danger. We want them to understand there are some deadly implications to this."[2]

The search for a solution to this problem actually began well over a decade earlier. In 1997, the Whirlpool Corporation approached the Baltimore-based

---

1. See media article above.
2. The *Bergen Record*, September 26, 2011.

Star-K kashrut agency to collaborate on a project to make ovens suitable for use on Shabbos and Yom Tov in a halachically permissible way. Just one year later, the company was awarded a patent for its "Sabbath mode," a system that surmounts the halachic obstacles posed by most modern ovens — namely, opening and closing the door does not activate fans, lights, or electronic displays. Of interest to us, however, is a different feature of the "Sabbath mode" — a system which, according to the Star-K, permits adjusting the oven's temperature on Yom Tov. When the oven runs in "Sabbath mode," the temperature adjustment does not occur immediately after the user presses the button; rather, it takes place only after a brief delay.[3] Based on a *psak* issued by Rav Moshe Heinemann, the Star-K authorized the use of this device on Yom Tov to raise or lower the oven's temperature.

Distinguishing Between Shabbos and Yom Tov

Rav Heinemann penned a responsum explaining his position, which the Star-K published on its website.[4] The ruling is based primarily on the fact that the delayed activation renders the situation one of גרמא — committing a halachic violation indirectly. One does not actually activate the oven's mechanism, but rather performs an act that will then cause the activation to occur.

The Rama rules (O.C. 334:22), based on the position of Rabbeinu Yoel, that performing a מלאכה in a manner of גרמא is forbidden on Shabbos, except when this is necessary to prevent a significant financial loss. The classic example of permissible גרמא is placing utensils with water in the line of a spreading fire in order to extinguish it, which is permissible on Shabbos in order to prevent loss or damage to property. When it comes to Yom Tov, however, the Chafetz Chayim rules (*Sha'ar Ha-Tziyun* 514:31), based on the *Ma'amar Mordechai*, that indirect מלאכה is permissible under all circumstances, even when this is not necessary to prevent the loss of property.

Rav Heinemann noted that although the *Kitzur Shulchan Aruch* (98:25) rules in accordance with the stringent view of the *Magen Avraham* (514:5), who maintains that Yom Tov is no different from Shabbos in this regard, the *Aruch Ha-Shulchan* (514:11) follows the *Ma'amar Mordechai*'s view. Rav Heinemann

---

3. Mr. Jonah Ottensoser, the Star-K's engineering consultant, wrote a detailed article explaining the "Sabbath mode" more fully, available at the organization's website, at http://www.star-k.org/articles/articles/kosher-appliances/483/the-sabbath-mode/.
4. http://www.star-k.org/articles/wp-content/uploads/2015/11/oventeshuva.pdf (retrieved November 15, 2015). The responsum was published with slight variations in *Yeshurun*, vol. 20, p. 503.

added that this also seems to have been the position of Rav Shlomo Zalman Auerbach (as implied in *Mevakshei Torah*, p. 18, ד"ה ועי"ז).

It should be noted, however, that in addition to the *Kitzur Shulchan Aruch*, several other *poskim* also forbid גרמא on Yom Tov, including the *Chayei Adam* (95:5), the *Shulchan Aruch Ha-Rav* (514:10), the *Chelkas Yaakov* (O.C. 72), and the *Chazon Ish* (38:6). Moreover, it seems clear that Rav Shlomo Zalman Auerbach, whom Rav Heinemann listed among those *poskim* who follow the *Ma'amar Mordechai*'s lenient ruling, would not permit adjusting the temperature in the "Sabbath mode" oven on Yom Tov.[5] In his *Minchas Shlomo* (2:22:2), Rav Shlomo Zalman writes as follows:

> ידוע שיש כאלו שמרתיחים ביו"ט מים שלא לצורך שתיה, אלא כדי לכבות את הגז בלבד, משום הפסד ממון. אבל לדעתי אין להתיר לעשות כן בקביעות, דכיון שהודלק לכתחילה על דעת כן לא חשיב במקום הפסד, כי ההיתר של גרמא הוא רק על דרך מקרה, אבל לא לנהוג כן בקביעות לכתחילה, אבל אם קרה ושכח לכבות את הגז בערב יו"ט ויש בזה הפסד ניכר, בזה יש להקל לגרום לכיבוי הגז, אבל צריך שיהא החימום לצורך שתיה. אבל להדליק לכתחילה על דעת לכבות על ידי גרמא אינו בכלל ההיתר של מקום ההפסד, דרק באופן שיש כבר דליקה התירו חז"ל לעשות מחיצה בכלים מלאים מים.

As is well-known, there are those who on Yom Tov boil water not for the purpose of drinking, but rather to extinguish the [flame over the] gas [when the water overflows the pot], because of the financial loss [they would otherwise incur by leaving the stove on]. In my view, this should not be allowed on a regular basis, because since it was lit from the outset with this intention, this is not considered a situation of financial loss. גרמא is permitted only on an occasional basis, but not as a regular practice planned from the outset. Only if it happened that one forgot to extinguish the gas on Erev Yom Tov, and this would cause a significant loss, in such a case one is allowed to indirectly cause the gas to be extinguished, but the heating [of the water] must be done for the purpose of drinking. However, kindling [the stove] from the outset with the intention of extinguishing it through a גרמא — this is not included in the law allowing [גרמא] in a situation of loss. Only in a case in which there is already a fire did the Sages allow making an obstruction with utensils filled with water.

Rav Shlomo Zalman explains that since several *poskim* — as noted above — do not permit גרמא on Yom Tov unless there is a significant financial loss at stake,

---

5. This point was made by Rav Shlomo Miller in an article published in *Yeshurun*, vol. 20, p. 509.

one should abide by this ruling and avoid גרמא on Yom Tov except in situations of potential financial loss. Clearly, then, Rav Shlomo Zalman maintained that one should follow the stringent position, and he thus cannot be relied upon as a basis for permitting operating an oven through a גרמא on Yom Tov.

Rav Moshe and the Shabbos Clock

Another reason to disallow use of the "Sabbath mode" on Yom Tov is a famous responsum of Rav Moshe Feinstein (*Iggeros Moshe*, O.C. 4:60) concerning the use of timers on Shabbos. Rav Moshe forbade the use of "Shabbos clocks," ruling that one may not set a timer before Shabbos to turn lights and appliances on and off during Shabbos. Although his ruling has not been accepted, and Shabbos clocks are indeed commonplace throughout the Jewish world, the rationale underlying his ruling is nevertheless very relevant to the issue of "Sabbath mode" ovens.

In his responsum, Rav Moshe presents two reasons for forbidding the use of Shabbos clocks. First, he writes that permitting Shabbos clocks for lights would result in permitting all *melachos* on Shabbos via automatic timers. Undoubtedly, Rav Moshe argues, if Shabbos clocks had been available in the time of *Chazal*, they would have forbidden using them for the same reason they forbade אמירה לנכרי, asking non-Jews to perform מלאכה on one's behalf. Rav Moshe goes so far as to suggest that setting a timer may actually be included under the prohibition of אמירה לנכרי, which, he explains, "forbids מלאכה performed by a Jew's word, not to mention by a Jew's actions." Second, Rav Moshe writes, using a timer is forbidden because of זילותא דשבת, belittling Shabbos and undermining the honor with which we are obligated to treat it.

Of course, as mentioned, the use of Shabbos clocks is widespread, despite Rav Moshe's ruling. Nevertheless, it could be argued that his ruling was not accepted only because the timer is set before Shabbos. This is much like placing a pot of food on a fire before Shabbos, which is permissible even if the cooking process actually begins after Shabbos has begun. (Rav Moshe distinguishes between the situation of cooking and that of a Shabbos clock, but, as mentioned, this distinction has not been generally accepted.) Since the action is done before Shabbos in the case of the Shabbos clock, one might argue that it differs significantly from אמירה לנכרי and does not infringe upon the honor of Shabbos. It would appear, however, that Rav Moshe's line of reasoning would apply to adjusting an oven's temperature on Yom Tov, as one performs an action on Yom Tov that demonstrably causes a מלאכה effect.

There is another ruling of Rav Moshe concerning Shabbos clocks that appears relevant to the "Sabbath mode" ovens as well. Rav Moshe ruled that if a timer was set before Shabbos, it is forbidden to adjust the timer so that the electric device will be activated or deactivated earlier or later than it would be on the current setting. He writes that aside for the prohibition of *muktzeh*, which forbids moving the pegs, delaying or advancing the effect might constitute a Torah violation, depending on the nature of the electrical device. If one changes the setting for turning on a light, for example, so that the light will turn on earlier or later than originally scheduled, this would constitute an outright מלאכה, just like directly turning on a light constitutes a מלאכה.[6] Elsewhere (O.C. 4:91), Rav Moshe applies this ruling to Yom Tov as well. Clearly, Rav Moshe maintained that the act of moving the pegs of a timer on Shabbos constitutes an act of מלאכה despite the fact that the effect does not occur immediately. This seems comparable to adjusting the temperature of an oven on "Sabbath mode," which would presumably be similarly forbidden despite the delayed effect.

Placing Wheat in a Water-Powered Mill

One might also challenge Rav Heinemann's ruling on the basis of Rav Chaim Ozer Grodzinsky's comments (*Achiezer* 3:60) regarding the case of one who places grain in a water-powered mill on Shabbos, indirectly causing them to be ground. The *Even Ha-Ozer*, as Rav Chaim Ozer cites, maintains that placing grain in a mill constitutes a Torah violation.[7] Rav Chaim Ozer explains that even if one performs a מלאכה indirectly, he nevertheless transgresses the Torah violation if this is the normal manner of performing that מלאכה.

The classic example is the case of winnowing on Shabbos, described by the Gemara (*Bava Kama* 60a) as זורה והרוח מסייעתו — one separates the chaff from the grain by throwing the raw grain into the air, allowing the wind to separate the various particles. Although the effect is brought about by the wind, and the person merely places the grain in a situation in which the wind can then separate the particles, he transgresses a Torah prohibition because he has performed this מלאכה in its usual fashion.

By the same token, Rav Chaim Ozer explains, one transgresses the Torah prohibition of grinding on Shabbos by placing the grain in the mill, even though he does not actually grind the grain, since this is the conventional method of grinding. This is quite different from the situation of גרם כיבוי — indirect extinguishing — in which one places water in the path of a fire, as this is not the conventional

---

6. Extinguishing might not constitute a Torah violation, as according to *Tosfos*, extinguishing a fire is forbidden only מדרבנן unless it is done to produce a coal.
7. This is in contrast to the view of the *Magen Avraham* (252:20), who maintains that this is forbidden only מדרבן.

manner of extinguishing, and it is therefore permissible on Shabbos (under certain circumstances). Rav Shlomo Zalman Auerbach (*Minchas Shlomo* 1:9) likewise asserts that an indirect מלאכה is considered no different from a direct מלאכה if it is performed in the conventional manner.[8]

Applying this to the case of the "Sabbath mode" oven, it would seem that adjusting the oven's temperature by pressing a button is the normal way of controlling the appliance, irrespective of the oven's delayed response. Therefore, this should seemingly be forbidden.[9]

Indiscernible מלאכה

In his *teshuva*, Rav Heinemann raises the possibility that use of "Sabbath mode" should be forbidden because of the electrical response that is triggered at the moment the button is pressed. Even if the actual effect is delayed, the user's command is registered by the oven's system immediately, and the system then "counts down" to the moment when the temperature is to be adjusted. Seemingly, this immediate response should suffice for us to forbid utilizing this mechanism on Yom Tov.

Rav Heinemann dismisses this argument, however, claiming that since the immediate response is not discernible by any of the five human senses, it does not violate Yom Tov. He explains:

> מיהו זהו דבר ידוע דכל איסורי תורה הם רק מה שבידינו להכיר ולעשות, דלא נתנה תורה למלאכי השרת ואין הקב"ה בא בטרוניא עם בריותיו, ולכן מותר לאכול גבינה אע"ג שנעשה ע"י חיידקים שאין בהם שום סימני כשרות משום שאינם נראים ע"י העיניים שנתן לנו הקב"ה אע"פ שיכולים לראותם ע"י זכוכית המגדלת ואנו יודעים בודאי שהם שם, מ"מ לא נאסרו...
>
> א"כ בנידן דידן, כשלוחצים על הכפתורים אין שום דבר נראה בשעת מעשה, ואין שום דבר מורגש או נשמע, וזולתי בכלים מיוחדים א"י לידע כלל ששום דבר נשתנה שאין כאן שום ניצוץ או קול, ואינו נקרא מלאכה אא"כ יכולים להרגיש הדבר ע"י חושים שנתן לנו הקב"ה שיש כאן השתנות.

However, it is well known that all of the Torah's prohibitions apply only to that which we are capable of discerning and doing, for "the Torah was not given to the ministering angels" and "the Almighty does not deal

---

8. This notion is also cited in the name of Rav Yosef Shalom Elyashiv. See *Shevus Yitzchak, Hilchos Gerama*, ch. 15, and *Ashrei Ha-Ish* 19:18, 37, 50.
9. This argument is advanced by Rav Shlomo Miller in the responsum cited above (n. 5). Rav Miller further notes that the *Yeshuos Yaakov* (334), explaining the comments of the *Shiltei Ha-Gibborim*, writes that גרם כיבוי is permitted only if the primary intention is not to extinguish the flame.

cruelly with His creatures." Therefore, it is permissible to eat cheese, even though it is produced through bacteria which have no kosher properties, because they cannot be seen with the eyes that the Almighty gave us. Although they can be seen under a microscope, and we know for certain that they are present, nevertheless, they are not forbidden…

And so in our case, when one presses the buttons, nothing visible occurs at that moment, and nothing is felt or heard. Without special instruments, it is impossible to know that anything has changed, for there is no spark or sound, and it is not considered a מלאכה unless it can be detected with the senses that the Almighty has given us that a change has occurred.

Rav Heinemann contends that pressing the button in "Sabbath mode" is permissible on Yom Tov because this act triggers an effect that is only later discernible to the human senses. Since the immediate electrical effect is indiscernible, even though we know with certainty that it occurred, the act is permissible. Rav Heinemann compares this indiscernible effect to bacteria in cheese, which are permitted for consumption because they are not visible to the naked eye.

Rav Heinemann cites in this context a ruling by Rav Moshe Feinstein (*Iggeros Moshe*, Y.D. 4:2) that worms that are too small to see with the naked eye are not forbidden for consumption. Another example brought by Rav Heinemann is that of two adjacent letters in a *sefer Torah* that appear connected. Even if a small space between the letters can be discerned through a magnifying glass, the *sefer Torah* is nevertheless invalid, since to the naked eye the letters touch one another. Conversely, if the two letters appear separated but a magnifying glass reveals a thin drop of ink that connects them, the *sefer Torah* is valid.

We might, however, challenge this assertion, in light of a clear distinction that exists between the cases noted by Rav Heinemann and the situation of the "Sabbath mode" oven. When a person presses the button on the oven, he does so for the specific purpose of triggering the electrical effect of raising or lowering the oven's temperature; his sole intention is to activate the oven. This is quite different from the situations of invisible bacteria or insects and the ink of the *sefer Torah*, regarding which we may invoke the rule of לא ניתנה תורה למלאכי השרת — that the Torah is meant to be observed by human beings with limited capabilities, and thus the *halacha* clearly depends on what can be seen with the naked eye. It does not seem plausible that pressing a button on an oven with the clear intention of triggering an electrical effect should be permitted only because the immediate effect is indiscernible.

Rav Heinemann proceeds to raise the question of why, according to his rationale, we would not permit typing on a computer on Yom Tov when the screen is turned off. In this instance as well, one performs an act that produces a מלאכה that is currently indiscernible, but whose effects will be seen later. Seemingly, if adjusting the temperature on the "Shabbos oven" is permitted because the immediate מלאכה effect is indiscernible, then typing on a computer should likewise be allowed when the screen is deactivated. Rav Heinemann, however, distinguishes between the two cases, noting that typing on a computer produces text that will later be visible, and thus violates the prohibition of תיקון מנא — creating or repairing something on Shabbos or Yom Tov — whereas the electrical effect of pressing the buttons on an oven does not constitute תיקון מנא.

This distinction, however, seems very difficult to understand. Once we accept the premise that *halacha* does not forbid an act that produces an indiscernible מלאכה effect, it should not make any difference whether the מלאכה effect involves תיקון מנא or any other Shabbos prohibition. Even if we can somehow formulate a fine distinction between the two, it seems hardly reasonable to issue a lenient ruling on this basis when a potential Torah violation is at stake.

Opening a Refrigerator

Rav Shlomo Zalman Auerbach, in a well-known ruling (*Minchas Shlomo* 1:10:6), permitted opening a refrigerator door on Shabbos, even when the motor is not running, despite the possibility that opening the door will cause a rise in the temperature in the refrigerator and could thus activate the motor. Rav Shlomo Zalman contended that this is permissible for two reasons. First, the main concern that arises when activating electricity on Shabbos is the *Chazon Ish*'s famous claim that activating electricity constitutes בונה, the Torah prohibition against building and creating. In the case of a refrigerator, Rav Shlomo Zalman argued, the structure is already fully built and functioning. The way a refrigerator operates is by turning itself on or off in response to temperature changes, and therefore by opening the refrigerator door, one does not "build" or "dismantle" anything; he is simply allowing the appliance to operate in its usual way.

Second, Rav Shlomo Zalman argued, it seems reasonable to assume that גרמא is forbidden on Shabbos only when one intends to produce the מלאכה effect. Rav Shlomo Zalman draws a comparison to the ruling of many *poskim* allowing one to tell a non-Jew on Shabbos to perform an act that unintentionally involves a מלאכה, such as opening a car door, which will have the effect of turning on the light. Although it is forbidden for a Jew to perform such an act on Shabbos if the מלאכה result is inevitable (פסיק רישא), one may ask a non-Jew to perform such an act. It appears that when it comes to אמירה לנכרי — the prohibition against asking non-Jews to perform מלאכה on one's behalf on Shabbos — the prohibition is limited to intentional מלאכה; it does not include actions that incidentally involve מלאכה. Rav Shlomo Zalman reasons that if this distinction applies to the prohibition of אמירה לנכרי, which is forbidden even when it is necessary to prevent a financial loss, then it should certainly apply to the more lenient prohibition of גרמא, which we allow for the sake of preventing a loss. Therefore, since one does not intend to activate the refrigerator's motor when he opens the door, this is permissible on Shabbos, as the מלאכה result is produced indirectly and is not intentional.

Neither of these arguments can be applied to the "Sabbath mode" oven. First, adjusting the oven's thermostat indeed results in a מלאכה, as the oven's mechanism works to raise or lower its temperature. This differs from the case of a refrigerator, regarding which, Rav Shlomo Zalman claimed, no actual מלאכה is involved. As for the second argument, one quite obviously presses the button with the clear intention of causing the temperature to change, and thus the מלאכה effect is not unintentional. Seemingly, therefore, the use of this mechanism is forbidden on Yom Tov, despite the delayed effect on the oven's temperature.

INTERVIEW

Rav Moshe Heinemann *shlit"a* on *Headlines with Dovid Lichtenstein**

On Yom Tov, there is an added feature [in the "Sabbath mode" oven] which I added into it, which works with גרמא based on the *Mishna Berura*, [who rules] that גרמא is permissible on Yom Tov. The reason why this is not considered as though you are doing something right away is because really you're sending a message to the computer, and the computer determines that whatever should happen, will happen after ten seconds or whenever it's going to happen. Since it's not possible for a person to recognize that anything has happened with his five senses, he is not considered to be doing anything right away. [By contrast,] typing on a computer with the screen turned off might be considered תיקון מנא, as if you've made something now which could be used at a later date.

Let me tell you about something very similar. In Baltimore, they put in new water meters which they do not need to send people to read. There is a digital display, and it sends a signal to the central system's computer. When they want to send you a bill, it is produced right away... This is a problem for Shabbos. We were able to reach an agreement with the city. We said that they should make a cover over the display, so they can check the display if there's a problem, but normally it cannot be seen. But there was still a problem with the message being sent to the computer. I went to Rav Chaim Kanievsky and asked him what he thought about it. I thought it was not a problem because you cannot see, feel, hear, taste, or smell anything — there is nothing we can notice with our five senses. He said he does not see any problem with it, because you're just sending a message.

* Broadcast aired 20 Tishrei, 5776 (October 3, 2015).

Research Confirms Next Generation Bioplastics Could Be Made From Trees

June 9, 2014

A research project led by Biome Bioplastics has demonstrated the feasibility of extracting organic chemicals from lignin for the manufacture of bioplastics.

The results stem from a grant from the UK's innovation agency, the Technology Strategy Board, awarded to a consortium led by Biome Bioplastics in early 2013 to investigate lignin as a new source of organic chemicals for bioplastics manufacture, which could significantly reduce costs and increase performance of these sustainable materials.

Lignin is a complex hydrocarbon that helps to provide structural support in plants and trees. As a waste product of the pulp and paper industry, lignin is a potentially abundant and low-cost feedstock for the high performance chemicals that could provide the foundation for the next generation of bioplastics.

The research was undertaken in conjunction with the University of Warwick's Centre for Biotechnology and Biorefining led by Professor Tim Bugg, whose team has been working to develop methods to control the breakdown of lignin using bacteria and extract these chemicals in significant quantities.

The project has successfully demonstrated that bacteria can be effective in the selective degradation of lignin, and that the breakdown pathway can be controlled and improved using synthetic biology. Crucially, several organic chemicals have been produced at laboratory scale in promising yields that have potential use in bioplastic manufacture.

Initial scale-up trials on several of these target chemicals have demonstrated the potential for them to be produced at industrial scale, suggesting the commercial feasibility of using lignin-derived chemicals as an alternative for their petrochemical counterparts. Biome Bioplastics has also transformed these chemicals into a material that shows promising properties for use as an advanced bioplastic.

Professor Tim Bugg, Director of the Warwick Centre for Biotechnology and Biorefining, explains: scientists have been trying to extract chemicals from lignin for more than 30 years. Previously, chemical methods have been used but these produce a very complex mixture of hundreds of different products in very small amounts. By using bacteria found in soil we can manipulate the lignin degradation pathway to control the chemicals produced. This is groundbreaking work. We've made great progress over the last year and the results are very exciting.

The next phase of the project will examine how the yields of these organic chemicals can be increased using different bacteria and explore options for further scale-up of this technology. The first commercial target is to use the lignin-derived chemicals to replace the oil-derived equivalents currently used to convey strength and flexibility in some of Biome Bioplastics' products, further reducing cost and enhancing sustainability.

Paul Mines, CEO of Biome Bioplastics, commented, "We are extremely pleased with the initial results of the feasibility study, which show strong promise for integration into our product lines. Looking ahead, we anticipate that the availability of a high performance polymer, manufactured economically from renewable sources, would considerably increase the bioplastic market."

Industrial biotechnology, the use of biological materials to make industrial products, is recognised by the UK government as a promising means of developing less carbon intensive products and processes, with an estimated value to the UK of between £4bn and £12bn by 2025.

Copyright © biomebioplastics.com

Bioplastic *Sechach*

In recent years, as part of the ongoing effort to reduce the use of petroleum and gas in industrial manufacturing, the bioplastics industry has emerged as a major player, seeking to replace ordinary plastic with plastic manufactured from organic materials. According to a report in 2010, an estimated 4% of the word's oil is used in the manufacture of ordinary plastic, and the amount of oil consumed in plastic packaging in the U.S. alone is estimated at 200,000 barrels of oil a day.[1] The manufacture of bioplastics from organic materials such as starches, sugarcane, and vegetation consumes 65% less energy than the manufacture of ordinary plastic, and produces 70% less greenhouse gas emissions. Bioplastic products are also biodegradable. According to a 2015 report by the Biopreferred program of the U.S. Department of the Agriculture, the use of biobased products displaces approximately 300 million gallons of petroleum each year in the United States, the rough equivalent of taking 200,000 cars off the road. The report also said that in 2013, the biobased product industry added over 4 million jobs in the United States, and some $369 billion to the nation's economy.[2]

From a halachic standpoint, the availability of plastic produced from vegetation challenges us to examine the status of these materials vis-à-vis the *mitzva* of *sukka*. One of the basic requirements of the *sukka* is that the *sechach*, which constitutes the rooftop, must be made from פסולת גורן ויקב — inedible vegetation.[3] Conceivably, then, bioplastic materials could perhaps be eligible for use as *sechach*, as they are grown from the ground.[4]

---

1. http://www.thomaswhite.com/global-perspectives/bioplastics-industry-emerges/.
2. http://www.biopreferred.gov/BPResources/files/EconomicReport_6_12_2015.pdf.
3. *Sukka* 12a.
4. One might argue that materials produced from edible substances, such as corn starch and sugarcane, should be disqualified for use as *sechach* because food may not be used as *sechach*. In truth, however, it is generally assumed that food may not be used as *sechach* because it is susceptible to טומאה, and one of the requirements of the *sechach* is that it must not have the ability to contract טומאה. But once an edible food has been transformed into an inedible substance — as is the case with bioplastics — it is no longer susceptible to טומאה, and thus may be used for *sechach* (see *Bikkurei Yaakov* 629:9.) It should be noted that the *Tosfos Rid* (*Sukka* 13b) offers a different reason for the disqualification of food products (דפסולת גורן ויקב אמר רחמנא ולא גורן ויקב עצמן), but even he indicates that only foods that are capable of becoming eligible to contract טומאה are included in this provision (כיון דראויין לקבל טומאה ע"י הכשר פסולין לסיכוך).

The *Peri Megadim* and Forest Glass

A possible halachic precedent for the use of such a product as *sechach* is *sechach* made from "forest glass," glass made primarily from plant ash.[5] The *Peri Megadim* (O.C. 629) rules — albeit controversially — that under extenuating circumstances, when no other options are available, one may use a slab of forest glass as *sechach*. He writes that even if materials other than plant ash (such as sand) are included in the manufacturing process, the product's status is nevertheless determined based on its majority ingredient. The *Peri Megadim* notes, however, that forest glass should be used only if conventional options are unavailable, because this is a situation of נשתנה צורתו — the product bears no resemblance at all to the vegetation from which it was made. Such a product is invalid for use as *sechach* מדרבנן (by force of Rabbinic enactment), and thus it should not be used unless no other options are available. But when a person has no other options, he may use such glass as *sechach*, and it appears from the *Peri Megadim* that one may even recite a *beracha* over the *mitzva* in such a case.

Seemingly, a bioplastic sheet is no different from forest glass, as both are manufactured from vegetation. In light of the *Peri Megadim*'s ruling, we should perhaps conclude that although a bioplastic sheet should not ordinarily be used as *sechach*, as it bears no resemblance to the original vegetation, nevertheless, when no other options are available, it may be used and a *beracha* may be recited.

However, the *Peri Megadim*'s contention is far from simple due to the apparent absence of one of the fundamental requirements of *sechach* — shade. *Halacha* requires that the area under the *sechach* have more shade than sunlight — צילתה מרובה מחמתה — and a transparent glass covering quite obviously provides no shade.

The Brisker Rav explained that the *Peri Megadim* understood the law of צילתה מרובה מחמתה as referring to the quantity of shade, not the quality or substance of shade. Even forest glass provides a slight degree of protection from the sun. Thus, as long as the majority of the *sukka* is under this thin layer of shade, the *Peri Megadim* maintains that the *sukka* is valid (when no other *sukka* is available).[6]

The *Chazon Ish*, however, seems to have disagreed. It is reported that the *Chazon Ish* was once asked whether glass should be treated as *sechach pasul* — material that is invalid for use as *sechach* — or as empty space in the *sukka*. An area of *sechach pasul* in the *sechach* invalidates the *sukka* only if the area is

---

5. Standard glass is clearly invalid for *sechach* because it is produced from sand. See *Bikkurei Yaakov* 632:7.
6. *Sukkas Rachel*, p. 5.

a size of four טפחים (handbreadths) or more, whereas empty space is permitted only if it extends no more than three handbreadths. Therefore, if glass is treated as *sechach pasul*, a piece of glass less than four טפחים may be placed within the *sechach*, but if we regard it as empty space, then the piece of glass must be less than three טפחים. The *Chazon Ish* replied that glass should be treated as empty space, since it does not provide shade. He was then asked whether, in light of this position, one may cover the entire *sukka* with glass and place *sechach* over it, and he responded that this *sukka* would be valid.[7] Since the glass is regarded as empty space and not invalid *sechach*, it does not disqualify the *sukka* if one sits underneath the *sechach*. In any event, it is clear that according to the *Chazon Ish*, transparent material may not be used as *sechach*. Indeed, he writes in his work (150:4), צל דק לא חשיב סכך, אלא בעינן צל חשוב שהאדם נהנה ממנו — "Thin shade is not considered *sechach*, because we require significant shade from which a person benefits."[8]

It thus emerges that in the case of a transparent bioplastic sheet, its validity as *sechach* hinges on this debate between the *Peri Megadim* and the *Chazon Ish*. The *Peri Megadim* would presumably permit the use of such a sheet as *sechach* in the absence of other options, just as he permits forest glass, whereas the *Chazon Ish* would not allow it because it does not provide shade. If the sheet is opaque, however, and it thus provides shade, it should seemingly be acceptable when no other options are available even according to the *Chazon Ish*, and it stands to reason that one may even recite a *beracha* in such a case.

Protecting the *Sukka* from the Rain

The more practical application of this discussion is the possibility of using a plastic sheet — either on its own as *sechach* or as a covering over the *sechach* — when rain falls on Sukkos. At first glance, such a situation qualifies as שעת הדחק — "extenuating circumstances" — when we would allow using a bioplastic covering as *sechach*, at least if it is opaque. Even if the sheet is transparent, one could seemingly place it on top of the ordinary *sechach* to protect the *sukka* from rain, in light of the *Chazon Ish*'s ruling noted above.

The source for this solution is the *Magen Avraham*'s ruling regarding the

---

7. *Orchos Rabbeinu*, vol. 2, p. 218. The only condition would be that the glass must have several holes to allow rain to penetrate, to satisfy the view mentioned below requiring that rain must be able to penetrate the *sechach*.
8. Earlier (143:4), however, the *Chazon Ish* writes that according to one view mentioned by *Tosfos* (*Eiruvin* 3a, ד"ה אי קלשת), there is no minimum required amount of shade, and even the thinnest layer of shade suffices. It would thus appear that this question hinges upon the two views mentioned there by *Tosfos*.

placement of a cloth sheet over or underneath the *sechach*. The *Shulchan Aruch* (O.C. 629:19) cites two views as to whether one may hang such a sheet over or underneath the *sechach* to protect the *sukka* from either the sunlight or from leaves falling from the *sechach*. According to Rashi, placing a sheet is permissible only if this is done for decoration and the sheet is positioned within four טפחים (handbreadths) of the *sechach*. If the sheet is spread for protection, then the *sukka* is invalid for the *mitzva*. Rabbeinu Tam, however, disagrees, ruling that one may place a sheet within four טפחים of the *sechach* even to protect the *sukka*, as long as the *sechach* is independently adequate for the *mitzva*. The *Mishna Berura* (629:58) writes that the *halacha* follows the stringent view of Rashi. However, the *Mishna Berura* adds — citing the *Magen Avraham* — that in light of Rabbeinu Tam's ruling, if one would otherwise be unable to eat in the *sukka*, then it is preferable to place a sheet. The *Mishna Berura* writes:

בשעת הדחק, שלא יוכל לאכול בסוכה ע"י העלין הנושרין לתוך המאכל **או ע"י הגשמים הנוטפין** או ע"י הרוח שמכבה הנרות, מוטב לפרוס סדין תחת הסכך בתוך ד' טפחים משיאכל חוץ לסוכה, אבל לא יברך ע"ז לישב בסוכה.

> Under extenuating circumstances, when one would be unable to eat in the *sukka* due to the leaves falling into the food, **or because of the dripping rain**, or because of the wind which would extinguish the candles, it is preferable to spread a sheet under the *sechach* within four handbreadths, rather than eat outside the *sukka*, although one should not recite in such a case the *beracha* of לישב בסוכה.

According to the *Magen Avraham*, when rain falls on Sukkos, it is preferable to spread a sheet[9] to protect the *sukka* so that one could fulfill the *mitzva* according to Rabbeinu Tam's view, rather than eat indoors. However, since this option is available only according to Rabbeinu Tam's view, and not according to Rashi, one should not recite a *beracha* in such a case, following the well-established rule of ספק ברכות להקל — we do not recite a *beracha* if there is some question regarding whether it is warranted. When rain falls, then, according to the *Magen Avraham* and *Mishna Berura*, one should spread a sheet to protect the *sukka* from the rain, and then eat in the *sukka* without a *beracha*.

In the case of a bioplastic sheet, however, one might argue that placing it over the *sukka* during rainfall allows one to eat in the *sukka* with a *beracha*, in light of the halachic concept of ספק ספיקא. According to some *poskim*, the rule

---

9. The *Magen Avraham* writes that one should spread a sheet underneath the *sechach*. Seemingly, it should make no difference whether the sheet is placed underneath the *sechach* or over the *sechach*. This point is noted by Rav Shimon Shapiro, cited by Rav Efrayim Greenblat in *Rivevos Efrayim* 3:515.

of ספק ברכות להקל does not apply if the uncertainty surrounding the *beracha*'s obligation hinges on two questions. In the case under discussion, the *beracha* is unwarranted only if we make two assumptions that are subject to controversy: 1) a bioplastic sheet is unsuitable for *sechach*; 2) a sheet that may not be used for *sechach* may also not be spread underneath or over the *sechach* for protection. The first assumption is challenged by the *Peri Megadim*, as noted above, and the second assumption is challenged by Rabbeinu Tam. Perhaps, then, given the two uncertainties involved, one should be allowed to recite a *beracha* when he has spread a bioplastic sheet over the *sukka* in the rain.

In truth, however, the issue of reciting ברכות in situations of ספק ספיקא is itself subject to a great deal of controversy. The *Peri Megadim*, in his introduction to *Hilchos Berachos*, seems to indicate that one should not recite a *beracha* in such a case, and he likewise writes in this regard elsewhere (*Mishbetzos Zahav*, Y.D. 28:16), טוב שלא לברך — "It is appropriate not to recite the *beracha*." This is also the view of the *Chayei Adam* (5:6).[10]

The *Shulchan Aruch*, however, appears to have ruled otherwise. In a famous passage (O.C. 489:8), the *Shulchan Aruch* writes that one who misses a day of counting the עומר continues to count without reciting a *beracha*, since some *poskim* maintain that the *mitzva* can no longer be performed after missing a day. But if one is uncertain as to whether he counted on a certain day, he continues counting with a *beracha*. The *Mishna Berura* (489:38) explains that this ruling stems from the rule of ספק ספיקא, as in this case there are two reasons why one would potentially be required to continue counting: 1) perhaps the person in fact counted on that day, and thus did not miss any days of counting; 2) perhaps the *halacha* follows the view that missing one day's counting does not affect the ספירת העומר obligation on the subsequent days. It thus appears that in the view of the *Shulchan Aruch*, one indeed recites a *beracha* in a situation of ספק ספיקא.[11]

We might conclude, then, that if rain falls on Sukkos, it would be preferable to spread a bioplastic sheet over the *sukka*, in which case he may even recite the *beracha* of לישב בסוכה.

It should be noted, however, that the *Peri Megadim* himself (*Eishel Avraham* 629:25) does not accept this line of reasoning. He writes that the *Shulchan Aruch*

---

10. The case under discussion is one in which a person ate a בריה — a complete item, such as a grape — and he is uncertain whether it was the quantity of a כזית. In such a case, there are two reasons why he potentially is required to recite a *beracha acharona*: 1) he may have eaten a כזית; 2) some *poskim* require reciting a *beracha acharona* after eating a בריה, regardless of its volume. See also *Michtam Le-David,* O.C. 3; *Sedei Chemed,* vol. 5, *Ma'areches Berachos* 1:18:10; and *Michtav Le-Chizkiyahu,* O.C. 1,3.

11. The *Mishna Berura*, however, appears to contradict this ruling, as elsewhere (215:20) he codifies the *Chayei Adam*'s position cited above.

ruled definitively in accordance with Rashi's view that spreading a sheet to protect the *sukka* invalidates it. Thus, Rabbeinu Tam's lenient position cannot be introduced to create a ספק ספיקא.

Nevertheless, we might still argue for a different reason that one could eat in the *sukka* with a *beracha* by spreading a transparent bioplastic sheet over the *sukka*. As we saw, even the *Chazon Ish*, who clearly did not accept the *Peri Megadim*'s ruling regarding glass, ruled that transparent glass may be treated as empty space. Thus, if *sechach* is placed over a sheet of glass on the *sukka*, the *sukka* is valid. If so, spreading a transparent bioplastic sheet over the *sechach* during rainfall should be acceptable according to all views. According to the *Peri Megadim*, the sheet is simply an extra layer of valid *sechach*, and according to the *Chazon Ish*, the sheet may be regarded as empty space, and thus ignored.

The Rainproof *Sukka*

This entire discussion, however, hinges upon the more general question as to whether one must, or may, undertake measures to make his *sukka* rainproof. Until now, we have worked on the assumption that if the inclement weather makes it impossible to eat in the *sukka*, but halachically acceptable measures can be taken to protect the *sukka* from the rain, then it would be preferable to take these measures.

However, Rabbeinu Tam, as cited by the *Tur* (O.C. 631), maintains that to the contrary, a *sukka* whose *sechach* cannot be penetrated by rain is invalid for the *mitzva*. The *Mishna Berura* (631:6) explains this *halacha* based on the concept of גזירת בית — *Chazal* disqualified a *sukka* that resembles a permanent home, given the concern that people might not recognize the difference between a *sukka* and their regular home, and would thus not build *sukkos*. A *sukka* with *sechach* so thick that it protects against the rain resembles a permanent home, and is therefore invalid. Rabbeinu Tam draws proof to his position from the fact that, as mentioned by the Mishna (*Ta'anis* 2a), rainfall on Sukkos is considered a "sign of curse" (סימן קללה), as it prevents us from performing the *mitzva*. If it is possible to construct a rainproof *sukka*, Rabbeinu Tam argues, then one can circumvent the halachic exemption granted when rain falls, and thus rain should not be viewed as a "curse." Evidently, a rainproof *sukka* is not acceptable, and rain must be able to penetrate the *sechach*.

The question thus arises as to how to reconcile the *Magen Avraham*'s ruling with this position of Rabbeinu Tam. According to Rabbeinu Tam, the *sechach* may not be impenetrable, and the *Magen Avraham* (631:2) cites this ruling (in the name of the *Levush* and *Bach*). How, then, can the *Magen Avraham* write that it is preferable to spread a sheet over the *sukka* to protect it from the rain?

Rav Moshe Feinstein briefly addresses this question in one of his posthumously-published responsa (*Iggeros Moshe*, O.C. 5:43:4). He suggests that the *Magen Avraham* proposed the solution of the sheet only as a חומרא בעלמא — a measure of stringency — in light of the fact that some *Rishonim* disputed Rabbeinu Tam's view and ruled that impenetrable *sechach* is acceptable.[12] This was not intended as an actual halachic ruling, but rather as a חומרא that one could choose to take on.[13]

On the other hand, it should be noted that the *Peri Megadim*, in his discussion of using glass as *sechach*, makes no mention whatsoever of the problem that a glass sheet does not allow rain to enter the *sukka*. Apparently, he did not follow Rabbeinu Tam's ruling, and permitted the use of rainproof *sechach*.[14]

Regardless, it is clear that the widespread custom does not follow the *Magen Avraham*'s view, as people do not spread out sheets or undertake other measures to rainproof their סוכות. Moreover, most *poskim* accept Rabbeinu Tam's ruling requiring that rain should be able to penetrate the *sukka*. Indeed, although the *Chazon Ish* rules that *sechach* may be placed over a sheet of transparent glass, as noted above, he required that holes be made in the glass to allow rain to penetrate the *sukka*. Therefore, a solid sheet of bioplastic should not be used as *sechach* unless one has no other options, in which case rainproof *sechach* may be used (*Mishna Berura* 631:6).

---

12. Rav Moshe notes the *Hagahos Maimoniyos* (*Hilchos Sukka* 5:9), which mentions that Rabbeinu Tam's brother-in-law, Rabbbenu Shimshon of Falaise, disagreed with this ruling. Furthermore, Rav Moshe adds, the Rambam makes no mention of this disqualification, indicating that he does not disqualify rainproof *sechach*.

13. Rav Moshe acknowledges the difficulty with this theory, as it fails to account for the *Magen Avraham*'s comment that one does not recite a *beracha* when eating in the *sukka* in such a case because ספק ברכות להקל. If the *Magen Avraham* advises spreading a sheet only as a חומרא, then it should be obvious that a *beracha* is not recited. Rav Moshe suggests that the *Magen Avraham* was imprecise in this instance, and ספק ברכות להקל is not the real reason why a *beracha* is not recited in such a case.

14. Rav Gavriel Ciner (*Nitei Gavriel, Sukkos*, p. 265) asserts that the *Magen Avraham*, who advises spreading a sheet to protect the *sukka* from the rain, disagrees with Rabbeinu Tam's ruling and maintains that the *sukka* may be rainproof. He suggests that the issue depends on the conceptual question surrounding the nature of the exemption from the *sukka* obligation during rainfall. If this exemption stems from the standard rule of מצטער פטור מן הסוכה — that one is exempt if the *sukka* causes him discomfort — then conceivably, one would be required to undertake reasonable measures to make the *sukka* comfortable, including protecting it from rain. Some *Acharonim*, however, explained that when rain falls, the *sukka* loses its halachic status as a *sukka* altogether. If so, then one is not required to protect the *sukka* from rain so that he can remain there during rainfall, since in any event it is not regarded as a halachic *sukka* as long as the rain is falling.

Conclusion

In principle, bioplastic materials may be used for *sechach* when one has no other options, although transparent materials would be invalid according to the *Chazon Ish*. As common practice requires using *sechach* that allows rain to enter the *sukka*, a solid sheet of plastic over the *sukka* should not be used. It would seem, however, that strips of opaque bioplastic, which allow rain to enter the *sukka*, would be acceptable when one has no other options.

HAARETZ

The Cost of Jewish Living: British Economists Create 'Kosher Chicken Index'

January 18, 2016

Maintaining a Jewish lifestyle in the U.K. costs an extra 12,700 pounds sterling per year, according to two researchers.

Maintaining a Jewish lifestyle in the United Kingdom costs a pretty penny — an extra 12,700 pounds sterling ($17,900) a year, to be exact, found two economists.

Anthony Tricot, a consultant for Ernst and Young, and Andrea Silberman, a British Treasury economist, published their findings at this year's Limmud conference. Their research was driven by a desire to quantify community concerns about the spiraling cost of Jewish living, they said.

"As economists, we wanted to see what actual data was available so we could encourage a more evidence-based debate on whether there is indeed a 'cost of Jewish living' crisis," they wrote in the Jewish Chronicle. Living Jewishly has several big-ticket expenses, they wrote. Observant Jews are likely to spend an extra 2,000 pounds a year or more just on food, their research shows.

Kosher meat costs on average twice that of non-kosher supermarket meat, they found. They based their comparison on five products at London kosher chain Kosher Deli versus similar products at Tesco. That premium works out to 500 pounds a year.

A kosher roasted chicken. Limor Laniado Tiroche

Those who buy only certified kosher food — and not just meat — are liable to spend even more.

Likewise, kosher Indian or Chinese restaurants cost 70% more than nonkosher restaurants. This is due to the higher material cost as well as supervision. There goes 1,500 pounds a year.

One of the biggest expenses of Jewish living is housing. In order to live Jewishly, Jews often choose to cluster in communities. One-fifth of Britain's Jews choose to concentrate in the north London borough of Barnet, where housing costs 150% more than the average, they noted.

"Kosher inflation" outpaces the country's inflation rate, according to the economists' findings. Kosher meat prices have doubled in a decade, compared to a 40% increase for other meat products. Likewise home prices in northwest London have jumped.

Other costs include synagogue membership, at 600–800 pounds per household. Some half of British Jewish households belong to a synagogue. And then there are religious state schools, which cost up to 2,000 pounds per child each year. However, that's cheaper than in the United States or France, where there are no state-funded religious schools, they noted.

Social pressure also makes life more expensive, they say. "Simchahs are a further significant cost, driven by the need to 'keep up with the Cohens,'" they write. Jews spend more than twice the U.K. average on weddings, and also pay for bar and bat mitzvahs...

They caution that the high cost of living Jewishly drives many observant Jews to seek charity, while it may push others away from tradition. They call on community leaders to take action: to increase transparency and to seek ways of becoming more efficient.

"Kashrut authorities need to value the interests of consumers over that of producers when deciding whether to license new stores or products. And communal organizations need to give greater consideration to inclusivity by offering activities and services at a wider range of price points," they conclude.

Copyright © haaretz.com

Is *Ben Pekua* Meat the Solution to Prohibitive Kosher Meat Prices?

It's no secret that kosher meat costs considerably more than ordinary meat, and that the high kosher meat prices contribute towards the high cost of Orthodox Jewish living. According to a report published in early 2016, kosher meat in Great Britain costs twice as much as non-kosher meat.[1] In the United States, the discrepancy is less stark, but still considerable, estimated at 20%.

The reason for the exorbitant prices can be attributed to the combination of three factors: waste, staff, and inefficiency.

Waste: Every animal must be inspected for טריפות — terminal medical conditions, as defined by *halacha* — before its meat can be sent to the kosher market. An estimated 20–30% of all animals that undergo kosher *shechita* are found to have טריפות, and must therefore be either discarded or shipped to the non-kosher market to recover some of the lost money. A staggering 40–50% of slaughtered animals fail to meet *glatt* standards, and are thus discarded. Moreover, the prohibition of *gid ha-nasheh* — the sciatic nerve — results in the impossibility of selling hind quarters on the kosher market, such that considerable portions of even non-טריפה animals cannot be sold. This immense volume of non-kosher animals and meat forces kosher meat producers to drive up prices in order to make the industry profitable.

Staff: Kosher meat requires not only qualified *shochtim* (slaughterers), but also experts to inspect the slaughtered animals and to perform ניקור — the removal of the *chelev* (forbidden fats) and other forbidden parts — as well as מליחה (salting the carcass to extract its blood).

Inefficiency: The obligatory inspections and supervision make the process lengthy and cumbersome, and large-scale production is therefore terribly inefficient. More time and work is needed to produce kosher meat than to produce non-kosher, resulting in higher costs for consumers.

The בן פקועה Solution

As early as 1975, Rabbi Avraham Korman proposed the idea of reducing kosher

---

1. See media article above.

meat costs by breeding בני פקועה, which eliminates the concern of טריפות, and perhaps even the need to remove the *chelev* and *gid ha-nasheh*.[2]

The *Shulchan Aruch* (Y.D. 13:2), following the majority view in the Mishna (*Chullin* 74a), writes that if a kosher pregnant animal is slaughtered, its fetus — called a בן פקועה — may, on the level of Torah law, be taken from the mother's carcass, alive or dead, and eaten even without *shechita*. By force of Rabbinic enactment, *shechita* is required if the fetus had been fully gestated at the time its mother was slaughtered and it had tread on the ground after being extracted from its mother. In such a case, the young animal must be slaughtered before it is eaten to avoid the misconception that eating ordinary animals without *shechita* is permissible.[3] Significantly, however, the *Shulchan Aruch* rules that in all cases of a בן פקועה, even if the fetus was fully gestated and had tread on the ground, the rules of טריפות do not apply. Since this animal is viewed as part of the mother, which had been properly slaughtered, it is permissible even if it suffers from a medical condition that would render an ordinary animal a טריפה.[4]

What makes the concept of בן פקועה a potential game-changer for the kosher meat industry is the *Shulchan Aruch*'s extraordinary ruling (13:4) that the offspring of two בני פקועה that mated is itself considered a בן פקועה. In the *Shulchan Aruch*'s words, this applies עד סוף כל הדורות — "until the end of all generations." Meaning, no matter how many generations removed an animal is from the original two animals that were extracted alive from their mothers after *shechita*, it still has the status of בן פקועה if its two parents had this status. This remarkable provision offers the possibility of breeding בני פקועה industrially in order to avoid the concern of טריפות. As long as fool-proof measures can be taken to ensure that no other animals enter the breeding ground, בני פקועה can be bred and thus used for meat. Although proper *shechita* would still be required, 100% of the animals would be kosher. No inspections would be necessary, and no meat would need to be discarded out of concern for טריפות. Moreover, producing meat from בני פקועה would eliminate the concern of mistakes and oversights in the inspection process. There would be no margin of error whatsoever, as every slaughtered animal can be 100% guaranteed טריפה-free.

This idea was proposed again in the 1990s by a group of ranchers who

---

2. In an article published in *Torah U-Madda* 5:1 (Shevat 5735).
3. An exception is made in a case of a בן פקועה with an unusual feature — or, according to some opinions, two unusual features — which distinguishes it from other animals, in which case *shechita* is not needed because people recognize that this animal is different. See *Shulchan Aruch* and its commentaries, Y.D. 13:2.
4. However, the *Aruch Ha-Shulchan* (Y.D. 13:7) qualifies this ruling and maintains that outwardly visible *tereifos* render a בן פקועה forbidden, for the same reason that *shechita* is required.

approached Israel's Chief Rabbinate seeking its approval for a בן פקועה herd. The Rabbinate, under the leadership of Rav Yisrael Meir Lau and Rav Eliyahu Bakshi-Doron, denied the request. The reasons for the Rabbinate's decision were noted and discussed by Rav Bakshi-Doron in an article on the subject published in the Israel-based journal *Techumin* (vol. 19).

The בן פקועה Controversy of 2015–2016

More recently, an Australian rabbi, Rabbi Meir Rabi of Melbourne, after extensive research, concluded that the idea should be put into practice, and he established Ben Pekuah Meats, a company that breeds herds of בני פקועה that are safely isolated. DNA testing is performed to ensure the offspring are pure-bred, and each animal is labeled. The company sells the meat without inspecting the animals for טריפות or removing the *chelev* and *gid ha-nasheh*. This enables them to keep their prices low and to market the hind quarters, which, as mentioned, are not available in the standard kosher meat industry.

Rabbi Rabi's enterprise, not surprisingly, has drawn considerable controversy. He published a thorough article on the subject in the 5775 (2015) edition of *Techumin* (vol. 35), which included a response by Rav Zev Weitman, the head of *kashrus* for the Tnuva food company and a renowned expert on *kashrus*. Rav Weitman challenged several of Rabbi Rabi's claims (as will be discussed below), while acknowledging the advantages of a בן פקועה farm and leaving open the question of whether such an operation is acceptable. In Australia, Rabbi Rabi's initiative was strongly condemned by a group of prominent Australian rabbis, who, on 7 Shevat, 5776 (January 17, 2016), signed a letter declaring that they "support and agree with the halachic ruling of the great Rabbis who have already expressed their adamant objection to the notion of raising herds of *bnei pakuos*…" In the United States, Rabbi Yair Hoffman authored a pair of articles in the *5 Towns Jewish Times* in which he expressed vehement opposition to Rabbi Rabi's operation.[5]

In the pages that follow, we will examine the arguments advanced against Rabbi Rabi's initiative in order to understand why it has met with such widespread opposition.

The Fully-Gestated Offspring of a Preemie

One apparent shortcoming of Rabbi Rabi's analysis is the assumption that

---

5. "The New Commercially Produced Ben Pekuah Meats," January 7, 2016; "The Ben P'kuah Controversy Rages On," January 13, 2016.

the *chelev* and *gid ha-nasheh* of all animals born in the בן פקועה herd are permissible.

The *Shulchan Aruch* (Y.D. 64:2) rules explicitly that if a בן פקועה was fully gestated at the time its mother was slaughtered, its *chelev* is forbidden for consumption. (According to one view cited by the *Shulchan Aruch*, this applies only if the בן פקועה treads on the ground before it is slaughtered.) Later, in discussing the laws of *gid ha-nasheh* (65:7), the *Shulchan Aruch* cites a view that the *gid ha-nasheh* of a fully-gestated בן פקועה is forbidden, and the Rama accepts this view as authoritative. Accordingly, it is only if a fetus was extracted from its slaughtered mother's body before reaching full gestation that its *chelev* and *gid ha-nasheh* are permissible for consumption. In other words, the *chelev* and *gid ha-nasheh* of a בן פקועה are permissible only when it does not require *shechita*. When, however, *shechita* is required due to the concern of מראית עין — the concern that observers might conclude that even ordinary animals do not require *shechita* — then its *chelev* and *gid ha-nasheh* are likewise forbidden.

In order to avoid these prohibitions, Rabbi Rabi's company is careful to extract the initial בני פקועה before full gestation.[6] Since these animals are בני ח' — prematurely born בני פקועה — their *chelev* and *gid ha-nasheh* are permissible for consumption. These animals are then bred, and their offspring are likewise treated as בני ח', even though they are born after full-term pregnancies. The underlying assumption is that when two בני פקועה mate and produce offspring, the offspring is the same kind of בן פקועה as the parents. If the parents were both בני ח', then the offspring also have the halachic properties of בני ח', even though they are themselves בני ט' — meaning, they were born after full gestation.

Clearly, however, this assumption is questionable. If *halacha* forbids the *chelev* and *gid ha-nasheh* of a בן פקועה born after full gestation, there seems to be little reason to assume that the same would not be true regarding a child produced by two בני פקועה. We might draw proof from the brief comment of the *Shach* (13:16) that the product of two בני פקועה requires *shechita*, כיוון שהפריסו על גבי קרקע — because it had tread upon the ground, and there is thus the concern of מראית עין. The clear implication of the *Shach*'s remark is that if one wishes to partake of the child of two בני פקועה right after birth, before the newborn animal had stood on the ground, *shechita* is not required. Even though the parents themselves require *shechita*, as they had been fully gestated before being extracted from their mother,[7] the newborn does not require *shechita*. This seems to prove

---

6. This was explained by Rabbi Rabi in a radio interview on *Headlines with Dovid Lichtenstein*, broadcast on 20 Teves, 5776 (January 16, 2016).
7. It is clear that the *Shach* is referring to a case in which the two בני פקועה parents had been fully gestated before being extracted from their parents, as the *Shach* makes his

that, at least according to the *Shach*, when two בני פקועה mate and produce a child, its status vis-à-vis *shechita* is determined based on its own properties, not its parents' properties. As Rav Yaakov Gezuntheit explains in reference to the *Shach*'s comment, in his *Tiferes Yaakov* (Y.D. 13:8, p. 50):

> כוונתו דס"ד דוקא בבן פקועה ראשון בלא הפריס מותר, אבל בנו כיון שהוא בא מכח האב, והאב צריך שחיטה, לא יהא כחו עדיף מכח האב להתירו בלא שחיטה. קמ"ל כיון דהכל משום מראית העין, והיכא דליכא [מראית העין] אינו צריך שחיטה כל שלא הפריס.

> [The *Shach*'s] intent is that we might have thought that specifically the initial בן פקועה is permissible [for consumption without *shechita*] if it had not stepped [on the ground], whereas [regarding] a child [of a בן פקועה], since its status [as a בן פקועה] comes [only] on account of the father, and the father requires *shechita*, its status cannot be greater than the status of the father, such that it is permissible without *shechita*. He [the *Shach*] therefore informs us that since it is all because of מראית העין, where there is no [concern for מראית העין], it does not require *shechita* if had not stepped [upon the ground].

In other words, while one might have assumed that two mating בני פקועה transfer their particular status to their young, in truth, the offspring's status is determined based on its own qualities.

It would thus stand to reason that the status of the product of two בני פקועה as a בן ט' or בן ח' depends on when it was born, and not when its parents were born. Even if its parents were extracted from their mothers before completing gestation, if it was born after full gestation, it is treated as a בן ט', and, as such, its *chelev* and *gid ha-nasheh* are forbidden for consumption.[8]

Rav Weitman raised a different objection to this policy, claiming that in today's day and age, a בן פקועה extracted before full gestation must be treated no differently than a fully-gestated בן פקועה. The reason why *halacha* treats a בן ח' differently, Rav Weitman asserts, is because in ancient times, an animal born in the eighth month was not expected to survive. The *Piskei Ha-Rid* (*Chullin* 72b) writes:

> עגל בן שמונה, אף על פי שיצא חי, אין במינו שחיטה והרי הוא כמת שחיותו אינו חיות.

---

    comment in reference to the ruling of the *Shulchan Aruch*, which deals with the case of two בני ט'.

8. Curiously, Rabbi Rabi's company treats their animals as בני ט' in that they make a point of slaughtering them with proper *shechita*, but the company permits the *chelev* and *gid ha-nasheh* as in בני ח', taking a seemingly self-contradictory stance in determining the animals' status.

A calf [extracted from its mother after] eight [months] — even though it left [its mother] alive, its type does not require slaughtering, and it is considered dead, because its life is not real life.

The *Shach* (Y.D. 13:9) similarly writes that a בן ח׳ is "considered dead" — חשוב כמת. Rav Weitman further notes that when the *Shulchan Aruch* discusses the status of the offspring of a בן פקועה, it speaks specifically of a fully-gestated fetus who grows and mates:

בן ט׳ חי שנמצא במעי שחוטה כשרה וגדל ובא על בהמה דעלמא...

There seems to be only one reason why the *Shulchan Aruch* speaks in this context about a בן ט׳ — because the author could not envision a situation of a בן ח׳ growing and reaching the age of reproduction. Nowadays, however, we know that a בן ח׳ is capable of living a long life, and Rav Weitman thus claims that a בן ח׳ would have the same status as a בן ט׳, both with regard to the requirement of *shechita*, and with regard to the prohibitions of *chelev* and *gid ha-nasheh*.

Therefore, even though the בן פקועה solution is, at least in principle, effective in avoiding the issue of טריפות, it does not allow for the consumption of the animals' *chelev* and *gid ha-nasheh*.[9]

Practical Considerations

The primary objection to the idea of a בן פקועה herd, however, has to do with the practical risks entailed.

The *Shulchan Aruch* rules explicitly (13:4), based on the Gemara (*Chullin* 75b), that if a בן פקועה mates with an ordinary animal, the offspring is forbidden for consumption, even after proper *shechita*.[10] The reason, as explained by Rashi in his commentary to the Gemara, is that the product of this union is halachically considered to have been partially slaughtered. Since one parent is a בן פקועה, an animal considered to have already undergone *shechita*, the part of the child produced by that parent is already "slaughtered," while the other part is not. The *shechita* of such an animal would thus be invalid in light of the rule

---

9. Rav Weitman concedes, however, that since the *chelev* and *gid ha-nasheh* of a בן פקועה are forbidden only מדרבנן — by force of Rabbinic enactment, as opposed to Torah law — we may permit the consumption of portions of the animals that are normally removed as a matter of custom, but are technically permissible.
10. The *Shulchan Aruch* addresses specifically the case of a male בן פקועה that impregnates a female animal, but the *Shach* and *Taz* note that this *halacha* applies also in the reverse case, in which an ordinary male animal impregnates a female בן פקועה.

of *shehiya*, which disqualifies *shechita* if there was a delay between the severing of the two pipes (the trachea and the esophagus).

This *halacha* turns the idea of a בן פקועה herd into a very risky operation. If a non-בן פקועה ever manages to mix in with the herd, its offspring is forbidden for consumption on the level of Torah prohibition. Yet, the staff will slaughter the offspring and sell its meat on the kosher market, unaware of the fact that it is forbidden.[11] Likewise, if a בן פקועה from the herd ever escapes and mates with an ordinary animal, the offspring will be forbidden for consumption without anyone realizing it.

Rabbi Rabi's company addresses this concern by ensuring maximum security and protection, as well as through DNA testing, which guarantees that all animals born in the herd are indeed products of other animals in the herd, and not from outside sources.

Another concern that has been noted is the eventuality that the company might one day close down, and the בן פקועה animals would be sold on the open market or released into the wild.[12] This would result in the birth of countless forbidden animals that would be treated as ordinary kosher animals. Thus, even if a foolproof method of safeguarding the herd could be implemented, there is no telling what might happen in the future, when בן פקועה animals might mix and be bred with other animals, creating a colossal halachic dilemma.

Notwithstanding these concerns, some have argued that since rabbinic scholars after the Talmudic era do not have the authority to legislate safeguards and forbid that which *halacha* permits, we do not have the right to object to בן פקועה meat due to practical concerns. The concept that rabbis no longer have the authority to introduce new safeguards to Torah law was developed at length by Rav Tzvi Pesach Frank in a famous responsum published in his *Har Tzvi* (2:2:24) regarding the Manhattan *eiruv*. Rav Frank wrote that while he could not issue a definitive ruling, since he did not actually see the *eiruv*, he felt compelled to denounce those who invalidated the *eiruv* out of the concern that people might conclude that carrying outdoors is permissible on Shabbos. Citing numerous sources, Rav Frank demonstrated that post-Talmudic rabbis do not have the authority to ban that which is permitted, and thus they cannot ban a halachically legitimate *eiruv*. This argument could seemingly be applied to בן פקועה meat as

---

11. Rav Bakshi-Doron also noted the fact that contemporary industrial breeding is generally done through artificial insemination, rather than by allowing the animals to naturally mate, and thus we would need to trust the hired staff that performs the procedure to ensure that all the sperm is taken from בני פקועה.
12. Rav Weitman wrote that in conversation with Rav Asher Weiss, Rav Weiss pointed to this concern as the reason for his stern objection to the idea of a בן פקועה herd.

well. Once the halachic obstacles have been overcome, perhaps rabbis do not have the authority to forbid the meat.

Rav Bakshi-Doron notes this argument and responds by drawing a clear distinction between enacting a safeguard and reaching a prudent public policy decision. The Rabbinate did not issue a ban against eating the meat of a בן פקועה, but rather decided, as a matter of policy, not to give its stamp of approval to the initiative to create a herd of בני פקועה, because it felt the idea was unwise. This is far different from enacting a prohibition against בן פקועה meat, and it is certainly well within the authority of a rabbinic body.[13]

רצון הבורא

Rav Shmuel Wosner addressed the issue of בני פקועה herds in the eighth volume of his *Shevet Ha-Levi* (178), where he dismisses the idea out of hand, calling the arguments in favor of such an enterprise פטפוטים בעלמא — "meaningless chatter." He writes that while it is true that בן פקועה herds allow us to avoid complications involving טריפות, the Torah specifically wants us to deal with these complex issues, rather than try to escape them:

דזה רצון הבורא ב"ה שינהוג שחיטה מן התורה ושינהגו בה עפ"י הלכה, וינהגו בה הפרישות מחששי טריפות...

> For this is the will of the Creator — that *shechita* should be observed on the level of Torah law and be conducted according to *halacha*, and that we act with restraint due to the concern of טריפות...

Rav Wosner cites the verse in *Sefer Vayikra* (11:47) in which the Torah concludes its discussion of forbidden foods by instructing us to distinguish between permissible and forbidden animals:

להבדיל בין הטמא ובין הטהור ובין החיה הנאכלת ובין החיה אשר לא תאכל.

> To distinguish between the impure and the pure; between an animal that may be eaten and an animal that may not be eaten.

Rashi explains this to mean that we are to carefully distinguish between animals that were properly slaughtered and those that were slaughtered improperly, and between animals that have symptoms of טריפות and those with conditions that do not qualify as טריפות. Rav Wosner proves on the basis of Rashi's comments

---

13. Rav Bakshi-Doron takes issue with Rav Tzvi Pesach Frank's letter concerning the Manhattan *eiruv*, arguing that it is within a rabbinical body's right to disapprove of an *eiruv* if it feels that this is the best policy.

that "the will of the Creator" is not to avoid the process of properly slaughtering and inspecting animals, but rather to undertake this responsibility, with all the challenges and complexities entailed. In his view, then, cultivating בן פקועה herds to avoid halachic complexities runs counter to the Torah's will, which requires us to address these complexities to the best of our ability, and not to try to escape from them.

In a somewhat similar vein, Rav Menashe Klein (*Mishneh Halachos* 16:130) raises the question of why בן פקועה herds were never before established as a way of avoiding the halachic prohibitions of טריפות. In particular, raising בני פקועה would allow us to drink milk without having to rely on the assumption that the cow from which it was taken is not a טריפה — something that cannot be definitively ascertained without slaughtering and inspecting it. *Halacha* permits relying on the statistical majority, and we may thus drink milk without first killing and inspecting the cow, but we might, at first glance, wonder whether it would be preferable to raise בני פקועה and use their milk in order to avoid the possibility of טריפות. Rav Klein writes:

אלקים עשה את האדם ישר וכן צותה לשתות חלב, וכל המוסיף גורע.

"God created man upright"[14] and [the Torah] likewise commanded to drink milk, and whoever adds in effect detracts.

In other words, we are expected to conduct our lives normally and to utilize familiar, traditional methods of preparing meat and milk; we should not be looking to outsmart the system through creative innovations.

Historical Precedent

Rabbi Rabi drew support for his idea by noting the precedent of Rav Sherira Gaon, who allegedly bred a herd of בני פקועה.[15] This claim is based on the account presented by the *Or Zarua* (1:440) describing how Rav Sherira Gaon killed בני פקועה without *shechita* and served the meat at a wedding.[16]

It should be noted, however, that there is no indication whatsoever that Rav

---

14. *Koheles* 7:29. The continuation of the *pasuk* reads, והמה בקשו חשבונות רבים — "but they have sought many calculations."
15. In the interview cited above, n. 6. Likewise, his company's website claims that Rav Sherira Gaon and his son, Rav Hai Gaon, "cultivated herds of *benei pekua* and actively took steps to promote its legitimacy by serving it at public functions." However, there is no indication in the *Or Zarua*'s account that the meat was served at a wedding in order to "promote its legitimacy."
16. Cited in *Hagahos Ashri*, *Chullin* 4:5.

Sherira raised herds of בני פקועה. The *Or Zarua* states simply that Rav Sherira had בני פקועה and once served them at a wedding. No mention is made of בני פקועה being bred together to produce a herd consisting exclusively of בני פקועה. The claim that Rav Sherira Gaon created בני פקועה herds is, at best, pure speculation, and thus cannot be advanced as a basis for dismissing legitimate practical concerns.

We might add that even if we accept the questionable assumption that Rav Sherira Gaon raised herds of בני פקועה, this would mark the glaring exception that proves the rule. The absence of any other documented account of such a practice in centuries' worth of halachic literature speaks far more loudly than this lone passage in the *Or Zarua*. If we would look to halachic precedent as a basis for affirming the legitimacy of this enterprise, the precedent of not raising בני פקועה is overwhelmingly stronger than the precedent possibly set by Rav Sherira Gaon.

Pareve Meat?

Rabbi Rabi also advanced the claim that the meat of a בן פקועה does not have the formal halachic status of meat, and therefore, in principle, it may be cooked and eaten with milk and dairy products. Although Rabbi Rabi does not believe that this should be allowed as a practical matter, he makes this point as an example of the unique status of בן פקועה meat.[17] The practical importance of this claim is that it offers yet another very significant advantage of Rabbi Rabi's initiative, as consumers who do not adhere to the halachic restrictions of בשר בחלב (eating milk with meat) would avoid this transgression when using בן פקועה meat.

The basis for this contention is a passage in Rav Meir Simcha Ha-Kohen's *Meshech Chochma* (*Bereishis* 18:8).[18] Rav Meir Simcha advances the theory that when Avraham hosted the three angels and served them meat, the meat he served was that of a בן פקועה. He then writes, ambiguously:

ושחיטה התירתו ואין בה משום בשר בחלב, דחלב שחוטה מותר, ועיין שער המלך.

Its slaughtering rendered it permissible, and it was not subject to בשר

---

17. In the interview cited above (n. 6), Rabbi Rabi said, "Absolutely, the meat is pareve. I don't like the idea of suggesting cooking בשר בחלב; this is not my intention at all. But I use this to highlight dramatically that בן פקועה is a מין בפני עצמו [its own type of entity]."
18. In his article in *Techumin*, Rabbi Rabi develops the theory that *halacha* does not treat בן פקועה as an animal; it is regarded instead as its own kind of creature. He explains on this basis the view he ascribes to the *Meshech Chochma*, that its meat is not halachically considered meat.

בחלב, because the milk of a slaughtered animal is permissible [with meat]; see *Sha'ar Ha-Melech*.

The source referenced here by Rav Meir Simcha is the *Sha'ar Ha-Melech* commentary on the Rambam's *Mishneh Torah*, written by Rav Yitzchak Nunis. In *Hilchos Issurei Mizbei'ach* (3:11), the *Sha'ar Ha-Melech* writes that just as milk extracted from an animal after its slaughtering may, strictly speaking, be consumed with meat,[19] the milk of a בן פקועה may similarly be consumed with meat.[20] A בן פקועה does not require *shechita* (on the level of Torah law) because it is covered by the *shechita* performed on its mother, and thus its milk has the status of חלב שחוטה — milk of a slaughtered animal — which is not subject to the restrictions of בשר בחלב.

Accordingly, the *Meshech Chochma* appears to claim that Avraham served his guests the meat of a בן פקועה together with its own milk. Since the milk was not subject to the prohibition of בשר בחלב, it was permissible according to Torah law to cook it and eat together with meat.[21]

However, Rav Yehuda Cooperman, in his annotated edition of the *Meshech Chochma*, understood this passage to mean that Avraham cooked the meat of a בן פקועה in milk because the meat is not subject to the prohibition of בשר בחלב. According to Rav Cooperman's reading, the *Meshech Chochma* drew a parallel between the milk of a בן פקועה and its meat. Thus, once the *Sha'ar Ha-Melech* established that the animal's milk may be consumed together with meat, it follows that its meat may be consumed together with milk.

As Rabbi Rabi noted, this is also how Rav Moshe Sternbuch understood the *Meshech Chochma*'s comments, in his explanation of this passage in his *Moadim U-Zemanim* (4:319): השחיטה מתיר בבן פקועה **ושרי בחלב** — "The slaughtering [of the mother] renders the בן פקועה permissible, and **it is permissible with milk**."

Whether or not this is the view of the *Meshech Chochma*, it is very difficult to accept. For one thing, the *Sha'ar Ha-Melech* — whom the *Meshech Chochma* cites as the source of his claim — states explicitly that a בן פקועה's milk may be consumed with meat only because it is treated as חלב שחוטה — milk taken from

---

19. *Chullin* 113b: בחלב אמו ולא בחלב שחוטה. Although such milk is permissible on the level of Torah law, it is nevertheless forbidden by force of Rabbinic enactment; see *Shach*, Y.D. 87:13.
20. This claim that the milk of a בן פקועה may be eaten with meat is made also by the Maharit Algazi, *Hilchos Bechoros* (1:2). A number of *Acharonim*, however, expressed some uncertainty regarding this matter. See Rabbi Akiva Eiger's notes to Y.D. 87:6; *Noda Be-Yehuda, Mahadura Tinyana*, Y.D. 36; and *Chasam Sofer*, Y.D. 14.
21. This is how Rav Shmuel Chaim Domb understood the *Meshech Chochma*'s comments in his annotated edition of the work.

an animal after it had undergone *shechita*. Since a בן פקועה is regarded as having already been slaughtered, its milk may be consumed with meat. This line of reasoning, quite obviously, cannot be applied to the animal's meat, which is forbidden for consumption with milk despite being taken after *shechita*. As such, there is no logical basis at all to consider a בן פקועה's meat pareve.[22]

We may also disprove this position from the Rambam's ruling in *Hilchos Ma'achalos Asuros* (9:7) that one who eats a שליל — an animal fetus — with milk violates the Torah prohibition of בשר בחלב. This ruling is based on the Gemara's comment (*Chullin* 113b) that a שליל is included under this prohibition. It is clear that the Rambam refers here to a case in which the mother had been properly slaughtered; otherwise, the fetus would be already forbidden due to its being part of a נבילה — the carcass of an animal that had not undergone proper *shechita*. As the Rambam rules in the immediately preceding passage, one who eats meat of a נבילה with milk is not liable for בשר בחלב, because the meat had already been forbidden for consumption before it was mixed with milk.[23] Necessarily, then, the Rambam speaks of a fetus found inside of an animal that had undergone proper *shechita* — meaning, a בן פקועה[24] — and he writes explicitly that eating or cooking it with milk transgresses the Torah violation of בשר בחלב.[25]

Finally, even if we accept the assumption that the *Sha'ar Ha-Melech*'s stance regarding the milk of a בן פקועה applies also to its meat, we cannot ignore the fact that several authorities question the status of the milk, and maintain (or at least suggest) that it is subject to the prohibition of בשר בחלב.[26] For this reason as well, we cannot consider permitting the consumption of a בן פקועה's milk with meat or viewing it as anything less than a Torah violation.

---

22. It should also be noted that the *Sha'ar Ha-Melech*'s comments would appear to disprove Rabbi Rabi's contention (mentioned above, n. 19) that a בן פקועה does not have the halachic status of an animal. If this were true, then the *Sha'ar Ha-Melech* would not have had to resort to the rule of חלב שחוטה to explain why the milk of a בן פקועה may be consumed with meat. If the בן פקועה is not halachically an animal, then its milk is not halachic milk, and the fact that the animal is considered to have undergone שחיטה is entirely irrelevant.
23. The basis of this ruling is the well-known principle of אין איסור חל על איסור — a food item forbidden due to one prohibition cannot then become forbidden again by force of a second prohibition.
24. Indeed, the Gemara in *Chullin* (74b) uses the term שליל in reference to a בן פקועה.
25. This can be proven from the Gemara's discussion there as well. Addressing the prohibition of eating a fetus's meat with milk, the Gemara writes that this prohibition would apply even according to the position that אין איסור חל על איסור (see Rashi, ד"ה אין איסור חל על איסור). This is possible only if the שליל was found inside a properly slaughtered animal, as otherwise, it would already be forbidden as נבילה, and thus the prohibition of בשר בחלב could not then take effect.
26. See n. 20.

Would You Eat AquAdvantage Salmon If Approved?

April 26, 2013
by Robynne Boyd

It's been a long battle for AquaBounty Technologies and its divisive fish. Twenty years in the making, the first transgenic animal created for consumption — a doubly fast growing salmon — is now in its last leg of the U.S. Food and Drug Administration approval process.

Regardless of the regulatory hoops AquAdvantage salmon must bound, it's the social hurdles that, in the end, may prove whether this fish will swim or sink.

The small, scaly fish has polarized people, sending fear, indifference and admiration throughout scientific and environmental communities, as well as the general public.

All this, even after a draft Environmental Assessment was done in the early months of 2012. The findings of which reaffirmed the FDA's previous conclusions that the genetically engineered (GE) salmon is as safe to eat as conventional farm-raised Atlantic salmon. The Assessment also says that it's very unlikely the GE salmon could escape into the environment, and even if by some odd chance it did, the salmon would be incapable of reproducing since they will be "effectively sterile."

The FDA's findings have not quelled the concerns of opponents. Food safety critics believe it's a Mad-Max test that could go disastrously wrong.

Genetically altered fish?

The Food and Drug Administration will decide whether Atlantic salmon genetically engineered to grow faster than their natural relatives can be allowed to be raised and sold as food in the U.S.

Bred to grow faster: Altered fish can reach adult size in 16-28 months instead of 36 months for normal Atlantic salmon

Both fish shown at 18 months of age

Length: 24 in. (61 cm)
Weight: 6.6 lb (3.0 kg)

Genetically altered

Length: 13 in. (33 cm)
Weight: 2.8 lb (1.3 kg)

The process
- Growth hormone from Chinook salmon (1) joins a "promoter" from an ocean pout (2), an eel-like fish
- Spliced into Atlantic salmon DNA (3); new growth hormone directs the gene to produce hormone all year round instead of only in summer

Pros
- GE salmon could help meet rising demand for fish
- Could reduce pressure on wild fish stocks
- Altered fish eats 25 percent less feed; could make fish farming more profitable

Cons
- Science on long-term effects of GE salmon is limited
- Fish could escape from farms, harm wild salmon populations
- Food safety activists and fisherman say GE salmon won't be properly labeled

Source: U.S. Food and Drug Administration, AquaBounty Technologies
Graphic: Melina Yingling   © 2013 MCT

Regardless of the regulatory hoops

...

In direct response to the FDA approval process, a new bill, the Genetically Engineered Food Right-to-Know Act, is circulating through congress. It would mandate any GM food ingredient be labelled. Also, the supermarkets Whole Foods, Trader Joes and Aldi, are a few on a list of food providers refusing to stock their shelves with transgenic food product.

AquaBounty's answer to naysayers is that the production of AquAdvantage salmon is in the interest of both the environment and consumers. On the company's website, it says that their objective is to use the technology of genetic engineering to "contribute to increasing aquaculture productivity in an efficient, safe and sustainable manner to meet the demand for high quality seafood from a growing world population." And demand is growing.

"Between 2000–2004, Americans alone ate an average of about 284,000 metric tons of salmon annually, of which two-thirds was farmed," states the FDA's Environmental Assessment.

Despite all the hubbub, the FDA is the final authority who will make the decision whether or not the first genetically engineered food animal will arrive in supermarkets across the country. According to AquaBounty's CEO Ronald Stotish, as quoted in the Guardian, the company should receive approval by the end of the year.

If Stotish's prediction is correct, what I want to know is would you eat the salmon?

Copyright © blogs.scientificamerican.com

Genetically Modified Organisms: Will this be the Greatest *Kashrus* Challenge of Modern Times?

On November 19, 2015, the United States Food and Drug Administration (FDA) announced that for the first time, it had approved a GMO — genetically modified organism — for commercial production and consumption. The approval was granted to AquAdvantage salmon, a product developed by the Massachusetts-based Aqua Bounty company, which calls it "the world's most sustainable salmon," touting the modified salmon as a game-changer in the seafood industry. The decision was issued twenty years after Aqua Bounty first applied for FDA approval, and it was accompanied by a great deal of controversy surrounding the safety of GMOs and the possible long-term environmental impact of genetic modification on an industrial scale.

The idea behind the so-called "super salmon" — derisively dubbed "frankenfish" by its opponents — is to accelerate the fish's growth through genetic modification. The modified salmon needs just about 18 months after hatching to reach market size, as opposed to the three years that salmon normally requires. And it can grow in habitats that would otherwise be inhospitable to salmon; specifically, it can grow in warmer waters. Currently, salmon is bred in waters in the North Atlantic and North Pacific, and has to be shipped to U.S. markets. The genetically engineered fish can be bred in land-based pools, significantly reducing shipping costs and delays.

Aqua Bounty alters the salmon by introducing to the fertilized eggs a growth-regulating gene from the Chinook salmon, which is known as the "king" of salmon, as it is the largest salmon in the Pacific. The gene is "turned on" and kept running by a "promoter" gene taken from the ocean pout, a fish that resembles an eel. The genetically altered eggs are then sold to salmon "farmers" who grow the fish for commercial sale.

Having received FDA approval, AquAdvantage salmon may very well transform the meat and fish industry much as the iPhone transformed the cellular communication industry. With the precedent of an FDA-approved GMO in place, the floodgates have been opened for other companies to genetically modify chickens, turkeys, and livestock, thereby revolutionizing the food market. Genetic modification could be used to accelerate growth, eliminate disease, and enhance reproduction capabilities, all of which will serve to increase availability and thereby lower prices. Thus, AquAdvantage salmon is poised to be a game-changer not only in the salmon industry, but in the entire food industry.

This specter presents us with what might very well turn out to be the greatest *kashrus* challenge of the 21st century. In the not-too-distant future, we might see companies altering cows with genes taken from pigs or other non-kosher animals to accelerate growth or enhance taste. What would be the halachic status of the meat produced from such a cow?

In the case of AquAdvantage salmon, as with other genetically modified products, this question is actually irrelevant. Although the ocean pout — one of the two fish from which genes are taken for modifying the salmon — is not kosher, the gene from the ocean pout is not actually injected into the salmon egg. Aqua Bounty uses a system called PCR (polymerase chain reaction), whereby synthetic copies of DNA strands are reproduced. As such, no actual substance from an ocean pout is implanted in the eggs of AquAdvantage salmon, and there is thus no reason to question the fish's halachic status. As long as this method remains as the standard genetic modification technique, we can rest assured that our kosher poultry and livestock are, indeed, kosher.

Nevertheless, the prospect of GMOs transforming the food industry compels us to consider the situation of modification through implantation of genes from one species to another. How would the introduction of a gene from a non-kosher organism in a kosher organism affect its halachic status? If the resulting fish, for example, has all the physical properties of a kosher fish, would it nevertheless be forbidden if it contains a gene originating from a non-kosher fish?[1]

This question hinges on two different issues. First, we must ask whether a non-kosher genetic source affects the status of a fish that contains the two identifying characteristics of a kosher fish — fins and scales. In the case of AquAdvantage, the modified salmon bears full physical resemblance to ordinary salmon. Perhaps, then, even if the AquAdvantage salmon would stem from actual non-kosher biological material, this material would have no effect on its halachic status, as the resulting fish features the physical properties of a kosher fish. Second, even if we must indeed take into account the non-kosher status of the fish's "parents" despite its kosher properties, the lone gene taken from a non-kosher fish might be subject to the rule of ביטול ("negation"), whereby

---

1. This question earned a great deal of attention in the early 2000s, when rumors circulated in Bnei-Brak that genetically altered poultry had infiltrated the kosher market. Rabbi J. David Bleich wrote an extensive essay on the topic in *Tradition* (37:2 [2003], pp. 72–80), surveying the rulings of several leading sages who addressed the issue.

a substance may be ignored due to its constituting an insignificant minority portion of a mixture.

I. Are Fins and Scales Enough?

Eggs and היוצא מן הטהור

The Gemara in *Maseches Nidda* (50b) establishes that a species of bird called תרנגול דאגמא is forbidden for consumption, whereas a different species called תרנגולתא דאגמא is permissible. The words תרנגול and תרנגולתא refer, respectively, to a rooster and a hen. It thus seems, at first glance, that the Gemara speaks here of a single species of bird, and establishes that the males are not kosher while the females are. This is, in fact, *Tosfos*' approach to explaining the Gemara. *Tosfos* (ד"ה תרנגולתא דאגמא) write that the males of this species do not have the physical properties required by the Torah for a bird to be permissible for consumption, but the females do, and thus only the females may be eaten.

This reading, however, gives rise to the question of why we do not apply to this species the rule of היוצא מן הטהור טהור — that something produced by a kosher animal is kosher. The Mishna in *Maseches Bechoros* (5b) establishes that if a kosher animal produces offspring with a genetic mutation, such that the offspring does not have the properties of a kosher animal, it is nevertheless permissible for consumption. Since it was born to a kosher animal, it is considered kosher regardless of its physical properties. Conversely, if a non-kosher animal gives birth to an animal that resembles a kosher animal, the offspring is forbidden for consumption despite featuring the physical characteristics of a kosher species. Since it was born to a non-kosher animal, it is not kosher. Seemingly, if we apply this rule to the תרנגול דאגמא, it should be permissible for consumption despite lacking the properties required for kosher birds. Since it was produced by a תרנגולתא דאגמא, which is a kosher bird, it should be kosher.

Tosfos answer this question by establishing that the rule of היוצא מן הטהור טהור applies to mammals, but not to fowl. The bird that emerges from an egg after hatching is not considered the halachic offspring of its mother, because its fetal development occurred outside of its mother's body. *Tosfos* write:

> האם לא ילדה האפרוח, אלא ביצים הטילה, והאפרוח מעפרא קא גדיל, ונאסר ממילא ע"י סימני טומאה.

> The mother did not give birth to the chick; rather, it laid eggs, and the chick grew from the earth, and is therefore forbidden by virtue of its non-kosher characteristics.

Since the chick develops outside the mother's body and does not emerge from the mother's body in its complete form, it does not fall under the category of היוצא מן הטהור. We view it as the product of the "earth," as its development takes place on the ground, and its kosher status is therefore determined by its own physical properties, and not by its mother's species. In the case of a תרנגול דאגמא, then, the bird is forbidden for consumption because it does not have the required characteristics of a kosher bird, despite its having been produced by a kosher bird.

A different view, however, is taken by *Tosfos* in *Maseches Chullin* (62b, ד"ה תרנגולתא דאגמא). There, *Tosfos* accept the argument that a bird with non-kosher physical characteristics is kosher if it was produced by a kosher bird. *Tosfos* are therefore compelled to advance an entirely different reading of the Gemara's ruling concerning תרנגול דאגמא and תרנגולתא דאגמא, and they claim that the Gemara refers to two distinct species with closely resembling names.

The Rambam appears to have followed the view taken by *Tosfos* in *Chullin*. In *Hilchos Ma'achalos Asuros* (3:11), the Rambam addresses the case of a chick that emerged from an egg laid by a *tereifa* — a bird that has a fatal wound and thus may not be eaten. Based on the Gemara in *Maseches Temura* (31a), the Rambam rules that the chick is permissible for consumption. The chick is not viewed as יוצא מן האסור — something which was produced by a forbidden creature — because, as the Gemara explains, it developed outside of the mother's body. When it left the mother bird's body, it was not yet a chick; it took form after the egg was laid, and thus the chick is not viewed as the product of the mother bird. However, the Rambam adds that the chick is permissible שאין מינו טמא — because it belongs to a kosher species of bird. In other words, if the mother bird that laid the egg belonged to a non-kosher species, then the chick would be forbidden for consumption even if it had the properties of a kosher bird.

According to the Rambam, a bird is not viewed as its mother's offspring with respect to the prohibition of *tereifa*, but it is considered its mother's offspring with regard to its species. Although the bird develops outside of the mother's body, nevertheless, its identity in terms of classification is determined by the mother's species, despite the fact that it is not assigned the mother's other halachic characteristics, such as *tereifa*.

Rav Chaim Soloveitchik of Brisk, commenting on the Rambam's ruling (in *Chiddushei Rabbeinu Chayim Ha-Levi*), explains the conceptual basis underlying this distinction. He writes that the rule of היוצא מן הטמא טמא actually encompasses two different principles, which apply in different contexts. The first is that an animal's identity and classification are determined based on its parents, and not based on its own properties. Thus, with regard to *halachos* that depend not on a certain characteristic, but rather on a creature's formal classification, the animal assumes the status of its parents. The second principle establishes that something produced by a creature that is forbidden for consumption is itself forbidden for consumption. This principle says nothing about identity; it rather introduces a prohibition against consuming something that was produced by a forbidden creature.

The Rambam distinguished in this regard between the prohibition of *tereifa* and the prohibition of eating a forbidden species. An animal becomes a *tereifa* not because of its essential nature, but rather due to a medical condition. As such, the offspring is forbidden only by force of the second rule of היוצא מן הטמא — namely, the rule that forbids that which emerges from something forbidden. In the case of a hatched egg, however, this rule does not apply, since the chick was not produced directly by the mother, and it is thus permissible. When it comes to the issue of forbidden species, however, the prohibition results not from the creature's having been produced by a forbidden creature, but rather from its species, and its species is determined based on its parents' species. Regarding this matter, the fact that a bird is not produced directly by its mother is of no consequence. Since it was, after all, created by its parents, it halachically belongs to its parents' species. Thus, if the mother belonged to a forbidden species of bird, then it is also forbidden.

The Rambam's view thus clearly reflects the position taken by *Tosfos* in *Maseches Chullin*, that a bird's status of *kashrus* is dependent upon the mother's species, regardless of the bird's physical properties.[2]

Rav Moshe Sternbuch, in a responsum published in *Teshuvos Ve-Hanhagos* (vol. 4, Y.D. 184), cites and follows the view of *Tosfos* in *Nidda* that a bird's kosher status depends on its own characteristics, rather than its parents' species. He thus rules that a chicken with all the properties of a kosher chicken is, strictly speaking, permissible for consumption even if it underwent genetic modification with genes from a non-kosher animal.[3]

Conceivably, this issue would directly affect the case of salmon genetically modified through the introduction of a gene from a non-kosher fish. Fish reproduce by laying eggs, and thus a fish, like a bird, is formed in an egg outside of its

---

2. This issue also comes to the fore in a responsum of the *Chasam Sofer* (Y.D. 74) regarding a chicken fathered by a non-kosher bird, giving rise to the question of whether the father's non-kosher status affects the status of the egg and chick. The *Beis Shlomo* (Y.D. 144) writes that this would depend on the debate between these two views of *Tosfos* as to whether a bird's status is determined based upon its own properties or the species of its parents.
3. Rav Sternbuch does, however, express concern that a non-kosher genetic source may yield an adverse spiritual effect on an animal's meat, which could, in turn, cause spiritual harm to those who eat it. He thus concludes that such food should be avoided.

mother's body.⁴ Hence, according to *Tosfos* in *Nidda*, we may discount the gene taken from a non-kosher source; a fish's identity is not determined based on its biological parents, as it does not grow inside of its mother.⁵ However, according to *Tosfos* in *Chullin* and the Rambam, we cannot necessarily disregard the fish's non-kosher source. Since a fish's species with respect to *kashrus* depends upon the mother's species, the fact that the fish is partially produced by an ocean pout could, at least in theory, render it forbidden.

סיבה or סימן

This question might hinge on a broader issue that a number of *Acharonim* have addressed regarding the nature of the סימני טהרה — the characteristics that determine a species' halachic status.⁶ Do these characteristics themselves determine the kosher status of an animal, or do these characteristics merely indicate that these species are permissible? In other words, should these characteristics be perceived as a סיבה — the reason why these species are deemed permissible for consumption — or as a סימן — an indicator that these species are halachically suitable for consumption?

According to the first approach, the determining factor is the creature's actual properties, irrespective of its origins. As such, a fish with fins and scales would be permissible even if it has undergone genetic modification through the introduction of a gene from a non-kosher fish. According to the second possibility, however, the fish's status depends on its formal classification, on whether or not it belongs to a kosher species, as the fins and scales are merely indicators of a kosher species. Hence, the presence of fins and scales on a genetically modified salmon would not necessarily mean that the fish is permissible.

As far as fish are considered, proof to the first possibility may perhaps be

---

4. The Gemara in *Maseches Avoda Zara* (40a) actually distinguishes in this regard between kosher fish and non-kosher fish, establishing that a kosher fish lays the egg before the fetus is developed, whereas the fetus of a non-kosher fish develops inside the mother's body and is then laid before hatching. Accordingly, a fish with fins and scales that was produced by non-kosher fish is forbidden for consumption according to all views. (This point was made by Rav Shlomo Zalman Auerbach in *Minchas Shlomo* 2:97:27.) In the case of genetically modified salmon, however, the eggs develop just like ordinary salmon's eggs, outside the mother's body, and thus according to *Tosfos* in *Nidda*, its kosher status depends on its own characteristics, and not those of its parents.
5. This point is made by the *Chasam Sofer* in his commentary to *Chullin* (66a).
6. *Tzofnas Panei'ach, Hilchos Ma'achalos Asuros*; Maharit 1:51. See also Rav Elchanan Wasserman's *Kovetz Shiurim* (vol. 2, *Kovetz Shemuos, Chullin* 62b, #27), where he suggests that the aforementioned debate between *Tosfos* in *Nidda* and *Tosfos* in *Chullin* hinges on this fundamental question.

drawn from the Gemara's discussion in *Maseches Nidda* (51b) concerning the properties of a kosher fish. The Mishna asserts that all fish with scales also have fins, raising the question of why the Torah bothered to identify both characteristics. Seemingly, it would have sufficed to inform us that any fish with scales is permissible for consumption. For what purpose, then, did the Torah mention fins? In response to this question, the Gemara invokes the *pasuk* (*Yeshayahu* 42:21), יגדיל תורה ויאדיר — in other words, the fins are mentioned only for the sake of glorifying Torah by adding more Torah material for us to study. But what value is there in adding unnecessary information? How is the Torah "glorified" by the addition of a superfluous word?

The likely explanation is that the Torah sought to instruct that it is these two features — the fins and the scales — that make a fish permissible.[7] If these features were merely physical signs that reflected the fish's kosher status, then there would be no purpose served by adding the requirement of fins. The Torah chose to mention fins because the presence of both fins and scales is the reason why such a fish is permissible for consumption. Indeed, the Ritva, commenting on the Gemara's discussion, writes, ואולי הוא ג"כ גורם טהרתו, ואע"פ שהוא לבדו אינו גורם טהרה — "Perhaps it [fins] also causes its [the fish's] kosher status, even though it independently does not cause its kosher status." These comments clearly suggest that the Ritva viewed fins and scales as the סיבה — the cause of the fish's kosher status — and not indicators of its kosher status.[8]

In truth, however, this discussion may not be relevant to the question of genetically modified salmon, for two reasons. First, the Maharit already noted that this conceptual question concerning the nature of the סימני טהרה seems to be answered by the aforementioned rule of היוצא מן הטהור טהור.[9] The very fact that a creature's status is determined by its mother's species, and not by its own physical properties, would seem to prove that the סימני טהרה do not create an animal's kosher status, but rather reflect the kosher status of its species. As such, we return to the aforementioned debate among the *Rishonim* as to whether the

---

7. See Rav Yeshaya Horowitz, *Shela, Amud Ha-Torah*.
8. This point was made by Rav Shmuel Baruch Deutsch in *Birkas Kohen, Parshas Shemini* (57). It is also cited by Rav Shlomo Zalman Auerbach (in the responsum cited above, n. 4) in the name of the *Mitzpeh Shmuel*. Rav Shlomo Zalman dismisses the relevance of this argument, however, writing, אין להסיק הלכה מזה, ובפרט שזה נעשה על ידי בני אדם ולא לסימנים כאלה נתכונה התורה — "We cannot establish the *halacha* on this basis, especially since this was done by human beings, and these are not the characteristics the Torah had in mind." In other words, even if we view fins and scales as the cause of a fish's kosher status, this is true only of fins and scales that appear naturally, and not through human manipulation, such as genetic engineering.
9. Cited above, n. 6. See also Rav Menachem Ziemba's *Zera Avraham* (13:14).

rule of היוצא מן הטהור טהור applies to creatures that reproduce by laying eggs. The discussion regarding the nature of the סימני טהרה is of no practical relevance, as this issue has been halachically resolved with regard to mammals and remains subject to debate in the context of fowl and fish, as we saw above.

Moreover, even if we view the סימני טהרה as indicators of kosher species, rather than as the reason for an animal's permissible status, we might still permit genetically modified salmon that feature fins and scales. The very fact that the scientists did not modify the fish to such an extent that it no longer has fins and scales demonstrates that the modified fish still belongs to a kosher species. The presence of fins and scales, even if it does not create the fish's kosher status, nevertheless indicates that this fish still belongs to the group of kosher fish, despite the introduction of a gene from a non-kosher species.

To illustrate this point, consider the example of a genetically modified kosher fish that no longer grows scales as a result of the modification. Undoubtedly, the absence of scales would render the fish forbidden, not because fins and scales are what make a fish kosher, but because the absence of scales testifies to the fact that the species has been altered and the new species is not a kosher species. By the same token, if a process of genetic modification did not eliminate the fins or scales, we may determine that the fish still belongs to a kosher species.

II. ביטול

Our entire discussion thus far has revolved around the question of whether or not we must take into account the non-kosher origins of genetically modified salmon, or whether we may deem the fish permissible due to its own physical properties, without looking at its genetic history. We will now turn our attention to the second question — namely, whether we may apply the rule of ביטול, and thus disregard the non-kosher gene. In other words, even if we must indeed take into account the fish's biological origins, and the presence of fins and scales thus does not suffice to render the fish permissible, may we nevertheless allow its consumption in light of the fact that the gene from the non-kosher species constitutes a minuscule percentage of the fish?[10]

This question is vitally important with respect to the status of genetically

---

10. It should be noted that if we permit genetically modified organisms solely on the basis of ביטול, then although the product is permissible for consumption, it would be forbidden for a Jew to perform the modification procedure for the purpose of preparing meat. The well-established rule of אין מבטלין איסור לכתחילה forbids adding a non-kosher substance into kosher foodstuff with the intention that it will be nullified and thus have no halachic effect on the food. Hence, if a kosher animal containing a non-kosher gene is deemed permissible solely on the basis of ביטול, then it would be forbidden for a Jew to knowingly

modified mammals. As noted above, the offspring of a non-kosher mammal is forbidden even if it has all the physical properties of a kosher animal. As such, if a gene is taken from a non-kosher mammal and implanted in the fertilized egg inside a kosher mammal, we might be compelled to forbid the offspring — unless we can apply the concept of ביטול, and thus ignore the offspring's non-kosher genetic origins.

מעורב בתחילתו

One argument against utilizing the concept of ביטול in this context is a significant restriction on the rule of ביטול imposed by the Mordechai (*Chullin* 737). The Mordechai asserts that ביטול does not apply in situations of מעורב בתחילתו — wherein the small portion of forbidden material was present from the inception of the item in question. If a food item contained a small forbidden component already at the time it came into existence, that component may not be ignored, even if it comprises a very small percentage of the food item. The law of ביטול, according to the Mordechai, applies only when two substances existed independently and were then mixed together. If one of the substances constitutes a small proportion (generally, one-sixtieth) of the mixture, then it is deemed "negated" and thus has no halachic impact upon the other food. If, however, a product from the outset consisted of two substances, they are both deemed halachically significant, regardless of their respective proportions. Thus, for example, the Mordechai rules that if a woman performing *chalitza* spits blood instead of saliva, the *chalitza*[11] is valid as long as even a minuscule amount of saliva is mixed with the blood. In such a case, we do not view the small portion of saliva as "negated" by the blood, since the liquid was produced in the woman's mouth from the outset with both fluids, and thus they are not subject to the provision of ביטול.

A number of *Acharonim*[12] drew proof to the Mordechai's position from the Gemara's discussion in *Maseches Chullin* (69a) concerning the law of בן פקועה — a living fetus removed from its mother's carcass after the mother was slaughtered. *Halacha* permits eating the fetus's meat without first slaughtering it, as it was covered by the slaughtering of the mother animal. However, if the mother had begun delivery before it was slaughtered, and part of the fetus — for

---

create such a situation. This point is made by Rav Yaakov Yisrael Fisher (*Even Yisrael* 8:55), as discussed by Rav Bleich in the article cited above, n. 1.

11. If a man dies without children, his widow must marry his brother, unless she performs the *chalitza* ritual, during which she spits in front of the brother.
12. Rav Moshe Katzenelenbogen, *Ohel Moshe* 22; and Rav Shimon Shkop, *Sha'arei Yosher* 3:26.

example, its leg — had exited the mother's body before slaughtering, that part of the fetus is forbidden for consumption.

The Gemara raises the question of whether one may eat an animal born from the union of two בני פקועה, one of which had a part of its body outside the womb before its mother was slaughtered. Does the forbidden portion of one of the two parents render the offspring forbidden? The Gemara concludes that the animal would be permissible, but not because we apply the concept of ביטול. Throughout its discussion of this case, the Gemara never proposes that the forbidden portion of one of the two parents should be negated by the majority and may thus be ignored. The reason, some *Acharonim* suggest, is that this animal came into existence as a "mixture" consisting of a small forbidden portion and a majority of permissible matter. Since the animal was מעורב בתחילתו — it consisted from the very outset of both permissible and forbidden portions — we cannot apply the rule of ביטול.

Returning to the case of a genetically modified organism, since the animal came into existence with a gene from a non-kosher source, it is seemingly not eligible for ביטול, and it should thus be forbidden.[13]

However, it seems likely that the Mordechai's qualification would not apply to this case. The *Noda Be-Yehuda* (*Mahadura Tinyana*, Y.D. 54), citing his son, asserts that the Mordechai established the exception of מעורב בתחילתו only with regard to certain forms of ביטול. A fundamental distinction exists between the application of ביטול in the context of מאכלות אסורות — the status of food products for consumption — and in other contexts. In other areas of *halacha*, the question that arises when two substances mix with one another is how to halachically define the mixture, given that it consists of two distinct components. The guiding principle in such situations, based upon the verse in *Sefer Shemos* (23:2), is אחרי רבים להטות — the mixture's identity is determined based upon the majority component. According to the *Noda Be-Yehuda*, it is with regard to these situations that the Mordechai establishes the rule of מעורב בתחילתו. Since the substance was made from the outset with both components, they are both

---

13. It should be noted, however, that even if we accept this line of reasoning, the prohibition might apply only on the level of דרבנן, a Rabbinic enactment. The *Minchas Kohen* (*Sefer Ha-Ta'arovos* 1:4) asserts that although the Torah prohibits eating even very small amounts of forbidden food, this does not apply to forbidden food mixed with permissible food. Even when ביטול does not occur and the mixture is forbidden, eating small quantities of the forbidden food would be prohibited only מדרבנן. (See *Peri Megadim*, *Sha'ar Ha-Ta'arovos* 2:2, who disputes this contention.) According to the *Minchas Kohen*, even if we cannot discount the gene taken from a non-kosher source, what's at stake is only a Rabbinic prohibition, giving us additional flexibility and grounds for relying on leniencies.

halachically significant and the minority component cannot be disregarded. Thus, for example, in the case of *chalitza*, where *halacha* requires the woman to expectorate saliva, the obligation is fulfilled as long as the substance that leaves her mouth includes even a small percentage of saliva.

When it comes to the consumption of food, however, ביטול operates much differently. The principle of טעם כעיקר establishes that a mixture containing forbidden food may not be eaten if it contains the taste of the forbidden food. The determining factor in such situations is not the formal identity of the mixture, but rather the presence or absence of the forbidden food's taste. Accordingly, the *Noda Be-Yehuda* contends, it makes no difference whether the product consisted from the outset of both components or if two separately preexisting entities mixed. Since the critical factor is the forbidden food's taste, the mixture cannot be prohibited if the forbidden food's taste cannot be discerned. As a practical matter, *halacha* generally presumes that a food's taste cannot be discerned when it constitutes a proportion of 1:60 or less. Thus, according to the *Noda Be-Yehuda*, even if a product consisted from the outset of a forbidden component, the product is permissible if the forbidden substance constitutes one-sixtieth or less of the entire product.

Quite obviously, a single gene constitutes far less than one-sixtieth of an organism, and the fish or animal should thus seemingly be permissible for consumption.

We might also add that our case might not even fall under the category of מעורב מתחילתו, since the gene from the non-kosher source is introduced to the egg and immediately "negated" by the majority at that point. Although the salmon emerges from the egg with this gene, that gene had already, halachically speaking, been "negated" the moment it was added to the egg. As such, the fish is entirely permissible.

עיקרו כך

One may, however, contend that ביטול cannot be applied in this case in light of a ruling of the Rashba in one of his responsa (3:214). The Rashba addresses a case in which a small amount of vinegar originating from non-Jewish wine was mixed with honey to produce medicine. This mixture is forbidden for consumption, the Rashba rules, despite the fact that the vinegar constitutes a small proportion of the mixture, because עיקרו כך — this is the ordinary way of making this product. Since the vinegar is supposed to be added to the honey, it cannot be considered "negated" by the honey, and the mixture is therefore forbidden.

We might argue, then, that once it becomes standard procedure to add a gene to modify a certain creature, this gene cannot be discounted, despite its constituting a minuscule proportion of the final product.

However, the *Noda Be-Yehuda* (*Mahadura Tinyana*, Y.D. 56) notes that many *Rishonim* do not accept the Rashba's position, and one may rely upon their lenient ruling. The *Noda Be-Yehuda* adds that even according to the Rashba, the mixture would be forbidden only מדרבנן — on the level of Rabbinic enactment, as opposed to Torah law — and thus there is certainly room to rely on the lenient position.[14]

דבר המעמיד

Another argument that one might advance to deny the possibility of ביטול in this case is the rule regarding דבר המעמיד — a stabilizing agent in a food product. If the stabilizer is forbidden for consumption, then the food containing the stabilizer is forbidden regardless of how small a proportion of the food the stabilizer comprises. The reason underlying this rule is that the stabilizer's presence is unmistakably discernible, as it lends the food its texture. Since its effects are clear and evident, it cannot be ignored, even if it constitutes a minuscule portion of the product.

At first glance, this principle should be applied to a foreign gene added for the purpose of accelerating growth. Although the forbidden gene comprises an infinitesimally small proportion of the organism, nevertheless, its effects are discernible in the creature's rapid growth. One might argue, then, that we cannot disregard the forbidden gene in light of its evident impact on the creature.

However, there is an important exception to the rule of דבר המעמיד that undermines this argument. The *Shulchan Aruch* (Y.D. 87:11) permits eating a food product with a non-kosher stabilizer (that comprises less than one-sixtieth of the product) if the product also contains another stabilizer that is permissible for consumption. The special stringency of דבר המעמיד applies only if the non-kosher stabilizer is the product's sole stabilizing agent. Accordingly, a non-kosher gene added to an organism should not render the organism forbidden, as it is not the only substance that causes the creature to grow. The gene combines with other material in the organism — which is, of course, entirely permissible — to advance its growth, and it is thus subject to the law of ביטול.

This argument, however, would not be valid if the genetic modification discernibly enhances the flavor of the meat. If, for example, manufacturers begin introducing the gene of pig into livestock to enhance the beef's flavor, it would be difficult to apply the rule of ביטול to permit the beef. Since the minute portion

---

14. For more on the *Noda Be-Yehuda*'s discussion, see Rav Yitzchak Weiss, *Minchas Yitzchak* (2:28:10).

of forbidden substance is clearly discernible, it cannot be overlooked, and thus the product would perhaps be forbidden.

Orla and the Grafted Branch

There may in fact be a compelling halachic precedent for applying ביטול to our situation and viewing the implanted gene as assuming the identity of the host organism.

The Gemara in *Maseches Sota* (43b) addresses the case of a branch taken from a tree within the first three years after its planting — whose fruit is forbidden due to the prohibition of *orla* — and grafted onto an older tree. The Gemara rules that all the fruit produced by the tree, including by the grafted branch, is permissible for consumption, because the grafted branch loses its identity and assumes the identity of the host tree. Even though the grafted branch likely affects certain biological properties of the host tree, nevertheless, since it has become part of the host tree, it loses its identity and is regarded as a branch of an older tree, which is not subject to the prohibition of *orla*.

Rav Sternbuch, in his aforementioned responsum, suggests drawing an analogy between this case and the situation of a genetically modified organism. In the case of the modified organism, a small portion of one species is implanted within another. Thus, just as the *orla* branch loses its original identity and the fruit it subsequently produces is not regarded as *orla*, similarly, a gene introduced into the egg of a different species should lose its identity and assume the identity of the host species. This analogy might prove that the concept of ביטול is applicable in the case of genetically modified organism, despite the effects of the implanted gene on the host organism.

חצי שיעור

In truth, even if we would conclude that the non-kosher gene cannot be negated through the concept of ביטול, we would still have good reason to permit the consumption of the genetically modified creature, due to a theory postulated by the *Noda Be-Yehuda* elsewhere in his writings concerning the prohibition of חצי שיעור — eating small quantities of forbidden food.

Although *beis din* would not administer corporal punishment to violators guilty of eating small quantities of forbidden food (generally, less than a *kezayis*), nevertheless, *halacha* forbids eating any amount. However, the *Tzelach* (written by the author of *Noda Be-Yehuda*), in *Maseches Pesachim* (44a ד"ה ועוד נלע"ד), makes an exception to this rule. He notes that the reason given for the law of חצי שיעור is the fact that it is חזי לאיצטרופי — the consumption of a small quantity of forbidden food could combine with food eaten subsequently to reach the amount which renders one liable to *malkos* (lashes). In other words, the consumption of small quantities is forbidden only because a small quantity could eventually combine with additional food to comprise the minimum amount that warrants *malkos*. Accordingly, the *Tzelach* contends, in a case in which there is no possibility of reaching the minimum quantity prohibited by the Torah, חצי שיעור is permitted.

The case he discusses is one who wishes to eat a small morsel of *chametz* in the final moments of Pesach. Since *chametz* will become permissible by the time one would be able to eat a *ke-zayis* of *chametz*, there should, in theory, be no reason to forbid the consumption of a small bit of *chametz* at this point. For this reason, the *Tzelach* contends, the Rambam (*Hilchos Chametz U-Matza* 1:7) cites a Biblical source for the prohibition of eating small amounts of *chametz*.[15] If this were forbidden solely because of חצי שיעור, then it would be permissible to eat a small portion of *chametz* in the final moments of Pesach. The Rambam therefore resorted to a Biblical source to establish that eating small amounts of *chametz* is intrinsically forbidden, and not merely due to the possibility of subsequently reaching the amount of a *ke-zayis*.

This theory of the *Tzelach* should conceivably apply also to situations of a food product containing a minuscule portion of forbidden food that is not, for whatever reason, subject to ביטול. *Beis din* can punish a sinner for eating forbidden food only if the violator partakes of a כזית בכדי אכילת פרס — a *ke-zayis* of forbidden food within the time-frame of אכילת פרס, which is commonly identified as anywhere from 4–9 minutes. According to the *Tzelach*, it would seem, in a case in which there is no theoretical possibility of consuming a *ke-zayis* of forbidden food within this time frame, such as if the forbidden substance constitutes a fractional portion of the food one eats, the food should be permissible.

This is certainly the case with regard to a kosher animal containing a single non-kosher gene. The amount of non-kosher substance in this animal's meat constitutes an infinitesimally small proportion of the meat. As such, even if ביטול cannot take effect, the meat should be permissible because one could not possibly partake of a *ke-zayis* of forbidden foodstuff within the period of אכילת פרס.

Conclusion

When it comes to fowl and fish, the status of a genetically modified organism that has kosher properties but contains a gene from a non-kosher species is subject to debate among the *Rishonim*. Mammals, according to all opinions,

---

15. לא יאכל חמץ (*Shemos* 13:3).

are forbidden if they were produced by non-kosher animals, regardless of their own physical characteristics.

Nevertheless, it seems likely that we may apply the rule of ביטול and thus overlook the forbidden element within a genetically modified kosher fish or animal. Even if ביטול does not apply in such a case, the forbidden gene constitutes such a small portion of the organism that there is no possibility of consuming a *ke-zayis* of the creature's forbidden substance within the period of אכילת פרס, and thus the fish or animal is permissible (according to the position of the *Tzelach*).

The New York Times

Whiskey Makers Court Jewish Market

June 4, 2013
Robert Simonson

For avid whiskey lovers, few events are more eagerly anticipated than WhiskyFest, an enormous tasting that touches down in several American cities throughout the year. But when sponsors of the New York festival suddenly moved it last year from Tuesday to Friday and Saturday, many regulars were unable to attend.

An alternative arrived suddenly in the form of a new one-night event, held on the eve of WhiskyFest. Despite little time to advertise, it drew a crowd of 250 to its unlikely Manhattan location: the West Side Institutional Synagogue.

These whiskey devotees, it turned out, were Jews shut out of the big event because they observe the Sabbath. And to drive home the point of the tasting, its founder, the fledgling Jewish Whisky Company, called it Whisky Jewbilee.

Whiskey has numerous fan bases, but few are more devoted — and arguably less noticed by the press and public — than Jews, particularly observant Jews. Synagogues are increasingly organizing events around whiskey, and whiskey makers are reaching out to the Jewish market.

Retailers have long recognized Jews as valuable customers. "Jewish men are very interested in the selection of whiskey available at a wedding or bar/bat mitzvah," said Jonathan Goldstein, vice president of Park Avenue Liquor Shop, a Manhattan

Some of the growing number of kosher whiskeys on the market, for sale at Park Avenue Liquor Shop in Manhattan. Credit: Ruth Fremson/The New York Times

store known for its whiskey selection. "They very often will pick up a special bottle to offer close friends or relatives." Of the Friday before the Jewish holiday of Purim, last February, he said, "It was like Christmas in here."

Part of the spirit's appeal to many Orthodox Jews is that most whiskey is naturally kosher. In contrast, wine, owing to its long connection to Jewish tradition, must satisfy many regulations to earn a hechsher, the symbol of kosher certification.

But that hasn't stopped prominent Scotch producers like Glenrothes, Glenmorangie, Ardbeg, Bowmore and Auchentoshan from courting the Jewish consumer by obtaining official kosher certification for certain bottlings.

Bourbon producers have even less to worry about, because by federal law their spirits must be aged in new casks, rather than in the sherry, port or wine barrels that some whiskey distillers use, and that give some kosher drinkers pause because of their exposure to wine. Yet the Buffalo Trace Distillery in Kentucky recently enlisted the help of the Chicago Rabbinical Council in laying down more than 1,000 barrels of three styles of whiskey, all certified kosher and set for release in five or six months.

In a smaller-scale but similar enterprise, the Royal Wine Corporation, a New York producer of kosher wine and grape juice, asked Wesley Henderson two years ago if he would be interested in making a kosher-certified version of his boutique bourbon, Angel's Envy. "We were looking for a bourbon line in general," said Shlomo S. Blashka, a wine and spirits educator at Royal, also the New York-area distributor of Angel's Envy. "The Jewish community is a very big bourbon community."

Mr. Henderson did not have to be told. "You'd have to be blind not to notice it," he said. "I thought, if you had a kosher bourbon, that would be a great thing. It seemed a no-brainer."

For the new whiskey, Angel's Envy was aged for six months in barrels that had held Kedem kosher port for 20 years. The run sold quickly, Mr. Henderson said, and may become a permanent addition to the bourbon maker's line.

In 2011, Jason Johnstone-Yellin and two partners founded the Jewish Whisky Company, which has bottled barrels from six Scotch distillers. "We had the opportunity to purchase casks, where not everybody would have that opportunity," said Mr. Johnstone-Yellin, who was born in Scotland and whose American wife is Jewish.

Single Cask Nation is produced by the Jewish Whisky Company. Credit: Jason Johnstone-Yellin

During a recent trip to the Victoria Whisky Festival in British Columbia, he said, he buttonholed a representative of a well-known international whiskey distillery and asked if it would let the Jewish Whisky Company bottle one of its casks. "The response was: 'We're very protective of our brand. We don't do that,'" said Joshua

Hatton, another partner in the business, who also founded a popular blog, Jewish Single Malt Whisky Society — now renamed Jewmalt.

Mr. Johnstone-Yellin, not giving up, gave the man his card and pointed to the word "Jewish." "This is our market," he said. "These are our customers and members."

The man paused, he said, then agreed to talk to them.

The bond with whiskey goes way back. Mr. Blashka said early Jewish immigrants to America, unable to trust the provenance of local wines, turned to certain distilled liquors, including whiskey. "Because the wine was an issue, typically spirits was their avenue for drinking," he said.

As recent decades have ushered in a revival in Scotch, bourbon and other whiskeys, Jews, like many other groups, have moved beyond the usual blends and have developed more sophisticated tastes. "Now we have many whiskeys that we know are kosher," said Rabbi Aaron Raskin of Congregation B'nai Avraham in Brooklyn Heights, whose preferred whiskey is the smoky Laphroaig, a single malt from Islay. "It is used to add to our joy."

"And it helps attendance at synagogues," he added.

Whiskey-centered events at temples are a lot more common than they used to be, said Joshua London, a lobbyist for the Zionist Organization of America who regularly writes about whiskey for Jewish publications.

...The extent of a congregation's, or congregant's, embrace of whiskey can vary. "It all depends on what rabbi you hold by," Rabbi Arian said. Some are content with whiskeys that are kosher by nature; others like the extra insurance of a hechsher. Aging or finishing in wine barrels will disqualify a bottle for one drinker, while another isn't troubled by the distinction.

For years, there was no greater yardstick of Jewish interest in whiskey than New York's WhiskyFest, sponsored by Whisky Advocate magazine.

"If you went years ago, you'd see that close to 50 percent of the people attending were wearing kippot," Mr. Blashka said, referring to skullcaps. When WhiskyFest became a two-day event in 2012, held during the Sabbath, many Jews who wanted to attend were not pleased. "I wish I could tell you the sheer number of e-mails I received from my readers, distributors, importers, distillers," Mr. Hatton said.

He said an importer and a distributor entreated him to assemble a pop-up festival for the disenfranchised customers and many producers in town for WhiskyFest.

Whisky Jewbilee will return this fall, at a larger site, and a second date in Westchester County will be added. "There were a couple distillers that we didn't reach out to" last fall, Mr. Johnstone-Yellin said. "They said, 'You will have us be part, won't you?' They're smart people. They know who's not going to be standing at their table on Friday and Saturday night."

Copyright © nytimes.com

Is Sherry Cask Whiskey Kosher?

Made from just barley, water, and yeast (and sometimes caramel coloring), whiskey[1] has generally been presumed free of *kashrus* concerns. In fact, it is claimed that the Jews' well-known affinity for whiskey originates with the early Jewish immigrants to America, who turned to whiskey for alcoholic drinking due to the unavailability of kosher wine.[2]

However, already in 1949, Rabbi Pinchas Teitz of Elizabeth observed that some blended whiskeys contained a small percentage of wine, which is forbidden due to the law of סתם יינם, which prohibits drinking the wine of non-Jews. Rabbi Teitz's inquiries determined that the maximum percentage of wine found in blended whiskeys was 2.5%. This meant that in some brands, the wine content comprised more than 1/60th (1.67%) of the product. Since ביטול — halachic "nullification" of a minority portion of a mixture — generally requires a proportion of 60:1 against the minority portion, it would seem that these brands were forbidden due to the wine content. Rabbi Teitz posed this question to Rav Moshe Feinstein, who devoted three responsa to the subject, which were published in his *Iggeros Moshe* (Y.D. 1:62–64).

For reasons that will be discussed below, Rav Moshe concluded that ביטול for non-kosher wine requires only a proportion of 6:1, not 60:1. As such, he ruled that blended whiskeys were permissible despite the 2.5% wine content. Rav Moshe did, however, qualify his ruling by stating that a בעל נפש — one who wishes to be especially scrupulous to satisfy all halachic opinions — should avoid blended whiskeys, as their permissibility hinges on a number of halachic debates.

Notwithstanding this significant qualification, many Jews have generally assumed that whiskey is permissible and may be consumed without any concern, in light of Rav Moshe's lenient ruling.

More recently, however, some kashrus professionals have questioned the

---

1. Formally, whiskey produced in Scotland is spelled "whisky," without an e, whereas the spelling "whiskey" is used in reference to other whiskeys. For the sake of simplicity, we will use the spelling "whiskey" generically, to refer to all brands.
2. See media article above.

status of sherry cask scotch, a type of whiskey that is aged[3] or finished[4] in oak casks that had previously stored sherry wine.[5]

The practice of aging whiskey in sherry casks actually began by accident. Spanish wine exporters would deliver barrels of sherry wine to England, and after the wine was bottled, Scottish whiskey companies would purchase the empty casks at a discounted price to use for aging their beverages. It was later discovered that the sherry flavor in the barrels enhanced the flavor of the whiskey, so the use of sherry casks for whiskey continued even after Spanish winemakers started bottling their wine before exporting it.

From a halachic standpoint, storing an otherwise kosher beverage in a utensil that had previously contained non-kosher wine generally renders the beverage forbidden for consumption, due to the non-kosher wine absorbed in the walls of the utensil, which is then absorbed by the beverage. The *Shulchan Aruch* (Y.D. 135) discusses at length the procedures required to permit the use of a utensil that had contained non-kosher wine, and quite obviously, these procedures are not followed by whiskey distilleries.[6] Hence, the use of sherry casks for aging whiskey would seem to make the whiskey forbidden due to the flavor of forbidden wine that it absorbs.

This issue was the subject of an impressive, thorough treatise prepared by Rabbi Akiva Niehaus of the Chicago Community Kollel, which published the monograph in 2012.[7] Based on extensive research into the process of producing scotch whiskey and of the relevant halachic sources, Rabbi Niehaus concluded that 100% sherry cask scotch — meaning, a bottle whose entire content had been aged in sherry casks — should be avoided, whereas whiskeys that contain only a portion of sherry cask scotch — such as most blended whiskeys — are permissible. He added that in light of the aforementioned ruling of Rav Moshe Feinstein regarding blended whiskeys, it would be appropriate for a בעל נפש to avoid most types of sherry cask scotch.

---

3. Whiskey undergoes aging, or "maturation," after distillation for at least three years, and usually for eight years or more.
4. "Sherry finish" whiskey is whiskey that was transferred to sherry casks for the final period — usually six months to two years — of the maturation process.
5. "Sherry wine" refers to wine produced from white grapes grown in the area of Jerez de la Frontera in Spain's Andalusia region.
6. It should be noted that according to the *Shach* (Y.D. 135:33), if non-kosher wine had been contained for twenty-four hours or more, then the utensil requires *hagala* (immersion in boiling hot water), which distilleries certainly do not do to their casks.
7. "Sherry Casks: A Halachic Perspective," available online at http://www.rccvaad.org/documents/SherryCasks.pdf.

In the pages that follow, we will briefly review Rabbi Niehaus' analysis and suggest that a different conclusion may be reached.

I. The Halachic Effects of a Sherry Cask

נותן טעם לפגם

The *Shulchan Aruch* (Y.D. 137:4) rules that wine placed in utensils that had previously contained non-kosher wine is forbidden for consumption; but other beverages stored in such utensils are permissible. As long as the barrel had been completely emptied and dried, it may be used for beverages such as water and beer. The *Tur* (cited by the *Taz*, 7) explains that the wine absorbed in the container has an adverse effect upon the beverage, and as such, its taste is not considered forbidden. The law of טעם כעיקר, which forbids consuming foodstuff that contains the flavor of non-kosher food, does not apply to a taste that negatively affects the mixture, a rule known as נותן טעם לפגם. Hence, since the wine absorbed in a utensil negatively affects the taste of the water or beer now stored in it, the taste of the wine is of no halachic consequence, and the beverage is permissible for consumption. This is in contrast to wine stored in such containers, whose taste is enhanced by the flavor of the wine absorbed in the walls of the container, and thus is forbidden.

Rabbi Niehaus cites several halachic authorities who rule that whiskey is an exception to this rule.[8] Absorbed wine enhances the flavor of whiskey, and thus cannot be disregarded on the grounds of נותן טעם לפגם. Rabbi Niehaus also notes seemingly contradictory statements of the *Noda Be-Yehuda* (*Mahadura Tinyana*, Y.D. 58, 67) in this regard. In any event, as Rabbi Niehaus concludes, it seems clear that if the manufacturer specifically stores the product in sherry casks in order to incorporate the taste of sherry in the beverage, this taste cannot possibly fall under the category of נותן טעם לפגם. Therefore, at least in principle, this taste can render the whiskey forbidden.

Additionally, while taste that is absorbed in walls of a utensil is generally considered stale (פגום) and thus negligible after twenty-four hours, the Rama (Y.D. 137:1) writes explicitly that this rule does not apply to wine, which improves with time.[9] Therefore, the wine absorbed by the cask should seemingly render the whiskey forbidden for consumption.

Rabbi Niehaus notes in this context the argument advanced by Rav Shlomo Miller suggesting that sherry may actually ruin the taste of the whiskey, but the

---

8. *Magen Avraham*, O.C. 451:40; *Chayei Adam* 125:15; *Maharsham* 3:150.
9. After twelve months, however, the absorbed wine may be disregarded, as we will discuss below.

distillers nevertheless use sherry casks for the benefit of the fragrance provided by the absorbed sherry:

> In a conversation with Harav Shlomo Miller *shlita*, he suggested that it is quite possible that the flavor contributed by the wine does indeed ruin (*pogem*) Scotch (just like wine ruins beer, as indicated by the Gemara's allowance to store beer in a non-kosher wine barrel). Nevertheless, it is possible that Scotch distillers specifically use wine barrels to allow the Scotch to absorb the wine's *fragrance*, and according to *halacha*, fragrance added by a non-kosher ingredient is insignificant (*reicha lav milsa* — Shach 108:14). Accordingly, the non-kosher wine *blios* [absorption] would not require nullification.[10]

Rabbi Niehaus rightly questions this contention, proceeding to extensively document experts who have written about the sherry's enhancement of the taste of whiskey.[11] He then adds that Rav Miller refuted the significance of the experts' claims with an astonishing assertion:

> Rav Miller countered in a follow-up letter that even taste stems from fragrance; this is proved by the fact that someone with a cold and is unable to smell has difficulty tasting food. Accordingly, the experts are merely experiencing the fragrance, which is negligible in *halacha*.

This attempt to distinguish between "real" taste and taste that is in truth a function of fragrance is nothing short of bizarre. If experts in the field determine empirically that the sherry impacts the taste of the whiskey, we cannot possibly ignore their claims based on a far-fetched, unsubstantiated theory.

ביטול

The question then becomes whether we may apply to sherry cask scotch the rule of ביטול, which allows us to disregard a small amount of forbidden substance mixed with a much larger quantity of permissible foodstuff. If the forbidden portion constitutes a small enough percentage of the mixture, then we view it as "negated" by the majority, and hence halachically irrelevant. In the case of sherry cask whiskey, we need to ask what percentage is needed for a small portion of sherry wine to be negated by the whiskey, and whether we may presume that this ratio is indeed present in contemporary whiskeys.

---

10. "Sherry Casks," n. 19.
11. Ibid., n. 20.

Generally speaking, the taste of a forbidden food is considered "negated" if it comprises one-sixtieth or less of the mixture. The *Rishonim* debate the question of whether this applies to forbidden wine as well. The Ramban and Ritva, in their respective commentaries to *Maseches Avoda Zara* (73b), maintain that *halacha* draws no difference in this regard between forbidden wine and other prohibited foods. Thus, forbidden wine must comprise one-sixtieth or less of a mixture in order for the mixture to be permissible. However, the Ra'avad and the Ri (cited by the *Tur*, Y.D. 134) claim that the rules of ביטול apply more leniently in the context of forbidden wine, and the wine is considered negated as long as it comprises no more than one-sixth of the mixture. The *Shulchan Aruch* (Y.D. 134:5) follows the lenient position, and this is indeed the accepted *halacha* (as noted by the *Shach*, 123:16).

The conventional explanation of this distinction is that wine cannot be formally considered "wine" when it is diluted to such an extent.[12] Whereas other forbidden foods may not be consumed as long as their taste can be discerned, forbidden wine becomes permissible once it loses the formal halachic status of "wine." When wine mixes with a quantity of water six or more times the wine's quantity, we do not view the mixture as water with a taste of wine. Rather, the wine loses its identity altogether, and thus the mixture is entirely permissible. Hence, even though one can taste the wine when he drinks the water, the water is nevertheless permissible for consumption.[13]

However, the applicability of this principle to whiskey hinges on a debate among the *Rishonim* concerning its scope. The Rama (Y.D. 114:4) writes that one may not buy a beverage that normally has wine added from gentiles, unless he can ascertain that the wine comprises one-sixtieth or less of the beverage. Curiously, the Rama here requires a ratio of 60:1 to overwhelm the non-kosher wine, and not 6:1. The *Shach* (in *Nekudos Ha-Kesef*, commenting on the *Taz* 114:4) explains that the Rama distinguishes in this regard between water and other beverages. It is only when wine mixes with water that a 6:1 ratio suffices to "negate" the wine. If, however, wine mixes with other beverages, then a proportion of 60:1 is needed for ביטול to apply. This is indeed the position of the *Issur Ve-Heter*, cited by the *Shach* elsewhere (134:21).

The *Taz* (114:4) rejects this distinction and rules that even when non-kosher wine mixes with beverages other than water, the mixture is permissible if the

---

12. See Rashba to *Avoda Zara* 73b and in *Toras Ha-Bayis* 5:6. Rav Moshe Feinstein elaborates on this point in *Iggeros Moshe*, Y.D. 1:62, ד"ה והנה.
13. Rav Moshe Feinstein (Y.D. 1:63) writes that for this reason, ביטול would apply even if the producers of the beverage introduce the small amount of wine specifically to contribute its flavor to the beverage, as is the case with sherry cask scotch.

wine comprises a portion of one-sixth or less. This is the view accepted by several *poskim* as well, including the *Peri Chadash* (114:10), *Chochmas Adam* (66:15), and *Magen Avraham* (204:16). More recently, Rav Yitzchak Weiss follows this view in *Minchas Yitzchak* (2:28:4), as does Rav Moshe Feinstein in *Iggeros Moshe* (Y.D. 1:62). Both Rav Weiss and Rav Feinstein propose that the *Shach* might concede that in the case of strong alcoholic beverages, wine is considered "negated" in a proportion of 6:1.

The consensus among the *poskim*, then, permits drinking a beverage with a small portion of non-kosher wine added, even if the wine's taste can be discerned, provided that the wine comprises no more than one-sixth of the beverage.

There is, however, a separate controversy that affects the manner in which the proportion is determined in the case of a barrel that had previously contained non-kosher wine. The *Shulchan Aruch* (Y.D. 135:13) rules that when a utensil stores non-kosher wine, wine is absorbed only in the surface layer of the utensil's wall (כדי קליפה); it does not extend throughout the entire thickness of the wall. As such, the *Shulchan Aruch* writes, if one chisels the wall to remove its surface layer, the container may then immediately be used for kosher wine. Since the wall does not absorb wine beyond the first layer, the container can be "*kashered*" through the removal of that first layer.

This ruling bears vital importance for the question surrounding sherry cask scotch, as it drastically increases the likelihood that the non-kosher wine absorbed in the barrel is "negated" by the whiskey. If wine is absorbed only in the surface of the barrel's interior, and not throughout the entire thickness of the wall, then this wine constitutes a minuscule quantity, which can be presumed to amount to less than one-sixth of the volume of whiskey in the barrel.

This conclusion, however, is subject to debate. The *Shach* (135:33) asserts that the *Shulchan Aruch* refers here only to situations of uncertainty, when it has not been verified that the utensil had stored wine for a period of twenty-four hours. In such a case, the *Shulchan Aruch* allows removing the surface layer as a means of "*kashering*" the utensil. If, however, the utensil had definitely contained non-kosher wine for a period of twenty-four hours, then the wine is absorbed throughout the entire thickness of the wall, and removing the surface layer would not suffice. Many halachic authorities, including the *Chochmas Adam* (81:11), *Kitzur Shulchan Aruch* (48:17), and *Imrei Eish* (Y.D. 44), concur with this stringent ruling of the *Shach*.

According to this view, the whiskey in the sherry cask must constitute six times the volume of the entire width of the wood of the barrel, and not merely six times the area of the surface layer.

Others dispute the *Shach*'s ruling and maintain that non-kosher wine stored in a barrel is absorbed only in the surface layer. These include the *Chacham Tzvi*

(75), *Machaneh Efrayim* (*Hilchos Ma'achalos Asuros* 11:15), *Chazon Ish* (55:6), *Chikrei Lev* (77), and *Yad Yehuda* (*Hilchos Melicha* 69:64). This lenient ruling would make it all but certain that sherry casks do not contain enough absorbed non-kosher wine to have a halachic effect on the whiskey. As Rabbi Niehaus observes (p. 43, note 59), several *poskim* establish that the volume of liquid in a container even constitutes more than sixty times the amount contained in the surface layer.[14]

However, Rabbi Niehaus cites the view of two contemporary *poskim* — Rav Moshe Heinemann and Rav Shlomo Miller — that it is proper to follow the stringent ruling of the *Shach*. Rav Heinemann asserts that conventional practice follows the *Shach*'s position, and Rav Miller posits that although, strictly speaking, the *halacha* follows the lenient view, it is preferable to assume that the wine is absorbed throughout the thickness of the wall.[15]

Rabbi Niehaus proceeds to present the results of measurements conducted with a barrel calculator of a barrel that had stored sherry wine, which was obtained from a Spanish barrel supplier. The calculator measured the barrel's internal dimensions (511.5 liters) and external dimensions (647.4 liters); the difference between them, 135.9 liters, amounts to 26.6% of the interior volume. This means that the volume of the walls of the barrel constitutes over one-quarter of the volume of the whiskey stored in the barrel, significantly exceeding the 1:6 proportion needed for ביטול.

Accordingly, Rabbi Niehaus concludes that 100% sherry whiskey, which has been stored entirely in sherry casks, should be avoided, as the small amount of wine in the beverage renders the product forbidden. Whiskeys that contain only a portion of sherry cask scotch — such as combinations of sherry cask and bourbon cask whiskey — may be drunk, as the wine absorbed from the sherry cask may be presumed to be "negated" by the rest of the beverage.

Rabbi Niehaus then notes Rav Moshe Feinstein's ruling that a בעל נפש should follow the stringent ruling of the *Shach* that ביטול for forbidden wine requires a proportion of 60:1 against the forbidden wine. Rav Moshe also maintained that a בעל נפש should avoid beverages containing even a slight proportion of non-kosher wine due to the ruling of the Rashba, in one of his responsa (3:214), that if wine is normally added to a beverage, it is not subject to ביטול in that beverage, regardless of its minuscule proportion. As such, according to Rav Moshe, those who seek to be especially scrupulous should avoid all sherry scotch.

---

14. *Shach* 69:65; *Binas Adam, Sha'ar Issur Ve-Heter* 43.
15. However, in footnote 61, Rabbi Niehaus cites these two *poskim* as permitting sherry scotch for other reasons, and he disputes their arguments.

II. Grounds for Leniency

It would seem, however, that a more lenient position can be formulated in light of the fact that the prohibition of סתם יינם — wine produced or owned by non-Jews — was enacted by the Sages, and does not constitute a Torah prohibition. When dealing with איסורים דרבנן — prohibitions enacted by *Chazal* — there is far greater room for leniency when halachic uncertainties arise. The famous rule of ספק דרבנן לקולא allows assuming the lenient possibility in situations of halachic doubt, and in the case of sherry whiskey, as we will now proceed to demonstrate, several such doubts arise, which, in the view of this author, suffice to permit its consumption.

1. כדי קליפה

One uncertainty has already been mentioned — namely, the question regarding the amount of non-kosher wine that can be assumed to have been absorbed by the cask. As we saw, several leading *poskim*, including the *Chacham Tzvi* and the *Chazon Ish*, rule against the *Shach*'s position that non-kosher wine is absorbed throughout the entire thickness of the container's walls. According to these authorities, the sherry absorbed by the whiskey is certainly "negated" by the whiskey, and thus has no halachic effect. While it may be true that the *Shach*'s stringency is generally accepted as the *halacha*, the opposing view can certainly be taken into account and combined with other uncertainties to establish grounds for leniency.

2. Subsequent Fills

The *Shulchan Aruch* (Y.D. 135:16) rules that once twelve months have passed from the time a container was emptied of its non-kosher wine, the barrel may then be used for kosher wine. After twelve months, any absorbed taste of the wine is presumed stale, and hence halachically negligible. The *Shulchan Aruch* adds that this applies even if the barrel was filled with water in the interim. In other words, the barrel does not have to remain unused for twelve months for it to become suitable for use with wine; as long as twelve months have passed since the non-kosher wine was removed, it may now be used, even if it had contained water in the interim.

Applying this *halacha* to sherry cask whiskey, we may arrive at yet another basis for leniency. Even if the "first fill" — the first whiskey stored in a barrel after the sherry wine had been removed — is forbidden for consumption, subsequent fills are seemingly permissible. Since whiskey is aged for several years, the sherry cask is permissible after the first fill, as more than twelve months have passed since the wine was removed. As noted, the presence of a different beverage in the utensil does not interfere with this twelve-month "kashering" process, and thus although the cask contains whiskey within twelve months of the wine's removal, the absorbed taste of the wine nevertheless becomes insignificant after twelve months.

The potential flaw in this argument relates to the fact that since the first fill becomes forbidden by the wine it absorbs from the walls of the barrel, it should then render the barrel forbidden anew. Since the entire vat of whiskey is forbidden for consumption and the walls of the barrel absorb this whiskey, the clock is restarted, so-to-speak, and we view the barrel as freshly absorbing forbidden wine throughout the period in which it contains the whiskey.

The basis for this claim is the halachic concept of חתיכה נעשית נבילה, often referred to by the acronym חנ״נ, which establishes that a piece of permissible food that absorbs the taste of forbidden food must be treated as entirely forbidden. If the proportion of permissible food to forbidden food is not large enough for ביטול to occur, then we must treat the entire piece of food as a נבילה — a piece of forbidden meat. As such, if that newly forbidden piece of meat mixes with permissible food, the mixture is forbidden unless the permissible food constitutes sixty times the volume of the entire forbidden piece that had mixed in. Even though that piece is forbidden only by virtue of a small portion of forbidden food that it contains, nevertheless, we must treat the piece as entirely forbidden, such that it forbids permissible food with which it mixes.

Applying this principle to whiskey in sherry casks, if we assume that the whiskey absorbs an amount of wine exceeding one-sixth of the total volume of the beverage, then all the whiskey in the cask must be treated as forbidden wine. As such, the cask absorbs forbidden wine anew over the course of the aging process, and thus even subsequent fills should be forbidden.

This conclusion, however, hinges on a number of debates among the *poskim*. First, the *Shulchan Aruch* (Y.D. 92:4) rules explicitly that the principle of חתיכה נעשית נבילה applies only in the very specific context of בשר בחלב — when meat mixes with milk. When it comes to all other areas of *halacha*, we do not treat the mixture as comprised entirely of forbidden foodstuff. According to this view, the first fill of whiskey, even if it is forbidden for consumption, does not have to be treated as forbidden wine that would then render the cask forbidden anew. Although the Rama disputes this ruling and maintains that חתיכה נעשית נבילה applies to all forbidden foods, the *Shach* (92:12) cites earlier *poskim* who assert that this applies only on the level of מדרבנן. As such, and particularly in light of the fact that the prohibition against drinking non-Jewish wine to begin with applies only מדרבנן, we certainly have room for leniency given the other uncertainties entailed.

Moreover, the Rama also cites an opinion that חתיכה נעשית נבילה applies only to a solid piece of food that absorbs a forbidden substance, but not when a permissible liquid is mixed with a forbidden liquid — such as in the case of whiskey and sherry wine. The Rama concludes that one may rely on this view (with respect to prohibitions other than בשר בחלב) when this is necessary to avoid a substantial financial loss (לצורך הפסד גדול), but not in other situations. The *Taz* (92:15), however, infers from the comments of the Maharshal (*Yam Shel Shlomo*, *Chullin*, 60) that one may rely on this opinion even when no financial loss is at stake.[16]

Another consideration is the ruling of the *Peri Chadash* (Y.D. 92:17), which he infers from the Rambam (*Hilchos Ma'achalos Asuros* 15:26–27), that the rule of חתיכה נעשית נבילה does not apply to any Rabbinic prohibitions. Since the prohibition of סתם יינם applies only on the level of Rabbinic enactment, the *Peri Chadash* would undoubtedly permit subsequent fills of sherry whiskey, as even if the first fill is forbidden for consumption, it does not then render the cask forbidden anew. The *Aruch Ha-Shulchan* (Y.D. 92:25) rules in accordance with this position of the *Peri Chadash*. Although others, including the *Peri Megadim* (*Mishbetzos Zahav*, Y.D. 92:11), reject this opinion, we may certainly take this view into account as yet another factor to consider.

This is true as well of a different ruling of the *Peri Chadash* (ibid.) limiting the rule of חתיכה נעשית נבילה to items that absorbed forbidden foodstuff specifically through the process of cooking. If a forbidden food was absorbed through the process of כבוש — soaking for a period of twenty-four hours or longer — then although it may not be eaten, it is not, according to the *Peri Chadash*, subject to the provision of חתיכה נעשית נבילה. The entire concern of sherry whiskey arises due to the concept of כבוש, and thus for this reason, too, the *Peri Chadash* would not apply the rule of חתיכה נעשית נבילה in the context of whiskey aged in sherry casks. As in regard to the earlier debate, many *poskim* disagree with the *Peri Chadash*.[17] Nevertheless, in light of all we have seen, there is clearly room to permit the consumption of sherry whiskey beyond the first fill, even if we concede that the first fill is forbidden. Hence, since any given bottle of whiskey may have been produced from a second or later fill, we may permit the bottle on the grounds of ספק דרבנן להקל.[18]

---

16. The exception, as the *Taz* notes, is when the two liquids were mixed דרך בישול — meaning, they were cooked together from the outset — which is clearly not relevant to our discussion.
17. See *Darchei Teshuva*, Y.D. 105:17.
18. The *Sedei Chemed* (vol. 7, Ma'areches Chametz U-Matza, 8:15) writes that according to the opinion that gentile wine is not subject to ביטול, a container that had been used for gentile wine does not become "kashered" after twelve months if it contained another

3. The Duration of the Shipping Process

We can also add to the equation the real possibility that any given barrel was filled with whiskey only twelve months or longer after the wine was removed. These barrels are shipped to Scotland from Spain after the sherry wine is removed from them, and we have no way of determining how much time passes from the moment they are emptied of wine until the Scotch distillers fill them with whiskey. It is certainly well within the realm of possibility that the process, at least in many cases, extends for over a year, in which case the wine absorbed in the barrels will have no halachic effect on the whiskey, even in the first fill.

4. Empirical Evidence

Rather than engage in speculation about the amount of sherry wine contained in sherry whiskey, I sent five bottles of different brands of whiskey — four of which were aged in sherry casks — to a laboratory for analysis. As I expected, the amount of wine contained in the whiskey constituted a minuscule proportion:

- Glenmorangie 12 (Sherry): 0.06%
- The Balvenie 17 (Sherry): Less than 0.01%
- Auchentoshan (Sherry): 0.13%
- Macallan 18 (Sherry): 0.05%
- Glenfiddich 14 (No Sherry): Less than 0.01%

The brand with the highest sherry content, Auchentoshan, contained sherry in a

---

liquid in the interim. The reason, he explains, is that the liquid becomes forbidden by absorbing the non-kosher wine from the walls of the barrel, and then the walls absorb anew this forbidden liquid. Seemingly, this ruling applies practically even though we accept the view that recognizes the possibility of ביטול for gentile wine. In a case in which the volume of liquid in the container does not suffice for ביטול, according to the *Sedei Chemed*, the liquid must be treated as entirely forbidden, and thus the container absorbs a forbidden beverage anew. If so, then in the case of sherry whiskey, the *Sedei Chemed* would forbid subsequent fills, since the first fill becomes entirely forbidden and is then absorbed into the cask.

In truth, however, a clear distinction can be drawn between our discussion and that of the *Sedei Chemed*. According to the view that gentile wine is not subject to ביטול, even the slightest quantity of gentile wine suffices to forbid an entire vat. Since ביטול does not occur, there will always remain a tiny element of prohibited wine that cannot be disregarded, and it will continue to be absorbed into the wall of the container, extracted into the new liquid, and then reabsorbed in the wall, *ad infinitum*. We, however, accept the view that ביטול occurs, and thus the question of whether the wall reabsorbs forbidden beverage hinges on the applicability of חתיכה נעשית נבילה, as discussed.

proportion of 1:769. The other brands contained a significantly lower proportion of sherry.

In light of these results, the question becomes whether we may rely on laboratory findings for the purpose of determining ביטול. The *Shulchan Aruch* (Y.D. 98:1) rules that when a small amount of forbidden food mixes with a different kind of permissible food, a gentile should be asked to taste the mixture and determine whether the forbidden food can be discerned. If the gentile says that no taste of the forbidden food can be discerned in the mixture, then the mixture is permissible. The only condition imposed by the *Shulchan Aruch* is that the gentile is unaware that he is being relied upon for matters of religious law, as if he is, then he might knowingly lie.

The Rama, however, citing the *Agur*, writes that the custom is not to rely on this method of determining the presence or absence of the taste of forbidden food. Instead, we make this determination solely on the basis of proportion. If the forbidden food constitutes one-sixtieth or less of the mixture, then we presume it imparts no taste into the mixture, but otherwise, we must assume that it does, and the mixture is forbidden.

In light of this custom, it would appear, at first glance, that in the case of sherry whiskey, the results of laboratory results are irrelevant, and the status of the whiskey is determined solely on the basis of the proportion of the volume of the cask's walls with respect to its content.

Upon further reflection, however, there is ample reason to accept the laboratory's findings as halachically authoritative.

Two reasons are given for the custom documented by the Rama. The first is that a gentile tasting the mixture cannot be trusted, given the hostility that some gentiles of that time showed to Jews. The *Shach* (98:5) infers this approach from the fact that the Rama ruled against relying on gentiles (אין נוהגין עכשיו לסמוך אעובד כוכבים), and not against relying on tasting in general. As such, the *Shach* rules that in situations in which it is possible for a Jew to taste the mixture and determine the presence or absence of forbidden taste, this solution may be used. One example noted by the *Shach* is a situation in which a Jew vowed to abstain from a certain food, and a small amount of that food fell into some other food. According to the *Shach*, another Jew may be invited to taste the mixture and determine whether he can discern the taste of the food from which the other fellow had vowed to abstain.

Rabbi Akiva Eiger (*chiddushim* to *Shulchan Aruch*) explained the custom differently, claiming that it evolved due to the concern that people might not detect a taste that is, in truth, present in the mixture. It is the concern for mistakes, not dishonesty, that gave rise to the practice not to rely on tasting. According to this explanation, this method should not be relied upon even if a Jew of presumed integrity does the tasting.[19]

According to both reasons, it would seem, conclusive results of laboratory tests should suffice to establish the proportion of a forbidden component of a mixture. When dealing with a professional laboratory that is paid for its services and, like any business, must remain competitive and maintain a reputation for accuracy and integrity, we may apply the well-known halachic principle, חזקה דאומן לא מרע לאומנותיה — a professional can be assumed not to risk his reputation by providing incorrect information. There is certainly no reason to suspect that a professional research laboratory would knowingly distort the results of a test commissioned by a customer. As for the possibility of error, it is difficult to imagine that a contemporary lab conducting a simple test identifying the respective proportions of a beverage's components would mistake a proportion of $1/6^{th}$ (or $1/60^{th}$) for $1/769^{th}$.

Indeed, Rav Shlomo Zalman Braun (*She'arim Ha-Metzuyanim Be-Halacha*, vol. 1, p. 260) cites several halachic authorities, including Rav Yosef Shaul Nathanson (*Shoel U-Meishiv* 3:1:317) and Rav Yitzchak Schmelkes (*Beis Yitzchak*, vol. 1, Y.D. 141), who allowed relying on laboratory tests — in conjunction with other considerations — to allay fears of the presence of pig fat in oil. More recently, Rav Moshe Sternbuch (*Teshuvos Ve-Hanhagos*, vol. 1, Y.D. 423) ruled that a laboratory test may be trusted, although he adds that the technician must be told that the sample is also being given to two other experts for testing, so that he realizes his reputation is on the line. Rav Sternbuch proceeds to note the practical problems on relying on lab tests for the purposes of formally certifying a certain product as kosher, given the possibility that the ingredients might change, as well as other pragmatic concerns.[20] In our case, however, we need only to ascertain that whiskey aged in sherry casks does not contain anywhere

---

19. Both these explanations have support from the Rama's own comments elsewhere in his writings. In one of his published responsa (54), the Rama addresses the case of wine barrels that were lined with oil, which some feared may have contained pig fat, and he rules that the wine is permitted for several reasons, including the fact that no one had ever detected the taste of pig fat in wine. This would suggest that a Jew's tasting may be relied upon to discount the presence of forbidden taste. In his *Toras Chatas* (61:1), however, the Rama writes explicitly that we do not rely on tasting דאין אנו בקיאין — because we lack the necessary skill to determine the presence or absence of a forbidden taste. For a resolution of these two sources, see *Yad Yehuda* (*Aruch*, 98:5).
20. For example, in situations of a forbidden food that is prohibited במשהו — meaning, in even the slightest quantity — a laboratory test may be insufficient to establish the absence of even a slight trace of the forbidden food.

near a significant quantity of wine. There is little reason to discount these laboratory findings, and thus sherry whiskey should be permitted.

We should also note that Rabbi Akiva Eiger, in his notes to the *Shulchan Aruch* (Y.D. 98:1), proposes that one may rely on a gentile's tasting a mixture in situations involving an איסור דרבנן. He writes that since the custom noted by the Rama evolved as a matter of stringency, in order to satisfy all opinions, it stands to reason that it should not apply if the prohibition at stake is Rabbinic in origin, as opposed to a Biblical command.

In light of these considerations, it seems clear that there is room to allow sherry cask scotch without any concern.[21] However, it must be emphasized that, as noted earlier, Rav Moshe Feinstein ruled that a בעל נפש should avoid blended whiskeys in light of the Rashba's ruling forbidding beverages to which any amount of gentile wine is added to enhance its taste. This ruling would seemingly apply to sherry whiskey as well, and thus those who wish to be stringent and satisfy the Rashba's view should avoid such whiskey.[22]

However, Rabbi Niehaus raised the possibility of distinguishing in this regard between blended whiskeys, into which wine was actually added, and sherry whiskey, which was aged in sherry-flavored casks.[23] One could argue, Rabbi Niehaus writes, that the Rashba's ruling applies only when wine was poured directly into a beverage, but not when a beverage was stored in a barrel to absorb the taste of the wine that previously occupied the barrel. Additionally, we might add, the Rashba might concede that even wine added for the purpose of enhancing taste can be ignored if it constitutes less than one-thousandth of the beverage (בטל באלף). As this is the case in the majority of brands of sherry whiskey, the slight amount of wine in the whiskey would not pose a problem even according to the Rashba. Hence, it is possible that even a בעל נפש would be allowed to consume sherry whiskey without any concern.

---

21. To this we might add that although Rabbi Niehaus refers to measurements done on a standard whiskey barrel, it is far from certain that every sherry cask used for whiskey is constructed in such a way that the volume of its wood exceeds one-sixth the volume of its content.
22. In light of what we have seen, Rav Moshe's other reason for why a בעל נפש should avoid blended whiskeys — to satisfy the *Shach*'s view, requiring a proportion of 60:1 against forbidden wine — does not apply to sherry scotch, as the proportion of wine is far below even one-sixtieth. Rav Moshe also noted the view of the *Mateh Yehonasan* that if wine enhances the beverage with which it is mixed, then a proportion of one-sixtieth is needed for ביטול to occur. Of course, this consideration also does not apply to sherry whiskey.
23. "Sherry Whiskey," note 50.

INTERVIEWS

Rav Ezra Schwartz
on *Headlines with Dovid Lichtenstein**

There certainly is על מי לסמוך to allow the majority of scotches. However, for those scotches that are aged exclusively in sherry casks, the *kula* is much more difficult. The sherry casks contribute flavor, and anything that contributes flavor is not going to be בטל, even were there to be a 6:1 ratio. There is a discussion in *Yoreh Dei'a* whether סתם יינם is בטל בשש or בטל בששים, but even if we accept the leniency that it is בטל בשש, when something is עבידא לטעמא — it contributes flavor — it is very difficult to be lenient. Rav Moshe does rule leniently, but he acknowledges that a בעל נפש should be stringent.

The reality is that it is not בטל בששים, and according to the Chicago kollel's book, it might not even be בטל בשש... In all likelihood, it is not בטל בשש unless it is blended, meaning, different types of scotch were mixed together. But if it's exclusively from sherry casks, we have the impression that this is not a legitimate ספק.

As to whether a year passes [between the time the barrel is emptied of its wine and it is filled with whiskey], the reality is that the transportation [process] does not work that way... The likelihood is that the trip from Spain takes maximum 6–8 months. The manufacturers want to do things as quickly as possible...

[Rabbi Niehaus'] calculation [of the proportion of wine in the whiskey] resonates with me; this barrel calculator seems accurate...

The more legitimate ספק is that maybe [the barrel absorbs] only כדי קליפה...

Some argue that the color of scotch aged in a sherry cask differs from that of scotch aged in a bourbon cask; it tends to be darker and more of an amber-like color. The *Shach* (102:5) paskens that something which is עבידא לחזותא (added for the sake of coloring) is not בטל. The *Taz* disagrees, as does the *Peri Megadim*, but the *Minchas Yaakov* says that if something is אסור בהנאה (forbidden for any kind of benefit, and not just for consumption), then it will not be בטל. And we are *machmir* that סתם יינם is אסור בהנאה. (Granted, the *Peri Chadash* says that when dealing with an איסור דרבנן, we are not concerned with חזותא.)

There are many types of scotch available that do not have this problem. The problem is only with the pure sherry, those matured exclusively in sherry casks. Regarding the others there is no concern. Even Rav Moshe said that a בעל נפש should try to avoid [blended whiskeys which contain a small amount of wine], and he praised Rav Teitz for putting on the market a type of whiskey which did not contain any wine.

[In response to the laboratory results, which found that pure sherry whiskey contains an infinitesimally small percentage of sherry:]

One of the more difficult questions that come up is that בליעת כלים — the notion that a utensil absorbs *treif* food and then imparts that taste [into the food cooked in it subsequently] — does not seem to exist in the real world. Many people who work with metal contend that there's no such thing. So what do we do about all of *Yoreh Dei'a*, if the realities of בליעת כלים do not seem to meet the halachic definitions? There are some nice articles in *Techumin*, vol. 35, in which the authors go back and forth and debate the issue. One Rosh Yeshiva in *Eretz Yisrael* takes this question into consideration as a factor in difficult cases involving *Yoreh Dei'a*. But most *poskim* with whom I have spoken feel that we need to deal with בליעת כלים based on what it says in the *Shulchan Aruch*. The entire volume of the walls of the utensil are absorbed with *issur* [forbidden foodstuff], and consequently, that full amount will come out in the next food [cooked in the utensil]. Most *poskim* say we cannot overturn all the laws in *Yoreh Dei'a*… בליעת כלים is less about *metzius* [actual reality] than it is a halachic construct…

There are many *poskim* who take different approaches to the Rama's ruling that nowadays we do not rely on a gentile tasting a mixture [and concluding that no forbidden taste is discernible]. The *Levush* assumes that כח הטעימה [the skill to discern taste] does not exist at all…

I acknowledge that certainly, according to standard approaches to *halacha*, we have many ספיקות. Nonetheless, the question is whether there is enough of a need to be lenient. So מעיקר הדין, there is certainly what to rely on [to permit sherry whiskey], but once we're coming from the perspective of a בעל נפש, I don't think it's an unreasonable stringency.

* Broadcast 10 Adar II, 5776 (March 19, 2016).

Rabbi Eli Gersten
on *Headlines with Dovid Lichtenstein**

The opinion of the poskim for the OU — Rav Yisrael Belsky *zt"l* and *ybl'ch* Rav Herschel Schachter — is that the OU should not certify scotches made in sherry casks, and that they should not be sold in restaurants or served by caterers certified by the OU. This is a matter of policy, the public position of the OU. As far as individuals are concerned, each person should ask his own מורה הוראה what to do.

There are blended whiskeys that have many whiskeys together. As long as it does not say "sherry cask," the OU would allow it to be sold and served. Blended whiskeys can have as many as 50 whiskeys mixed together, so only a minimal amount was aged in sherry casks. As long as it is not known how much was aged in sherry casks, it's permissible.

The wine casks [used for sherry whiskey] contained non-kosher wine for many years. To use them for kosher wine gives rise to the question of אין מבטלין איסור לכתחילה (the prohibition against knowingly mixing a small amount of forbidden foodstuff into kosher food, even if the proportion is small enough for ביטול to occur). When it comes to giving a *hechsher*, certifying a bottle of scotch that is known to have been made with wine barrels is not permitted. The OU does not certify products made through ביטול. The factory has to be kashered first, and all the ingredients must be kosher. This is not the case with these wine barrels. Giving it a *hechsher* would be an issue of אין מבטלין איסור לכתחילה. Rav Moshe has a *teshuva* in which he writes that a Jewish company cannot ask a non-Jew to make food relying on ביטול, and even if the non-Jew is making the food anyway, it's מכוער הדבר (something inappropriate); a *hashgacha* should not allow this. Even though strictly speaking, this is not ביטול איסור לכתחילה [since the ביטול is being done by a non-Jew, who is not doing it at a Jew's behest], it nevertheless falls under the category of מכוער; it's not in the spirit of the law. We should not certify and give our stamp of approval to a product that would be forbidden for a Jew to make. All *hashgachos* accept this. People expect more when they buy a certified product. Therefore, we kasher every factory we go to.

Additionally, in his *teshuva* about whiskey, Rav Moshe was not referring to בליעת כלים. He was referring to בעין (actual wine added to the whiskey), which is much easier to calculate; you just look at the recipe. When it comes to בליעת כלים, we have to calculate based on the thickness or the קליפה of the barrel… *Chazal* required us to evaluate this in its entirety.

Moreover, sherry is not regular wine; it's fortified wine, meaning that alcohol is added. Sherry is 20–22 percent alcohol, which means they could be adding 10 percent wine alcohol to the wine. When dealing with a regular wine barrel, there are certain familiar *halachos* that apply; it becomes permitted even without kashering after twelve months [have passed since the wine was removed]. This is not necessarily true if you were to put alcohol into a barrel. The *Darkei Teshuva* (end of 135) brings from the *Yad Yehuda* that [a period of] twelve months does not help if the barrel held wine alcohol. Sherry is somewhere on the spectrum between wine and alcohol, somewhere between schnapps and wine. If you define it as schnapps, then you get into trouble, and twelve months does not help. And, you have to be concerned with not just כדי קליפה, but with the whole thickness of the barrel, all of which becomes non-kosher. Also, the issue of 6:1 or 60:1 could change if it's alcohol. Rav Moshe has a *teshuva* about wine alcohol which was turned into vinegar, and he writes that you need a proportion of 60:1 for it to be בטל.

The laboratory won't be able to tell you about the alcohol. If the barrel is saturated with wine alcohol, no lab will be able to tell you where the alcohol is coming from… A laboratory can provide information from an allergen standpoint, and say there is no grape [in the whiskey], but it cannot tell you which part of the product is made from grape. And my guess is that when a barrel is saturated with alcohol, much of it will come out into the whiskey. We cannot make any assumptions when it comes to ביטול.

[Also,] when *Chazal* said that we have to be concerned with the entire בליעה of utensils, and we could perhaps rely on a קפילא for this — [in the case of a laboratory] they're not tasting, which is what *Chazal* required.

* Broadcast 10 Adar II, 5776 (March 19, 2016).

The New York Times

Butcher Is Accused of Passing Off Chicken as Kosher

September 6 2006
Fernanda Santos

MONSEY, N.Y., Sept. 6 — Since sundown on Saturday — when the Jewish Sabbath ended — men, women and children have been scrubbing kitchen counters and stoves, and dipping pots and utensils in scalding water.

"My husband and I had to leave everything we were doing," said Esther Herzl, 61, a Hasidic grandmother who lives here, "and all we did was scrape and scrape and scrape — from the cutlery to the glassware to the countertops, oven and stove. I'm beat. We're truly religious, so we don't cheat in the cleaning."

The cleansing ritual, which is prescribed by Jewish law, became necessary after a Hasidic butcher was accused of stocking the shelves of a kosher grocery store here with nonkosher chicken and selling it to thousands of Orthodox Jewish families.

Now a group of rabbis is debating the fate of the butcher.

Last week, the state's Department of Agriculture and Markets seized 15 cases of chicken from the store, Hatzlocha Grocery, where the butcher sold chicken and other meats from rented shelf space to test it for salt, a key ingredient in kosher food.

The state agency and the rabbis, who represent several Hasidic congregations in Monsey and elsewhere in Rockland County, are trying to determine the origin of the chicken, whose package carried the stickers of two area kosher meat plants that

Kitchenware being cleansed at the Belzer Shul in Ramapo, N.Y., in response to concerns that chicken had illegitimately been sold as kosher. Credit: Alan Zale for The New York Times

had ceased supplying to the butcher after he failed to pay them, according to a local rabbi and an employee at the store.

"To sell nonkosher as kosher is one of the biggest acts of betrayal that a Jewish person can do to another," said Rabbi Menachem Meir Weissmandel of Chemed Shul, a local synagogue. "This is the darkest day in the history of our community since we settled in this area many years ago."

The butcher, Moshe Finkel, owns Shevach Meats, which buys kosher chicken and other meats in bulk, and then slices, packages and sells it at the grocery store and to wedding halls, religious schools and Hasidic camps in the Catskill Mountains.

Attempts to reach Mr. Finkel, who lives in Monsey, by telephone were unsuccessful on Wednesday. Rabbi Weissmandel said that Mr. Finkel was banned from Hatzlocha Grocery last Wednesday, as soon as the store owners uncovered his alleged transgression.

He said the store owners confronted Mr. Finkel after they noticed the shelves lined with kosher meats, even though his usual suppliers had not made a delivery. Almost immediately, leaflets lined Hatzlocha's windows, telling patrons in Hebrew that Shevach Meats had been caught selling nonkosher chicken. At synagogues and on the street, rabbis instructed the faithful to throw out the meat and cleanse their kitchens to make them kosher again.

The matter has been the talk of Jewish Web logs. One of them, Vos Iz Neias, announced it under the banner headline "Butcher Sells Treifa Chicken as Kosher." (Nonkosher food, or food that is not in accord with Jewish dietary laws, is called treif, which derives from the Hebrew word teref, or torn.) The posting generated 440 comments in two days.

Rabbinical panels often work in secret, so it is hard to figure out when the rabbis here will reach a decision or what it will be.

As for the state, a spokeswoman for the Agriculture Department said investigators were trying to determine if the chicken was ever certified as kosher and advertised as such at the store. She said violators are subject to fines of up to $1,000.

Copyright © nytimes.com

Are *Treif* Utensils Really *Treif*?

I. Introduction

The primary distinguishing feature of the kosher kitchen since time immemorial has been the separation between meat and dairy utensils. We are not only careful to avoid mixing meat and dairy, but also to handle, prepare and eat them with separate utensils. And when a dairy utensil is used with meat, or vice versa, or if one discovers after cooking that the food was non-kosher, then, in many circumstances, *halacha* will require either "kashering" the utensil — meaning, purging it of its absorbed non-kosher substance — or discarding it.

In extreme cases, when one learns that a food product which he had purchased was falsely labelled as kosher, the entire kitchen might require kashering. Case in point, in a widely publicized incident in 2006, a certified kosher butcher shop in Monsey was found to have sold non-kosher chickens, and a group of twenty local rabbis issued a ruling that those who had purchased chickens from the shop in the period in question, and used them, must kasher their utensils. The story was picked up by *The New York Times*,[1] which began its report by describing how "men, women and children have been scrubbing kitchen counters and stoves, and dipping pots and utensils in scalding water."

The source for this requirement to kasher utensils that had been used with non-kosher food is a pair of verses towards the end of *Sefer Bamidbar* (31:22–23) in which instructions are given after *Bnei Yisrael*'s war with Midyan regarding utensils seized as spoils of war. Elazar, the *Kohen Gadol* at the time, informed the soldiers that they may use these utensils only after purging them of the taste of non-kosher food with which they had been used. The commonly accepted understanding is that the Torah here indicates that not only is non-kosher food itself forbidden for consumption, but even the taste absorbed by the utensils in which it was used is likewise forbidden. A utensil that had been used with non-kosher food, even after it is cleaned, retains the taste of that food, and this taste is extracted from the walls of the utensil when the utensil is subsequently used for cooking. The taste then blends with the kosher food being cooked, which thus becomes forbidden for consumption unless the absorbed forbidden taste comprises such a small proportion of the food that it cannot be discerned.[2]

---

1. See media article above.
2. A vast literature exists concerning the precise source, nature and parameters of this concept of טעם כעיקר — that a food's taste is treated by *halacha* as the food itself. For

The basic principle outlined by Elazar — known as כבולעו כך פולטו — is that taste absorbed in a utensil is extracted through the same means through which it had been absorbed. Hence, if non-kosher food was prepared in a utensil directly over a fire, as in the case of a spit used for roasting, the utensil must be exposed directly to fire to expunge the absorbed taste of non-kosher food before it may be used with kosher food. If the non-kosher food was absorbed through boiling hot liquid, then it is expunged through *hag'ala* — immersion in boiling hot water. If the utensil was used only with cold non-kosher food, then it may be assumed to have not absorbed any taste, and it thus needs only to be thoroughly cleaned.

Interestingly, the *Semak* (198) lists the requirement to immerse utensils as a *mitzvas asei*, an independent Biblical command introduced by the Torah in the aforementioned verses in *Sefer Bamidbar*. This would imply that according to the *Semak*, a utensil that had been used with non-kosher food requires kashering irrespective of the need to purge it of the taste of non-kosher food. However, all other *Rishonim* who listed the Torah's 613 commands do not assign a separate command to kashering utensils, indicating that kashering is required strictly as a practical necessity, to avoid eating food that had absorbed the taste of non-kosher products.

II. Distinguishing Between Ancient and Modern-Day Kitchens

Why Don't We Taste Our Lunch in Our Dinner?

In recent years, a number of articles[3] have surfaced addressing the question of whether the principle of בליעת כלים — that the taste of food cooked in a utensil remains in the utensil even after it is cleaned, and will impact food subsequently cooked in the utensil — is applicable to modern-day kitchenware. Perhaps the clearest indication that our utensils do not absorb and expunge taste the way described by our ancient halachic sources is empirical evidence from everyday

---

our purposes, however, it suffices to acknowledge that a utensil can absorb taste which can then halachically impact upon food subsequently placed in that utensil, unless the taste has been extracted in the interim through kashering. See Rashi and Ramban to *Bamidbar* 31:22–23; Mishna, *Avoda Zara* 75b; Rashi, *Pesachim* 45a, ד"ה ור"ע; Rambam, *Hilchos Ma'achalos Asuros*, 17:3; *Shulchan Aruch*, O.C. 451:5, Y.D. 121:1; Ra'a, *Bedek Ha'bayis* 4:1; *Peri Megadim* — *Sifsei Da'as*, 93:3.

3. See, for example, Rav Roi Sitton, "*Od Be-Inyan Beli'a Be-Keilim Be-Yameinu*," *Ha-Ma'ayan*, Nissan, 5773; Rav Yair Frank and Rav Dr. Dror Fixler, "*Beli'a U-Pelita Be-Keilim Le-Or Totza'ot Ha-Mivchan Ha-Mada'i*," *Techumin*, vol. 34; Rav Yitzchak Devir, "*Beli'at Keilim Be-Yameinu*," *Techumin*, vol. 35.

use. If we boil roast beef in a typical stainless steel pot, wash it, and then boil a vegetable soup in the same pot, nobody would discern the taste of beef in the soup. Simply put, if we use a pot to prepare our lunch, and after cleaning it we use it to prepare dinner, we do not taste the food served at lunch in our dinner. This would seem to prove that modern-day utensils do not absorb the taste of food with which they are used.

To further verify this point, Rav Roi Sitton[4] writes that he conducted an experiment with a clean, stainless steel pot. He boiled coffee in the pot and then thoroughly cleaned it with soap and cold water. Immediately afterward, he boiled water in the pot. After the water cooled, it was completely transparent, without any coffee coloring, and no taste of coffee whatsoever was discernible in the water. He then took a pot which had been used for boiling eggs, and had a layer of white film stuck to the surface which could not be removed with washing and scrubbing. He then repeated the previous experiment with this pot: he boiled coffee in the pot, washed it with soap and cold water, and then boiled water in it. When he poured water from the pot into a clear cup, he noticed that the water was slightly colored, and when he drank it, he discerned a certain taste. Rav Sitton concluded that the film on the utensil absorbed the taste of the coffee, and that taste was then absorbed by the water. However, when a perfectly clean pot — which, of course, is what we generally use when cooking — is used, no taste is absorbed in the wall of utensil.

Rav Sitton further reported that he discussed this issue with numerous chemists and chemical engineers, all of whom agreed that any absorption of food during the cooking process is infinitesimally small, amounting to one in several hundred thousandths of the volume of the utensil. This comes nowhere remotely near the 1/60th proportion that *Chazal* determined as capable of imparting taste, in consideration of which utensils must be kashered.[5]

How do we reconcile this empirical evidence with the halachic principle of בליעת כלים and the requirement to kasher utensils that had been used with non-kosher food?

Rav Sitton attributes the discrepancy to two factors: the quality of modern-day utensils, and the quality of modern-day cleaning agents. In ancient times, it seems, utensils were not perfectly smooth, and had small cracks and crevices, which resulted in tiny food particles being trapped in the walls. Nowadays, our utensils are perfectly smooth and cannot be penetrated, and it is thus difficult

---

4. In the article referenced above.
5. See sections 4–5 of the article by Rav Yair Frank and Rav Dr. Dror Fixler referenced above, note 3, for a detailed presentation of the various scientific experiments that have been conducted to determine whether *beli'a* actually occurs in modern-day utensils.

to imagine any significant absorption of taste into the walls.⁶ Secondly, we may reasonably assume that in the times of *Chazal*, it was all but impossible to thoroughly remove residue from a used utensil. A layer of residue likely remained on the wall of a utensil even after it was thoroughly cleaned by ancient standards, and this layer had to be expunged through kashering, as it would otherwise impact upon the taste of the food subsequently cooked in the utensil. In modern times, when we have running water, strong soaps and efficient sponges and scrubbers, our utensils are thoroughly cleaned, and nobody uses a utensil until all residue from its previous use has been entirely removed.⁷ These two factors, seemingly, combine to create a fundamental halachic difference between modern-day kitchens and the kitchens in the times of *Chazal*.

A review of several halachic sources relevant to the principle of בליעת כלים reinforces the assumption that our utensils do not absorb taste the way utensils did in ancient times.⁸

קוניא

The Gemara in *Maseches Avoda Zara* (33b) records an exchange that took place revolving around the status of קוניא, a type of glazed earthenware utensil. As the utensil's surface was smooth, it was questionable whether it was forbidden for use on Pesach after having been used with *chametz*, since it seemingly was incapable of absorbing any food. Mereimar concluded that such a utensil may

---

6. Rav Sitton cites the work *Madrich Ha-Kashrus Ha-Ma'asi* (p. 149) which tells that Rav Aharon Pfeuffer once raised a question concerning the requirement when kashering through *libun* (direct exposure to fire) to keep the utensil in fire until it produces sparks. Today, Rav Pfeuffer observed, it is very rare for sparks to be produced when exposing metal utensils to fire, yet it seems that this was fairly common in *Chazal*'s time. He consulted with an expert in metals, who responded that metals in ancient times were porous and thus absorbed a significant quantity of the food prepared in them, and this absorbed food would produce sparks. Nowadays, the scientist said, metals are far more compressed such that only an infinitesimally small amount of food is absorbed.
7. This point is also noted by Rav Eliezer Melamed, in his article on the subject published on the Arutz Sheva website (available at http://www.inn.co.il/News/News.aspx/329723). Rav Melamed writes that he discussed the issue of בליעת כלים with several chemists, who felt that even in ancient times, it is unlikely that metal utensils actually absorbed taste in their walls, as food molecules are significantly larger than any pores that may have existed in metal utensils. These scientists contended that when *Chazal* spoke of *beli'a*, they referred to residue that could not be removed. (See also below, note 9.)
8. Several of the sources cited below are noted by Rav Yitzchak Dvir, in his article on the topic published on the website of the Kosharot organization (http://www.kosharot.co.il/show_hadracha.asp?id=61685).

not be used on Pesach, based on empirical evidence. He noted that visible signs of absorption are present when this utensil is used, and so if it had been used with *chametz*, it may not be used on Pesach. Rashi and the Ran (*Pesachim* 9a in the Rif) explain that Mereimar saw moisture on the exterior of the utensil, which proved the occurrence of absorption, whereas the Ritva and Meiri understood Mereimar's comment to mean that the exterior surface darkened somewhat. According to either explanation, it is clear that in Talmudic times, the process of *beli'a* (absorption) had a discernible effect upon the utensil. No such manifestations of *beli'a* are seen in today's utensils, suggesting that the process of *beli'a* described in halachic sources does not take place in modern-day kitchenware.[9]

The Discolored *Hag'ala* Water

Perhaps even more compelling proof may be found in the comments of the Ran (*Chullin*, 44a in the Rif) warning against kashering a large number of utensils in a single pot:

צריך ליזהר שלא להגעיל כלים יותר מדאי ביורה אחת עד שנשתנה צורת המים מחמת פליטת הכלים, דהוה ליה מגעיל ברוטב.

> One must ensure not to immerse too many utensils in the same pot such that the water's appearance changes as a result of the [substances] expunged from the utensils, as he is then immersing in gravy [as opposed to water].

The Ran cautions that kashering a large number of utensils one after the other in the same pot of boiling water will eventually cause the water to change color, to the point where it loses its halachic identity as water suitable for *hag'ala*. (The Ran's ruling is codified by the Rama, O.C. 452:5.) In his experience, it seems, the particles expelled from the walls of utensils during kashering gradually accumulate in the pot until the water becomes discolored. Despite the fact that utensils must be thoroughly cleaned before they can be kashered, utensils in the Ran's time expunged actual residue into the water during the process of *hag'ala*. Needless to say, as anyone who has been involved in public *hag'ala* facilities before Pesach can testify, this does not happen nowadays. This would seem to

---

9. The Ran understood the Gemara's discussion differently, as revolving not around the question of whether קוניא absorbs, but rather around the question of whether it can be purged of absorbed taste, and Mereimar concluded on the basis of empirical evidence that the utensil cannot be purged. Regardless, the Gemara clearly makes mention of physical changes that do not occur to modern-day pot.

prove that our utensils do not absorb or expel food particles as utensils did even as late as the times of the Ran (14th century, Spain).

Shedding further light on the Ran's comments is a ruling of the *Machzor Vitri* which would initially strike a contemporary Orthodox Jew as startling. In discussing the guidelines for kashering utensils for Pesach, the *Machzor Vitri* writes: שוטפן ומדיחן יפה, ואין צורך לגוררן — one must rinse the utensils thoroughly in preparation for *hag'ala*, but there is no need to scrape the residue stuck onto the utensils' surface. It might sound astonishing to us that Jews would kasher their utensils for Pesach with *chametz* residue stuck onto the utensils, but upon further reflection, this is perfectly reasonable. As mentioned earlier, people centuries ago were not always able to thoroughly eliminate residue from their utensils, and thus *hag'ala* was often done with some food stuck onto the utensils. This is very likely the reason why, as the Ran describes, the water would change colors when *hag'ala* was done repeatedly in the same pot, as the hot water dissolved the food substance stuck onto the utensils, which was then released into the water.[10]

III. Halachic Reality or Physical Reality?

Having demonstrated that modern-day utensils do not absorb taste the way ancient utensils did, the question now becomes whether this matters. One might argue that the prohibition of טעם כעיקר, which establishes the prohibition against ingesting kosher food that has a taste of non-kosher food, refers to halachic טעם — "taste" as defined in halachic terms. According to this perspective, the question of whether one actually tastes during lunch the non-kosher food that had been cooked in this pot for breakfast is immaterial, since the laws of בליעת כלים define the halachic reality of טעם, which differs from the physical reality of טעם which we can discern and which scientists can identify in a laboratory. The fundamental question that needs to be addressed, then, is whether we define טעם for the purposes of this *halacha* based upon the actual presence or absence of taste, or based upon the formal guidelines established by *Chazal*, irrespective of the physical reality. According to the second viewpoint, the difference between

---

10. This point is made by Rav Sitton, in the article referenced in note 3. Rav Sitton also cites a passage from the *Tosfos Rid* (*Pesachim* 30a) addressing the question of why a clean utensil may not be used for meat after it had been used for dairy, given the negligible amount of food that is actually absorbed in the wall of the utensil. The *Tosfos Rid* answers that this is forbidden because of the residue which cannot be removed from the utensil through washing, which imparts taste into food subsequently cooked in the utensil. This, too, demonstrates that utensils in ancient times could not be thoroughly cleaned, and that this is the basis underlying the concept of בליעת כלים.

our utensils and those of *Chazal* have no impact whatsoever on the halachic status of utensils that had been used with non-kosher food.

The Radbaz's Porcelain Experiment

The first approach, that the laws of בליעת כלים hinge upon the physical reality of absorption of taste, seems to be reflected in several sources. Firstly, as noted earlier, Mereimar determined the halachic status of קוניא based on empirical evidence of absorption. He reached his conclusion not on the basis of formal halachic rules and definitions, but rather through experimentation.

Another example of experimentation used to determine a utensil's halachic status appears in a responsum of the Radbaz (3:401). Writing in 16th century Egypt, the Radbaz addressed the question surrounding the status of porcelain utensils, which had evidently begun to be imported to the Middle East at that time. To determine whether or not such utensils may be used after having been used with non-kosher food, the Radbaz conducted two experiments. First, he took a fragment of porcelain and briefly placed it fire. He noticed that the piece of porcelain produced a flame כדרך הכלים הבלועים — as is characteristic of utensils that had absorbed food. The fragment's ability to catch fire, the Radbaz reasoned, testified to the presence of food particles absorbed in its walls. For his second experiment, the Radbaz again placed the fragment in fire and left it there to be completely purged. He then weighed it with a very precise scale. After noting the fragment's precise weight, he inserted it into a pot of boiling food, and left it there for about a half-hour. He then thoroughly washed and dried the piece of porcelain to ensure it was as clean and dry as when he had initially weighed it. When he weighed it a second time, he found that its weight after being in the pot slightly exceeded its initial weight — proving that it had absorbed some of the food or liquid in the pot. The Radbaz thus concluded that porcelain utensils absorb some of the food cooked within them.

Ironically, other *poskim* reached the opposite conclusion regarding porcelain on the basis of empirical evidence. Rav Yaakov Emden, in his *Mor U-Ketzi'a* (451), ruled that although porcelain utensils are made from earth, they differ from standard earthenware with respect to בליעת כלים. As cited earlier, Mereimar determined that קוניא, glazed earthenware, absorbs food based on the evidence of absorption on the utensil's exterior. These signs of absorption are not seen in porcelain utensils, thus proving that *beli'a* does not occur. It seems clear that Rav Yaakov Emden accepts the premise underlying the Radbaz's ruling, that the phenomenon of בליעת כלים can be determined based on empirical evidence, only they disagree as to whether Mereimar's method of detecting *beli'a* is the only way to make this determination.

The Radbaz's experimentation was invoked as a precedent by Rav Chizkiya Medini, in his *Sedei Chemed*,[11] for permitting the use of iron utensils without kashering. Noting the practice among Ashkenazim to be lenient in this regard, Rav Medini speculated that they perhaps conducted experiments similar to those conducted by the Radbaz, and determined on this basis that iron utensils do not absorb. Rav Medini clearly works off the assumption that experimentation is a valid means of determining a material's status vis-à-vis בליעת כלים.

Dentures and Fillings

This assumption comes to the fore in the universally accepted practice to eat both milk and meat with fillings and dentures in one's mouth. Nobody would think to change their fillings or dentures in between meat and milk, despite the possibility that they absorb taste of the food one eats and then expel that taste into the food one eats later in the day. This issue was addressed already by Rav Tzvi Hersh Shapiro of Munkatch, in his *Darchei Teshuva* (Y.D. 89:11). Rav Shapiro notes the widespread practice to allow eating both meat and dairy foods with the same dental implants, and he upholds the validity of this practice. One of the reasons he gives for permitting the use of dental implants with meat and dairy food is the presumption that they are impenetrable, and do not absorb any food. Rav Shapiro adds that he consulted with an expert dentist in Vienna, who told him that the material used for dentures is incapable of absorbing, and in fact this particular material was used (and was especially imported from the United States for this purpose) because if it absorbed any food or liquid, it would cause decay which would, in turn, result in serious illness. Rav Shapiro clearly relied on scientific proof that *beli'a* does not occur to allow the use of a "utensil" for both meat and milk. His ruling is approvingly cited by several later *poskim*, including Rav Ovadia Yosef[12] and Rav Eliezer Waldenberg.[13]

Barrels Lined With Pig Fat

Further proof may be drawn from the *Shulchan Aruch*'s ruling (Y.D. 98:1), based on the Gemara (*Chullin* 97a), that if a small portion of non-kosher food mixes with kosher food, the mixture should be fed to a non-Jewish expert — קפילא — to determine whether the non-kosher substance imparts taste in the mixture. If the קפילא tastes the non-kosher food in the mixture, then it may not be eaten. If no such expert is available, then this determination is made based on the

---

11. אסיפת דינים, מערכה ה׳, אות כא.
12. *Yechaveh Da'as* 1:9.
13. *Tzitz Eliezer* 9:25.

proportion of the non-kosher food, on the assumption that unless the non-kosher food constitutes one-sixtieth or less of the mixture, it will impart its taste and thus render the mixture forbidden. Although the Rama notes the prevalent custom not to rely on a קפילא, and to instead determine the mixture's status based solely on the proportion,[14] he might nevertheless accept the basic premise of the *Shulchan Aruch*'s ruling. The *Shach* explains this custom as based upon the concern that a non-Jewish קפילא may not be trustworthy, whereas Rabbi Akiva Eiger claims that people at some point lost the skill to discern tastes. According to both approaches, it seems likely that the Rama would accept the results of a laboratory test as sufficient evidence of the presence or absence of a non-kosher food's taste. The *Peri Megadim* (*Sifsei Da'as*, Y.D. 98:29), however, explains that the custom not to rely on a קפילא stems from the view among the *Rishonim* that the determination of a קפילא is halachically significant only as a matter of stringency. That is, if a קפילא discerns the taste of forbidden food in a mixture, then the mixture is prohibited for consumption even if the forbidden food constitutes a very small proportion that we might have assumed renders it inconsequential. But in the opposite scenario, when a קפילא determines that the taste of a forbidden food that constitutes more than one-sixtieth of a mixture cannot be discerned, the mixture remains forbidden, despite the presumed absence of taste. According to this understanding of the Rama, we might conclude that the prohibition of טעם indeed depends upon formal, abstract halachic categories, and not on the physical presence or absence of taste.

In truth, however, we do not need to speculate about the Rama's view on this matter, because he lays it out quite clearly for us in a separate context. In one of his published responsa (54), the Rama addresses the question that arose concerning barrels of olive oil which were found to have been greased with lard (pig fat) before being filled with olive oil. The Rama permits the use of this oil, asserting that the thin layer of lard undoubtedly constitutes less than one-sixtieth of the oil. Additionally, he writes, no gentiles who consume this oil taste any lard in their oil, and they have even explicitly acknowledged such. The Rama then adds that we may permit the oil even according to the position that we cannot rely on non-Jewish experts to make this determination, because אנו בעצמנו טעמנו אותו כמה פעמים ולא טעמנו בו כלום — "we ourselves have tasted it on several occasions, and we tasted nothing in it." Once it has been empirically determined that the quantity of forbidden food in a mixture is too small to impart taste, we may rely on this conclusion. It seems that although the Rama does not allow relying on a קפילא to ascertain the absence of forbidden taste in a mixture, he does permit

---

14. This custom has since become generally accepted among Sephardim, as well. See, for example, *Kaf Ha-Chaim*, Y.D. 98:2.

mixtures in which it is widely and definitively known that no forbidden taste exists.[15] We may reasonably argue that if the Rama permits consuming oil stored in barrels greased with pig fat on the basis of empirical evidence, then he would certainly permit eating kosher food cooked in a clean pot that had been used with non-kosher food based on scientific evidence that *beli'a* does not occur in modern-day utensils.

The Glassware Controversy

This conclusion, however, must be tested against the longstanding practice among Ashekanzic Jewry to use separate glassware for meat and dairy products, and to use separate glassware for Pesach.

The status of glassware is subject to a famous controversy that dates back to the *Rishonim*. The Rashba, in one of his responsa (1:233), rules that glassware does not require kashering because the surface is perfectly solid without any cracks, and thus incapable of absorbing any food. He draws upon the Gemara's discussion of glazed earthenware, where these utensils are assumed not to absorb by virtue of their perfectly solid surface, and because they have no external signs of absorption. The Rashba applies the Gemara's conclusion to glassware, as well, and thus rules that glass utensils do not have to be kashered. The Rashba makes reference to the Mishna in *Avos De-Rabbi Nasan* (41), which states explicitly that glass utensils neither absorb nor expunge the taste of food that is cooked in them. This view is taken by numerous other *Rishonim*, as well, including the Re'avya (*Pesachim*, 464), Rabbeinu Tam (*Tosfos, Avoda Zara* 33b), *Sefer Ha-Michtam* (*Pesachim* 30b), Rabbeinu Yerucham (5:2), and the Ran (*Pesachim* 30b), among others. By contrast, Rabbeinu Yechiel of Paris, cited by the Mordechai (*Pesachim*, 574), ruled that since glass is produced from sand, it is halachically equivalent to earthenware, and is therefore assumed to absorb and to be incapable of being completely purged of absorbed taste. This is also the view of the Ritva (*Avoda Zara* 33b), *Shibolei Ha-Leket* (207), and other *Rishonim*.

---

15. In his *Toras Chatas* (61:1), the Rama writes that the prevalent practice was not to allow relying on somebody tasting a mixture to ascertain the absence of forbidden taste, "because we are not proficient" in discerning subtle tastes. This remark seems, at first glance, to contradict the Rama's comments permitting the use of oil stored in barrels greased with lard on the grounds that the lard's taste is not discernible in the oil. The likely answer, as noted by the *Yad Yehuda* (98:5), is that the Rama distinguished between a lone individual tasting a mixture to determine the presence of a slight taste of forbidden food, and something that is universally consumed without anybody detecting the taste of lard.

As for the practical *halacha*, Ashkenazic and Sephardic traditions are split in this regard. Sephardim, following the ruling of the *Shulchan Aruch* (O.C. 451:26), allow using one's ordinary glassware on Pesach provided they are thoroughly cleaned, as glass is assumed incapable of absorbing. Ashkenazim, however, following the custom observed by the Rama, forbid using on Pesach glassware that had been used with *chametz*.

At first glance, these two traditions reflect the two fundamentally different perspectives on the concept of *beli'a*. Sephardic practice, it would seem, adopts the position that the prohibition of טעם relates to the physical reality of discernible taste. As such, since glass is incapable of absorbing or imparting taste, there is no need to kasher glassware and it may be used with both meat and dairy, and both during the year and on Pesach. The Ashkenazic tradition, by contrast, appears to accept the view that the laws of טעם and *beli'a* work on the basis of formal halachic guidelines that do not depend on the actual presence or absence of taste. According to this view, halachically-defined טעם can exist without the physical presence of טעם. Therefore, despite the fact that glass does not absorb taste, nevertheless, it is formally classified under the halachic category of earthenware and must be treated accordingly.

If so, then the status of modern-day utensils, which, practically speaking, resemble glassware used by the *Rishonim*, would depend upon these two customs. Quite simply, Sephardim would not be required to kasher even metal utensils nowadays, as our utensils do not absorb taste, whereas Ashkenazim must treat modern-day metal utensils like the metal utensils of yesteryear, despite the fact that *beli'a* does not occur in reality.

In truth, however, there is ample reason to absolve even Ashkenazim of the need to kasher modern-day utensils, at least in many circumstances.

For one thing, the Rama writes in *Darchei Moshe* (O.C. 451:19) that although Ashkenazic practice follows the stringent position that glass utensils absorb, בדיעבד אין להחמיר כולי האי — "after the fact, one need not be so stringent." Meaning, the Rama maintained that Ashkenazic practice requires following the stringent view and disallowing the use of one's regular glassware on Pesach, but allows relying on the lenient position after the fact. This would seem to mean that if one prepared food on Pesach in a glass utensil that had been used with *chametz*, the food may be eaten on Pesach, despite the fact that glassware ought to be kashered before Pesach. This is, indeed, the way the *Taz* (O.C. 451:30) understood the Rama's remark. Returning, then, to our proposed analogy between glassware and modern-day utensils, this would mean that after the fact, if one mistakenly cooked meat in a dairy pot, or vice versa, or if one mistakenly cooked non-kosher meat in a pot and then used it with kosher food, the food does not have to be discarded, and it may be eaten. It must be noted, however, that even according to this reading of the Rama's comment, the pot must be kashered. Although the Rama permits food cooked in the glass utensil before it was kashered, he still requires kashering the utensil in deference to the stringent view.

The *Magen Avraham* (O.C. 451:49) and *Chok Yaakov* (451:68), however, read the Rama's comment differently. In their view, the Rama permits the food prepared in a glass utensil only if that utensil had been kashered. In other words, the Rama forbids using for Pesach glassware that had been used with *chametz*, even after kashering the glassware, but if one kashered a glass utensil and then used it on Pesach, the food may be eaten. This position is accepted by the *Mishna Berura* (451:155). Applying this view to modern-day metal utensils, there would be no room, seemingly, to permit food cooked in a pot that had been used with non-kosher food and had not been kashered in the interim.

This conclusion, however, is not necessarily correct. The *Peri Megadim* (*Eishel Avraham*, 451:49) asserted that the *Magen Avraham* and *Chok Yaakov* stated their view only with regard to the prohibition of *chametz* on Pesach. This prohibition is unique in that it is not subject to *bittul* ("nullification"); that is to say, it is forbidden even when it constitutes an infinitesimal proportion of a mixture. Whereas mixtures containing other forbidden foods may be eaten if the forbidden foods comprise too small a proportion to impart taste, mixtures containing even a very small proportion of *chametz* may not be eaten on Pesach. The *Peri Megadim* thus explained that according to the *Magen Avraham* and *Chok Yaakov*, glass is capable of absorbing very small amounts of taste of food with which they are used, and therefore, food prepared in them on Pesach is forbidden, unless they had been kashered in the interim. If so, then even according to this reading of the Rama, if a modern-day pot had been used with non-kosher food, and is then used with kosher food, or it had been used with meat and then dairy food (or vice versa), the food in the pot may be eaten, despite the fact that the utensil requires kashering.

Moreover, many *Acharonim* maintained that the stringent practice of the Ashkenazim applies only to Pesach in the first place. The Rama made his comment concerning the use of glassware only in the context of the laws of Pesach, in reference to the *Shulchan Aruch*'s ruling that glass utensils that had been used during the year may be used on Pesach. But the *Shulchan Aruch* returns to this issue again in a different context — in regard to utensils used to store non-Jewish wine (Y.D. 135:8). There, too, the *Shulchan Aruch* codifies the lenient position, writing that glassware that had been used with non-Jewish wine, even for long-term storage, may be used with kosher wine and does not require any kashering. Curiously, the Rama makes no comment in this context, seemingly suggesting that he accepts this ruling even as normative practice for Ashkenazim. As many

Acharonim noted,¹⁶ it is likely that Ashkenazic custom follows the stringent position regarding glassware only with regard to the prohibition of *chametz* on Pesach, due to the uniquely stringent status of this prohibition, but not in regard to other *halachos*. Accordingly, when it comes to other halachic matters — such as non-kosher products, and the mixture of meat and dairy foods — glassware may be assumed not to absorb. Hence, our modern-day utensils, too, should perhaps be allowed for use with both and meat and dairy products, and after being used with non-kosher food, without any requirement of kashering.

What's more, it is possible that the Ashkenazic practice stems from a purely practical concern, and has nothing at all to do with the nature of בליעת כלים. As cited earlier, Rav Chizkiya Medini, in *Sedei Chemed*,¹⁷ noted that although the Ashkenazic *poskim* (to whom he refers as חכמי וורשא — "the scholars of Warsaw") forbid the use of glassware for meat and milk, they permit the use of iron utensils, without requiring kashering. He explains that the Ashkenazic custom to treat glassware as though it absorbs stems from the concern that one might use imitation glassware that is actually produced from earth, as opposed to sand.¹⁸ Meaning, both Ashkenazim and Sephardim fully accept the view that glass is incapable of absorbing, and so in principle, glassware may be used for both meat and milk, during the year and on Pesach, and so on. However, Ashkenazic communities adopted the practice to treat glassware as earthenware to avoid the risk of mistakenly treating an earthenware utensils as glassware, given that some earthenware utensils are deceptively marketed as glassware.

According to Rav Medini's understanding, then, the controversy surrounding glassware has no bearing whatsoever on the status of modern-day utensils, which have been shown to be incapable of absorbing. As this quality is shared by all utensils produced nowadays, there is no need to treat our utensils stringently as a safeguard against forbidden use of utensils which are capable of absorbing.

Interim Summary

Thus far, we have shown that:

1. The amount of food absorbed and expunged by the surfaces of modern-day utensils is infinitesimally small, far less than the process of *beli'a* spoken of by *Chazal*.

---

16. *Kenneses Ha-Gedola* (Y.D. 121:25), *Shoel U-Meishiv* (2:91), *Chelkas Yaakov* (44), and *Seridei Eish* (1:45).
17. In the passage reference above, note 11.
18. ובהכרח לומר שחשו חכמים הראשונים, לקדושינים אשר בארץ המה, שמא יש כלים הדומים להם ומזייפים בהם לערב משאר עפר, או שעושים מעפר אחר ממש ומתקנים אותם ודומים לאלו ממש.

2. The evidence overwhelmingly supports the conclusion that the prohibition of טעם depends upon the physical reality of taste, and thus since we do not taste in our food the taste of food with which the utensils had been used earlier, that food has no halachic bearing on the status of the utensils. In light of the Ashkenazic practice concerning glassware, we might, at most, forbid for Ashkenazim the use of year-round utensils on Pesach. According to the *Sedei Chemed*'s understanding of this practice, we may be lenient even with regard to Pesach.

IV. Reasons for Stringency

Nevertheless, despite what we have seen, several factors need to be considered which may lead us to a different conclusion.

אין מבטלין איסור לכתחילה

As noted earlier, scientific data shows that modern-day utensils do, indeed, absorb a minuscule quantity of food, and then expunge it during subsequent use, but this amount is far too small to impart taste. Seemingly, these findings should suffice to permit the consumption of the food prepared in a utensil that had previously been used with non-kosher food, but not to permit from the outset the use of this utensil without first kashering it. The well-established rule of אין מבטלין איסור לכתחילה, which is codified by the *Shulchan Aruch* (Y.D. 99:5), forbids knowingly effecting the process of *bittul*. The concept of *bittul*, which allows us to overlook an insignificantly small quantity of forbidden food in a mixture, applies only after the fact; one may not intentionally mix forbidden food with a much larger quantity of permissible food in order to bring about the process of *bittul*. It would thus appear that even if we definitively conclude that modern-day utensil do not absorb and expunge enough to impart taste, kashering would nevertheless be required to avoid violating the law of אין מבטלין איסור לכתחילה.

This conclusion would likely hinge on a debate among the *poskim* regarding a possible exception to this prohibition. The *Shulchan Aruch* (Y.D. 99:7), based on a controversial ruling of the Rashba (*Toras Ha-Bayis Ha-Aroch*, 4:4), writes that if a utensil is used exclusively with large quantities of food, and it happened to have absorbed a very small amount of non-kosher food, it may be used without kashering. Since the absorbed quantity of food will never be capable of imparting taste, given the fact that the utensil is used strictly for large quantities, the prohibition of אין מבטלין איסור לכתחילה does not apply. The *Shulchan Aruch*'s ruling is disputed by several later *poskim*, including the *Bach* (Y.D. 122), the *Taz*

(Y.D. 99:7) and the *Shach* (Y.D. 122:3). The Vilna Gaon, by contrast, accepted this leniency (*Bei'ur Ha-Gra*, Y.D. 122:15).[19] We might assume that those who dispute the *Shulchan Aruch*'s ruling would not permit using modern-day utensils for meat after they had been used with dairy foods, or vice versa, or using a utensil that had been used with non-kosher food.

On the other hand, there is evidence that a utensil that had absorbed an infinitesimally small quantity of forbidden food may be used without kashering. The Ran (*Pesachim* 9a in the Rif), articulating the view permitting the use of year-round glassware on Peach, explains that בליעתם מעוטה מכל הכלים — glassware absorbs far less than all other utensils. The clear implication of the Ran's remark is that glass does, in fact, absorb some quantity of food, but this quantity is so small as to be halachically meaningless. The assumption seems to be that an infinitesimally small proportion of forbidden food is negligible even with respect to the rule of אין מבטלין איסור לכתחילה, and this would, conceivably, apply to modern-day utensils in light of the scientific data noted earlier.[20]

It must be emphasized that this discussion relates only to the permissibility of using a utensil that had been used with non-kosher food without kashering. Even according to the stringent view, if such a utensil was used, the food would be permissible after the fact.

Are Our Utensils Really Different?

Rav Eitam Henkin *Hy"d*, in a letter printed in *Ha-Ma'ayan* (Teives, 5774),[21] questions the basic assumption that our utensils do not absorb to the same extent as

---

19. An intermediate position is taken by the *Kaf Ha-Chayim*, who writes that although one should preferably follow the stringent opinion, one may be lenient once twenty-four hours had passed since the utensil had been used with non-kosher food.
20. Indeed, Rav Dov Lior, in a letter published in *Techumin* (vol. 34, pp. 127–128), asserted that even according to those who dispute the *Shulchan Aruch*'s ruling, the amount of absorbed food in modern-day utensils is not subject to the rule of אין מבטלין איסור לכת-חילה, though he does not explain the rationale for this claim. By contrast, Rav Eliezer Melamed, in his article on the subject published on the Arutz Sheva website (available at http://www.inn.co.il/News/News.aspx/329723), ruled that the principle of אין מבטלין איסור לכתחילה is applicable, and thus modern-day utensils must be kashered in between uses for meat and milk.

    Another consideration, as noted by Rav Yitzchak Dvir (in an article published on the website of the Kosharot organization, available at *http://www.kosharot.co.il/show_hadracha.asp?id=61685*), is the fact that even after *hag'ala*, a minuscule amount of food remains absorbed in the utensil, and yet the utensil may be used. This, too, would support the contention that exceedingly low quantities of absorbed food may be overlooked with regard to the law of אין מבטלין איסור לכתחילה.
21. The letter was written in response to Rav Sitton's article, referenced above (note 3), and

the utensils in the times of *Chazal* and the *Rishonim*. He contends that scientific experimentation on modern-day utensils is significant only if experimentation can also be conducted on the kinds of utensils used in ancient times, and it verifies the occurrence of *beli'a*. In other words, the methods by which science shows that our utensils do not absorb must also show that ancient utensils did absorb. If these methods cannot confirm the occurrence of *beli'a* in ancient utensils, we must consider the possibility that the halachic phenomenon of *beli'a* cannot be discerned through these methods, and so the recent scientific experiments are halachically inconsequential. We must first verify that our methods of experimentation can affirm the occurrence of *beli'a* in ancient utensils before we can rely on these methods to affirm that *beli'a* does not occur in our utensils.[22]

One might respond, however, that the accounts cited above of external signs of *beli'a*, such as in the case of קוניא, as described in the Gemara, and the darkened color of the water used for *hag'ala*, as reported by the Ran, suffice as proof to the drastic difference between our utensils and those of ancient times. This, coupled with the reality that we do not taste in our food the food with which had previously been prepared in the utensil, would be compelling evidence that *beli'a* does not occur.

מנהג ישראל

Another concern relates to the prospect of overhauling an entire section of the *Shulchan Aruch* and discarding one of the primary defining features of a kosher home. *Halacha* is, by nature, conservative and resistant to change, and the longstanding tradition to decide matters involving בליעת כלים on the basis of halachic principles, rather than scientific findings, perhaps suffices to dismiss the possibility of ignoring בליעת כלים in our time. Suddenly changing *kashrus*

---

is available at http://www.machonso.org/hamaayan/?gilayon=32&id=1067.

22. Rav Henkin proceeds to postulate that people in ancient times were far more sensitive to variations in taste than they are now, and this explains why *Chazal* assumed that taste could be discerned in a proportion higher than 1:60, even though we cannot detect any taste in such mixtures. To substantiate his claim, Rav Henkin experimented with utensils made of wood, which clearly absorb liquid, even nowadays. He stirred two identical cups of tea with two different wooden spoons, one of which had been used several minutes earlier to stir boiling hot milk. Halachically speaking, the tea stirred with that spoon must be treated as dairy. However, Rav Henkin reported, neither he nor any of his family members noticed any difference between the tastes of the two cups of tea. Conceivably, then, it is possible that the ancients would discern in our food the taste of food prepared previously in the pot, even though we do not discern any such taste.

protocol in such a drastic fashion, it has been argued, is not in the best interests of Torah observance.[23]

This point was made by Rav Asher Weiss, in a letter to Rabbi Dr. Dror Fixler that was printed in *Techumin* (vol. 34, p. 128). Rav Weiss noted that the Radbaz's use of experimentation with porcelain was the exception, rather than the rule. The conventional, accepted approach is to determine the presence or absence of *beli'a* by analyzing the relevant halachic guidelines, and not based on science, and this is the method that we should continue to follow.

Practical Concerns

Finally, several contemporary *poskim* warned of the practical complications that could arise if we allow using utensils for both meat and dairy foods. Specifically, if a utensil is not properly cleaned, and it contains residue of a dairy food with which was used, meat prepared subsequently in that utensil would clearly be forbidden for consumption.[24] Interestingly, Rav Nachum Rabinovitch, in a letter published in the aforementioned volume of *Techumin* (p. 127), speculates that this might be the reason for why Ashkenazic communities forbade the use of glass utensils for both meat and dairy foods, despite the fact that glass does not absorb. This practice was perhaps instituted as a safeguard against problems that could arise if utensils are not thoroughly washed.

Moreover, Rav Rabinovitch noted that permitting the use of utensils with both meat and dairy foods would likely lead people to wash dishes used with one together with those used with the other. If this is done with hot water, or in a dishwasher, it might very well violate the Torah prohibition against cooking meat with milk.

Another concern that has been noted is the possibility of new kinds of utensils being produced in the future. If we grow accustomed to using utensils for

---

23. We might note that several leading 20th century *poskim* addressed the question of the status of plastic utensils with regard to בליעת כלים, and none of them suggested laboratory testing to determine whether plastic absorbs. See, for example, *Minchas Yitzchak* 3:67, *Seridei Eish* 1:46, *Iggeros Moshe* E.H. 4:7, *Lehoros Nasan* 6:69.
24. This point is made by Rav Eliezer Melamed, in the article referenced above, note 19. Rav Melamed elsewhere (http://ph.yhb.org.il/plus/17-12-07/) noted the widespread custom mentioned by the Rama (Y.D. 89:4), and discussed more elaborately by the *Aruch Ha-Shulchan* (Y.D. 89:16), to keep separate utensils for meat and dairy foods, and to label them accordingly. It stands to reason, Rav Melamed contends, that this custom developed not only due to the food absorbed by these utensils, but also due to the concern of residue that had not been removed through washing, and thus the custom applies even to utensils that do not absorb.

both meat and dairy foods, we will likely continue doing so even when realities change and utensils that are subject to *beli'a* become common.

In light of these concerns, there is no doubt that the time-honored tradition to keep separate utensils for meat and dairy foods, and to kasher utensils that had been used with non-kosher food, should be maintained. However, some *poskim* have suggested that there is room for leniency after the fact, if one mistakenly prepared dairy food in a meat utensil, or vice versa. Similarly, if one discovered that food he had been purchasing was non-kosher, and kashering his entire kitchen and replacing utensils would entail a great expense and inconvenience, it seems reasonable that one may rely on the assumption that modern-day utensils do not absorb.[25]

A more stringent ruling is cited in the name of Rav Shlomo Zalman Auerbach, who reportedly allowed introducing this factor as a consideration when addressing questions involving *beli'a*. Although he did not, as a rule, permit food prepared in a utensil that had not been kashered, nevertheless, he said that if it is uncertain whether the food is truly forbidden, we may rule leniently in consideration of the fact that taste of the forbidden food cannot actually be discerned.[26]

INTERVIEW

Rabbi Yitzchok Berkovits on *Headlines with Dovid Lichtenstein**

It is known that Rav Shlomo Zalman Auerbach used to say that one of the things *Mashiach* will do is determine that there are no *bli'os* in stainless steel pots. Rav Shlomo Zalman wasn't ready to determine this, but he did add this [as a factor] where there were a couple of other reasons to be lenient.

Once, when I was teaching איסור והיתר to a group, we had a food scientist who was part of the *chabura*... He told us that the fragrant oil that carries טעם does get absorbed into pots, even stainless steel pots. It is very subtle, most of us cannot taste it, but when there is some kind of clash — two chemicals that don't

---

25. This is the ruling of Rav Rabinovitch and Rav Melamed. By contrast, Rav Asher Weiss, as well as Rav Yaakov Ariel (in a letter appended to Rabbi Dr. Dror Fixler's aforementioned article in *Techumin*), rejected the entire premise and insisted that we must treat modern-day utensils as though they absorb.
26. This ruling was reported by Rav Uriel Eisenthal, in his *Megilas Sefer* (p. 104).

"get along" — there are people in the business who know that you cannot use the same pot for these two things. There are enough traces in it to ruin a different kind of food... If you boil milk in a pot, even if you wash it well, and then you put corned beef there, it would interfere. He said this was a fact.

Another time when I taught a *chabura* they decided to get in touch with the chief scientist for a company that made dental equipment, and he told them that the silver in fillings is totally non-porous and absorbs nothing, whereas stainless steel used for pots is slightly porous, and it does absorb, though very little. This means that in reality, there is probably a little bit of *beli'a*, and we do not know what the amount is. And since we do not rely on a Jew's tasting, we have no way of knowing... Once you start telling me that there are very small traces, I don't know how to evaluate when it has טעם and when it does not. But Rav Shlomo Zalman would add this to other reasons for leniency, and said that when *Mashiach* comes, we'll know better.

* Broadcast on 14 Tishrei, 5777 (October 15, 2016).